Microsoft®
OFFICE 2000

ADVANTAGE
S E R I E S

Microsoft®
OFFICE 2000

Sarah E. Hutchinson

Glen J. Coulthard

Irwin
McGraw-Hill

Boston   Burr Ridge, IL   Dubuque, IA   Madison, WI   New York   San Francisco   St. Louis
Bangkok   Bogotá   Caracas   Lisbon   London   Madrid   Mexico City
Milan   New Delhi   Seoul   Singapore   Sydney   Taipei   Toronto

McGraw-Hill Higher Education ⤴

*A Division of The **McGraw-Hill** Companies*

MICROSOFT® OFFICE 2000

This book is printed on acid-free paper.

1 2 3 4 5 6 7 8 9 0 WEB/WEB 9 0 4 3 2 1 0 9

ISBN 0-07-233793-1

Vice president/Editor in chief: *Michael W. Junior*

Publisher: *David Brake*

Sponsoring editor: *Trisha O'Shea*

Developmental editor: *Kyle Thomes*

Senior marketing manager: *Jodi McPherson*

Project manager: *Christina Thornton-Villagomez*

Production supervisor: *Debra R. Benson*

Designer: *A.M. Design*

Supplement coordinator: *Carol Loreth*

Compositor: *GTS Graphics*

Typeface: *11/13 Stone Serif*

Printer: *Webcrafters, Inc.*

Library of Congress Cataloging-in-Publication Data

Hutchinson, Sarah E.
    Microsoft Office 2000 / Sarah E. Hutchinson, Glen J. Coulthard.
       p. cm. — (The advantage series for computer education)
    Includes index.
    ISBN 0-07-233793-1
    1. Microsoft Office.   2. Business—Computer programs.
  I. Coulthard, Glen J. II. Title. III. Series.
  HF5548.4.M525H8818 2000
  005.369—dc21   99-15465

http://www.mhhe.com

At McGraw-Hill Higher-Education, we publish instructional materials targeted at the higher-education market. In an effort to expand the tools of higher learning, we publish texts, lab manuals, study guides, testing materials, software and multimedia products.

At Irwin/McGraw-Hill (a division of McGraw-Hill Higher Education), we realize that technology will continue to create new mediums for professors and students to manage resources and communicate information with one another. We strive to provide the most flexible and complete teaching and learning tools available and offer solutions to the changing world of teaching and learning.

Irwin/McGraw-Hill is dedicated to providing the tools for today's instructors and students to successfully navigate the world of Information Technology.

- **Seminar Series**—Irwin/McGraw-Hill's Technology Connection seminar series offered across the country every year, demonstrates the latest technology products and encourages collaboration among teaching professionals.

- **Osborne/McGraw-Hill**—A division of The McGraw-Hill Companies known for its best-selling Internet titles *Harley Hahn's Internet & Web Yellow Pages* and the *Internet Complete Reference*, offers an additional resource for certification and has strategic publishing relationships with corporations such as Corel Corporation and America Online. For more information visit Osborne at www.osborne.com.

- **Digital Solutions**—Irwin/McGraw-Hill is committed to publishing Digital Solutions. Taking your course online doesn't have to be a solitary venture, nor does it have to be a difficult one. We offer several solutions, which will let you enjoy all the benefits of having course material online. For more information visit www.mhhe.com/solutions/index.mhtml.

- **Packaging Options**—For more information about our discount options, contact your local Irwin/McGraw-Hill Sales representative at 1-800-338-3987 or visit our Website at www.mhhe.com/it.

Preface The Advantage Series

Goals/Philosophy

The Advantage Series presents the **What, Why, and How** of computer application skills to today's students. Each lab manual is built upon an efficient learning model, which provides students and faculty with complete coverage of the most powerful software packages available today.

Approach

The Advantage Series builds upon an efficient learning model, which provides students and faculty with complete coverage and enhances critical thinking skills. This case-based, "problem-solving" approach teaches the What, Why, and How of computer application skills.

The Advantage Series introduces the **"Feature-Method-Practice"** layered approach. The **Feature** describes the command and tells the importance of that command. The **Method** shows students how to perform the feature. The **Practice** allows students to apply the feature in a keystroke exercise.

About the Series

The Advantage Series offers *three levels* of instruction. Each level builds upon the previous level. The following are the three levels of instructions:

Brief: covers the basics of the application, contains two to four chapters, and is typically 120–190 pages long.

Introductory: includes the material in the Brief lab manual plus two to three additional chapters. The Introductory lab manuals are approximately 300 pages long and prepare students for the *Microsoft Office User Specialist Proficient Exam (MOUS Certification).*

Complete: includes the Introductory lab manual plus an additional five chapters of advanced level content. The Complete lab manuals are approximately 600 pages in length and prepare students to take the *Microsoft Office User Specialist Expert Exam (MOUS Certification).*

About the Book

Each lab manual features the following:

- ***Learning Objectives:*** At the beginning of each chapter, a list of action-oriented objectives is presented detailing what is expected of the students.

- ***Chapters:*** Each lab manual is divided into chapters.

- ***Modules:*** Each chapter contains three to five independent modules, requiring approximately 30–45 minutes each to complete. Although we recommend you complete an entire chapter before proceeding, you may skip or rearrange the order of these modules to best suit your learning needs.

Case Study

- ***Case Studies:*** Each chapter begins with a Case Study. The student is introduced to a fictitious person or company and their immediate problem or opportunity. Throughout the chapter students obtain the knowledge and skills necessary to meet the challenges presented in the Case Study. At the end of each chapter, students are asked to solve problems directly related to the Case Study.

- ***Feature-Method-Practice:*** Each chapter highlights our **unique** **"Feature-Method-Practice"** layered approach. The ***Feature*** layer describes the command or technique and persuades you of its importance and relevance. The ***Method*** layer shows you how to perform the procedure, while the ***Practice*** layer lets you apply the feature in a hands-on step-by-step exercise.

- ***Instructions:*** The numbered step-by-step progression for all hands on examples and exercises are clearly identified. Students will find it surprisingly easy to follow the logical sequence of keystrokes and mouse clicks, and no longer worry about missing a step.

In Addition

- ***In Addition Boxes:*** These content boxes are placed strategically throughout the chapter and provide information on advanced topics that are beyond the scope of the current discussion.

- ***Self-Check Boxes:*** At the end of each module, a brief self-check question appears for students to test their comprehension of the material. Answers for these questions appear in the Appendix.

- ***Chapter Review:*** The *Command Summary* and *Key Terms* provide an excellent review of the chapter content and prepare students for the short-answer, true-false, and multiple-choice questions at the end of each chapter.

Easy ●
Moderate ■
Difficult ◆

- ***Hands-On Projects:*** Each chapter concludes with six hands-on projects that are rated according to their difficulty level. The *easy* and *moderate* projects use a running-case approach, whereby the same person or company appears at the end of each chapter in a particular tutorial. The two *difficult* or *on your own* projects provide greater latitude in applying the software to a variety of creative problem-solving situations.

- ***Appendix: Microsoft Windows Quick Reference:*** Each lab manual contains a Microsoft Windows Quick Reference. This Quick Reference teaches students the fundamentals of using a mouse and a keyboard, illustrates how to interact with a dialog box, and describes the fundamentals of how to use the Office 2000 Help System.

Features of This Lab Manual

Instructions: The numbered step-by-step progression for all hands-on examples and exercises are clearly identified. Students will find it surprisingly easy to follow the logical sequence of keystrokes and mouse clicks, and no longer worry about missing a step.

8 To return to a multicolumn list format:
CLICK: down arrow beside the Views button
CHOOSE: List

9 Let's open one of the documents in the list area:
DOUBLE-CLICK: WRD140
The dialog box disappears and the document is loaded into the application window. (*Note:* The "WRD140" filename reflects that this document is used in module 1.4 of the Word learning guide.)

10 Close the document before proceeding.

In Addition Boxes: These content boxes are placed strategically throughout the chapter and provide information on topics that are beyond the scope of the current discussion.

In Addition
Storing and Retrieving Files on Web Servers

With the appropriate network connection, you can open and save Word documents on the Internet. In the Open or Save As dialog boxes, click the Web Folders button (⬛) in the Places bar or select an FTP Internet site from the *Look in* drop-down list. This feature allows you to share and update Word documents with users from around the world.

Self-Check Boxes: At the end of each module, a brief self-check question appears for students to test their comprehension of the material. Answers for these questions appear in the Appendix.

1.4 Self Check In the Open and Save As dialog boxes, how do the List and Details views differ?

1.5 Previewing and Printing

This module focuses on outputting your document creations. Most commonly, you will print a document for inclusion into a report or other such document.

1.5.1 Previewing a Document

Feature-Method-Practice: Each chapter highlights our unique "Feature-Method-Practice" layered approach. The *Feature* layer describes the command or technique and persuades you of its importance and relevance. The *Method* layer shows you how to perform the procedure, while the *Practice* layer lets you apply the feature in a hands-on step-by-step exercise.

FEATURE
Before sending a document to the printer, you can preview it using a full-page display that closely resembles the printed version. In this Preview display mode, you can move through the document pages, and zoom in and out on desired areas.

METHOD
CLICK: Print Preview button (⬛), or
CHOOSE: File, Print Preview

PRACTICE
You will now open a relatively large document and then preview it on the screen.

Case Studies: Each chapter begins with a case study. Throughout the chapter students obtain the knowledge and skills necessary to meet the challenges presented in the case study. At the end of each chapter students are asked to solve problems directly related to the case study.

Chapters: Each lab manual is divided into chapters. Each chapter is composed of 2–5 **Modules.** Each module is composed of one or more **lessons.**

New Design: The **new** Advantage Series design offers a shaded area where the Feature-Method-Practice and numbered step-by-step instructions maintain the focus of the student.

Case Study   1-on-1 Tutoring Services

Dean Shearwater is helping to pay his university tuition by tutoring other university and high school students. Over the last two years, he has developed an excellent reputation for making complex topics simple and easy to remember. While he is an excellent tutor, last year he didn't earn as much as he had expected.

Dean thinks his lackluster earnings can be attributed to poor advertising and inadequate record keeping. This year, he has decided to operate his tutoring services more like a real business. His first priority is to learn how to use Microsoft Word so that he can prepare advertising materials, send faxes and memos, and organize his student notes.

In this chapter, you and Dean learn how to create simple documents from scratch, use built-in document templates, edit documents, and use the Undo command. You also learn how to preview and print your work.

1.1 Getting Started with Word

Microsoft Word 2000 is a **word processing** program that enables you to create, edit, format, and print many types of documents including résumés and cover letters, reports and proposals, World Wide Web pages, and more. By the time you complete this learning guide, you will be skilled in creating all types of documents and in getting them to look the way you want. In this module, you load Microsoft Word and proceed through a guided tour of its primary components.

1.1.1 Loading and Exiting Word

FEATURE
You load Word from the Windows Start menu, accessed by clicking the Start button (Start) on the taskbar. Because Word requires a significant amount of memory, you should always exit the application when you are finished doing your work. Most Windows applications allow you to close their windows by clicking the Close button (X) appearing in the top right-hand corner.

Teaching Resources

The following is a list of supplemental material, which can be used to teach this course.

Skills Assessment

Irwin/McGraw-Hill offers two innovative systems that can be used with the Advantage Series, ATLAS and **SimNet,** which take skills assessment testing beyond the basics with pre- and post-assessment capability.

- **ATLAS—(Active Testing and Learning Assessment Software)**—Atlas is our **live** in the application skills assessment tool. ATLAS allows Students perform tasks while working *live* within the office applications environment. ATLAS is web-enabled and customizable to meet the needs of your course. Atlas is available for Office 2000.
- SimNet—(Simulated Network Assessment Product)—SimNet permits you to test the actual software skills students learn about the Microsoft Office Applications in a **simulated** environment. Sim-Net is web-enabled and is available for Office 97 and Office 2000.

Instructor's Resource Kits

The Instructor's Resource Kit provides professors with all of the ancillary material needed to teach a course. Irwin/McGraw-Hill is committed to providing instructors with the most effective instructional resources available. Many of these resources are available at our **Information Technology Supersite** www.mhhe.com/it. Our Instructor's Resource Kits are available on CD-ROM and contain the following:

- **Diploma by Brownstone**—is the most flexible, powerful, and easy to use computerized testing system available in higher education. The Diploma system allows professors to create an exam as a printed version, as a LAN-based Online version and as an Internet version. Diploma includes grade book features, which automates the entire testing process.
- **Instructor's Manual**—Includes:
  —Solutions to all lessons and end of chapter material
  —Teaching Tips
  —Teaching Strategies
  —Additional exercises
- **Student Data Files**—To use the Advantage Series, students must have data files to complete practice and test sessions. The instructor and students using this text in classes are granted the right to post the student files on any network or stand-alone computer, or to distribute the files on individual diskettes. The student files may be downloaded from our IT Supersite at www.mhhe.com/it.
- **Series Web Site**—Available at www.mhhe.com/cit/apps/adv/.

Digital Solutions

PageOut Lite—allows an instructor to create their own basic Web site hosted by McGraw-Hill. PageOut Lite includes three basic templates that automatically convert typed material into html Web Pages. Using PageOut Lite an instructor can set up a homepage, Web links, and a basic course syllabus and lecture notes.

PageOut—is Irwin/McGraw-Hill's Course Webster Development Center. Pageout allows an instructor to create a more complex course Webster with an interactive syllabus and some course management features. Like PageOut Lite, PageOut converts typed material to html. For more information please visit the Pageout Web site at www.mhla.net/pageout.

OLC/Series Web Sites—Online Learning Centers (OLC's)/Series Sites are accessible through our Supersite at www.mhhe.com/it. Our OLC/Series Sites provide pedagogical features and supplements for our titles online. Students can point and click their way to key terms, learning objectives, chapter overviews, PowerPoint slides, exercises, and Web links.

The McGraw-Hill Learning Architecture (MHLA)—is a complete course delivery system. MHLA gives professors ownership in the way digital content is presented to the class through online quizzing, student collaboration, course administration, and content management. For a walkthrough of MHLA, visit the MHLA Web site at www.mhla.net.

Packaging Options

For more information about our discount options, contact your local Irwin/McGraw-Hill Sales representative at 1-800-338-3987 or visit our Web site at www.mhhe.com/it.

Acknowledgments

This series of tutorials is the direct result of the teamwork and heart of many people. We sincerely thank the reviewers, instructors, and students who have shared their comments and suggestions with us over the past few years. We do read them! With their valuable feedback, our tutorials have evolved into the product you see before you.

Many thanks go to Kyle Lewis, Trisha O'Shea, Kyle Thomes, and Carrie Berkshire from Irwin/McGraw-Hill whose management helped to get this book produced in a timely and efficient manner. Special recognition goes to all of the individuals mentioned in the credits at the beginning of this tutorial. And finally, to the many others who weren't directly involved in this project but who have stood by us the whole way, we appreciate your encouragement and support.

The Advantage Team
Special thanks go out to our contributing members on the Advantage team.

Verlaine Murphy
Walt Musekamp
Ingrid Neumann
Catherine Schuler

Write to Us
We welcome your response to this tutorial, for we are trying to make it as useful a learning tool as possible. Please contact us at

Sarah E. Hutchinson—sclifford@mindspring.com
Glen J. Coulthard—glen@coulthard.com

Visit www.mhhe.com/it
THE ONLY SITE WITH ALL YOUR CIT AND MIS NEEDS.

Contents—Word

Contents—Excel

Contents—PowerPoint

CREATING A PRESENTATION — CHAPTER 1

DEVELOPING A PRESENTATION — CHAPTER 2

Contents—Access

ORGANIZING AND RETRIEVING DATA CHAPTER 3

PRESENTING AND MANAGING DATA CHAPTER 4

Contents—Integrating

EXTENDING MICROSOFT OFFICE TO THE WEB   CHAPTER 3

CONTENTS—END MATTER

ADVANTAGE
S E R I E S

Microsoft®
OFFICE 2000

MICROSOFT WORD 2000
Creating a Document

CHAPTER

O N E

Chapter Outline

Learning Objectives

After reading this chapter, you will be able to:

- Identify the different components of the application window

- Select commands and options using the Menu bar and right-click menus

- Create and edit documents

- Start a new document

- Save, open, and close a document

- Preview and print a document

Case Study

1-on-1 Tutoring Services

Dean Shearwater is helping to pay his university tuition by tutoring other university and high school students. Over the last two years, he has developed an excellent reputation for making complex topics simple and easy to remember. While he is an excellent tutor, last year he didn't earn as much as he had expected.

Dean thinks his lackluster earnings can be attributed to poor advertising and inadequate record keeping. This year, he has decided to operate his tutoring services more like a real business. His first priority is to learn how to use Microsoft Word so that he can prepare advertising materials, send faxes and memos, and organize his student notes.

In this chapter, you and Dean learn how to create simple documents from scratch, use built-in document templates, edit documents, and use the Undo command. You also learn how to preview and print your work.

1.1 Getting Started with Word

Microsoft Word 2000 is a **word processing** program that enables you to create, edit, format, and print many types of documents including résumés and cover letters, reports and proposals, World Wide Web pages, and more. By the time you complete this learning guide, you will be skilled in creating all types of documents and in getting them to look the way you want. In this module, you load Microsoft Word and proceed through a guided tour of its primary components.

1.1.1 Loading and Exiting Word

FEATURE

You load Word from the Windows Start menu, accessed by clicking the Start button (Start) on the taskbar. Because Word requires a significant amount of memory, you should always exit the application when you are finished doing your work. Most Windows applications allow you to close their windows by clicking the Close button (x) appearing in the top right-hand corner.

METHOD
- To load Word:
  CLICK: Start button (🏁 Start)
  CHOOSE: Programs, Microsoft Word
- To exit Word:
  CLICK: Close button (☒) appearing in the top right-hand corner, or
  CHOOSE: File, Exit from Word's Menu bar

PRACTICE
You will now load Microsoft Word using the Windows Start menu.

Setup: Ensure that you have turned on your computer and that the Windows desktop appears. If necessary, refer to the Preface for additional instructions.

1 Position the mouse pointer over the top of the Start button (🏁 Start) and then click the left mouse button once. The Start pop-up menu appears.

2 Point to the Programs cascading command using the mouse. Notice that you do not need to click the left mouse button to display the list of programs in the fly-out or cascading menu.

3 Move the mouse pointer horizontally to the right until it highlights an option in the Programs menu. You can now move the mouse pointer vertically within the menu to select an option.

4 Point to the Microsoft Word menu item and then click the left mouse button once to execute the command. After a few seconds, the Microsoft Word screen appears.

5 An Office Assistant character, like "Rocky" (shown at the right), may now appear. You learn how to hide this character in lesson 1.1.2.

In Addition
Switching Among
Applications

Each application that you are currently working with is represented by a button on the taskbar. Switching among open applications on your desktop is as easy as clicking the appropriate taskbar button, like switching channels on a television set.

1.1.2 Touring Word

FEATURE
The Word **application window** acts as a container for your document. As with other Microsoft Office 2000 applications, the application window contains the primary interface components for working in Word including the *Windows icons, Menu bar, Toolbars,* and *Status bar.* It also includes several tools specific to Word including the *Ruler, Scroll bars,* and *View buttons.* Figure 1.1 identifies several components of Word's application window.

PRACTICE
In a guided tour, you will now explore the features of Word's application window.

Setup: Ensure that you've loaded Word.

1

Word's application window is best kept maximized to fill the entire screen, as shown in Figure 1.1. As with most Windows applications, you use the Title bar icons—Minimize (⬜), Maximize (□), Restore (⧉), and Close (✕)—to control the display of a window using the mouse. Familiarize yourself with the components labeled in Figure 1.1.

Figure 1.1

Word's application window

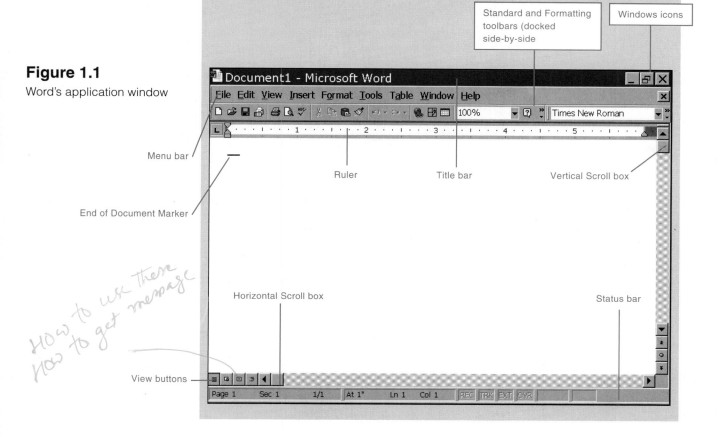

Standard and Formatting toolbars (docked side-by-side

Windows icons

Menu bar

End of Document Marker

Ruler   Title bar   Vertical Scroll box

Horizontal Scroll box   Status bar

View buttons

2 The Menu bar contains the Word menu commands. To execute a command, you click once on the desired Menu bar option and then click again on the command. Commands that appear dimmed are not available for selection. Commands that are followed by an ellipsis (...) will display a dialog box.

To practice working with the Word Menu bar:
CHOOSE: Help
This instruction tells you to click the left mouse button once on the Help option appearing in the Menu bar.

3 To display other pull-down menus, move the mouse to the left over other options in the Menu bar. As each option is highlighted, a pull-down menu appears with its associated commands.

4 To leave the Menu bar without making a command selection:
CLICK: in a blank area of the Title bar

5 Word provides context-sensitive *right-click menus* for quick access to menu commands. Rather than searching for the appropriate command in the Menu bar, you can position the mouse pointer on any object, such as a graphic or toolbar button, and right-click the mouse to display a list of commonly selected commands.

To display a document's right-click menu:
RIGHT-CLICK: in the blank document area
The pop-up menu at the right should appear.

6 To remove the right-click menu from the screen:
PRESS: ESC

7 If an Office Assistant character currently appears on your screen, do the following to hide it from view:
RIGHT-CLICK: *the character*
CHOOSE: Hide *character* from the right-click menu
(*Note:* The character's name will appear in the command, such as "Hide Rocky.")

1.1.3 Customizing Menus and Toolbars

FEATURE

Some people argue that software becomes more difficult to learn and use with the addition of each new command or feature. In response to this sentiment, Microsoft developed **adaptive menus** that display only the most commonly used commands. By default, Office 2000 ships with the adaptive menus feature enabled. However, you may find this dynamic feature confusing and choose to turn off the adaptive menus. Likewise, the Standard and Formatting toolbars are positioned side-by-side in a single row by default. Again, you may find it easier to locate buttons when these toolbars are positioned on separate rows.

METHOD

To disable the adaptive menus feature:

1. CHOOSE: Tools, Customize
2. CLICK: *Options* tab
3. SELECT: *Menus show recently used commands first* check box, so that no "✔" appears
4. CLICK: Close command button

To display the Standard and Formatting toolbars on separate rows:

1. CHOOSE: Tools, Customize
2. CLICK: *Options* tab
3. SELECT: *Standard and Formatting toolbars share one row* check box, so that no "✔" appears.
4. CLICK: Close command button

PRACTICE

After a brief tour of Word's adaptive menus, you will disable the adaptive menus feature. At the same time, you will display the Standard and Formatting toolbars on separate rows.

Setup: Ensure that you've completed the previous lesson.

1 Let's display the Tools menu.
CHOOSE: Tools
The Tools menu (shown on the right) should now appear. When a desired command does not appear on a menu, you can extend the menu to view all of the commands either by waiting for a short period or by clicking the downward pointing arrows (also called *chevrons*) at the bottom of a pull-down menu. You can also double-click a menu option to display the entire list of commands immediately.

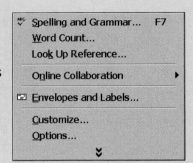

2 Let's display the entire list of commands in the Tools menu by double-clicking:
DOUBLE-CLICK: Tools in the Menu bar
The menu should now contain a complete list of options.

3 Let's turn off the adaptive menus feature and ensure that the Standard and Formatting toolbars appear on separate rows. Do the following:
CHOOSE: Customize from the Tools pull-down menu
CLICK: *Options* tab
The Customize dialog box should now appear similar to Figure 1.2.

Figure 1.2

Customize dialog box

4 SELECT: *Menus show recently used commands first* check box, so that no "✔" appears

5 SELECT: *Standard and Formatting toolbars share one row* check box, so that no "✔" appears

6 To proceed:
CLICK: Close command button
Your screen should now appear similar to Figure 1.3.

IMPORTANT: *For the remainder of this learning guide, we assume that the adaptive menus feature has been disabled and that the Standard and Formatting toolbars are positioned on separate rows.*

Figure 1.3

The Standard and Formatting toolbars are now positioned on separate rows

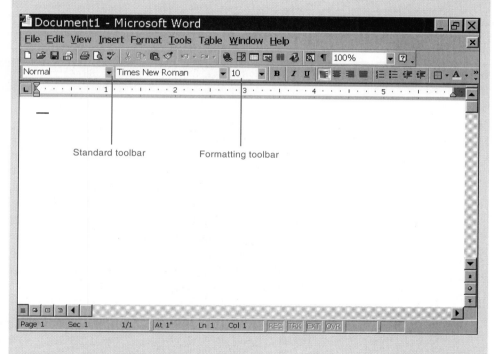

Standard toolbar   Formatting toolbar

7 To display additional toolbars, you select the desired options from a right-click menu. For example:
RIGHT-CLICK: *any button* on the Standard toolbar
Notice that the Standard and Formatting options are currently selected, as illustrated by the check marks in the pop-up menu.

8 To display the Picture toolbar:
CHOOSE: Picture from the pop-up menu
Another toolbar should appear in the application window.

To remove or hide the Picture toolbar:
RIGHT-CLICK: *any button on any toolbar*
CHOOSE: Picture
The toolbar disappears from the application window.

In Addition
Moving Toolbars

You can move toolbars around the Word application window using the mouse. A *docked* toolbar appears attached to one of the window's borders. An *undocked* or *floating* toolbar appears in its own window, complete with a Title bar and Close button. To float a docked toolbar, drag the Move bar (|) at the left-hand side toward the center of the window. To re-dock the toolbar, drag its Title bar toward a border until it attaches itself automatically.

1.1 Self Check   How do you remove a right-click menu from view?

1.2 Creating Your First Document

Creating a document in Word is easy. You type information onto the screen, save the document to the disk, and, if desired, send it to the printer. Before you begin typing, make sure that you have a blinking **insertion point** in the upper left-hand corner of the document window. This marks the location where text is inserted. Below the insertion point, you may see a horizontal black bar called the **End of Document Marker.** As you enter information, this marker automatically moves downward.

In the next few lessons, you will create the paragraph appearing in Figure 1.4.

Figure 1.4

Sample document

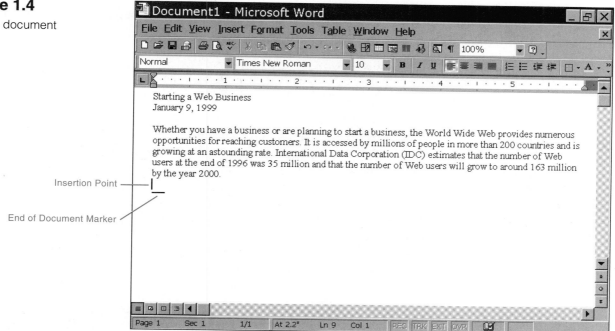

1.2.1 Inserting and Deleting Text

FEATURE

You create and edit documents by inserting and deleting text.

METHOD
- To insert text, begin typing. Insert spaces by pressing the Space Bar and insert blank lines by pressing (ENTER).
- To toggle between Insert and Overtype modes, double-click the OVR indicator in the Status bar.
- Press (DELETE) to delete text to the right of the insertion point. Press (BACKSPACE) to delete text to the left of the insertion point.

PRACTICE

Next, you practice the basics of inserting and deleting text.

Setup: Ensure that you've completed the previous lesson and that a blank document appears.

1 TYPE: Web Business

The insertion point appears one character to the right of the word "Business."

2 To move the insertion point back to the beginning of the line:
PRESS: HOME
The insertion point should now appear to the left of the "W" in "Web Business."

3 Make sure that the letters OVR in the Status bar appear dimmed. This tells you that Word's current mode is Insert mode and not Overtype mode. If the letters OVR are not dim, double-click the letters in the Status bar before continuing. Type the following, exactly as it appears:
TYPE: STarting
PRESS: Space Bar
Notice that Word's AutoCorrect feature automatically corrected your capitalization error at the beginning of the word. Also, the Insert mode let you insert text and spaces at the current position by simply typing the characters and pressing the Space Bar. The existing information was pushed to the right. By default, Word operates in Insert mode.

4 To demonstrate the difference between Insert mode and Overtype mode, position the insertion point to the left of the letter "W" in the word "Web." (*Note:* The insertion point may already be in the correct position.)

5 Locate OVR, the abbreviation for Overtype mode, on the Status bar.
DOUBLE-CLICK: OVR
The letters OVR appear highlighted (not dimmed) in the Status bar.

6 TYPE: a
PRESS: Space Bar
The letter "a" and following space overwrite the first two characters of "Web." The line should now look like the following:

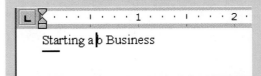

7 To toggle back to Insert mode:
DOUBLE-CLICK: OVR in the Status bar
The letters OVR should now appear dimmed.

8   Let's complete the phrase:
TYPE: **We**
The line should now look like the following:

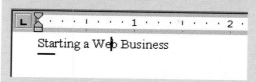

9   The (ENTER) key inserts blank lines into a document and signifies the end of a paragraph. To illustrate, position the insertion point to the left of the "B" in the word "Business."

10   PRESS: (ENTER) four times
The word "Business" moves down with the insertion point and blank lines are inserted into the document. Your document should now look like the following:

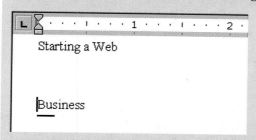

11   To quickly move to the top of the document:
PRESS: (CTRL) + (HOME)
This instruction tells you to press and hold down the (CTRL) key and tap (HOME) once. You then release both keys. The insertion point jumps to the left side of the first line in the document.

12   To move to the end of the line:
PRESS: (END)

13   In order to get the word "Business" back to its original location, you must delete the blank lines.
PRESS: (DELETE) four times

14   To illustrate the use of the (BACKSPACE) key, ensure that the insertion point is positioned to the left of the word "Business."

15   PRESS: (BACKSPACE) four times
The word "Web" and the space are deleted. The text now reads "Starting a Business."

To put the word "Web" back in the line:
TYPE: Web
PRESS: Space Bar

 To move the insertion point down one line without moving the text:
PRESS: ⌈END⌉ to move to the end of the line
PRESS: ⌈ENTER⌉ once
The insertion point is now in the correct position for you to insert the current date in the next lesson. Your document should now look like the following:

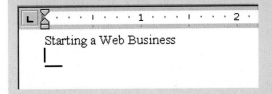

1.2.2 Inserting the Date and Time

FEATURE
To insert the current date and time in a document, simply choose Insert, Date and Time from the menu and select how you want the date and/or time to appear. Not only does this command save time, it also reduces the possibility of typing errors.

METHOD
1. CHOOSE: Insert, Date and Time
2. SELECT: a format in the *Available formats* list box
   CLICK: OK command button

PRACTICE
You will now insert the current date in a document.

Setup: Ensure that you've completed the previous lesson. The insertion point should be positioned one line below the title.

 CHOOSE: Insert, Date and Time
The Date and Time dialog appears, as shown in Figure 1.5.

Figure 1.5

Date and Time dialog box

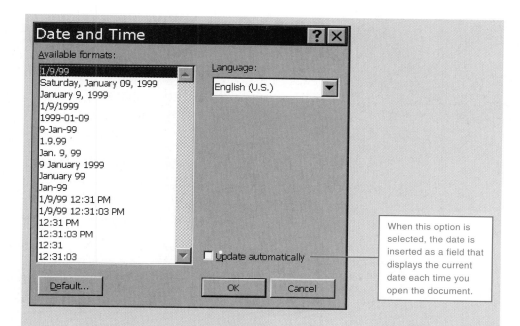

When this option is selected, the date is inserted as a field that displays the current date each time you open the document.

2 SELECT: the "Month ##, 199#" format (depicted as "January 9, 1999" in Figure 1.5)
CLICK: OK command button
The date was inserted in the document.

3 To insert two blank lines below the date:
PRESS: (ENTER) twice
Your document should now appear similar to the following, but with a more recent date.

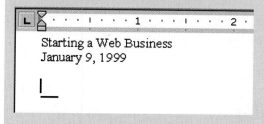

1.2.3 Putting "Word Wrap" to Work

FEATURE
The **word wrap** feature of Word allows you to continuously type without having to press the (ENTER) key at the end of each line.

METHOD
When typing a paragraph, do not press the (ENTER) key at the end of each line. The (ENTER) key is used only to end a paragraph or to insert a blank line in a document.

PRACTICE
You will now complete the sample document.

Setup: Ensure that you've completed the previous lesson. The insertion point should be positioned two lines below the date.

1 TYPE: Whether you have a business or are planning to start a business, the World Wide Web provides numerous opportunities for reaching customers. It is accessed by millions of people in more than 200 countries and is growing at an astounding rate. International Data Corporation (IDC) estimates that the number of Web users at the end of 1996 was 35 million and that the number of Web users will grow to around 163 million by the year 2000.

2 PRESS: (ENTER)
Your screen should now appear similar to Figure 1.4, shown earlier.

3 To conclude this module, you will close the document without saving changes. From the Menu bar:
CHOOSE: File, Close

4 In the dialog box that appears:
CLICK: No command button
There should be no documents open in the application window.

1.2 Self Check   How would you insert a word in the middle of a sentence?

1.3   Editing Your Work

What if you type a word into a document and then decide it needs to be changed? Both novices and experts alike make data entry errors when creating documents. Fortunately, Word provides several features for editing information that has already been entered. One of Word's most popular commands is the Undo command, because it lets you start over by undoing your most recent actions. Another popular feature is the spelling and grammar checker, which scans your documents for errors as you type. We describe these features in the following lessons.

1.3.1   Using the Undo, Redo, and Repeat Commands

FEATURE

The **Undo command** enables you to cancel the last several commands you performed in a document. The **Redo command** enables you to redo one or more actions after they have been undone. The **Repeat command** repeats the last action you performed in the document, such as inserting or deleting text, or using a menu command.

METHOD

- To undo or redo the last action:
  CLICK: Undo button (⟳▾) on the Standard toolbar, or
  CLICK: Redo button (⟳▾) on the Standard toolbar
- To undo or redo the last several actions:
  CLICK: down arrow next to the Undo button (⟳▾), or
  CLICK: down arrow next to the Redo button (⟳▾)
- To repeat the last action:
  CHOOSE: Edit, Repeat

PRACTICE
You will now practice using the Undo, Redo, and Repeat commands.

Setup: Ensure that no documents are displaying in the application window.

1 To display a new document for use in this module:
CLICK: New button (⬜) on the Standard toolbar
A new document, entitled Document#, appears in the document area. (*Note:* The name "Document#" is provided as a temporary name until you name the document yourself.)

2 TYPE: Your First Document

3 To undo the typing you just performed:
CLICK: Undo button (↩)
(*CAUTION:* Place the tip of the mouse pointer over the curved arrow on the left side of the button, as opposed to the downward pointing arrow, before clicking the left mouse button.) The title should have disappeared.

4 Using the Redo command, you can reinsert the title back in the document.
CLICK: Redo button (↪)

5 In this step, you retype the title and perform several actions.
PRESS: [ENTER] twice
PRESS: [⬆] twice to move to the top of the document
PRESS: [DELETE] four times to delete the characters "Your"
TYPE: My
The title should now read "My First Document."

6 To view all the actions that you can undo:
CLICK: down arrow beside the Undo button (↩)
Your screen should now appear similar to Figure 1.6.

Figure1.6

Using the Undo command

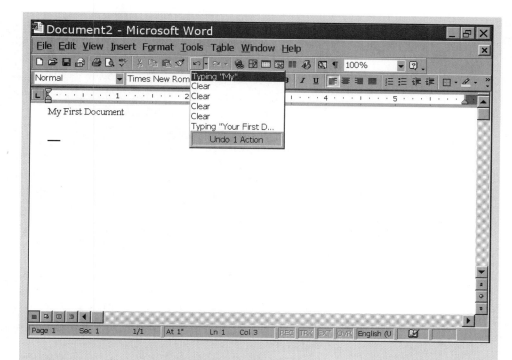

7 To exit the drop-down list without selecting an item:
CLICK: the Title bar

8 To illustrate the use of the Repeat command:
CHOOSE: Edit, Repeat from the Menu bar
Because the last action you performed was to type the word
"My" in your document, "My" appears at the insertion point.

9 To remove the duplicate "My" from the document:
CLICK: Undo button (⟲)

1.3.2 Correcting Mistakes As You Type

FEATURE
By default, Word checks your documents for spelling and grammar
errors as you type. Word marks spelling errors with a red wavy
underline and grammar errors with a green wavy underline. You
have the choice of accepting or ignoring Word's suggestions.

METHOD
To correct spelling and grammar errors:

1. Point to a word with a wavy red or green underline and then right-click with the mouse.
2. Choose Word's suggestion from the right-click menu, choose the Ignore All or Ignore Sentence command if no error has been made, or edit the error yourself.

PRACTICE
You will now practice correcting a spelling error.

Setup: Ensure that you've completed the previous lesson. The text "My First Document" should be displaying.

1 In this step, force an intentional spelling error by deleting the "o" of "Document."

2 To register the error with Word, you must move the insertion point.
PRESS: ⬇
Note that a red wavy underline appears beneath the misspelled word.

3 To correct the word, point to the word and then right-click using the mouse. Your screen should now appear similar to Figure 1.7.

Figure 1.7

The Spelling right-click menu

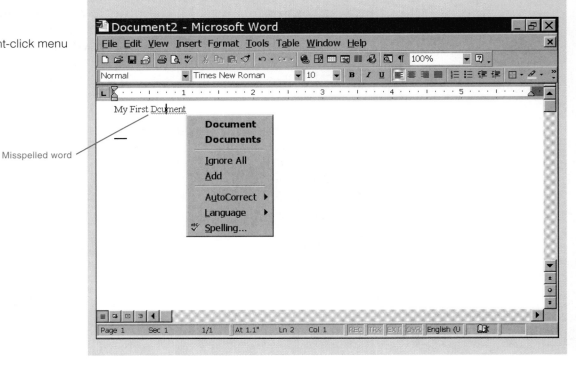

Misspelled word

4 Using the mouse, choose the word "Document" in the menu. The word "Document" should have replaced "Dcument" in the document.

5 To conclude this module, you will close the document without saving changes. From the Menu bar:
CHOOSE: File, Close
CLICK: No command button

1.3 Self Check   What procedure enables you to undo several actions at once?

1.4 Managing Files

Managing the document files that you create is an important skill. When you are creating a document, it exists only in the computer's RAM (random access memory), which is highly volatile. In other words, if the power to your computer goes off, your document is lost. For safety and security, you need to save your document permanently to the local hard disk, a network drive, or a floppy diskette.

Saving your work to a named file on a disk is similar to placing it into a filing cabinet. For important documents (ones that you cannot risk losing), you should save your work at least every 15 minutes, or whenever you're interrupted, to protect against an unexpected power outage or other catastrophe. When naming your document files, you can use up to 255 characters, including spaces, but it's wise to keep the length under 20 characters. Furthermore, you cannot use the following characters in naming your documents:

$$\backslash \quad / \quad : \quad ; \quad * \quad ? \quad " \quad < \quad > \quad |$$

In the following lessons, you practice several file management procedures including creating a new document, saving and closing documents, and opening existing documents.

Important: In this guide, we refer to the files that have been created for you as the **student data files.** *Depending on your computer or lab setup, these files may be located on a floppy diskette, in a folder on your hard disk, or on a network server. If necessary, ask your instructor or lab assistant where to find these data files. To download the Advantage Series' student data files from the Internet, visit McGraw-Hill's Information Technology Web site at:*

http://www.mhhe.com/it

You will also need to identify a personal storage location for the files that you create, modify, and save.

1.4.1 Beginning a New Document

FEATURE
There are three ways to start creating a new document. First, you can start with a blank document and then create the document from scratch. Next, you can select a document **template** that provides preexisting data and design elements. And, lastly, you can employ a **wizard** to help lead you step-by-step through creating a particular type of document.

METHOD
- To display a new blank document:
  CLICK: New button (⬜)
- To begin a document using a template or wizard:
  CHOOSE: File, New

PRACTICE
In this example, you use a template and a wizard.

Setup: Ensure that no documents are open in the application window.

A document template is a model that you can use to create new documents. By its very nature, a template is a time-saver that promotes consistency in both design and function. To view the templates that are available to you, do the following:
CHOOSE: File, New
The "Blank Document" template icon appears on the *General* tab of the New dialog box. This document template is used by Word when you click the New button (⬜) on the Standard toolbar.

2 The custom templates that are shipped with Word and that have been installed onto your system appear on the other tabs. To display a selection of templates for creating résumés:
CLICK: *Other Documents* tab
Your screen should now appear similar, but not identical, to Figure 1.8.

Figure 1.8
Displaying document templates

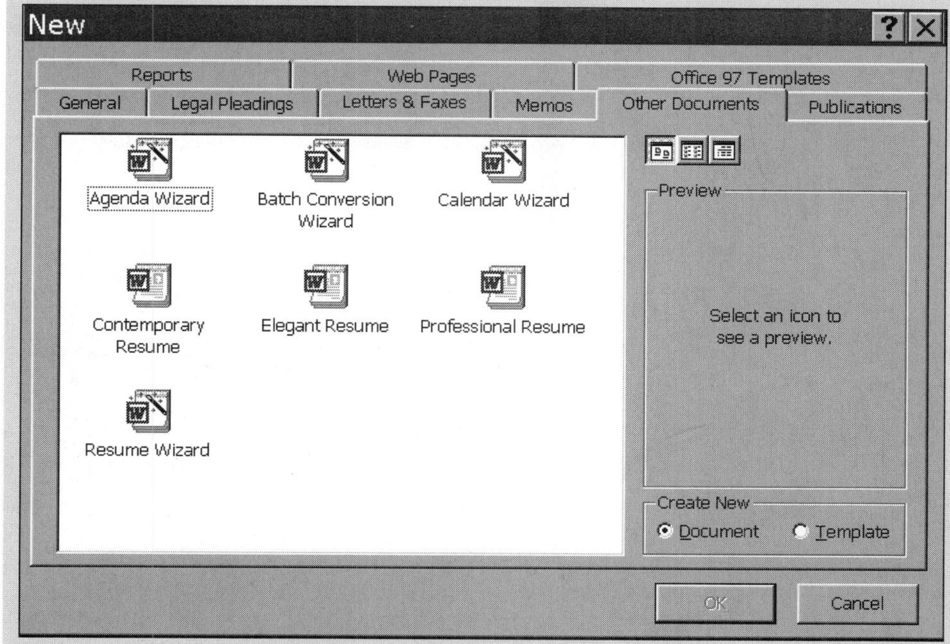

3 To create a new document based on the "Professional Resume" template:
DOUBLE-CLICK: Professional Resume template icon
(*Note*: If your lab administrator has not installed the document templates, skip to step 5.) You should now see the Professional Resume template, as shown in Figure 1.9.

Figure 1.9

New document based on the
Professional Resume
template

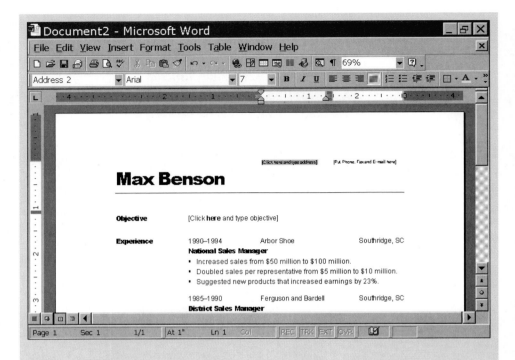

4 Rather than editing this document now, let's close the document and continue our discussion of file management.
CHOOSE: File, Close
CLICK: No command button, if asked to save the changes

5 To create a document from a wizard:
CHOOSE: File, New
CLICK: *Letters & Faxes* tab
DOUBLE-CLICK: Letter Wizard icon

6 The *Send one letter* option is selected in the opening dialog box.
To proceed:
CLICK: OK command button

7 The *Letter Format* tab is currently selected in the Letter Wizard dialog box. To proceed without making any changes:
CLICK: Next command button
The *Recipient Info* tab is now selected.

8 TYPE: *any name* in the *Recipient's name* text box
TYPE: *any address* in the Delivery address text box
CLICK: Next command button

9 To bypass the *Other Elements* tab without making any changes:
CLICK: Next command button

10 The *Sender Info* tab is now selected.
TYPE: *your name* in the *Sender's name* text box
TYPE: *your address* in the *Return address* text box

WORD

11 To display the letter:
CLICK: Finish command button
At this point, you would continue editing the body of the letter.

12 Let's close the current document:
CHOOSE: File, Close
CLICK: No command button, if asked to save the changes

13 To create a new document from scratch:
CLICK: New button (▢)

14 Let's enter some text into this document:
TYPE: Amazon.com
PRESS: ENTER twice
TYPE: On May 15, 1997, Amazon.com Inc. made
headlines when it went public and became valued
at $438 million. Mr. Jeff Bezos, the company's
founder, is now one of the richest Internet
entrepreneurs given that he and his family
control 52 percent of the company's common stock.

15 Keep this document open for use in the next lesson.

1.4.2 Saving and Closing

FEATURE
You can save the currently displayed document by updating an existing file on the disk, by creating a new file, or by selecting a new storage location. The File, Save command and the Save button (▣) on the toolbar allow you to overwrite a disk file with the latest version of a document. The File, Save As command enables you to save a document to a new filename or storage location. When you are finished working with a document, ensure that you close the file to free up valuable RAM.

METHOD
- To save a document:
  CLICK: Save button (▣), or
  CHOOSE: File, Save, or
  CHOOSE: File, Save As
- To close a document:
  CHOOSE: File, Close

PRACTICE
You will now practice saving and closing a document.

Setup: Ensure that you have completed the previous lesson. You will also need to identify a storage location for your personal document files. If you want to use a diskette, place it into the diskette drive now.

1 If you are working in a new document that has not yet been saved, Word displays the Save As dialog box (Figure 1.10), regardless of the method you choose to save the file. To demonstrate:
CLICK: Save button ()
(*Note*: The filenames and directories that appear in your Save As dialog box may differ from those shown in Figure 1.10.) The **Places bar,** located along the left border of the dialog box, provides convenient access to commonly used storage locations.

Figure 1.10

Save As dialog box

Lists the files that you have most recently worked with

Lists files in Word's default working folder

Lists common desktop shortcuts

Lists shortcuts to your favorite files

Lists files and folders stored on your Intranet or Internet Web server

2 In the next few steps, you practice navigating your computer's disks. To begin, let's view a list of the files that you've worked with recently:
CLICK: History button () in the Places bar

3 To browse the files in your "My Documents" folder:
CLICK: My Documents button ()

4 Let's browse the local hard disk:
CLICK: down arrow attached to the *Save in* drop-down list box
SELECT: Hard Disk C: ()
(*Note:* Your hard drive may have a different name.) The list area displays the folders and files stored in the root directory of your local hard disk.

5 To drill down into one of the folders:
DOUBLE-CLICK: Program Files folder
(*Note:* If the Program Files folder isn't located on your local hard disk, select an alternate folder to open.) This folder contains the program files for several applications.

6 Let's drill down one step further:
DOUBLE-CLICK: Microsoft Office folder
This folder contains the Microsoft Office program files.

7 To return to the previous display:
CLICK: Back button (⬅) in the dialog box
(*Note:* The button is renamed "Program Files," since that is where you will end up once the button is clicked.)

8 To return to the "My Documents" display:
CLICK: Back button (⬅) twice
(*Hint:* You could have also clicked the My Documents button in the Places bar.)

9 Now, using either the Places bar or the *Save In* drop-down list box:
SELECT: *a storage location for your personal files*
(*Note:* In this guide, we save files to the My Documents folder.)

10 Next, you need to give the document file a unique name. Let's replace the existing name with one that is more descriptive. Do the following:
DOUBLE-CLICK: the *document name* appearing in the *File name* text box to select it
TYPE: Amazon Success Story

11 To save your work:
CLICK: Save command button
Notice that the document's name now appears in the Title bar.

12 Move the insertion point to the bottom of the document.

13 To insert a blank line and then type your name:
PRESS: (ENTER)
TYPE: *your name*

14 To save the updated document:
CLICK: Save button (▣)
There are times when you may want to save an existing document under a different filename. For example, you may want to keep different versions of the same document on your disk. Or, you may want to use one document as a template for future documents that are similar in style and format. To do this, save the document under a different name using the File, Save As command.

15 Let's save a copy of the "Amazon Success Story" document to your personal storage location and name the copy "Backup Document."
CHOOSE: File, Save As
TYPE: `Backup Document` to replace the existing filename
CLICK: Save command button
The document was saved as "Backup Document" to your personal storage location.

16 To close the document:
CHOOSE: File, Close

1.4.3 Opening an Existing Document

FEATURE
You use the Open dialog box to search for and retrieve existing documents that are stored on your local hard disk, a floppy diskette, a network server, or on the Web. If you want to load Word and an existing document at the same time, you can use the Open Office Document command on the Start menu. Or, if you have recently used the document, you can try the Documents command on the Start menu, which lists the 15 most recently used files.

METHOD
- CLICK: Open button (▣), or
- CHOOSE: File, Open

PRACTICE
You will now open a document announcing an upcoming snowboard vacation.

Setup: Ensure that you have completed the previous lesson and that no documents are displaying. You will also need to know the storage location for the student data files.

1 To display the Open dialog box:
CLICK: Open button (📂)

2 Using the Places bar and the *Look in* drop-down list box, locate the folder containing the student data files. (*Note*: In this guide, we retrieve the student data files from a folder named "Student.")

3 To view additional information about each file:
CLICK: down arrow beside the Views button
CHOOSE: Details
Each document is presented on a single line with additional file information, such as its size, type, and date it was last modified, as shown in Figure 1.11.

Figure 1.11

Open dialog box

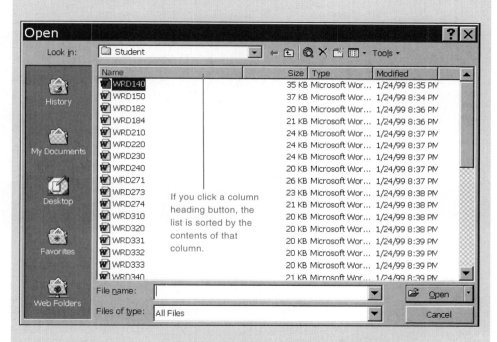

4 To alphabetically sort the list of files displayed in the Open dialog box:
CLICK: Name button in the column heading area

5 When you click the same column heading a second time, the order of the listing is reversed. To illustrate:
CLICK: Name button

6 To sort the list by size:
CLICK: Size button in the column heading area

7 To chronologically sort the file list by the date of modification:
CLICK: Modified button

8 To return to a multicolumn list format:
CLICK: down arrow beside the Views button
CHOOSE: List

9 Let's open one of the documents in the list area:
DOUBLE-CLICK: WRD140
The dialog box disappears and the document is loaded into the application window. (*Note:* The "WRD140" filename reflects that this document is used in module 1.4 of the Word learning guide.)

10 Close the document before proceeding.

In Addition
Storing and Retrieving Files on Web Servers

With the appropriate network connection, you can open and save Word documents on the Internet. In the Open or Save As dialog boxes, click the Web Folders button (🏠) in the Places bar or select an FTP Internet site from the *Look in* drop-down list. This feature allows you to share and update Word documents with users from around the world.

1.4 Self Check In the Open and Save As dialog boxes, how do the List and Details views differ?

1.5 Previewing and Printing

This module focuses on outputting your document creations. Most commonly, you will print a document for inclusion into a report or other such document.

1.5.1 Previewing a Document

FEATURE
Before sending a document to the printer, you can preview it using a full-page display that closely resembles the printed version. In this Preview display mode, you can move through the document pages, and zoom in and out on desired areas.

METHOD
CLICK: Print Preview button (), or
CHOOSE: File, Print Preview

PRACTICE
You will now open a relatively large document and then preview it on the screen.

Setup: Ensure that no documents are displaying in the application window.

1 Open the WRD150 data file.

2 Before continuing, let's save the file using a new filename:
CHOOSE: File, Save As
TYPE: For Printing

3 Using the *Save in* drop-down list box or the Places bar:
SELECT: *your storage location*
CLICK: Save command button

4 To preview how the document will appear when printed:
CLICK: Print Preview button ([Q])
Your screen should now appear similar to Figure 1.12.

Figure 1.12

Previewing a document

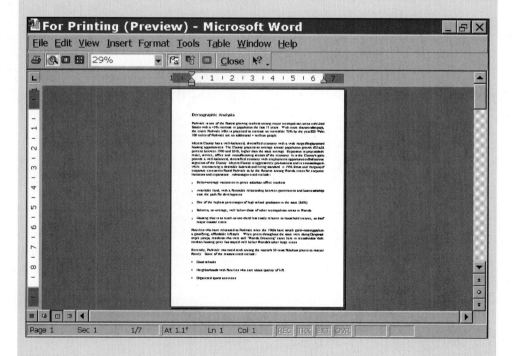

5 To display multiple pages at once:
CLICK: Multiple Pages button in the toolbar
CHOOSE: 2 x 2 from the drop-down menu
Small representations (called *thumbnails*) of the first four pages now appear in the Preview window.

6 To redisplay a single page:
CLICK: One Page button in the toolbar

7 To zoom in on the document, move the magnifying glass mouse pointer over the document area and then click once.

8 To zoom out on the display, click the mouse pointer once again.

9 CLICK: Close button on the Print Preview toolbar

1.5.2 Printing a Document

FEATURE
When you're satisfied with a document's appearance, it's time to send it to the printer.

METHOD
CLICK: Print button (🖨), or
CHOOSE: File, Print

PRACTICE
You will now send the "For Printing" document to the printer.

Setup: Ensure that you've completed the previous lesson and that the "For Printing" document is displaying in the application window.

1 Assuming that you are satisfied with the layout of the document, let's send it to the printer. Do the following:
CHOOSE: File, Print
The dialog box displayed in Figure 1.13 appears. You can use this dialog box to specify what to print and how many copies to produce. (*Note*: The quickest method for sending the current document to the printer is to click the Print button (🖨) on the Standard toolbar.)

Figure 1.13

Print dialog box

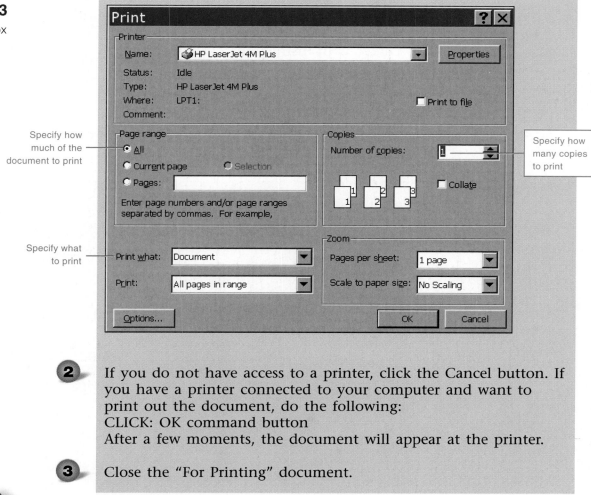

2   If you do not have access to a printer, click the Cancel button. If you have a printer connected to your computer and want to print out the document, do the following:
CLICK: OK command button
After a few moments, the document will appear at the printer.

3   Close the "For Printing" document.

1.5 Self Check   What is the procedure for printing your work?

1.6 Chapter Review

To create a basic document in Word, you simply begin typing after loading the application. Keep in mind that when the end of the current line is reached, the feature called *word wrap* automatically moves the insertion point to the beginning of the next line. You can easily remove characters from a document using (DELETE) and (BACKSPACE), and insert blank lines using (ENTER). Word provides several tools to help you create error-free documents including an undo feature and automatic spelling and grammar checking.

Besides creating documents, it is important to know how to execute common file management procedures including starting new documents, saving, and opening and closing documents. This chapter concluded with instructions on how to preview and print a document.

1.6.1 Command Summary

Many of the commands and procedures appearing in this chapter are summarized in the following table.

Skill Set	To Perform This Task . . .	Do the Following . . .
Using Word	Launch Microsoft Word	CLICK: Start button (Start) CHOOSE: Programs, Microsoft Word
	Exit Microsoft Word	CLICK: its Close button (☒), or CHOOSE: File, Exit
Working with Text	Correct spelling and grammar errors as you type	RIGHT-CLICK: any word or phrase with a wavy red or green underline CHOOSE: an option from the right-click menu
	Insert the date and time	CHOOSE: Insert, Date and Time
	Insert blank lines	PRESS: ENTER
	Toggle between Insert and Overtype modes	DOUBLE-CLICK: OVR in the Status bar
	Delete text to the right of the insertion point	PRESS: DELETE
	Delete text to the left of the insertion point	PRESS: BACKSPACE
	Undo or redo your last action	CLICK: Undo button (⌐), or CLICK: Redo button (⌐)
	Undo or redo the last several actions	CLICK: down arrow next to the Undo button (⌐), or CLICK: down arrow next to the Redo button (⌐)
	Repeat the last action	CHOOSE: Edit, Repeat

Continued

Skill Set	To Perform This Task . . .	Do the Following . . .
Working with Files	Save a document with the same name	CLICK: Save button (🖫)
	Save a document with a different name or to a different location	CHOOSE: File, Save As
	Close a document	CLICK: Close button (☒) of the document window, or CHOOSE: File, Close
	Begin a new blank document	CLICK: New button (🗅)
	Begin a new document from a wizard or template	CHOOSE: File, New
	Open a document	CLICK: Open button (🗁), or CHOOSE: File, Open
Working with Documents	Preview a document	CLICK: Print Preview button (🔍), or CHOOSE: File, Print Preview
	Print a document	CLICK: Print button (🖨), or CHOOSE: File, Print

1.6.2 Key Terms

This section specifies page references for the key terms identified in this chapter. For a complete list of definitions, refer to the Glossary provided immediately after the Appendix in this learning guide.

application window, *p. 5*

End of Document Marker, *p. 10*

insertion point, *p. 10*

Places bar, *p. 25*

Redo command, *p. 17*

Repeat command, *p. 17*

template, *p. 22*

Undo command, *p. 17*

wizard, *p. 22*

word processing, *p. 3*

word wrap, *p. 16*

1.7   Review Questions

1.7.1   Short Answer

1. What is the difference between a wizard and a template?
2. What is the difference between clicking the New button (□) and choosing File, New?
3. How can you leave a menu without making a command selection?
4. How do you delete the character to the right of the insertion point?
5. What happens if you press [ENTER] when the insertion point is in the middle of a paragraph?
6. How do you delete a single character to the left of the insertion point?
7. What can you do to remove a red wavy underline from a document?
8. What is *word wrap*?
9. Without leaving Word, how could you make a copy of the currently displayed document for storage onto a diskette?
10. How do you close a document without saving it?

1.7.2   True/False

1. __X__ You can include spaces in filenames.
2. _____ To permanently save your work, you must save it to a disk.
3. _____ Using the Open dialog box, you can sort a file listing.
4. __X__ To exit Word, you must choose File, Close.
5. __X__ The insertion point marks the location where text is inserted.
6. __X__ When you press the [HOME] key, the insertion point moves to the beginning of the line.
7. __X__ To move to the top of the document, press [CTRL] + [HOME].
8. __X__ To switch between Insert and Overtype modes, double-click the OVR indicator on the Status bar.
9. _____ To delete the character to the left of the insertion point, press [DELETE].
10. _____ To move the insertion point to the end of the document, press [END].

1.7.3 Multiple Choice

1. Which of the following procedures is the most like placing your work in a filing cabinet?
   a. opening
   b. closing
   c. saving
   d. printing

2. When you create a document, it exists:
   a. in the Clipboard
   b. in the Open dialog box
   c. on disk
   d. in the computer's RAM

3. To display an option in the Menu bar, you must _____ the option.
   a. click
   b. right-click
   c. Both a and b
   d. None of the above

4. Which of the following keys deletes the character to the right of the insertion point?
   a. [DELETE]
   b. [BACKSPACE]
   c. [HOME]
   d. [END]

5. Which of the following can you use to close the application window?
   a. [_]
   b. [□]
   c. [×]
   d. [▣]

6. To save a document using a different name, choose

   _____
   a. File, Save
   b. File, Save As
   c. File, Print
   d. All of the above

7. To leave the Menu bar without making a selection, click:
   a. any option in the pull-down menu
   b. Office Assistant character
   c. Title bar
   d. All of the above

8. The _____ feature enables you to type continuously
    without having to press (**ENTER**) at the end of each line.
    a. Office Assistant
    b. Undo
    c. AutoCorrect
    ✓d. word wrap

9. To correct a spelling error that Word has marked with a red
    wavy underline, you can _____ the word and then
    choose the correct spelling from the displayed menu.
    a. click
    b. double-click
    ✓c. right-click
    d. None of the above

10. Which of the following starts a new document?
    a. CHOOSE: File, Open
    ✗b. CLICK: Open button (⌸)
    c. CLICK: Views button (⌸▾)
    ✓d. CLICK: New button (⌸)

1.8 Hands-On Projects

● ## 1.8.1 Sandra Baker: Thank You Letter

This exercise practices creating, editing, and saving the document pictured in Figure 1.14.

Figure 1.14

"Baker Thanks" document

> April 5, 1999
>
>
> Ms. Carolyn Spencer
> Taylor Supplies, Inc.
> 12 Ocean Avenue
> Seattle, WA 93456
>
>
> Dear Ms. Spencer:
>
> Thank you for taking the time last week to talk with me about the receptionist position at your Tacoma branch.
>
> Our interview confirmed my impression that I would very much enjoy working at Taylor Supplies. It was delightful to meet such a friendly and cooperative group of people. I'd like to be a part of that!
>
> I look forward to hearing from you when you have made a final decision. Once again, thank you for your time and interest.
>
>
> Sincerely,
>
>
> Sandra Baker

1. Load Microsoft Word.
2. To insert the date at the top of the blank document:
   CHOOSE: Insert, Date and Time
   SELECT: the appropriate format in the *Available formats* list box
   CLICK: OK command button
3. To position the insertion point before typing the name and address information:
   PRESS: `ENTER` three times
4. TYPE: Ms. Carolyn Spencer
   PRESS: `ENTER`
   TYPE: Taylor Supplies, Inc.
   PRESS: `ENTER`
   TYPE: 12 Ocean Avenue
   PRESS: `ENTER`
   TYPE: Seattle, WA 93456
5. To position the insertion point before typing the salutation:
   PRESS: `ENTER` three times
   TYPE: Dear Ms. Spencer:
   PRESS: `ENTER` twice
6. TYPE: Thank you for taking the time last week to talk with me about the receptionist position at your Tacoma branch.
   PRESS: `ENTER` twice
7. TYPE: *the next paragraph beginning with "Our interview ..."*
   PRESS: `ENTER` twice

8. TYPE: *the next paragraph beginning with "I look forward..."*
   PRESS: ENTER three times
9. To complete the letter:
   TYPE: `Sincerely,`
   PRESS: ENTER three times
   TYPE: `Sandra Baker`
10. Save the letter as "Baker Thanks" to your personal storage location.
11. Preview and print the letter.
12. Close the document.

1.8.2 Clearwater Systems Inc: Account Letter

In this exercise, you open an existing document and then edit and save the document.

1. Open the WRD182 data file.
2. Save the document as "Clearwater Account" to your personal storage location.
3. Let's change the payment amount in the second paragraph from $2,345.32 to $50. To begin, position the insertion point to the left of dollar sign ($).
4. To delete the current number and then type in the new number:
   PRESS: DELETE nine times
   TYPE: `$50`
5. Let's add the following paragraph to the end of the last paragraph. Before typing, position the insertion point at the end of the last paragraph (to the right of the word "agreement.").
6. TYPE: `Our products are under a full warranty for a period of one year from the date of installation. Problems caused by staff members adjusting the internal settings are not covered by this warranty and will be billed in the future at our regular rates.`
7. Preview and print the document.
8. Save and then close the document.

1.8.3 Norstorm Systems: Fax

You will now practice creating a fax using the "Contemporary Fax" template.

1. To launch the template:
   CHOOSE: File, New
   CLICK: *Letters & Faxes* tab
   DOUBLE-CLICK: Contemporary Fax
2. Click in the upper-right corner of the document where it says "Click here and type address."

3. Type the following name and address:
   ```
   Norstorm Systems Ltd.
   9090 Seascape Blvd.
   Fort Worth, TX 98720
   ```
4. Complete the fax so that it includes the details shown below:

   To: James Wiggins
   From: Janet Burbury
   Fax: 314-893-5446
   Re: Conference Call

   The conference call on the ACEC training program setup is scheduled for April 3rd at 9am Pacific Standard Time and is expected to last 2 hours. Please notify Regional Headquarters whether your office will participate in the call. Also, please provide me with the name of your representative.

   Standard conference protocol will be in effect.

5. Save the document as "Norstorm Fax" to your personal storage location.
6. Print and then close the document.

1.8.4 Aardvark Enterprises: Memo

You will now open a memo that was created previously and then edit and save the document.

1. Open the WRD184 data file.
2. Save the document as "Aardvark Memo" to your personal storage location.
3. Change the addressee from "Administrators" to "District Coordinators."
4. Add the following paragraph to the end of the memo before the "Thank you:"
   ```
   If you know at this point that your
   schedule allows for partial attendance
   (or no attendance) at a show because of
   prior commitments, please let me know.
   ```
5. Save the revised memo.

1.8.5 On Your Own: Letter to a Friend

To practice creating and editing a new document, use Word to write a letter to a friend. This document should begin with the current date and include at least three paragraphs. In the first paragraph, share your excitement about the courses you're taking this semester. In the second paragraph, describe some of the extra-curricular activities you're currently involved in. Insert a few closing remarks in the final paragraph. The letter should end with your name in the closing. Review the document for spelling errors before saving it as "My Letter" to your personal storage location.

1.8.6 On Your Own: Book Sale Notice

Use your knowledge of Word to create, print, and save a notice to advertise the sale of several new and used textbooks, similar to the sample in Figure 1.15.

Figure 1.15

"Book Sale Notice" document

```
*** TEXT BOOKS ARE FOR SALE ***

New and nearly new 1998 Science and Math text books for
Sale.

New Books:
Introduction to Biology–J. S. Stillwell
Invertebrate Biology–Maxwell B. Baker
Cell Biology–Susan B. Fredericks
Organic Chemistry–J. Taylor
Fundamentals of Chemical Equation–Clyde G. Matthews
Advanced Calculus–Janice Underbaer

Used Books:
Biology Laboratory Manual–David Eaton
Chemistry, An Introduction–Eldon G. Appley
Experiments in Physics–J. G. Nelson & R. Sampson
Differential Equations–Wilson Smith

For more information, contact your name
McDougal Residence #1105
Phone: 314-8923 (evenings)
Message: 314-2883 (before 6pm)
```

Your notice should include your list of books, your name, and your contact information. Save the completed document as "Book Sale Notice" to your personal storage location.

1.9   Case Problems: 1-on-1 Tutorial Services

Now that Dean has completed the first chapter of this learning guide, he decides that he can start using Word to organize his business. He realizes that he still has minimal skills, but decides to begin preparing the documents that he needs. He'll format them later, once he masters some basic formatting skills.

In the following case problems, assume the role of Dean and perform the same steps that he identifies. You may want to re-read the chapter opening before proceeding.

1.   Dean has decided to prepare notices to be posted on bulletin boards around the college. He found an old copy of the notice that he used last year (shown below), and decides that he will use Word to create the same notice for this term. He then saves his work as "DS Notice."

   1-on-1 Tutoring Services

   Personal tutoring, lab prep, and review services available in the following subjects:

   Computer Science 101, 102, and 201
   Biology 101, 104
   Chemistry 102, 103, 201, and 204
   Physics 101

   Reasonable rates (both individuals and groups)

   For more information, call:
   Dean Shearwater
   Phone: 319-4234
   Email: dshearwater@sitsom.net

2. After completing the notice for the college bulletin boards, Dean shows the notice to his friend Glen for feedback. Glen reminds him that before a notice can be posted in the Student Union building, it must be submitted to the Student Union office for review. Dean decides to use a Word template to create a memo to accompany the notice. He uses the "Contemporary Memo" template and creates a memo that includes the information shown below. After saving the memo as "DS Memo," he sends a copy to the printer.

    To: SouthWestern Student Union Association
    From: Dean Shearwater
    Re: Tutoring Advertisement

    Attached is a copy of the posting that will be placed on all bulletin boards on September 10th. I request that a copy of this posting be placed on the Student Union bulletin boards.

3. Dean decides that he should also place an advertisement in the *SouthWestern Banner*, the student newspaper. After phoning to determine the rates and get a price for his ad, he arranges to fax a copy by tomorrow morning. Dean opens the original notice file saved earlier as "DS Notice" and edits the document to resemble the following:

    Personal tutoring, lab prep, and review services available.
    Computer Science 101, 102, 201
    Biology 101, 104
    Chemistry 102, 103, 201, 204
    Physics 101
    Reasonable rates
    For info call Dean Shearwater 319-4234
    Email: dshearwater@sitsom.net

    He then saves the document again and assigns the new name of "DS Notice (Short)." Finally, he prints a copy of the revised document.

4. Dean arranges to fax the advertisement to the newspaper in order to meet tomorrow morning's deadline. He drafts an outline of the fax on his way home.

1-on-1 Tutorial Services
302-1011 College Circle,
Dayton, Ohio 53345

To: Melody Baker
From: Dean Shearwater
Fax: 319-1234
Re: Advertisement
Pages: 1

Attached is a copy of the advertisement to be posted in the September 12th edition of the Banner and repeated again in the September 26th edition. I have already given you my charge card information and agree to be billed immediately in the amount of $13.57.

He creates a new fax document based on the "Contemporary Fax" template. He particularly likes the box that allows him to include his business information in the top-right corner. Once completed, he checks the "Urgent" box, saves his document as "DS Fax," and prints the document.

Notes

MICROSOFT WORD 2000
Changing the Look of Text

CHAPTER
TWO

Chapter Outline

Learning Objectives

After reading this chapter, you will be able to:

- Move the insertion point through a document

- Select blocks of text

- Enhance the appearance of text using character-formatting commands

- Indent and align paragraphs, create bulleted and numbered lists, vary line spacing, and set tabs

Case Study

Ards County Humane Society

The Ards County Humane Society in Willow Tree, Kansas, has recently purchased a computer system and software for their office. Janice French, a volunteer with the society, has offered to use her recently acquired word processing skills to convert many of the current type-written letters and printed forms to Microsoft Word documents.

Janice has already used Word to prepare several rather plain documents for the center. She is looking forward to learning how to use Word's formatting features to add impact to her work and to make more efficient use of her time.

In this chapter, you and Janice learn how to move through a document, select text, and change the look of text using character and paragraph formatting commands.

2.1 Moving Through a Document

Before inserting or changing text in a document, you must position the insertion point using the mouse or keyboard. Like many procedures in Word, the mouse provides the easiest method for moving through a document. To position the insertion point, you scroll the document window until the desired text appears and then click the I-beam mouse pointer in the text. Contrary to what you might think, scrolling the document window does not automatically move the insertion point. If you forget to click the mouse and start typing or press an arrow key, Word takes you back to the original location of the insertion point before you started scrolling.

Common methods for scrolling the document window are described below:

To scroll the window . . .	*Do this . . .*
One line at a time	Click the up (▲) and down (▼) arrowheads on the vertical scroll bar.
One screen at a time	Click the vertical scroll bar itself, above and below the scroll box (▢).
One page at a time	Click on these scroll bar symbols to move to the previous page (▣) or to the next page (▣) in a document.
Pages at a time	Drag the scroll box (▢) along the vertical scroll bar.

In addition to the above methods, you can opt to browse through a specific type of object using the Select Browse Object button (⊙) on the vertical scroll bar. When used in conjunction with the Next Page (▼) and Previous Page (▲) buttons you can browse through specific types of objects such as endnotes, footnotes, headings, sections, graphics, or tables.

2.1.1 Positioning the Insertion Point

FEATURE
It is important to position the insertion point before inserting and changing text. Several methods exist for positioning the insertion point using the mouse or keyboard.

METHOD
Some common methods for positioning the insertion point using the keyboard include:

- ⬆ or ⬇ to move up or down one line
- ⬅or ➡ to move to the previous or next character
- END to move to the end of the current line
- HOME to move to the beginning of the current line
- PgUp or PgDn to move up or down one screen
- CTRL+HOME to move to the beginning of the document
- CTRL+END to move to the end of the document

PRACTICE
You will now open a two-page document that discusses how computers are used in the field of manufacturing. You will then practice positioning the insertion point and using the Go To command.

Setup: Ensure that you've loaded Word and that you've disabled the adaptive menus feature as described in Chapter 1. Also, ensure that the Standard and Formatting toolbars are positioned on separate rows.

1 Open the WRD210 data file. (*Hint:* Choose File, Open and then locate the file using the *Look in* drop-down list or the Places bar.)

2 Save the file as "Manufacturing" to your personal storage location. (*Hint:* Choose File, Save As.) Your screen should now appear similar to Figure 2.1. Note that the insertion point is positioned at the beginning of the document.

Figure 2.1

"Manufacturing" document

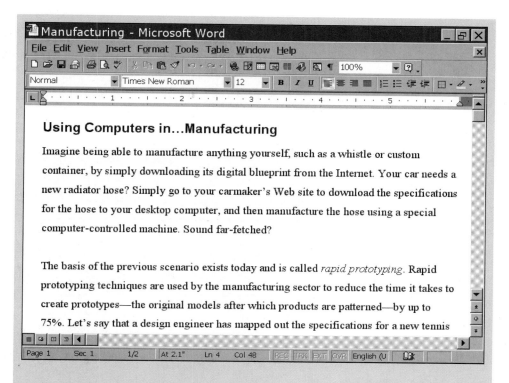

3 To move down through the document one screen at a time:
CLICK: below the scroll box on the vertical scroll bar repeatedly

4 To move to the top of the document:
DRAG: the scroll box to the top of the vertical scroll bar
Note that as you drag the scroll box along the scroll bar, Word
displays the current page number.

5 To move the insertion point directly to the bottom of the document using the keyboard:
PRESS: CTRL + END

6 To move back to the top of the document using the keyboard:
PRESS: CTRL + HOME

7 To move to the end of the current line:
PRESS: END

8 To move to the beginning of the current line:
PRESS: HOME

9 To move to the top of the second page in the document:
CLICK: Next Page button (⊡) on the vertical scroll bar
The insertion point automatically moves to the first line of
page 2.

10 To practice using the Go To dialog box:
CHOOSE: Edit, Go To
Other methods for displaying the Go To dialog box include double-clicking the page area—"Page 2"—in the Status bar or pressing **F5** . Your screen should now appear similar to Figure 2.2.

Figure 2.2

The Go to dialog box

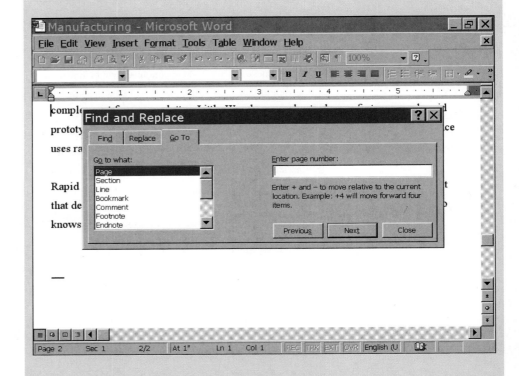

11 TYPE: **P1L8**
CLICK: Go To command button
The "P" tells Word that the following number is a page number, and the "L" tells Word that the next number is a line number. The letters can be typed in either uppercase or lowercase characters. In this step, the insertion point is moved to line 8 on page 1.

12 CLICK: Close command button

13 To move to the top of the document:
PRESS: **CTRL** + **HOME**

14 Close the "Manufacturing" document.

2.1 Self Check   How do you move directly to the end of a document using the keyboard?

2.2 Selecting Text

Once text has been typed into a document, you make formatting enhancements by selecting the text and then issuing the appropriate command. Word provides an invisible column in the extreme left margin of the document window called the **Selection bar.** When the mouse is moved into this area, the pointer changes from an I-beam to a right-pointing diagonal arrow ( ). The Selection bar provides shortcut methods for using the mouse to select text, as summarized in Table 2.1 along with other selection methods.

Table 2.1

Selecting text
using the mouse

To select this...	Do this...
Single Letter	Position the I-beam pointer to the left of the letter you want to select. Press down and hold the left mouse button as you drag the mouse pointer to the right.
Single Word	Position the I-beam pointer on the word and double-click the left mouse button.
Single Sentence	Hold down CTRL and click once with the I-beam pointer positioned on any word in the sentence.
Block of Text	Move the insertion point to the beginning of the block of text and then position the I-beam pointer at the end of the block. Hold down SHIFT and click once.
Single Line	Move the mouse pointer into the Selection bar, beside the line to be selected. Wait until the pointer changes to a right-pointing arrow and then click once.
Single Paragraph	Move the mouse pointer into the Selection bar, beside the paragraph to be selected. Wait until the pointer changes to a right-pointing arrow and then double-click.
Entire Document	Move the mouse pointer into the Selection bar. Wait until the pointer changes to a right-pointing arrow and then hold down CTRL and click once.

2.2.1 Selecting Text Using the Mouse

FEATURE
A selection of text may include letters, words, lines, paragraphs, or even the entire document. Many Word procedures require that you begin by making a text selection.

METHOD
The methods for selecting text are summarized in Table 2.1. To de-select text, click once in the text area.

PRACTICE
You will now open an existing two-page document and practice selecting text and deleting a block of text.

Setup: Ensure that you've loaded Word and that the application window is maximized.

1 Open the WRD220 data file.

2 Save the file as "Technology" to your personal storage location.

3 To select the word "Computers" in the title, first position the I-beam mouse pointer on the word.

4 DOUBLE-CLICK: Computers
The word and its trailing space should be highlighted in reverse video. Your screen should now appear similar to Figure 2.3. (*Note:* Unless a font color has been applied to text, selected text always appears in reverse video, with white text on a black background.)

Figure 2.3

The word "Computers" is selected

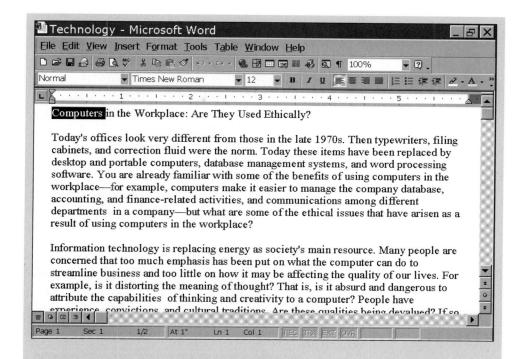

5 To select the letters "Work" in the word "Workplace," you must first position the I-beam pointer to the left of the "W" in "Workplace."

6 PRESS: left mouse button and hold it down
DRAG: I-beam to the right until "Work" is highlighted

7 To select the first sentence in the first paragraph below the title, first position the I-beam pointer on the word "offices." (*Note:* The mouse pointer can be placed over any word in the sentence.)

8 PRESS: CTRL and hold it down
CLICK: left mouse button once
The first sentence, including the period and spaces, is highlighted.

9 To select only the third line in the first paragraph, position the mouse pointer to the left of the line in the Selection bar. The mouse pointer should change from an I-beam to a right-pointing diagonal arrow.

10 CLICK: the Selection bar beside the third line

11 To select the entire first paragraph:
DOUBLE-CLICK: the Selection bar beside the first paragraph
(*Note*: You can also position the I-beam pointer on any word in the paragraph and triple-click the left mouse button to select the entire paragraph.)

12 To delete the selected paragraph:
PRESS: DELETE
The entire paragraph was removed from the document.

13 To undo the previous action:
CLICK: Undo button (⟲)

14 To select the entire document:
PRESS: CTRL and hold it down
CLICK: once anywhere in the Selection bar
(*Note*: You can also position the mouse pointer in the Selection bar and triple-click the left mouse button to select the entire document.) Your screen should now appear similar to Figure 2.4.

Figure 2.4

Selecting the entire document

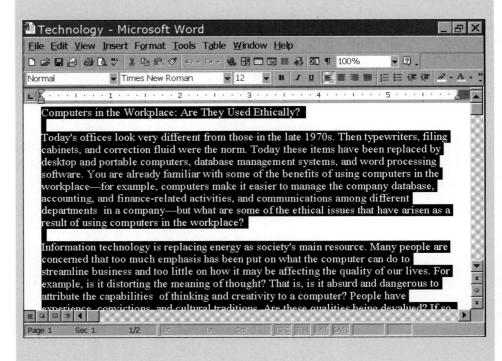

15 To remove highlighting from the text:
CLICK: once anywhere in the text area

16 To return the insertion point to the top of the document:
PRESS: CTRL + HOME

17 Close the document.

2.2 Self Check   What is the procedure for selecting the entire document?

2.3 Enhancing Text

In word processing, enhancing the appearance of text is called *character formatting* and involves selecting typefaces, font sizes, and attributes for text. Word's character formatting commands are accessed through the Font dialog box (Figure 2.5), the Formatting toolbar, or by using shortcut keyboard combinations. Since many of the features are accessible from the Formatting toolbar and shortcut keys, you may never need to use the Format, Font menu command except to select a special character attribute in the dialog box. Table 2.2 summarizes some common mouse and keyboard methods for choosing character formatting commands.

Figure 2.5

Font dialog box

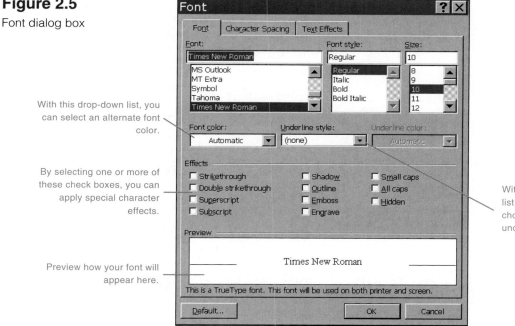

With this drop-down list, you can select an alternate font color.

By selecting one or more of these check boxes, you can apply special character effects.

Preview how your font will appear here.

With this drop-down list, you can choose from over 15 underline styles.

Table 2.2

Character formatting summary

Toolbar Button	Keyboard Shortcut	Description
B	CTRL + b	Makes the selected text **bold**
I	CTRL + i	*Italicizes* the selected text
U	CTRL + u	Applies a <u>single underline</u>
A ·		Changes the font color
Times New Roman	CTRL + SHIFT + f	Specifies a font or typeface
10	CTRL + SHIFT + p	Specifies a point size for the font
	CTRL + [	Decreases the point size by 1 point
	CTRL +]	Increases the point size by 1 point
	CTRL + SHIFT + a	CAPITALIZES the selection
	SHIFT + F3	Changes the case of the selection
	CTRL + Space Bar	Removes all character formatting

2.3.1 Bolding, Italicizing, and Underlining

FEATURE
The bold, italic, and underline attributes help to emphasize important text.

METHOD
- To make selected text bold, click the Bold button (B) or press CTRL + b
- To italicize selected text, click the Italic button (I) or press CTRL + i
- To underline selected text, click the Underline button (U) or press CTRL + u

PRACTICE
You will now open an existing document and practice applying boldface, italic, and underlines.

Setup: No documents should be open in the application window.

1 Open the WRD230 student file. (*Note:* This file is similar to the WRD220 student file.)

2 Save the file as "Computers" to your personal storage location.

3 To insert a new line between the title and the first paragraph:
PRESS: (END)
PRESS: (ENTER)

4 To add an italicized subtitle for this document:
CLICK: Italic button (I) on the Formatting toolbar
TYPE: The Information Age and the Age of Humanity

5 To stop typing in italic:
CLICK: Italic button (I)

6 To select this subtitle, position the mouse pointer in the Selection bar to the left of the line and click the left mouse button once.

7 Make the subtitle bold and underlined using the buttons on the Formatting toolbar:
CLICK: Bold button (B)
CLICK: Underline button (U)

8 To deselect the text to better see the changes you've made:
CLICK: anywhere in the text area

9 Make the following formatting changes in the first paragraph using either the Formatting toolbar buttons or the keyboard shortcuts.

Text to be formatted	*Formatting to apply*
computers	italic and bold
database management systems	italic
word processing software	italic

Your screen should now appear similar to Figure 2.6.

Figure 2.6

Bolding, italicizing, and underlining text

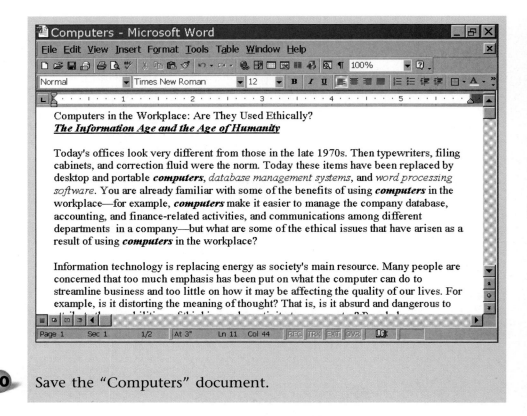

10 Save the "Computers" document.

2.3.2 Changing Fonts, Font Sizes, and Colors

FEATURE

A **font** is defined as all the symbols and characters of a particular style of print. Font size is measured in *points*. By selecting fonts and font sizes, you provide your document with the right tone for your message. Also, by selecting colors other than black for typed text, you visually enhance your documents.

METHOD
- To select a typeface:
  CLICK: Font drop-down arrow ( )
  SELECT: the desired font
- To change the font size:
  CLICK: Font Size drop-down arrow ( )
  SELECT: the desired point size
- To change the font color:
  CLICK: Font Color button ( ) to select the most recently used color
  CLICK: Font Color drop-down arrow ( ) to display a palette of colors that you can choose from

PRACTICE

You will now change some of the fonts, point sizes, and font colors in the "Computers" document.

Setup: Ensure that you've completed the previous lesson and that the "Computers" document is displaying.

1 SELECT: the main title on the first line

2 To display a list of the available fonts:
CLICK: Font drop-down arrow (Times New Roman ▾)
One example of the Font drop-down list appears below. The list on your computer may be different.

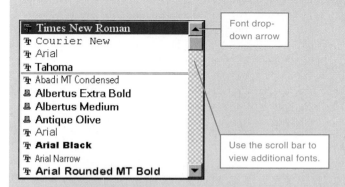

Font drop-down arrow

Use the scroll bar to view additional fonts.

3 Scroll through the font choices by clicking the up and down arrows on the drop-down list's scroll bar or by dragging the scroll box.

4 SELECT: Arial (or a font that is available on your computer)
(*Hint:* You select a font from the drop-down list by clicking on it.)

5 To display the range of available font sizes:
CLICK: down arrow beside the Font Size drop-down list (10 ▾)

6 SELECT: 16-point font size
CLICK: Bold button (**B**)
CLICK: in the document to deselect the text
The title and formatted subtitle should appear similar to the following:

The main title is now formatted with a 16-point Arial font.

Computers in the Workplace: Are They Used Ethically?
The Information Age and the Age of Humanity

7 Let's apply a different font color to the title and subtitle.
SELECT: the title and subtitle
CLICK: Font Color drop-down arrow (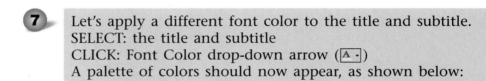)
A palette of colors should now appear, as shown below:

8 CLICK: Blue in the color palette
CLICK: in the document to deselect the text
Your screen should now appear similar to Figure 2.7. The Font Color button now displays blue because this was the most recently applied color.

Figure 2.7

Changing font color

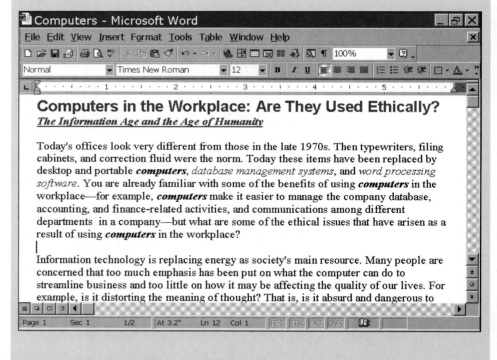

9 Save and then close the document.

2.3 Self Check   How would you boldface and underline existing text?

2.4 Formatting Paragraphs

Paragraph formatting involves changing alignment, line spacing, indentation, and tab settings for a paragraph. To apply paragraph formatting commands to a paragraph, position the insertion point anywhere in the paragraph—you do not need to select any text—and then issue the desired command.

Paragraph formatting commands are accessed through the Paragraph dialog box, from the Formatting toolbar, using the mouse, and using keyboard shortcut combinations. The Paragraph dialog box (Figure 2.8) is useful for entering specific measurements and accessing the full gamut of paragraph formatting options.

Figure 2.8

Paragraph dialog box

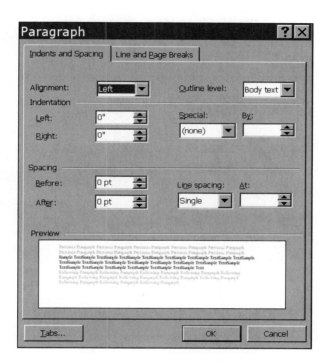

2.4.1 Displaying Paragraph Marks

FEATURE

Word stores paragraph formatting information in the (¶), which is inserted at the end of a paragraph when you press ENTER . By default, paragraph marks and other nonprinting characters are hidden from view. By revealing these codes, you can more thoroughly check a document for errors.

METHOD
To display paragraph marks and all other nonprinting characters:
CLICK: Show/Hide button (¶) on the Formatting toolbar

PRACTICE
You will now open a document that discusses how to use the Web to sell products and services. You will then practice displaying paragraph marks and other nonprinting characters, and a Help bubble showing formatting characteristics.

Setup: Ensure that no documents are displaying in the application window.

1 Open the WRD240 data file.

2 Save the document as "Commerce" to your personal storage location.

3 If not already displayed, show the document's nonprinting characters by doing the following:
CLICK: Show/Hide button (¶)
Your screen should now appear similar to Figure 2.9.

Figure 2.9
Displaying paragraph marks and other nonprinting characters

Characters like this won't appear in your printed document

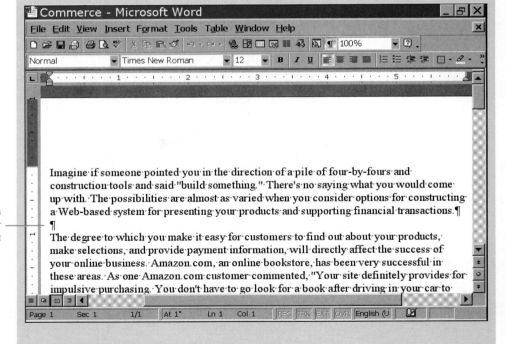

4 Before proceeding, let's hide the symbols:
CLICK: Show/Hide button (¶)

WORD

5 Another useful procedure for reviewing a document's formatting involves choosing Help, What's This? from the Menu bar. To illustrate:
CHOOSE: Help, What's This?

6 Position the question mark mouse pointer over any letter in the second paragraph:
CLICK: left mouse button once
Your screen should now appear similar to Figure 2.10.

Figure 2.10

Help bubble for showing formatting charcteristics

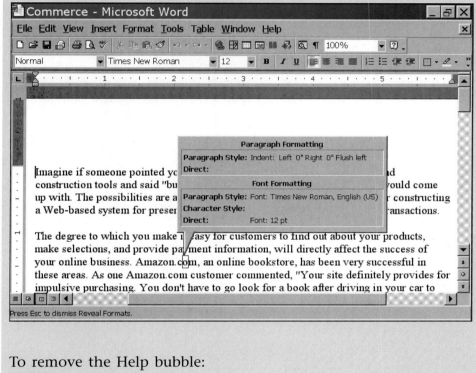

7 To remove the Help bubble:
PRESS: ESC

2.4.2 Changing Paragraph Alignment

FEATURE
Justification refers to how text aligns within the margins. *Left justification* aligns text on the left but leaves jagged right edges as a typewriter does. New Word documents are left-justified by default. *Center justification* centers the line or paragraph between the left and right margins. *Right justification* positions text flush against the right margin. *Full justification* provides even text columns at the left and right by automatically spacing words on the line.

METHOD
- To apply left justification:
  CLICK: Align Left button (▤), or press CTRL+l
- To apply center justification:
  CLICK: Center button (▤), or press CTRL+e
- To align text against the right margin:
  CLICK: Align Right button (▤), or press CTRL+r
- To justify text between the margins:
  CLICK: Justify button (▤), or press CTRL+j

PRACTICE
You will now practice changing justification.

Setup: Ensure that you've completed the previous lesson and that the "Commerce" document is displaying.

1 Position the insertion point anywhere in the first paragraph.

2 CLICK: Center button (▤)
The paragraph is immediately centered between the left and right margins.

3 CLICK: Align Right button (▤)
The paragraph is positioned flush against the right margin.

4 CLICK: Justify button (▤)
The paragraph is positioned flush against both the left and right margins.

5 To move the paragraph back to its original position:
CLICK: Align Left button (▤)

2.4.3 Indenting Paragraphs

FEATURE
Indenting a paragraph means to move a body of text in from the normal page margins. When you indent a paragraph, you temporarily change the text's positioning relative to the left and right margins. You can indent a paragraph on the left side only, right side only, or on both sides.

METHOD

- To increase or decrease the left indent of an entire paragraph:
  CLICK: Increase Indent button (⊞), or
  CLICK: Decrease Indent button (⊞)
- To customize the left and right indents:
  DRAG: the indent markers on the Ruler

PRACTICE

You will now practice indenting text.

Setup: Ensure that you completed the previous lessons in this module and that the "Commerce" document is displaying.

1 To begin, position the insertion point in the second paragraph.

2 To add a left indent to this paragraph:
CLICK: Increase Indent button (⊞)
The paragraph moves to the right 0.5 inches to the next tab stop. You can also customize your indents by dragging the indent markers on the Ruler. We label these markers below and describe them in Table 2.3.

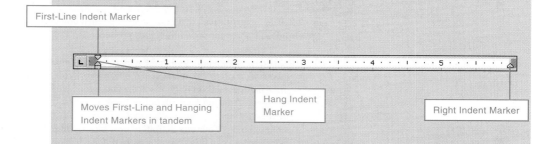

Table 2.3

Indent markers

Type	Description
First-Line Indent Marker	This indent marker moves only the first line of a paragraph in from the left margin. This paragraph format is often used in documents to avoid having to press the ⟨TAB⟩ key at the start of each new paragraph.
Hanging Indent Marker	This indent marker moves all but the first line of a paragraph in from the left margin, leaving the first-line indent marker in its current position.

Continued

Type	Description
Left Indent Marker	The Left Indent Marker moves the First-Line and Hanging Indent Markers in tandem.
Right Indent Marker	The Right Indent Marker moves the body of the entire paragraph in from the right margin. Left and right indents are often used together to set quotations apart from normal body text in a document.

3   To indent the paragraph 1 inch from the right margin:
DRAG: right indent marker to the left by 1 inch (to 5 inches on the Ruler)
Your screen should now appear similar to Figure 2.11.

Figure 2.11

Indenting paragraphs

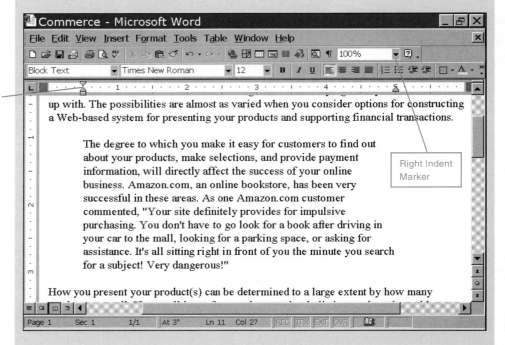

First-Line and Hanging Indent Markers

Right Indent Marker

4   To remove the left indent:
CLICK: Decrease Indent button ([image])
Notice that this button has no effect on the right indent marker.

5   To remove the right indent:
DRAG: right indent marker back to the right margin (at 6 inches on the Ruler)

6   Move the insertion point to anywhere in the last paragraph of the "Commerce" document.

WORD

7 To indent the last paragraph by 1 inch:
CLICK: Increase Indent button (⬚) twice

8 A handy keystroke to remember is CTRL+q; it removes all paragraph formatting characteristics from the current paragraph.
To demonstrate:
PRESS: CTRL+q

9 Move to the end of the document and insert a new blank line.

10 In this next step, you insert a hanging indent where the first line of the paragraph lines up with the left margin and the remainder of the paragraph is indented. To begin:
DRAG: Hanging Indent Marker to 1 inch on the Ruler
(*Caution:* Make sure that the tip of your mouse pointer points to the triangle and not to the bottom rectangle when dragging.) If performed correctly, the Ruler should now appear similar to the following:

11 TYPE: Summary
PRESS: TAB

12 TYPE: For your online business to be successful, your Web site must be easy to use for first-time visitors.
Your screen should now appear similar to Figure 2.12.

Figure 2.12

Creating a hanging indent in the "Commerce" document

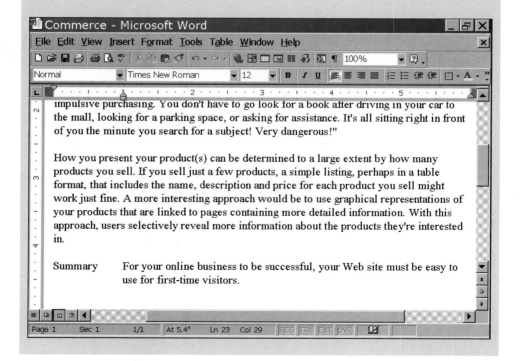

13 Save the "Commerce" document.

14 In preparation for the next lesson:
CLICK: New button (⬜) to start a new document

2.4.4 Creating Bulleted and Numbered Lists

FEATURE
Word provides a utility for automatically creating lists with lead-ing **bullets** or numbers. Although round circles are the standard shape for bullets, you can select shapes from a variety of symbols. Numbered lists can use numbers, numerals, or letters.

METHOD
- To create a bulleted list:
  CLICK Bullets button (▤)
- To create a numbered list:
  CLICK Numbering button (▤)
- To modify the bullet symbols or numbering scheme:
  CHOOSE: Format, Bullets and Numbering

PRACTICE
You will now begin a new document and then create bulleted and numbered lists.

Setup: Ensure that you completed the previous lessons and that a blank document is displaying.

1 TYPE: To Do List
PRESS: ENTER twice

2 To create a bulleted list:
CLICK: Bullets button (▤)
A bullet appears and the indent markers are moved on the Ruler.

3 Enter the following text, pressing ENTER at the end of each line:
Pick up dry cleaning
Meet Jesse at the gym
Go grocery shopping
Mail letter to Mom

4 You will notice that Word automatically starts each new line with a bullet when you press (ENTER). To turn off the bullets, ensure that your insertion point is on the line below "Mail letter to Mom" and then:
PRESS: (ENTER)
Because the previous line was empty, Word automatically turned off bullet formatting. You could also have clicked the Bullets button (📋) to turn off bullet formatting. The document should now appear similar to the following:

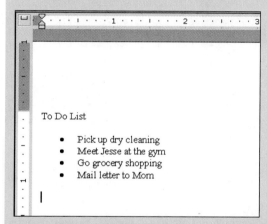

5 In this next example, you create a numbered list after you've already entered information into your document. To begin:
TYPE: Travel Itinerary
PRESS: (ENTER) twice

6 Enter the following lines of text, as before:
Aug 12: Flight 455 to Sydney.
Aug 28: Flight 87 to Auckland.
Aug 29: Flight A101 to Christchurch.
Sep 11: Flight 110 to Vancouver.

7 Using the mouse pointer in the Selection bar, select the text that you entered in step 6.

8 CLICK: Numbering button (📋)
The selected text is automatically numbered and indented.

9 To use letters rather than numbers for the list:
CHOOSE: Format, Bullets and Numbering
Your screen should now appear similar to Figure 2.13.

Figure 2.13

Bullets and Numbering
dialog box: *Numbered* tab

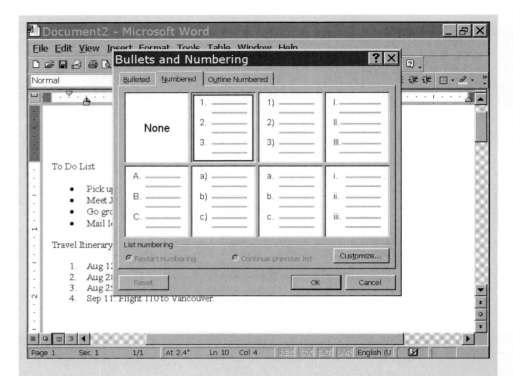

10 Ensure that the *Numbered* tab is selected in the dialog box.

11 SELECT: the option that shows a), b), and c)

12 CLICK: OK command button
CLICK: anywhere in the document to remove the highlighting
Your document should now appear similar to Figure 2.14.

Figure 2.14

Numbered and bulleted lists

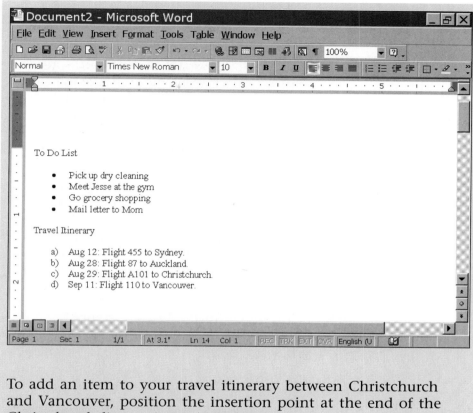

13 To add an item to your travel itinerary between Christchurch and Vancouver, position the insertion point at the end of the Christchurch line or item c), and press **ENTER**.

14 TYPE: **Sep 10: Flight 904 to Seattle.**
Notice that Word automatically renumbers, or in this case re-letters, the list for you when you insert new entries.

15 Save the document as "To Do List" to your personal storage location.

16 Close the document.

2.4.5 Changing Line Spacing

FEATURE
Sometimes changing the line spacing in a document makes it easier to read. The standard options for line spacing are single- and double-spaced, but your choices aren't limited to these.

METHOD
- To single-space a paragraph, select the text, press `CTRL`+1
- To space a paragraph by 1.5 lines, press `CTRL`+5
- To double-space a paragraph, press `CTRL`+2
- To select a specific line spacing option:
  CHOOSE: Format, Paragraph
  CLICK: down arrow beside the *Line Spacing* drop-down list box
  SELECT: *the desired spacing*
  CLICK: OK command button

PRACTICE
You will now practice changing line spacing.

Setup: Ensure that you've completed the previous lessons in this module and that the "Commerce" document is displaying.

1 Move the insertion point into the first paragraph.

2 To double-space this paragraph:
PRESS: `CTRL`+2
Notice that only the first paragraph is double-spaced (Figure 2.15).

Figure 2.15

Changing line spacing

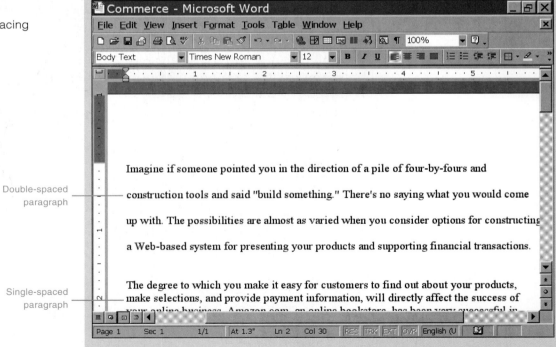

Double-spaced paragraph

Single-spaced paragraph

3 To apply 1.5-line spacing:
PRESS: `CTRL`+5

4 To return the paragraph to single spacing:
PRESS: CTRL +1

5 To double-space the entire document, you must first select the document. Move the mouse pointer into the Selection bar and triple-click the left mouse button. (*Note:* Pressing CTRL +a also selects the entire document.) The entire document should be highlighted in reverse video before proceeding.

6 PRESS: CTRL +2
The entire "Commerce" document is now double-spaced.

7 With the document still selected, let's use the Paragraph dialog box to return the document to single spacing.
CHOOSE: Format, Paragraph
SELECT: *Line spacing* drop-down list
Your screen should now appear similar to Figure 2.16.

Figure 2.16

Using the Paragraph dialog box to change line spacing

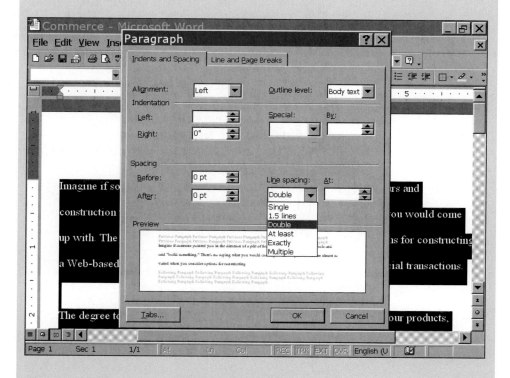

8 CHOOSE: Single from the drop-down list
CLICK: OK command button

9 CLICK: anywhere in the document to remove the current selection

10 Close the "Commerce" document without saving changes.

2.4.6 Setting Tabs

FEATURE

Tabs enable you to neatly arrange text and numbers on a page. The four basic types of tabs are left, center, right, and decimal. (By default, Word supplies left-aligned tabs every .5 inch.) You can also create tab **leaders,** which are dotted, dashed, or solid lines that fill the space between text and tab stops. Leaders are commonly used in tables of contents to visually join the section headings with the page numbers.

METHOD

- To select a tab:
  CLICK: the Tab Alignment button (⬡) until the tab symbol you want appears
  CLICK: the desired location on the Ruler to set the tab stop
- To remove a tab:
  DRAG: the tab stop down and off the Ruler
- To create a custom tab that includes a tab leader:
  CHOOSE: Format, Tabs to display the Tabs dialog box

PRACTICE

In this lesson, you create an itinerary for a trip to the Baltic States and Russia.

Setup: Ensure that you've completed the previous lessons in this module. No documents should be displaying.

1 To begin a new document:
CLICK: New button (⬡)

2 TYPE: Dear Friends,
PRESS: ENTER twice

3 TYPE: We are pleased to offer this long-anticipated tour to the Baltic States and Russia. Once hidden together behind the Iron Curtain, the Baltic nations of Lithuania, Latvia, and Estonia now stand independently in sharp cultural contrast to the former Soviet Union and to each other. This in-depth tour enables you to learn how these distinct countries, while in the lingering shadow of Russia, have embraced their new freedom. The tour involves visits to the following cities:
PRESS: ENTER twice
In the next few steps, you set tabs and type text so that your document resembles Figure 2.17 when completed.

Figure 2.17

"Baltic" document

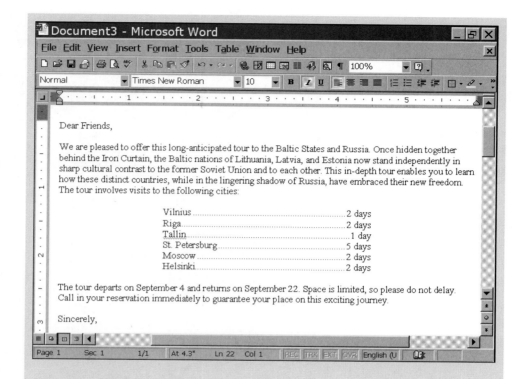

4 To specify a tab position for the city names:
CLICK: Tab Alignment button until the left-aligned tab symbol (⊥)
appears (*Note:* This left-aligned symbol may already be displaying.)

5 To specify a tab position for the city names:
CLICK: 1.5 inches on the Ruler
(*Hint:* If the tab stop is not correctly positioned, drag it along the
Ruler using the mouse. You can also remove a tab by dragging it
down and off the Ruler.)

6 To specify a tab type and position for the number of days:
SELECT: Tab Alignment button until the right-aligned tab symbol
(⊥) appears
CLICK: 4.5 inches on the Ruler
The Ruler should now appear similar to the following:

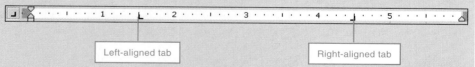

Left-aligned tab   Right-aligned tab

7 Now let's edit the right-aligned tab to be a dot leader.
CHOOSE: Format, Tabs
SELECT: 4.5 inches in the *Tab stop position* list box
SELECT: 2 in the *Leader* area
The dialog box should now appear similar to Figure 2.18.

Figure 2.18

Tabs dialog box

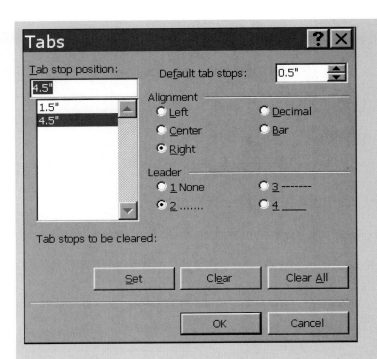

8 CLICK: OK command button

9 To keep track of your keystrokes:
CLICK: Show/Hide button (¶)

10 Now let's enter the first row of information.
PRESS: TAB to move the insertion point to the first tab stop on the Ruler
TYPE: Vilnius
PRESS: TAB to move the insertion point to the next tab stop on the Ruler
TYPE: 2 days
PRESS: ENTER
Notice that each press of the TAB key results in the tab symbol (→).

11 Enter the following information in the city and number of days columns, using the TAB key to position the insertion point:
Riga . . . . 2 days
Tallinn . . . . 1 day
St. Petersburg . . . . 5 days
Moscow . . . . 2 days
Helsinki . . . . 2 days

12 To continue:
PRESS: ENTER twice

13 Before typing the rest of the letter, remove the two tabs you inserted in steps 4 and 5 by dragging them down and off the Ruler.

14 TYPE: The tour departs on September 4 and returns on September 22. Space is limited, so please do not delay. Call in your reservation immediately to guarantee your place on this exciting journey.
PRESS: ENTER twice
TYPE: Sincerely,
PRESS: ENTER three times
TYPE: *your name*
PRESS: ENTER
TYPE: Director of Travel

15 Let's remove the hidden codes from view.
CLICK: Show/Hide button (¶)

16 Save the document as "Baltic" to your personal storage location.

17 Close the document.

2.4 Self Check   How do you display a document's hidden symbols?

2.5 Chapter Review

Two procedures that you should know about before changing the look of text are how to position the insertion point and select text. As with most Windows programs, Word is based upon a "Select and then Do" approach to formatting and editing. Therefore, the proper selection of text is extremely important for executing commands and working effectively with Word.

Word's formatting commands can be used to your advantage to create compelling documents. The bold, italic, and underline attributes are useful for emphasizing important text and your selection of fonts, font sizes, and colors contribute to the overall tone of your message. You can also use paragraph formatting commands to give your document a more professional look. This chapter explored indenting paragraphs, creating bulleted and numbered lists, aligning text, and setting tabs.

2.5.1 Command Summary

Many of the commands and procedures appearing in this chapter are summarized in the following table.

Skill Set	To Perform This Task . . .	Do the Following . . .
Working with Text	Bold text	CLICK: Bold button ([**B**])
	Italicize text	CLICK: Italic button ([*I*])
	Underline text	CLICK: Underline button ([U̲])
	Select a font	CLICK: Font drop-down arrow ([Times New Roman ▼])
	Change the font size	CLICK: Font Size drop-down arrow ([10 ▼])
	Change the font color	CLICK: Font Color button ([A ▾]) to apply the most recently-selected color, or CLICK: Font Color drop-down arrow ([A ▾]) to choose from a palette of colors
Working with Paragraphs	Show/Hide paragraph marks	CLICK: Show/Hide button ([¶])
	Left-align a paragraph	CLICK: Align Left button ([≡])
	Center-align a paragraph	CLICK: Center button ([≡])
	Right-align a paragraph	CLICK: Align Right button ([≡])
	Justify a paragraph	CLICK: Justify button ([≡])
	Increase indentation	CLICK: Increase Indent button ([≣])
	Decrease indentation	CLICK: Decrease Indent button ([≣])
	Customize the left and right indents	DRAG: indent markers on the Ruler
	Create a first-line or hanging indent	DRAG: Hanging Indent Marker on the ruler to the right

Continued

Skill Set	To Perform This Task . . .	Do the Following . . .
	Create a bulleted list	CLICK: Bullets button (▤)
	Create a numbered list	CLICK: Numbering button (▤)
	Specify bullet symbols or numbering schemes	CHOOSE: Format, Bullets and Numbering
	Single-space a paragraph	PRESS: CTRL +1
	Space a paragraph by 1.5 lines	PRESS: CTRL +5	
	Double-space a paragraph	PRESS: CTRL +2
	Set tabs	SELECT: a tab type using the Tab Alignment button (L) CLICK: the desired location on the Ruler to set the tab stop
	Create a tab leader	CHOOSE: Format, Tabs
	Remove tabs	DRAG: tab stop down and off the Ruler

2.5.2 Key Terms

This section specifies page references for the key terms identified in this chapter. For a complete list of definitions, refer to the Glossary provided immediately after the Appendix in this learning guide.

Bullets, *p. 68*   leaders, *p. 74*

font, *p. 55*   paragraph, *p. 61*

justification, *p. 63*   Selection bar, *p. 51*

2.6   Review Questions

2.6.1   Short Answer

1. Describe four types of tabs you can include in a document.
2. How would you set line spacing to 1.5 lines?
3. What is the procedure for right-aligning a paragraph?
4. What is the significance of the paragraph symbol?
5. What procedure would you use to move the insertion point efficiently to page 2, line 16?
6. How would you go about selecting a single sentence?
7. What is a tab leader?
8. What procedure would you use to select an entire document?
9. How would you go about changing the font and point size of a selection of text?
10. What procedure would you use to change the color of a selection of text to red?

2.6.2   True/False

1. __T__ To move to the end of a document, press **END**.
2. _____ Pressing **CTRL** + **HOME** will move the insertion point to the top of the document.
3. _____ Scrolling moves the insertion point.
4. _____ You can preview your font selections in the Font dialog box.
5. __T__ To delete a selected block of text, press **DELETE**.
6. __T__ To number text after it has been typed, you must select it and then click the Numbering button (▤).
7. __F__ To customize a numbering scheme, you must use the Bullets and Numbering dialog box.
8. __T__ One method to create a hanging indent involves dragging the Hanging Indent marker on the ruler.
9. _____ The scroll bar provides buttons for moving to the next page and previous page.
10. _____ By default, tabs display with a dot leader.

2.6.3 Multiple Choice

1. Character formatting involves choosing:
   a. typefaces
   b. font sizes
   c. text attributes
   d. All of the above

2. To increase a paragraph's indentation level, click:
   a.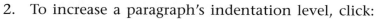
   b.
   c.
   d. None of the above

3. To double-space a paragraph, press:
   a. CTRL +1
   b. CTRL +q
   ✓c. CTRL +2
   d. CTRL + F2

4. To remove paragraph formatting, press:
   a. CTRL +1
   ✗b. CTRL +q
   c. CTRL +2
   d. CTRL + F2

5. To remove a tab stop from the Ruler:
   a. Drag the tab stop down and off the ruler
   b. Select the tab stop and press DELETE
   c. Position the insertion point to the right of the tab stop and press BACKSPACE
   d. All of the above

6. To create a tab leader, you must use the:
   a. Tabs dialog box
   b. Ruler
   c. period (.) key
   d. All of the above

7. You can select a word by _____.
   a. single-clicking
   b. double-clicking
   c. Both a and b
   d. None of the above

8. Which of the following can't be selected?
   a. letter
   b. word
   c. line
   d. Selection bar

9. To display a document's paragraph marks:
   a. CHOOSE: File, Marks
   b. CLICK: Show/Hide button
   c. Both a and b
   d. None of the above

10. To align text so that it is even on both the left and right margins, you must click the _____.
    a. Center button
    b. Justify button ✓
    c. Align Right button
    d. Both a and b

2.7 Hands-On Projects

2.7.1 Sandra Baker: Application Letter

In this exercise, you practice formatting an existing document and using Word's proofing tools.

1. Open the WRD271 data file.
2. Save a copy of the document as "Baker Letter" to your personal storage location.
3. Let's select the entire document and then set the font formatting for the entire document to 11 points, Times New Roman.
   PRESS: CTRL and hold it down
   CLICK: once anywhere in the Selection bar
   SELECT: Times New Roman from the Font drop-down list (Times New Roman ▾)
   SELECT: 11 from the Font Size drop-down list (10 ▾)
4. To insert Sandra's name above her return address at the top of the letter, move the insertion point to the top of the document and then press ENTER.
5. PRESS: ⬆ to move the insertion point to the first line
   TYPE: Sandra Baker
6. Let's format Sandra's name using an Arial, 16 point font.
   SELECT: Sandra Baker
   SELECT: Arial from the Font drop-down list (Times New Roman ▾)
   SELECT: 16 from the Font Size drop-down list (10 ▾)

7. To format Sandra's address using an Arial, 9 point font:
   SELECT: the three address lines
   SELECT: Arial from the Font drop-down list (Times New Roman ▾)
   SELECT: 9 from the Font Size drop-down list (10 ▾)
8. Underline the words "Sales Rep Position" in the subject line.
9. Preview and print the letter.
10. Save and then close the revised document.

2.7.2 Clearwater Systems Inc: Memo

In this exercise, you practice setting tabs and applying paragraph formatting. You will create a memo similar to the one in Figure 2.19 and then print it so that it can be photocopied and completed with a pen.

Figure 2.19
"Clearwater Memo" document

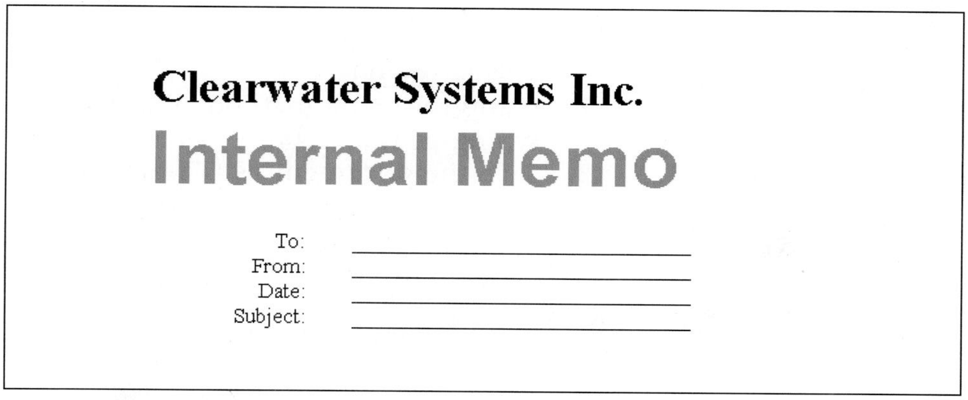
Clearwater Systems Inc.

Internal Memo

To: ______________
From: ______________
Date: ______________
Subject: ______________

1. Create a new blank document.
2. TYPE: `Clearwater Systems Inc.`
   PRESS: ENTER
3. TYPE: `Internal Memo`
   PRESS: ENTER twice
4. Format the company name using Times New Roman, 22 points, and the bold attribute.
5. Format the words "Internal Memo" using Arial, 36 points, and the bold attribute.
6. Change the color of the text "Internal Memo" to red.
7. To move to the end of the document:
   PRESS: CTRL + END
   The insertion point is now positioned two lines below the text "Internal Memo."

8. To insert a right tab at position 1 inch and left tabs at positions 1.25 inches and 3.5 inches:
SELECT: Right-aligned tab (⬛) using the Tab Alignment button
CLICK: 1 inch on the Ruler
SELECT: Left-aligned tab (⬛) using the Tab Alignment button
CLICK: 1.25 inches on the Ruler
CLICK: 3.5 inches on the Ruler
9. Let's format the tab in position 3.5 inches to include a line leader.
CHOOSE: Format, Tabs
SELECT: 3.5 inches in the *Tab stop position* list box
SELECT: 4 in the *Leader* area
CLICK: OK command button
10. To begin typing the "To:" line of the memo, do the following:
PRESS: [TAB] to move the insertion point to the next tab stop
TYPE: To:
PRESS: [TAB] twice to move the insertion point to the last tab stop on the Ruler
PRESS: [ENTER]
11. Using the same method as in the previous step, proceed by typing in the "From", "Date", and "Subject" lines.
12. Save the document as "Clearwater Memo" to your personal storage location.
13. Print the document.

2.7.3 Norstorm Systems: Memo Form

You will now practice applying character and paragraph formatting commands.

1. Open the WRD273 data file.
2. Save the document as "Norstorm Memo" to your personal storage location.
3. Format the business name and location using an Arial font.
4. Format the business name using a 16-point font size, and apply the bold, italic, and underline effects.
5. Format the word "Memorandum" to include a 28-point font size.
6. Apply blue to the text "Memorandum."
7. Format the remaining lines in the document using an Arial, 10 point font and then apply the bold effect.
8. Select the word "Date" and any text that appears below.
9. Create a hanging indent in position 1 inch.
10. Save the revised document.
11. Preview and print the document.

2.7.4 Aardvark Enterprises: Bulletin

In this exercise, you open a draft copy of a news bulletin. You then practice several formatting techniques.

1. Open the WRD274 data file.
2. Save a copy of the document as "Aardvaark Bulletin" to your personal storage location.
3. Change the formatting of the entire document to 12-point Times New Roman.
4. Format the words "News Report" to include a 20-point font size.
5. Format the business name to include the bold and underline effects.
6. Change the color of the business name to a shade of green.
7. Format the first two paragraphs of the document so they are fully justified between the margins.
8. Apply bullets to the city and date lines.
9. Fully justify the final paragraph of the document.
10. Save and then print the document.

2.7.5 On Your Own: Garage Sale Notice

In this exercise, you must use your formatting skills to create a garage sale notice to be posted on notice boards throughout your neighborhood. Your notice should detail the time and location of the sale and include a list of some of the key items you hope to sell quickly. After preparing your notice, apply attention-grabbing formatting. Save your work as "Garage Sale" to your personal storage location.

2.7.6 On Your Own: Itinerary

To practice applying character and paragraph formatting, create an itinerary describing a vacation in a city you have never been to but would like to visit. For each day in your weeklong vacation, detail the types of activities that you will be doing, such as taking a tour or visiting a monument. Give the itinerary a professional look using character and paragraph-formatting commands. Save the document as "Itinerary" and then print the document.

2.8 Case Problems: Ards County Humane Society

Now that Janice has learned some techniques for creating professional-looking documents, she decides to tackle those documents in her office that will benefit the most from her newly attained skills. Among the documents she creates are a letter to the general membership, a notice about upcoming society events, and a thank you note.

In the following case problems, assume the role of Janice and perform the same steps as she would perform to complete these tasks.

1. Janice begins her work by preparing a letter to the general membership about this year's fund-raising campaign. After creating the letter shown in Figure 2.20, she saves the letter as "Ards Letter."

Figure 2.20

"Ards Letter" document

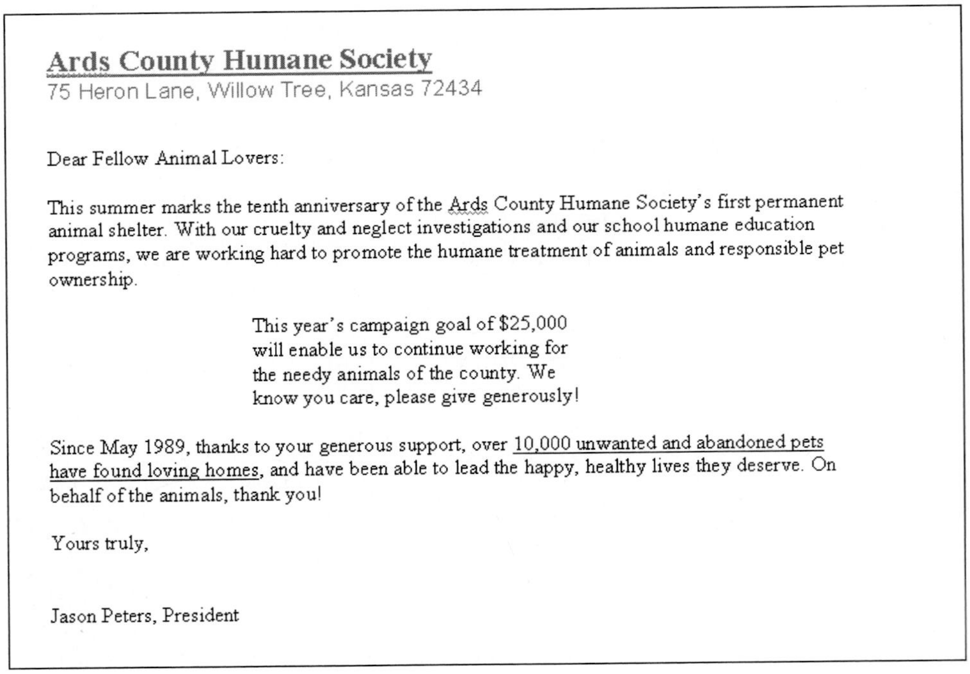

> ## Ards County Humane Society
> 75 Heron Lane, Willow Tree, Kansas 72434
>
> Dear Fellow Animal Lovers:
>
> This summer marks the tenth anniversary of the Ards County Humane Society's first permanent animal shelter. With our cruelty and neglect investigations and our school humane education programs, we are working hard to promote the humane treatment of animals and responsible pet ownership.
>
> > This year's campaign goal of $25,000
> > will enable us to continue working for
> > the needy animals of the county. We
> > know you care, please give generously!
>
> Since May 1989, thanks to your generous support, over 10,000 unwanted and abandoned pets have found loving homes, and have been able to lead the happy, healthy lives they deserve. On behalf of the animals, thank you!
>
> Yours truly,
>
> Jason Peters, President

2. Janice decides to prepare the notice pictured in Figure 2.21 listing the upcoming events organized by society members. The heading and subheading are centered between the margins. Janice must insert bullets and indent text in order to achieve the desired results. She then saves the notice as "Ards Notice."

Figure 2.21

"Ards Notice" document

Ards County Humane Society
We speak for those who cannot speak for themselves

UPCOMING EVENTS AT A GLANCE

- *May 3*
  10th Anniversary of the shelter construction and launch of annual fundraising appeal

- *May 24*
  Second Annual Book Sale at Baker Place

- *June 5*
  Coldstream Pet Walk-a-Thon

- *June 20*
  Farmer's Market Bake Sale

- *July 8*
  Taylor Park Pet Look-Alike Contest

Volunteers needed for all events. Please call 948-3728.

3. David Green, the center manager, has asked Janice to create a document that can be used as an advertisement in the local newspaper. The purpose of the advertisement is to give thanks to several companies for contributing to the center. To create the document, Janice must set a dot-leader tab in position 3.5 inches and create a hanging indent in position 3.5 inches. Janice saves the document as "Ards Thanks" and then prints the document. The completed document is pictured in Figure 2.22.

Figure 2.22

"Ards Thanks" document

Ards County Humane Society
We speak for those who cannot speak for themselves

ACHS THANKS YOU!!

Amigos Pet Food & Feed Store .... for your donation of Science Diet food

Betterson Elementary School Students .... for your donation of fundraising proceeds to the ACHS shelter

Kalamalka Business Students .... for donating your profits to the shelter

Intra Travel .... for sponsoring our ACHS display during the DVA Sunshine Festival and raising $305 for the shelter

Landscaping Volunteers .... for sowing grass, weeding, nurturing trees, and transforming our former landfill site

Mae's Meats .... for holding a ACHS Benefit Barbecue

The Hanson Family .... for providing the entertainment for the shelter's open house

4. Janice needs to prepare a list of the Board of Directors for posting on the ACHS bulletin board. She starts by creating a document with the information shown below. After formatting the first three lines similar to other ACHS documents, she uses a line-leader tab to separate each director's name from his/her corresponding title. Janice applies 1.5 line spacing to the list of directors and uses character formatting commands to give the listing a more professional look. After saving the document as "Ards Board," she prints the document.

Ards County Humane Society
Willow Tree, Kansas
1998–1999 Board of Directors

Alfred Baker President
Claire Dangerfield Vice-President
Eldon Frank Treasurer
Gloria Holdings Secretary
Ivan Jackson Past President
Kelly Lingren Director-at-Large Area E
Mark Neilson Director-at-Large Area D
Olivia Peters Regional District Representative

Notes

Notes

MICROSOFT WORD 2000
Modifying a Document

CHAPTER
THREE

Chapter Outline

Learning Objectives

After reading this chapter, you will be able to:

- Customize the application window to your preferred way of working

- Search for and replace words and phrases

- Copy and move information within the same document and among documents

- Check for spelling and grammar errors

- Put Word's AutoCorrect feature to work for you

Cottage Crafts

Nigel Needlebaum is the owner of Cottage Crafts, a crafts and antiques store on Main Street in Opelousas, Louisiana. Nigel's store is divided into sections that he rents to talented folk who sell their wares. For example, Freda Morris rents the corner space, where she displays antique kitchen items such as cooking utensils and pots and pans. Angel Romstrom's nook is covered with picture frames that she hand-paints. Other tenants include Abel, the rock painter; Roger, the furniture refinisher; and Dorris, the doll-maker. In addition to collecting rent from these people, Roger takes a small slice off the top of any sales made in the store.

Nigel recently purchased a computer that came with a preinstalled copy of Microsoft Word 2000. For the last few months he has been using any slow hours at the store to learn more about Word and has even posted several promotional documents on the store's bulletin board. One of his tenants pointed out several improvements that Nigel could make in the posted documents. Nigel agrees, but is unsure of how to proceed.

In this chapter, you and Nigel learn how to customize your work area, find and replace text, copy and move information, and proof your work. You will also learn how to use and customize Word's Auto-Correct feature.

3.1　Customizing Your Work Area

Word provides four primary views for working with documents: Normal, Web Layout, Print Layout, and Outline. While each view has its own advantages, it is their combination that gives you the best overall working environment. In addition, for optimal viewing, Word lets you zoom in and out on a document, increasing and decreasing its display size.

3.1.1 Selecting a View

FEATURE
Your selection of a view depends on the type of work you are performing. You will want to perform most of your work in Normal view. In this view mode, your document displays without headers, footers, and columns. Whereas Print Layout view lets you see how text and graphics will appear on the printed page, Web Layout view enables you to see how a document will look in a Web browser. In these two view modes, you can also take advantage of Word's new **Click and Type** feature, which lets you position the insertion point by simply double-clicking in a blank area of your document. Finally, Outline view provides a convenient environment for organizing a document.

METHOD
To change a document's display view:

- CHOOSE: View, Normal (or click ▤)
- CHOOSE: View, Web Layout (or click ▣)
- CHOOSE: View, Print Layout (or click ▣)
- CHOOSE: View, Outline (or click ▣)

PRACTICE
You will now practice switching views using a two-page newsletter.

Setup: Ensure that no documents are displaying in the application window.

1 Open the WRD310 data file.

2 Save a copy as "Newsletter" to your personal storage location.
The "Newsletter" document should be displaying in Print Layout view. The blank space at the top of the document corresponds to the top margin.

3 Let's try out Word's new Click and Type feature. This feature is useful for inserting and aligning text and graphics. To begin:
PRESS: CTRL + END to move the insertion point to the end of the document.

4 To position the insertion point in the blank area that appears at the bottom of the document:
DOUBLE-CLICK: anywhere in the blank area
The insertion point should have moved to the new location.

WORD

5 To switch to Normal view:
CHOOSE: View, Normal
(*Note:* You can also click the Normal View button (☰), located to the left of the horizontal scroll bar.) Your screen should now appear similar to Figure 3.1. Note that you no longer see the space allotted for the top margin.

Figure 3.1

Normal view

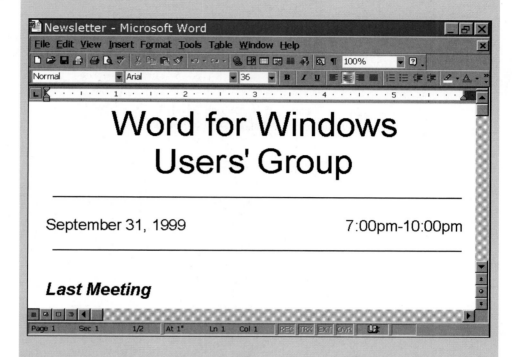

6 To switch to Web Layout view:
CHOOSE: View, Web Layout
In this mode, you see how your document will look when viewed in a Web browser.

7 Let's view the document in outline view.
CHOOSE: View, Outline
The Outlining toolbar is now positioned below the Formatting toolbar.

8 To view just the main headings in the document:
CLICK: Show Heading 1 button (1) on the Outlining toolbar
Your screen should now appear similar to Figure 3.2. In this view mode, it's easy to organize the different parts of your document.

Figure 3.2

Outline view

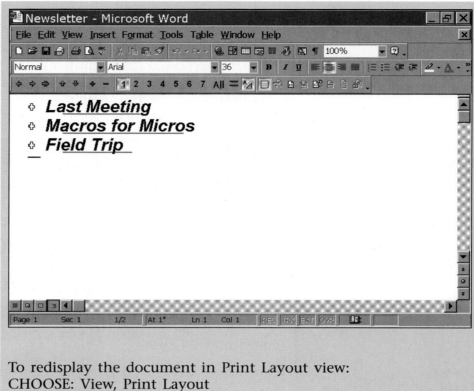

9   To redisplay the document in Print Layout view:
CHOOSE: View, Print Layout

3.1.2   Zooming the Display

FEATURE
Regardless of the view you select, Word lets you zoom in and out on a document, increasing and decreasing its display size. For example, you may want to enlarge Word's Normal view to 200% of its original size when working with detailed graphics.

METHOD
- CLICK: Zoom drop-down arrow (100%), or
- CHOOSE: View, Zoom

PRACTICE
You will now practice zooming the display.

Setup: Ensure that you've completed the previous lesson and that the "Newsletter" document is displaying.

WORD

1 To zoom the document to 200% of its original size:
CLICK: Zoom drop-down arrow on the Standard toolbar
The drop-down menu, shown on the right, should now appear.

2 From the drop-down list:
CHOOSE: 200%
Your screen should now appear similar to Figure 3.3. The document is immediately magnified to twice its original size.

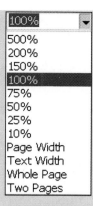

Figure 3.3

Increasing the zoom factor to 200%

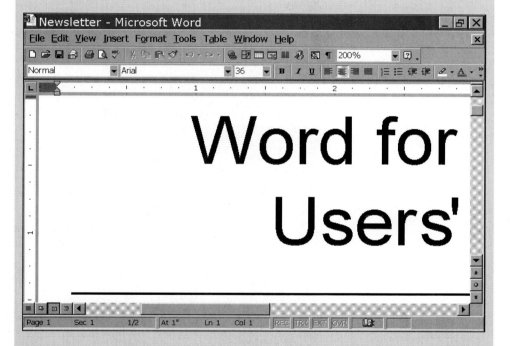

3 To find the best-fit magnification:
CLICK: Zoom drop-down arrow
SELECT: Page Width from the drop-down list
The view is zoomed to the best fit for your screen's resolution.

4 To conclude this module, you will close the document.
CHOOSE: File, Close
There should be no documents open in the application window.

3.1 Self Check What is the different between Normal and Print Layout view?

3.2 Finding and Replacing Text

Imagine that you have just completed a 200-page proposal support-ing the importation of llamas as household pets in North America. As you are printing the final pages, a colleague points out that you spelled *llama* with one *l* throughout the document. The Spell Checker didn't catch the error since both *llama*, the animal, and *lama*, the Tibetan monk, appear in Word's dictionary. Therefore, you must use another of Word's editing features—the Find and Replace utility—to correct your mistake.

3.2.1 Finding Text

FEATURE
The **Find** command enables you to search for text, nonprinting characters like the Paragraph Symbol (¶), and formatting charac-teristics. This tool is also useful for quickly finding your place in a document.

METHOD
1. CHOOSE: Edit, Find
2. TYPE: *the text you're looking for* in the *Find what* text box
3. CLICK: More button to refine your search (optional)
4. SELECT: Find Next

PRACTICE
In this lesson, you practice finding text.

Setup: Ensure that Word is loaded and that the application window is maximized.

1 Open the WRD320 data file.

2 Save the file as "Dentistry" to your personal storage location.

3 To begin a search for a word or phrase in a document:
CHOOSE: Edit, Find
Your screen should now appear similar to Figure 3.4.

WORD

Figure 3.4

Find and Replace dialog box:
Find tab

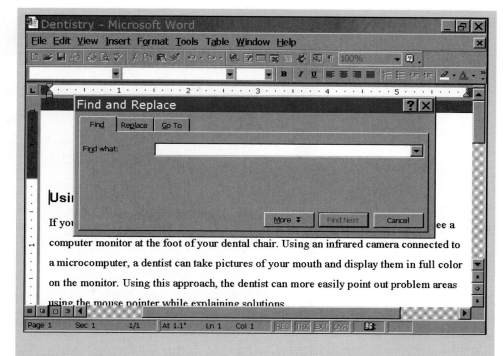

4 ▸ With the insertion point in the *Find what* text box:
TYPE: monitor

5 ▸ In this step, you instruct Word to only retrieve whole words.
That is, you don't want Word to retrieve all words containing
the letters "monitor," such as *monitor*ing or *monitor*s. To do this,
you must click the More button.
CLICK: More button in the Find and Replace dialog box
SELECT: *Find whole words only* check box in the *Search Options*
area
Your screen should appear similar to Figure 3.5.

Figure 3.5

Find and Replace dialog box:
Displaying additional options

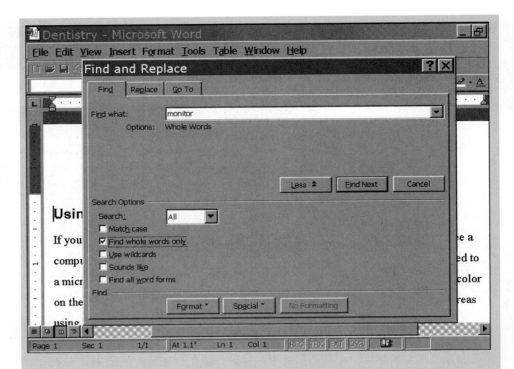

6 To display less information in the Find and Replace dialog box:
CLICK: Less button

7 To tell Word to begin the search:
CLICK: Find Next command button

8 Word stops at the first occurrence of "monitor." (*Note:* You may
have to drag the dialog box downward to see that "monitor" is
now selected in your document.) To continue the search:
CLICK: Find Next command button
Word stops at the second occurrence of "monitor."

9 To continue the search:
CLICK: Find Next command button
The following dialog box appears, indicating the search is com-
plete:

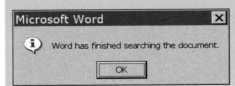

10 To continue:
CLICK: OK command button

11 To close the Find and Replace dialog box:
CLICK: Cancel command button

3.2.2 Replacing Text

FEATURE
The **Replace** command enables you to search for and replace text, nonprinting characters, and formatting characteristics. This command is extremely useful when you've made the same error repeatedly throughout a document.

METHOD
1. CHOOSE: Edit, Replace
2. TYPE: *the text you're looking for* in the *Find what* text box
3. TYPE: *the replacement text* in the *Replace with* text box
4. CLICK: More button to refine your search (optional)
5. CLICK: Replace, Replace All, or Find Next command button

PRACTICE
You will now replace the word "monitor" with "screen" throughout the "Dentistry" document.

Setup: Ensure that you've completed the previous lesson and that the "Dentistry" document is open in the application window. Also, make sure that the insertion point is positioned at the beginning of the document.

1 CHOOSE: Edit, Replace
Note that the word "monitor" already appears in the *Find what* text box from the last time you performed the Edit, Find command.

2 To enter the replacement text, click the I-beam mouse pointer in the *Replace with* text box to position the insertion point.

3 TYPE: screen
Your screen should now appear similar to Figure 3.6.

Figure 3.6

Find and Replace dialog box:
Replace tab

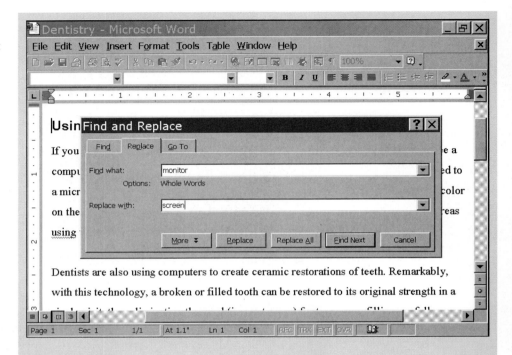

4 To execute the replacement throughout the document:
CLICK: Replace All command button
The following dialog box appears informing you that two
replacements were made in the document:

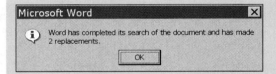

5 To close the dialog boxes:
CLICK: OK command button
CLICK: Close command button

6 Now let's make all occurrences of the word "screen" bold:
CHOOSE: Edit, Replace

7 In the *Find what* text box:
TYPE: screen

8 Position the insertion point in the *Replace With* text box by clicking the I-beam mouse pointer in the text box.

9   Since the word "screen" already appears in this text box, you need only specify the bold formatting option. To do this:
CLICK: More command button
CLICK: Format command button
CHOOSE: Font from the menu
SELECT: Bold in the Font Style list box
CLICK: OK command button
Note that the text "Format: Font: Bold" appears below the *Replace with* text

10   To perform the replacement:
CLICK: Replace All command button
Similar to last time, two replacements are made in the document.

11   To close the dialog boxes:
CLICK: OK command button
CLICK: Close command button
If you browse through the document, you will notice that all occurrences of the word "screen" are now bold.

12   Save and then close the "Dentistry" document.

In Addition Finding and Replacing Formats and Other Items	In addition to text, the Find and Replace dialog box can be used to find and replace formatting characteristics, special codes, and characters. To find and replace formatting characteristics, click the More command button in the Find and Replace dialog box and then click the Format command button. Next, choose the formats you want from the menu. To find and replace other items, such as page breaks and paragraph marks, click the More command button and then the Special command button. Then, choose the items you want from the menu.

3.2 Self Check   What is the procedure for replacing text in a document?

3.3 Copying and Moving Information

In Word, it's easy to copy and move information within the same document and among documents. Like all Office 2000 applications, Word provides several methods for copying and moving information. First, you can cut or copy a single piece of data from any application and store it on the **Windows Clipboard.** Then, you can paste the data into any other application. Second, you can use the new **Office**

Clipboard to collect up to 12 items and then paste the stored data singularly or as a group into any one of the Office 2000 applications. You can also use **drag and drop** to copy and move cell information using the mouse. Lastly, you can use the **Format Painter** to copy formatting attributes.

3.3.1 Copying Formatting Attributes

FEATURE
The **Format Painter** enables you to copy the formatting styles and attributes from one area in your document to another. Not only does this feature speed formatting operations, it ensures consistency among the different areas in your document.

METHOD
To copy formatting to another area in your document:

1. SELECT: the text with the desired formatting characteristics
2. CLICK: Format Painter button (⊠) on the Standard toolbar
3. SELECT: the text that you want to format

To copy formatting to several areas in your document:

1. SELECT: the text with the desired formatting characteristics
2. DOUBLE-CLICK: Format Painter button (⊠)
3. SELECT: the text that you want to format
4. Repeat step 3, as desired.
5. CLICK: Format Painter button (⊠) to deselect it

PRACTICE
You will now practice using the Format Painter on a document that describes one of Microsoft's operating systems.

Setup: Ensure that Word is loaded and that the application window is maximized.

1 Open the WRD331 data file.

2 Save the file as "Paint" to your personal storage location.

3 SELECT: the heading entitled "Features"

4 To format the heading:
CLICK: Bold button ([B])
CLICK: Italic button ([I])
SELECT: Arial font from the Font drop-down list ([Times New Roman ▾])
SELECT: 14-point size from the Font Size drop-down list ([10 ▾])
(*Note:* If you don't have the Arial font on your computer, select an alternate font.) Your screen should now appear similar to Figure 3.7.

Figure 3.7

"Paint" document

Using the Format Painter, you can copy the formatting of this selection to another location, such as to the "Future Expectations" heading.

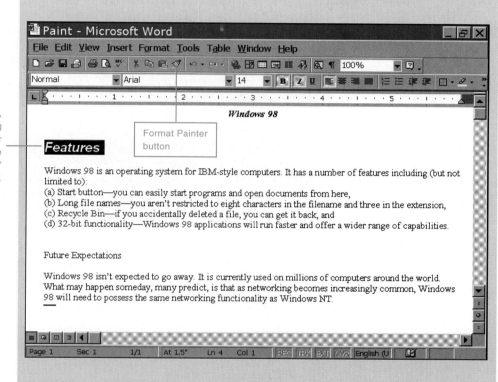

5 To copy the formatting characteristics of the selected text "Features":
CLICK: Format Painter button ([◌]) on the Standard toolbar

6 Move the mouse pointer into the document area. Note that it becomes an I-beam attached to a paintbrush.

7 To copy the formatting to the second heading:
DRAG: mouse pointer over the subheading "Future Expectations"
When you release the mouse button, the second heading is formatted with the same characteristics as the first heading.

8 To format "Windows 98" in the first sentence (not in the title):
SELECT: Windows 98

9 CLICK: Bold button ([B])
CLICK: Italic button ([I])

10 To copy this formatting to several areas in the document:
DOUBLE-CLICK: Format Painter button (🖌)

11 Using the I-beam paintbrush mouse pointer, select all occurrences of "Windows 98" and "Windows NT" in the document. (*Tip:* You can double-click words as you would with the regular I-beam mouse pointer to apply the formatting.)

12 To finish using the paintbrush mouse pointer:
CLICK: Format Painter button (🖌)

13 To deselect the current text and move the insertion point to the beginning of the document:
PRESS: CTRL + HOME
Your screen should now appear similar to Figure 3.8.

Figure 3.8

The Format Painter was used to apply formatting to this document

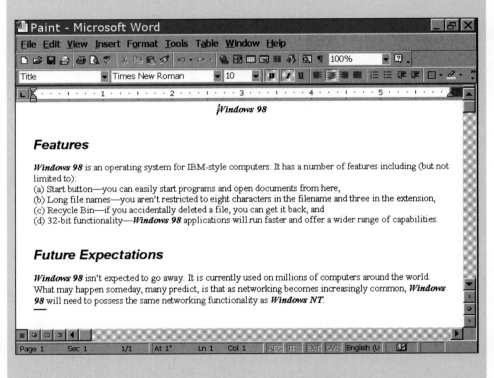

14 Save and then close the document.

WORD

3.3.2   Using the Clipboards

FEATURE

You use the Windows and Office Clipboards to copy and move information within Word and among other applications. The Windows Clipboard can store a single item of data from any application, while the Office Clipboard can store up to 12 items. (*Note*: The last item that you cut or copy to the Office Clipboard will appear as the one item stored on the Windows Clipboard.) When working in any one of the Office 2000 applications, such as Word, you can display the Office Clipboard toolbar for use in copying, managing, and pasting information.

METHOD

- To view and manage data stored on the Office Clipboard:
  CHOOSE: View, Toolbars, Clipboard
- To move selected information to the Clipboards:
  CLICK: Cut button (✂), or press CTRL + x
- To copy selected information to the Clipboards:
  CLICK: Copy button (📋), or press CTRL + c
- To paste information into your document:
  CLICK: Paste button (📋), or press CTRL + v

PRACTICE

You will now open a document that warns about the effects of extreme temperatures on computer systems. You will then practice using the Windows and Office Clipboards.

Setup: Ensure that you have completed the previous lesson and that no documents are open in the application window.

1 Open the WRD332 data file.

2 Save the file as "Hardware" to your personal storage location.

3 To copy the phrase "Computer systems" from the first sentence to the top of the document, first you must select the text:
SELECT: Computer systems

In this step, you selected the text you want to copy or move.

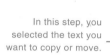

Computer systems should be kept i
Microcomputers tend to have the most

4 To copy the selection to the Clipboard:
CLICK: Copy button (📋) on the Standard toolbar

5 PRESS: ⬆ twice

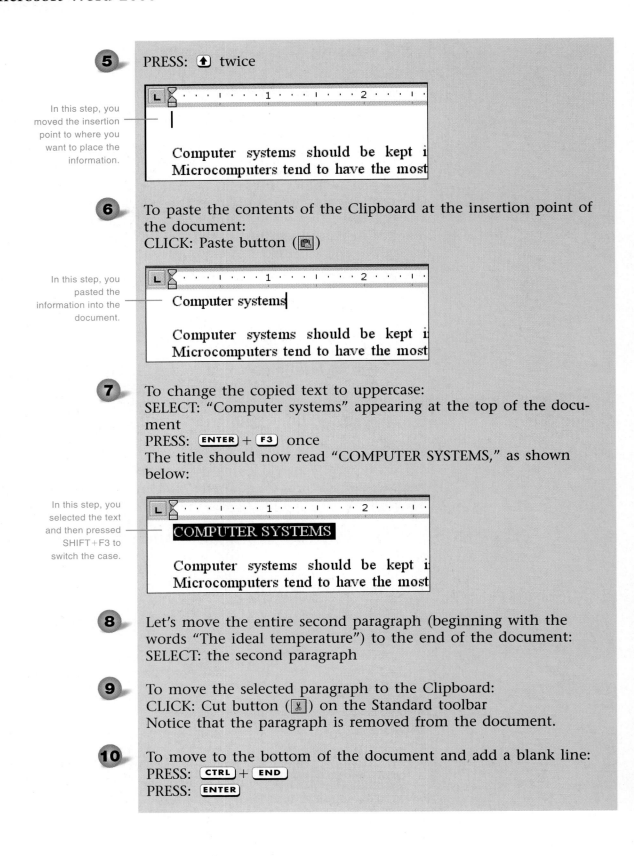

In this step, you moved the insertion point to where you want to place the information.

6 To paste the contents of the Clipboard at the insertion point of the document:
CLICK: Paste button (🔳)

In this step, you pasted the information into the document.

Computer systems

Computer systems should be kept i
Microcomputers tend to have the most

7 To change the copied text to uppercase:
SELECT: "Computer systems" appearing at the top of the document
PRESS: ENTER + F3 once
The title should now read "COMPUTER SYSTEMS," as shown below:

In this step, you selected the text and then pressed SHIFT+F3 to switch the case.

COMPUTER SYSTEMS

Computer systems should be kept i
Microcomputers tend to have the most

8 Let's move the entire second paragraph (beginning with the words "The ideal temperature") to the end of the document:
SELECT: the second paragraph

9 To move the selected paragraph to the Clipboard:
CLICK: Cut button (✂) on the Standard toolbar
Notice that the paragraph is removed from the document.

10 To move to the bottom of the document and add a blank line:
PRESS: CTRL + END
PRESS: ENTER

WORD

11 To paste the contents of the Clipboard at the insertion point of the document:
CLICK: Paste button (📋)
The paragraph is inserted at the bottom of the document.

12 When information is placed in the Clipboard, it can be pasted multiple times. To illustrate:
PRESS: [ENTER]
CLICK: Paste button (📋)
Note that the same paragraph has been pasted twice.

13 Let's view the contents of the Office Clipboard:
CHOOSE: View, Toolbars, Clipboard
The Office Clipboard should now appear similar to the following:

14 The Office Clipboard contains the most recent item you copied to the Clipboard. To insert a blank line and then paste this item into your document, do the following:
PRESS: [ENTER]
CLICK: 📄 in the Clipboard dialog box

15 To close the Office Clipboard:
CHOOSE: View, Toolbars, Clipboard
(*Note:* You could have also clicked ☒ in the Office Clipboard window.)

16 Close the document without saving.

3.3.3 Using Drag and Drop

FEATURE
You can use the mouse (and bypass the Clipboards altogether) to **drag and drop** information from one location in your document to another. Although you cannot perform multiple pastes, the drag and drop method provides the easiest and fastest way to copy and move selected text and graphics short distances.

METHOD
To copy or move text using the drag and drop method:

1. SELECT: the text that you want to copy or move
2. If you want to perform a copy operation, hold down the
    CTRL key.
3. DRAG: the selection to the target destination
4. Release the mouse button and, if necessary, the CTRL key.

PRACTICE
You will now open an existing document and then practice using drag and drop.

Setup: Ensure that you have completed the previous lessons and that no documents are open in the application window.

1 Open the WRD333 data file. (*Note:* This data file is similar to the WRD332 data file you opened earlier.)

2 Save the file as "Hardware2" to your personal storage location.

3 Select the first sentence of the first paragraph by positioning the I-beam mouse pointer over any word in the sentence, holding down the CTRL key, and clicking once.

4 Position the mouse pointer over the selected text. Notice that the pointer shape is a left-pointing diagonal arrow and not an I-beam. To move this sentence using drag and drop:
CLICK: left mouse button and hold it down
The mouse pointer changes shape to include a phantom insertion point at the end of the diagonal arrow. This dotted insertion point indicates where the selected text will be inserted.

5 Drag the phantom insertion point into the second paragraph and position it immediately *before* the second sentence (to the left of the letter "B" in the word "But").

6 Release the left mouse button. Note that the sentence is inserted at the mouse pointer, causing the existing text to wrap to the next line. Your screen should now appear similar to Figure 3.9.

Figure 3.9

The selected sentence was
moved using drag and drop

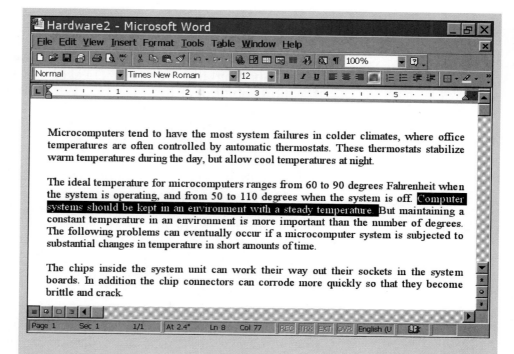

7 To deselect the text and move the insertion point to the top of
the document:
PRESS: CTRL + HOME

8 The drag and drop method can also be used to copy text. To
illustrate:
SELECT: the words "system failures" in the first paragraph

9 To copy these words into the title area:
PRESS: CTRL and hold it down

10 Position the mouse pointer over the highlighted word and then
drag the selection to the first blank line at the top of the document.

11 Release the left mouse button and then the CTRL key.

12 The copied text is currently selected. To change the copied text
to uppercase:
PRESS: SHIFT + F3 twice
The title should now read "SYSTEM FAILURES."

13 Close the document without saving the changes.

3.3 Self Check   How would you go about moving text to the Clipboard?

3.4 Proofing a Document

Although there's no substitute for reading a document carefully, Word's Spelling and Grammar checker can help you locate some of the more obvious errors quickly. When Word performs a spelling check, it begins by comparing each word to entries in Word's main dictionary, which contains well over 100,000 words. If a word cannot be found, the Spell checker attempts to find a match in a custom dictionary that you may have created. Custom dictionaries usually contain proper names, abbreviations, and technical terms.

Word's Grammar checker contains grammatical rules and style considerations for every occasion. Word offers the following styles of grammar checking: Casual, Standard (the default setting), Formal, Technical, and Custom. You can also customize Word to check only for specific rules and wording styles.

Two additional tools are useful when proofing a document. The Thesaurus feature helps you pinpoint the most effective words for getting your message across. For those documents that will be proofed by others online, you can use the Highlight tool to draw attention to the parts of your document that need special focus.

3.4.1 Checking Spelling and Grammar

FEATURE
The **Spelling and Grammar command** analyzes your document all at once for spelling and grammar errors and reports the results. It is important to use this command as a final check before submitting a document to others.

METHOD
1. CLICK: Spelling and Grammar button (🔤), or
    CHOOSE: Tools, Spelling and Grammar
2. When a misspelled word is found, you can accept Word's suggestion, change the entry, ignore the word and the suggested alternatives provided by Word, or add the term to the AutoCorrect feature or custom dictionary. When a grammar error is detected, you can accept Word's suggestion, change the entry, or ignore the sentence.

PRACTICE

In this lesson, you will perform a spelling and grammar check and display some statistics about your document.

Setup: Ensure that Word is loaded and that the application window is maximized.

1 Open the WRD340 data file.

2 Save the document as "Legal" to your personal storage location.

3 To start the spelling check:
CLICK: Spelling and Grammar button (⟨ABC⟩)
When Word finds the first misspelled word, it displays a dialog box (Figure 3.10) and waits for further instructions. In the dialog box, Word applies red to spelling selections and green to grammar selections.

Figure 3.10
Spelling and Grammar dialog box

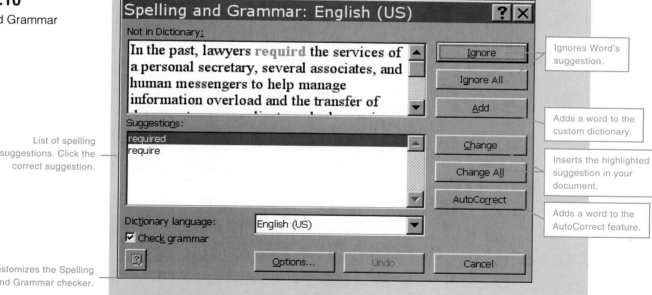

List of spelling suggestions. Click the correct suggestion.

Customizes the Spelling and Grammar checker.

Ignores Word's suggestion.

Adds a word to the custom dictionary.

Inserts the highlighted suggestion in your document.

Adds a word to the AutoCorrect feature.

4 To correct the misspelled word "requird," ensure that the correct spelling of the word appears in the *Suggestions* text box and then:
CLICK: Change command button

5 Word has now detected a grammar error (Figure 3.11). The dialog box shows the offending phrase and suggests why it was flagged. In this case, Word suggests that the sentence's subject and verb don't agree. Word also provides two suggestions for how the sentence might be reworded. To accept the selected suggestion:
CLICK: Change command button

Figure 3.11

Checking for grammar

Reason the phrase was flagged.

Suggestions for how the sentence might be improved.

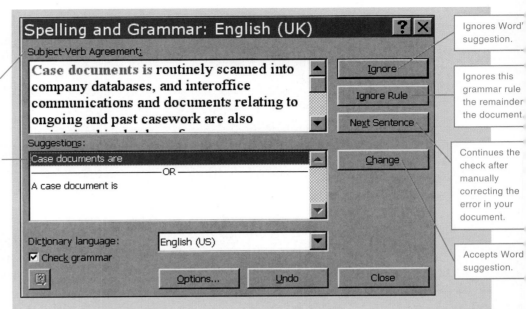

Ignores Word' suggestion.

Ignores this grammar rule the remainder the document.

Continues the check after manually correcting the error in your document.

Accepts Word suggestion.

6 On your own, continue the spelling and grammar check for the rest of the document. A message dialog box will appear when it is finished. To clear this dialog box:
CLICK: OK command button

7 The Word Count command is another useful tool that provides some basic document statistics. To display the Word Count dialog box:
CHOOSE: Tools, Word Count

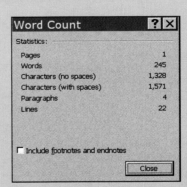

8 To close the Word Count dialog box:
CLICK: Close command button

9 Save the document.

3.4.2 Using the Thesaurus

FEATURE
A **thesaurus** provides quick access to synonyms (words with similar meanings) and antonyms (words with opposite meanings) for a given word or phrase. Word provides a built-in thesaurus for those times when you've found yourself with the "perfect" word at the tip of your tongue—only to have it stay there.

METHOD
1. SELECT: a word to look up in the Thesaurus
2. CHOOSE: Tools, Language, Thesaurus (or press (SHIFT) + (F7))
3. SELECT: the desired word in the *Replace with Synonym* list box
4. SELECT: Replace command button

PRACTICE
You will now practice using the Thesaurus.

Setup: Ensure that you've completed the previous lesson and that the "Legal" document is displaying.

1 Using the mouse, select the word "massive" in the first sentence.

2 CHOOSE: Tools, Language, Thesaurus
The Thesaurus dialog box should now appear, as shown in Figure 3.12.

Figure 3.12
Thesaurus dialog box

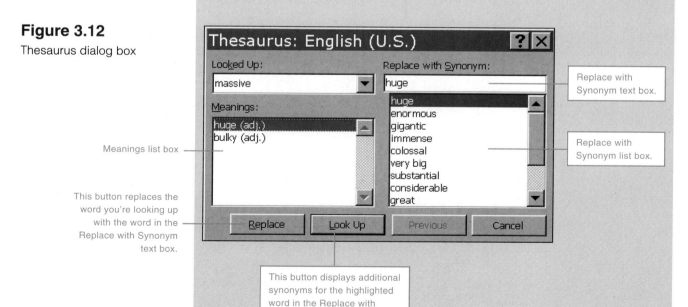

3 To replace the word "massive" with "enormous:"
SELECT: "enormous" in the *Replace with Synonym* list box
CLICK: Replace command button

4 Let's find a synonym for the word "big," appearing at the beginning of the first sentence in the second paragraph. To begin:
SELECT: "big"

5 PRESS: `SHIFT` + `F7`

6 In the *Replace with Synonym* list box:
SELECT: "large"

7 To look up synonyms for "large:"
CLICK: Look Up command button

8 To display the previous list of synonyms:
CLICK: Previous command button

9 To replace the word "big" with "large:"
SELECT: "large" in the *Replace with Synonym* list box
CLICK: Replace command button

10 Save "Legal" to your personal storage location.

3.4.3 Highlighting Text for Review

FEATURE
When others will be reviewing your document online, you may want to highlight those elements that deserve special attention. You can access Word's Highlight tool (🖊▾) from the Formatting toolbar and select an alternate highlight color using the Highlight drop-down arrow. Keep in mind that if your intention is to print your document, you should stick with lighter highlight colors so that your text isn't obscured.

METHOD
- To activate the highlighter:
  CLICK: Highlight button (🖊▾)
- To change the highlight color:
  CLICK: Highlight drop-down arrow (🖊▾)
  CHOOSE: None (no color) or an alternate highlight color

WORD

PRACTICE

You will now practice highlighting text.

Setup: Ensure that you've completed the previous lessons in this module and that the "Legal" document is displaying.

1 Let's begin by selecting a color for the highlighter:
CLICK: Highlight drop-down arrow (⬚⬚▾)
SELECT: red
Word's Highlight tool is now activated, as indicated by the highlighter mouse pointer.

2 With the Highlight tool activated, you simply select the text you want to highlight.
SELECT: the first sentence in the first paragraph
The sentence now appears highlighted in red.

3 SELECT: the third sentence in the first paragraph
Your screen should now appear similar to Figure 3.13.

Figure 3.13

Highlighting text

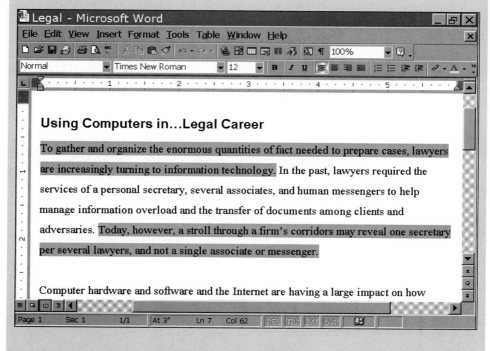

4 To deactivate the Highlight tool:
CLICK: Highlight button

5   To remove highlighting from the first paragraph:
SELECT: the entire first paragraph
CLICK: Highlight drop-down arrow
CHOOSE: None

6   Save and then close the "Legal" document.

3.4 Self Check   What is the procedure for adding a word to Word's custom dictionary?

3.5 Using AutoCorrect

Word's **AutoCorrect** feature works on your behalf to correct common capitalization, spelling, and grammatical errors as you type. For example, AutoCorrect will automatically replace "teh" with "the," "firts" with "first," and "sPorting" with "Sporting." AutoCorrect is preinstalled with over 500 entries that you can add to or change to complement your individual typing habits. In this module, we explore using Word's AutoCorrect feature.

3.5.1 Applying AutoCorrect Entries

FEATURE
It couldn't be easier to apply AutoCorrect entries. Simply type words followed by the desired punctuation, such as a space, period (.) or comma (,) and AutoCorrect will correct any errors that you make.

PRACTICE
You will now type a few words to see AutoCorrect in action.

Setup: Ensure that no documents are open in the application window.

1   Start a new blank document.

2   Type the following sentence, exactly as it appears below.
TYPE: cureously, teh snake slithered awya.
Thanks to our AutoCorrect partner, the sentence should now read "Curiously, the snake slithered away."

3   PRESS: ENTER to insert a blank line

4   Continue to the next lesson.

3.5.2 Adding and Deleting AutoCorrect Entries

FEATURE

If the current list of AutoCorrect entries doesn't include all the entries you want, you can easily add new entries. You can also delete existing AutoCorrect entries.

METHOD

1. CHOOSE: Tools, AutoCorrect
2. TYPE: a word that you often misspell in the *Replace* text box
3. TYPE: the correct spelling in the *With* text box
4. CLICK: Add command button

To add an AutoCorrect entry for inserting text and graphics:

1. SELECT: the text or graphic you want to add
2. CHOOSE: Tools, AutoCorrect
3. TYPE: a name for the entry in the *Replace* text box
4. SELECT: *Plain text* or *Formatted text* option button
5. CLICK: Add command button

To delete an AutoCorrect entry:

1. CHOOSE: Tools, AutoCorrect
2. TYPE: the entry name in the *Replace* text box
3. CLICK: Delete command buttton

PRACTICE

You will now practice adding and deleting AutoCorrect entries.

Setup: Ensure that you completed the previous lesson and that the insertion point is positioned on the second line.

1   What if you frequently type "bak" instead of "back." To instruct Word to correct this mistake automatically, you must add "bak" to the list of AutoCorrect entries. Do the following:
CHOOSE: Tools, AutoCorrect
The AutoCorrect dialog box should now appear (Figure 3.14).

Figure 3.14

AutoCorrect dialog box

These four check boxes affect capitalization corrections.

When this check box is selected, Word will automatically correct and replace text as you type.

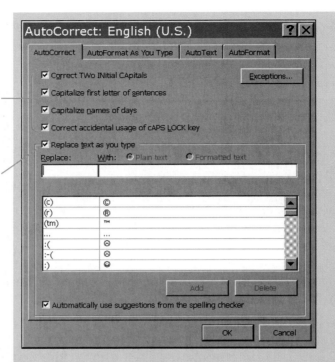

2 Review the existing capitalization check boxes. With these check boxes selected, Word corrects most capitalization errors. Also, drag the dialog box's vertical scroll bar downward to get a feel for the current list of AutoCorrect entries.

3 To insert the word "bak" as an AutoCorrect entry:
TYPE: bak in the *Replace* text box
TYPE: back in the *With* text box
CLICK: Add
CLICK: Close command button

4 To test the new entry:
TYPE: I'll be right bak!
"Back" should have replaced "bak" automatically.

5 Let's create an AutoCorrect entry for inserting your name and address.
PRESS: ENTER twice
TYPE: *your name*
PRESS: ENTER
TYPE: *your street address*
PRESS: ENTER
TYPE: *your city, state, and zip code*
PRESS: ENTER

6 SELECT: the three lines containing your name and address

7 To add the current selection as an AutoCorrect entry, do the following:
CHOOSE: Tools, AutoCorrect
Your name and address should now appear in the *With* text box.

8 TYPE: myinfo in the *Replace* text box
Your screen should now appear similar, but not identical, to Figure 3.15.

Figure 3.15

Creating an AutoCorrect entry for your name and address

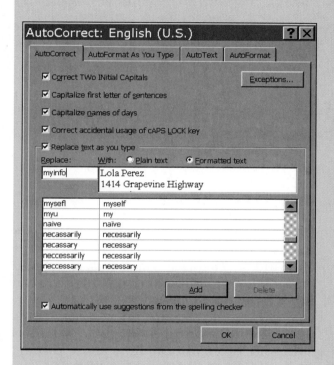

9 To add the entry to the current list of entries:
CLICK: Add command button
CLICK: Close command button

10 Let's insert a blank line at the bottom of the document and then type "myinfo."
PRESS: CTRL + END
PRESS: ENTER
TYPE: myinfo
PRESS: ENTER to activate the AutoCorrect command
The word "myinfo" should have been replaced by your name and address.

To practice deleting entries, let's delete the "bak" and "myinfo" entries you created in this lesson.
CHOOSE: Tools, AutoCorrect
TYPE: bak in the *Replace* text box
CLICK: Delete command button
TYPE: myinfo in the *Replace* text box
CLICK: Delete command button

12 Before continuing to the next lesson:
CLICK: Close command button

13 Close the document without saving.

3.5 Self Check   What is the procedure for adding AutoCorrect entries?

3.6 Chapter Review

Word includes a powerful set of features for modifying your work. The techniques for switching views and changing the zoom factor let you customize your view of the document to suit the current task. The Find and Replace commands simplify the process of locating the information you need and making multiple changes at once throughout a document. The ability to Cut, Copy, and Paste using the Clipboards is highly useful when reorganizing a document or reusing parts of a document elsewhere. Word also includes the capability to drag and drop information short distances and copy formatting attributes using the Format Painter.

The Spelling and Grammar checker tool provides excellent assistance when proofing a document for errors and the Thesaurus helps you find just the right word to convey your message. Finally, Word's Auto-Correct feature helps ensure that common typing mistakes don't creep into your documents.

3.6.1 Command Summary

Many of the commands and procedures appearing in this chapter are summarized in the following table.

Skill Set	To Perform This Task . . .	Do the Following . . .
Working with Text	Find text	CHOOSE: Edit, Find
	Replace text	CHOOSE: Edit, Replace
	Copy formatting options to another area	CLICK: Format Painter button (☑)
	Copy formatting options to several areas	DOUBLE-CLICK: Format Painter button (☑)
	Copy text to the Clipboard	CLICK: Copy button (🖺)
	Move text to the Clipboard	CLICK: Cut button (✂)
	Paste text from the Clipboard	CLICK: Paste button (🖺)
	Drag and drop text (copy)	PRESS: CTRL and then drag the selected text to a new location
	Drag and drop text (move)	DRAG: the selected text to a new location
	Check a document for spelling and grammar errors	CLICK: Spelling and Grammar button (🔤)
	Use the thesaurus	CHOOSE: Tools, Language, Thesaurus
	Highlight text	CLICK: Highlight button (🖊▾)
	Customize AutoCorrect	CHOOSE: Tools, AutoCorrect
Working with Documents	Switching views	CHOOSE: View, Normal, or CHOOSE: View, Web Layout, or CHOOSE: View, Print Layout, or CHOOSE: View, Outline
	Zooming the display	CLICK: Zoom drop-down arrow (100% ▾), or CHOOSE: View, Zoom

3.6.2 Key Terms

This section specifies page references for the key terms identified in this chapter. For a complete list of definitions, refer to the Glossary provided immediately after the Appendix in this learning guide.

AutoCorrect, *p. 116*

Click and Type, *p. 96*

drag and drop, *p. 107*

Format Painter, *p. 101*

Office Clipboard, *p. 104*

Spelling and Grammar command, *p. 110*

thesaurus, *p. 113*

Windows Clipboard, *p. 104*

3.7 Review Questions

3.7.1 Short Answer

1. What are the two methods for copying and moving information?
2. How do you apply AutoCorrect entries?
3. What procedure enables you to get a closer look at your document?
4. Besides a word count, what other statistics appear in the Word Count dialog box?
5. What is the purpose of Web Layout view?
6. What is the procedure for highlighting document text?
7. In Word, when might you want to use the Thesaurus?
8. What is an AutoCorrect *exception?*
9. What menu command enables you to replace text in a document?
10. What is the Format Painter used for?

3.7.2 True/False

1. __F__ When replacing text in Word, you can instruct Word to retrieve whole words.
2. __T__ Double-clicking the Format Painter button enables you to copy formatting attributes to multiple locations.
3. __F__ To move a selection of text using drag and drop, hold down (CTRL) before dragging.
4. __T__ AutoCorrect is preinstalled with over 500 entries that you can add to or change.
5. _____ Outline view describes in outline form how your document will appear in your Web browser.

6. __T__ Drag and drop is used for moving text between documents.
7. __F__ In Word, you can search for words, but not phrases.
8. __T__ Word's Grammar Checker offers several styles of grammar checking.
9. __T__ A thesaurus provides quick access to synonyms.
10. __T__ Once information is placed in the Clipboard, it can be pasted multiple times.

3.7.3 Multiple Choice

1. In _____, you can see how text and graphics will appear on the printed page.
   a. Normal view
   b. Web Layout view
   c. Print Layout view
   d. Outline view

2. Which of the following simplifies the process of formatting text if the same formatting is required in more than one location?
   a. AutoText
   b. Format Painter
   c. Font dialog box
   d. None of the above

3. Which of the following is best for quick "from-here-to-there" copy operations?
   a. Windows Clipboard
   b. Cut, copy, and paste
   c. drag and drop
   d. AutoText

4. Which of the following operations moves text from the Clipboard?
   a. cut
   b. copy
   c. paste
   d. drag and drop

5. Which of the following provides a list of synonyms?
   a. Find command
   b. Replace command
   c. Thesaurus
   d. Spelling and Grammar command

6. Which of the following enables you to paste data multiple times?
   a. Windows Clipboard
   b. Office Clipboard
   c. drag and drop
   d. Both a and b

7. To display statistics about a document:
   a. CHOOSE: Insert, Statistics
   b. CHOOSE: Tools, Spelling and Grammar
   c. CHOOSE: Tools, Statistics
   d. CHOOSE: Tools, Word Count

8. Which of the following helps reduce the number of errors you make in a document?
   a. Spelling and Grammar checker
   b. AutoCorrect
   c. Highlight tool
   d. Both a and b

9. Which of the following enables you to make multiple changes in a document at once?
   a. Find command
   b. Replace command
   c. drag and drop
   d. Copy command

10. Which of the following commands should you always use before submitting a document to others?
    a. Find
    b. Replace
    c. Spelling and Grammar
    d. Thesaurus

3.8 Hands-On Projects

3.8.1 Sandra Baker: Interview Request

In this exercise, you practice using the Find and Replace command and Word's proofing tools.

1. Open the WRD381 data file.
2. Save the document as "Baker Request" to your personal storage location.
3. To replace every occurrence of "Manager" with "Sales Manager," do the following:
   CHOOSE: Edit, Replace
   TYPE: **Manager** in the *Find what* text box
   TYPE: **Sales Manager** in the *Replace with* text box
   CLICK: Replace All command button
   Word should have made two replacements.
4. To proceed:
   CLICK: OK command button
   CLICK: Close to leave the Find and Replace dialog box
5. After moving the insertion point to the top of the document, let's check the document for spelling and grammar errors.
   CLICK: Spelling and Grammar button ()
6. During the spelling and grammar check, do the following:
   - Change "respnse" to "response"
   - Change "apealing" to "appealing"
   - Change "hav" to "have"
   - Change "som" to "some"
   - Delete the second occurrence of "my"
7. At the completion of the spelling and grammar check, press ENTER.
8. Find a different word for the word "appealing" in the first paragraph.
9. Print the document.
10. To display statistics about this document:
    CHOOSE: Tools, Word Count
11. Write the statistics that relate to words, characters (no spaces), and paragraphs near the bottom of your printout. When you're finished, click the Close command button to leave the Word Count dialog box.
12. Save and then close the document.

3.8.2 Clearwater Systems Inc: Report

In this exercise, you open a document and then practice applying formatting commands, using the Format Painter, and using the Replace command.

1. Open the WRD382 data file.
2. Save a copy of the file as "Clearwater Report" to your personal storage location.
3. Insert a blank line at the very top of the document and then position the insertion point on the blank line.
4. To insert a new title:
    TYPE: `Clearwater Systems Inc.—A History`
    PRESS: ENTER
5. Format the title using a Times New Roman, 18 point font.
6. Format the "The First Fifty Years" title with the bold attribute and an Arial, 11 point font.
7. Let's use the Font dialog box to apply the Small-Cap effect to the topic line "The First Fifty Years." Ensure that the topic line is still selected.
    CHOOSE: Format, Font
    SELECT: *Small Caps* check box
    CLICK: OK command button
8. Let's use the Format Painter feature to copy the topic line formatting to the remaining four topic lines. Ensure that the topic line is still selected.
    DOUBLE-CLICK: Format Painter button (⊿)
    SELECT: "The European Connection" topic line
    SELECT: "The Roots of Mail Order" topic line
    SELECT: "Direction vs. Management" topic line
    SELECT: "A Time for Reflection" topic line
    CLICK: Format Painter button (⊿) to deactivate the Format Painter
9. To use the Replace command to italicize the business name "Clearwater Systems" throughout the document, but not in the title, do the following:
    PRESS: CTRL + HOME to move the insertion point to the top of the document
    CHOOSE: Edit, Replace
    TYPE: `Clearwater Systems` in the *Find what* text box
    TYPE: `Clearwater Systems` in the *Replace with* text box
    PRESS: CTRL +i to apply italic formatting to the replacement text using the keyboard shortcut
10. To begin making replacements:
    CLICK: Find Next command button
11. The text "Clearwater Systems" in the title should now be selected. Since we don't want to change the title:
    CLICK: Find Next command button

12. Continue by clicking the Replace command button to replace all remaining occurrences of the text "Clearwater Systems."
13. To conclude the replacement procedure:
    CLICK: OK command button
    CLICK: Close button
14. Proof the document for spelling and grammar errors.
15. Save, print, and then close the document.

3.8.3 Norstorm Systems: Memo Update

You will now practice copying text and using the Format Painter.

1. Open the WRD383 data file.
2. Save the document as "Norstorm Update" to your personal storage location.
3. Format the word "Date:" to include a 14 point font size.
4. Use the Format Painter to apply this formatting to the remaining lines in the document.
5. Using drag and drop, change the order of the information lines to reflect the following: Date, RE, To, From, Cc, and Priority.
6. Copy the entire memo to the Clipboard, then paste the text below the existing memo to create two memos on a single page.
7. Save the revised document.
8. Preview, print, and then close the document.

3.8.4 Aardvark Enterprises: Bulletin Update

In this exercise, you open a formatted news bulletin and then practice moving text, proofing the document, and customizing Auto-Correct.

1. Open the WRD384 data file.
2. Save the document as "Aardvark Update" to your personal storage location.
3. Rearrange the order of the information sessions so that they are arranged in chronological order.
4. Use the Thesaurus to find alternative words for "council" and "attitude" in the first paragraph.
5. Add "aaardvark" as an AutoCorrect entry that includes "aardvark" as the replacement text.
6. To test your AutoCorrect addition, move to the end of the document and then type `Aaardvark Industries.`
7. Check the document for spelling and grammar errors.
8. Save, print, and then close the document.

3.8.5 On Your Own: Hobby Description

In a one- to two-page document, describe your hobby or favorite pursuit. Create a formatted cover page that includes the title for your document, your name, and the current date. Apply interesting formatting to the title-page text and then create an AutoCorrect entry for your name and the current date. Using the AutoCorrect feature, include your name and the current date in the closing of the document. Check your document for spelling and grammar errors before saving the document. Save the document as "Hobby Description" to your personal storage location and then print the document.

3.8.6 On Your Own: Upcoming Event Flyer

Using techniques you've learned in this and previous chapters, design a one-page flyer that describes an upcoming event, such as an auto show or school picnic. The objective of the flyer is to get the word out about the event and to motivate people to attend. Include your name at the end of the flyer as the contact person for the event. Apply compelling formatting and use the thesaurus to find effective words. Check your document for spelling and grammar errors before saving the document. Save the flyer as "Upcoming Event" to your personal storage location and then print the flyer.

3.9 Case Problems: Cottage Crafts

Now that Nigel has learned several techniques for modifying documents, he decides to make changes to the documents he posted on the store's bulletin board.

In the following case problems, assume the role of Nigel and perform the same steps he would perform to complete these tasks. You may want to re-read the chapter opening before proceeding.

1. Nigel begins by opening the WRD391 data file and saving it as "Intro to Antiques" to his personal storage location. He then switches to Normal view and zooms the display to 150% so that he doesn't have to strain his eyes when looking at the screen. Next, he replaces every occurrence of the word "breakable" with the word "collectible." (*Note:* If "Font: Italic" appears below the *Replace with* text box, use the Format command button to reverse this setting. Otherwise, "collectible" will appear italicized throughout the document.) In the final step before saving and printing the document, he proofs the document using the Spelling and Grammar checker.

2. One of Nigel's tenants pointed out to him that the "Intro to Antiques" document should be rearranged. The tenant thinks that the sections in the beginning of the document should be arranged so that the "Introduction" section comes first, the "Getting Started" section comes second, and the "Who are the Collectors" section comes next. Nigel implements these changes by opening the "Intro to Antiques" document and using the Clipboard. He then saves the revised document to his personal storage location.

3. Nigel thinks that the Format Painter tool could help him greatly in formatting the WRD393 document, which contains a glossary of terms. After opening the document, he saves it as "Antique Dictionary" to his personal storage location. Nigel increases the formatting of the first term (Alexandrite) to 12 points. He then increases the amount of space that appears above the term using the following procedure:
   a. CHOOSE: Format, Paragraph
   b. CLICK: *Indents and Spacing* tab
   c. SELECT: "0" in the *Before* spin box
   d. TYPE: **3**
   e. CLICK: OK command button
   Now Nigel uses the Format Painter to apply the same formatting he used on the first term to the remaining terms in the document. After performing a spelling and grammar check, Nigel then saves, prints, and closes the document.

4. Nigel decides to improve the appearance of the WRD394 document and then proof the document. After opening the document, he saves it as "Weights and Measures" to his personal storage location. He then increases the font size of the entire document to 12 points and applies an Arial font. Next, he increases the point size of the document's main title to 20 points and the subtitle to 16 points. He then centers the title and subtitle. Next, he uses the Replace command to replace the phrase "text file" with "document." Nigel then saves and prints the document. With thumbtacks in hand, Nigel marches over to the bulletin board and posts his revised documents.

Notes

Notes

Notes

MICROSOFT WORD 2000
Finalizing Your Work

CHAPTER
FOUR

Chapter Outline

Learning Objectives

After reading this chapter, you will be able to:

- Change margins and page orientation, and align text vertically

- Insert page numbers and create headers and footers

- Add shading to words and paragraphs and add a page border

- Save a document to HTML for publishing on the World Wide Web

WORD

Case Study

Green Thumb Yard Design

Jean and David Bellows of Florence, North Dakota, operate a small landscaping business called Green Thumb Yard Design. Jean is widely recognized for her creative flair and innovative use of materials. David laughingly admits that he provides the labor behind their efforts and that his creative bent is best applied to managing the paperwork and administration needed to run a successful enterprise.

David is enthusiastic about computers and is currently enrolled in a Word 2000 course. His objective is to use his word processing skills to create professional-looking documents that can be published in print form and on his company's Web site.

In this chapter, you and David learn how to finalize a document's layout by changing margins and page orientation, and aligning text vertically on the page. You also learn how to create headers and footers, apply shading to words and paragraphs, and add a page border. Finally, you learn how to save a document to HTML for publishing on the World Wide Web.

4.1 Adjusting the Layout of Your Document

Now that you know how to create, edit, and apply character and paragraph formatting commands, it's time to think about publishing your work for others to see. To present your work in the most flattering way, you may want to change the layout of your document before printing.

Your document's page layout is affected by many factors, including the margins or white space desired around the edges of the page, the size of paper you are using, and the page orientation. Fortunately for us, Word provides a single dialog box, called the Page Setup dialog box, for controlling all of these factors. This module includes lessons on setting margins, changing page orientation, and aligning text vertically on the page. You also learn how to insert page breaks.

4.1.1 Changing Margins

FEATURE
Word allows you to set the top, bottom, left, and right margins for a page. In addition, you can set a gutter margin to reserve space for binding a document. The **gutter** is where pages are joined in the center of the binding or hole-punched for a ring binder. Word provides default settings of 1.25 inches for the left and right margins and 1 inch for the top and bottom margins. The gutter margin is initially set at 0 inches, as most documents are not bound.

METHOD
1.   CHOOSE: File, Page Setup
2.   CLICK: *Margins* tab to display the settings page for margins
3.   Specify a gutter margin if binding the document, as well as the top, bottom, left, and right margins.

PRACTICE
You will now open a long document and then practice changing margins.

Setup: Ensure that no documents are open in the application window.

1 Open the WRD410 student file.

2 Save a copy as "Demographic Analysis" to your personal storage location.

3 To change the margins from the default settings to an even 1 inch around the entire page:
CHOOSE: File, Page Setup
CLICK: *Margins* tab
The Page Setup dialog box should now appear, as shown in Figure 4.1.

Figure 4.1

Page Setup dialog box:
Margins tab

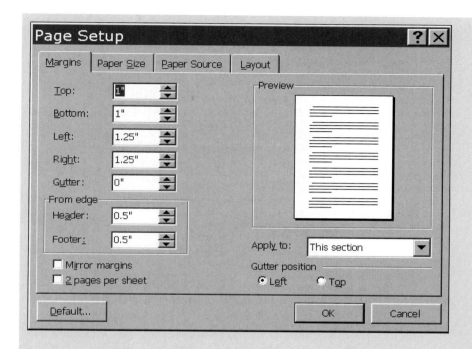

4 To change the left and right margins to 1 inch:
CLICK: down arrow beside the *Left* margin spin box repeatedly,
until the value decreases to 1 inch
CLICK: down arrow beside the *Right* margin spin box repeatedly,
until the value decreases to 1 inch
(*Note:* As you click the symbols, the *Preview* area at the right-
hand side shows the effect of the change on your document.)

5 To illustrate the use of a gutter, increase the counter in the *Gutter*
text box to 0.5 inches:
CLICK: up arrow beside the *Gutter* text box repeatedly, until the
value increases to 0.5 inches
(*Note:* The shaded area in the *Preview* area represents the binding.)

6 Reset the Gutter margin to 0 inches.

7 To leave the Page Setup dialog box:
CLICK: OK command button

8 Save the document.

4.1.2   Changing Page Orientation

FEATURE
If you consider your typical document printed on an 8.5-inch by 11-inch piece of paper, text usually flows across the 8.5-inch width of the page. In this case, your document is said to have a **portrait orientation** (8.5-inches wide and 11-inches tall). When text flows across the 11-inch side of the page, the document is said to have a **landscape orientation** (11-inches wide and 8.5 inches tall). In Word, it's easy to switch between portrait and landscape orientation.

METHOD
1.   CHOOSE: File, Page Setup
2.   CLICK: *Paper Size* tab
3.   CLICK: *Portrait* or *Landscape* option button in the *Orientation* area

PRACTICE
You will now practice displaying your document using a landscape orientation.

Setup: Ensure that you've completed the previous lesson. The "Demographic Analysis" document should be open in the application window.

To specify a landscape orientation:
CHOOSE: File, Page Setup
CLICK: *Paper Size* tab
Your screen should now appear similar to Figure 4.2.

Figure 4.2

Page Setup dialog box:
Paper Size tab

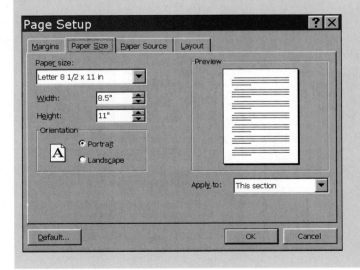

2 SELECT: *Landscape* option button in the *Orientation* area
Notice that the *Preview* area changes with your selection.

3 To proceed:
CLICK: OK command button

4 When you return to the document, the page may be too wide to
fit in the current view. To remedy this problem:
CLICK: Print Layout button (📄) located to the left of the hori-
zontal scroll bar
CLICK: Zoom drop-down arrow (100% ▾) on the Standard
toolbar
CHOOSE: Page Width
Your screen should now appear similar to Figure 4.3.

Figure 4.3

Print Layout view with a
landscape orientation

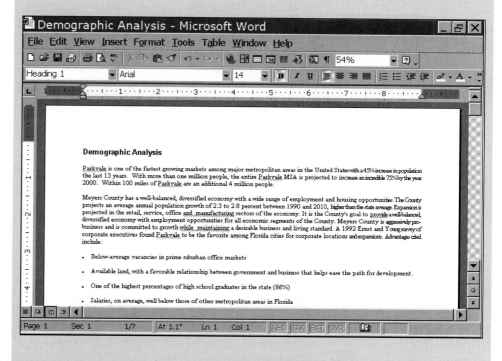

5 Let's return your document to a portrait orientation.
CHOOSE: File, Page Setup
CLICK: *Paper Size* tab
SELECT: *Portrait* option button in the *Orientation* area
CLICK: OK command button

6 Proceed to the next lesson.

4.1.3 Aligning Text Vertically

FEATURE
When you begin typing in a new document, the first line of text prints near the top of the page. In some cases, such as when inserting a cover page or table of data in your document, you may want to center or justify text between the top and bottom margins. You can choose to align a selection of text or the entire document.

METHOD
1. CHOOSE: File, Page Setup
2. SELECT: *Layout* tab
3. SELECT: an alignment option in the *Vertical alignment* drop-down list
4. SELECT: what you want to align in the *Apply to* drop-down list
5. CLICK: OK command button

PRACTICE
You will now start a new document and then vertically align a selection of text.

Setup: Ensure that you've completed the previous lessons in this module.

1 Start a new blank document.

2 TYPE: `Finalizing Your Work`
PRESS: [ENTER] twice
TYPE: `By your name`

3 With the text selected that you typed in the previous step, increase the point size to 26 points and then click the Center button (≡) to align the text between the left and right margins.

4 Let's pretend that the text we typed in step 2 will be used for the title page of a multipage report. As such, let's center the text between the top and bottom margins.
CHOOSE: File, Page Setup
SELECT: *Layout* tab
Your screen should now appear similar to Figure 4.4. Notice that the document's *Vertical alignment* setting is currently set to "Top."

Figure 4.4

Page Setup dialog box: *Layout* tab

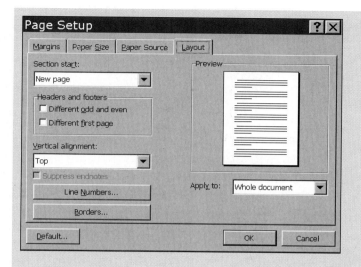

5. To change the vertical alignment to center:
SELECT: *Vertical alignment* drop-down arrow
SELECT: Center

6. To apply this setting to the current selection:
SELECT: *Apply to* drop-down arrow
SELECT: Selected Text from the drop-down menu

7. To proceed:
CLICK: OK command button
The text is now centered both horizontally and vertically on the page.

8. Preview and then close the document without saving.

4.1.4 Forcing a Page Break

FEATURE
Word automatically repaginates a document as you change your page-layout settings and insert and delete text. In Word's Normal view, a dotted line appears wherever Word begins a new page, sometimes splitting an important paragraph or a list of items. Rather than leaving the text on separate pages, you can instruct Word to start a new page at the insertion point by inserting a hard page break. The quickest way to force a hard page break is to press CTRL + ENTER.

METHOD
1. Position the insertion point at the beginning of the line that you want moved to the top of the next page.
2. PRESS: `CTRL` + `ENTER`, or
   CHOOSE: Insert, Break and select the *Page Break* option button

PRACTICE
You will now practice inserting a page break.

Setup: Ensure that you've completed the previous lessons in this module and that the "Demographic Analysis" document is displaying.

1 So that your screen matches ours, let's change the zoom factor and switch to Normal view.
CLICK: Zoom drop-down arrow (`100% ▾`)
CHOOSE: 100%
CHOOSE: View, Normal

2 Position the insertion point near the bottom of page 1, to the left of the paragraph that begins with "Recently, Parkvale was...".

3 To insert a page break at this location:
PRESS: `CTRL` + `ENTER`
Your screen should now appear similar to Figure 4.5. Notice that a dotted line, containing the words "Page Break," now appears above the insertion point. Also, notice that the insertion point is now positioned at the top of page 2.

WORD

Figure 4.5

Inserting a page break

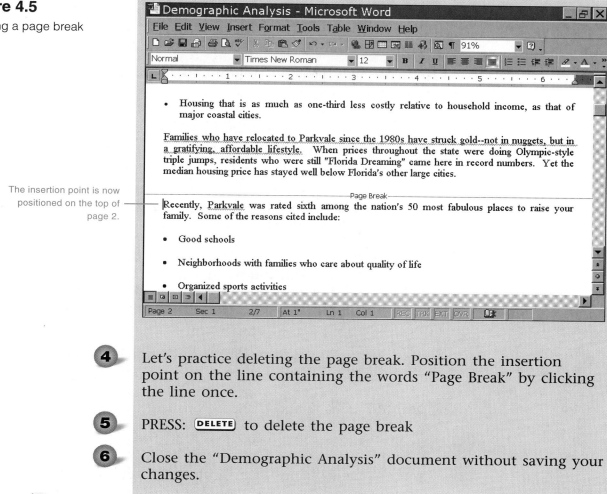

The insertion point is now positioned on the top of page 2.

4 Let's practice deleting the page break. Position the insertion point on the line containing the words "Page Break" by clicking the line once.

5 PRESS: DELETE to delete the page break

6 Close the "Demographic Analysis" document without saving your changes.

4.1 Self Check   In inches, how wide are the left and right margins by default?

4.2   Inserting Headers and Footers

A document **header** and **footer** appear at the top and bottom of each page. The header often contains the title or section headings for a document while the footer might show the page numbers or copyright information. Adding a header or footer produces a more professional-looking document and makes longer documents easier to read.

4.2.1 Inserting Page Numbers

FEATURE
In Word, you position page numbers in a document's header or footer. You can align the page number with the left, center, or right margins. To view inserted page numbers, you must preview or print the document or switch to Print Layout view.

METHOD
1. CHOOSE: Insert, Page Numbers
2. SELECT: an option from the *Position* drop-down list box
3. SELECT: an option from the *Alignment* drop-down list box
4. To specify an alternate number format (optional):
   CLICK: Format command button
   SELECT: an option from the *Number format* drop-down list
   CLICK: OK command button
5. CLICK: OK command button to close the Page Numbers dialog box

PRACTICE
You will now insert page numbers in an existing three-page document.

Setup: No documents should be open in the application window.

1 Open the WRD420 student file.

2 Save the file as "Consumer Confidence" to your personal storage location.

3 CHOOSE: Insert, Page Numbers
The dialog box in Figure 4.6 should appear on your screen. (*Note:* Figure 4.6 also shows the dialog box for changing the numbering format from standard numbers to letters or Roman numerals.)

WORD

Figure 4.6

Page Numbers dialog box

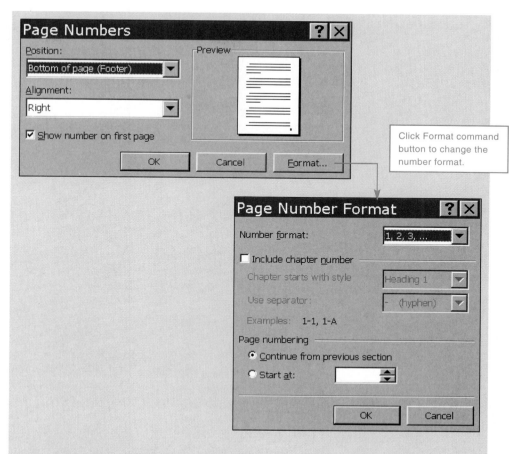

Click Format command button to change the number format.

4 Notice that "Bottom of page (Footer)" is selected in the *Position* box and "Right" is selected in the *Alignment* box. To insert the page number with these default settings:
CLICK: OK command button

5 You can only view inserted page numbers in Print Layout view, the current view mode. To view the page number on the bottom on page 1, do the following:
DRAG: the horizontal scroll box to the bottom of page 1
If you look closely, you'll see the page number in the bottom-right corner of the page. (*Note:* The page number only appears dimmed on screen; it won't appear dimmed in the printed document.)

6 To change the format of the page numbers from numbers to letters:
CHOOSE: Insert, Page Numbers
CLICK: Format command button
CHOOSE: "A, B, C, ..." from the *Number format* drop-down list
CLICK: OK command button to close the Page Number Format dialog box
CLICK: OK command button to close the Page Numbers dialog box
Notice that the page number has changed to a letter in your document.

7 To change the format of the page numbers back to numbers:
CLICK: Undo button (⌐◦⌐)

8 Save the revised document.

9 To prepare for the next lesson:
PRESS: CTRL + HOME to move the insertion point to the top of the document

4.2.2 Creating Headers and Footers

FEATURE
By default, the information that you include in a header or footer prints on every page in your document.

METHOD
1. CHOOSE: View, Header and Footer
2. Edit and format the header and footer using regular formatting commands and the buttons on the Header and Footer toolbar.
3. CLICK: Close button on the Header and Footer toolbar

PRACTICE
You will now create a header in the "Consumer Confidence" document. You will also edit the footer to include additional information.

Setup: Ensure that you've completed the previous lesson in this module. The "Consumer Confidence" document should be displaying in Print Layout view.

1 To edit the document's header:
CHOOSE: View, Header and Footer
Upon choosing this command, Word displays the Header and Footer toolbar, creates a framed editable text area for the header and footer, and dims the document's body text. Your screen should now appear similar to Figure 4.7. Figure 4.8 identifies the buttons in the Header and Footer toolbar.

Figure 4.7

Viewing a doucment's header and footer

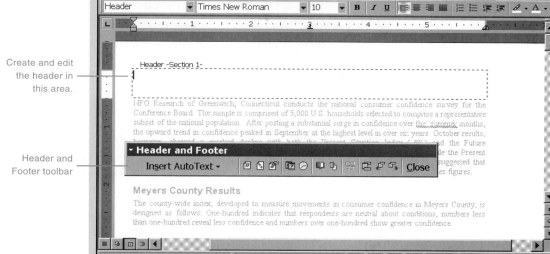

Create and edit the header in this area.

Header and Footer toolbar

Figure 4.8

Header and Footer toolbar

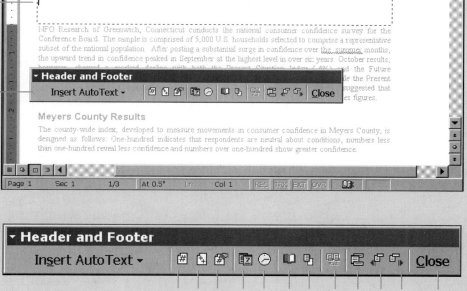

> **2** The insertion point is blinking in the document's header area.
> TYPE: Annual Consumer Confidence Survey

> **3** To format the header, do the following:
> SELECT: header text
> CHOOSE: Arial from the Font drop-down list
> CHOOSE: 14 from the Font Size drop-down list
> CLICK: Bold button (B)
> CLICK: Center button (≡)

> **4** To view the footer:
> CLICK: Switch Between Header and Footer button (国) on the Header and Footer toolbar

5 The page number, inserted in the last lesson, appears at the far right-hand side of the first line in the footer area. Your insertion point should appear flashing at the left edge. Let's now enter information about when the document was last printed.
TYPE: Printed on
PRESS: Space Bar

6 To place the date and time in the footer and have them automatically updated when you print the document:
CLICK: Insert Date button (🖾) on the Header and Footer toolbar
PRESS: Space Bar
TYPE: at
PRESS: Space Bar
CLICK: Insert Time button (🕒) on the Header and Footer toolbar

7 To format the footer, you must first select the text in the footer. Because the footer includes inserted fields, the easiest way to do this is to use the Edit, Select All command.
CHOOSE: Edit, Select All to select the footer text

8 Issue the following character formatting commands:
SELECT: Arial from the *Font* drop-down list (Times New Roman ⏷)
CLICK: Bold button (**B**)
Congratulations, you've finished creating and formatting a header and footer. Your screen should now appear similar to Figure 4.9 (with a different date and time in the footer, of course).

Figure 4.9

Completing the footer

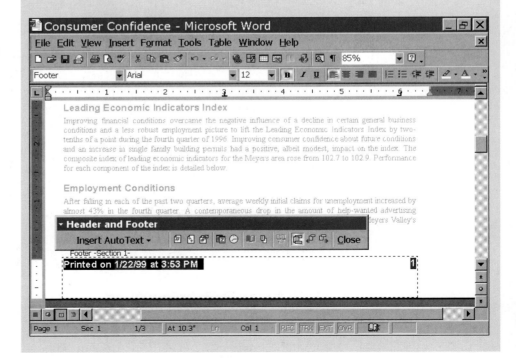

9 To finish editing the footer and return to your document:
CLICK: Close button on the Header and Footer toolbar

10 Scroll through the document to view the headers and footers.
(*Tip:* To switch back to the header and footer in Print Layout
view, you double-click its dimmed text.)

11 Save and then close the document.

3.2 Self Check   How do you insert page numbers in a document?

4.3   Adding Shading and Page Borders

Documents that incorporate interesting visual effects do a better job
of engaging readers than those that use plain formatting. You already
know how to use character formatting commands to add visual
emphasis to words and paragraphs. Shading and page borders can
make your documents even more visually interesting.

4.3.1 Shading Words and Paragraphs

FEATURE
Shading provides another means for emphasizing text. Just make
sure that your shading color doesn't match your text color too
closely. Otherwise, your text will be difficult to read.

METHOD
1. CHOOSE: Format, Borders and Shading
2. CLICK: *Shading* tab
3. CLICK: a color in the *Fill* palette or choose an option from
    the *Style* drop-down list
4. SELECT: Text or Paragraph in the *Apply to* drop-down list
5. CLICK: OK command button

PRACTICE
You will now open an existing flier and then apply shading to
words and paragraphs.

Setup: Ensure that no documents are open in the application window.

1 Open the WRD430 student file.

2 Save the document as "Sleepy Hollow" to your personal storage location.

3 Drag the vertical scroll bar downward until you see the three dates and times. In the next few steps, you're going to shade this information so that it will stand out on the printed flier.

4 SELECT: Saturday, 8am–noon

5 To shade the text selection:
CHOOSE: Format, Borders and Shading
CLICK: *Shading* tab
Your screen should now appear similar to Figure 4.10. (*Note:* The Preview area on the right side of the dialog box may appear different on your computer.)

Figure 4.10

Borders and Shading dialog box: *Shading* tab

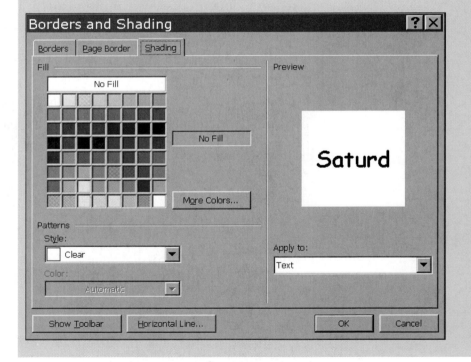

WORD

6 In the *Fill* palette:
CLICK: Yellow

7 Next, take a look at the setting in the *Apply to* drop-down list. When "Text" is selected, the shading only covers the selected letters. When "Paragraph" is selected, the shading will extend from the left to the right margin of the page. If "Paragraph" isn't currently selected:
SELECT: Paragraph from the *Apply to* drop-down list
CLICK: OK command button
The date and time, as well as a line that extends from the left to the right margin, should now appear shaded.

8 To repeat the same shading for the next date:
SELECT: Tuesday-Thursday, 8am-7pm
CHOOSE: Edit, Repeat Borders and Shading
(*Note:* You could have also pressed CTRL+y.)

9 Using the same procedure as in step 8, repeat the shading for the "Monday and Friday, 8am-5pm" date.

10 CLICK: away from the shaded text so that no text is selected
Your screen should now appear similar to Figure 4.11.

Figure 4.11

Shading document text

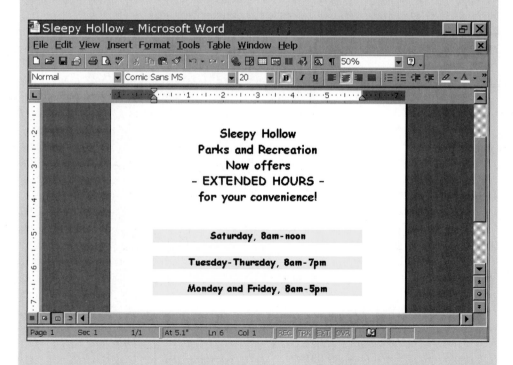

11 Save the revised document.

4.3.2   Creating a Page Border

FEATURE
Page borders add visual interest to title pages, flyers, and newsletters. Your borders can consist of a solid line or a graphic that is repeated around the page.

METHOD
1. CHOOSE: Format, Borders and Shading
2. CLICK: *Page Border* tab
3. CLICK: an option in the *Setting* area, or
    CHOOSE: a graphic from the *Art* drop-down list
4. Optionally:
    SELECT: a color from the *Color* drop-down list
    SELECT: a width from the *Width* drop-down list
5. CLICK: OK command button

PRACTICE
You will now add a page border to the Sleepy Hollow flier.

Setup: Ensure that you've completed the previous lesson and that the "Sleepy Hollow" document is displaying.

1 To insert a page border:
CHOOSE: Format, Borders and Shading
SELECT: *Page Border* tab

2 Let's see what happens when we click the *Box* graphic in the *Setting* area.
CLICK: *Box* graphic in the *Setting* area
Your screen should now appear similar to Figure 4.12. The result of your selection displays in the *Preview* area to the right.

Figure 4.12

Borders and Shading dialog
box: *Page Border* tab

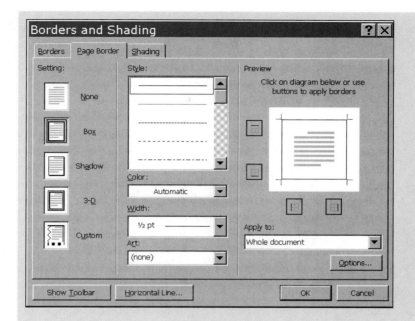

3 Let's increase the width of the line.
CLICK: *Width* drop-down arrow
CHOOSE: 3 pt from the drop-down list

4 To experiment with changing the border style:
CLICK: Shadow graphic in the *Setting* area

5 Let's select a graphic for the border.
CLICK: *Art* drop-down arrow
DRAG: the menu's vertical scroll box down until you see a row
of green trees
CHOOSE: tree graphic

6 To continue:
CLICK: OK command button
Your screen should now appear similar to Figure 4.13.

Figure 4.13

Creating a graphic border

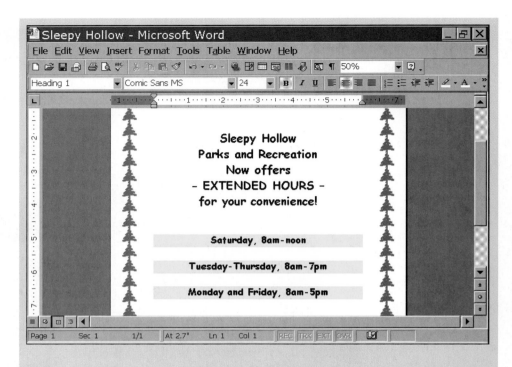

⑦ If you drag the document's vertical scroll bar up and down, you'll see that the border surrounds all four sides of the page.

⑧ Save and then close the "Sleepy Hollow" document.

4.3 Self Check   What are page borders used for?

4.4 Publishing to the Web

For those of you new to the online world, the **Internet** is a vast collection of computer networks that spans the entire planet, made up of many smaller networks connected by standard telephone lines, fiber optics, and satellites. The term **Intranet** refers to a private and usually secure local or wide area network that uses Internet technologies to share information. To access the Internet, you need a network or modem connection that links your computer to your account on the university's network or an Independent Service Provider (ISP).

Once you are connected to the Internet, you can use Web browser software, such as Microsoft Internet Explorer or Netscape Navigator, to access the **World Wide Web.** The Web provides a visual interface for the Internet and lets you search for information by simply clicking on highlighted words and images, known as **hyperlinks.** When you click a link, you are telling your computer's Web browser to retrieve a page from a Web site and display it on your screen. Not only can you publish your documents on the Web, you can incorporate hyperlinks directly within a document to facilitate navigating between documents.

4.4.1 Saving a Document to HTML

FEATURE

Word makes it easy to convert a document for display on the World Wide Web. The process involves saving the document to **HTML** (Hypertext Markup Language) format for publishing to a Web server. Once saved using the proper format, you may upload the files to your company's Intranet or to a Web server.

METHOD

- To preview how a document will appear as a Web page:
  CHOOSE: File, Web Page Preview
- To save a document into HTML format for Web publishing:
  CHOOSE: File, Save as Web Page

PRACTICE

You will now practice saving an existing document for publishing to the Web.

Setup: No documents should be displaying in the application window.

1 Open the WRD440 student file.

2 Save the file as "Organic Coffee" to your personal storage location.

3 To preview your document as a Web page:
CHOOSE: File, Web Page Preview
Figure 4.14 shows the document displayed using Internet Explorer.

Figure 4.14

Using Web Page Preview mode

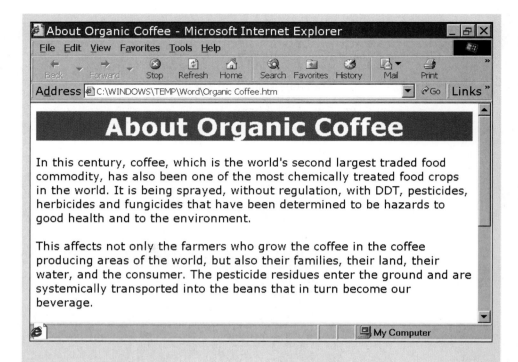

4   To close the Internet Explorer window:
CLICK: its Close button (⊠)

5   To save the current document as a Web page:
CHOOSE: File, Save as Web Page
The Save As dialog box appears with some additional options.
Notice that "Web Page" appears as the file type in the *Save as type* drop-down list box.

6   Using the *Save in* drop-down list box or the Places bar:
SELECT: *your storage location*, if not already selected
(*Note:* To publish or post your document Web page to an Intranet or to the Internet, you can click the Web Folders button (⌂) in the Places bar and then select a server location.)

7   To proceed with the conversion to HTML:
CLICK: Save command button
The document is saved as "*Web Page Name*.htm" to your personal storage location.

8   To close the Web browser window:
CLICK: its Close button (⊠)

Close the "Organic Coffee" document without saving the changes.

 To exit Microsoft Word:
CHOOSE: File, Exit

4.4 Self Check   Why might you want to convert a Word document to HTML?

4.5 Chapter Review

Depending on your output requirements, you may want to change one or more page-layout settings before printing. Using the Page Setup dialog box, you can change margins, switch between portrait and landscape modes, and align text vertically on the page. Headers, footers, and page numbers, which are printed in the top and bottom margins of the page, help provide a structure for your document in order to keep your audience focused.

When used wisely, such effects as shading and page borders make your document more visually appealing. Once your document looks the way you want, you can print it or even publish it on your personal or company Web site. Before publishing a document to a Web site, you must save it to HTML.

4.5.1 Command Summary

Many of the commands and procedures appearing in this chapter are summarized in the following table.

Skill Set	To Perform This Task . . .	Do the Following . . .
Working with Text	Insert a page break	Press: CTRL + ENTER , or CHOOSE: Insert, Break
Working with Paragraphs	Shade selected words and paragraphs	CHOOSE: Format, Borders and Shading CLICK: *Shading* tab
Working with Documents	Change margins	CHOOSE: File, Page Setup CLICK: *Margins* tab
	Change page orientation	CHOOSE: File, Page Setup CLICK: *Paper Size* tab CLICK: *Portrait* or *Landscape* option button in the *Orientation* area
	Align text vertically	CHOOSE: File, Page Setup CLICK: *Layout* tab SELECT: an option in the *Vertical alignment* drop-down list
	Insert page numbers	CHOOSE: Insert, Page Numbers
	Create a header or footer	CHOOSE: View, Header and Footer
	Create a page border	CHOOSE: Format, Borders and Shading CLICK: *Page Border* tab
Working with	Save a document to HTML Page	CHOOSE: File, Save as Web **Files**
	Preview a Web page	CHOOSE: File, Web Page Preview

4.5.2 Key Terms

This section specifies page references for the key terms identified in this chapter. For a complete list of definitions, refer to the Glossary provided immediately after the Appendix in this learning guide.

footer, *p. 147*   Internet, *p. 158*

gutter, *p. 140*   Intranet, *p. 158*

header, *p. 147*   landscape orientation, *p. 142*

HTML, *p. 159*   portrait orientation, *p. 142*

hyperlink, *p. 158*   World Wide Web, *p. 158*

4.6 Review Questions

4.6.1 Short Answer

1. How do you create a Web document from a standard Word document?
2. What is the difference between a document that prints with a portrait orientation versus one that prints with a landscape orientation?
3. When might you want to use Word's vertical alignment feature?
4. What is a page break?
5. How do you create a page border?
6. How is the term *gutter* used in Word?
7. What is the difference between the Internet and an Intranet?
8. What is the procedure for viewing headers and footers on the screen?
9. Why might it be a good idea to include shading in a document?
10. How wide are a document's top and bottom margins by default?

4.6.2 True/False

1. _____ Using the Insert, Page Numbers command, page numbers are inserted in the header or footer area.
2. _____ The Header and Footer toolbar automatically appears when you create a header or footer.
3. _____ Clicking the Align Vertical button on the Formatting toolbar aligns text vertically between the top and bottom margins.
4. _____ Once inserted, it's not possible to apply character formatting to a page number.
5. _____ By default, a footer appears at the top of the page.
6. _____ It's possible to change the width of a page border, but not its color.
7. _____ Page breaks are always used when printing documents in a landscape orientation.
8. _____ You can delete a page break by positioning the insertion point on the break and pressing (DELETE).
9. _____ You can align page numbers with the left, center, and right margins.
10. _____ In Word, you can format headers and footers using regular formatting commands.

4.6.3 Multiple Choice

1. Which of the following are commonly found on Web pages?
   a. hyperlinks
   b. Internet
   c. Intranet
   d. All of the above

2. Which of the following do you use to change margins?
   a. Standard toolbar
   b. Formatting toolbar
   c. Page Setup dialog box
   d. Paragraph dialog box

3. To force a page break, press:
   a. (CTRL) + (BREAK)
   b. (CTRL) + (ALT)
   c. (CTRL) + (ENTER)
   d. None of the above

4. To create a footer, choose:
    a. View, Footer
    b. View, Header and Footer
    c. Insert, Header and Footer
    d. Both a and b

5. To shade words and paragraphs in Word, choose:
    a. Insert, Shading
    b. Format, Borders and Shading
    c. View, Shading
    d. None of the above

6. To view headers and footers, you must switch to:
    a. Normal view
    b. Print Layout view
    c. Print Preview mode
    d. Both b and c

7. Which of the following can you change using the Page Setup dialog box?
    a. margins
    b. page orientation
    c. vertical alignment
    d. All of the above

8. By default, your documents print with:
    a. 1 inch top and bottom margins
    b. 1.25 inches left and right margins
    c. a portrait orientation
    d. All of the above

9. Switching between portrait and landscape modes involves the:
    a. Print Layout view
    b. Page Setup dialog box
    c. Header and Footer toolbar
    d. None of the above

10. By default, the information you store in a header or footer prints:
    a. on just the first page
    b. on every other page
    c. on every page
    d. None of the above

4.7 Hands-On Projects

4.7.1 Sandra Baker: Résumé

This exercise practices changing margins, inserting and modifying a header, and applying a page border. You will begin by opening a model for a sample résumé.

1. Open the WRD471 data file.
2. Save the document as "Baker Résumé" to your personal storage location.
3. To set the left and right margins to .5 inch:
   CHOOSE: File, Page Setup
   CLICK: *Margins* tab
   CLICK: down arrow beside the *Left* margin text box until the value decreases to .5 inch
   CLICK: down arrow beside the *Right* margin text box until the value decreases to .5 inch
   CLICK: OK command button
4. In this step, you insert a header that includes Sandra's name and address.
   CHOOSE: View, Header and Footer
   TYPE: Sandra Baker in the Header area
   PRESS: (ENTER)
   TYPE: 4344 Mission Road
   PRESS: (ENTER)
   TYPE: Oakland, CA 95622
   PRESS: (ENTER)
   TYPE: (415) 212-6822
5. To apply a larger point size and right-align the name and address lines:
   SELECT: the name and address lines
   SELECT: 14 from the Font Size drop-down list
   CLICK: Align Right button (▤) on the Formatting toolbar
   CLICK: Close on the Header and Footer toolbar
6. Do the following to apply a solid page border to the document:
   CHOOSE: Format, Borders and Shading
   CLICK: *Page Borders* tab
   CLICK: Box in the *Setting* area
   CHOOSE: 1½ pt from the *Width* drop-down list
   CLICK: OK command button
7. Let's edit the header so that it is centered between the margins.
   CHOOSE: View, Header and Footer
   SELECT: the name and address lines
   CLICK: Center button (▤) on the Formatting toolbar
   CLICK: Close on the Header and Footer toolbar

8. Let's increase the left margin to .75 inches.
    CHOOSE: File, Page Setup
    CLICK: *Margins* tab
    SELECT: the value in the *Left* margin text box
    TYPE: **.75**
    CLICK: OK command button
9. Save the revised document.
10. Preview and print the document.

4.7.2 Clearwater Systems Inc: Letterhead

In this exercise, you practice creating a header and applying shading. You will create the letterhead stationery shown in Figure 4.15.

Figure 4.15

"Clearwater Letterhead" document

1. Create a new blank document.
2. To open the header section of the document:
    CHOOSE: View, Header and Footer
    DRAG: the center tab down and off the Ruler
3. Do the following to begin creating the header:
    PRESS: `TAB` to move to the center tab position
    TYPE: Clearwater Systems, Inc.
    PRESS: `ENTER`
    PRESS: `TAB` to move to the center tab position
    TYPE: 3402 South Border Blvd
    PRESS: `ENTER`
    PRESS: `TAB` to move to the center tab position
    TYPE: Santa Clara, CA 94532
    PRESS: `ENTER`
    PRESS: `TAB` to move to the center tab position
    TYPE: Phone (913) 234-2321
    PRESS: `ENTER`
    PRESS: `TAB` to move to the center tab position
    TYPE: Fax (913) 543-5324
    PRESS: `ENTER` twice
4. To complete typing the header text:
    PRESS: `TAB` to move to the center tab position
    TYPE: St. Louis
    PRESS: Space bar five times
    TYPE: San Diego
    PRESS: Space bar five times
5. Continue typing the remaining city names (Seattle, Charleston, Portland, Las Vegas) using the same procedure as in the previous step. Don't press the Space Bar after typing the final city (Las Vegas).
6. Format the company name using Times New Roman, 22 points, and the bold attribute.
7. Format the address and business locations using Arial, 8 points, and the bold attribute.
8. To apply blue shading to the entire header:
    CHOOSE: Edit, Select All
    CHOOSE: Format, Borders and Shading
    CLICK: *Shading* tab
    CLICK: royal blue in the *Fill* color palette
    CLICK: OK command button
9. With the contents of the header still selected, apply white as the font color.
10. Save the document as "Clearwater Letterhead" to your personal storage location.
11. Print the document.

4.7.3 Norstorm Systems: Report

You will now practice changing margins, inserting headers and footers, and applying shading to a previously created report.

1. Open the WRD473 data file.
2. Save the document as "Norstorm Report" to your personal storage location.
3. Set the top and bottom margins to 1 inch, the left margin to 1.5 inches, and the right margin to 1.25 inches.
4. Insert a header that displays the words "Annual Report" aligned to the left.
5. Apply the bold attribute to the header text.
6. Apply 15% gray shading to the header text, making sure that the shading stretches from the left to the right margin.
7. Add a footer that includes a page number centered between the margins and then close the Header and Footer toolbar
8. Save the revised document as "Norstorm Report," replacing the previous version.
9. Preview and print the revised report.

4.7.4 Aardvark Enterprises: Advertisement

In this exercise, you will practice applying shading, creating a page border, changing margins and page orientation, and aligning text vertically to modify an advertisement created previously.

1. Open the WRD474 data file.
2. Save the document as "Aardvark Advertisement" to your personal storage location.
3. Set the top and bottom margins to .5 inches and the left and right margins to 1 inch.
4. Change the orientation of the document from portrait to landscape.
5. Align all the text in this document vertically between the top and bottom margins.
6. Apply yellow shading to title, subtitle, and date that appear at the top of the document. The shading should span from the left to the right margin.
7. Apply yellow shading to the last two lines of the document. The shading should span from the left to the right margin.
8. Insert a solid page border that is 6 points wide and uses the *Shadow* setting.
9. Save the revised document.
10. Preview and print your work.

4.7.5 On Your Own: Budget

This exercise practices using some commands from previous chapters as well as several page layout commands.

1. Start a new document and then switch to Normal view.
2. Set the following page dimensions:
Paper Orientation:	Portrait
Top Margin:	1 inch
Bottom Margin:	1 inch
Left Margin:	1 inch
Right Margin:	1 inch
3. Enter the information in Figure 4.16. (*Hint*: Use tabs.)

Figure 4.16

"Budget 2K" revised

document

```
                        ABC REALTY INC.


                                                        2000
          Revenue
             Commercial Properties          $125,500,000
             Residential Properties           35,000,000
             Leased Properties                   875,000

          Total Revenue                     $161,375,000


          Expenses
             Insurance                           $50,000
             Salaries                            750,000
             Commissions                      15,500,000
             Office Supplies                      25,000
             Office Equipment                     20,000
             Utilities                            15,000
             Leased Automobiles                   50,000
             Travel                              250,000
             Advertising & Promotion         25,000,000


          Total Expenses                      41,660,000

          Net Income                        $119,715,000
```

4. Align all the text vertically between the top and bottom margins.

5. Apply the shading of your choice to the title "ABC Realty Inc.".
6. Save the document as "Budget2K" to your personal storage location.
7. Preview and print the document.
8. Save the document to HTML for posting on the company's Web site.

4.7.6 On Your Own: Newsletter

In this exercise, you will open the WRD476 student file and format it to create a presentable newsletter. The newsletter should have a landscape orientation and a page break before the "Our Mandate" heading. It should include the text "Twin Valley Banner" in the header and the header text should appear in a large, boldfaced font with 15% shading. The footer should include the current date in the left-aligned position and the current page number in the right-aligned position. All the headings in the newsletter should include yellow shading that spans from the left to the right margin. The newsletter should also include a blue page border. Preview and print your work and save the document as "Twin Valley Banner."

4.8 Case Problems: Green Thumb Yard Design

Now that David has learned how to change page layout, create headers and footers, and add shading and page borders, he is ready to finalize some of the draft documents that he had prepared previously.

In the following case problems, assume the role of David and perform the same steps he would perform to complete these tasks. You may want to re-read the chapter opening before proceeding.

1. David decides to add some finishing touches to a document he likes to send out to new customers about maintaining a healthy lawn. After opening the WRD481 data file, he saves it as "Green Thumb Lawn" to his personal storage location. He begins by creating a centered footer that reads "Article courtesy of the Toro Company" and applies the bold attribute. Next, he inserts a page break before the "What does fertilizer do for my lawn?" heading. David then applies black paragraph shading to the title and changes the font color to white. After saving the revised document, he previews the document as a Web page. Satisfied with its appearance in his Web browser, he then saves it to HTML for later posting on his company's Web site.

2. David decides that his business's letterhead stationery should include a listing of some of the services that his business provides. He drafts several designs to discuss with Jean, then develops and prints a copy of his favorite design (shown below). (*Hint:* He inserts the letterhead information in a header and sets center tabs in positions 1.75, 3, and 4.5 inches. He also sets a right tab in position 6 inches.) He saves this file as "Green Thumb Letterhead."

Figure 4.17

"Green Thumb Letterhead"

Green Thumb Yard Design
12348 Main St., Florence, ND 68345
Phone: 542-3457 Fax: 542-3458

CUTTING & RAKING	WEED CONTROL	FERTILIZING	PEST CONTROL	AERATING
DETHATCHING	LANDSCAPING	PRUNING	PLANTING	SEEDING

3. Green Thumb could use a more professional-looking invoice. David determines what information should be included and drafts a design that looks clean and readable. He includes all the text at the top of the document in the header, down to and including the word "INVOICE." He then changes the margins of the invoice to 1 inch on all sides. He prepares, previews and prints his new document, then saves it as "Green Thumb Invoice."

Figure 4.18

"Green Thumb Invoice"

Green Thumb Yard Design   Landscaping
                                               Water Gardens
                                               Free Estimates

INVOICE

                              DATE: _____
                         INVOICE NO.   _____

            CLIENT: _____
            STREET: _____
        CITY/STATE: _____
         ZIP CODE: _____

The following work was completed on _____ .

_____

_____

              AMOUNT DUE: _____
                              PAYABLE UPON RECEIPT

4. David wants to begin distributing a newsletter to his customers. He opens the document named WRD484 that he prepared previously and then makes some changes to his work. He includes his bulletin name **Green Thumb Gardens** centered on the first line of the header, his slogan **Growing in Excellence** centered on the second line, the text **Issue #1** aligned to the left on the third line, and the date aligned to the right on the third line. He then applies green shading to the entire header, changes the font color of the header text to white, applies the bold attribute, and enlarges the font size of the bulletin name to 16 points. He adds a footer that displays the business name, address, and phone numbers on separate lines, centered between the left and right margins.

Next, David inserts a page break before the "FALL" heading and inserts an extra line at the top of page 2 so that there is space between the heading and the header information. Finally, David applies a thick green page border to the document. After he has previewed and printed his bulletin, he saves it as "Green Thumb Bulletin."

Notes

Notes

Notes

ADVANTAGE
SERIES

MICROSOFT®
EXCEL 2000

BRIEF EDITION

MICROSOFT EXCEL 2000
Creating a Worksheet

CHAPTER
ONE

Chapter Outline

Learning Objectives

After reading this chapter, you will be able to:

- Describe the different components of the application and workbook windows

- Select commands using the Menu bar and right-click menus

- Enter text, dates, numbers, and formulas in a worksheet

- Edit and erase cell data

- Use the Undo and Redo commands

- Start a new workbook

- Save, open, and close a workbook

EXCEL

Case Study

Rain Coast Air

Rain Coast Air is a small, privately owned airline charter company operating in the Pacific Northwest. The company's typical charter business consists of flying tourists to remote fishing lodges and transporting geological and forestry survey crews. Earlier this year, Rain Coast added a third aircraft to their fleet of float planes and retained two full-time and three part-time pilots. Along with the pilots, Rain Coast employs a dock hand and a mechanic. Hank Frobisher, the general manager, started the company and oversees all aspects of its operation.

To date, Rain Coast has been operating with a bare minimum of paperwork and manual record-keeping. All bookings are hand-written into a scheduling chart and the pilots fill out trip logs at the end of each flight. Invoices and receipts are simply turned over to a bookkeeping service as Hank cannot afford a staff accountant. Just lately, however, Hank is finding it increasingly difficult to obtain the information he needs to make key business decisions. To remedy this, he hired Jennifer Duvall, the daughter of one of his pilots, as an office assistant. Jennifer is enrolled in a Microsoft Excel course at the local community college and has expressed some enthusiasm in setting up worksheets for Rain Coast Air.

In this chapter, you and Jennifer learn how to work with Microsoft Excel. Specifically, you create new worksheets from scratch and enter text, numbers, dates, and formulas. Then you learn how to edit and modify cell entries and even practice using the Undo command. To complete the chapter, you practice saving and opening workbooks.

1.1 Getting Started with Excel

Microsoft Excel 2000 is an electronic spreadsheet program that enables you to store, manipulate, and chart numeric data. Researchers, statisticians, and business people use spreadsheet software to analyze and summarize mathematical, statistical, and financial data. Closer to home, you can use Excel to create a budget for your monthly living expenses, analyze returns in the stock market, develop a business plan, or calculate the loan payment required to purchase a new car.

Excel enables you to create and modify worksheets—the electronic version of an accountant's ledger pad—and chart sheets. A **worksheet** (Figure 1.1) is divided into vertical columns and horizontal rows. The rows are numbered and the columns are labeled from A to Z, then AA to AZ, and so on to column IV. The intersection of a column and a row is called a **cell.** Each cell is given a **cell address,** like a post office box number, consisting of its column letter followed by its row number (for example, B4 or FX400). Excel allows you to open multiple worksheets and chart sheets within its application window.

Figure 1.1

An electronic worksheet

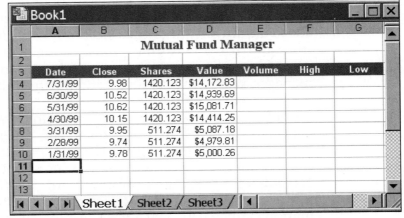

Numba Crunchers

A **chart sheet** (Figure 1.2) displays a chart graphic that is typically linked to data stored in a worksheet. When the data is changed, the chart is updated automatically to reflect the new information. Charts may also appear alongside their data in a worksheet.

Figure 1.2

A chart sheet

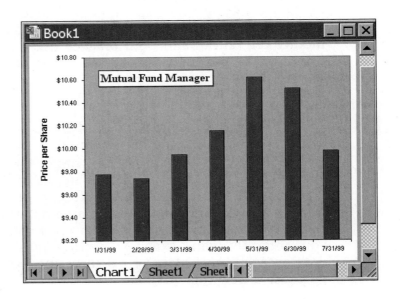

Related worksheets and chart sheets are stored together in a single disk file called a **workbook.** You can think of an Excel workbook as a three-ring binder with tabs at the beginning of each new page or sheet. In this module, you load Microsoft Excel and proceed through a guided tour of its application and document windows.

EXCEL

1.1.1 Loading and Exiting Excel

FEATURE
You load Excel from the Windows Start menu, accessed by clicking the Start button (⬛Start) on the taskbar. Because Excel requires a significant amount of memory, you should always exit the application when you are finished doing your work. Most Windows applications allow you to close their windows by clicking on the Close button (☒) appearing in the top right-hand corner.

METHOD
- To load Excel:
  CLICK: Start button (⬛Start)
  CHOOSE: Programs, Microsoft Excel
- To exit Excel:
  CHOOSE: File, Exit from Excel's Menu bar

PRACTICE
You will now load Microsoft Excel using the Windows Start menu.

Setup: Ensure that you have turned on your computer and that the Windows desktop appears.

1 Position the mouse pointer over the Start button (⬛Start) appearing in the bottom left-hand corner of the Windows taskbar and then click the left mouse button once. The Start pop-up menu appears as shown here.

2 Position the mouse pointer over the Programs menu option. Notice that you do not need to click the left mouse button to display the list of programs in the fly-out or cascading menu.

3 Move the mouse pointer horizontally to the right until it highlights an option in the Programs menu. You can now move the mouse pointer vertically within the menu to select an option.

4 Position the mouse pointer over the Microsoft Excel menu option and then click the left mouse button once. After a few seconds, the Excel application window appears.

6 An Office Assistant character, like "Rocky" (shown at the right), may now appear. You will learn how to hide this character in lesson 1.1.2.

In Addition
Switching Among
Applications

Each application that you are currently working with is represented by a button on the taskbar. Switching between open applications on your desktop is as easy as clicking the appropriate taskbar button, like switching channels on a television set.

1.1.2 Touring Excel

FEATURE
The Excel **application window** acts as a container for the worksheet and chart windows. It also contains the primary interface components for working in Excel, including the *Windows icons, Menu bar, Toolbars, Name box, Formula bar,* and *Status bar.* The components of a worksheet **document window** include *Scroll bars, Sheet tabs, Tab Split box,* and *Tab Scrolling arrows.* Figure 1.3 identifies several of these components.

PRACTICE
In a guided tour, you will now explore the features of the Excel application and document windows.

Setup: Ensure that you've loaded Excel.

1 Excel's application window is best kept maximized to fill the entire screen, as shown in Figure 1.3. As with most Windows applications, you use the Title bar icons—Minimize (▭), Maximize (▢), Restore (▣), and Close (☒)—to control the display of a window using the mouse. Familiarize yourself with the components labeled in Figure 1.3.

Figure 1.3

Excel's application window

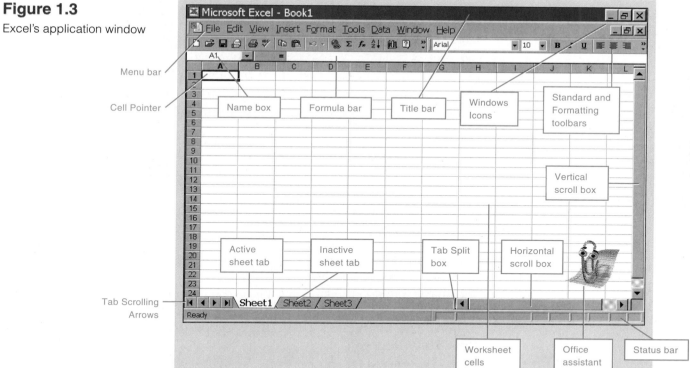

EXCEL

2 The Menu bar contains the Excel menu commands. To execute a command, you click once on the desired Menu bar option and then click again on the command. Commands that appear dimmed are not available for selection. Commands that are followed by an ellipsis (...) will display a dialog box. Pull-down menus that display a chevron ( ) at the bottom display further menu options when selected.

To practice working with the Excel Menu bar:
CHOOSE: Help
This instruction tells you to click the left mouse button once on the Help option appearing in the Menu bar. (*Note:* All menu commands that you execute in this guide begin with the instruction "CHOOSE.")

3 To display other pull-down menus, move the mouse to the left over other options in the Menu bar. As each option is highlighted, a pull-down menu appears with its associated commands.

4 To leave the Menu bar without making a command selection:
CLICK: in a blank area of the Title bar

5 Excel provides context-sensitive *right-click menus* for quick access to menu commands. Rather than searching for the appropriate command in the Menu bar, you can position the mouse pointer on any object, such as a cell, graphic, or toolbar button, and right-click the mouse to display a list of commonly selected commands.

To display a cell's right-click menu:
RIGHT-CLICK: cell A1
The pop-up menu at the right should appear.

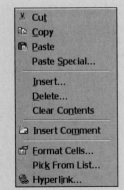

6 To remove the cell's right-click menu from the screen:
PRESS: (ESC)

7 If an Office Assistant character currently appears on your screen, do the following to hide it from view:
RIGHT-CLICK: *the character*
CHOOSE: Hide from the right-click menu
(*Note:* The character's name may appear in the command, such as "Hide Rocky.")

1.1.3 Customizing Menus and Toolbars

FEATURE

Some people argue that software becomes more difficult to learn and use with the addition of each new command or feature. In response to this sentiment, Microsoft developed **adaptive menus** that display only the most commonly used commands. By default, Microsoft Office 2000 ships with the adaptive menus feature enabled. However, you may find this dynamic feature confusing and choose to turn off the adaptive menus. Likewise, the Standard and Formatting toolbars are positioned side-by-side in a single row by default. Again, you may find it easier to locate buttons when these toolbars are positioned on separate rows.

METHOD

To disable the adaptive menus feature:
1. CHOOSE: Tools, Customize
2. SELECT: *Menus show recently used commands first* check box, so that no "✔" appears

EXCEL

To display the Standard and Formatting toolbars on separate rows:
1. CHOOSE: Tools, Customize
2. SELECT: *Standard and Formatting toolbars share one row* check box, so that no "✔" appears

PRACTICE
In this lesson, you disable the adaptive menus feature and display the Standard and Formatting toolbars on separate rows.

Setup: Ensure that you've completed the previous lesson.

1 To begin, display the Tools menu:
CHOOSE: Tools
You should now see the Tools pull-down menu. When a desired command does not appear on a menu, you can extend the menu to view all of the available commands by waiting for a short period, by clicking on the chevron (⟱) at the bottom of the pull-down menu, or by double-clicking the option in the Menu bar.

2 Let's turn off the adaptive menus feature and customize the Standard and Formatting toolbars. Do the following:
CHOOSE: Customize from the Tools pull-down menu
The Customize dialog box should now appear (Figure 1.4.)

Figure 1.4
Customize dialog box

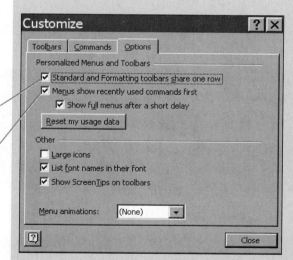

Customize toolbars

Customize Menu bar

3 SELECT: *Menus show recently used commands first* check box, so that no "✔" appears

4 SELECT: *Standard and Formatting toolbars share one row* check box, so that no "✔" appears

5

To proceed:
CLICK: Close button

Figure 1.5 displays the Standard and Formatting toolbars as they should now appear on your screen. The Standard toolbar provides access to file management and editing commands, in addition to special features such as wizards. The Formatting toolbar lets you access cell formatting commands.

IMPORTANT: *For the remainder of this learning guide, we assume that the adaptive menus feature has been disabled and that the Standard and Formatting toolbars are positioned on separate rows.*

Figure 1.5

Standard toolbar

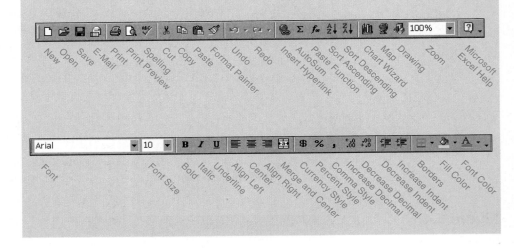

Formatting toolbar

| **In Addition** | You can move toolbars around the Excel application window using the |
| Moving Toolbars | mouse. A *docked* toolbar appears attached to one of the window's borders. An *undocked* or *floating* toolbar appears in its own window, complete with a Title bar and Close button. To float a docked toolbar, drag the Move bar (▌) at the left-hand side toward the center of the window. To redock the toolbar, drag its Title bar toward a border until it attaches itself automatically. |

1.1 Self Check   How do you turn the adaptive menus feature on or off?

1.2 Creating Your First Worksheet

You create a worksheet by entering text labels, numbers, dates, and formulas into the individual cells. To begin entering data, first move the cell pointer to the desired cell in the worksheet. Then type the information that you want to appear in the cell. And finally, complete the entry by pressing (ENTER) or by moving the cell pointer to another cell. In this module, you learn how to navigate a worksheet, enter several types of data, and construct a simple formula expression.

1.2.1 Moving the Cell Pointer

FEATURE
You move the **cell pointer** around a worksheet using the mouse and keyboard. When you first open a new workbook, the cell pointer is positioned on cell A1 in the Sheet1 worksheet. Excel displays the current cell address in the **Name box,** appearing at the left-hand side of the Formula bar.

METHOD
Some common keystrokes for navigating a worksheet include:
- (↑), (↓), (←), and (→)
- (HOME), (END), (PgDn), and (PgDn)
- (CTRL) + (HOME) to move to cell A1
- (CTRL) + (END) to move to the last cell in the active worksheet area
- (F5) GoTo key for moving to a specific cell address

PRACTICE
You will now practice moving around an empty worksheet.

Setup: Ensure that Excel is loaded and a blank worksheet appears.

1 With the cell pointer in cell A1, move to cell D4 using the following keystrokes:
PRESS: (→) three times
PRESS: (↓) three times
Notice that the cell address, D4, is displayed in the Name box and that the column (D) and row (4) headings in the frame area appear boldface.

2 To move to cell E12 using the mouse:
CLICK: cell E12
(*Hint*: Position the cross mouse pointer over cell E12 and click the left mouse button once.)

3   To move to cell E124 using the keyboard:
PRESS: `PgDn` until row 124 is in view
PRESS: `↑` or `↓` to select cell E124
(*Hint*: The `PgUp` and `PgDn` keys are used to move up and down a worksheet by as many rows as fit in the current document window.)

4   To move to cell E24 using the mouse, position the mouse pointer on the vertical scroll box and then drag the scroll box upwards to row 24, as shown in Figure 1.6. Notice that a yellow Scroll Tip appears identifying the current row. When you see "Row: 24" in the Scroll Tip, release the mouse button. Then click cell E24 to select the cell.

Figure 1.6

Dragging the vertical
scroll bar

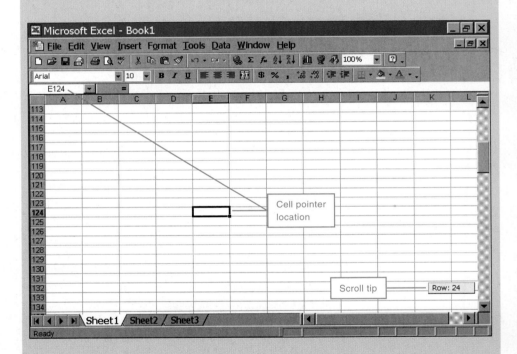

5   To move quickly to a specific cell address, such as cell AE24:
CLICK: once in the Name box
TYPE: ae24
PRESS: `ENTER`
The cell pointer scoots over to cell AE24. (*Hint*: Because cell addresses are not case sensitive, you need not use capital letters when typing a cell address.)

EXCEL

6 To move the cell pointer in any direction until the cell contents change from empty to filled, filled to empty, or until a border is encountered, press CTRL with an arrow key. For example:
PRESS: CTRL + ➡ to move to column IV
PRESS: CTRL + ⬇ to move to row 65536
The cell pointer now appears in the bottom right-hand corner of the worksheet.

7 To move back to cell A1:
PRESS: CTRL + HOME

1.2.2 Entering Text

FEATURE
Text labels are used to enhance the readability of a worksheet by providing headings, instructions, and descriptive information. Although a typical worksheet column is only eight or nine characters wide, a single cell can hold thousands of characters. With longer entries, the text simply spills over the column border into the next cell, if it is empty.

METHOD
TYPE: *a text string*
PRESS: ENTER

PRACTICE
In this example, you begin a simple worksheet by specifying text labels for the row and column headings.

Setup: Ensure that the cell pointer is positioned in cell A1 of the Sheet1 worksheet.

1 Let's begin the worksheet by entering a title. As you type the following entry, watch the Formula bar:
TYPE: Income Statement

2 To accept an entry, you press ENTER or click the Enter button (☑) in the Formula bar. To cancel an entry, you press ESC or click the Cancel (☒) button. To proceed:
PRESS: ENTER
Notice that the entry does not fit in a single column and must spill over into column B. This is acceptable as long as you don't place an entry into cell B1. Otherwise, you need to increase the width of column A.

After you press (ENTER), you may notice that the cell pointer moves to the next row. (*Note:* If your cell pointer remains in cell A1, choose Tools, Options from the Menu bar and click the *Edit* tab in the Options dialog box. Ensure that there is a check mark in the *Move selection after Enter* check box, as shown in Figure 1.7.)

Figure 1.7

Options dialog box: *Edit* tab

Ensure that this check box is selected and that the *Direction* drop-down list box displays Down.

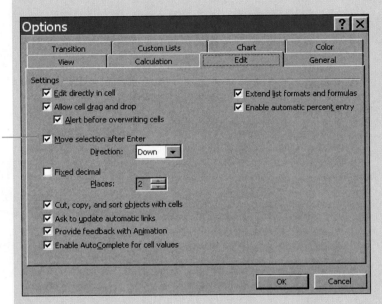

3 Move the cell pointer to cell B3.

4 Enter the following text label:
TYPE: **Revenue**
PRESS: ⊕
Notice that pressing ⊕ provides the same result as pressing (ENTER).

5 To complete entering the row labels:
TYPE: **Expenses**
PRESS: ⊕
TYPE: **Profit**
PRESS: (ENTER)
All of the text data has now been entered into the worksheet.

EXCEL

1.2.3 Entering Dates

FEATURE

You enter dates into a cell using one of the common date formats recognized by Excel, such as mm/dd/yy (12/25/99) or dd-mmm-yy (25-Dec-99). Excel treats a date (or time) as a formatted number or value. Consequently, you can use date values to perform arithmetic calculations, such as finding out how many days have elapsed between two calendar dates.

METHOD

TYPE: *a date*, using a recognized date format
PRESS: ENTER

PRACTICE

You will now add date values as column headings.

Setup: Ensure that you have completed the previous lesson.

1   Move to cell C2.

2   To enter a month and year combination as a date value, you use the format mmm-yy. For example:
TYPE: Sep-99
PRESS: →
(*Note:* Pressing → moves the cell pointer one cell to the right.)

3   In cell D2, do the following:
TYPE: Oct-99
PRESS: →
TYPE: Nov-99
PRESS: →
TYPE: Dec-99
PRESS: ENTER
Your worksheet should now appear similar to Figure 1.8.

Figure 1.8

Entering date values into a worksheet

(handwritten: Date under formula)

	A	B	C	D	E	F	G
1	Income Statement						
2			Sep-99	Oct-99	Nov-99	Dec-99	
3		Revenue					
4		Expenses					
5		Profit					
6							

4   Move the cell pointer to cell C2. Looking in the Formula bar, notice that the entry reads "9/1/1999" and not "Sep-99." As shown here, a cell's appearance on the worksheet can differ from its actual contents.

1.2.4 Entering Numbers

FEATURE
Numbers are entered into a worksheet for use in performing calculations, preparing reports, and creating charts. You can enter a raw or unformatted number, like 3.141593, or a formatted number, such as 37.5% or $24,732.33. It is important to note that phone numbers, Social Security numbers, and zip codes are not treated as numeric values, since they are never used in performing mathematical calculations. Numbers and dates are right-aligned when entered as opposed to text, which aligns with the left border of a cell.

METHOD
TYPE: *a number*, using recognized symbols
PRESS: ENTER

PRACTICE
You will now add some numbers to the worksheet.

Setup: Ensure that you have completed the previous lesson.

1 Move to cell C3.

2 To enter a value for September's revenue, do the following:
TYPE: 112,500
PRESS: ➡
Notice that you placed a comma (,) in the entry to separate the thousands from the hundreds. Excel recognizes symbols such as commas, dollar signs, and percentage symbols as numeric formatting.

3 In cell D3, do the following:
TYPE: 115,800
PRESS: ➡
TYPE: 98,750
PRESS: ➡
TYPE: 112,830
PRESS: ENTER

4 Move the cell pointer to cell C3. Notice that the Formula bar reads "112500" without a comma separating the thousands. Similar to date values, numeric values may be formatted to display differently on the worksheet than the actual value stored.

1.2.5 Entering Formulas

FEATURE
You use formulas to perform calculations, such as adding a column of numbers. A **formula** is an expression, containing numbers, cell references, and/or mathematical operators, that is entered into a cell in order to display a result. The basic mathematical operators ("+" for addition, "-" for subtraction, "/" for division, and "*" for multiplication) and rules of precedence from your high school algebra textbooks apply to an Excel formula. In other words, Excel calculates what appears in parentheses first, multiplication and division operations (from left to right) second, and, lastly, addition and subtraction (again from left to right.)

METHOD
1. SELECT: the cell where you want the result to appear
2. TYPE: = (an equal sign)
3. TYPE: *the desired expression*, such as A4+B4
4. PRESS: ENTER

PRACTICE
You will now enter formulas into the worksheet that multiply the Revenue values by 60% to yield the related Expenses.

Setup: Ensure that you have completed the previous lesson.

1 Move to cell C4. Notice that the first step in entering a formula is to move to the cell where you want the result to display.

2 To inform Excel that you will be entering a formula, you type an equal sign. Do the following:
TYPE: =

3 In order to calculate September's expenses as 60% of the month's revenue, you multiply the cell containing the revenue value (cell C3) by 60%. Do the following:
TYPE: c3*60%
PRESS: ➡
The result, 67500, appears in the cell.

4 In cell D4, you will use a method called *pointing* to enter the required formula. With pointing, you use the mouse or keyboard to point to the cell reference that you want included in an expression. To illustrate:
TYPE: =
PRESS: ⬆
Notice that a dashed marquee appears around cell D3 and that the value "D3" appears in the Formula bar.

5 To finish entering the formula:
TYPE: *60%
PRESS: ➡
The result, 69480, appears in the cell.

6 For November's calculation, you will use the mouse to point to the desired cell reference. Do the following:
TYPE: =
CLICK: cell E3
Notice that cell E3 displays a dashed marquee to denote its selection.

7 To complete the row:
TYPE: *60%
PRESS: ➡
The result, 59250, appears.

8 Lastly, enter the formula for December by typing:
TYPE: =f3*.6
PRESS: ENTER
The result, 67698, appears in cell F4. Notice that you used the value .6 instead of 60% to yield this result. Your worksheet should now appear similar to Figure 1.9.

Figure 1.9

Entering formulas into a worksheet

	A	B	C	D	E	F	G
1	Income Statement						
2			Sep-99	Oct-99	Nov-99	Dec-99	
3		Revenue	112,500	115,800	98,750	112,830	
4		Expenses	67500	69480	59250	67698	
5		Profit					
6							

9 To illustrate the true power of Excel, you can change a cell's value and all the formulas in the worksheet that reference that cell are updated automatically. Do the following:
ELECT: cell F3
TYPE: 100,000
PRESS: ENTER
Notice that the Expense calculation for Dec-99 (cell F4) is immediately updated to display 60000.

10 To conclude this module, you will close the worksheet without saving the changes. From the Menu bar:
CHOOSE: File, Close

11 In the dialog box that appears:
CLICK: No command button
There should be no workbooks open in the application window.

EXCEL

 To display a new workbook and worksheet for use in the next module:
CLICK: New button ( ) on the Standard toolbar
A new workbook, entitled Book2, appears in the document area.

1.2 Self Check Explain why a phone number is not considered a numeric value in an Excel worksheet.

1.3 Editing Your Work

What if you type a label, a number, or a formula into a cell and then decide it needs to be changed? Both novices and experts alike make data entry errors when creating a worksheet. Fortunately, Excel provides several features for editing information that has already been entered. In this module, you learn how to modify existing cell entries, erase the contents of a cell, and undo a command or typing error.

1.3.1 Editing a Cell's Contents

FEATURE
You can edit information either as you type or after you have entered data into a cell. Effective editing of a worksheet is an extremely valuable skill. In fact, few worksheets are created from scratch in favor of simply revising older worksheets. And, as a relatively new user of Excel, you will often find yourself engaged in modifying and maintaining worksheets created by other people.

METHOD
- To edit data as you type, press (BACKSPACE) and then correct the typographical error or spelling mistake.
- To replace a cell's contents entirely, select the cell and then type over the original data.
- To edit a cell whose contents are too long or complicated to retype, double-click the cell to perform **in-cell editing.** In this mode, the flashing insertion point appears ready for editing inside the cell. Alternatively, you can press the (F2) EDIT key or click in the Formula bar to enter Edit mode, in which case you edit the cell's contents in the Formula bar. Regardless, once the insertion point appears, you perform your edits using the arrow keys, (DELETE), and (BACKSPACE).

PRACTICE
In this lesson, you create a simple inventory worksheet. Then, you practice modifying the data stored in the worksheet cells.

Setup: Ensure that a blank worksheet appears in the application window.

1 SELECT: cell A1
(*Note:* For the remainder of this guide, you may use either the keyboard or mouse to move the cell pointer.)

2 Let's enter a title for this worksheet:
TYPE: Staples Food Supplies
PRESS: ⬇
TYPE: Inventory List
PRESS: ENTER

3 SELECT: cell A4

4 Now let's add some column headings:
TYPE: Code
PRESS: ➡
TYPE: Product
PRESS: ➡
TYPE: Quantity
PRESS: ➡
TYPE: Price
PRESS: ENTER

5 On your own, complete the worksheet as displayed in Figure 1.10. If you make a typing error, use BACKSPACE to correct your mistake prior to pressing ENTER or an arrow key.

Figure 1.10

Creating an inventory worksheet

	A	B	C	D	E
1	Staples Food Supplies				
2	Inventory List				
3					
4	Code	Product	Quantity	Price	
5	AP01B	Apples	200	0.17	
6	DM21P	Milk	40	2.28	
7	DB29G	Butter	35	3.91	
8	FL78K	Flour	78	1.25	
9	RS04G	Sugar	290	7.23	
10					
11					

EXCEL

6 As the editor for this worksheet, you've noticed that the column heading in cell D4 should read "Cost" and not "Price." To replace this entry:
SELECT: cell D4
TYPE: Cost
PRESS: ENTER
Notice that the new entry overwrites the existing entry.

7 You activate in-cell editing by double-clicking a cell. To practice, let's change the quantity of butter from 35 to 350 packages:
DOUBLE-CLICK: cell C7

Notice that the Status bar now reads "Edit" in the bottom left-hand corner, instead of the word "Ready." A flashing insertion point should also appear inside the cell.

8 To add a "0" to the end of the cell's contents:
PRESS: END to move the insertion point to the far right
TYPE: 0
PRESS: ENTER
Notice that the Status bar once again reads "Ready."

9 You can also activate Edit mode by pressing the F2 EDIT key or by clicking the I-beam mouse pointer inside the Formula bar. In this step, you edit one of the product codes. Do the following:
SELECT: cell A6
Notice that the text "DM21P" appears in the Formula bar.

10 To modify the "DM" to read "DN," position the I-beam mouse pointer over the Formula bar entry, immediately to the left of the letter "M." Click the left mouse button and drag the mouse pointer to the right until the "M" is highlighted. Now that the desired letter is selected:
TYPE: N
PRESS: ENTER
The letter "N" replaces the selected letter in the Formula bar.

1.3.2 Erasing a Cell

FEATURE
You can quickly erase a single cell, a group of cells, or the entire worksheet with a few simple keystrokes. To erase a cell's contents, select the cell and then press DELETE. If you would like to delete other characteristics of a cell, such as formatting attributes or attached comments, choose the Edit, Clear command from the Menu bar.

METHOD

After choosing the Edit, Clear command, select one of the following:

- *All*   Removes the cell contents, formatting, and comments
- *Formats*   Removes the cell formatting only
- *Contents* Removes the cell contents only; same as pressing `DELETE`
- *Comments* Removes the cell comments only

PRACTICE

You will now practice erasing information that is stored in the inventory worksheet.

Setup: Ensure that you have completed the previous lesson.

1 SELECT: cell A2

2 To delete the subtitle:
PRESS: `DELETE`
Notice that you need not press `ENTER` or any other confirmation key. Pressing `DELETE` removes the contents of the cell immediately.

3 SELECT: cell A9

4 In order to delete a group of cells, you must first select the cells. In this step, you select the inventory line item for Sugar. Do the following:
PRESS: `SHIFT` and hold it down
CLICK: cell D9
RELEASE: `SHIFT`
The four cells should now appear highlighted, as shown in Figure 1.11.

Figure 1.11

Selecting a group of cells to erase

	A	B	C	D	E
1	Staples Food Supplies				
2					
3					
4	Code	Product	Quantity	Cost	
5	AP01B	Apples	200	0.17	
6	DN21P	Milk	40	2.28	
7	DB29G	Butter	350	3.91	
8	FL78K	Flour	78	1.25	
9	RS04G	Sugar	290	7.23	
10					

5 To erase all of the cell information:
CHOOSE: Edit, Clear from the Menu bar
CHOOSE: All from the cascading menu

6 PRESS: (CTRL) + (HOME) to move the cell pointer to cell A1

1.3.3 Using Undo and Redo

FEATURE
The **Undo command** allows you to cancel up to your last 16 actions. The command is most useful for immediately reversing a command or modification that was mistakenly performed. If an error occurred several steps before, you can continue "undoing" commands until you return the worksheet to its original state prior to the mistake. Although somewhat confusing, you can undo an Undo command. The **Redo command** allows you to reverse an Undo command that you performed accidentally.

METHOD
To reverse an action or command:
- CLICK: Undo button (◀), or
- CHOOSE: Edit, Undo, or
- PRESS: (CTRL) + z

To reverse an Undo command:
- CLICK: Redo button (▶)

PRACTICE
Let's practice reversing common editing procedures using the Undo command.

Setup: Ensure that you have completed the previous lesson.

1 SELECT: cell A5

2 In order to practice using the Undo command, let's delete the contents of the cell:
PRESS: (DELETE)

3 To undo the last command or action performed:
CLICK: Undo button (◀) on the Standard toolbar
(*CAUTION*: The tip of the mouse pointer should be placed over the curved arrow and not on the attached down arrow.)

4 SELECT: cell C5

5 To modify the quantity of Apples:
TYPE: 175
PRESS: (ENTER)

6 To undo the last entry using a keyboard shortcut:
PRESS: CTRL + z
The value 175 is replaced with 200 in cell C5. (*Hint:* This short-cut keystroke allows you to continue entering data without having to reach for the mouse or choose a menu command.)

7 Let's view the commands that Excel has been tracking for the Undo command. To begin, position the mouse pointer over the down arrow attached to the Undo button (⟲▾) on the Standard toolbar. Then click the down arrow once to display the drop-down list of "undoable" or reversible commands.

8 Move the mouse pointer slowly downward to select multiple commands. Your screen should appear similar to Figure 1.12.

Figure 1.12

Displaying reversible
commands

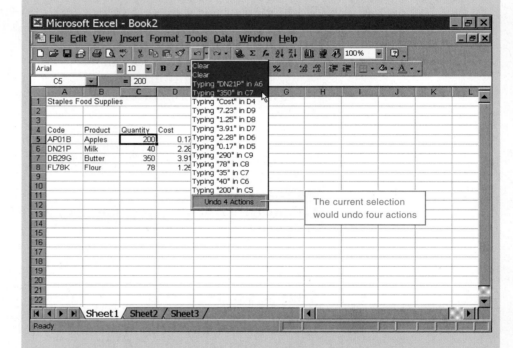

9 To remove the drop-down list without making a selection:
CLICK: down arrow attached to the Undo button (⟲▾)
(*Hint:* You can also click the Title bar, which provides a larger mouse target than the button's down arrow.)

10 To conclude this module, close the worksheet without saving the changes. Do the following:
CHOOSE: File, Close
CLICK: No command button

1.3 Self Check   Why is worksheet editing such a valuable skill?

1.4 Managing Files

Managing the workbook files that you create is an important skill. When you are creating a workbook, it exists only in the computer's RAM (random access memory), which is highly volatile. If the power to your computer goes off, your workbook is lost. For security, you need to save your workbook permanently to the local hard disk, a network drive, or a floppy diskette.

Saving your work to a named file on a disk is similar to placing it into a filing cabinet. For important workbooks (ones that you cannot risk losing), you should save your work at least every 15 minutes, or whenever you're interrupted, to protect against an unexpected power outage or other catastrophe. When naming your workbook files, you can use up to 255 characters, including spaces, but it's wise to keep the length under 20 characters. Furthermore, you cannot use the following characters in naming your workbooks:

$$\backslash \quad / \quad : \quad ; \quad * \quad ? \quad " \quad < \quad > \quad |$$

In the following lessons, you will practice several file management procedures, including creating a new workbook, saving and closing workbooks, and opening existing workbooks.

Important: *In this guide, we refer to the files that have been created for you as the* **student data files.** *Depending on your computer or lab setup, these files may be located on a floppy diskette, in a folder on your hard disk, or on a network server. If necessary, ask your instructor or lab assistant where to find these data files. You will also need to identify a storage location for the files that you create, modify, and save. To download the Advantage Series' student data files from the Internet, visit McGraw-Hill's Information Technology Web site at:*

http://www.mhhe.com/it

1.4.1 Beginning a New Workbook

FEATURE
There are three ways to start creating a new workbook. First, you can start with a blank workbook and then enter all of the data from scratch. Next, you can select a workbook **template** that provides pre-existing data and design elements. A template is a time-saver that promotes consistency in both design and function. And, lastly, you can employ a **wizard** to help lead you step-by-step through creating a particular type of workbook.

METHOD
- To display a new blank workbook:
  CLICK: New button (🗅)
- To begin a workbook using a template or wizard:
  CHOOSE: File, New

PRACTICE
In this example, you use one of Excel's prebuilt templates to create a new workbook for an invoicing application.

Setup: Ensure that no workbooks are displayed in the application window.

1 To view the templates that are available:
CHOOSE: File, New
The blank "Workbook" template icon appears on the *General* tab of the New dialog box. This workbook template is used by Excel when you click the New button (🗅) on the Standard toolbar.

2 The custom templates that are shipped with Excel and that have been installed onto your system appear on the next tab:
CLICK: *Spreadsheet Solutions* tab
Your screen should appear similar to Figure 1.13.

Figure 1.13

Displaying custom workbook templates

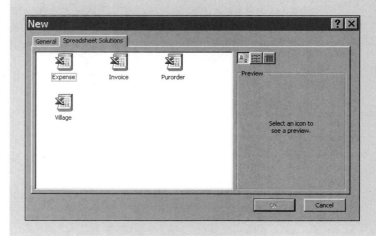

EXCEL

3 To create a new workbook based on the "Invoice" template:
DOUBLE-CLICK: Invoice template icon (🖳)
(*Note:* If you or your lab administrator has not installed the
workbook templates, you must skip to step 7.)

4 A warning dialog box may appear stating that the template may
contain a **macro virus.** A virus is a hostile program that is
secretly stored and shipped inside of another program or document. As this template is provided by Microsoft and not from an
unknown source, you can safely enable the macros and continue:
CLICK: Enable Macros

5 If other warning dialog boxes appear, click the appropriate command buttons to remove them from the screen. You should now
see the Invoice template, as shown in Figure 1.14.

Figure 1.14

New workbook based on the
Invoice template

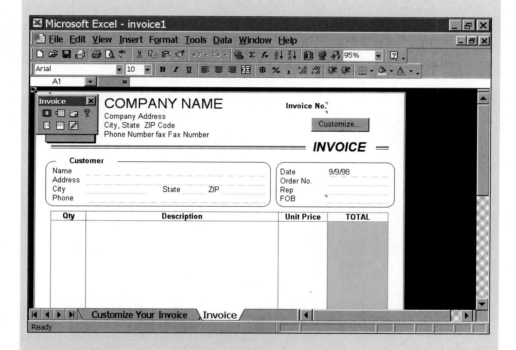

6 The workbook templates provided by Excel contain many
advanced features. Rather than introducing these features now,
let's close the workbook and continue our discussion of file management.
CHOOSE: File, Close
CLICK: No command button, if asked to save the changes

1.4.2 Saving and Closing

FEATURE
There are many options available for saving a workbook to a permanent storage location. The File, Save command and the Save button (◫) on the toolbar allow you to overwrite an existing disk file with the latest version of a workbook. The File, Save As command enables you to save a workbook to a new filename or storage location. Once you have finished working with a workbook, you close the file to free up valuable system resources (RAM).

METHOD
- To save a workbook:
  CLICK: Save button (◫), or
  CHOOSE: File, Save, or
  CHOOSE: File, Save As
- To close a workbook:
  CLICK: its Close button (☒), or
  CHOOSE: File, Close

PRACTICE
You will now practice saving and closing a workbook.

Setup: Identify a storage location for your personal workbook files. If you want to use a diskette, place it into the diskette drive now.

1 To create a new workbook from scratch:
CLICK: New button (▢)
TYPE: My Library into cell A1
PRESS: ENTER

2 To save the new workbook:
CLICK: Save button (◫)

(*Note:* If you have not yet saved a workbook, Excel displays the Save As dialog box regardless of the method you chose to save the file. The filenames and directories that appear in your Save As dialog box may differ from those shown in Figure 1.15.)

Figure 1.15

Save As dialog box

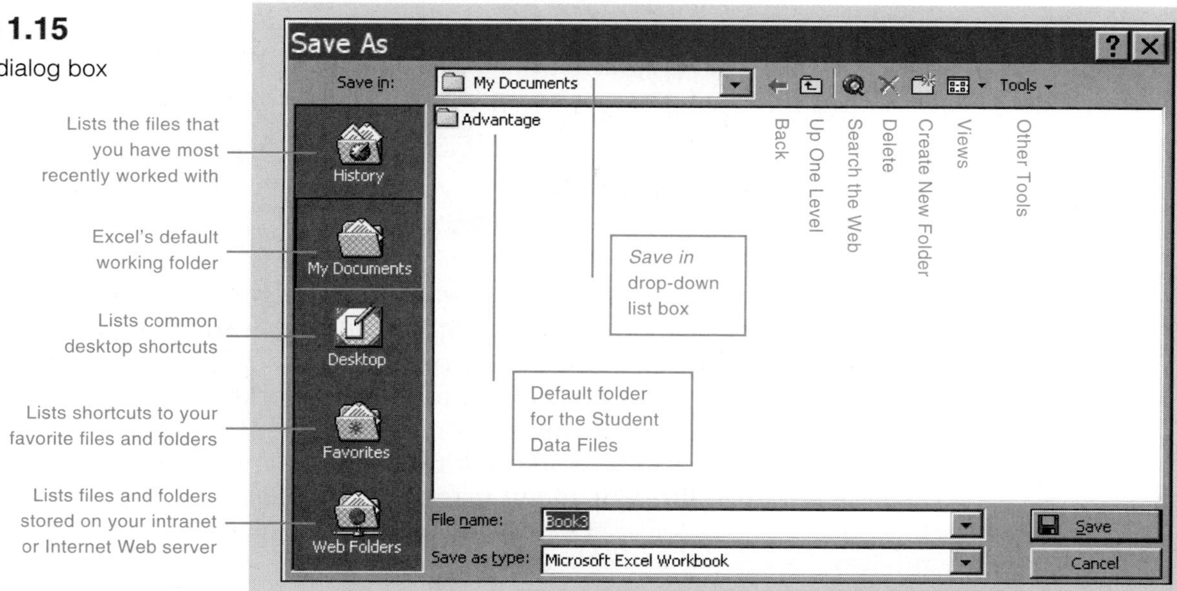

Lists the files that you have most recently worked with

Excel's default working folder

Lists common desktop shortcuts

Lists shortcuts to your favorite files and folders

Lists files and folders stored on your intranet or Internet Web server

3 The **Places bar,** located along the left border of the dialog box, provides convenient access to commonly used storage locations. To illustrate, let's view the files in your "My Documents" folder:
CLICK: My Documents button (🏠) in the Places bar

4 Let's browse the local hard disk:
CLICK: down arrow attached to the *Save in* drop-down list box
SELECT: Hard Disk C:
The list area displays the folders and files stored in the root directory of your local hard disk.

5 To drill down into one of the folders:
DOUBLE-CLICK: Program Files folder
This folder contains the program files for several applications.

6 To return to the previous display:
CLICK: Back button (⬅) in the dialog box

7 Now, using either the Places bar or the *Save In* drop-down list box:
SELECT: *a storage location for your personal files*
(*Note:* In this guide, we save files to the My Documents folder.)

8 Let's give the workbook file a unique name. Do the following:
DOUBLE-CLICK: the *workbook name* appearing in the *File name* text box to select it
TYPE: My Library

9 To complete the procedure:
CLICK: Save command button
Notice that the workbook's name now appears in the Title bar.

10 Let's close the workbook:
CHOOSE: File, Close

There are times when you'll want to save an existing workbook under a different filename. For example, you may want to keep different versions of the same workbook on your disk. Or, you may want to use one workbook as a template for future workbooks that are similar in style and format. Rather than retyping an entirely new workbook, you can retrieve an old workbook file, edit the information, and then save it under a different name using the File, Save As command.

In Addition Creating a New Folder	Folders can help you organize your work. They also make it easier to find documents and back up your data. For example, you can use a folder to collect all of the workbooks related to a single fiscal period. You can also specify a folder to hold all of your personal documents, such as resumes and expense reports. While the Windows Explorer should be used for most folder management tasks, Excel allows you to create a new folder from the Save As dialog box. After you navigate to where you want the folder to appear, click the Create New Folder button (🗀). In the New Folder dialog box, type a name for the folder and press **ENTER**.

1.4.3 Opening an Existing Workbook

FEATURE
You use the Open dialog box to search for and retrieve existing workbooks that are stored on your local hard disk, a floppy diskette, a network server, or on the Web. If you want to load Excel and an existing workbook at the same time, you can use the Open Office Document command on the Start menu. Or, if you have recently used the workbook, you can try the Start, Documents command, which lists the 15 most recently used files.

METHOD
- CLICK: Open button (🖻), or
- CHOOSE: File, Open

EXCEL

PRACTICE

You will now retrieve a student data file named EXC140 that displays the market penetration for snowboard sales by Canadian province.

Setup: Ensure that you have completed the previous lesson. There should be no workbooks displayed in the application window. You will also need to know the storage location for the student data files.

1 To display the Open dialog box:
CLICK: Open button (🗁)

2 Using the Places bar and the *Look in* drop-down list box, locate the folder containing the student data files. (*Note:* In this guide, we retrieve the student data files from a folder named "Advantage.")

3 To view additional information about each file:
CLICK: down arrow beside the Views button (▦▾)
CHOOSE: Details
Each workbook is presented on a single line with additional file information, such as its size, type, and date, as shown in Figure 1.16. (*Hint:* You can sort the filenames in this list area by clicking on one of the column heading buttons.)

Figure 1.16

Open dialog box

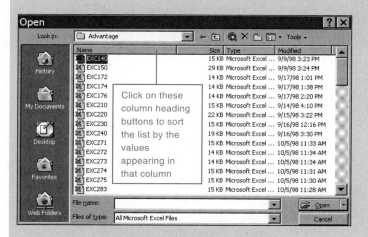

4 To return to a multicolumn list format:
CLICK: down arrow beside the Views button
CHOOSE: List

5 Let's open one of the workbooks in the list area:
DOUBLE-CLICK: EXC140
The dialog box disappears and the workbook is loaded into the
application window. (*Note:* The "EXC140" filename reflects that
this workbook is used in module 1.4 of the Excel learning guide.)

6 Now close the EXC140 workbook without saving the changes.

7 To exit Microsoft Excel:
CHOOSE: File, Exit

In Addition
Opening and Saving
Files of Different
Formats

In the Open and Save As dialog boxes, you will notice a drop-down list box
named *Files of type* and *Save as type* respectively. These list boxes allow
you to select different file formats for opening and saving your files. For
instance, you can save a workbook so that users with an earlier version of
Excel are able to open and edit its contents. You can also open a file that
was created using another spreadsheet software program, such as Lotus or
Quattro Pro.

1.4 Self Check   In the Open and Save As dialog boxes, how do the List and Details
views differ? What two other views are accessible from the Views
button?

1.5 Chapter Review

This chapter introduced you to using Microsoft Excel 2000, an electronic spreadsheet program. Spreadsheet software is used extensively
in business and other industries for performing statistical analyses
and summarizing numerical data for inclusion into reports. In the
first module, you learned about worksheets and were led on a guided
tour of the primary components in Excel. Next, you created a worksheet from scratch by entering text, numbers, dates, and formulas.
The third module spent time explaining the importance of editing a
worksheet effectively. In the last module, you learned how to create,
save, and open workbook files.

1.5.1 Command Summary

Many of the commands and procedures appearing in this chapter are summarized in the following table.

Skill Set	To Perform This Task . . .	Do the Following . . .
Using Excel	Launch Microsoft Excel	CLICK: Start button (🏁Start) CHOOSE: Programs, Microsoft Excel
	Exit Microsoft Excel	CLICK: its Close button (☒), or CHOOSE: File, Exit
	Close a workbook	CLICK: its Close button (☒), or CHOOSE: File, Close
	Customize menus and toolbars	CHOOSE: Tools, Customize
Managing Files	Create a new workbook	CLICK: New button (▢), or CHOOSE: File, New
	Use a template to create a new workbook	CHOOSE: File, New CLICK: *Spreadsheet Solutions* tab DOUBLE-CLICK: *a template*
	Locate and open an existing workbook	CLICK: Open button (📂), or CHOOSE: File, Open
	Open files of different formats	SELECT: a format from the *Files of type* drop-down list box in the Open dialog box
	Save a workbook	CLICK: Save button (💾), or CHOOSE: File, Save
	Save a workbook using a different filename, location, or format	CHOOSE: File, Save As
	Create a new folder while displaying the Save As dialog box	CLICK: Create New Folder button (📁)

Continued

Skill Set	To Perform This Task . . .	Do the Following . . .
Using Excel	Launch Microsoft Excel	CLICK: Start button (🏁 Start) CHOOSE: Programs, Microsoft Excel
Working with Cells	Navigate to a specific cell	CLICK: in the Name box TYPE: *the desired cell address*
	Enter text labels, numbers, and dates	TYPE: *the desired entry*
	Enter a formula	TYPE: *=expression*
	Replace a cell's contents with new data	TYPE: *a new entry*
	Activate Edit mode to revise a cell's contents	DOUBLE-CLICK: the desired cell, or CLICK: in the Formula bar, or PRESS: **F2** EDIT key
	Delete cell contents	PRESS: **DELETE**
	Delete all information associated with a cell	CHOOSE: Edit, Clear, All
	Reverse or undo a command or series of commands	CLICK: Undo button (↶▾), or CHOOSE: Edit, Undo, or PRESS: **CTRL** + z
	Reverse or undo an Undo command	CLICK: Redo button (↷▾)

1.5.2 Key Terms

This section specifies page references for the key terms identified in this chapter. For a complete list of definitions, refer to the Glossary provided in the Appendix.

adaptive menus, *p. 10*

application window, *p. 8*

cell, *p. 5*

cell address, *p. 5*

cell pointer, *p. 13*

chart sheet, *p. 6*

document window, *p. 8*

formula, *p. 19*

in-cell editing, *p. 21*

macro virus, *p. 29*

Name box, *p. 13*

Places bar, *p. 31*

Redo command, *p. 25*

template, *p. 28*

Undo command, *p. 25*

wizard, *p. 28*

workbook, *p. 6*

worksheet, *p. 5*

1.6   Review Questions

1.6.1 Short Answer

1.   Explain the difference between an application window and a document window.
2.   What is the difference between a toolbar and the Menu bar?
3.   What is the fastest method for moving to cell DF8192?
4.   What is significant about how dates are entered into a worksheet?
5.   How do you enter a formula into a cell? Provide an example.
6.   With respect to entering a formula, explain the term *pointing*.
7.   How would you reverse the last three commands executed?
8.   How do you create a new workbook based on a template?
9.   How would you save a copy of the currently displayed workbook onto a diskette?
10. How would you save a workbook in Excel using the Lotus spreadsheet file format?

1.6.2   True/False

T 1. ___F___ The cell reference "100AX" is an acceptable cell address.

2. ___T___ Pressing CTRL + HOME moves the cell pointer to cell A1.

3. ___T___ An Excel worksheet contains over 64,000 rows.

4. ___F___ Once a formula has been entered into a cell, you cannot edit the expression.

5. ___T___ A formula may contain both numbers and cell references, such as A1*B7-500.

6. ___T___ Pressing DELETE erases the contents of a cell.

7. ___F___ Pressing CTRL +x will undo the last command executed.

8. ___T___ You can create a new folder from within the Save As dialog box.

9. ___F___ You access Excel's workbook templates using the File, Open command.

10. ___T___ You can open files in Excel that have been created using different application software programs.

1.6.3   Multiple Choice

1. Which mouse shape is used to select cells in a worksheet?
   a. arrow
   b. cross
   c. hand
   d. hourglass

2. Excel displays the current cell address in the:
   a. Name box
   b. Status bar
   c. Title bar
   d. Standard toolbar

3. Using a mouse, you move around a worksheet quickly using the:
   a. Status bar
   b. Tab Scrolling arrows
   c. Tab Split bar
   d. Scroll bars

4. When you enter a text label, Excel justifies the entry automatically between the cell borders as:
   a. left-aligned
   b. centered
   c. right-aligned
   d. fully justified

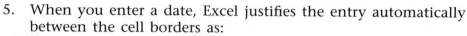

5. When you enter a date, Excel justifies the entry automatically between the cell borders as:
   a. left-aligned
   b. centered
   c. right-aligned
   d. fully justified

6. Which keyboard shortcut lets you modify the contents of a cell?
   a. CTRL
   b. SHIFT
   c. F2
   d. F5

7. Which is the correct formula for adding cells B4 and F7?
   a. =B4*F7
   b. +B4+F7
   c. $B4:F7
   d. =B4+F7

8. To save the current workbook using a different filename:
   a. CHOOSE: File, Save
   b. CHOOSE: File, Save As
   c. CLICK: Save button (⊡)
   d. CLICK: File, Rename

9. To open a new blank workbook:
   a. CLICK: New button (◻)
   b. CHOOSE: File, Open
   c. CHOOSE: File, Blank
   d. CHOOSE: File, Template

10. To reverse an Undo command:
    a. CHOOSE: Edit, Go Back
    b. CHOOSE: File, Reverse Undo
    c. CLICK: Reverse button (↺▾)
    d. CLICK: Redo button (↻▾)

EXCEL

1.7 Hands-On Projects

1.7.1 Grandview College: Semester Information

This exercise lets you practice fundamental worksheet skills, such as moving around a worksheet and entering text labels.

1. Load Microsoft Excel and ensure that a blank worksheet is displayed.
2. To enter a title label for the worksheet:
   SELECT: cell A1
   TYPE: Grandview Community College
   PRESS: ENTER
3. In cell A2:
   TYPE: Enrollment Statistics
   PRESS: ↓ twice
   The cell pointer should now appear in cell A4.
4. Let's add some row heading labels:
   TYPE: Courses
   CLICK: cell A7
   Notice that when you click a new cell location, the contents are moved from the Formula bar into the cell as if you had pressed ENTER.
5. TYPE: Instructors
   CLICK: cell A10
6. TYPE: Students
   PRESS: ENTER
7. On your own, enter the following text labels:

Move to cell	TYPE:
B5	credit
B6	non-credit
B8	salaried
B9	contract
B11	full-time
B12	part-time

8. To quickly move the cell pointer to the first column heading:
   CLICK: the Name box
   TYPE: c4
   PRESS: ENTER

9. In cells C4 and D4, enter the following column headings:
   TYPE: **Fall-99**
   PRESS: ➡
   TYPE: **Spring-00**
   PRESS: **ENTER**
10. To move the cell pointer to cell A1:
    PRESS: **CTRL** + **HOME**
11. Save the workbook as "Grandview Stats" to your personal storage location. (*Hint:* If you are unsure of where to store your personal files, select the "My Documents" folder.)
12. Close the workbook before proceeding.

1.7.2 Fast Forward Video: Store Summary

In this exercise, you will edit text labels in an existing worksheet, enter numbers and dates, and practice using the Undo command.

1. Open the data file named EXC172.
2. Save the workbook as "Video Stores" to your personal storage location.
3. To change the "Store" column heading to read "Location:"
   SELECT: cell B3
   TYPE: **Location**
   PRESS: **ENTER**
4. To correct a spelling mistake that occurs in the first location's name:
   DOUBLE-CLICK: cell B5
   PRESS: **END**
   PRESS: ⬅
   TYPE: **w**
   PRESS: **ENTER**
   The entry should now read "Downtown."
5. To expand upon the abbreviation used for the second location's name:
   SELECT: cell B6
   PRESS: **F2**
   PRESS: **BackSpace** to remove the last letter
   TYPE: **ream**
   The location name should now read "Coldstream."

6. To correct an error appearing in the second column heading:
   SELECT: cell D3
7. Position the I-beam mouse pointer to the right of the text in the formula bar and click the left mouse button once. The flashing insertion point should appear at the end of the word "Hour." Then do the following:
   TYPE: s
   PRESS: (ENTER)
   The entry now reads "Hours."
8. On your own, change the column heading "Tapes" to "Videos" and then correct the last heading so that it reads "Games."
9. Now let's put the current date on the worksheet:
   SELECT: cell D1
   TYPE: *the current date* using the format dd/mm/yy
10. Complete the following worksheet as shown in Figure 1.17.

Figure 1.17

Entering values into the Video Stores workbook

	A	B	C	D	E	F	G
1	Fast Forward Video			12/25/99			
2							
3		Location		Hours	Staff	Videos	Games
4							
5		Downtown		68	7	2,325	
6		Coldstream		68	5	1,790	
7		Westside		62	3	857	
8		Sahali Mall		74	9	2,114	
9							
10							

11. To delete the last column heading:
    SELECT: cell G3
    PRESS: (DELETE)
12. Now let's select the information for the Sahali Mall location:
    SELECT: cell D8
    PRESS: (SHIFT) and hold it down
    CLICK: cell F8
13. To erase all of the information in the selected cells:
    CHOOSE: Edit, Clear from the Menu bar
    CHOOSE: All from the cascading menu
14. To undo the deletion of the previous step:
    CLICK: Undo button (⟲) on the Standard toolbar
15. Save and then close the workbook.

1.7.3 Sun Valley Frozen Foods: Variance Analysis

You will now practice creating a worksheet from scratch that includes text, values, and formulas.

1. To display a new workbook and a blank worksheet:
    CLICK: New button (▢)
2. Enter the company name in cell A1:
    TYPE: **Sun Valley Frozen Foods**
    PRESS: ⬇
    TYPE: **Today is:**
    PRESS: ➡
3. Enter today's date in cell B2:
    TYPE: *the current date* using the format dd-mmm-yy
    (*Hint:* The date 9/24/99 would be entered as 24-Sep-99.)
4. Complete the worksheet as shown in Figure 1.18.

Figure 1.18

Entering data into a blank worksheet

	A	B	C	D	E	F
1	Sun Valley Frozen Foods					
2	Today is:	25-Dec-99				
3				Budget	Actual	Variance
4	Income					
5		Sales		43,000	41,380	
6		Service		17,500	19,620	
7						
8						
9	Expenses					
10		Materials		11,500	12,340	
11		Fixed Overhead		6,700	6,700	
12		Other Costs		12,500	12,975	
13						
14						

5. To calculate the Sales variance:
    SELECT: cell F5
    TYPE: **=e5-d5**
    PRESS: (ENTER)
    The value –1620 appears in the worksheet.
6. Using the same method, calculate the remaining variances for cells F6, F10, F11, and F12.

7. SELECT: cell C7
    TYPE: **Total**
    SELECT: cell C13
    TYPE: **Total**
    PRESS: (ENTER)
8. To sum the Income and Expenses columns:
    SELECT: cell D7
    TYPE: =
    SELECT: cell D5
    TYPE: +
    SELECT: cell D6
    PRESS: (ENTER)
9. Using either the typing or pointing method, enter addition formulas in the remaining cells of row 7 and row 13.
10. Save the workbook as "Sun Variance" and then close the workbook.

1.7.4 Lakeside Realty: Current Listing Report

This exercise lets you practice adding and modifying text, numbers, and formulas in an existing workbook.

1. Open the data file named EXC174.
2. Save the workbook as "Lakeside Listings" to your personal storage location.
3. In cell C7, you will now construct a formula to calculate the "Total Current Listings." Do the following:
    SELECT: cell C7
    TYPE: = **c3+c4-c5-c6**
    PRESS: (ENTER)
4. In cell A14, change the label from "Undeveloped" to read "Undeveloped Commercial."
5. In cell D14, you will enter the number of Undeveloped Commercial listings. As you do so, watch the formula in cell D16 recalculate after you press (ENTER). Do the following:
    TYPE: **19**
    PRESS: (ENTER)

6. The formula appearing in cell D16 for "Total Residential" incorrectly sums both the "Commercial" and "Undeveloped Commercial" listings. Therefore, you must edit the formula:
    SELECT: cell D16

7. Position the I-beam mouse pointer to the right of the formula in the Formula bar. Then, do the following:
    CLICK: the left mouse button and hold it down
    DRAG: the I-beam mouse pointer to the left to select "+D13+D14"

8. Once the selection is made, release the mouse button. Then:
    PRESS: [DELETE]

9. To complete the entry:
    PRESS: [ENTER]

10. In cell D18, enter a formula that adds up the Commercial (cell D13) and Undeveloped Commercial (cell D14) listings.

11. The Market Share column shows the proportional value of a particular row category as compared to either the Total Residential or Total Commercial results. To examine the formula used to calculate the Market Share for Single Family Houses, do the following:
    SELECT: cell F9
    Notice the expression displayed in the Formula bar.

12. Enter formulas in cells F10, F11, and F12 that calculate their respective market shares of the residential listings. (*Hint:* Divide each row value in column D by the Total Residential value in cell D16.)

13. Enter formulas in cells F13 and F14 that calculate their respective market shares of the commercial listings. (*Hint:* Divide each row value in column D by the Total Commercial value in cell D18.)

14. Save and then close the workbook.

1.7.5 On Your Own: Personal Monthly Budget

To practice working with text, values, and formulas, ensure that Excel is loaded and then display a blank workbook. You will now begin creating a personal budget. Enter a title that contains the words "My Monthly Budget." Under this title include your name and the current month. Now enter the following expense categories and a reasonable amount for each:

- Rent/Mortgage
- Food
- Clothing
- Car expenses
- Utilities
- Education
- Entertainment

In the same column as the labels, enter the words "Total Expenses." Then, beneath the column of numbers, enter a formula that sums the column. Now add a new column next to these budget figures that displays the percentage share for each budget category of the total expenses. For example, you would divide the value for Food by the Total Expenses value to calculate its share of the budget. Experiment with increasing and decreasing the budget expense figures to see their effect on the percentage share calculations. When completed, save the workbook as "My Budget" to your personal storage location and then close the workbook.

1.7.6 On Your Own: Personal Grade Book

To practice working with data and formulas, open the EXC176 workbook. Before continuing, save the workbook as "My Grades" to your personal storage location. Enter sample marks into column D of the worksheet.

Enter formulas that calculate the percentage grade for each test or assignment by dividing the "Mark" column by the "Out Of" column. Then, enter formulas that calculate the Term Percentages for display in cells F8 and F15. (*Hint:* Divide the total course marks achieved by the total marks possible.) Finally, enter a formula that calculates the average percentage of both courses for display in cell F17. Adjust some of the sample marks to ensure that the formulas are working correctly.

Save the workbook to your personal storage location. And, lastly, close the workbook and exit Microsoft Excel.

1.8　Case Problems: Rain Coast Air

Rain Coast Air, a small airline charter business on the West coast, is in the process of modernizing how it tracks and analyzes its business data. As an initial step, the new office assistant, Jennifer Duvall, is learning how to use Microsoft Excel. Her boss, Hank Frobisher, wants Jennifer to create a worksheet that will enable him to compare the monthly efficiency of each of his three planes. You see, Hank has an opportunity to purchase an additional float plane for well below market value. And, as a cost-conscious businessman, Hank wants to have a clear understanding of how his current equipment is performing before deciding to spend any money.

In the following case problems, assume the role of Jennifer and perform the same steps that she identifies. You may want to re-read the chapter opening before proceeding.

1.　Jennifer decides to create a new worksheet that she can use as a template for each month's report. She begins by loading Microsoft Excel and displaying a blank workbook. Her first step will be to enter the title and the row and column headings. Then, the workbook needs to be saved to disk so that it can be later retrieved as a starting point for the monthly reports.

   Jennifer creates the worksheet shown in Figure 1.19 and then saves it as "Aircraft Stats" to her personal storage location.

Figure 1.19

The Aircraft Stats worksheet

	A	B	C	D	E	F	G	H
1	Monthly Aircraft Performance							
2								
3	Month:	Sep-99						
4								
5	Aircraft	Revenue	Expenses	Net Rev.	Flight Hrs	Rev/Hour	Exp %	
6								
7	XL-3079							
8	RB-2100							
9	DZ-514							
10								
11	Total							
12								
13								

2. Satisfied that this format will provide Hank with the information he needs, Jennifer begins to fill in the first month's figures. Then, she enters the formulas required to summarize each aircraft's performance. Most of the data she uses is taken directly from the monthly revenue and expense summaries prepared by the bookkeeping service. The pilots' trip logs provide the rest of the data. After entering the data in Figure 1.20, Jennifer saves the workbook as "September Stats" to her personal storage location.

Figure 1.20

September's aircraft
performance report

	A	B	C	D	E	F	G	H
1	Monthly Aircraft Performance							
2								
3	Month:	Sep-99						
4								
5	Aircraft	Revenue	Expenses	Net Rev.		Flight Hrs	Rev/Hour	Exp %
6								
7	XL-3079	15,326	4,259			87		
8	RB-2100	17,210	3,876			95		
9	DZ-514	9,845	2,633			53		
10								
11	Total							
12								
13								

3. Now, Jennifer tackles entering the formulas for the worksheet:

- She constructs formulas for display in row 11 that add the values appearing in the Revenue, Expenses, and Flight Hrs columns. The three formulas are entered into cells B11, C11, and E11.
- She enters formulas in cells D7, D8, D9, and D11 that calculate the Net Revenue by subtracting the Expenses for an aircraft from the Revenue it generated.
- She calculates and displays the Net Revenue per Hour in cells F7, F8, F9, and F11. The calculation she uses is simply the Net Revenue from column D divided by the Flight Hours in column F.
- Lastly, she calculates the Exp % column, which divides the Expenses by the Revenue and then multiples the result by 100. She places the results in cells G7, G8, G9, and G11.

Unfortunately, Hank has already gone home. Jennifer decides to call it a day; she saves and closes the workbook. She is already looking forward to showing off her new creation to Hank in the morning.

4.　The next morning, Jennifer opens the "September Stats" workbook and asks Hank to take a look at it. He is very pleased with the report and amazed at how quickly Excel can perform the calculations. Hank asks Jennifer what it would take to produce this report for another month. She explains that all she needs to do is enter the month's revenues, expenses, and flight hours into the appropriate cells; Excel then recalculates the worksheet automatically. Hank is outwardly impressed, realizing that he will finally have some decent information on which to base business decisions.

After mulling over the worksheet, Hank decides it would be prudent to purchase the fourth aircraft. With some minor modifications to the worksheet, he realizes that this information would come in handy during his meeting with the bank's loan officer. Hank calls Jennifer over to his desk and explains the revisions he wants her to make.

- The title of the report, explains Hank, should read "Rain Coast Air." And the aircraft should be identified by their names instead of their registration numbers. For example, the aircraft names are Eagle (XL-3079), Wanderer (RB-2100), and Sky Spirit (DZ-514).
- An upholstery repair bill for $262 was accidentally charged against the Wanderer, when it was actually for the Eagle. Therefore, the expense figures need to be adjusted accordingly. (*Hint:* To change the cell entry from a value to a formula, edit the cell contents by inserting an equal sign (=) at the front of the entry and "-262" at the end of the entry. You need an equal sign to convert the cell contents from a value to a formula.)

Jennifer makes the requested changes. She then saves the workbook as "Sept 99 Stats" and closes the workbook. As a last step, she exits Microsoft Excel.

MICROSOFT EXCEL 2000
Modifying a Worksheet

CHAPTER
TWO

Chapter Outline

Learning Objectives

After reading this chapter, you will be able to:

- Use several "Auto" features provided by Excel for entering and editing data and formulas

- Copy and move information with the Windows and Office Clipboards, and by using drag and drop

- Use the AutoFill feature and Fill commands to duplicate and extend data and formulas

- Insert and delete cells, rows, and columns

- Hide, unhide, and adjust rows and columns

Case Study

Granby Insurance Agency

The Granby Insurance Agency, located at the corner of 43rd and Main in Middleton's business district, is the city's largest private insurance company. Granby Insurance has always maintained a high profile in the community by sponsoring youth programs and providing assistance to the local charities. This sense of community was one of the main attractions for Scott Allenby, who recently joined the agency as their internal business manager.

Just last week, one of the agency partners purchased a new computer for Scott and made him personally responsible for generating the company's monthly profitability reports. With an increased workload, Scott knows that he must streamline operations and find a more efficient method for summarizing the data he receives. Fortunately, the computer came with Microsoft Excel installed and, after only a few days, Scott is now creating his own worksheets. Far from being comfortable with Excel's vast number of features, Scott has asked a knowledgeable friend to help construct a few simple workbooks for him to use.

In this chapter, you and Scott learn to modify and manipulate worksheet data. In addition to copying and moving information, you are introduced to inserting and deleting cells, rows, and columns. You also learn how to hide specific columns before generating reports.

2.1 Entering and Reviewing Data

Even novice users find it easy to build and use simple worksheets. In this module, you are introduced to some popular tools that can help speed your learning and improve your efficiency. Specifically, Excel provides three "Auto" features that may be used to enter repetitive data and perform calculations. Once you've practiced selecting ranges, you learn to use these three "Auto" features, called *AutoComplete*, *AutoCalculate*, and *AutoSum*.

2.1.1 Selecting Cells and Ranges

FEATURE
A **cell range** is a single cell or rectangular block of cells. Each cell range has a beginning cell address in the top left-hand corner and an ending cell address in the bottom right-hand corner. To use a cell range in a formula, you separate the two cell addresses using a colon. For example, the cell range B4:C6 references the six cells shown shaded below. Notice that the current or active cell, B4, is not shaded in this graphic.

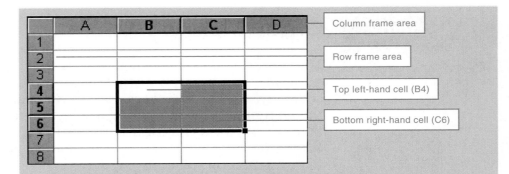

METHOD
To select a cell range using the mouse:
1. CLICK: the cell in the top left-hand corner
2. DRAG: the mouse pointer to the cell in the bottom right-hand corner

 To select a cell range using the keyboard:
1. SELECT: cell in the top left-hand corner
2. PRESS: (SHIFT) and hold it down
3. PRESS: *an arrow key* to extend the range highlighting
4. RELEASE: (SHIFT)

PRACTICE
In this exercise, you open a workbook, save it to your personal storage location, and practice selecting single and multiple cell ranges.

Setup: Ensure that Excel is loaded.

1 Open the data file named EXC210.

2 In the next two steps, you will save the file as "My Gift List" to your personal storage location. Do the following:
CHOOSE: File, Save As
TYPE: My Gift List (but do not press (ENTER))

3 Using the *Save in* drop-down list box or the Places bar:
SELECT: *your storage location* (for example, the "My Documents" folder)
CLICK: Save command button
(*Note:* Most lessons in this guide begin by opening a student data file and then saving it immediately using a new filename.)

4 Let's practice selecting cell ranges. To begin:
SELECT: cell A3
(*Hint:* The word SELECT tells you to place the cell pointer at the identified cell address using either the keyboard or the mouse.)

5 To select the range from cell A3 to E3 using the keyboard:
PRESS: (SHIFT) and hold it down
PRESS: ➡ four times
Although not explicitly stated in the above instruction, you release the (SHIFT) key once the range is selected.

6 The (CTRL) + (HOME) combination moves the cell pointer to cell A1. Pressing (HOME) by itself moves the cell pointer to column A within the same row. To move the cell pointer back to cell A3:
PRESS: (HOME)

7 To select the same cell range, but faster and more efficiently:
PRESS: (SHIFT) and hold it down
PRESS: (CTRL) + ➡ together
Notice that the entire range is selected. You may remember from the last chapter that the (CTRL) +arrow combination moves the cell pointer until the cell contents change from empty to filled or filled to empty.

8 To select a cell range using the mouse:
CLICK: cell C6 and hold down the left mouse button
DRAG: the mouse pointer to E8 (and then release the button)
Notice that the column letters and row numbers in the frame area appear bold for the selected cell range, as shown in Figure 2.1.

Figure 2.1

Selecting a cell range

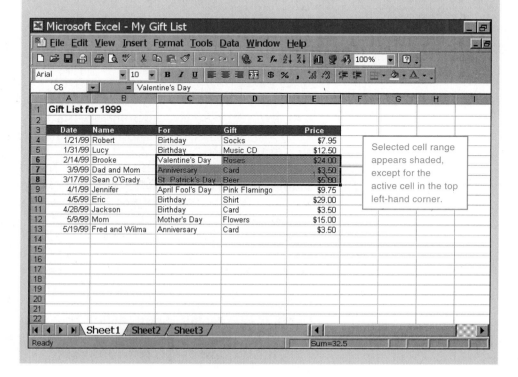

9 There is an easier method for selecting cell ranges for novice mouse users. To demonstrate, let's select the cell range from B10 to D13:
CLICK: cell B10
PRESS: (SHIFT) and hold it down
CLICK: cell D13
The range between the two cells should now appear highlighted. (*Note:* Remember to release the (SHIFT) key after the last selection is made.)

10 You can also select multiple cell ranges on a worksheet. To begin:
DRAG: from cell A6 to cell E6
PRESS: (CTRL) and hold it down
DRAG: from cell A9 to cell E9
You should see two separate cell ranges highlighted on the worksheet.

11 To select a third cell range:
PRESS: (CTRL) and hold it down
DRAG: from cell A12 to cell E12
(*Note:* Release the (CTRL) key after the last selection is made.)

12 To move the cell pointer to cell A1:
PRESS: (CTRL) + (HOME)

2.1.2 Entering Data Using AutoComplete

FEATURE
The **AutoComplete** feature second-guesses what you are typing into a worksheet cell and suggests how to complete the entry. After analyzing your first few keystrokes and scanning the same column for similar entries, AutoComplete tacks on the remaining letters when it thinks it has found a match. You can accept the Auto-Complete entry, or you can ignore its suggestion and continue typing. This feature can greatly reduce the number of repetitive entries you make in a worksheet.

METHOD
By default, the AutoComplete feature is turned on. If, however, you view its helpfulness as an intrusion, you can turn it off. To do so:
1. CHOOSE: Tools, Options
2. CLICK: *Edit* tab in the dialog box
3. SELECT: *Enable AutoComplete for cell values* check box to toggle AutoComplete on and off

EXCEL

PRACTICE

You will now practice using Excel's AutoComplete feature to enter data.

Setup: Ensure that the "My Gift List" workbook is displayed.

1 SELECT: cell A14

2 To add a new entry to the worksheet:
TYPE: 6/2/99
PRESS: ➡
TYPE: Anda
PRESS: ➡

3 You will now enter the word "Birthday" into cell C14. After typing the first letter, Excel notices that there is only one other entry in the column that begins with the letter "B" and, thus, makes the assumption that this is the word you want to enter. To demonstrate:
TYPE: B
Notice that Excel completes the word "Birthday" automatically.

4 To accept the completed word:
PRESS: ➡

5 For the remaining cells in the row:
TYPE: Shoes
PRESS: ➡
TYPE: $19.95
PRESS: ENTER
PRESS: HOME
Your cell pointer should now appear in cell A15.

6 Let's add another entry to the worksheet. Do the following:
TYPE: 6/5/99
PRESS: ➡
TYPE: Trevor and Ann
PRESS: ➡

7 You can use Excel's AutoComplete feature to display a sorted list of all the unique entries in a column. To illustrate:
RIGHT-CLICK: cell C15 to display its shortcut menu
CHOOSE: Pick From List
AutoComplete generates the list and then displays its results in a pop-up list box, as shown in Figure 2.2.

Figure 2.2

Entering data using the
AutoComplete pick list

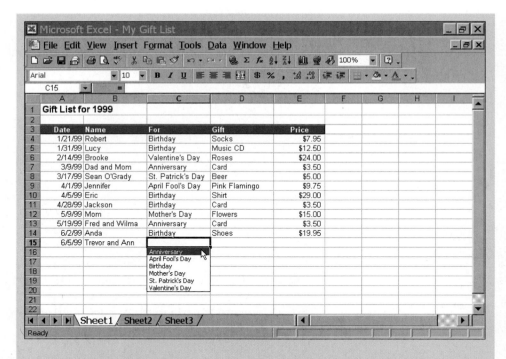

8 To make a selection:
CLICK: Anniversary in the pick list
(*Hint:* As a shortcut, press <kbd>ALT</kbd> + <kbd>↓</kbd> in a cell to display a column's pick list.)

9 To complete the row:
CLICK: cell D15
TYPE: `Picture Frame`
PRESS: <kbd>→</kbd>
TYPE: `$15.00`
PRESS: <kbd>ENTER</kbd>

10 Save the workbook and keep it open for use in the next lesson.
(*Hint:* The fastest methods for saving a workbook include clicking the Save button (<kbd>🖫</kbd>) or pressing <kbd>CTRL</kbd> + s.)

2.1.3   Using AutoCalculate and AutoSum

FEATURE
The **AutoCalculate** feature allows you to select a range of values and view their sum in the Status bar. This feature is useful for checking the result of a calculation without having to store its value in the worksheet. If, on the other hand, you need to store a result, click the **AutoSum** button (Σ) on the Standard toolbar. Excel reviews the surrounding cells, guesses at the range you want to sum, and then places a SUM function (described later in this book) into the current or active cell.

METHOD
- To use the AutoCalculate feature:
  SELECT: the range of values that you want to sum
- To use the AutoSum feature:
  SELECT: the cell where you want the result to appear
  CLICK: AutoSum button (Σ)

PRACTICE
Using the same worksheet, you will now practice viewing Auto-Calculate results and entering an addition formula using AutoSum.

Setup: Ensure that you have completed the previous lessons in this module and that the "My Gift List" workbook is displayed.

1 Let's say you want to know how much money to set aside for gifts in April. To find the answer, do the following:
SELECT: cell range from E9 to E11
Notice that only the April values are selected in the "Price" column.

2 Review the Status bar information. Notice that "Sum=$42.25" now appears near the right-hand side of the Status bar.

3 Let's perform another calculation:
SELECT: cell E4
PRESS: SHIFT and hold it down
PRESS: CTRL + ↓
All of the cells under the "Price" column heading should now appear selected. Assuming that you completed the previous lessons, the Status bar will now display "Sum=$148.65," as shown in Figure 2.3.

Figure 2.3

Adding values using
AutoCalculate

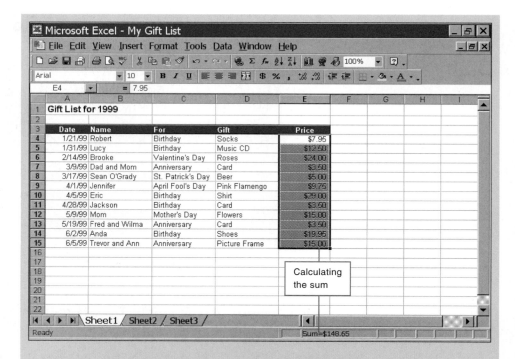

4 SELECT: cell D16

5 Let's enter a text label for the next calculation:
TYPE: Total Cost
PRESS: ➡

6 The quickest way to sum a row or column of values is using the
AutoSum button (Σ) on the Standard toolbar. To demonstrate:
CLICK: AutoSum button (Σ) once
A built-in function called SUM is entered into the cell, along
with the range that Excel assumes you want to sum. Notice that
this cell range is also highlighted by a dashed marquee.

7 To accept the highlighted cells as the desired range:
CLICK: AutoSum button (Σ) again
The result, $148.65, now appears in cell E16. (*Note:* You could
just as easily have pressed ENTER to accept the AutoSum entry.)

8 Perhaps you made a mistake in one of the column entries. To
correct the mistake, do the following:
SELECT: cell E14
TYPE: $119.95
PRESS: ENTER
Notice that the AutoSum result in cell E16 now reads $248.65.

9 Save the workbook by clicking the Save button (🖫).

EXCEL

2.1.4   Inserting and Deleting Cells

FEATURE
You can insert a cell or cell range in the middle of existing data by moving the data that is there into the cells immediately below or to the right of the current selection. Likewise, you can delete a cell or cell range and close up the gap that is normally left when you clear the contents of a range.

METHOD
To insert a cell or cell range:
1.   SELECT: the desired cell or cell range
2.   CHOOSE: Insert, Cells
3.   SELECT: *Shift cells right* or *Shift cells down* option button
4.   CLICK: OK command button

To delete a cell or cell range:
1.   SELECT: the desired cell or cell range
2.   CHOOSE: Edit, Delete
3.   SELECT: *Shift cells left* or *Shift cells up* option button
4.   CLICK: OK command button

PRACTICE
You will now practice inserting and deleting cells.

Setup: Ensure that the "My Gift List" workbook is displayed.

1   Let's insert a new item into the worksheet list. To begin:
SELECT: cell range from A9 to E9

2   To insert a new range of cells:
CHOOSE: Insert, Cells
Your screen should now appear similar to Figure 2.4.

Figure 2.4

Inserting a range of cells

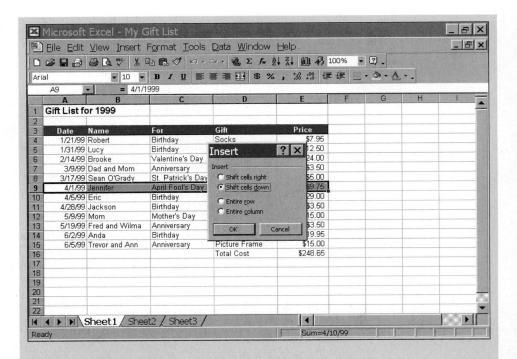

3 To complete the procedure, ensure that the *Shift cells down* option is selected and then do the following:
CLICK: OK command button
The existing data is pushed down to make space for the new cells.

4 Keep the cell range from A9 to E9 selected and enter a new item:
TYPE: 3/31/99
PRESS: ENTER
Notice that the cell pointer moves to the next cell in the selected range.

5 To complete the row item with an Anniversary entry:
TYPE: Tim and Starr
PRESS: ENTER
TYPE: An
PRESS: ENTER
TYPE: Mirror
PRESS: ENTER
TYPE: $37.00
PRESS: ENTER
Notice that the cell pointer wraps around to the beginning of the selected range and that the "Total Cost" value in cell E17 is updated.

6 Now let's remove an item from the list:
SELECT: cell range from A12 to E12

7 To delete the selected cells:
CHOOSE: Edit, Delete
The Delete dialog box appears similar to the Insert dialog box shown in Figure 2.3.

8 To complete the procedure, ensure that the *Shift cells up* option is selected and then do the following:
CLICK: OK command button
The remaining cells slide up one row to close the gap and the "Total Cost" value in cell E16 is updated to $282.15.

9 PRESS: CTRL + HOME to move to cell A1

10 Save and then close the workbook.

2.1 Self Check　Which of the "Auto" features enables you to sum a range of values and display the result in the Status bar?

2.2　Copying and Moving Data

Excel provides tools for copying, moving, and pasting data. Like the "Auto" features, these tools can help you reduce the number of repetitive entries you are required to make. For example, once you enter a formula to sum one column of values, you can duplicate that formula to sum the adjacent columns. There are three methods for copying and moving data. First, you can cut or copy a single piece of data from any application and store it on the **Windows Clipboard.** Then, you can paste the data into any other worksheet, workbook, or application. Second, you can use the new **Office Clipboard** to collect up to 12 items and then paste the stored data singularly or as a group into any other Office 2000 application. Lastly, you can use **drag and drop** to copy and move cell information short distances using the mouse. In this module, you practice duplicating cell contents and extending data and formulas in a worksheet range.

2.2.1 Using the Clipboards

FEATURE

You use the Windows and Office Clipboards to copy and move information within Excel and among other applications. The Windows Clipboard can store a single item of data from any application, while the Office Clipboard can store up to 12 items. (*Note:* The last item that you cut or copy to the Office Clipboard will appear as the one item stored on the Windows Clipboard.) When working in an Office 2000 application, such as Excel, you display the Office Clipboard toolbar by choosing the View, Toolbars, Clipboard command.

METHOD

Task Description	Menu Command	Toolbar Button	Keyboard Shortcut
Move data from the worksheet to the Clipboard	Edit, Cut	✂	CTRL + X
Place a copy of the selected data on the Clipboard	Edit, Copy	📋	CTRL + C
Insert data stored on the Clipboard into the worksheet	Edit, Paste	📋	CTRL + V

PRACTICE

Using the Clipboards, you will now practice copying data in a worksheet. The steps for moving data are identical to copying, except you use the Cut command instead of Copy.

Setup: Ensure that no workbooks are displayed in the application window.

1 Open the data file named EXC220.

2 Save the file as "Sales Forecast" to your personal storage location.

3 Let's sum the product values for entry into the Total row:
SELECT: cell range from B6 to D6
CLICK: AutoSum button (Σ)
The results appear immediately in the selected range.

4 You will now use the Copy command to duplicate data in the worksheet. To demonstrate:
SELECT: cell range from A2 to D6
Notice that all the data is selected, except for the title in cell A1.

5 To copy the range selection to both Clipboards:
CLICK: Copy button (▣) on the Standard toolbar
(*Note:* The range that you want to copy appears surrounded by a dashed marquee.)

6 You must now select the top left-hand corner of the location where you want to place the copied data. Do the following:
SELECT: cell A9

7 To complete the copy operation:
CLICK: Paste button (▣)
The Paste button (▣) places the contents of the Windows Clipboard into the selected cell. The data, however, remains on both Clipboards.

8 Let's continue pasting the copied data into your worksheet:
SELECT: cell A16
CLICK: Paste button (▣)
A second copy appears beneath the original data.

9 To demonstrate using the Office Clipboard toolbar:
SELECT: cell A1
CHOOSE: View, Toolbars, Clipboard
Your screen should now appear similar to Figure 2.5. (*Hint:* Unlike the Windows Clipboard, remember that the Office Clipboard can store up to 12 items and then paste them all at the same time.)

EXCEL

Figure 2.5

Displaying the Office Clipboard toolbar

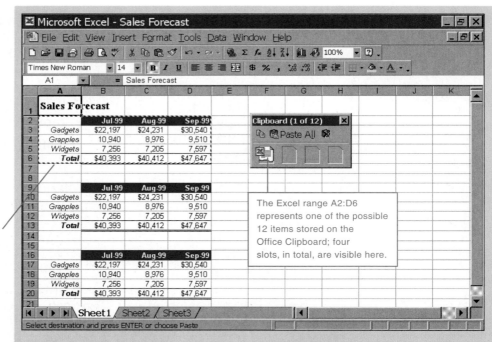

A dashed marquee appears around the range that has been copied to the Clipboard.

The Excel range A2:D6 represents one of the possible 12 items stored on the Office Clipboard; four slots, in total, are visible here.

10 To clear the contents of the Office Clipboard:
CLICK: Clear Clipboard button (⊠) on the Clipboard toolbar
Notice that the dashed marquee around the range also disappears.

11 To add data items to the Office Clipboard:
SELECT: cell A3
CLICK: Copy button (🗈) on the Clipboard or Standard toolbars
SELECT: cell B3
CLICK: Copy button (🗈)
SELECT: cell C3
CLICK: Copy button (🗈)
SELECT: cell D3
CLICK: Copy button (🗈)
Depending on your screen resolution, your Office Clipboard may expand to display an additional row of placeholders.

12 Position the mouse pointer over one of the data icons (🗐) in the toolbar. A ToolTip will appear displaying the value stored in the slot. Drag the mouse pointer over the other icons to see their values. The data elements are stored in the order that they were collected. You can paste a single item by selecting a target cell and then clicking an icon in the toolbar. You can also paste all of the items into a column format, as demonstrated in the next step.

13 To paste all of the collected data elements into the worksheet:
SELECT: cell F9
CLICK: Paste All button ([Paste All])
(*Note:* You may need to move the Office Clipboard
window by dragging its Title bar before you can
select cell F9.) The contents of the Office Clipboard
are pasted into a single column in the worksheet;
each data element is placed into its own row, as
shown here.

Gadgets
$22,197
$24,231
$30,540

14 Let's prepare for another copy operation:
CLICK: Clear Clipboard button ([⊠])

15 In this step, you want to collect, reorder, and then paste informa-
tion from Rows 3 through 5. The key to this step is to collect the
data in the order that you want to paste it later. For example:
SELECT: cell range A5 through D5
PRESS: (ENTER) + c
SELECT: cell range A3 through D3
PRESS: (ENTER) + c
SELECT: cell range A4 through D4
PRESS: (ENTER) + c
You should now see three occupied slots on the Clipboard
toolbar.

16 Let's paste the results over top of an existing data area in the
worksheet. Do the following:
SELECT: A10
CLICK: Paste All button ([Paste All])
Notice that you need only select the top left-hand corner of the
desired target range. Your screen should now appear similar to
Figure 2.6.

17 CLICK: Close button ([⊠]) on the Office Clipboard toolbar

18 Save the workbook and keep it open for use in the next lesson.

Figure 2.6

Collecting and pasting
multiple items

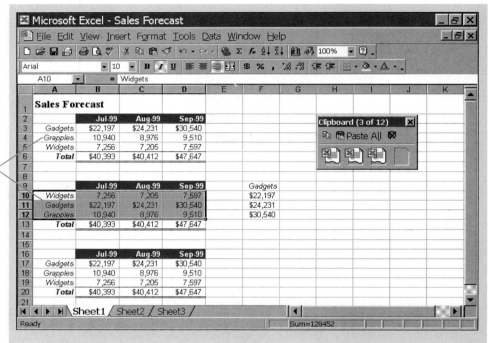

You can use the Office
Clipboard toolbar to
change the layout of
data in the worksheet.

2.2.2   Using Drag and Drop

FEATURE

You can use the mouse (and bypass the Clipboards altogether) to drag and drop data from one location in your worksheet to another. Although you cannot perform multiple pastes, the drag and drop method provides the easiest and fastest way to copy and move cell information short distances.

METHOD

1.   SELECT: the cell range that you want to copy or move
2.   Position the mouse pointer over any border of the cell range, until a white arrow pointer appears.
3.   If you want to perform a copy operation, hold down the CTRL key.
4.   DRAG: the cell range by the border to the target destination
5.   Release the mouse button and, if necessary, the CTRL key.

PRACTICE

Using a mouse, you will now practice dragging and dropping a cell range in the worksheet.

Setup: Ensure that you have completed the previous lesson and that the "Sales Forecast" workbook is displayed.

EXCEL

1 Let's practice moving the data that was copied to column F in the previous lesson. Do the following:
SELECT: cell range from F9 to F12

2 Position the mouse pointer over a border of the selected cell range until a white diagonal arrow appears.

3 CLICK: left mouse button and hold it down
DRAG: mouse pointer upwards until the ToolTip displays "F2:F5"
Your screen should now appear similar to Figure 2.7.

4 Release the mouse button to complete the drag and drop operation.

Figure 2.7

Using drag and drop to move cell data

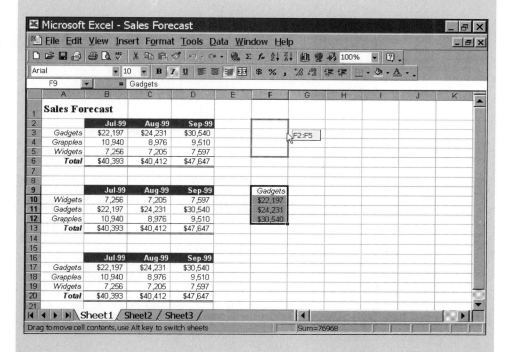

5 To copy a cell range using drag and drop:
SELECT: cell range from D9 to D13

6 Position the mouse pointer over a border of the cell range until a white diagonal arrow appears. Then, do the following:
PRESS: CTRL and hold it down
You should notice a plus sign is added to the mouse pointer.

7 CLICK: left mouse button and hold it down
DRAG: mouse pointer right to E9:E13

8 Release the mouse button and CTRL key to complete the copy operation. Notice that there are now two "Sep-99" columns.

9 SELECT: cell E9
TYPE: Oct-99
PRESS: ENTER
In one simple drag and drop operation, you successfully created a new data column with the same formatting specifications as the other monthly columns in the table.

10 Save and then close the workbook.

2.2.3 Creating a Series Using AutoFill

FEATURE
Excel's **AutoFill** feature allows you to enter a data series into a worksheet. Whether a mathematical progression of values (1, 2, 3,...) or a row of date headings (Jan, Feb, Mar,...), a **series** is a sequence of data that follows a pattern.

METHOD
1. SELECT: the cell range containing the data you want to extend
2. DRAG: the **fill handle,** which is a black square that appears in the lower right-hand corner of the cell range to extrapolate the series
3. Release the mouse button to complete the operation.

PRACTICE
In this exercise, you create a new workbook and then extend the contents of cells using the fill handle and the AutoFill feature.

Setup: Ensure that no workbooks appear in the application window.

1 To display a new workbook:
CLICK: New button (🗋)

2 Let's enter some source data from which you will create a series:
SELECT: cell A3
TYPE: Jan
PRESS: ⬇
TYPE: Period 1
PRESS: ⬇
TYPE: Quarter 1
PRESS: ENTER
Each of these entries will become the starting point for creating a series that extends across their respective rows.

3 To extend the first entry in row 3:
SELECT: cell A3

4 Position the mouse pointer over the small black square (the fill handle) in the bottom right-hand corner of the cell pointer. The mouse pointer will change to a black cross when positioned correctly. (*Hint:* Figure 2.8 identifies the fill handle and mouse pointer.)

Figure 2.8

Using a cell's fill handle

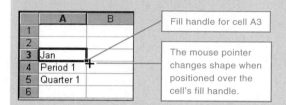

5 CLICK: left mouse button and hold it down
DRAG: the mouse pointer to column F, until the ToolTip displays "Jun"

6 Release the mouse button to complete the AutoFill operation.

7 Let's extend the next two rows:
SELECT: cell A4
DRAG: fill handle for cell A4 to column F
SELECT: cell A5
DRAG: fill handle for cell A5 to column F
(*Note:* Always release the mouse button after dragging to the desired location.) In the above example, notice that Excel recognizes the word Quarter; it resumes at Quarter 1 after entering Quarter 4.

8 You can also extend a date series using the fill handle:
SELECT: cell A7
TYPE: Sep-99
PRESS: ➡
TYPE: Dec-99
PRESS: ENTER

9 To extend the range using the same increment, you select both cells and then drag the range's fill handle. Do the following:
SELECT: cell range from A7 to B7
DRAG: fill handle for the range to column F
The quarterly values to Dec-00 appear.

10 You can also extract a nonlinear series from a range of values:
SELECT: cell A9
TYPE: **12**
PRESS: ➡
TYPE: **15**
PRESS: ➡
TYPE: **17**
PRESS: (ENTER)
Notice that there isn't a static incrementing value in this example.

11 To continue this range of values:
SELECT: cell range from A9 to C9
DRAG: fill handle for the range to column F
Excel calculates a "best guess" for the next few values. Your screen should now appear similar to Figure 2.9.

12 Save the workbook as "My Series" and then close the workbook.

Figure 2.9

Creating data series using
the AutoFill feature

	A	B	C	D	E	F	G
1							
2							
3	Jan	Feb	Mar	Apr	May	Jun	
4	Period 1	Period 2	Period 3	Period 4	Period 5	Period 6	
5	Quarter 1	Quarter 2	Quarter 3	Quarter 4	Quarter 1	Quarter 2	
6							
7	Sep-99	Dec-99	Mar-00	Jun-00	Sep-00	Dec-00	
8							
9	12	15	17	19.66667	22.16667	24.66667	
10							
11							

Fill Handle

2.2.4 Extending a Cell's Contents

FEATURE
You use the Edit, Fill commands to extend a formula across a row or down a column. These commands allow you to copy a cell's contents to its adjacent cells in a single step. If you prefer using the mouse, you can also extend a cell's contents using its fill handle.

METHOD
1. SELECT: the desired cell range, ensuring that the data you want to copy is located in the top left-hand corner
2. CHOOSE: Edit, Fill, Right (or Left) to copy across a row
   CHOOSE: Edit, Fill, Down (or Up) to copy down (or up) a column

EXCEL

PRACTICE

In this exercise, you open a cash flow worksheet and then copy and extend the formulas that are stored therein.

Setup: Ensure that no workbooks appear in the application window.

1 Open the data file named EXC224.

2 Save the file as "Filling Cells" to your personal storage location.

3 To extend the date headings using the AutoFill feature:
SELECT: cell B1
DRAG: fill handle for cell B1 to column E
When you release the mouse button, the formatted date headings are entered into the columns.

4 In this worksheet, the beginning balance for a new month is the ending balance from the previous month. To enter this formula into column C:
SELECT: cell C2
CLICK: Bold button ([B]) to apply boldface to the cell
TYPE: =b11
PRESS: [ENTER]

5 To copy and extend this formula to the right:
SELECT: cell range from C2 to E2
Notice that the top left-hand cell in the selected range contains the formula (and formatting) that you want to copy.

6 CHOOSE: Edit, Fill, Right
For the moment, only zeroes will appear in the cells.

7 To extend the formulas for multiple ranges:
SELECT: cell range from B6 to E6
PRESS: [CTRL] and hold it down
SELECT: cell range from B10 to E10
SELECT: cell range from B11 to E11
When all the ranges are highlighted, release the [CTRL] key.

8 To fill each row with their respective formulas stored in column B:
CHOOSE: Edit, Fill, Right
Your worksheet should now appear similar to Figure 2.10.

Figure 2.10

Filling ranges with formulas
stored in the leftmost column

	A	B	C	D	E	F
1	Cash Flow	Sep-99	Oct-99	Nov-99	Dec-99	
2	Beg Balance	125,349	106,093	106,093	106,093	
3	*Add:*					
4	Cash Sales	45,000				
5	Receivables	15,234				
6	Total	60,234	0	0	0	
7	*Subtract:*					
8	Cash Exp	27,490				
9	Payables	52,000				
10	Total	79,490	0	0	0	
11	End Balance	106,093	106,093	106,093	106,093	
12						

9 On your own, enter sample values into the worksheet and witness how the formulas recalculate the totals.

10 Save and then close the workbook.

2.2 Self Check Which method would you use to copy several nonadjacent worksheet values for placement into a single column?

2.3 Modifying Rows and Columns

By adjusting the row heights and column widths in a worksheet, you can enhance its appearance for both viewing and printing—similarly to how a textbook employs white space or a document uses double-spacing to make the text easier to read. You can also reorganize or modify the structure of a worksheet by inserting and deleting rows and columns. This module shows you how to manipulate the appearance and structure of a worksheet.

2.3.1 Changing Column Widths

FEATURE

You can increase and decrease the width of your worksheet columns to allow for varying lengths of text labels, numbers, and dates. To speed the process, you can select and change more than one column width at a time. Excel can even calculate the best or **AutoFit** width for a column based on its existing entries. The maximum width for a column is 255 characters.

EXCEL

METHOD
- To change a column's width using the mouse:
  DRAG: its right borderline in the frame area
- To change a column's width using the menu:
  SELECT: a cell in the column that you want to format
  CHOOSE: Format, Column, Width
  TYPE: *the desired width*
- To change a column's width to its best fit:
  DOUBLE-CLICK: its right borderline in the frame area, or
  CHOOSE: Format, Column, AutoFit Selection

PRACTICE
In this lesson, you open a workbook used to summarize the income earned by organizers of a craft fair. Then you practice changing the worksheet's column widths to better view the data stored therein.

Setup: Ensure that no workbooks are open in the application window.

1 Open the data file named EXC230.

2 Save the file as "Craft Fair" to your personal storage location.

3 In columns D and E of the worksheet, you will notice that some cells contain a series of "#" symbols. These symbols inform you that the columns are not wide enough to display the contents. Let's adjust the width of column D using a command from the Menu bar:
SELECT: cell D1
Notice that you need not select the entire column to change its width; in fact, you can choose any cell within the column.

4 CHOOSE: Format, Column, Width
The Column Width dialog box appears, as shown here. Notice that 8.43 characters is the default column width.

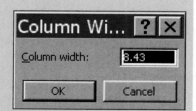

Column Wi... ? ×
Column width: 8.43
OK   Cancel

5 Enter the desired width as measured in characters:
TYPE: 12
PRESS: **ENTER** or CLICK: OK
All of the values stored in column D should now be visible.

6 Now let's adjust the width for column E. In the frame area, position the mouse pointer over the borderline between columns E and F. The mouse pointer changes shape when positioned correctly, as shown in Figure 2.11.

7 CLICK: the borderline and hold down the mouse button
DRAG: the mouse pointer to the right to increase the width to
12.00
Notice that the width (in characters and pixels) is displayed in a
ToolTip. Your screen should now appear similar to Figure 2.11.

Figure 2.11

Changing a column's width

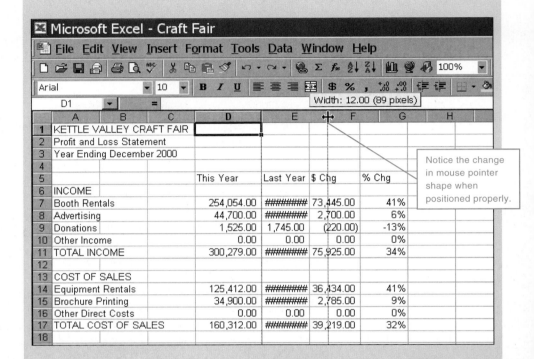

8 Remember to release the mouse button to finalize the new column width setting.

9 The AutoFit feature enables you to find the best width for a column based on its existing entries. To adjust column A, let's select
the entire column as the basis for the width calculation. Do the
following:
SELECT: column A
(*Hint:* This instruction tells you to move the mouse pointer over
the "A" in the column frame area and click once. When done
properly, the entire column will appear highlighted.)

10 CHOOSE: Format, Column, AutoFit Selection
Notice that the width has been adjusted so that it can comfort-
ably hold the longest entry in the column.

2.3.2 Changing Row Heights

FEATURE

You can change the height of any worksheet row to customize the borders and line spacing in a worksheet. What's more, a row's height is adjusted automatically when you increase or decrease the font size of information appearing in the row. A row's height is measured in points, where 72 points is equal to one inch. The larger the font size that you select for a given cell, the larger its row height.

METHOD

- To change a row's height using the mouse:
  DRAG: its bottom borderline in the frame area
- To change a row's height using the menu:
  SELECT: a cell in the row that you want to format
  CHOOSE: Format, Row, Height
  TYPE: *the desired height* in points
- To change a row's height to its best fit:
  DOUBLE-CLICK: its bottom borderline in the frame area, or
  CHOOSE: Format, Row, AutoFit

PRACTICE

You will now change some row heights in a worksheet to improve the spacing between data.

Setup: Ensure that you have completed the previous lesson and that the "Craft Fair" workbook is displayed.

1 SELECT: cell A1

2 In the next two steps, you will change the line spacing for the entire worksheet. As with most formatting commands, you must first select the object for which you want to apply formatting. In this case, you need to select the entire worksheet. To begin:
CLICK: Select All button (☐), as shown below

Click here to select the entire worksheet.

	A
1	KETTLE VALLEY CRAFT FAIR
2	Profit and Loss Statement
3	Year Ending December 2000

3 With the entire worksheet highlighted:
CHOOSE: Format, Row, Height
The following dialog box appears.

4 In the *Row height* text box, enter the desired height as measured in points:
TYPE: **20**
PRESS: (ENTER) or CLICK: OK
Notice that the rows are enlarged, providing more white space.

5 To remove the selection highlighting:
CLICK: cell A1

6 Let's change the height of row 4 using the mouse. To do so, position the mouse pointer over the borderline between rows 4 and 5. Then:
CLICK: the borderline and hold down the mouse button
DRAG: the mouse pointer up to decrease the height to 9.00 points
Similar to changing the column width, the mouse pointer changes and a yellow ToolTip appears with the current measurement.

7 Release the mouse button to finalize the new setting.

8 Let's practice adjusting a row to its best height:
SELECT: row 5
(*Hint:* This instruction tells you to move the mouse pointer over the "5" in the row frame area and click once. When done properly, the entire row will appear highlighted.)

9 CHOOSE: Format, Row, AutoFit
The row height is adjusted automatically.

10 Save the workbook and keep it open for use in the next lesson.

2.3.3 Inserting and Deleting Rows and Columns

FEATURE
You insert and delete rows and columns to affect the structure of a worksheet. But in doing so, you must be careful not to change other areas in your worksheet unintentionally. Deleting column B, for example, removes all of the data in the entire column, not only the cells that are currently visible on your screen.

METHOD

- To insert or delete a row:
  RIGHT-CLICK: a *row number* in the frame area
  CHOOSE: Insert or Delete
- To insert or delete a column:
  RIGHT-CLICK: a *column letter* in the frame area
  CHOOSE: Insert or Delete

PRACTICE

In this lesson, you will practice inserting and deleting rows and columns.

Setup: Ensure that you have completed the previous lessons and that the "Craft Fair" workbook is displayed.

1 After adjusting the width for column A earlier in the module, you may have noticed that columns B and C do not contain any data. Before deleting rows or columns, however, it is always wise to check your assumptions. To do so:
CLICK: cell B1
PRESS: CTRL + ↓
The cell pointer scoots down to row 65536. If there were data in the column, the cell pointer would have stopped at the cell containing the data.

2 To check whether there is any data in column C:
PRESS: →
PRESS: CTRL + ↑
The cell pointer scoots back up to row 1, unencumbered by any cells containing data.

3 Now that you are sure that these columns are indeed empty, let's delete them from the worksheet. To begin, select both of the columns:
CLICK: column B in the frame area
DRAG: the mouse pointer right to also highlight column C
Release the mouse button after the two columns appear highlighted.

4 To delete these two columns:
RIGHT-CLICK: column C in the frame area
Notice that you need only right-click one of the selected column letters. Your screen should now appear similar to Figure 2.12.

Figure 2.12

Displaying the right-click
menu for selected columns

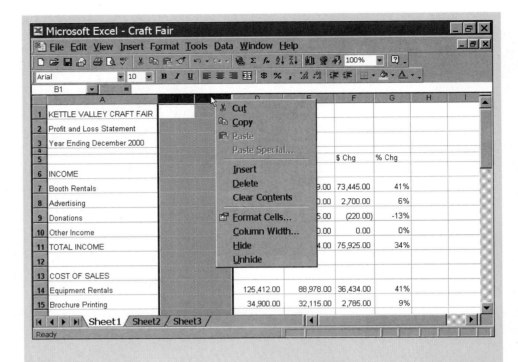

5 From the right-click menu:
CHOOSE: Delete
The column selection remains highlighted in case you want to
apply additional formatting commands.

6 To insert a row:
RIGHT-CLICK: row 8 in the frame area
CHOOSE Insert
A new row is inserted at row 8; pushing down the existing rows.

7 To enter some new information:
SELECT: cell A8
TYPE: Food Pavilion
PRESS: ➡
TYPE: 55800
PRESS: ➡
TYPE: 43750
PRESS: ENTER

8 To copy the formulas for calculating the annual increase:
SELECT: cell range D7 to E8
CHOOSE: Edit, Fill, Down
The results, 12,050.00 and 28%, now appear in row 8.

EXCEL

2.3.4 Hiding and Unhiding Rows and Columns

FEATURE

Rather than deleting a row or column, you can modify a worksheet so that not all of the data is displayed. For example, you may want to hide rows and columns that contain sensitive data, such as salaries or commissions. You can even hide detailed information temporarily that you do not want included in a particular report.

METHOD

To hide a row or column:
1. RIGHT-CLICK: the desired row or column
2. CHOOSE: Hide

To unhide a row or column:
1. SELECT: the rows or columns on either side of the hidden row or column
2. RIGHT-CLICK: the selected rows or columns
3. CHOOSE: Unhide

PRACTICE

In this lesson, you practice hiding and unhiding worksheet information.

Setup: Ensure that you have completed the previous lessons and that the "Craft Fair" workbook is displayed.

1 Let's hide columns D and E from displaying. Do the following:
CLICK: column D in the frame area
DRAG: the mouse pointer right to also highlight column E

2 To hide the selected columns:
RIGHT-CLICK: column E in the frame area
CHOOSE: Hide
Notice that the column frame area now shows A, B, C, and then F.

3 To hide several rows in the worksheet:
SELECT: rows 7 through 11 in the frame area
RIGHT-CLICK: row 7 in the frame area
CHOOSE: Hide
PRESS: CTRL + HOME to move the cell pointer
The row frame area now displays a gap between row 6 and row 12. Your screen should now appear similar to Figure 2.13.

Figure 2.13

Hiding columns and rows

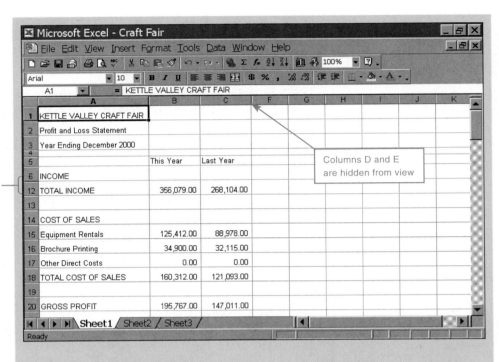

Rows 7 through 11 are hidden from view.

 4 To unhide columns D and E, you must select the columns on either side. For example:
CLICK: column C in the frame area
DRAG: the mouse pointer right to also highlight column F

5 Let's use the Menu bar to unhide the columns:
CHOOSE: Format, Column, Unhide
The columns reappear on the worksheet.

6 To unhide the rows:
SELECT: rows 6 through 12
CHOOSE: Format, Row, Unhide
The rows reappear on the worksheet.

7 Save and then close the workbook.

8 Exit Microsoft Excel.

2.3 Self Check   Why must you be careful when deleting rows or columns?

2.4 Chapter Review

This chapter introduced you to some common procedures for modifying the contents and structure of a worksheet. In the first module, you entered data and formulas using Excel's special "Auto" features, including AutoComplete and AutoSum. Then you learned how to use the Windows and Office Clipboards and Excel's drag and drop features for moving, copying, and pasting data. You also practiced using the AutoFill feature by dragging a cell range's fill handle to extend a data series. As for modifying a worksheet's structure, you inserted and deleted cells, rows, and columns. And lastly, you practiced hiding, unhiding, and changing the height and width of rows and columns.

2.4.1 Command Summary

Many of the commands and procedures appearing in this chapter are summarized in the following table.

Skill Set	To Perform this Task . . .	Do the Following . . .
Using Functions	Entering the SUM function using the AutoSum button	SELECT: a cell to place the result CLICK: AutoSum button (Σ)
	Displaying the sum result of a calculation using AutoCalculate	SELECT: a cell range and view the result in the Status bar
Working with Cells	Insert a cell or cell range	SELECT: the desired cell range CHOOSE: Insert, Cells
	Delete a cell or cell range	SELECT: the desired cell range CHOOSE: Edit, Delete
	Insert data using AutoComplete	RIGHT-CLICK: the desired cell CHOOSE: Pick From List SELECT: the desired data
	Copy or move data using the toolbar	SELECT: the desired cell or range CLICK: Copy or Cut SELECT: the target cell or range CLICK: Paste button
	Move data using drag and drop	SELECT: the desired cell or range DRAG: the selection by its border

Continued

Skill Set	To Perform this Task . . .	Do the Following . . .
	Copy data using drag and drop	SELECT: the desired cell or range PRESS: CTRL and hold it down DRAG: the selection by its border
	Display the Office Clipboard	CHOOSE: View, Toolbars, Clipboard
	Clear the Office Clipboard	CLICK: Clear Clipboard button (🗷)
	Create a series using the fill handle	SELECT: the desired range DRAG: the fill handle
	Copy a formula across a row or down a column	SELECT: the range to fill; with the formula in the top left-hand corner CHOOSE: Edit, Fill, Right (or Down)
Formatting Worksheets	Change a cell's column width	CHOOSE: Format, Column, Width TYPE: *width* in characters
	Change a cell's row height	CHOOSE: Format, Row, Height TYPE: *height* in points
Modifying Worksheets	Insert and delete columns	RIGHT-CLICK: a column's frame area CHOOSE: Insert or Delete
	Insert and delete rows	RIGHT-CLICK: a row's frame area CHOOSE: Insert or Delete
	Hide a row or column	RIGHT-CLICK: in the frame area CHOOSE: Hide
	Unhide a row or column	SELECT: rows or columns on either side of the hidden row or column RIGHT-CLICK: the frame selection CHOOSE: Unhide

2.4.2 Key Terms

This section specifies page references for the key terms identified in this chapter. For a complete list of definitions, refer to the Glossary provided in the Appendix.

AutoCalculate, *p. 59*

AutoComplete, *p. 56*

AutoFill, *p. 70*

AutoFit, *p. 74*

AutoSum, *p. 59*

cell range, *p. 53*

drag and drop, *p. 63*

fill handle, *p. 70*

Office Clipboard, *p. 63*

series, *p. 70*

Windows Clipboard, *p. 63*

2.5 Review Questions

2.5.1 Short Answer

1. What visible feature differentiates the active cell in a selected cell range?
2. How do you select more than one cell range in a worksheet?
3. Where does Excel's AutoComplete feature get the values for displaying in a pick list?
4. What are the two choices for moving existing data when you insert a new cell or cell range?
5. Name the two types of Clipboards and explain how they differ.
6. What is the primary difference between using the Clipboards and using the drag and drop method to copy information?
7. What is the fastest way to place five year's worth of quarterly headings at the top of your worksheet (i.e., Jan-00, Mar-00, Jun-00,...)?
8. What does "########" in a cell indicate?
9. What is meant by a "best fit" or "AutoFit" column width?
10. In what circumstances might you hide a row or column?

2.5.2 True/False

1. _F_ You use <kbd>ALT</kbd> to select a range of cells using the keyboard.
2. _T_ Excel's AutoComplete feature allows you to sum a range of values and place the result into a worksheet cell.
3. _T_ You use the Edit, Clear command to delete the contents of a cell and the Edit, Delete command to delete the actual cell.
4. _T_ You can collect up to 12 items for pasting using the Office Clipboard.
5. _F_ You can collect up to four items for pasting using the Windows Clipboard.
6. _T_ When you drag and drop using the <kbd>CTRL</kbd> key, a plus sign appears indicating that you are using the copy feature.
7. _T_ To copy and extend a formula to adjacent cells, you can use either the fill handle or the Edit, Fill, Right command.
8. _F_ When you insert a column, the existing column is pushed left.
9. _T_ When you insert a row, the existing row is pushed down.
10. _F_ You unhide rows and columns using the Window, Unhide command.

2.5.3 Multiple Choice

1. You hold down the following key to select multiple cell ranges using the mouse.
   a. <kbd>ALT</kbd>
   b. <kbd>CTRL</kbd>
   c. <kbd>SHIFT</kbd>
   d. <kbd>PRTSCR</kbd>

2. This feature allows you to view the sum of a range of values without entering a formula into a worksheet cell.
   a. AutoCalculate
   b. AutoComplete
   c. AutoTotal
   d. AutoValue

3. The AutoSum feature enters this function into a cell to sum a range of values:
   a. ADD
   b. SUM
   c. TOTAL
   d. VALUE

4. If you want to delete cells from the worksheet, you select the desired range and then choose the following command:
   a. Edit, Clear, All
   b. Edit, Clear, Cells
   c. Edit, Cells, Delete
   d. Edit, Delete

5. To perform a drag and drop operation, you position the mouse pointer over the selected cell or cell range until it changes to this shape.
   a. 
   b. 
   c. 
   d. 

6. What menu command allows you to copy a formula in the active cell to a range of adjacent cells in a row?
   a. Edit, Fill, Down
   b. Edit, Fill, Right
   c. Edit, Copy, Right
   d. Edit, Extend, Fill

7. To select an entire column for editing, inserting, or deleting:
   a. PRESS: ALT + ↓ with the cell pointer in the column
   b. DOUBLE-CLICK: a cell within the column
   c. CLICK: the column letter in the frame area
   d. CHOOSE: Edit, Select Column

8. The height of a row is typically measured using these units.
   a. Characters
   b. Fonts
   c. Picas
   d. Points

9. To change a column's width using the mouse, you position the mouse pointer into the column frame area until it changes to this shape.
   a. 
   b. 
   c. 
   d. 

10. Row 5 is hidden on your worksheet. To unhide the row, you must make this selection before issuing the appropriate menu command.
    a. rows 4 and 6
    b. rows 1 through 4
    c. row 4
    d. row 6

2.6 Hands-On Projects

2.6.1 Grandview College: Course List

In this exercise, you practice using Excel's "Auto" features to enter information and calculate results.

1. Load Microsoft Excel.
2. Open the data file named EXC261.
3. Save the workbook as "Course List" to your personal storage location.
4. To complete this worksheet, you must enter some additional information for "Intermediate French." To begin:
   SELECT: cell B9
   TYPE: L
   PRESS: (ENTER)
   Notice that the word "Languages" is inserted automatically.
5. To enter some data for the "Writer's Workshop," do the following:
   RIGHT-CLICK: cell B10
   CHOOSE: Pick From List
   CLICK: English in the pick list
6. To use AutoComplete with the keyboard:
   SELECT: cell C10
   PRESS: (ALT) + (↓)
   PRESS: (↓) four more times to highlight "Molina"
   PRESS: (ENTER)
7. Now let's use the AutoCalculate feature to sum the total number of hours without placing an entry into the worksheet. Do the following:
   SELECT: cell range from D5 to D10
   Notice that the Status bar now displays 169.

EXCEL

8. You will now enter a total formula for the Hours column:
   SELECT: cell D12   _=Sum(D5:D11_
   CLICK: AutoSum button (Σ)
   CLICK: AutoSum button (Σ) a second time to accept the cell range
   The answer, 169, now appears in the cell.
9. On your own, place a total formula in cell E12 for the Credits column.
10. Save and then close the workbook.

2.6.2 Fast Forward Video: Top Five Rentals

You will now practice copying and moving data using Excel's AutoFill feature, drag and drop, and the Windows and Office Clipboards.

1. Open the data file named EXC262.
2. Save the workbook as "Top Five" to your personal storage location.
3. Let's use the AutoFill feature to extend the heading to column C:
   SELECT: cell B1
   DRAG: fill handle for cell B1 to column C
   Notice that the text entry becomes "Week-2" and that the formatting is also copied.
4. On your own, extend the column heading for Week-2 in row 8.
5. You will now extend the row labels for "Videos" in column A. Do the following:
   SELECT: cell range from A2 to A3
   DRAG: fill handle for the selected cell range to row 6
6. On your own, extend the row labels for "Games" in column A.
7. Using the Windows Clipboard, copy the first two videos from Week-1 (Rocky: the Next Generation and Lethal Instinct) to the same positions in Week-2:
   SELECT: cell range from B2 to B3
   CLICK: Copy button () on the Standard toolbar
   SELECT: cell C2
   CLICK: Paste button ()
   PRESS: ESC to remove the dashed marquee
8. Using drag and drop, copy the number 3 video of Week-1 (Rent: the Movie) to the number 5 position of Week-2:
   SELECT: cell B4

Autofill +

9. Position the mouse pointer over the border of the selected cell so that a white diagonal arrow appears. Then, do the following:
PRESS: (CTRL) and hold it down
DRAG: mouse pointer to cell C6

10. Release the mouse button and then the (CTRL) key to complete the copy operation.

11. Using drag and drop, copy the cell range B5:B6 (X-Files 2 and Wild and Crazy Guys) to cells C4:C5.

12. You will use the Office Clipboard to modify the Games order from Week-1 to Week-2. First, display the Office Clipboard toolbar and clear its existing contents:
CHOOSE: View, Toolbars, Clipboard
CLICK: Clear Clipboard button (🗷) on the Clipboard toolbar

13. Now, add the Games to the Office Clipboard:
SELECT: cell B12
CLICK: Copy button (📄) on the Clipboard or Standard toolbars
SELECT: cell B9
CLICK: Copy button (📄)
SELECT: cell B10
CLICK: Copy button (📄)
SELECT: cell B13
CLICK: Copy button (📄)
SELECT: cell B11
CLICK: Copy button (📄)

14. Now, paste all of the data elements into the Week-2 column:
SELECT: cell C9
CLICK: Paste All button (📋Paste All)
Your screen should now appear similar to Figure 2.14.

15. Lastly, remove the range selection highlighting and close the Office Clipboard toolbar:
PRESS: (CTRL) + (HOME)
CLICK: Close button on the Office Clipboard toolbar

16. Save and then close the "Top Five" workbook.

Figure 2.14

Pasting data from
the Office Clipboard

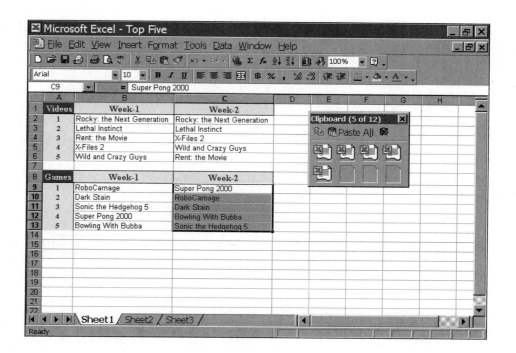

2.6.3 Sun Valley Frozen Foods: Sales Force

In this exercise, you practice modifying an existing worksheet that is used to track sales representatives for Sun Valley Frozen Foods.

1. Open the data file named EXC263.
2. Save the workbook as "Sales Force" to your personal storage location.
3. You may have noticed that the title in cell A1 is difficult to read. Adjust the height for row 1 to its "best fit" or "AutoFit" height.
4. The sales representatives' names are truncated by the "Location" entries in column B. Therefore, adjust the width of column A to ensure that all the names are visible.
5. Change the column width for columns B through D to 8 characters.
6. Change the column width for columns E through G to 10 characters.
7. Change the height of rows 2 through 15 to 15.00.
8. In cell F4, enter a commission rate of 5%.
9. In cell G4, multiple the commission rate (F) by the Revenue (E).
10. Copy the entries in cells F4 and G4 down the column to row 15.
11. Remove the Route information by deleting column C.
12. Remove the information for Bruce Towne by deleting the cell range A8 to F8 and then closing up the gap.

*[handwritten annotations: = E4 * F4, .05, Rev Box * X, Comission Box]*

13. Hide the two end columns used in calculating and displaying a sales rep's commission.
14. Without placing a formula on the worksheet, calculate the total Revenue collected by these sales reps. What is this value?
15. Save and then close the workbook.

2.6.4   Lakeside Realty: Sales Projections

In this exercise, you practice copying data and modifying a worksheet.

1. Open the data file named EXC264.
2. Save the workbook as "Sales Volume" to your personal storage location.
3. Increase the width of column A to 12 characters.
4. Use the AutoSum button to sum the values for columns B through D and display the results in row 9.
5. To extend the table to project values for the years 2000, 2001, and 2002, select the cell range from B4 to D9.
6. Drag the fill handle of the selected range to column G. When you release the mouse button, the range is filled with projected results. These results are based on the trends calculated from the selected columns of data. Notice that you did not enter any formulas into the worksheet, other than using AutoSum to provide a totals row.
7. Use the Office Clipboard to collect and sort data from the worksheet and then paste the results into the area below the table. Specifically, replicate the result shown in Figure 2.15.

Figure 2.15

Using the Office Clipboard to organize data

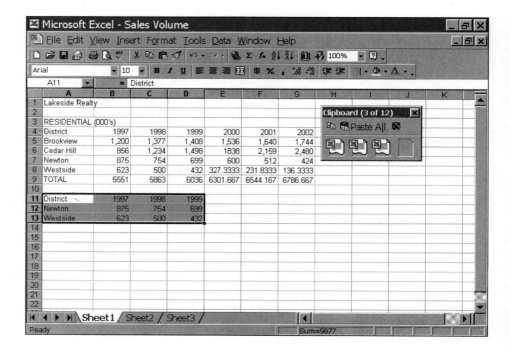

EXCEL

8. Clear the Clipboard contents and then close the Clipboard toolbar.
9. Hide rows 4 through 8.
10. Save and then close the workbook.

2.6.5 On Your Own: Blue Zone Personnel

A friend of yours has just accepted a position at Blue Zone Personnel. In addition to her general administrative duties, she must help the accountant prepare monthly income statements. Since she seemed quite nervous about the new position, you offered to help her develop an Excel worksheet. You open the EXC265 workbook that she has been using and save it as "Blue Zone" to her personal storage location.

After adjusting the column widths, you review the structure of the worksheet. To begin, you insert a row above EXPENSES and label it Total Revenue. Then, you use the AutoSum feature to sum the revenues for September and October. Continuing in this manner, you adjust and insert rows, data, and formulas so that the worksheet appears similar to Figure 2.16. Then, you save and close the workbook.

Figure 2.16

Modifying a worksheet's structure and appearance

	A	B	C	D
1	Blue Zone Personnel			
2				
3	REVENUE	Sep-99	Oct-99	
4	Programming	12,400	13,100	
5	Service Calls	450	540	
6	Technical Support	225	330	
7	Total Revenue	13,075	13,970	
8	EXPENSES			
9	Advertising	200	250	
10	Bank Charges	25	25	
11	Depreciation	2,400	2,400	
12	Payroll Costs	10,000	10,000	
13	Telephone	275	275	
14	Total Expenses	12900	12950	
15	PROFIT	175	1,020	
16				

— AutoSum formula (row 7)

— New row inserted (row 9)

— AutoSum formula (row 14)

— Subtraction formula (row 15)

2.6.6 On Your Own: Running Diary

It's May and you're finally getting around to that New Year's resolution of getting into shape. To motivate yourself, you decide to create a running diary using Microsoft Excel. Open the data file named EXC266 and then save it as "My Running Diary" to your personal storage location.

Given your current statistics, you'd like to project how long it will take you to reach 10 miles. To do so, you select the cell range from B4 through B12. Then drag the fill handle for the range downward until the ToolTip displays a value over 10. You then press CTRL + HOME to return to the top of the worksheet. To make it easier to count the number of runs, you insert a new column A and then number each run in the column using the fill handle. *How many runs will it take you to reach 10 miles?* You then use Excel's AutoCalculate feature to determine how many total miles you have run as of May 23rd. *How many miles have you run thus far?* Impressed with your computer knowledge, your running partner asks you to track her running statistics also. Rather than create a new worksheet, you copy and paste the column headings beside your own, so that they begin in column H. Lastly, you save and close the workbook and then exit Excel.

2.7 Case Problems: Granby Insurance Agency

Scott Allenby, the business manager for the Granby Insurance Agency, is responsible for generating monthly profitability reports. One of the key business areas for Granby involves a long-standing agreement with a local car dealer to manage their financing, insurance, and after-market sales. Upon reviewing some of the past data from the dealership, Scott identifies an opportunity to use Microsoft Excel for generating their reports.

In the following case problems, assume the role of Scott and perform the same steps that he identifies. You may want to re-read the chapter opening before proceeding.

1. Scott decides to focus his attention on one report that is generated for the car dealership at the end of each month. He calls a good friend, whom he knows has several months experience using Excel, and describes what he needs over the phone. He then sends him a fax of the actual report to help clarify the discussion. The next day, Scott receives a diskette from his friend which contains a workbook called EXC271. He opens the workbook and then saves it as PROFIT to his personal storage location.

The PROFIT report, which is the car dealer's own abbreviation for a Performance Review of Finance and Insurance Totals, summarizes the number of new and used cars that are sold in a given month, including the number of financing, insurance, warranty, and rust protection packages. After reviewing the worksheet, Scott decides to make a few additions and modifications.

- In cell A1, edit the title to read "Profitability Review of Finance and Insurance Totals."
- In cells G3 and H3, enter the headings "Total Cars" and "Revenue," respectively.
- In cell G5, enter a formula that adds the number of new car sales to the number of used car sales.
- In cell H5, enter a formula that adds the revenue for new car sales to the revenue for used car sales.
- Using the fill handle, copy the formulas in cells G5 and H5 down their respective columns to row 9.
- Using the AutoSum feature, sum the values in columns C through H and place the results in row 10.

Save the workbook and keep it open for use in the next problem.

2. Wednesday morning does not start out well for Scott. The owner of the dealership calls to request that Granby Insurance no longer track the sale of "Rust Protection" packages. He also asks Scott to hide the "Used Car" columns in the report. Fortunately, Scott remembers how to remove and hide cells, rows, and columns. He also feels that this is a great opportunity to adjust some of the worksheet's column widths and row heights. Specifically, Scott performs the following steps:

- Select the "best fit" or "AutoFit" width for column A. Notice that the width is adjusted to handle the length of the title in cell A1.
- Specify a column width of 18 characters for column A.
- Specify a column width of 9 characters for columns C through H.
- Specify a row height of 7.50 points for row 4.
- Ensure that column B is empty. Then delete the entire column.
- Select the cell range (A8:G8) for Rust Protection. Then choose the Edit, Delete command to remove the cells from the worksheet and shift the remaining cells upward.
- Select columns D and E. Then hide the columns from displaying.

Your screen should now appear similar to Figure 2.17. Save the workbook and keep it open for use in the next problem.

Figure 2.17

Manipulating columns and rows in a worksheet

	A	B	C	F	G	H
1	Profitability Review of Finance and Insurance Totals					
2						
3	Product Category	New Cars	Revenue	Total Cars	Revenue	
4						
5	Retail Sales	20	492,000	35	630,000	
6	Life Ins. Policies	4	1,250	6	3,750	
7	Option Packages	5	2,150	5	2,150	
8	Ext. Warranties	1	375	2	715	
9	Totals	30	495775	48	636615	
10						

3. Scott decides that it would be helpful to develop a projection for next month's PROFIT report. Rather than create a new worksheet, he unhides columns D and E and then copies the data from cells A3 through G9 to the Windows Clipboard. He moves the cell pointer to cell A12 and then pastes the data. In order to start with a clean slate, Scott selects cells B14 through G17 and erases the cell contents in the range. Then he selects cell B14 and enters a formula that shows an increase of 20% over the value stored in cell B5. In other words, he multiplies the value in cell B5 by 1.2. Lastly, Scott copies the formula to the remaining cells in the range. The workbook appears similar to Figure 2.18. To ensure that the projection area works properly, Scott changes some of the values in the top table area. Satisfied that the bottom table area updates automatically, he saves and closes the workbook.

Figure 2.18

Creating a projection based on an existing range of cells

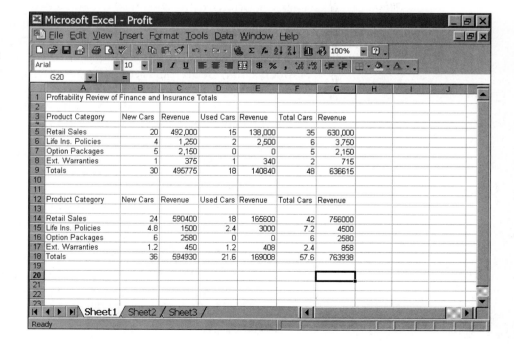

4. Scott opens a second workbook that he receives from his friend called EXC274. He then saves the workbook as "Car Buyers" to his personal storage location. This particular workbook stores customer information from each sale made in the month.

Scott reviews the worksheet and decides to make a few changes. First, he inserts a new column A and then enters 1 into cell A4 and 2 into cell A5. Using the mouse, he selects both cells and then drags the range's fill handle downward to continue numbering the customers. *What is the number of the last customer, Heidi Buehre?* He then moves to cell E12 and displays the Auto-Complete pick list. *What vehicles are listed in the pick list and in what order do they appear?* To remove the pick list, Scott presses the ⌷ESC⌷ key. Lastly, Scott uses Excel's AutoCalculate feature to sum the purchase price of all vehicles sold in January without having to enter a formula into the worksheet. *What is the total value of vehicles purchased?*

Ready to go home for the day, Scott saves and then closes the workbook. Then he exits Microsoft Excel.

Notes

MICROSOFT EXCEL 2000
Formatting and Printing

CHAPTER
THREE

Chapter Outline

Learning Objectives

After reading this chapter, you will be able to:

- Format cell entries to appear boldface or italic and with different typefaces and font sizes

- Format numeric and date values

- Format cells to appear with borders, shading, and color

- Preview and print a worksheet

- Publish a worksheet to the World Wide Web

- Define page layout options, such as margins, headers, and footers, for printing your worksheets

Case Study

Marvin's Music

Marvin's Music is an independently owned sidewalk store that is located in the downtown core of Randall, Virginia. Established in 1974, Marvin's has successfully sold record albums, 8-track tapes, cassettes, and audio CDs. And, just recently, they began stocking movie videos and DVDs. For the past 25 years, Marvin's most prominent business strategy has been a commitment to stocking a large selection of music that appeals to a broad audience. They have always taken pride in their large inventory and in providing personalized customer service.

Stacey Marvin, the store's owner and general manager, is concerned for her business. She recently read in the newspaper that a large discount superstore is planning to move into the area. In a meeting with Justin Lee, her senior sales associate, she discussed some possible advertising ideas for combating the new competitor. For the past 18 months, Justin has been acting as Stacey's right hand. He handles much of the purchasing and receiving duties and is the primary contact person for Marvin's suppliers. Justin is also familiar with using the custom accounting software and Microsoft Excel, both of which are loaded on the office's personal computer.

In this chapter, you and Justin learn more about working with Excel worksheets. First, you learn how to format a worksheet to make it appear more attractive and easier to read. After previewing and printing a worksheet, you learn to save it as an HTML document for publishing to a Web site. Lastly, you customize several layout options, such as margins and headers, for more effective printing.

3.1 Enhancing a Worksheet's Appearance

Most people realize how important it is to create worksheets that are easy to read and pleasing to the eye. Clearly, a visually attractive worksheet will convey information better than an unformatted one. With Excel's formatting capabilities, you can enhance your worksheets for publishing online or to print. In addition to choosing from a variety of fonts, styles, and cell alignments, you can specify decimal places and add currency and percentage symbols to values. The combination of these features enables you to produce professional-looking spreadsheet reports and presentations.

3.1.1 Applying Fonts, Font Styles, and Colors

FEATURE

Applying **fonts** to titles, headings, and other worksheet cells is often the most effective means for drawing a reader's attention to specific areas in your worksheet. You can also specify font styles, like boldface and italic, adjust font sizes, and select colors. Do not feel obliged, however, to use every font that is available to you in a single worksheet. Above all, your worksheets must be easy to read—too many fonts, styles, and colors are distracting. As a rule, limit your font selection for a single worksheet to two or three **typefaces**, such as Times New Roman and Arial.

METHOD

To apply character formatting, select the desired cell range and then:

- CLICK: Font list box ([Arial ▼])
- CLICK: Font Size list box ([10 ▼])
- CLICK: Bold button (**B**)
- CLICK: Italic button (*I*)
- CLICK: Underline button (U)
- CLICK: Font Color button (A ▾)

To display the *Font* formatting options:
1. SELECT: cell range to format
2. CHOOSE: Format, Cells
3. CLICK: *Font* tab in the Format Cells dialog box
4. SELECT: the desired font, font style, size, color, and effects

PRACTICE

In this lesson, you open and format a workbook that tracks a mutual fund portfolio.

Setup: Ensure that Excel is loaded.

1 Open the data file named EXC310.

2 Save the file as "My Portfolio" to your personal storage location.

3 Your first step is to select the cell range to format. Do the following to begin formatting the column labels:
SELECT: cell range from A3 to G3

4 Let's make these labels bold and appear with underlining:
CLICK: Bold button (B)
CLICK: Underline button (U)

5 Now you will format the title labels in cells A1 and A2. To begin:
SELECT: cell range from A1 to A2

6 To change the typeface used in the cells:
CLICK: down arrow attached to the Font list box (Arial ▾)
Your screen should now appear similar but not identical to Figure 3.1.

Figure 3.1

Selecting a typeface from the Font list box

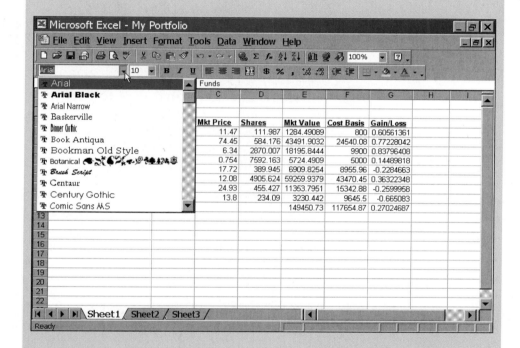

7 Using the scroll bars attached to the drop-down list box:
SELECT: Times New Roman

8 To increase the font size:
CLICK: down arrow attached to the Font Size list box (10 ▾)
SELECT: 14
The cells now appear formatted using a 14-point, Times New Roman typeface; the row heights have also been adjusted automatically.

9 You can also use the Format Cells dialog box to apply formatting to the selected cell range. Do the following:
SELECT: cell A1
CHOOSE: Format, Cells
CLICK: *Font* tab
Your screen should now appear similar to Figure 3.2.

Figure 3.2

Format Cells dialog
box: *Font* tab

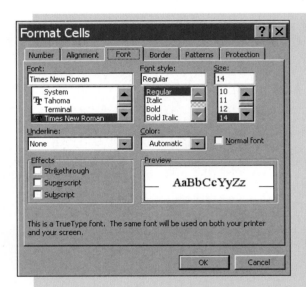

10 To add some additional flare to the title:
SELECT: *any typeface* from the *Font* list box
SELECT: Bold in the *Font style* list box
SELECT: 16 in the *Size* list box
SELECT: Blue from the *Color* drop-down list box
CLICK: OK
The title in cell A1 should now stand out from the rest of the
data.

11 You can also use shortcut keys to apply formatting:
SELECT: cell range from A12 to G12
PRESS: (CTRL)+b to apply boldface

12 Save the workbook and keep it open for use in the next lesson.

3.1.2 Formatting Numbers and Dates

FEATURE
Numeric formats improve the appearance and readability of numbers in a worksheet by inserting dollar signs, commas, percentage symbols, and decimal places. Although a formatted number or date appears differently on the worksheet, the value that is stored and displayed in the Formula bar does not change. Excel stores date and time entries as values and, therefore, allows you to customize their display as you do numbers.

METHOD
To apply number formatting, select the desired cell range and then:
- CLICK: Currency Style button (📰)
- CLICK: Percent Style button (💥)
- CLICK: Comma Style button (🔲)
- CLICK: Increase Decimal button (🔲)
- CLICK: Decrease Decimal button (🔲)

To display the *Number* formatting options:
1. SELECT: cell range to format
2. CHOOSE: Format, Cells
3. CLICK: *Number* tab
4. SELECT: a number or date format from the *Category* list box
5. SELECT: formatting options for the selected category

PRACTICE
You will now apply number, currency, percentage, decimal place, and date formatting to the worksheet.

Setup: Ensure that you have completed the previous lesson and that the "My Portfolio" workbook is displayed.

1 Columns B and G in the worksheet contain data that is best represented using a percent number format. First, column B displays the proportional share of an investment compared to the total portfolio. Column G calculates the gain or loss performance. To display these calculated results as percentages, do the following:
SELECT: cell range from B4 to B11
PRESS: CTRL and hold it down
SELECT: cell range from G4 to G12

2 Release the CTRL key after the last range is selected. Notice that these two ranges are highlighted independently—ready for formatting. (*Hint:* You will no longer be reminded to release the CTRL key when dragging the cell pointer over a range.)

3 To apply a percent style:
CLICK: Percent Style button (💥)

4 To display the percentages with two decimal places:
CLICK: Increase Decimal button (🔲) twice

5 Let's apply some further number formatting:
SELECT: cell range from C4 to F11
CHOOSE: Format, Cells
CLICK: *Number* tab

6 In the Format Cells dialog box that appears:
SELECT: Number in the *Category* list box
SELECT: 2 in the *Decimal places* text box
SELECT: *Use 1000 Separator (,)* check box
SELECT: Black (1,234.10) in the *Negative numbers* list box
Your screen should now appear similar to Figure 3.3.

Figure 3.3

Format Cells dialog
box: *Number* tab

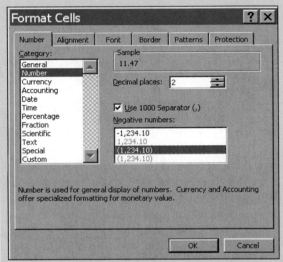

7 To apply the formatting options:
CLICK: OK

8 To increase the decimal places in the Shares column:
SELECT: cell range from D4 to D11
CLICK: Increase Decimal button (⊞)

9 To format the summary values using the Currency style:
SELECT: cell range from E12 to F12
CLICK: Currency Style button (⊞)

10 Depending on your system, the columns may not be wide
enough to display the formatted values. With the two cells still
selected:
CHOOSE: Format, Column, AutoFit Selection
You should now see all the data appearing in the column.

11 Let's develop a notes area:
SELECT: cell A14
TYPE: Notes
PRESS: ⬇

12 To enter the first note or comment:
TYPE: 31-Aug-99
PRESS: ➡
TYPE: The market rebounded from a low of 9,200 in
June.
PRESS: ENTER

13 SELECT: cell A15
In the Formula bar, notice that the date reads 8/31/1999.

14 To format the date to appear differently on the worksheet:
CHOOSE: Format, Cells
Notice that "Date" is already selected in the *Category* list box and that the current date format appears highlighted in the *Type* list box.

15 To apply a new format, you select one of the listed versions:
SELECT: "March 14, 1998" in the *Type* list box
CLICK: OK command button
(*Note*: The *Type* list box displays the date formats for March 14, 1998. Keep in mind that you are selecting a display format and not a date value to insert into the worksheet.) Your screen should now appear similar to Figure 3.4.

Figure 3.4

Applying number and date formats

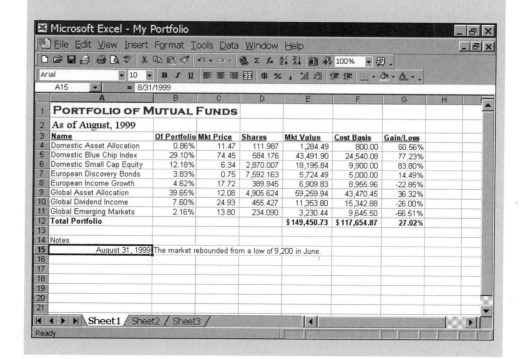

Microsoft Excel - My Portfolio

	A	B	C	D	E	F	G	H
1	**PORTFOLIO OF MUTUAL FUNDS**							
2	As of August, 1999							
3	**Name**	**Of Portfolio**	**Mkt Price**	**Shares**	**Mkt Value**	**Cost Basis**	**Gain/Loss**	
4	Domestic Asset Allocation	0.86%	11.47	111.987	1,284.49	800.00	60.56%	
5	Domestic Blue Chip Index	29.10%	74.45	584.176	43,491.90	24,540.08	77.23%	
6	Domestic Small Cap Equity	12.18%	6.34	2,870.007	18,195.84	9,900.00	83.80%	
7	European Discovery Bonds	3.83%	0.75	7,592.163	5,724.49	5,000.00	14.49%	
8	European Income Growth	4.62%	17.72	389.945	6,909.83	8,955.96	-22.85%	
9	Global Asset Allocation	39.65%	12.08	4,905.624	59,259.94	43,470.45	36.32%	
10	Global Dividend Income	7.60%	24.93	455.427	11,353.80	15,342.88	-26.00%	
11	Global Emerging Markets	2.16%	13.80	234.090	3,230.44	9,645.50	-66.51%	
12	**Total Portfolio**				**$149,450.73**	**$117,654.87**	**27.02%**	
13								
14	Notes							
15	August 31, 1999	The market rebounded from a low of 9,200 in June.						
16								

Sheet1 / Sheet2 / Sheet3 /

Ready

3.1.3 Aligning and Merging Cells

FEATURE
You can change the **cell alignment** for any type of data entered into a worksheet. By default, Excel aligns text against the left edge of a cell and values against the right edge. Not only can you change these default alignments, you can also merge or combine data across cells.

METHOD

To align and merge data, select the desired cell range and then:
- CLICK: Align Left button (☰)
- CLICK: Center button (☰)
- CLICK: Align Right button (☰)
- CLICK: Merge and Center button (☷)

To display the *Alignment* formatting options:
1. SELECT: cell range to format
2. CHOOSE: Format, Cells
3. CLICK: *Alignment* tab
4. SELECT: to align or merge cells

PRACTICE

You will now practice aligning cell information and merging cells.

Setup: Ensure that you have completed the previous lessons in the module and that the "My Portfolio" workbook is displayed.

1 You align the contents of a cell using buttons on the Formatting toolbar. Let's manipulate the "Notes" title in cell A14:
SELECT: cell A14
CLICK: Bold button (B)
CLICK: Underline button (U)

2 To practice changing a cell's alignment:
CLICK: Align Right button (☰)
CLICK: Align Left button (☰)
CLICK: Center button (☰)
Notice the change in alignment that takes place with each mouse click.

3 You can change the cell alignment for number and date values also:
SELECT: cell A15
CLICK: Center button (☰)
The date appears centered under the column heading for "Notes."

4 A little more interesting is the ability to merge cells together and center the contents. Do the following:
SELECT: cell range from A1 to G1
CLICK: Merge and Center button (☷)
Notice that the title is now centered over the table area. (*Note*: The merged cell is considered cell A1. The next cell in the row is cell H1.)

5 Let's merge and center the subtitle in cell A2 using the dialog box:
SELECT: cell range from A2 to G2
CHOOSE: Format, Cells
CLICK: *Alignment* tab
Your screen should now appear similar to Figure 3.5.

Figure 3.5

Format Cells dialog box: *Alignment* tab

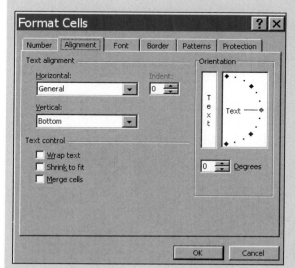

6 In the Format Cells dialog box:
SELECT: Center from the *Horizontal* drop-down list box
SELECT: *Merge cells* check box
CLICK: OK command button

7 Let's practice splitting up a merged cell without using the Undo command:
SELECT: cell A2 (which now covers the area to G2)
CHOOSE: Format, Cells
The last tab that was selected in the dialog box (*Alignment*) is displayed automatically.

8 To remove the merged cell:
SELECT: *Merge cells* check box so that no "✔" appears
CLICK: OK command button
The entry remains centered, but only between column A's borders.

9 Save the workbook and keep it open for use in the next lesson.

3.1.4 Adding Borders and Shading

FEATURE
As with the other formatting options, you use borders, patterns, shading, and colors to enhance a worksheet's readability. The gridlines that appear in the worksheet window are nonprinting lines, provided only to help you line up information. Borders can be used to place printed gridlines on a worksheet and to separate data into logical sections. These formatting options also enable you to create professional-looking invoice forms, memos, and tables.

METHOD
To apply borders or coloring, select the desired cell range and then:
- CLICK: Borders button (⊞)
- CLICK: Fill Color button (▨)

To display the Border and Patterns formatting options:
1. SELECT: cell range to format
2. CHOOSE: Format, Cells
3. CLICK: *Border* or *Patterns* tab
4. SELECT: borders or pattern, shading, and fill color options

PRACTICE
In this exercise, you further format the worksheet by applying borders and fill coloring to selected cell ranges.

Setup: Ensure that you have completed the previous lessons in the module and that the "My Portfolio" workbook is displayed.

1 In order to better see the borders that you will apply in this lesson, let's remove the **gridlines** from the worksheet display:
CHOOSE: Tools, Options
CLICK: *View* tab
SELECT: *Gridlines* check box, so that no check mark appears
CLICK: OK

2 Now let's apply some borders:
SELECT: cell range from A12 to G12
CLICK: down arrow attached to the Borders button (⊞)
A drop-down list of border options appears, as shown on the next page.

EXCEL

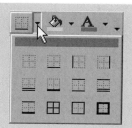

3 From the drop-down list that appears:
SELECT: Top and Double Bottom Border button (⊞)
CLICK: cell A1 to remove the highlighting
A nice border now separates the data from the summary information. You may have noticed that clicking the Underline button (U) underlines only the words in a cell, while applying borders underlines the entire cell.

4 Let's apply a new fill color (sometimes called *shading*) to emphasize the title in cell A1:
CLICK: down arrow attached to the Fill Color button (⬛▾)
A drop-down list of colors appears, as shown below.

5 SELECT: a dark blue color from the drop-down list
The title should now appear on a colored background.

6 To see the title, you need to adjust the text color:
CLICK: down arrow attached to the Font Color button (A▾)
SELECT: white from the drop-down list
Your screen should now appear similar to Figure 3.6.

Figure 3.6

Applying borders and colors to a worksheet

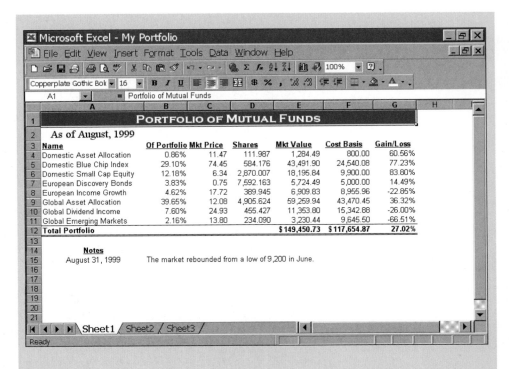

7 To turn the worksheet gridlines back on:
CHOOSE: Tools, Options
CLICK: *View* tab
SELECT: *Gridlines* check box, so that a "✔" appears
CLICK: OK

8 On your own, apply a border underline and a light gray shading (fill color) to the cell range A2 to G2. You can see how a subtle use of color can produce a truly professional-looking worksheet.

9 Save and then close the workbook.

3.1 Self Check What is the basic difference between using the Underline button (⬚) and the Borders button (⬚)?

3.2 Applying and Removing Formatting

Excel 2000 provides a wealth of formatting commands for improving the appearance of a worksheet, its individual cells, and the contents within those cells. In addition to selecting formatting options individually, you can use the Format Painter button (⬚) and the Edit, Paste Special command to copy formatting characteristics. These tools, along with Excel's AutoFormat feature, can help you apply formatting commands to a worksheet consistently and more efficiently. In this module, you work with these tools as well as learn how to remove formatting characteristics from a worksheet.

3.2.1 Using Format Painter

FEATURE
You use the **Format Painter** feature to copy formatting styles and attributes from one area in your worksheet to another. Not only does this feature speed formatting procedures, it ensures formatting consistency among cells in your worksheet.

METHOD
To copy formatting from one cell range to another:
1. SELECT: the cell range whose formatting you want to copy
2. CLICK: Format Painter button (🖊) on the Standard toolbar
3. SELECT: the cell range that you want to format

PRACTICE
You will now use Format Painter to copy formatting from one area of a worksheet to another.

Setup: Ensure that no workbooks are open in the application window.

1 Open the data file named EXC320.

2 Save the file as "ABC Retailers" to your personal storage location.

3 You will now apply formatting commands to the first journal entry in the worksheet. Then, once the formatting is completed, you will copy the set of formatting options to the other journal entries. To begin:
SELECT: cell A5

4 To change the date formatting:
CHOOSE: Format, Cells
CLICK: *Number* tab
SELECT: Date in the *Category* list box
SELECT: 3/14/1998 in the *Type* list box
CLICK: OK command button
The cell entry now appears as 10/10/1999.

5 To emphasize the account numbers and explanation:
SELECT: cell range from C5 to C6
CLICK: Bold button (🅱)
SELECT: cell B7
CLICK: Italic button (🅸)
SELECT: Green from the Font Color button (🄰▾)

6 To show the values in the Amount column as currency:
SELECT: cell range from D5 to E6
CLICK: Currency Style button (🅂)
CLICK: Decrease Decimal button (🖳) twice
The journal entry now appears formatted. (*Hint*: If necessary, increase the width of columns D and E to display the currency values.)

7 Using Format Painter, you will copy the formatting from this journal entry to another journal entry in the worksheet. Do the following:
SELECT: cell range from A5 to E7

8 To copy the formatting attributes:
CLICK: Format Painter button (🖋) on the Standard toolbar
Notice that a dashed marquee appears around the selected range.

9 To apply the formatting to the next journal entry:
CLICK: cell A9
Notice that you need only click the top left-hand cell in the target range. Your screen should now appear similar to Figure 3.7.

Figure 3.7

Applying a formatting coat
using Format Painter

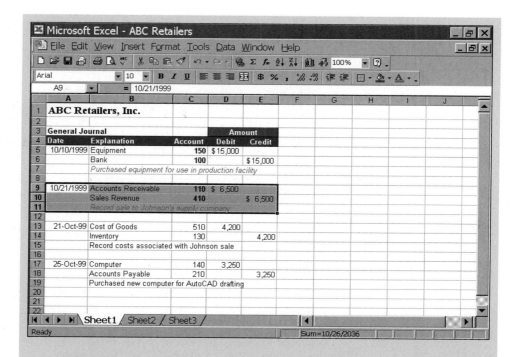

10 You can apply more than one coat using Format Painter. To demonstrate, ensure that the cell range A9 through E11 remains highlighted and then do the following:
DOUBLE-CLICK: Format Painter button (⬦)
Double-clicking the toolbar button will make the button stay active even after you apply the first coat to a target cell range.

11 With the Format Painter button (⬦) toggled on, you can apply multiple formatting coats. Do the following:
CLICK: cell A13
CLICK: cell A17
The remaining journal entries have been formatted.

12 To toggle this feature off:
CLICK: Format Painter button (⬦)

13 To better view your handiwork, do the following:
PRESS: (CTRL) + (HOME)

14 Save the workbook and keep it open for use in the next lesson.

3.2.2   Removing Formatting Attributes

FEATURE
You can safely remove a cell's formatting without affecting the contents of the cell. The easiest method, of course, is to click the Undo button (⟳) immediately after choosing a formatting command. You can also remove formatting characteristics by choosing the Edit, Clear, Formats command.

METHOD
To remove all formatting from a cell range:
1. SELECT: the desired cell range
2. CHOOSE: Edit, Clear, Formats

PRACTICE
You will now practice removing formatting characteristics from a cell range.

Setup: Ensure that you have completed the previous lessons in the module and that the "ABC Retailers" workbook is displayed.

1 Let's demonstrate the effects of entering data into a formatted cell. In this example, you will attempt to enter a value into a cell that is formatted to display a date. Do the following:
SELECT: cell A17
TYPE: 1000
PRESS: ENTER
The cell displays 9/26/1902.

2 You will now remove the formatting from this cell:
SELECT: cell A17
CHOOSE: Edit, Clear, Formats
The cell now displays the correct value, 1000.

3 The Edit, Clear, Formats command removes all formatting from a cell or cell range. To remove a single formatting characteristic, you can simply modify that characteristic. You will now remove the green color from the journal entry's explanatory note. To do so:
SELECT: cell B19
CLICK: down arrow attached to the Font Color button (▲⋮)
SELECT: Automatic from the drop-down list
The text retains the italic formatting but changes to the default black color.

EXCEL

4 To remove all of the formatting characteristics for the last two journal entries, do the following:
SELECT: cell range from A13 to E19
CHOOSE: Edit, Clear, Formats
Notice that the date in cell A13 is actually stored as a value, 36454. In the next lesson, you will reapply formatting to the journal entries.

3.2.3 Using the Paste Special Command

FEATURE
The Edit, Paste Special command allows you to copy portions or characteristics of a cell or cell range to another area. Some of these characteristics include cell values, formulas, comments, and formats. Like the Format Painter feature, this command is useful for copying formatting options from one cell range to another.

METHOD
To copy and paste formatting characteristics:
1. SELECT: the cell whose formatting you want to copy
2. CLICK: Copy button ()
3. SELECT: the cells where you want to apply the formatting
4. CHOOSE: Edit, Paste Special
5. SELECT: *Formats* option button
6. CLICK: OK command button

PRACTICE
In this exercise, you practice copying and pasting formatting characteristics using the Edit, Paste Special command.

Setup: Ensure that you have completed the previous lessons in the module and that the "ABC Retailers" workbook is displayed.

1 In order to paste formatting characteristics, you must first copy them to the Clipboard. Do the following:
SELECT: cell range from A9 to E11
CLICK: Copy button ()
A dashed marquee appears around the selected range.

2 To display the Paste Special dialog box:
SELECT: cell A13
CHOOSE: Edit, Paste Special
The dialog box shown in Figure 3.8 is displayed. (*Note*: There are several intermediate and advanced features accessible from this dialog box. For now, you need only focus on the *Formats* option button.)

Figure 3.8

The Paste Special dialog box

To find out more about the features of this dialog box, click the question mark button and then click on one of the option buttons. A brief ToolTip will appear. Click again to remove the ToolTip.

3 To paste the formatting:
SELECT: *Formats* option button
CLICK: OK
The formatting is applied.

4 To format the last journal entry:
SELECT: cell A17
CHOOSE: Edit, Paste Special
SELECT: *Formats* option button
CLICK: OK

5 Save and then close the workbook.

EXCEL

3.2.4 Using the AutoFormat Command

FEATURE
Rather than spend time selecting formatting options, you can use the **AutoFormat** feature to quickly apply an entire group of formatting commands to a cell range. The AutoFormat command works best when your worksheet data is organized using a table layout, with labels running down the left column and across the top row. After you specify one of the predefined table formats, Excel proceeds to apply fonts, number formats, alignments, borders, shading, and colors to the selected range. It is an excellent way to ensure consistent formatting across worksheets.

METHOD
1. SELECT: cell range to format
2. CHOOSE: Format, AutoFormat
3. SELECT: an option from the *Table format* list box

PRACTICE
You will now apply a predefined table format to a portfolio tracking worksheet.

Setup: Ensure that no workbooks are open in the application window.

1 Open the data file named EXC324.

2 Save the workbook as "Sandy's" to your personal storage location.

3 To apply an AutoFormat style to specific cells in a worksheet, select the cell range that you want to format. Do the following:
SELECT: cell range from A3 to F10
(*Hint*: As long as the table layout does not contain blank rows or columns, you can simply place the cell pointer within the table.)

4 To display the AutoFormat options:
CHOOSE: Format, AutoFormat
The AutoFormat dialog box appears as shown in Figure 3.9.

Figure 3.9

AutoFormat dialog box

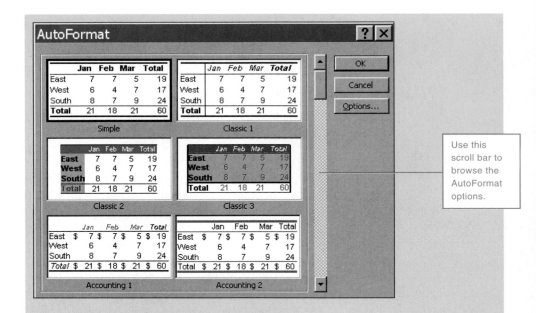

⑤ After scrolling the list in the AutoFormat dialog box, do the following:
SELECT: Colorful 2 option
CLICK: OK

⑥ To remove the cell highlighting:
CLICK: any cell outside of the highlighted range
Your worksheet should now appear similar to Figure 3.10.

Figure 3.10

Applying an AutoFormat

	A	B	C	D	E	F	G
1	**Sandy's Appliance Department**						
2							
3		*Qtr 1*	*Qtr 2*	*Qtr 3*	*Qtr 4*	*Total*	
4	*Dishwasher*	5,764	6,409	6,390	7,255	25,818	
5	*Dryer*	8,331	12,259	10,668	10,871	42,129	
6	*Microwave*	2,980	3,310	1,872	2,390	10,552	
7	*Refrigerator*	35,400	42,810	46,230	35,788	160,228	
8	*Stove/Range*	24,767	28,105	27,492	21,560	101,924	
9	*Washer*	12,890	16,881	12,452	13,700	55,923	
10	**Total**	90,132	109,774	105,104	91,564	396,574	
11							
12							

⑦ On your own, place the cell pointer within the table area and then apply some of the other AutoFormat options, such as Classic 2.

⑧ Save and then close the workbook.

3.2 Self Check How might you ensure formatting consistency among related worksheets and workbooks?

3.3 Printing and Web Publishing

This module focuses on outputting your worksheet creations. Most commonly, you will print a worksheet for inclusion into a report or other such document. However, the Internet is a strong publishing medium unto itself. With the proper access, anyone can become an author and publisher. This lesson introduces you to previewing and printing workbooks using traditional tools, but also publishing workbooks electronically on the World Wide Web.

For those of you new to the online world, the **Internet** is a vast collection of computer networks that spans the entire planet. This worldwide infrastructure is made up of many smaller networks connected by standard telephone lines, fiber optics, cable, and satellites. The term **Intranet** refers to a private and usually secure local or wide area network that uses Internet technologies to share information. To access the Internet, you need a network or modem connection that links your computer to your account on the university's network or an Independent Service Provider (ISP).

Once you are connected to the Internet, you can use Web browser software, such as Microsoft Internet Explorer or Netscape Navigator, to access the **World Wide Web**. The Web provides a visual interface for the Internet and lets you search for information by simply clicking on highlighted words and images, known as **hyperlinks**. When you click a link, you are telling your computer's Web browser to retrieve a page from a Web site and display it on your screen. Not only can you publish your workbooks on the Web, you can incorporate hyperlinks directly within a worksheet to facilitate navigating between documents.

3.3.1 Previewing and Printing a Worksheet

FEATURE

Before sending a worksheet to the printer, you can preview it using a full-page display that will resemble the printed version. In this Preview display mode, you can move through the workbook pages, zoom in and out on desired areas, and modify page layout options, such as margins. When satisfied with its appearance, you can send it to the printer directly.

METHOD

- To preview a workbook:
  CLICK: Print Preview button (🔍), or
  CHOOSE: File, Print Preview
- To print a workbook:
  CLICK: Print button (🖨), or
  CHOOSE: File, Print

PRACTICE

You will now open a relatively large workbook, preview it on the screen, and then send it to the printer.

Setup: Ensure that no workbooks are displayed in the application window.

1 Open the data file named EXC330.

2 Save the workbook as "Published" to your personal storage location.

3 To preview how the workbook will appear when printed:
CLICK: Print Preview button (🔍)
Your screen should now appear similar to Figure 3.11.

EXCEL

Figure 3.11

Previewing a workbook

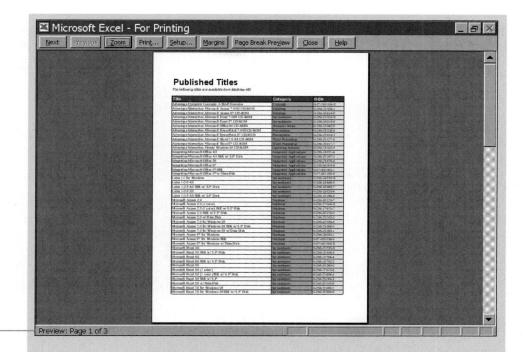

Identifies that you are in Preview mode and viewing "Page 1 of 3" total pages

4 To display the next page:
CLICK: Next button in the toolbar

5 To return to the first page:
CLICK: Previous button

6 To zoom in on the worksheet, move the magnifying glass mouse pointer over the worksheet area and then click once.

7 To zoom out on the display, click the mouse pointer once again.

8 On your own, practice zooming in and out on different areas of the page. You can also use the scroll bars to position the window.

10 Assuming that you are satisfied with the worksheet:
CLICK: Print button
The dialog box displayed in Figure 3.12 appears. You can use this dialog box to specify what to print and how many copies to produce. (*Note:* The quickest method for sending the current worksheet to the printer is to click the Print button (🖨) on the Standard toolbar.)

Figure 3.12

Print dialog box

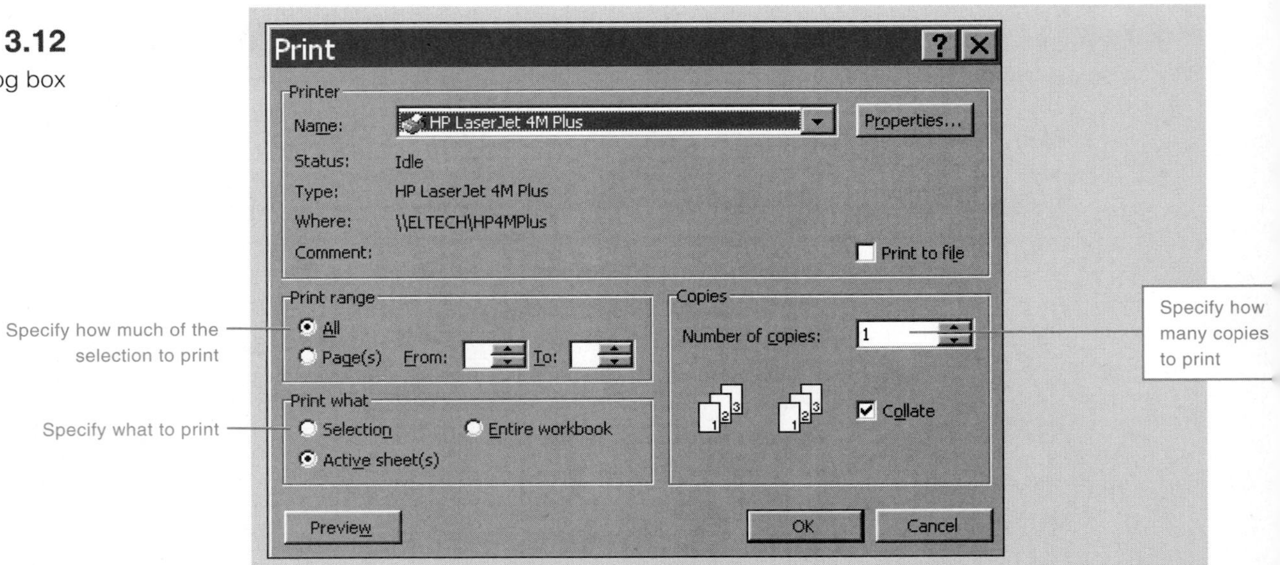

Print   ? X

Printer
Name: HP LaserJet 4M Plus   ▼   Properties...
Status: Idle
Type: HP LaserJet 4M Plus
Where: \\ELTECH\HP4MPlus
Comment: ☐ Print to file

Specify how much of the —— Print range   Copies
selection to print   ⦿ All   Number of copies: 1   ⬍   —— Specify how
                                ○ Page(s) From: ⬍ To: ⬍   many copies
                                                                                       to print
Specify what to print —— Print what
                                ○ Selection   ○ Entire workbook
                                ⦿ Active sheet(s)   ☑ Collate

Preview   OK   Cancel

10 If you do not have access to a printer, click the Cancel button and proceed to the next lesson. If you have a printer connected to your computer and want to print out the worksheet, do the following:
CLICK: OK
After a few moments, the worksheet will appear at the printer.

3.3.2 Previewing and Publishing to the Web

FEATURE
Excel makes it easy to convert a workbook for display on the World Wide Web. The process involves saving the workbook in **HTML** (Hypertext Markup Language) format for publishing to a Web server. You can choose to publish a single worksheet or an entire workbook, complete with graphics and hyperlink objects. Once saved using the proper format, you may upload the files to your company's intranet or to a Web server.

METHOD
- To save a worksheet as a Web page:
  CHOOSE: File, Save as Web Page
- To view a worksheet as a Web page:
  CHOOSE: File, Web Page Preview

PRACTICE
You will now practice saving and viewing a worksheet as an HTML Web document.

Setup: Ensure that you have completed the previous lesson and that the "Published" workbook is displayed.

1 To save the current worksheet as a Web page:
CHOOSE: File, Save as Web Page
The Save As dialog box appears with some additional options, as shown in Figure 3.13. Notice that "Web Page" appears as the file type in the *Save as type* drop-down list box.

Figure 3.13
Save As dialog box
for a Web page

Ensure that the "Web Page" option is selected in this drop-down list box

Save the Web page directly to a Web server on the Internet

2 Using the *Save in* drop-down list box or the Places bar:
SELECT: *your storage location,* if not already selected
(*Note:* To publish or post your workbook Web page to an intranet or to the Internet, you can click the Web Folders button (🖳) in the Places bar and then select a server location.)

3 To proceed with the conversion to HTML:
CLICK: Save command button
The workbook document is saved as "Published.htm" to your personal storage location.

4 To preview how the workbook will appear in a Web browser:
CHOOSE: File, Web Page Preview
After a few moments, the workbook appears displayed in a Web browser window. Figure 3.14 shows the document displayed using Internet Explorer.

Figure 3.14

Viewing a worksheet
as a Web page

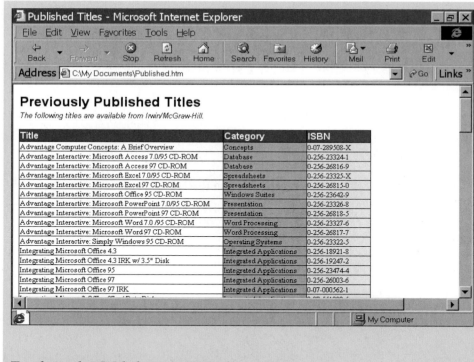

⑤ To close the Web browser window:
CLICK: its Close button ([x])

⑥ Close the "Published" workbook without saving the changes.

3.3 Self Check   How does the Print Preview display mode differ from the Web Page
Preview display mode?

3.4 Customizing Print Options

To assume control over how your workbooks will appear when
printed, you define page layout settings using the File, Page Setup
command. In the dialog box that appears, you may specify **margins,
headers, footers,** and whether gridlines or row and column headings should appear on the final printed output. To make the process
more manageable, Excel organizes the page layout settings under four
tabs (*Page, Margins, Header/Footer,* and *Sheet*) in the Page Setup dialog
box. The features and settings accessible from these tabs are discussed
in the following lessons.

3.4.1 Adjusting Page and Margin Settings

FEATURE
You use the *Page* tab in the Page Setup dialog box to specify the paper size, print scale, and print orientation (for example, portrait or landscape) for a workbook. The *Margins* tab allows you to select the top, bottom, left, and right page margins, and to center the worksheet both horizontally and vertically on a page. You can also manipulate the page margins while viewing a worksheet in Print Preview mode.

METHOD
1. CHOOSE: File, Page Setup
2. CLICK: *Page* and *Margins* tabs
3. SELECT: the desired page layout options

PRACTICE
In this lesson, you open and print a workbook that summarizes a company's amortization expense.

Setup: Ensure that no workbooks are open in the application window.

1 Open the data file named EXC340.

2 Save the file as "CCA Schedule" to your personal storage location.

3 To begin, let's display the worksheet using Print Preview mode:
CLICK: Print Preview button (🔍)

4 Practice zooming in and out on the worksheet using the Zoom command button and the magnifying glass mouse pointer.

5 To view the second page of the printout:
CLICK: Next command button
Notice that the worksheet does not fit for printing on a single page.

6 To exit from Print Preview mode:
CLICK: Close button

7 Let's adjust some page layout settings. Do the following:
CHOOSE: File, Page Setup
CLICK: *Page* tab
Your screen should now appear similar to Figure 3.15.

Figure 3.15

Page Setup dialog
box: *Page* tab

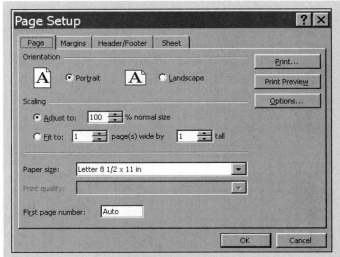

8 In the *Orientation* area:
SELECT: *Landscape* option button

9 To center the worksheet between the left and right margins:
CLICK: *Margins* tab

10 In the *Center on page* area:
SELECT: *Horizontally* check box
CLICK: Print Preview command button
You should now see the entire worksheet appear on a single
printed page and centered between the margins.

3.4.2 Inserting Headers and Footers

FEATURE
You can place descriptive information, such as the current date, in
the header and footer of a page. The contents of a header or footer
repeat automatically for each page that is printed. Some suggestions include using these areas for displaying your name, copyright
information, the words "confidential" or "first draft," or page numbering. You may simply want to place the workbook's filename in
the header so that you can easily find it again on your hard disk.

METHOD
1. CHOOSE: File, Page Setup
2. CLICK: *Headers/Footers* tab
3. SELECT: a predefined header or footer, or
    CLICK: Custom Header button to design a new header, or
    CLICK: Custom Footer button to design a new footer

EXCEL

PRACTICE

You will now add a custom header and footer to the worksheet.

Setup: Ensure that you have completed the previous lesson and that the "CCA Schedule" workbook is displayed in Print Preview mode.

1 To return to the Page Setup dialog box from Print Preview mode:
CLICK: Setup command button
The dialog box appears displaying the last tab that was selected.

2 To add headers and footers to the page:
CLICK: *Header/Footer* tab

3 First, select an existing footer for printing at the bottom of each page:
CLICK: down arrow attached to the *Footer* drop-down list
SELECT: "CCA Schedule, Page 1" option
Once selected, you should see the workbook's filename "CCA Schedule" appear centered in the footer preview area, and the words "Page 1" appear right-aligned.

4 To create a custom header:
CLICK: Custom Header command button
Figure 3.16 shows the Header dialog box and labels the buttons used for inserting information into the different sections.

Figure 3.16

Custom Header
dialog box

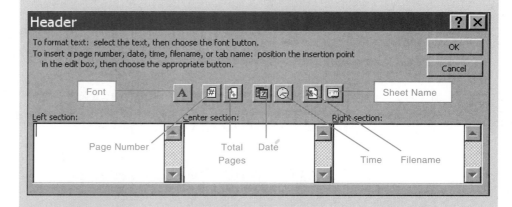

5 To create a header that prints the current date against the right margin:
CLICK: the mouse pointer in the *Right section* area
TYPE: Printed on:
PRESS: Space bar once
CLICK: Date button (🔲) as labeled in Figure 3.16
CLICK: OK
You will see the custom header appear in the preview area.

6 To return to Print Preview mode:
CLICK: OK
Your screen should now appear similar to Figure 3.17. Notice the header in the top right-hand corner and the footer along the bottom.

7 To exit from Print Preview mode:
CLICK: Close button

Figure 3.17

Previewing the CCA Schedule worksheet

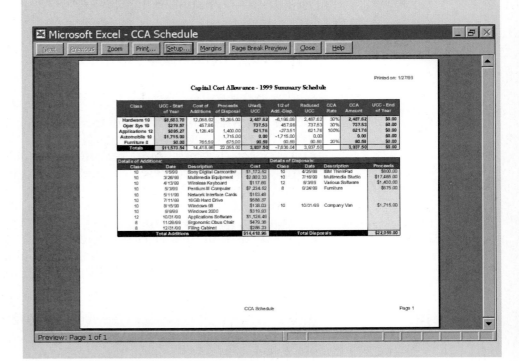

3.4.3 Selecting Worksheet Content to Print

FEATURE
From the Print dialog box, you can choose to print an entire workbook, a single worksheet, or a specified cell range. Alternatively, you can preselect a cell range to print by first specifying the print area. Other print options are available from the Page Setup dialog box, where you can choose to print the worksheet gridlines or row and column headings.

METHOD
To specify a print area:
1. SELECT: a cell range
2. CHOOSE: File, Print Area, Set Print Area

To select from the general print options:
1. CHOOSE: File, Print
2. SELECT: one of the following *Print what* option buttons—*Selection, Active Sheet(s),* or *Entire Workbook*
3. SELECT: *Number of copies* to print

To specify whether to print gridlines or row and column headings:
1. CHOOSE: File, Page Setup
2. CLICK: *Sheet* tab
3. SELECT: *Gridlines* check box to toggle the printing of gridlines
4. SELECT: *Row and column headings* check box to print the frame area

PRACTICE
In this lesson, you practice selecting print options and setting print areas. Lastly, you have the opportunity to print the worksheet.

Setup: Ensure that you have completed the previous lesson and that the "CCA Schedule" workbook is displayed.

1 You will often find the need to print specific ranges in a worksheet, rather than the entire workbook. This need is solved by first setting a print area. To practice selecting a cell range for printing:
SELECT: cell range from A1 (a merged cell) to J12
CHOOSE: File, Print Area, Set Print Area

2 Now that you have defined a specific cell range as the print area:
CLICK: Print Preview button ([📄])
Notice that only the selected range is previewed for printing.

3 To return to the worksheet:
CLICK: Close command button

4 To return to printing the entire worksheet:
CHOOSE: File, Print Area, Clear Print Area
This command removes the print area definition.

5 Let's view some other print options:
CHOOSE: File, Page Setup
CLICK: *Sheet* tab
Your screen should now appear similar to Figure 3.18.

Figure 3.18

Page Setup dialog
box: *Sheet* tab

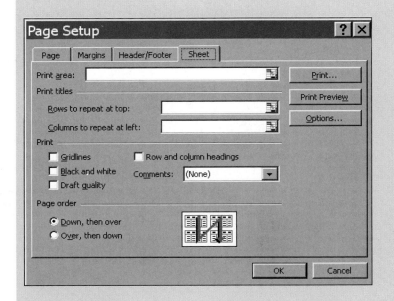

6 Sometimes printing the gridlines or row and column headings is useful for reviewing a worksheet for errors. To demonstrate:
SELECT: *Gridlines* check box in the *Print* area
SELECT: *Row and column headings* check box
CLICK: Print Preview
The printed worksheet now looks similar to the screen display, with the exception of the header and footer. (*Note*: All page setup options are saved along with the workbook file.)

7 If you have a printer connected to your computer, perform the following steps. Otherwise, proceed to the next step.
CLICK: Print command button
CLICK: OK, when the Print dialog box appears

8 If necessary, close the Print Preview window. Then save and close the "CCA Schedule" workbook.

9 Exit Microsoft Excel.

In Addition
Sending the Screen to
the Printer

Did you know that you can capture a screen image using the **PRTSCR** key on your keyboard? When you press **PRTSCR**, the current screen image is copied to the Windows Clipboard. You can then paste this image into a document or workbook for printing.

3.4 Self Check   How would you create a custom footer that displayed your name against the left page border and your company's name against the right page border?

3.5 Chapter Review

The majority of this chapter described common methods for enhancing the appearance of your worksheets. You were introduced to several of Excel's formatting capabilities and commands. Specifically, you applied fonts, number formats, cell alignments, borders, colors, and predefined table formats to a worksheet. You also learned how to print and electronically publish your worksheets for printing and display on the World Wide Web. Lastly, you were introduced to several of Excel's page layout options for controlling and customizing how a worksheet prints.

3.5.1 Command Summary

Many of the commands and procedures appearing in this chapter are summarized in the following table.

Skill Set	To Perform This Task . . .	Do the Following . . .
Formatting Worksheets	Apply font typefaces, font sizes, and font styles	CHOOSE: Format, Cells CLICK: *Font* tab
	Apply number formats	CHOOSE: Format, Cells CLICK: *Number* tab
	Increase and decrease decimal places	CLICK: Increase Decimal button (⊞) CLICK: Decrease Decimal button (⊞)
	Modify a cell's alignment	CHOOSE: Format, Cells CLICK: *Alignment* tab
	Merge a range of cells	CHOOSE: Format, Cells CLICK: *Alignment* tab SELECT: *Merge cells* check box

Continued

Skill Set	To Perform This Task . . .	Do the Following . . .
	Add borders, patterns, and shading	CHOOSE: Format, Cells CLICK: *Border* or *Patterns* tab
	Copy formatting from one range to another using the toolbar	SELECT: the desired range CLICK: Format Painter button (⬦) SELECT: the target range
	Copy formatting from one range to another using the Clipboard	SELECT: the desired range CLICK: Copy button (▤) SELECT: the target range CHOOSE: Edit, Paste Special SELECT: *Formats* option button
	Clear formatting that appears in a range	SELECT: the desired range CHOOSE: Edit, Clear, Formats
	Use AutoFormats	CHOOSE: Format, AutoFormat SELECT: *a predefined format*
Page Setup and Printing	Preview a worksheet	CLICK: Preview button (▦), or CHOOSE: File, Print Preview
	Print a worksheet	CLICK: Print button (🖨), or CHOOSE: File, Print
	Preview worksheet as a Web page	CHOOSE: File, Web Page Preview
	Print the selected cell range, active worksheet, or the entire workbook	CHOOSE: File, Print SELECT: *the desired option button*
	Set the worksheet area to print workbook	SELECT: the desired range CHOOSE: File, Print Area, Set Print Area
	Clear the selected print area	CHOOSE: File, Print Area, Clear Print Area
	Specify page orientation and paper size	CHOOSE: File, Page Setup CLICK: *Page* tab
	Specify print margins and placement on a page	CHOOSE: File, Page Setup CLICK: *Margins* tab

Continued

EXCEL

Skill Set	To Perform This Task . . .	Do the Following . . .
	Define headers and footers for printing	CHOOSE: File, Page Setup CLICK: *Header/Footer* tab
	Print the screen	PRESS: PRTSCR key
Managing Files	Save worksheet as an HTML document	CHOOSE: File, Save as Web Page

3.5.2 Key Terms

This section specifies page references for the key terms identified in this chapter. For a complete list of definitions, refer to the Glossary provided in the Appendix.

AutoFormat, *p. 119*   HTML, *p. 124*

cell alignment, *p. 107*   hyperlinks, *p. 121*

fonts, *p. 102*   Internet, *p. 121*

footers, *p. 126*   Intranet, *p. 121*

Format Painter, *p. 113*   margins, *p. 126*

gridlines, *p. 110*   typefaces, *p. 102*

headers, *p. 126*   World Wide Web, *p. 121*

3.6   Review Questions

3.6.1 Short Answer

1. Why should you limit the number of typefaces used in a worksheet?
2. Name two methods for specifying decimal places in a worksheet.
3. How do you split a merged cell?
4. How do you apply multiple coats using the Format Painter tool?
5. Name two color settings that you can change in a worksheet.

6. How do you turn off gridlines from displaying in a worksheet?
7. How do you turn on gridlines for printing on a worksheet?
8. What should you do prior to sending a worksheet to the printer?
9. Name the tabs in the Page Setup dialog box.
10. How do you create a Web document from a standard Excel worksheet?

3.6.2　True/False

1. _F_ The **B** button stands for bold. The **U** button stands for underline. The **I** button stands for incline.
2. _T_ You use the *Number* tab in the Format Cells dialog box to select date and time formatting options.
3. _F_ Whenever you merge cells, the contents must also be centered.
4. _F_ You can remove formatting from a cell range by choosing the Edit, Clear, Special command.
5. _T_ The AutoFormat command works best when your data is organized using a table layout.
6. _T_ You can zoom in and out on a worksheet using Print Preview mode.
7. _T_ You can view a worksheet as it would appear in a Web browser, prior to saving it as a Web page.
8. _F_ The two page orientation options are *Picture* and *Landscape.*
9. _T_ You can access the Page Setup dialog box directly from Print Preview mode.
10. _T_ To convert a worksheet for display on the World Wide Web, you save the workbook into HTML format.

3.6.3 Multiple Choice

1. To change the text color of a cell entry:
    a. CLICK: Fill Color button (　)
    b. CLICK: Font Color button (　)
    c. CLICK: Text Color button (　)
    d. You cannot change the text color of a cell entry.

2. Excel stores date and time entries as:
    a. formats
    b. formulas
    c. labels
    d. values

3. To merge a range of cells, you select the *Merge cells* check box on this tab of the Format Cells dialog box:
    a. *Number* tab
    b. *Alignment* tab
    c. *Margins* tab
    d. *Merge* tab

4. To remove a cell's formatting, you can:
    a. CHOOSE: Edit, Clear, Formats
    b. CHOOSE: Edit, Formats, Clear
    c. CHOOSE: Format, Cells, Clear
    d. CHOOSE: Format, Clear

5. To copy a cell's formatting characteristics to another cell, you can:
    a. Use the AutoFormat feature
    b. Use the AutoPainter feature
    c. Use the Format Painter feature
    d. Use the Edit, Paste Formats command

6. To select one of Excel's prebuilt table formats:
    a. CHOOSE: Format, AutoTable
    b. CHOOSE: Format, TableFormat
    c. CHOOSE: Format, AutoFormat
    d. CHOOSE: Format, Table

7. To produce gridlines on your printed worksheet:
    a. SELECT: *Gridlines* check box in the Page Setup dialog box
    b. CLICK: Gridline button (　) on the Formatting toolbar
    c. CLICK: Underline button (　) on the Formatting toolbar
    d. Both a and b above

8. To identify a specific cell range on the worksheet for printing:
    a. CHOOSE: File, Print Range
    b. CHOOSE: File, Print Area, Set Print Area
    c. CHOOSE: File, Set Print Area
    d. CHOOSE: File, Set Print Range

9. To print data at the top of each page, you create the following:
    a. footer
    b. footnote
    c. headline
    d. header

10. To save the current worksheet as a Web page:
    a. CLICK: Save button (🖫)
    b. CHOOSE: File, Save as Web Page
    c. CHOOSE: File, Save as HTML
    d. CHOOSE: File, Publish to Web

3.7 Hands-On Projects

3.7.1 Grandview College: Bookstore Inventory

In this exercise, you practice using Excel's formatting commands to enhance the appearance of a monthly bookstore report.

1. Load Microsoft Excel.
2. Open the data file named EXC371.
3. Save the workbook as "Bookstore" to your personal storage location.
4. Let's start by formatting the worksheet's title:
    SELECT: cell A1
    CHOOSE: Format, Cells
    CLICK: *Font* tab in the dialog box
5. In the Format Cells dialog box, make the following selections:
    SELECT: Times New Roman in the *Font* list box
    SELECT: Bold Italic in the *Font style* list box
    SELECT: 16 in the *Size* list box
    SELECT: Dark Red in the *Color* drop-down list box
    Notice that the *Preview* area in the dialog box displays all of your choices.

6. To accept the dialog box selections:
   CLICK: OK
7. Let's center the title across the width of the worksheet:
   SELECT: cell range from A1 to G1
   CLICK: Merge and Center button (⊞)
8. To apply percentage formatting:
   SELECT: cell range from D4 to D9
   CLICK: Percent Style button (%)
   CLICK: Increase Decimal button (🔢) twice
9. To apply currency formatting:
   SELECT: cell range from C4 to C10
   CLICK: Currency Style button ($)
   (*Hint*: You include cell C10 in the range so that you can later copy this column's formatting to other ranges in the worksheet.)
10. Let's copy this column's formatting to the other columns. With the range still selected, do the following:
    DOUBLE-CLICK: Format Painter button (🖌)
    CLICK: cell E4 to apply one formatting coat
    CLICK: cell G4 to apply another formatting coat
    CLICK: Format Painter button (🖌) to toggle the feature off
    (*Note*: Don't bother changing the column widths just yet.)
11. Now apply an AutoFormat to the data area:
    SELECT: cell range from A3 to G10
    CHOOSE: Format, AutoFormat

12. In the AutoFormat dialog box:
    SELECT: Classic 2
    CLICK: OK
13. To better see the results of the formatting:
    CLICK: cell A1
    A much nicer looking report!
14. Save and then close the workbook.

3.7.2 Fast Forward Video: Sales Analysis

You will now practice enhancing the layout of an existing worksheet by adjusting rows and columns and by formatting its text labels, numbers, and headings.

1. Open the data file named EXC372.
2. Save the workbook as "Video Sales" to your personal storage location.
3. To begin, adjust the width of column C to 5 characters:
    SELECT: cell C1
    CHOOSE: Format, Column, Width
    TYPE: **5**
    CLICK: OK
4. Now, delete row 3 using the following steps:
    RIGHT-CLICK: row 3 in the frame area
    CHOOSE: Delete
5. To format the headings:
    SELECT: cell A4
    PRESS: CTRL and hold it down
    CLICK: cell A9
    CLICK: Bold button (B)
    Remember to release the CTRL when you are finished.
6. To format the "Total Sales" label with boldface and italic:
    SELECT: cell A14
    CLICK: Bold button (B)
    CLICK: Italic button (I)
7. To format the two column headings:
    SELECT: cell range from D3 to E3
    PRESS: CTRL + b to apply boldface
    PRESS: CTRL + u to underline the contents
8. To format the values in the Amount column:
    CLICK: cell D5
    PRESS: SHIFT and hold it down
    CLICK: cell D14
    All of the cells between these two should now appear highlighted.
9. To apply currency formatting:
    CLICK: Currency Style button ($)
10. To apply percent formatting to the values in the adjacent column:
    SELECT: cell range from E5 to E12
    CLICK: Percent Style button (%)
    CLICK: Increase Decimal button twice

11. To format all of the category labels at the same time:
SELECT: cell range from B5 to B8
PRESS: CTRL and hold it down
SELECT: cell range from B10 to B12 by dragging with the mouse
There should now be two highlighted ranges on the worksheet.
12. To italicize the data and align it to the right:
CLICK: Italic button (*I*)
CLICK: Align Right button (≣)
13. Finally, let's format the titles in rows 1 and 2. Do the following:
SELECT: cell range from A1 to A2
CLICK: Bold button (**B**)
CLICK: down arrow attached to the Font list box ([Arial ▼])
SELECT: Times New Roman
CLICK: down arrow attached to the Font Size list box ([10 ▼])
SELECT: 14
14. To center the titles across the active area:
SELECT: cell range from A1 to E1
CLICK: Merge and Center button (▦)
SELECT: cell range from A2 to E2
CLICK: Merge and Center button (▦)
Your worksheet should now appear similar to Figure 3.19.
15. Save and then close the workbook.

Figure 3.19

Formatting the Sales Analysis worksheet

	A	B	C	D	E	F
1		Fast Forward Video				
2		Sales Analysis				
3				Amount	Pct of Total	
4	Rentals					
5		New Releases		$1,071.35	43.79%	
6		Weekly Movies		$ 826.00	33.76%	
7		Games		$ 549.10	22.44%	
8		Total Rentals		$2,446.45	84.63%	
9	Retail Sales					
10		Videos		$ 132.50	29.83%	
11		Snacks		$ 311.65	70.17%	
12		Total Retail		$ 444.15	15.37%	
13						
14	Total Sales			$2,890.60		
15						

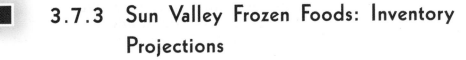

3.7.3 Sun Valley Frozen Foods: Inventory Projections

Incorporating some skills learned in Chapter 2, you will now practice modifying a worksheet and applying formatting commands.

1. Open the workbook named EXC373.
2. Save the workbook as "Sun Seasonal" to your personal storage location.
3. Adjust the width of column A to 18 characters.
4. Delete column B.
5. Adjust columns B through E to their best-fit widths.
6. Format the headings in row 1 to appear boldface and centered in their respective columns.
7. Format the "Total" label in cell A7 to appear boldface and italic.
8. Insert two rows at the top of the worksheet for entering a title. (*Hint*: Rather than performing the Insert command twice to insert two rows, you can select rows 1 and 2 first and then perform the command once.)
9. Enter a title for the worksheet:
    SELECT: cell A1
    TYPE: `Seasonal Inventory Projections`
    PRESS: `ENTER`
10. Merge and center the title in cell A1 between columns A and E.
11. Format the title to appear with a larger and more unique font. Also, apply a dark blue color to the font text on a light yellow background fill. Then, surround the merged cell with a Thick Box border.
12. To bring out the Total row, apply a Top and Double Bottom border to cells A9 through E9. With the cell range highlighted, assign a light gray background fill color.

13. To remove the highlighting:
    CLICK: cell A1
14. Save and then close the workbook.

3.7.4 Lakeside Realty: Listing Summary

In this exercise, you use the AutoFormat command and modify the page layout in an existing workbook.

1. Open the workbook named EXC374.
2. Save the workbook as "Listing Summary" to your personal storage location.
3. Apply the "Classic 3" AutoFormat style to the cell range from A3 to K10.

4. PRESS: HOME to remove the highlighting
5. Format the worksheet title in cell A1 to make it stand out from the table information.
6. Use the Page Setup dialog box to change the page orientation to *Landscape.*
7. Use the Page Setup dialog box to center the worksheet horizontally on the page.
8. Add a footer that prints the workbook's filename aligned left and the page number aligned right.
9. Add a header that shows the company name, "Lakeside Realty," aligned left and the current date aligned right.
10. Preview the worksheet. Your screen should now appear similar to Figure 3.20.

EXCEL

Figure 3.20

Previewing a
formatted worksheet

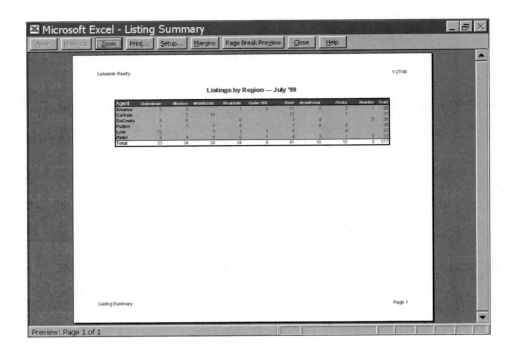

11. Print a copy of the worksheet.
12. Save and then close the workbook.

3.7.5 On Your Own: Financial Data Table

To practice formatting and manipulating data, open the workbook named EXC375. Then make a copy of the file by saving the workbook as "Financial Data" to your personal storage location. On your own, resize all of the columns to ensure that the data is visible. Insert a new row at the beginning of the worksheet and enter the worksheet title "United Consolidated Group." Using fonts, colors, alignment, and background fills, format the titles in rows 1 and 2 to stand out from the rest of the data.

Format the data in columns B through D with currency formatting and two decimal places, except for the date headings. Format the data in column E with percent formatting and two decimal places. Center and apply boldface to the column headings in row 3. Then apply boldface and italics to the cell range from A4 to A9. Before proceeding, adjust the column widths and row heights as required. When satisfied, preview and print the worksheet. Lastly, save and then close the workbook.

3.7.6 On Your Own: Personal Expense Comparison

To practice working with formatting and page layout options, use Excel to create a monthly expense comparison worksheet. After displaying a blank workbook, enter the following column headings in a single row: **Expense**, **January**, **February**, and **Change**. Then enter the following expense categories in a single column under the "Expense" heading.

- Rent/Mortgage
- Food
- Clothing
- Transportation
- Utilities
- Education
- Entertainment

For both the January and February columns, enter some reasonable data. Add the label "Total" below the last expense category and then use AutoSum to calculate totals for the monthly columns. Create formulas to calculate the difference for each expense category. Lastly, use the AutoFormat "Accounting 2" option to format the worksheet.

For printing purposes, add a custom footer that prints the current date, your name, and the page number at the bottom of each page. When you are finished, save the workbook as "My Expenses" to your personal storage location. Preview and print the worksheet, and then close the workbook and exit Excel.

3.8 Case Problems: Marvin's Music

Marvin's Music store is facing increased competitive pressures with the recent announcement that a discount superstore chain is moving into the area. Stacy Marvin realizes that in order to stay competitive, she needs to be able to track and analyze her inventory costs, stock levels, and sales trends quickly and accurately. Fortunately, her senior sales associate, Justin Lee, has explained how he can use Excel to create worksheets that will make these tasks easier.

In the following case problems, assume the role of Justin and perform the same steps that he identifies. You may want to re-read the chapter opening before proceeding.

1. Stacey asks Justin to prepare a worksheet that will summarize Marvin's current stock levels. He begins by launching Microsoft Excel so that a new blank workbook is displayed. As shown in Figure 3.21, he enters the worksheet title, row and column labels, and inventory values for each category.

Figure 3.21

Creating an inventory worksheet

	A	B	C	D	E
1	Inventory by Category				
2		CDs	Tapes	Total	
3	Pop	18500	6500		
4	Rock	23600	15350		
5	Dance	19000	9200		
6	Country	15420	8670		
7	Easy Listening	11330	3200		
8	Classical	5680	1340		
9	Soundtracks	4200	1030		
10	Total				
11					

Using the AutoSum feature, Justin has Excel calculate totals for both the row and column values. He then selects the cell range from A2 to D10 and applies the "Classic 2" AutoFormat style. Not yet satisfied, he merges and centers the title between columns A and D, and then applies formatting to make it appear consistent with the rest of the worksheet. Justin saves the workbook as "MM Inventory1" to his *personal storage location* and then prints a copy to show to Stacey.

2. After reviewing the worksheet, Stacey asks Justin to make the following adjustments:

- Insert a new row for "World Music" at row 9, enter 4100 for CDs and 3500 for Tapes, and ensure the totals are updated.
- Adjust the width of column A to 15 characters and then change the height of row 1 to 24 points.
- Make the values appear with dollar signs and commas, but with no decimal places.
- Adjust the width of columns B, C, and D to be larger than they presently appear and ensure that they are all the same width.

When Justin finishes customizing the worksheet to appear similar to Figure 3.22, he saves the workbook as "MM Inventory2" to the same location.

Figure 3.22

Customizing the
inventory worksheet

	A	B	C	D	E
1	Inventory by Category				
2		CDs	Tapes	Total	
3	Pop	$18,500	$6,500	$25,000	
4	Rock	$23,600	$15,350	$38,950	
5	Dance	$19,000	$9,200	$28,200	
6	Country	$15,420	$8,670	$24,090	
7	Easy Listening	$11,330	$3,200	$14,530	
8	Classical	$5,680	$1,340	$7,020	
9	World Music	$4,100	$3,500	$7,600	
10	Soundtracks	$4,200	$1,030	$5,230	
11	Total	$101,830	$48,790	$150,620	
12					

3. The next day, Stacey assigns Justin the task of completing the company's Advertising Schedule worksheet that she started a few days earlier. Justin opens the workbook named EXC383 and then saves it as "MM Ad Schedule" to his *personal storage location*. According to the sticky notes attached to Stacey's printout of the worksheet, Justin needs to enter the following three new promotions:

Back-to-School—1 newspaper ad on August 27th for $500
Rocktober Blitz—6 radio spots on October 11th for $2900
Christmas—3 TV ads starting Dec 1st for $9000

Using the toolbar, Justin formats the worksheet by applying the Currency style to the "Cost" column and then decreases the decimal places shown to 0. He adjusts the width of column F to show all of the information displayed. Then he uses the Format Cells dialog box to change the date values to appear using a "dd-mmm-yy" format. Again, he adjusts the column width as necessary.

Noticing that Stacey placed an extra column between the "Theme" and "Date" columns, Justin deletes column B and then resizes column A to display using its best-fit width. He also selects a new typeface and font size for the column headings, and modifies the alignment of the titles. Justin prints, saves, and then closes the workbook.

4. Having completed his work for Stacey, Justin opens one of his pet worksheet projects named EXC384. This workbook contains a sales transaction analysis that summarizes information from the store's point-of-sale equipment. He immediately saves the workbook as "MM Daily Sales" to his *personal storage location*.

To speed the formatting process, Justin uses the AutoFormat feature to apply a combination of table formatting attributes to the worksheet. Then, to distinguish the cells containing the times of day from the rest of the worksheet area, Justin applies a dark red fill color to the background of row 1 and makes the font color white. Next he increases the width for all of the columns to give the worksheet a more spacious look. At the top of the worksheet, Justin inserts a new row and then enters the title "Sales Transactions by Time Period." He merges and centers the title over the columns and then applies formatting to make the title stand out from the data.

To prepare for printing, Justin adds a custom header that places the company name at the center of the page. He then adds a custom footer that contains the words "Prepared by *your name*" on the right, the date in the center, and the page number on the right-hand side. Next, he adjusts the page setup so the worksheet is centered horizontally on the page. Justin then saves the workbook as a Web page and views it using his Web browser. Satisfied that he's put in a full day, Justin saves and closes the workbook. Then he exits Microsoft Excel.

MICROSOFT EXCEL 2000
Analyzing Your Data

CHAPTER
FOUR

Chapter Outline

Learning Objectives

After reading this chapter, you will be able to:

- Create, modify, remove, and apply range names

- Understand absolute and relative cell addresses

- Use natural language formulas in a worksheet

- Use mathematical and statistical functions, such as SUM, AVERAGE, COUNT, MIN, and MAX

- Use date functions, such as NOW and TODAY

- Embed, move, and size a chart on a worksheet

- Preview and print a chart

Case Study

Interior Hockey Association

The Interior Hockey Association consists of eight junior hockey teams in as many communities. The IHA is run by a small group of dedicated volunteers who handle everything from coaching to administration. An ex-player himself, Brad Stafford has volunteered for the organization for the past four years. In addition to fundraising, Brad is responsible for keeping records and tracking results for all of the teams in the league.

Shortly after the end of the season, the IHA publishes a newsletter that provides various statistics and other pertinent information about the season. In the past, this newsletter required weeks of performing manual calculations, followed by days of typing results into a word processor. Having enrolled in an Excel course last month, Brad now realizes that worksheets and charts can help him to complete his upcoming tasks.

In this chapter, you and Brad learn about using ranges and functions in Excel worksheets. First, you use named ranges to create formula expressions that are easier to understand. Then you practice using Excel's built-in functions to perform calculations. Lastly, you learn how to plot and print your worksheet data in a chart.

4.1 Working with Named Ranges

In its simplest form, a cell range is a single cell, such as B4. Still, the term *cell range* is more commonly used to describe a "from here to there" area on a worksheet. A range can also cover a three-dimensional area, crossing more than one worksheet within a workbook. In a new workbook, Excel provides three worksheets named *Sheet1, Sheet2,* and *Sheet3.* It may help you to think of a worksheet as a tear-off page on a notepad—the notepad representing the workbook. You access the worksheets in a workbook by clicking on the tabs appearing along the bottom of the document window.

A **range name** is a nickname given to a group of cells that can later be used in constructing formulas. For example, the formula expression =Revenue-Expenses is far easier to understand than =C5-C6. Working with cell references from more than one worksheet adds another level of complexity. For example, if the value for Revenue is stored on Sheet1 and the value for Expenses is stored on Sheet2, the formula would read =Sheet1!C5-Sheet2!C6. Notice that the worksheet name is separated from the cell address using an exclamation point (!). By default, range names already contain this information, making them far easier to remember than these cryptic expressions.

In this module, you learn how to name ranges and how to work with different types of cell references.

4.1.1 Naming Cell Ranges

FEATURE
By naming parts of a worksheet, you make it (and the formulas contained therein) much easier to read and construct. There are two ways to name cell ranges. First, click in the Name box, located at the far left of the Formula bar, and then type a unique name with no spaces. Second, use a menu command to create names automatically from the row and column headings appearing in a worksheet.

METHOD
To name a cell range using the Name box:
1. SELECT: the desired range
2. CLICK: in the Name box
3. TYPE: *a range name*

To name a cell range using the Menu bar:
1. SELECT: the desired range, including the row and column headings
2. CHOOSE: Insert, Name, Create

PRACTICE
You will now name cell ranges appearing in an existing worksheet using the two methods described above.

Setup: Ensure that Excel is loaded

1 Open the data file named EXC410.

2 Save the workbook as "Salaries" to your personal storage location.

3 To increase Matthew's salary by the growth factor appearing in cell B3, perform the following steps:
SELECT: cell C6
TYPE: =b6*(1+b3)
PRESS: ENTER
The answer, 41400, appears in cell C6. In order for another user to understand this calculation, they would need to track down each cell address in the formula.

4 A better approach is to name the cells that you often refer to in formulas. Let's name the cell containing the growth factor before entering a formula to increase Jennifer's salary:
SELECT: cell B3
CLICK: in the Name box with the I-beam mouse pointer
TYPE: Growth (as shown below)

Type the desired range name in the Name box ⎯

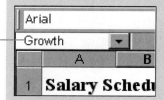

5 PRESS: ENTER
You have now created a named range called "Growth" that you can use in place of the cell address when entering formulas.

6 To use the range name:
SELECT: cell C7
TYPE: =b7*(1+Growth)
PRESS: ENTER
The answer, 53820, appears. A new user reading this formula would now be able to decipher its objective.

7 You can also use range names to navigate within your worksheet:
CLICK: down arrow attached to the Name box
SELECT: Growth in the drop-down list that appears
The cell pointer moves immediately to cell B3.

8 Now update the growth factor:
TYPE: 5%
PRESS: ENTER
The worksheet cells containing formulas are updated.

9 Another method for creating range names uses the existing heading labels in your worksheet. You can use this method effectively when the data is organized in a table layout. To demonstrate:
SELECT: cell range from A5 to D9
Notice that the selected range includes the fiscal years across the top row and the employee names down the leftmost column.

10 To specify that the heading labels be used in naming the ranges:
CHOOSE: Insert, Name, Create

11 In the Create Name dialog box, ensure that the *Top row* and *Left column* check boxes appear selected as shown in Figure 4.1.

Figure 4.1

Creating range names
from worksheet values

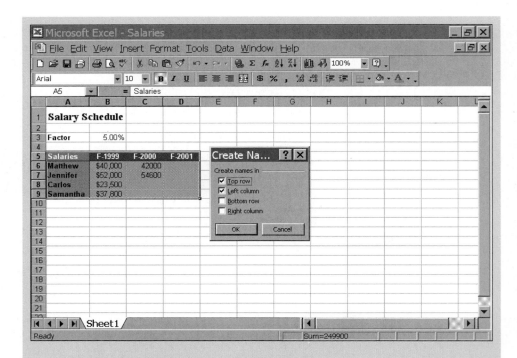

12 To complete the operation:
CLICK: OK

13 Now let's practice selecting named ranges:
CLICK: down arrow attached to the Name box
Many range names now appear in the drop-down list.

14 To move the cell pointer to one of the row ranges:
CLICK: Jennifer in the drop-down list
The cell range from B7 to D7 appears selected.

15 To display one of the column ranges:
CLICK: down arrow attached to the Name box
CLICK: F_2001 in the drop-down list
(*Note:* The label "F-2001" is used as the column heading instead
of the value 2001, since Excel can only create range names from
labels. You must also beware of conflicts with cell addresses. For
example, the range name F2001 is unacceptable because it refers
to a cell address.)

16 Lastly, let's select the entire data area in the table:
CLICK: down arrow attached to the Name box
CLICK: Salaries in the drop-down list

17 PRESS: `CTRL`+`HOME` to remove the highlighting

18 Save the workbook and keep it open for use in the next lesson.

4.1.2 Managing Range Names

FEATURE
Once created, you can easily modify and delete range names using the Define Name dialog box. Another useful feature is the ability to paste a list of the existing range names into your worksheet. Refer to this list when you are building formula expressions or when you need to jump to a particular spot in the worksheet.

METHOD
To display the Define Name dialog box:
• CHOOSE: Insert, Name, Define

To paste range names into the worksheet:
• CHOOSE: Insert, Name, Paste

PRACTICE
You will now practice deleting and pasting range names.

Setup: Ensure that you have completed the previous lesson and that the "Salaries" workbook is displayed.

You manipulate range names using the Define Name dialog box. To illustrate, let's delete the yearly range names that were created in the last lesson. Do the following:
CHOOSE: Insert, Name, Define
The dialog box in Figure 4.2 should now appear on the screen.

Figure 4.2

The Define Name dialog box

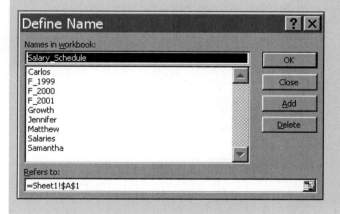

2 To remove the "F_1999" range name:
SELECT: F_1999 in the *Names in workbook* list box
Notice that the range address "=Sheet1!$B$6:$B$9" appears in the *Refer to* text box. (*Note:* If necessary, you can edit the cell references appearing in this text box. The significance of dollar signs in the range address is discussed in the next lesson.)

3 CLICK: Delete command button

4 To remove the remaining yearly range names:
SELECT: F_2000 from the list box
CLICK: Delete command button
SELECT: F_2001 from the list box
CLICK: Delete command button

5 To dismiss the dialog box:
CLICK: Close command button

6 To help you document and double-check the cell references in a worksheet, Excel enables you to paste a list of the existing named ranges into the worksheet. To demonstrate this technique:
SELECT: cell A12
CHOOSE: Insert, Name, Paste
CLICK: Paste List command button

7 To remove the highlighting:
PRESS: CTRL + HOME
Your screen should now appear similar to Figure 4.3.

8 Save the workbook and keep it open for use in the next lesson.

Figure 4.3

Pasting a list of range names into the worksheet

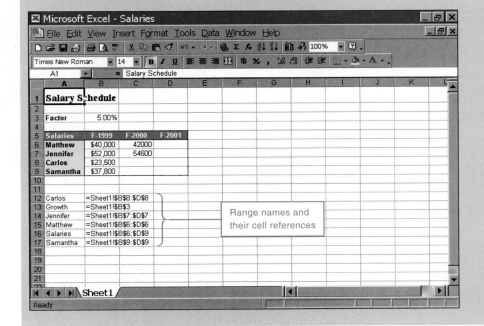

4.1.3 Using References in Formulas

FEATURE

There are two types of cell references that you can enter into formulas: *relative* and *absolute*. The difference between the two types becomes especially important when you start copying and moving formulas in your worksheet. A **relative cell address** in a formula adjusts itself automatically when copied, since the cell reference is relative to where it sits in the worksheet. An **absolute cell address** always refers to an exact cell location.

METHOD

The formulas that you have entered so far have all used relative cell references—Excel's default method. To specify an absolute reference, you precede each column letter and row number in a cell address with a dollar sign. For example, to make cell B5 an absolute cell reference, you type $B$5. A **mixed cell address,** on the other hand, locks only a portion of a cell address by placing the dollar sign ($) before either the address's column letter or row number, such as B$5. Sometimes it helps to vocalize the word "absolutely" as you read a cell address, whereby $B$5 would be read as "absolutely column B and absolutely row 5."

PRACTICE

In this lesson, you practice using relative and absolute cell addressing in performing simple copy and paste operations.

Setup: Ensure that you have completed the previous lesson and that the "Salaries" workbook is displayed.

1 Let's begin by reviewing the formula in cell C6:
SELECT: cell C6
Review the expression "=B6*(1+B3)" in the Formula bar. You can vocalize this formula as "take the value appearing to my left and then multiply it by 1 plus the value appearing three rows up and one column to the left." Notice that you need a point of reference for this formula to make any sense, which is the location of the cell pointer in cell C6.

2 Let's copy the formula in cell C6 to cell D6:
CLICK: Copy button (🖺) on the Standard toolbar
SELECT: cell D6
CLICK: Paste button (🖺)
PRESS: ESC to remove the dashed marquee
The result, 42000, appears in cell D6. This, however, is not the desired result. The value has not been incremented by the growth factor.

3 In the Formula bar, notice that the formula "=C6*(1+C3)" no longer performs the correct calculation. Copying and pasting has modified the cell addresses by automatically adjusting the column letters.

4 If you want to ensure that Excel does not change a cell address during a copy operation, you need to make it absolute:
PRESS: DELETE
SELECT: cell C6

5 Position the I-beam mouse pointer over the cell address B3 in the Formula bar and then click the left mouse button once.

6 To change the growth factor reference into an absolute address, you type dollar signs in front of the column letter and row number. Or, you can do the following:
PRESS: F4 ABS key (ABS stands for absolute)
Notice that B3 now appears as $B$3, as shown below.

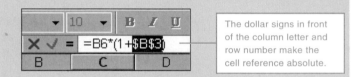

The dollar signs in front of the column letter and row number make the cell reference absolute.

7 Continue pressing F4 to see how Excel cycles through possible combinations of relative, absolute, and mixed cell addressing.

8 Before proceeding, ensure that $B$3 appears in the Formula bar and then press ENTER.

9 Copy and paste the formula into cell D6 again. The correct result, 44100, now appears in the cell.

10 Remember that you used a range name in constructing the formula for cell C7. On your own, copy the formula in cell C7 to cell D7. Notice that the formula calculates correctly because range names, such as Growth, are defined using absolute cell addresses.

11 To continue:
PRESS: ESC to remove the marquee
PRESS: CTRL + HOME

12 Save and then close the worksheet.

4.1.4 Entering Natural Language Formulas

FEATURE
Another alternative to using cell references is to enter a special type of expression called a **natural language formula.** Similar to using range names, a natural language formula allows you to build a formula using the row and column labels from the active worksheet. In order for natural language formulas to work effectively, the worksheet should be organized using a table format with distinctly labeled rows and columns.

METHOD
1. SELECT: the cell where you want the result to appear
2. TYPE: = (an equal sign)
3. TYPE: *an expression*, using row and column labels
4. PRESS: ENTER

PRACTICE
You will now use natural language formulas to calculate an expression in a worksheet.

Setup: Ensure that no workbooks are open in the application window.

1 Open the data file named EXC414.

2 Save the workbook as "Natural" to your personal storage location.

3 Before you begin, you'll need to review some configuration settings:
CHOOSE: Tools, Options
CLICK: *Calculation* tab
This tab, as shown in Figure 4.4, enables you to specify calculation options and dictate whether Excel recognizes labels in formulas.

Figure 4.4

Options dialog box:
Calculation tab

Select this option to have
Excel recalculate the formulas
in your worksheet whenever
you change a value.

Ensure that this check box is
selected before attempting to
enter a natural language
formula.

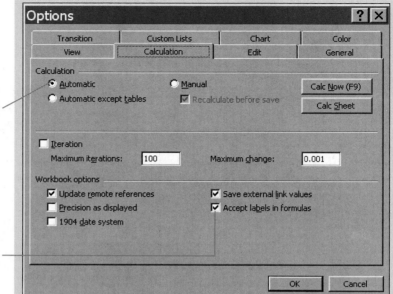

4 On the *Calculation* tab of the Options dialog box:
SELECT: *Automatic* option button
SELECT: *Accept labels in formulas* check box so that a "✔" appears
CLICK: OK command button

5 To calculate the profit for Q1 using a natural language formula:
SELECT: cell B6
TYPE: =Revenue-Expenses
PRESS: ➡
The result, 32500, appears in the cell. (*CAUTION:* You cannot
mix labels with cell references in a natural language formula. For
example, the formula =Revenue-B5 does not compute.)

6 To proceed, enter the same natural language formula into cells
C6, D6, and E6. Notice that Excel calculates the results correctly.

7 Save and then close the workbook.

4.1 Self Check   Why is "AD1999" an unacceptable name for a cell range?

4.2 Using Built-In Functions

This module introduces you to Excel's built-in **functions.** Don't let the word *function* conjure up visions of your last calculus class; functions are shortcuts that you use in place of entering lengthy and complicated formulas. Functions are incredible time-savers that can increase your productivity in creating worksheets.

There are several methods for entering a function into a worksheet cell. To begin with, you can type a function name, preceded by an equal sign (=), and then enter its **arguments** (labels, values, or cell references). Many functions are quite complex, however, and all require that you remember the precise order, called **syntax,** in which to enter arguments. An easier method is to select a function from the Paste Function dialog box shown in Figure 4.5. You access this dialog box by choosing the Insert, Function command or by clicking the Paste Function button (☰). In addition to organizing Excel's functions into tidy categories (further described in Table 4.1), the Paste Function dialog box lets you view a function's syntax, along with a brief description.

Figure 4.5

Paste Function
dialog box

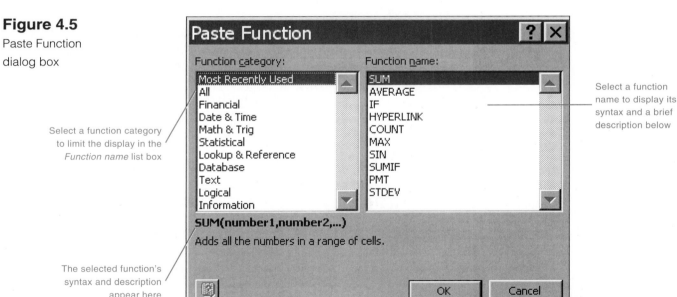

Select a function category
to limit the display in the
Function name list box

Select a function
name to display its
syntax and a brief
description below

The selected function's
syntax and description
appear here

Table 4.1

Function Categories

Category	Description
Financial	Determine loan payments, present and future values, depreciation schedules, and rates of return
Date & Time	Perform date and time calculations; input the current date and/or time into a cell
Math & Trig	Sum a range of values; perform trigonometric calculations; determine absolute and rounded values
Statistical	Determine the average, median, minimum, and maximum values for a range; calculate statistical measures, like variance and standard deviation
Lookup & Reference	Look up and select values from a range; return the active cell's column letter and row number
Database	Perform mathematical and statistical calculations on worksheet values in a table or list format
Text	Manipulate, compare, format, and extract textual information; convert values to text (and vice versa)
Logical	Perform conditional calculations using IF statements; compare and evaluate values
Information	Return information about the current environment; perform error-checking and troubleshooting

4.2.1 Adding Values (SUM)

FEATURE

You use the SUM function to add together the values appearing in a range of cells. SUM is the most frequently used function in Excel, saving you from having to enter long addition formulas such as =A1+A2+A3 . . . +A99. The AutoSum button ([Σ]) inserts the SUM function into a worksheet cell automatically, guessing at the range argument to use.

METHOD

=SUM(range)

PRACTICE

You will now practice entering the SUM function.

Setup: Ensure that no workbooks appear in the application window.

1 Open the data file named EXC420.

2 Save the workbook as "Functions" to your personal storage location. Your screen should now appear similar to Figure 4.6.

Figure 4.6

The "Functions" workbook

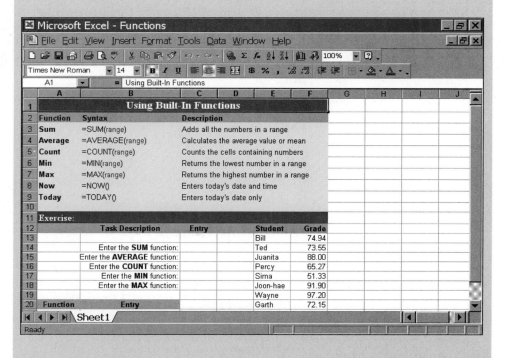

3 Let's total the grade values in column F. Do the following:
SELECT: cell C14

4 To enter the SUM function:
TYPE: `=sum(f13:f22)`
PRESS: `ENTER`
The result, 761.51, appears in the cell. (*Note:* You can enter a function's name and arguments using either lowercase or uppercase letters. Ensure that there are no blank spaces entered mistakenly.)

5 Let's change Percy's grade:
SELECT: cell F16

6 To enter the revised grade:
TYPE: `75.27`
PRESS: `ENTER`
The new SUM result displays 771.51 in cell C14.

7 Save the workbook and keep it open for use in the next lesson.

4.2.2 Calculating Averages (AVERAGE)

FEATURE
You use the AVERAGE function to compute the average value (sometimes called the arithmetic mean) for a range of cells. This function adds together all of the numeric values in a range and then divides the sum by the number of cells used in the calculation.

METHOD
`=AVERAGE(range)`

PRACTICE
In this exercise, you calculate the average value for a named range in a worksheet.

Setup: Ensure that you have completed the previous lesson and that the "Functions" workbook is displayed.

1 To make it easier to enter functions, you can name the cell ranges on your worksheet. Let's name the range that contains the grade values:
SELECT: cell range from E12 to F22
Notice that you include the column headings, Student and Grade, in the selection.

2 CHOOSE: Insert, Name, Create

3 In the Create Name dialog box:
SELECT: *Top row* check box, if not already selected
SELECT: *Left column* check box, if not already selected
CLICK: OK command button

4 To view the range names that have been created:
CLICK: down arrow attached to the Name box
Your screen should now appear similar to Figure 4.7.

Figure 4.7

Viewing a worksheet's range names

The Name Box displays the range names created from the worksheet selection

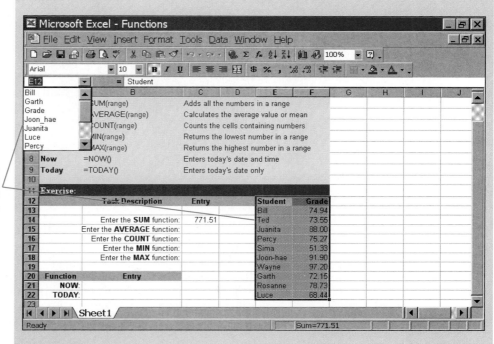

5 In the drop-down list box that appears:
CLICK: Garth
Your cell pointer should now be positioned in cell F20. Notice also that the Name box displays the name "Garth."

6 To select the entire "Grade" range:
CLICK: down arrow attached to the Name box
CLICK: Grade in the drop-down list
The cell range from F13 to F22 is selected.

7 Let's use the range name to calculate the average grade:
SELECT: cell C15
TYPE: =average(grade)
PRESS: ENTER
The result, 77.151, appears in the cell.

8 To determine the average of a list of nonadjacent values, separate the items in the list using commas. To illustrate:
SELECT: cell D15
TYPE: =average(Bill,Ted,Sima,Rosanne)
PRESS: (ENTER)
The result, 69.6375, appears as the average of only these students' grades.

4.2.3 Counting Values (COUNT)

FEATURE
The COUNT function counts the number of cells in a range that contain numeric or date values. This function ignores cells containing text labels.

METHOD
=COUNT(*range*)

PRACTICE
You will now enter the COUNT function in the "Functions" workbook.

Setup: Ensure that you have completed the previous lessons and that the "Functions" workbook is displayed.

1 Move the cell pointer to where you want the result to appear:
SELECT: cell C16

2 You will now use the mouse to help you count the number of entries in a range. To begin:
TYPE: =count(

3 Using the mouse, position the cell pointer over cell F13. Then:
CLICK: cell F13 and hold down the left mouse button
DRAG: mouse pointer to cell F22
Notice that as you drag the mouse pointer, the range is entered into the function as an argument. When you reach cell F22, the argument displays the range name "Grade."

4 Release the mouse button.

5 To complete the function entry:
TYPE:)
PRESS: (ENTER)
The result, 10, appears in cell C16.

EXCEL

6 Save the workbook and keep it open for use in the next lesson.

4.2.4 Analyzing Values (MIN and MAX)

FEATURE
You use the MIN and MAX functions to determine the minimum (lowest) and maximum (highest) values in a range of cells.

METHOD
=MIN(*range*)
=MAX(*range*)

PRACTICE
In this lesson, you practice using the **Formula Palette** to calculate the minimum and maximum grades in a range. The Formula Palette provides a helpful dialog box for selecting and entering function arguments in the correct order.

Setup: Ensure that you have completed the previous lessons in this module and that the "Functions" workbook is displayed.

1 To calculate the lowest grade achieved:
SELECT: cell C17
TYPE: =min(grade)
PRESS: ➡
The result, 51.33, appears.

2 To find the lowest grade achieved among three students:
TYPE: =min(Wayne,Garth,Luce)
PRESS: ENTER
The result, 68.44, appears.

3 You will now use Excel's Formula Palette to calculate the maximum value in a range. Do the following:
SELECT: cell C18
TYPE: =max(
Ensure that you include the open parentheses "(" at the end of the function name.

4 To display the Formula Palette:
CLICK: Edit Formula button () in the Formula bar
The Formula Palette appears under the Formula bar, as shown in Figure 4.8. (*Note:* You can ignore the Assistant character that may appear on your screen. He, she, or it will go away after you complete the next few steps.)

Figure 4.8

Formula Palette:

Entering the MAX function

You use the Formula Palette
when you need assistance
entering a function.

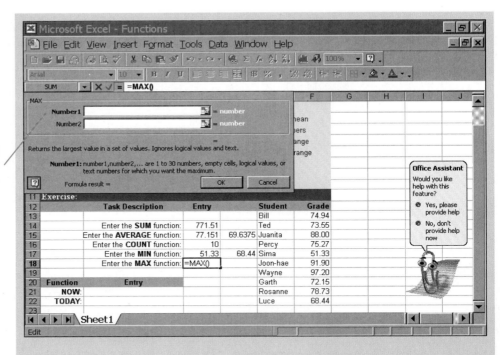

5 In the *Number1* argument text box:
TYPE: grade
Notice that the actual cell contents appear at the right of the
text box and that the result is calculated immediately and shown
below.

6 To complete the entry:
CLICK: OK command button

7 To find the maximum grade achieved among three students:
SELECT: cell D18
TYPE: =max(
CLICK: Edit Formula button (=)

8 In the Formula Palette:
TYPE: Juanita
PRESS: TAB
TYPE: Ted
PRESS: TAB
TYPE: Luce
Notice that the Formula bar displays the function as you build it
in the Formula Palette.

9 To complete the entry:
CLICK: OK command button
The result, 88, appears in the cell.

10 Save the workbook and keep it open for use in the next lesson.

EXCEL

4.2.5 Calculating Dates (NOW and TODAY)

FEATURE
You use the NOW and TODAY functions to display the current date and time. The NOW function returns the current date and time as provided by your computer's internal clock. The TODAY function provides the current date only. Neither of these functions require any arguments.

METHOD
=NOW()
=TODAY()

PRACTICE
In this exercise, you insert the NOW and TODAY functions into the worksheet.

Setup: Ensure that you have completed the previous lessons in this module and that the "Functions" workbook is displayed.

1 To insert the current date and time into the worksheet, do the following:
SELECT: cell B21
TYPE: =now()
PRESS: ENTER
The date is displayed using the "mm/dd/yy" format (depending on your default settings), while the time is typically displayed using the "hh:mm" 24-hour clock format.

2 To display only the time in the cell, you must format the entry:
SELECT: cell B21
CHOOSE: Format, Cells
CLICK: *Number* tab

3 You must now select a time format:
SELECT: Time in the *Category* list box
SELECT: 1:30:55 PM in the *Type* list box
CLICK: OK command button

4 To recalculate the NOW function:
PRESS: F9 CALC key
You should see the cell value change to the current time. (*Hint:* You can use ENTER to recalculate all formulas and functions in a worksheet.)

5   To enter the current date only:
SELECT: B22
TYPE: =today()
PRESS: [ENTER]
The current date should now appear in the worksheet.

6   On your own, format the current date to display using the "14-Mar-98" format option.

7   Save and then close the workbook.

4.2 Self Check   When might you use the Formula Palette or Paste Function dialog box to enter a function into the worksheet?

4.3 Creating an Embedded Chart

Since the earliest versions of spreadsheet software, users have been able to display their numerical data using graphs and charts. While acceptable for in-house business presentations and school projects, these graphics often lacked the depth and quality required by professional users. Until now! You can confidently use Excel to produce visually stunning worksheets and charts that are suitable for electronic business presentations, color print masters, Internet Web pages, and 35mm slide shows.

There are many types of charts available for presenting your worksheet data to engineers, statisticians, business professionals, and other audiences. Some popular business charts—line chart, column chart, pie chart, and XY scatter plot diagram—are described below.

- **_Line Charts_**   When you need to plot trends or show changes over a period of time, the **line chart** is the perfect tool. The angles of the line reflect the degree of variation, and the distance of the line from the horizontal axis represents the amount of the variation. An example of a line chart appears in Figure 4.9, along with some basic terminology.

Figure 4.9

A line chart

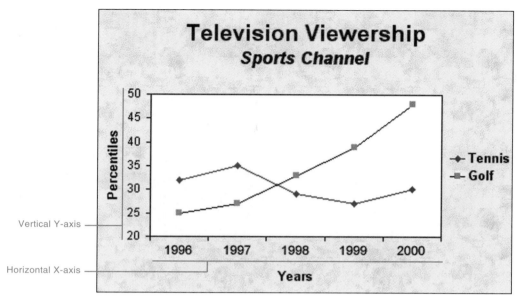

- ***Bar or Column Charts***   When the purpose of the chart is to compare one data element with another data element, a **column chart** is the appropriate form to use. A column chart (Figure 4.10) shows variations over a period of time, similarly to a line chart. A **bar chart** also uses rectangular images, but they run horizontally rather than vertically.

Figure 4.10

A column chart

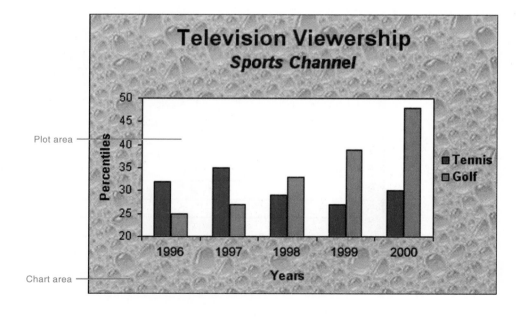

- ***Pie Charts***   A **pie chart** shows the proportions of individual components compared to the total. Similar to a real pie (the baked variety), a pie chart is divided into slices or wedges. (In Excel, you can even pull out the slices from the rest of the pie.) An example of a pie chart appears in Figure 4.11.

Figure 4.11

A pie chart

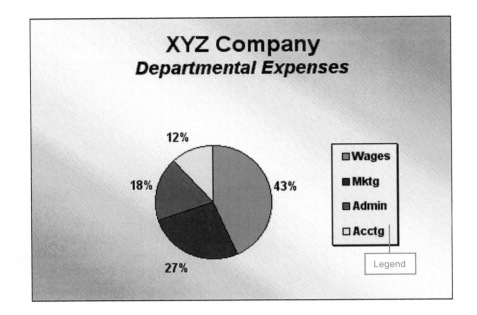

• **Scatter Plot Charts**   **XY charts,** which are commonly referred to as *scatter plot diagrams,* show how one or more data elements relate to another data element. Although they look much like line charts, XY charts show the correlation between elements and include a numeric scale along both the X and Y axes. The XY chart in Figure 4.12 shows that worker productivity diminishes as stress levels increase.

Figure 4.12

An XY chart

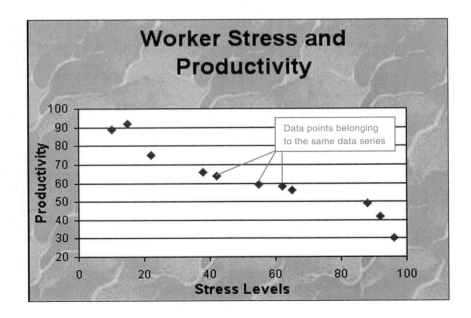

There are two methods for creating a chart in Excel, differing primarily in the way the chart is stored and printed. First, you can create a new chart as a separate sheet in a workbook. This method works well for printing full-page charts and for creating computer-based presentations or electronic slide shows. Second, you can create an **embedded chart** that is stored on the worksheet. Embed a chart when you want to view or print the chart alongside the worksheet data. Whichever method you choose, use the step-by-step features in Excel's **Chart Wizard** to construct a chart from existing worksheet data.

In this module, you learn how to create and print an embedded chart.

4.3.1 Creating a Chart Using the Chart Wizard

FEATURE
You create a chart by selecting a range of cells to plot and then launching the Chart Wizard. The wizard examines the selected range and then displays its dialog box. You make selections, such as choosing a chart type, and then proceed through the steps to embed the chart on the worksheet. An embedded chart is actually placed over—not entered into—a cell range. Once embedded, you can move, size, and delete the chart.

METHOD
1. SELECT: the cell range to plot in a chart
2. CLICK: Chart Wizard button (▦)
3. Complete the steps in the Chart Wizard.

PRACTICE
You will now create and embed a new chart onto a worksheet.

1 Open the data file named EXC430.

2 Save the workbook as "Cruising" to your personal storage location.

3 Let's plot the worksheet's demographic data. To begin, select both the headings and the data:
SELECT: cell range from A2 to D5

4 To start the Chart Wizard:
CLICK: Chart Wizard button (▦) on the Standard toolbar
Your screen should now appear similar to Figure 4.13. (*Note:* If the Assistant appears, right-click it and choose the Hide command.)

Figure 4.13

Chart Wizard: Step 1 of 4

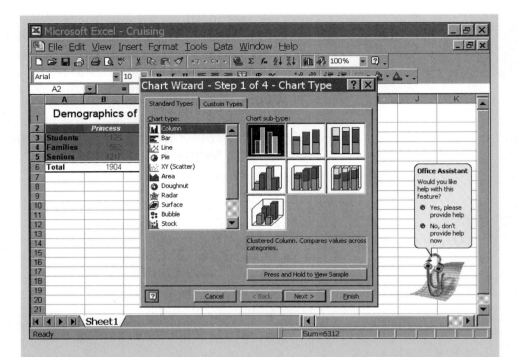

5 To see a sample of how Excel will plot this data:
CLICK: "Press and Hold to View Sample" command button
(*Note:* You must hold down the left mouse button to see the
chart inside the *Sample* preview window. When finished viewing,
release the mouse button.)

6 Let's select a different chart sub-type that amalgamates (adds
together) the two data series in a column. Do the following:
SELECT: Stacked Column in the *Chart sub-type* area
When you click on a chart sub-type, the chart's name and
description appear above the "Press and Hold to View Sample"
command button.)

7 Once again, preview a sample of the chart:
CLICK: "Press and Hold to View Sample" command button

8 To continue creating the chart:
CLICK: Next > to proceed to Step 2 of 4
CLICK: Next > to proceed to Step 3 of 4

9 In Step 3 of 4 of the Chart Wizard:
TYPE: Cruise Lines into the *Category (X) axis* text box
TYPE: Passengers into the *Value (Y) axis* text box
(*Hint:* Click the I-beam mouse pointer into a text box and then
type the appropriate text. You can also press TAB to move forward through the text boxes.) Notice that the preview area is
immediately updated to display the new titles, as shown in Figure 4.14.

Figure 4.14

Chart Wizard:

Step 3 of 4

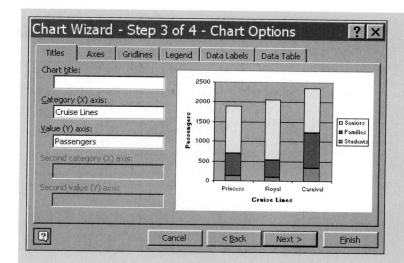

10. To proceed to the final step:
CLICK: Next >

11. In Step 4 of 4, you specify where you want to store the chart. To create an embedded chart:
SELECT: *As object in* option button, if it is not already selected
Notice that the current worksheet's name, Sheet1, already appears in the drop-down list box next to the option button.

12. To complete the Chart Wizard:
CLICK: Finish
The embedded chart appears in the application window. (*Note:* You may also see Excel's Chart toolbar appear.)

13. The black selection handles that surround the chart indicate that it is currently selected. Using the mouse, you can size the embedded chart by dragging these handles. On your own, practice sizing the chart.

14. You can also move the chart by dragging the object using the mouse. Position the white mouse arrow over a blank portion of the chart's background area. Then, drag the chart into position. Practice moving and sizing the chart to appear similar to Figure 4.15.

Figure 4.15

Moving and sizing an
embedded chart object

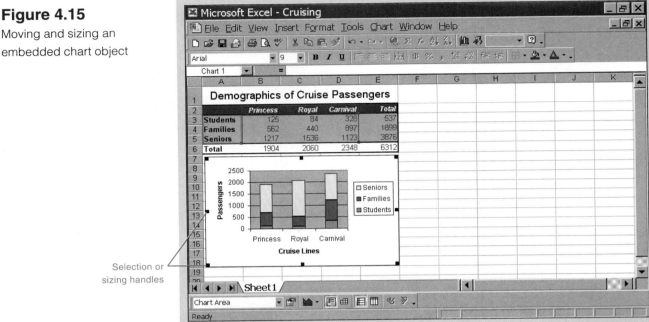

Selection or
sizing handles

15 To return focus to the worksheet:
CLICK: any visible cell in the worksheet area, such as cell F1
Notice that the Chart toolbar and the selection boxes around the
chart both disappear.

16 The embedded chart is dynamically linked to the information
stored in the worksheet. To demonstrate, let's update the "Carni-
val" column in the embedded chart:
SELECT: cell D5
TYPE: 123
PRESS: ENTER
The chart is updated immediately to reflect the new data.

17 To undo the last change:
CLICK: Undo button ( )

18 Save the workbook and keep it open for use in the next lesson.

4.3.2 Previewing and Printing an Embedded Chart

FEATURE
One of the primary reasons for embedding a chart on a worksheet is to view and print it alongside its worksheet data. You must ensure that the print area (or range), however, includes the entire chart object. And, as before, remember to preview your worksheet and chart prior to printing.

METHOD
1. SELECT: a cell range that includes the chart
2. CHOOSE: File, Print Area, Set Print Area
3. CHOOSE: File, Print or
   CHOOSE: File, Print Preview

PRACTICE
In this lesson, you preview and print an embedded chart along with its worksheet data.

Setup: Ensure that you have completed the previous lesson and that the "Cruising" workbook is displayed.

1 To print the worksheet and embedded chart on the same page:
SELECT: cell range from A1 to F20
(*Note:* Depending on the size and placement of your chart object, you may need to increase or decrease this print range. Make sure that the entire object is covered in the highlighted range.)

2 CHOOSE: File, Print Area, Set Print Area

3 To preview the worksheet and chart:
CLICK: Print Preview button

4 To zoom in on the preview window:
CLICK: Zoom command button

5 On your own, scroll the preview window to appear similar to Figure 4.16. Notice that the chart is printed immediately and seamlessly below the worksheet data.

Figure 4.16

Previewing an
embedded chart

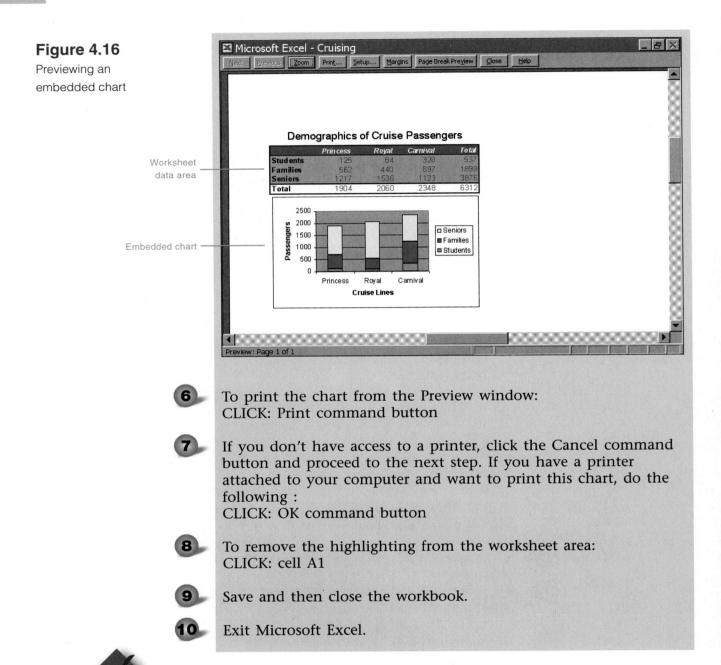

Worksheet
data area

Embedded chart

6 To print the chart from the Preview window:
CLICK: Print command button

7 If you don't have access to a printer, click the Cancel command button and proceed to the next step. If you have a printer attached to your computer and want to print this chart, do the following :
CLICK: OK command button

8 To remove the highlighting from the worksheet area:
CLICK: cell A1

9 Save and then close the workbook.

10 Exit Microsoft Excel.

4.3 Self Check   What must you do when selecting the print range for a worksheet that contains an embedded chart?

4.4 Chapter Review

This chapter introduced you to some powerful tools for analyzing and summarizing data. You learned how to name cells and ranges and how to use these names in constructing expressions and navigating the worksheet. The first module also discussed the differences between absolute and relative cell addresses. An absolute cell address appears with dollar signs ($), which serve to anchor an address to an exact location on the worksheet. The second module focused on Excel's built-in functions. These functions, such as SUM and AVERAGE, are used as shortcuts to performing complex or lengthy calculations. Remember to use the Formula Palette and Paste Function feature when you need assistance entering the arguments for a function. In the last module, you learned to create an embedded chart using the Chart Wizard and to position and print the chart alongside its worksheet data.

4.4.1 Command Summary

Many of the commands and procedures appearing in this chapter are summarized in the following table.

Skill Set	To Perform This Task . . .	Do the Following . . .
Working with Named Ranges	Name a cell range	SELECT: the desired range CLICK: in the Name box TYPE: a range name
	Create range names from labels appearing on the worksheet	SELECT: the desired range CHOOSE: Insert, Name, Create
	Modify and delete range names	CHOOSE: Insert, Name, Define
	Paste a list of range names onto the worksheet	CHOOSE: Insert, Name, Paste
Working with Formulas	Modify and use cell references (absolute, relative, and mixed)	SELECT: the desired cell CLICK: in the cell address in the Formula bar PRESS: F4 to apply reference type
	Recalculate formulas in a worksheet	PRESS: F9 CALC key

Continued

Skill Set	To Perform This Task . . .	Do the Following . . .
Using Functions	Use the Formula Palette to enter a function and its arguments	CLICK: Edit Formula button ([=])
	Insert a function using the Paste Function dialog box	CLICK: Paste Function button ([_fx_]) SELECT: a category and function

	Use basic functions:
	  Sum a range of values
	  Average a range of values
	  Count the numeric and date
	  values in a range
	  Find the lowest value in a range
	  Find the highest value in a range
		
		=SUM(*range*)
		=AVERAGE(*range*)
		
		=COUNT(*range*)
		=MIN(*range*)
		=MAX(*range*)

	Use date functions:
	  Enter the current date and time
	  Enter today's date
		
		=NOW( )
		=TODAY( )

Using Charts and Objects	Use the Chart Wizard to create a chart	SELECT: the cell range to plot CLICK: Chart Wizard button ([▥])
	Preview and print an embedded chart	SELECT: the desired range CHOOSE: File, Print Area, Set Print Area CLICK: Print Preview ([▣]) or Print ([▤])

4.4.2 Key Terms

This section specifies page references for the key terms identified in this chapter. For a complete list of definitions, refer to the Glossary provided in the Appendix.

absolute cell address, *p. 157*

arguments, *p. 161*

barchart, *p. 171*

Chart Wizard, *p. 173*

column chart, *p. 171*

embedded chart, *p. 173*

Formula Palette, *p. 167*

functions, *p. 161*

line chart, *p. 170*

mixed cell address, *p. 157*

natural language formula, *p. 159*

pie chart, *p. 171*

range name, *p. 151*

relative cell address, *p. 157*

scatter plot charts, *p. 172*

syntax, *p. 161*

XY charts, *p. 172*

4.5 Review Questions

4.5.1 Short Answer

1. Why would you want to name a range of cells?
2. How do you place a list of range names into the worksheet?
3. Name the two primary types of cell references and explain how they differ.
4. In order for natural language formulas to work effectively, how should the worksheet be organized?
5. Which function would you use to extract the highest value from a range named "salary?" How would you enter the function?
6. Which function would you use to place only the current time in your worksheet? What else might you want to do?
7. What is the name of the dialog box that you can use to select functions from categories? How do you access this dialog box?

8. What is the name of the dialog box that can help you to enter a function's arguments correctly? How do you access this dialog box?
9. Describe the four steps in creating a chart using the Chart Wizard.
10. What are the black boxes called that surround an embedded chart? What are they used for?

4.5.2 True/False

1. __T__ Range names that you create use absolute cell references.
2. __T__ Cell addresses that you enter into formulas use, by default, relative cell references.
3. __F__ The "&s" in the cell reference &D&5 indicate an absolute cell reference.
4. __F__ You cannot mix labels, such as "Revenue," with cell references in a natural language formula.
5. __F__ You enter a function using parentheses instead of the equal sign.
6. __F__ The SUM function appears in the Statistical function category of the Paste Function dialog box.
7. __F__ You must use the Formula Palette to enter the COUNT function.
8. __F__ The TODAY function updates the computer's internal clock to the current date and time.
9. __T__ A pie chart shows the proportions of individual components compared to the total.
10. __T__ You can move and size an embedded chart once it is placed on the worksheet.

EXCEL

4.5.3 Multiple Choice

1. What menu command allows you to create range names using the labels that already appear in the worksheet?
    a. Edit, Name, Create
    b. Range, Name, Create
    c. Insert, Name, Create
    d. Insert, Name, Define

2. Which of the following symbols precedes an absolute cell reference?
    a. $
    b. @
    c. &
    d. #

3. Which key do you press to change a cell address to being absolute, relative, or mixed?
    a. F2
    b. F3
    c. F4
    d. F9

4. Which key do you press to recalculate or update a worksheet?
    a. F2
    b. F3
    c. F4
    d. F9

5. Which is the correct expression for adding the values stored in the cell range from A1 to A20?
    a. =ADD(A1+A20)
    b. =SUM(A1:A20)
    c. =SUM(A1+A20)
    d. =AutoSUM(A1,A20)

6. Which is the correct expression for determining the average of a range named "Units"?
    a. =AVG(Units)
    b. =UNITS(Average)
    c. =AVERAGE(Units)
    d. =SUM(Units/Average)

7. What does the COUNT function actually count?
    a. All of the cells in a range
    b. All of the cells containing data in a range
    c. Only those cells containing text and numbers
    d. Only those cells containing numeric or date values

8. Which button do you click to display the Formula Palette?
   a. `=`
   b. ▣
   c. Σ
   d. ƒ

9. What is the name of the step-by-step charting tool provided by Excel?
   a. Chart Master
   b. Chart Wizard
   c. Plot Master
   d. Plot Wizard

10. A chart may be created as a separate chart sheet or as an embedded object. In which step of the Chart Wizard do you specify how a chart is created and stored?
    a. Step 1
    b. Step 2
    c. Step 3
    d. Step 4

4.6   Hands-On Projects

4.6.1   Grandview College: Enrollment Statistics

In this exercise, you practice creating and working with named cell ranges and constructing formulas using absolute and relative cell addresses.

1. Open the data file named EXC461.
2. Save the workbook as "Enrollment" to your personal storage location.
3. You will now name a cell range on the worksheet. To begin:
   SELECT: cell B8
   CLICK: in the Name box
   TYPE: Total
   PRESS: [ENTER]
   You have successfully named this cell "Total."
4. To create a set of range names using existing worksheet labels:
   SELECT: cell range from A2 to B7
   CHOOSE: Insert, Name, Create
   CLICK: OK command button

5. To view the list of range names that you just created:
   SELECT: cell E2
   CHOOSE: Insert, Name, Paste
   CLICK: Paste List command button
   SELECT: cell A1 to remove the highlighting
   (*Note:* The list is pasted in alphabetical order.)
6. To enter a formula using named cell ranges:
   SELECT: cell B10
   TYPE: =
   CLICK: cell B3
   TYPE: +
   CLICK: cell B7
   Notice that the expression "`=Continuing_Ed+Vocational`" appears in the Formula bar.
7. To complete the formula entry:
   PRESS: [ENTER]
8. On your own, enter a formula in cell B11 that totals the rest of the departments not included in the previous step.
9. Let's calculate the enrollment percentage for each department. Starting in cell C2, you will enter a formula that can be later used for copying. To do so, you need to specify an absolute cell reference for the Total value and a relative cell reference for the Arts value. To illustrate:
   SELECT: cell C2
   TYPE: `=b2/total`
   PRESS: [ENTER]
   (*Note:* A range name provides an absolute cell reference. Therefore, you cannot use the range name "Arts" in the formula expression.)
10. To copy the formula to the remaining departments:
    SELECT: cell C2
    DRAG: the fill handle for cell C2 to cell C8
    (*Hint:* The fill handle for a cell or cell range is the small black box in the bottom right-hand corner of the range selection.)
11. On your own, select the cells in the range C2:C8 and view the contents in the Formula bar. Notice that the relative cell references (B2, B3,... B8) adjust automatically. The range name "Total" remained absolute.
12. Save and then close the "Enrollment" workbook.

4.6.2 Fast Forward Video: Rental Category Chart

You will now practice creating a chart using Excel's Chart Wizard.

1. Open the data file named EXC462.
2. Save the workbook as "Video Chart" to your personal storage location.
3. To begin, select the cell range that contains the data for plotting:
   SELECT: cell range A3 to G5
   Notice that you did not include the "Total" row or "Total" column.
4. Launch the Chart Wizard:
   CLICK: Chart Wizard button () on the Standard toolbar
5. To display the two categories, New Release and Weekly, side by side:
   SELECT: Column as the *Chart type*
   SELECT: Clustered Column as the *Chart sub-type*
   CLICK: Next > to proceed to Step 2 of 4
   CLICK: Next > to proceed to Step 3 of 4
6. On the *Titles* tab of Step 3 in the Chart Wizard:
   TYPE: Income by Category into the *Chart title* text box
   TYPE: Movie Category into the *Category (X)* axis text box
   TYPE: Rental Income into the *Value (Y)* axis text box
   CLICK: Next >
7. To embed the chart in the worksheet:
   SELECT: *As object* in option button, if it is not already selected
   CLICK: Finish
   The chart object appears in the middle of the application window.
8. To move the embedded chart, position the mouse pointer on an empty portion of the chart's background. Then do the following:
   DRAG: the chart below the data area
9. To size the embedded chart, position the mouse pointer over the selection handle in the bottom right-hand corner. Then:
   DRAG: the selection handle down and to the right to enlarge the chart

10. On your own, finalize the size and placement of the embed-ded chart so that it appears similar to Figure 4.17.

Figure 4.17

Sizing and moving an embedded chart

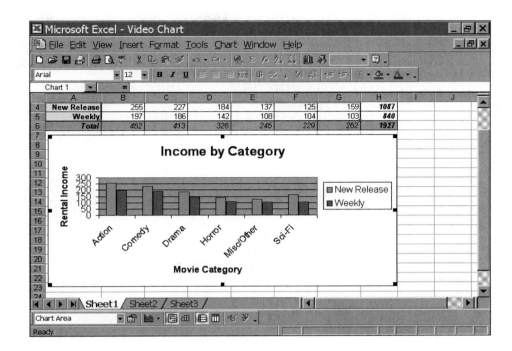

11. You've just received word that some information in the work-sheet has been entered incorrectly. Study the Misc/Other cate-gory columns on the chart. Now, update the worksheet:
    SELECT: cell F4
    TYPE: 104
    PRESS: ⬇
    TYPE: 175
    PRESS: (ENTER)
    Notice that the chart has been updated to reflect the new values.
12. Save and then close the "Video Chart" workbook.

4.6.3 Sun Valley Frozen Foods: Daily Production

You will now practice using some of Excel's built-in functions in an existing worksheet. You will also use the AutoFill feature to create a series and then the Fill command to copy formulas.

1. Open the data file named EXC463.
2. Save the workbook as "Sun Daily" in your personal storage location.

3. Use the fill handle to complete a series listing the days of the week (Monday through Friday) in cells A3 to A7.

4. In cell B9, enter the following function to calculate the minimum production amount for corn:
   TYPE: `=min(b3:b7)`
   PRESS: `ENTER`

5. Using the same approach as before, enter formulas in cells B10 and B11 to calculate the maximum and average production for corn.

6. Select the cell range from B9 to E11 and then use the Edit, Fill, Right command to copy the formulas to columns C, D, and E.

7. Select the cell range from A2 to E7 and then use the Insert, Name, Create command to assign range names using the existing labels.

8. To calculate the total production for Corn:
   SELECT: cell B13
   TYPE: `=sum(corn)`
   PRESS: `ENTER`

9. Using the same technique, calculate the totals for the Peas, Beans, and Other columns. (*Note:* You cannot use the Edit, Fill, Right command since the named range "Corn" uses an absolute cell reference.)

10. Save and then close the "Sun Daily" workbook.

4.6.4 Lakeside Realty: Mortgage Rate Chart

In this exercise, you create an embedded chart and then print it alongside the worksheet data.

1. Open the data file named EXC464.

2. Save the workbook as "Mortgage Chart" to your personal storage location.

3. Select the cell range from A2 to G8.

4. Launch the Chart Wizard.

5. In the *Chart type* and *Chart sub-type* list boxes, select a line chart with markers displayed at each data value. Then proceed to the third step.

6. In step 3 of the Chart Wizard, add the title "Average Mortgage Rates" to appear at the top of the chart. Then proceed to the next step.
7. Save the chart as an object in Sheet1 and then click the Finish command button.
8. Size and move the embedded chart so that it covers the range from cell A13 to G27.
9. Update July's six-month rate to 6.00 in the worksheet.
10. Set the print area to cover the range from A1 to H28.
11. Preview and then print the selected print area.
12. Save and then close the "Mortgage Chart" workbook.

4.6.5 On Your Own: Auto Fuel Comparison

This exercise lets you practice naming ranges and entering functions. To begin, open the EXC465 workbook and then save it as "Auto Fuel" to your personal storage location.

To begin, let's create some range names. Assign the name "Capacity" to the cell range B2:B7. Assign the name "City" to the cell range C2:C7. Assign the name "Hwy" to the cell range D2:D7. Paste a list of the range names in column F. In row 8, calculate the average for each column using their respective range names and the AVERAGE function. For more practice, enter a function in cell B10 that returns a count of the number of numerical entries in the "Capacity" range. In cell C10, display the minimum miles per gallon city rating. In cell D10, display the maximum miles per gallon highway rating.

When you are finished, save and then close the "Auto Fuel" workbook.

4.6.6 On Your Own: Personal Expense Chart

For additional practice creating charts, open the EXC466 data file. Before continuing, save the workbook as "Expense Chart" to your personal storage location. Then complete the worksheet by inputting your monthly expenses into the appropriate cells.

Using the Chart Wizard, create a pie chart of these expenses. Do not add a title to the chart and save it as an embedded object in the worksheet. Once it appears on the worksheet, size the chart so that the information is easily read. Lastly, position the chart to the right of the worksheet data. Print the worksheet data and the chart on the same page. Remember to use the Set Print Area command and Print Preview to ensure that your settings are correct. When you are satisfied with the results, send the worksheet and embedded chart to the printer.

Save and then close the "Expense Chart" workbook. Then, exit Excel.

4.7 Case Problems: Interior Hockey Association

The Interior Hockey Association is a junior hockey league that is just finishing its current season. As one of the many volunteers that keep the IHA going, Brad Stafford has the task of summarizing various statistics for inclusion into the season-end newsletter. Brad has recently learned how to use ranges and functions in Excel and now wants to use them to produce worksheets that can be incorporated into the newsletter.

In the following case problems, assume the role of Brad and perform the same steps that he identifies. You may want to re-read the chapter opening before proceeding.

1. It's 8:00 P.M. on a Sunday evening when Brad decides to sit down at his home computer and spend some time working on the IHA newsletter. After loading Excel, he opens the EXC471 workbook that he has been using to project next year's attendance levels. Brad wants to communicate the fine growth in attendance that the IHA has been experiencing. Before continuing, he saves the workbook as "IHA Attendance" to his personal storage location.

   Having learned about range names, Brad's first step is to use the Name box and apply a range name of "Factor" to cell C12. Then, he selects the cell range A2:B10 and uses the Insert, Name, Create command to create range names from the selection's row and column labels. To verify that the range names are correct, Brad selects cell E1 in the worksheet and then pastes a list of all existing named ranges.

   Brad remembers that to calculate next year's attendance using a growth factor formula, he will have to use both relative and absolute cell addresses. Otherwise, when he performs a copy operation, the formula's cell addresses will be adjusted automatically. Brad wants to ensure that the formulas always use the value in cell C12 as the growth factor. Fortunately, Brad also remembers that a named range is, by default, an absolute reference. Therefore, using a relative cell address and the "Factor" range name, he can complete his task. To begin, he enters the formula **=b3*(1+Factor)** into cell C3. Notice that Brad typed "b3" and not "Bristol" into the cell. (*Hint:* The range name "Bristol" refers to the absolute cell address $B$3 and not the relative cell address that is required for this calculation.) This formula calculates next year's projected attendance for Bristol.

Brad uses Excel's AutoFill feature to extend the formula in cell C3 for the rest of the teams. Finally, he uses the Format Painter to copy the formatting from column B to the new results in column C. Brad saves and then closes the workbook.

2. Brad Stafford is constructing a worksheet that shows the team standings at the end of the IHA's regular season play. To review the worksheet, he opens the EXC472 file and then saves it as "IHA Standings" to his personal storage location.

   With the teams already in the proper order, Brad wants to chart their results. He selects the cell range B2:C10 and then launches the Chart Wizard. In the first step, Brad selects a "Clustered bar with a 3-D visual effect" chart. Then he clicks the Finish command button. When the embedded chart appears in the application window, Brad sizes it so that all the team names are visible on the vertical axis. He then moves the chart below row 14, as shown in Figure 4.18.

Figure 4.18

Analyzing data using an embedded chart

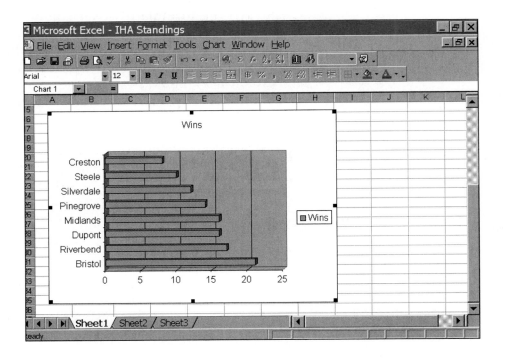

Continuing his work, Brad enters a formula into cell C12 that averages the values in that column. He uses the Fill, Right command to extend the formula across to column F. Lastly, Brad saves, prints, and then closes the workbook.

3. With the deadline for the season-end newsletter fast approaching, Brad is determined to finish the Team Goal Statistics worksheet. He opens the EXC473 data file and then saves it as "Goal Table" to his personal storage location.

   After double-checking to make sure that the formulas in column D are correct, Brad copies the formula from cell D3 to the cell range D14:D21. He then enters SUM functions into cells C11 and C22 that sum the goals for Offense and Defense, respectively. In column G, Brad uses Excel's built-in functions to find the highest, lowest, and average number of goals for both Offense and Defense. He names the two data ranges and then enters the functions into the appropriate cells. When he is finished, Brad saves and then closes the workbook.

4. The final worksheet that Brad needs to compile is for the "Scoring by Periods" statistics. He opens the EXC474 data file and saves it as "IHA Scoring" in his personal storage location.

   Using one of Excel's built-in functions, Brad calculates and displays the total goals scored by the first team in column F. After entering the function, he uses AutoFill to extend the formula to the rest of the teams. Next, he uses the appropriate function in row 11 to calculate the average for the first period. He formats the result to display using a single decimal place and then extends the formula to cover columns C through F.

   Brad completes the worksheet using the MIN and MAX functions to calculate the high and low scores for each period. As before, he extends these functions to cover the remaining columns. Lastly, Brad saves and closes the workbook and then exits Excel.

MICROSOFT®

POWERPOINT® 2000

BRIEF EDITION

MICROSOFT POWERPOINT 2000
Creating a Presentation

CHAPTER
ONE

Chapter Outline

1.1 Getting Started with PowerPoint

1.2 Creating a New Presentation

1.3 Managing Files

1.4 Previewing and Printing

1.5 Chapter Review

1.6 Review Questions

1.7 Hands-On Projects

1.8 Case Problems

Learning Objectives

After reading this chapter, you will be able to:

- Describe the different components of the application window

- Select commands using the Menu bar and right-click menus

- Begin a new presentation using the AutoContent Wizard or a design template

- Insert text in Slide and Outline views

- Save, open, close, and print a presentation

POWERPOINT

Case Study   Tristar Development

Tina Pusch is a public relations coordinator for Tristar Development, a large firm in New York. Earlier this morning Tina received a request from an important client to create a PowerPoint presentation summarizing the status of one of their projects. Then, during her coffee break, she received an e-mail message with a PowerPoint attachment from Kenyon, her sixth-grade nephew in Canada. Frustrated that she doesn't yet know how to use PowerPoint, Tina decides to roll up her sleeves and learn how to use this clearly popular tool.

In this chapter, you and Tina learn how to load Microsoft PowerPoint and open, close, and view existing presentations. You will create new presentations using the AutoContent Wizard and design templates, insert text, and insert and delete slides. You will also learn how to preview a presentation using grayscale tones and how to print.

1.1 Getting Started with PowerPoint

Microsoft PowerPoint 2000 is a presentation graphics program that enables you to create on-screen presentations, Web presentations, overhead transparencies, and 35mm slides. Even if you don't consider yourself a speechwriter or graphics designer, you can still create informative and attractive presentations using PowerPoint. In this module, you load Microsoft PowerPoint and proceed through a guided tour of its primary components.

1.1.1 Loading PowerPoint

FEATURE

You load PowerPoint from the Windows Start menu, accessed by clicking the Start button (Start) on the taskbar. Because PowerPoint requires a significant amount of memory, you should always exit the application when you are finished doing your work. Most Windows applications allow you to close their windows by clicking the Close button (x) appearing in the top right-hand corner.

METHOD

- To load PowerPoint:
  CLICK: Start button (Start)
  CHOOSE: Programs, Microsoft PowerPoint
- To exit PowerPoint:
  CHOOSE: File, Exit from PowerPoint's Menu bar

PRACTICE

You will now load Microsoft PowerPoint using the Windows Start menu.

Setup: Ensure that you have turned on your computer and that the Windows desktop appears. If necessary, refer to the Preface for additional instructions.

1 Position the mouse pointer over the top of the Start button (Start) and then click the left mouse button once. The Start pop-up menu appears.

2 Point to the Programs cascading command using the mouse. Note that you do not need to click the left mouse button to display the list of programs in the fly-out or cascading menu.

3 Move the mouse pointer horizontally to the right until it highlights an option in the Programs menu. You can now move the mouse pointer vertically within the menu to select an option.

4 Point to the Microsoft PowerPoint menu item and then click the left mouse button once to execute the command. After a few seconds, the Microsoft PowerPoint screen appears.

5 An Office Assistant character, like "Clippit" (shown at the right), may now appear. You learn how to hide this character in lesson 1.1.2.

6 Unless the feature has been disabled, a startup dialog box similar to the one shown in Figure 1.1 appears. This dialog box is used to determine how you want to proceed when PowerPoint is first loaded. If the dialog box appears on your screen, do the following:
CLICK: Cancel command button

Figure 1.1

PowerPoint startup
dialog box

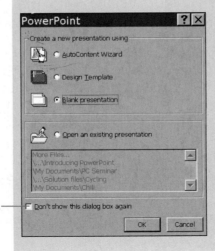

Select this check box
if you don't want the
startup dialog box to
display the next time
you load PowerPoint.

In Addition
Switching Among
Applications

Each application that you are currently working with is represented by a button on the taskbar. Switching between open applications on your desktop is as easy as clicking the appropriate taskbar button, like switching channels on a television set.

1.1.2   Touring PowerPoint

FEATURE
The PowerPoint **application window** acts as a container for your presentation. It also contains the primary interface components for working in PowerPoint, including the *Windows icons, Menu bar, Toolbars,* and *Status bar.* Figure 1.2 identifies several of these components.

PRACTICE
In a guided tour, you will now explore the features of the PowerPoint application window.

Setup: Ensure that you've loaded PowerPoint and that the application window is empty.

1   PowerPoint's application window is best kept maximized to fill the entire screen, as shown in Figure 1.2. As with most Windows applications, you use the Title bar icons—Minimize (▭), Maximize (☐), Restore (▣), and Close (☒)—to control the display of a window using the mouse. Familiarize yourself with the components labeled in Figure 1.2.

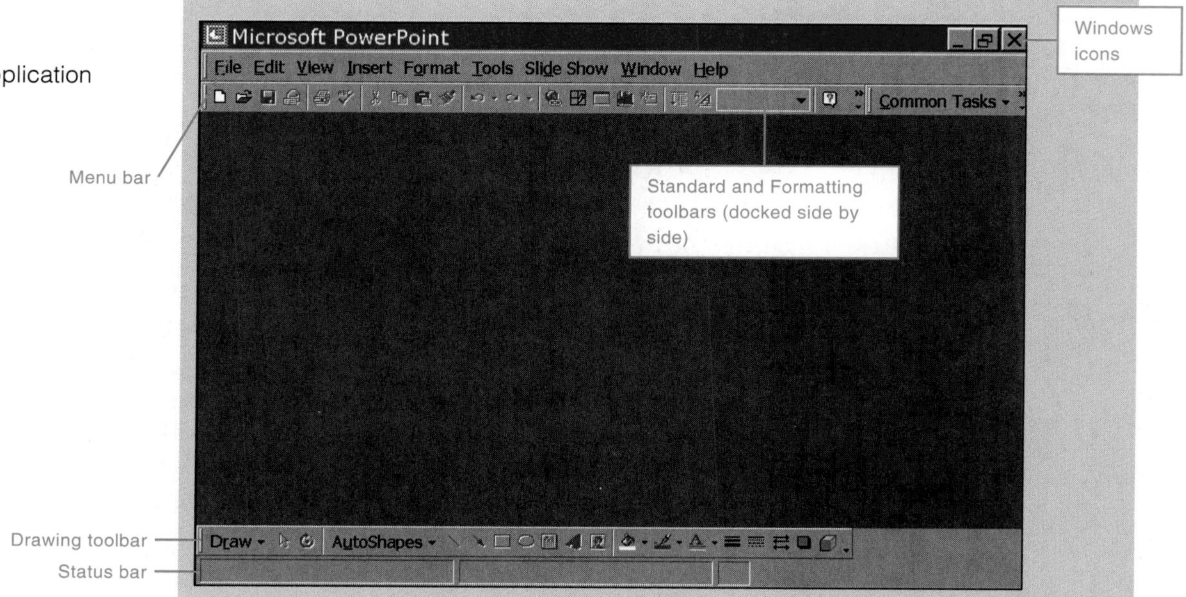

Figure 1.2
PowerPoint's application window

Windows icons

Menu bar

Standard and Formatting toolbars (docked side by side)

Drawing toolbar

Status bar

2 The Menu bar contains the PowerPoint menu commands. To execute a command, you click once on the desired Menu bar option and then click again on the command. Commands that appear dimmed are not available for selection. Commands that are followed by an ellipsis (...) will display a dialog box.

To practice working with the PowerPoint Menu bar:
CHOOSE: Help
This instruction tells you to click the left mouse button once on the Help option appearing in the Menu bar.

3 To display other pull-down menus, move the mouse to the left over other options in the Menu bar. As each option is highlighted, a pull-down menu appears with its associated commands.

4 To leave the Menu bar without making a command selection:
CLICK: in a blank area of the Title bar

5 PowerPoint provides context-sensitive *right-click menus* for quick access to menu commands. Rather than searching for the appropriate command in the Menu bar, you can position the mouse pointer on any object, such as a graphic or toolbar button, and right-click the mouse to display a list of commonly selected commands.

If an Office Assistant character currently appears on your screen, do the following to hide it from view:
RIGHT-CLICK: *the character*
CHOOSE: Hide from the right-click menu

1.1.3 Customizing Menus and Toolbars

FEATURE
Some people argue that software becomes more difficult to learn and use with the addition of each new command or feature. In response to this sentiment, Microsoft developed **adaptive menus** that display only the most commonly used commands. By default, Office 2000 ships with the adaptive menus feature enabled. However, you may find this dynamic feature confusing and choose to turn off the adaptive menus. Likewise, the Standard and Formatting toolbars are positioned side-by-side in a single row by default. Again, you may find it easier to locate buttons when these toolbars are positioned on separate rows.

METHOD

To disable the adaptive menus feature:
1. CHOOSE: Tools, Customize
2. CLICK: *Options* tab
3. SELECT: *Menus show recently used commands first* check box, so that no "✔" appears
4. CLICK: Close command button

To display the Standard and Formatting toolbars on separate rows:
1. CHOOSE: Tools, Customize
2. CLICK: *Options* tab
3. SELECT: *Standard and Formatting toolbars share one row* check box, so that no "✔" appears.
4. CLICK: Close command button

PRACTICE

After a brief tour of PowerPoint's adaptive menus, you will disable the adaptive menus feature. At the same time, you will display the Standard and Formatting toolbars on separate rows.

Setup: Ensure that you've completed the previous lesson.

1 Let's display the Tools menu.
CHOOSE: Tools
The Tools menu (shown on the right) should now appear. When a desired command does not appear on a menu, you can extend the menu to view all of the commands either by waiting for a short period or by clicking the downward pointing arrows (also called *chevrons*) at the bottom of a pull-down menu. You can also double-click a menu option to display the entire list of commands immediately.

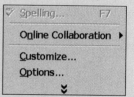

2 Let's display the entire list of commands in the Tools menu by double-clicking:
DOUBLE-CLICK: Tools in the Menu bar
The menu should now contain a complete list of options.

3 Let's turn off the adaptive menus feature and ensure that the Standard and Formatting toolbars appear on separate rows. Do the following:
CHOOSE: Customize from the Tools pull-down menu
CLICK: *Options* tab
The Customize dialog box should now appear similar to Figure 1.3.

Figure 1.3

Customize dialog box

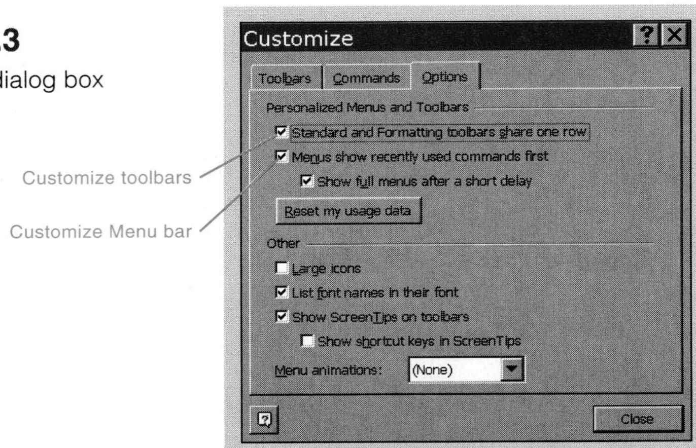

Customize toolbars

Customize Menu bar

4 SELECT: *Menus show recently used commands first* check box, so that no "✔" appears

5 SELECT: *Standard and Formatting toolbars share one row* check box, so that no "✔" appears

6 To proceed:
CLICK: Close command button
Your screen should now appear similar to Figure 1.4.

IMPORTANT: For the remainder of this learning guide, we assume that the adaptive menus feature has been disabled and that the Standard and Formatting toolbars are positioned on separate rows.

Figure 1.4

The Standard and Formatting toolbars are now positioned on separate rows

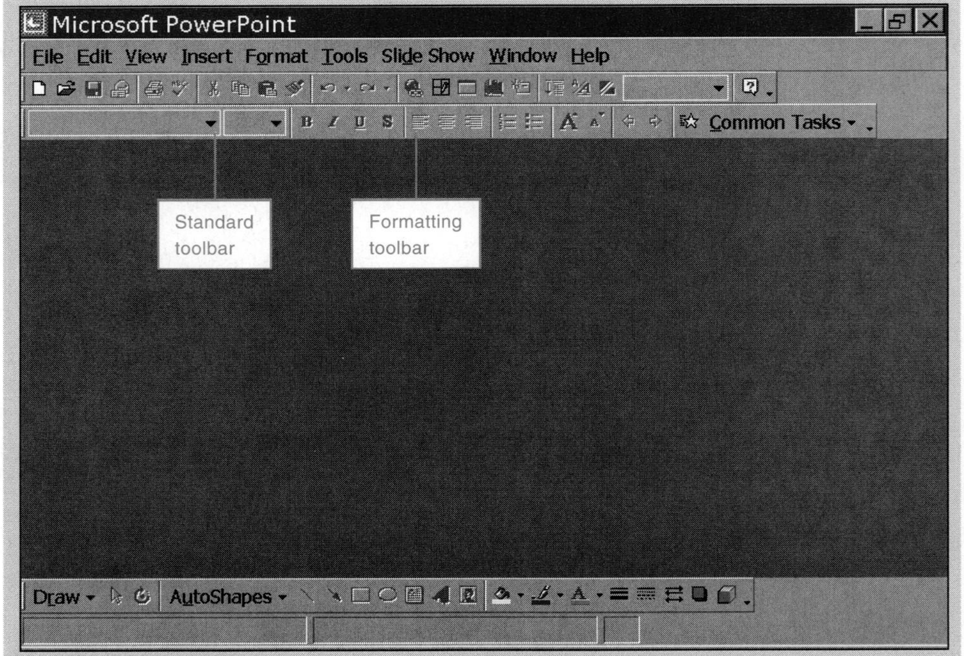

7 To display additional toolbars, you select the desired options from a right-click menu. For example:
RIGHT-CLICK: *any button* on the Standard toolbar
Notice that the Standard, Formatting, and Drawing options are currently selected, as illustrated by the check marks in the pop-up menu.

8 To display the Picture toolbar:
CHOOSE: Picture from the pop-up menu
You should see another toolbar appear in the application window.

9 To remove or hide the Picture toolbar:
RIGHT-CLICK: *any button on any toolbar*
CHOOSE: Picture
The toolbar disappears from the application window.

1.1 Self Check   What is an adaptive menu?

POWERPOINT

1.2 Creating a New Presentation

The **AutoContent Wizard** provides the quickest and easiest method for beginning a new presentation by providing content and design suggestions. AutoContent presentations, consisting of 5 to 10 slides each, are available on a range of topics. Once created, you simply edit the text of the presentation to meet your needs.

If you want suggestions on the design of your presentation, but not on its content, consider beginning a new presentation from a design template. A **design template** determines the look of your presentation by defining its color scheme, background, and use of fonts. If neither the AutoContent Wizard nor a design template sounds tempting, you can always start a presentation from scratch by clicking the New button ().

1.2.1 Creating a Presentation Using the AutoContent Wizard

FEATURE
If you're finding it difficult to organize and write down your thoughts, consider letting the AutoContent Wizard be your guide. After progressing through the Wizard's dialog boxes, you'll have a skeletal framework for building a complete presentation.

METHOD
1. To launch the AutoContent Wizard:
   CHOOSE: File, New
   CLICK: *General* tab
   DOUBLE-CLICK: AutoContent Wizard
2. To proceed through the AutoContent Wizard, responding to its questions:
   CLICK: Next command button
3. To complete the Wizard:
   CLICK: Finish command button

PRACTICE
You will now practice launching the AutoContent Wizard from the New dialog box.

Setup: Ensure that PowerPoint is loaded. If the PowerPoint startup dialog box is displayed, click its Cancel command button.

1 CHOOSE: File, New from the Menu bar
CLICK: *General* tab
DOUBLE-CLICK: AutoContent Wizard icon

2 The AutoContent Wizard is launched and presents the initial AutoContent Wizard screen. The left side of the dialog box shows the steps the wizard will go through in order to format the final presentation. To proceed to the next step, do the following:
CLICK: Next command button

3 In this step, you select the type of presentation you're going to give (Figure 1.5). When you click a category option button, a list of related presentations appears in the list box to the right.

Figure 1.5

Selecting a presentation type

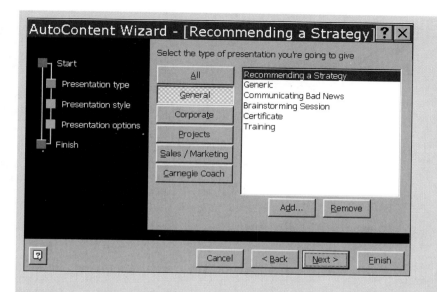

Do the following:
CLICK: Corporate button
SELECT: Company Meeting in the list box
CLICK: Next command button

4 You must now select an output option for the presentation:
SELECT: *On-screen presentation* option
CLICK: Next command button
Your screen should now appear similar to Figure 1.6.

Figure 1.6

Defining the opening slide

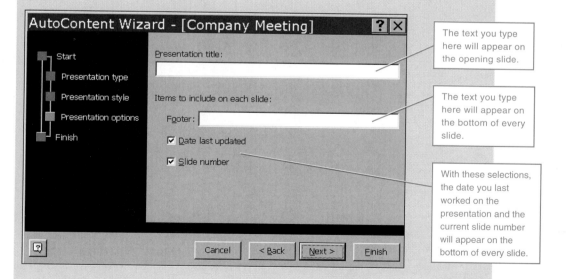

The text you type here will appear on the opening slide.

The text you type here will appear on the bottom of every slide.

With these selections, the date you last worked on the presentation and the current slide number will appear on the bottom of every slide.

5 In this step, you enter the information you want to appear on the opening slide of your presentation.
CLICK: in the *Presentation title* text box
TYPE: Effective Communication Skills

6 If you wish, you can review your selections by clicking the Back command button. Otherwise, do the following to proceed:
CLICK: Next command button
CLICK: Finish command button
At this point, as shown in Figure 1.7, the presentation is compiled with some content suggestions that you can edit to meet your needs. This view of your presentation is called **Normal view** and provides one place for building the different parts of your presentation. The **Outline pane** is used for typing text and rearranging your presentation. The **Slide pane** is used for seeing how your slide will look and for editing slides directly. The **Notes pane** provides a location for typing reminder notes and additional information that you want to share with your audience. We discuss switching views in lesson 1.2.5.

Figure 1.7

An AutoContent presentation

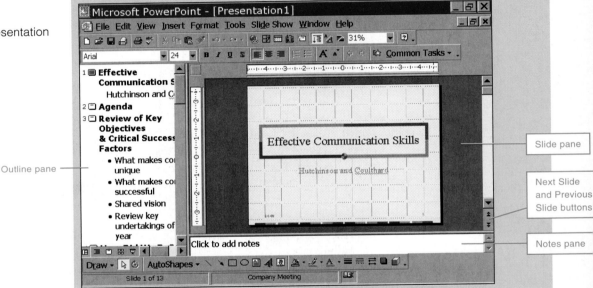

7 The Next Slide (▼) and Previous Slide (▲) buttons on the vertical scroll bar enable you to navigate through your presentation. To illustrate:
CLICK: Next Slide button (▼) to view the second slide
CLICK: Previous Slide button (▲) to view the first slide

8 Advance through the entire presentation using the Next Slide button (▼).

9 To close the presentation, without saving:
CHOOSE: File, Close
CLICK: No when asked whether you want to save the presentation

1.2.2 Creating a Presentation from a Design Template

FEATURE

One of the problems with the advent of presentation software programs like PowerPoint is that the presentation author has been hurled into the role of graphic designer. Many people who are skilled writers and content researchers find it difficult to take on these additional responsibilities. Fortunately, PowerPoint provides a selection of design templates that you can use to start new presentations.

METHOD

To start a new presentation from a design template:
1. CHOOSE: File, New
2. CLICK: *Design Templates* tab
3. DOUBLE-CLICK: a design template

PRACTICE

You will now practice applying design templates.

Setup: Ensure that PowerPoint is loaded and that no presentations are open.

1 Your first step is to display the New Presentation dialog box:
CHOOSE: File, New

2 To select a design template:
CLICK: *Design Templates* tab
The New Presentation dialog box should now appear.

3 To view the design templates in a list:
CLICK: List button (▦) in the dialog box

4 To display a preview of a design template, you click once on the template name.
CLICK: Citrus template
Your screen should now appear similar to Figure 1.8. (*Note:* On your computer, different design templates may appear in the list box.)

POWERPOINT

Figure 1.8

New Presentation dialog
box: *Design Templates* tab

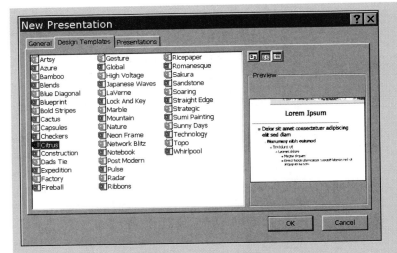

5 Let's open the "Citrus" design template:
DOUBLE-CLICK: Citrus
The New Slide dialog box should now appear (Figure 1.9). When
you add a new slide to a presentation, you will always be
prompted to select a slide type, called an **AutoLayout,** in the
New Slide dialog box. PowerPoint provides 24 AutoLayouts from
which you can choose.

Figure 1.9

New Slide dialog box

The Title Slide
AutoLayout is
currently
selected.

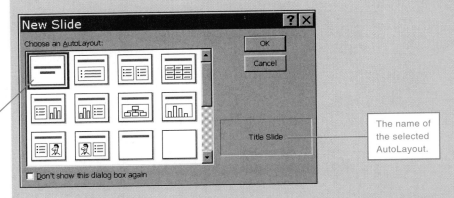

The name of
the selected
AutoLayout.

6 Let's create a title slide. Since the Title Slide AutoLayout is
already selected:
CLICK: OK command button
A new slide appears, complete with a background design (Citrus)
and areas, called *placeholders*, for entering a title and a subtitle.
Placeholders mark the location of slide objects and provide
instructions for editing them. Your screen should now appear
similar to Figure 1.10.

Figure 1.10

Citrus design template

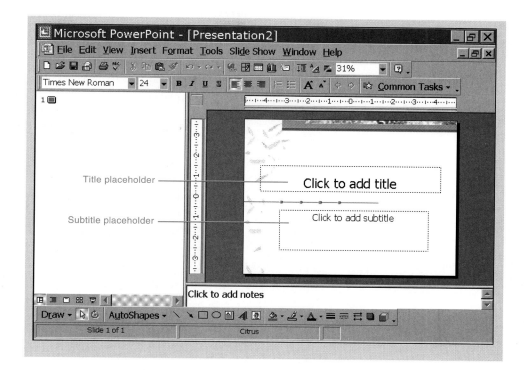

1.2.3 Adding Text

FEATURE

In most cases, the easiest way to add text to slides is to type it directly into a text placeholder in the Slide pane. If you type more text than can fit in the placeholder, PowerPoint's **AutoFit feature** will automatically resize the placeholder to accommodate the text. You can also insert text by typing in the Outline pane.

METHOD

To add text in the Slide pane:

CLICK: in a text placeholder and then begin typing

To add text in the Outline pane:

- CLICK: to the right of the slide number and icon to type title text
- PRESS: ⟮ENTER⟯ to insert a new slide or continue typing at the same heading level
- PRESS: ⟮TAB⟯ to begin typing at a demoted (lower) outline level
- PRESS: ⟮SHIFT⟯ + ⟮TAB⟯ to begin typing at a promoted (higher) outline level

PRACTICE
You will now practice adding text using the Slide and Outline panes.

Setup: Ensure that you've completed the previous lessons in this module and that a presentation based on the Citrus design template is open in the application window.

1 Let's practice using the Slide pane. To type text into the title placeholder:
CLICK: in the title placeholder, marked by the text "Click to add title"
The insertion point should be blinking in the title placeholder.

2 TYPE: Getting Started with PowerPoint
Notice that the title text appears in the Outline pane also.

3 To type text into the subtitle placeholder:
CLICK: in the subtitle placeholder, marked by "Click to add subtitle"

4 TYPE: By *your name*
Note that the subtitle text also appears in the Outline pane. Your screen should now appear similar to Figure 1.11.

Figure 1.11

Adding text

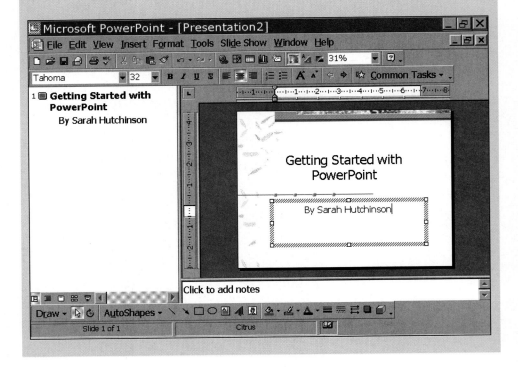

5 Now let's practice using the Outline pane. Let's edit the title text. In the Outline pane:
SELECT: the text "Getting Started with" by dragging with the mouse over the text
The selected text should be highlighted in reverse video.

6 TYPE: Introducing
The title should now read "Introducing PowerPoint" in both the Outline pane and the Slide pane.

7 CLICK: to the right of the subtitle text in the Outline pane

8 Let's see what happens when we press (ENTER).
PRESS: (ENTER)
In the Outline pane, the insertion point moved down to the next line in the subtitle.

9 TYPE: your school or business name
The subtitle now contains two lines of text.

10 PRESS: (ENTER)
In the Outline pane, the insertion point is now blinking on the third line of the subtitle.

11 To type at a promoted level:
PRESS: (SHIFT) + (TAB)
Since you're promoting the outline to the highest level, Power-Point added another slide and is waiting for you to insert a title. PowerPoint automatically inserted a slide that uses the Bulleted List AutoLayout.

12 Note that the insertion point is blinking to the right of the slide number and icon in the Outline pane.
TYPE: PowerPoint lets you create:
PRESS: (ENTER)
Note that PowerPoint inserted another slide.

13 In this step, you demote the outline level so that you can type a bulleted list on slide 2.
PRESS: (TAB) to demote the current outline level
TYPE: On-screen presentations
PRESS: (ENTER)
TYPE: Web presentations
PRESS: (ENTER)
TYPE: Overhead transparencies
PRESS: (ENTER)
TYPE: 35mm slides
Your screen should now appear similar to Figure 1.12.

POWERPOINT

Figure 1.12

Typing a bulleted
list in the Outline pane

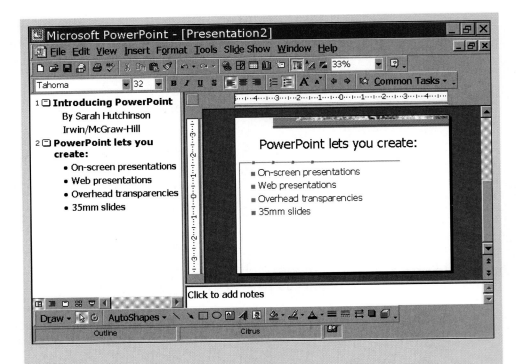

 As one final step, let's use the Slide pane to add an additional item to the bulleted list.
CLICK: to the right of the last bulleted item in the Slide pane
PRESS: `ENTER`
TYPE: `Audience handouts`
As you can see, the Outline pane and the Slide pane can be used interchangeably for entering and editing text.

1.2.4 Inserting and Deleting Slides

FEATURE
The most common method for inserting new slides involves clicking the New Slide button (□) on the Standard toolbar, however you can also insert slides while working in the Outline pane. New slides are inserted after the current, or displayed, slide. You can delete slides using the Menu bar or by selecting the slide in the Outline pane and pressing `DELETE`.

METHOD
- To insert a new slide:
  CLICK: New Slide button (⬚) on the Standard toolbar
  SELECT: an AutoLayout format
  PRESS: ENTER
- To delete an existing slide:
  CHOOSE: Edit, Delete Slide, or
  SELECT: the slide in the Outline panel and then press DELETE

PRACTICE
You will now practice inserting and deleting slides.

Setup: Ensure that you've completed the previous lessons in this module and that the "PowerPoint lets you create" slide is displaying in the Slide pane.

1 To insert a new slide after the current slide:
CLICK: New Slide button (⬚) on the Standard toolbar
SELECT: Text & Clip Art layout (located in the third row)
CLICK: OK command button
Your screen should appear similar to Figure 1.13. The presentation now includes three slides. Note that the Outline pane also includes three slide icons.

Figure 1.13

Inserting a new slide

To display an alternate slide in the Slide pane, click its icon in the Outline pane.

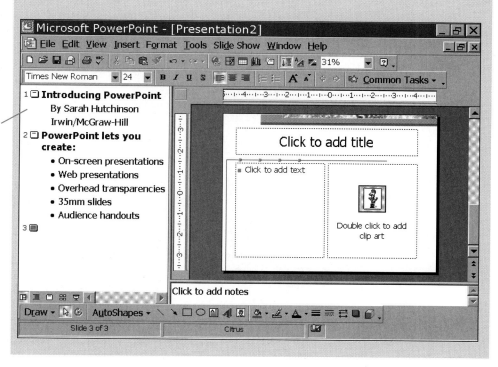

POWERPOINT

To delete the newly inserted third slide:
CHOOSE: Edit, Delete Slide
(*Note:* You could have also clicked the slide 3 icon in the Outline pane and then pressed DELETE.)

1.2.5 Switching PowerPoint Views

FEATURE
PowerPoint provides several ways to view a presentation to suit your preferred way of working. You switch views using the View command on the Menu bar or by clicking the View buttons located near the bottom-left corner of the application window. The active view of your presentation before being saved or closed becomes the default view when it is subsequently opened.

METHOD
- To switch views using the Menu bar:
  CHOOSE: View from the Menu bar
  CHOOSE: Normal, Slide Sorter, or Slide Show from the drop-down menu
- To switch views using the View buttons, located near the bottom-left corner of the application window:
  CLICK: Normal (▣), Outline (▤), Slide (▢), Slide Sorter (▦), or Slide Show (▽) button

PRACTICE
You will now practice switching views.

Setup: Ensure that you've completed the previous lessons in this module and that a two-slide presentation is displaying in the application window.

 In Normal view, as we described in lesson 1.2.1, you see the Outline pane, Slide pane, and Notes pane for the convenient editing of several parts of your presentation at once. You've been using Normal view until now in this chapter. To enlarge the Outline pane and reduce the size of the Slide and Notes pane:
CLICK: Outline View button (▤) in the bottom-left corner of the application window
Outline view, which displays the titles and main text of your presentation, is ideal for typing the text of your presentation and rearranging bulleted lists, paragraphs, and slides.

2 To enlarge the Slide pane, reduce the Outline pane, and remove the Notes pane:
CLICK: Slide View button (⬜) in the bottom-left of the application window
Slide view enlarges the Slide pane for easier viewing of the object placeholders. This mode is ideal for building a presentation by editing placeholders directly or fine-tuning the position of graphics.

3 To display the presentation in Slide Sorter view:
CHOOSE: View, Slide Sorter
Your screen should now appear similar to Figure 1.14. In **Slide Sorter view,** you view multiple slides at once using small thumbnail representations. Slide Sorter view gives you an immediate feeling for the continuity or flow of a presentation.

Figure 1.14
Slide Sorter view

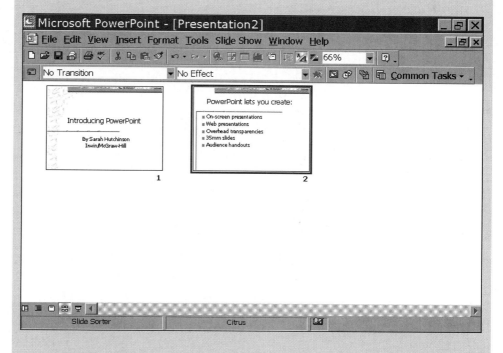

4 To view the presentation in Slide Show view:
CHOOSE: View, Slide Show
In **Slide Show view,** the presentation is displayed as an on-screen slide show, complete with transitions and special effects.

5 To proceed to the next slide in the presentation:
CLICK: left mouse button once
Your screen should now appear similar to Figure 1.15.

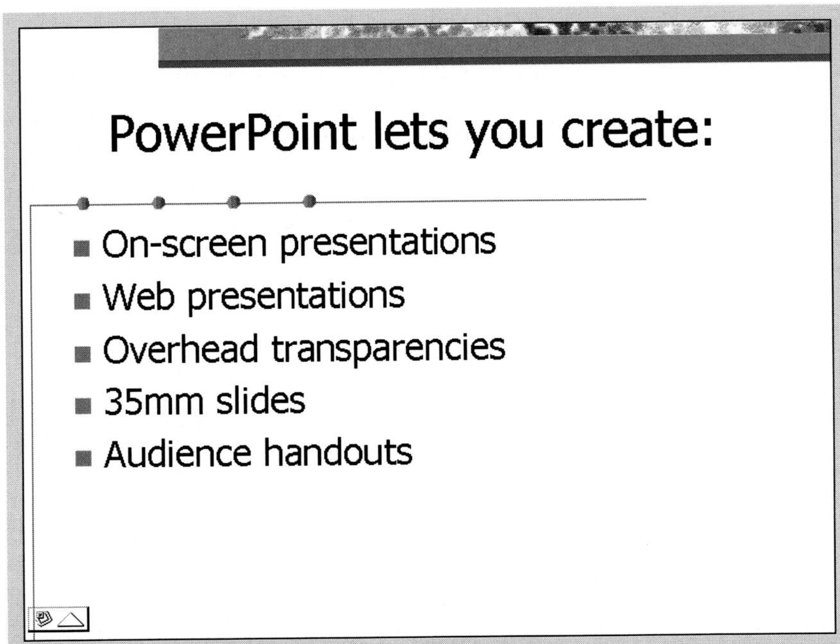

Figure 1.15

Slide Show view

PowerPoint lets you create:

- On-screen presentations
- Web presentations
- Overhead transparencies
- 35mm slides
- Audience handouts

6 The most common methods for controlling a presentation's display while in Slide Show view appear in Table 1.1. You can also use the right-click menu to display similar options for navigating through a presentation.

Table 1.1

Controlling a Slide
Show Presentation

Task Description	Keyboard and Mouse Methods
Go to the next slide	CLICK: left mouse button, or PRESS: PgDn, →, ↓, ENTER, or Spacebar
Go to the previous slide	PRESS: PgUp, ←, or ↑
Go to a specific slide	TYPE: *desired slide number*, and then PRESS: ENTER
Go to the first slide	PRESS: HOME
Go to the last slide	PRESS: END
Blank the screen to black	PRESS: b to blank screen to black PRESS: b again to unblank screen

| Blank the screen to white | PRESS: w to blank screen to white
PRESS: w again to unblank screen |
| Exit the slide show | PRESS: ESC |

To proceed to the next slide in the presentation:
CLICK: left mouse button once

7 To return to the previous slide using the keyboard:
PRESS: ⬆

8 To display the next slide using the keyboard:
PRESS: Spacebar

9 To exit Slide Show view:
PRESS: ESC

10 To return to Normal view:
CHOOSE: View, Normal

11 To close the presentation, without saving:
CHOOSE: File, Close
CLICK: No when asked whether you want to save the presentation

1.2 Self Check   What is the difference between Slide Sorter and Slide Show view?

1.3 Managing Files

Managing the presentations that you create is an important skill. When you are creating a presentation, it exists only in the computer's RAM (random access memory), which is highly volatile. In other words, if the power to your computer goes off, your presentation is lost. For safety and security, you need to save your presentation permanently to the local hard disk, a network drive, or a floppy diskette.

Saving your work to a named file on a disk is similar to placing it into a filing cabinet. For important presentations (ones that you cannot risk losing), you should save your work at least every 15 minutes, or whenever you're interrupted, to protect against an unexpected power outage or other catastrophe. When naming your presentation files, you can use up to 255 characters, including spaces, but it's wise to keep the length under 20 characters. Furthermore, you cannot use the following characters in naming your presentations:

$$\backslash \quad / \quad : \quad ; \quad * \quad ? \quad " \quad < \quad > \quad |$$

In the following lessons, you practice several file management procedures, including saving and closing presentations, and opening existing presentations.

Important: *In this guide, we refer to the files that have been created for you as the* **student data files.** *Depending on your computer or lab setup, these files may be located on a floppy diskette, in a folder on your hard disk, or on a network server. If necessary, ask your instructor or lab assistant where to find these data files. To download the Advantage Series' student data files from the Internet, visit McGraw-Hill's Information Technology Web site at:*

http://www.mhhe.com/it

You will also need to identify a personal storage location for the files that you create, modify, and save.

1.3.1 Saving and Closing

FEATURE
You can save the currently displayed presentation by updating an existing file on the disk, by creating a new file, or by selecting a new storage location. The File, Save command and the Save button (🖫) on the toolbar allow you to overwrite a disk file with the latest version of a presentation. The File, Save As command enables you to save a presentation to a new filename or storage location. When you are finished working with a presentation, ensure that you close the file to free up valuable RAM.

METHOD
- To save a presentation:
  CLICK: Save button (🖫), or
  CHOOSE: File, Save, or
  CHOOSE: File, Save As
- To close a presentation:
  CLICK: its Close button (☒), or
  CHOOSE: File, Close

PRACTICE

You will now practice saving and closing a presentation.

Setup: Ensure that PowerPoint is loaded. If the PowerPoint startup dialog box is displayed, click its Cancel command button. You will also need to identify a storage location for your personal document files. If you want to use a diskette, place it into the diskette drive now.

So that we have a presentation to save, let's create a quick Auto-Content presentation.
CHOOSE: File, New
CLICK: *General* tab
DOUBLE-CLICK: AutoContent Wizard
CLICK: Finish button
A presentation should now appear in the application window.

When you are working in a new presentation that has not yet been saved, PowerPoint displays the Save As dialog box (Figure 1.16), regardless of the method you choose to save the file. To demonstrate:
CLICK: Save button (🖫)
(*Note:* The filenames and directories that appear in your Save As dialog box may differ from those shown in Figure 1.16.) The **Places bar,** located along the left border of the dialog box, provides convenient access to commonly used storage locations.

Figure 1.16

Save As dialog box

Lists the files that you have most recently worked with

Lists files in PowerPoint's default working folder

Lists common desktop shortcuts

Lists shortcuts to your favorite files

Lists files and folders stored on your Intranet or Internet Web server

3 In the next few steps, you practice navigating your computer's disks. To begin, let's view a list of the files that you've worked with recently:
CLICK: History button (⊞) in the Places bar

4 To browse the files in your "My Documents" folder:
CLICK: My Documents button (⊞)

5 Let's browse the local hard disk:
CLICK: down arrow attached to the *Save in* drop-down list box
SELECT: Hard Disk C: (⊟)
(*Note:* Your hard drive may have a different name.) The list area displays the folders and files stored in the root directory of your local hard disk.

6 To drill down into one of the folders:
DOUBLE-CLICK: Program Files folder
(*Note:* If the Program Files folder isn't located on your local hard disk, select an alternate folder to open.) This folder contains the program files for several applications.

7 Let's drill down one step further:
DOUBLE-CLICK: Microsoft Office folder
This folder contains the Microsoft Office program files.

8 To return to the previous display:
CLICK: Back button (⊞) in the dialog box
(*Note:* The button is renamed "Program Files," since that is where you will end up once the button is clicked.)

9 To return to the "My Documents" display:
CLICK: Back button (⊞) twice
(*Hint:* You could have also clicked the My Documents button in the Places bar.)

10 Now, using either the Places bar or the *Save In* drop-down list box:
SELECT: *a storage location for your personal files*
(*Note:* In this guide, we save files to the My Documents folder.)

11 Next, you need to give the presentation file a unique name. Let's replace the existing name with one that is more descriptive. Do the following:
DOUBLE-CLICK: the *presentation name* appearing in the *File name* text box to select it
TYPE: Practice Presentation

12 To save your work:
CLICK: Save command button
Note that the presentation's name now appears in the Title bar.

13 In this step, let's insert a title on the first slide.
CLICK: the title placeholder
TYPE: Increasing Business Revenues

14 To save the revised presentation:
CLICK: Save button (⬛)
There are times when you may want to save an existing presentation under a different filename. For example, you may want to keep different versions of the same presentation on your disk. Or, you may want to use one presentation as a template for future presentations that are similar in style and format. To do this, you can retrieve the original presentation file, edit the information, and then save it again under a different name using the File, Save As command.

15 Let's close the presentation:
CHOOSE: File, Close

POWERPOINT

1.3.2 Opening an Existing Presentation

FEATURE
You use the Open dialog box to search for and retrieve existing presentations that are stored on your local hard disk, a floppy diskette, a network server, or on the Web. If you want to load PowerPoint and an existing presentation at the same time, you can use the Open Office Document command on the Start menu. Or, if you have recently used the presentation, you can try the Start, Documents command, which lists the 15 most recently used files.

METHOD
To open an existing presentation:
- CLICK: Open button (📰), or
- CHOOSE: File, Open

PRACTICE
You will now open an existing file that addresses the topic of buying a personal computer.

Setup: Ensure that you've completed the previous lesson and that no presentations are displaying. Also, you should know the storage location for the student data files.

1 To display the Open dialog box:
CLICK: Open button (📂)

2 Using the Places bar and the *Look in* drop-down list box, locate the folder containing the student data files. (*Note:* In this guide, we retrieve the student data files from a folder named "Student.")

3 To view additional information about each file:
CLICK: down arrow beside the Views button
CHOOSE: Details
Each presentation is presented on a single line with additional file information, such as its size, type, and date it was last modified, as shown in Figure 1.17.

Figure 1.17

Open dialog box in Details view

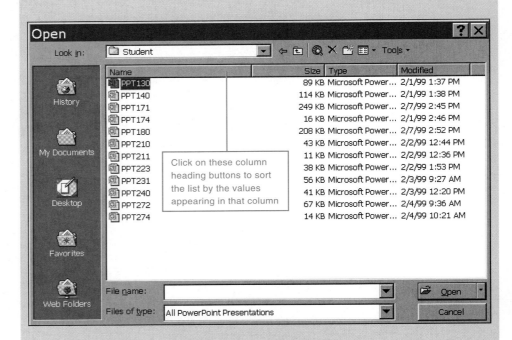

4 To alphabetically sort the list of files displayed in the Open dialog box:
CLICK: Name button in the column heading area

5 To sort the list by file size:
CLICK: Size button in the column heading area

6 To sort the list by when the file was last modified:
CLICK: Modified button

7 To return to a multicolumn list format:
CLICK: down arrow beside the Views button
CHOOSE: List

8 Let's open one of the presentations in the list area:
DOUBLE-CLICK: PPT130
The dialog box disappears and the presentation is loaded into the application window. (*Note:* The "PPT130" filename reflects that this presentation is used in module 1.3 of the PowerPoint learning guide.)

9 Close the presentation before proceeding.

In Addition	With the appropriate network connection, you can open and save PowerPoint
Storing and Retrieving	presentations on the Internet. In the Open or Save As dialog boxes, click the
Files on Web Servers	Web Folders button (🏠) in the Places bar or select an FTP Internet site from
	the *Look in* drop-down list. This feature allows you to share and update
	PowerPoint presentations with users from around the world.

1.3 Self Check   In the Save As dialog box, what is the Places bar used for?

1.4 Previewing and Printing

When you're satisfied with your presentation's appearance, you can send it to the printer. Most commonly, you will print a presentation for inclusion in a report or audience handout.

1.4.1 Previewing a Presentation in Black and White

FEATURE
Before printing to a noncolor printer, you may want to preview how your presentation's colors will convert to black, white, and shades of gray.

METHOD
CLICK: Grayscale Preview button (🔳) on the Standard toolbar

PRACTICE
You will now open a four-slide presentation and then preview it in black, white, and shades of gray.

POWERPOINT

Setup: Ensure that no presentations are open in the application window.

1 Open the PPT140 data file.

2 Before continuing, let's save the file using a new filename:
CHOOSE: File, Save As
TYPE: Chili

3 Using the *Save in* drop-down list box or the Places bar:
SELECT: *your storage location*
CLICK: Save command button

4 On your own, view the entire presentation using Slide Show view.

5 Let's preview the presentation using the Grayscale Preview button (▣).
CLICK: Grayscale Preview button (▣) on the Standard toolbar
Figure 1.18 shows the first slide of your presentation using a selection of grayscales.

Figure 1.18

Grayscale preview

6 To redisplay the presentation in color:
CLICK: Grayscale Preview button (▣)

1.4.2 Printing a Presentation

FEATURE

Whereas clicking the Print button (🖨) sends your presentation directly to the printer, choosing File, Print displays the Print dialog box for customizing one or more print options. For example, you can select what to print (audience handouts, notes pages, or your presentation's outline), whether you want to print your presentation using shades of gray or black and white, and how many copies to print.

METHOD

- To send a presentation directly to the printer:
  CLICK: Print button (🖨)
- To customize one or more print settings:
  CHOOSE: File, Print

PRACTICE

You will now send a presentation to the printer.

Setup: Ensure that you've completed the previous lesson and that the "Chili" presentation is open in the application window.

1 Let's send the "Chili" presentation to the printer. Do the following:
CHOOSE: File, Print
The dialog box displayed in Figure 1.19 appears. (*Note:* The quickest method for sending the current presentation to the printer is to click the Print button (🖨) on the Standard toolbar.)

POWERPOINT

Figure 1.19

Print dialog box

Specify how much of the
presentation to print.

Specify what to print.

Clear this check box to
print a color presentation.

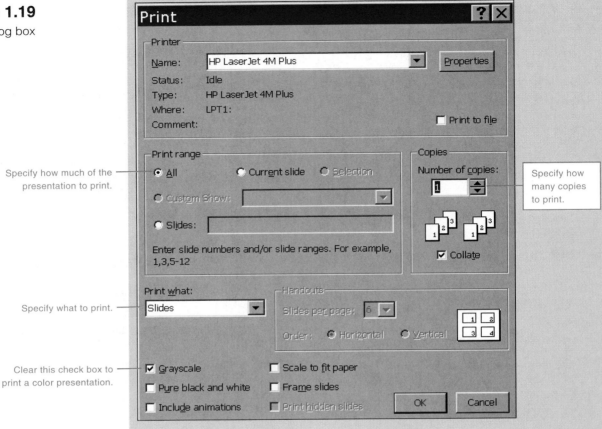

2   Note that "Slides" is the current selection in the *Print what* drop-down list. Let's see what the other options are:
CLICK: *Print what* drop-down arrow
Note the additional options of Handouts, Notes Pages, and Outline View.

3   To remove the drop-down list:
PRESS: ESC

4   If you do not have access to a printer, click the Cancel button. If you have a printer connected to your computer and want to print the presentation, do the following:
CLICK: OK command button
After a few moments, the presentation will appear at the printer.

5   Close the "Chili" presentation without saving the changes.

6   To exit Microsoft PowerPoint:
CHOOSE: File, Exit

1.5 Chapter Review

You have several options when starting a new presentation. For content and design suggestions, consider starting a presentation using the AutoContent Wizard. For design (and no content) suggestions, consider starting a presentation from a design template. You can also choose to begin a blank presentation, in which you ignore Power-Point's content and design suggestions altogether.

To assist you in the way you work, PowerPoint lets you customize how you view a presentation. By default, a presentation appears in Normal view, which displays the Outline pane, Slide pane, and Notes pane. Other view modes include Outline, Slide, Slide Sorter, and Slide Show view.

After inserting a new slide, you can add text to it by clicking a text placeholder or by typing in the Outline pane. Besides creating presentations, it is important to know how to execute common file management procedures including saving, opening, and closing presentations. This chapter concluded with instructions on how to preview a presentation in black and white and how to print.

1.5.1 Command Summary

Many of the commands and procedures appearing in this chapter are summarized in the following table.

Skill Set	To Perform This Task . . .	Do the Following . . .
Creating a presentation	Launch the AutoContent Wizard	CHOOSE: File, New CLICK: *General* tab DOUBLE-CLICK: AutoContent Wizard
	Choose a design template	CHOOSE: File, New CLICK: *Design Templates* tab DOUBLE-CLICK: a design template
	Begin a blank presentation	CLICK: New button (▢)
	Insert slides	CLICK: New Slide button (▣) DOUBLE-CLICK: an AutoLayout format

Continued

POWERPOINT

Skill Set	To Perform This Task . . .	Do the Following . . .
Creating a presentation (*cont.*)	Delete a selected slide	CHOOSE: Edit, Delete Slide
	Switch to Normal view	CHOOSE: View, Normal, or CLICK: Normal View button (⊡)
	Switch to Slide Sorter view	CHOOSE: View, Slide Sorter, or CLICK: Slide Sorter View button (⊞)
	Switch to Slide Show view	CHOOSE: View, Slide Show, or CLICK: Slide Show View button (▽)
	Switch to Outline view	CLICK: Outline View button (☰)
	Switch to Slide view	CLICK: Slide View button (▣)
Working with Text	Add text in Slide view	CLICK: in a text placeholder
	Add text in Outline view	CLICK: to the right of a slide icon in the Outline pane to type title text PRESS: ENTER to insert a new slide or continue typing at the same level PRESS: TAB to begin typing at a demoted (lower) level PRESS: SHIFT + TAB to begin typing at a promoted (higher) level
Managing Files	Save a presentation	CLICK: Save button (▣)
	Save as a new presentation	CHOOSE: File, Save As
	Close a presentation	CLICK: Close button (✕), or CHOOSE: File, Close
	Open an existing presentation	CLICK: Open button (🖫), or CHOOSE: File, Open

Continued

Skill Set	To Perform This Task . . .	Do the Following . . .
Creating Output	Print a presentation	CLICK: Print button (▣), or CHOOSE: File, Print
	Print a color presentation	CHOOSE: File, Print and then make sure that the *Grayscale* and *Black and White* check boxes aren't selected
	Print slides in a variety of formats	CHOOSE: File, Print SELECT: an option from the *Print what* drop-down list
	Preview a presentation using grayscale colors	CLICK: Grayscale Preview button (▣)

POWERPOINT

1.5.2 Key Terms

This section specifies page references for the key terms identified in this chapter. For a complete list of definitions, refer to the Glossary provided immediately after the Appendix in this learning guide.

application window, *p. 7*   Outline pane, *p. 12*

adaptive menus, *p. 8*   Outline view, *p. 22*

AutoFit feature, *p. 17*   placeholder, *p. 16*

AutoLayout, *p. 16*   Places bar, *p. 27*

AutoContent Wizard, *p. 11*   Slide pane, *p. 12*

design template, *p. 11*   Slide view, *p. 23*

Normal view, *p. 12*   Slide Show view, *p. 23*

Notes pane, *p. 12*   Slide Sorter view, *p. 23*

1.6 Review Questions

1.6.1 Short Answer

1. In Slide Show view, how do you proceed to the next slide?
2. Describe the procedure for inserting a new slide in a presentation.
3. How does starting a presentation from a design template differ from starting a presentation using the AutoContent Wizard?
4. How would you go about deleting the current slide?
5. What are the characteristics of Normal view?
6. What is an AutoLayout?
7. When opening a file, what is the History button used for?
8. What is the difference between choosing File, Print and clicking the Print button (🖨)?
9. What is the purpose of the PowerPoint's startup dialog box?
10. What happens when you click the New button (🗋)?

1.6.2 True/False

1. _F_   In Normal view, the Outline pane is larger than the Slide pane.
2. _F_   Placeholders are inserted on slides when you choose a slide layout.
3. _T_   Clicking the New button (🗋) starts a presentation from a design template.
4. _T_   In Slide Sorter view, thumbnail representations of your presentation appear.
5. _F_   To create a blank presentation, choose File, New.
6. _T_   It is possible to change the layout of a slide.
7. _T_   You can delete the current slide using the Menu bar or the Outline pane.
8. _T_   PowerPoint's AutoFit feature automatically resizes placeholders to accommodate typed text.
9. _F_   You can add text in both the Outline and Slide panes.
10. _T_   To close a presentation, choose File, Exit from the Menu bar.

POWERPOINT

1.6.3 Multiple Choice

1. Which of the following provides the best environment for creating a presentation?
   a. Normal view
   b. Slide Sorter view
   c. Slide Show view
   d. Outline view

2. Which of the following enables you to exit Slide Show view?
   a. View, Exit
   b. File, Close
   c. File, Exit
   d. ESC

3. In Slide Show view, which of the following displays the previous slide?
   a. PgUp
   b. ⬅
   c. ⬆
   d. All of the above

4. Which of the following provides design and content suggestions?
   a. design template
   b. AutoContent Wizard
   c. blank presentation
   d. Slide Show view

5. The New Slide dialog box provides:
   a. design suggestions
   b. AutoLayout options
   c. content suggestions
   d. All of the above

6. Which of the following marks the location of slide objects?
   a. HTML
   b. placeholders
   c. hyperlinks
   d. fonts

7. Which of the following must you choose when you insert a new slide?
   a. AutoContent Wizard
   b. AutoLayout option
   c. AutoFormat option
   d. None of the above

8. In Normal view, which of the following panes would you use to type in reminder notes?
   a. Slide pane
   b. Outline pane
   c. Notes pane
   d. None of the above

9. The Places bar is useful when _____.
   a. saving and opening
   b. formatting text
   c. inserting slides
   d. All of the above

10. In _____, your presentation displays with transitions and special effects.
    a. Slide view
    b. Outline view
    c. Normal view
    d. Slide Show view

1.7 Hands-On Projects

1.7.1 Outdoor Adventure Tours: Company Profile

This exercise practices opening an existing presentation and saving it to a new location, viewing the presentation using the Menu bar and View buttons, editing text, and deleting a slide.

1. Open the PPT171 presentation.
2. Save the presentation as "Outdoor" to your personal storage location. (*Hint:* Choose File, Save As.)
3. To view the presentation in Slide Sorter view:
   CHOOSE: View, Slide Sorter
4. To view the presentation in Slide Show view:
   CHOOSE: View, Slide Show
   CLICK: the left mouse button to advance through the entire presentation
5. To view the presentation in Normal view:
   CLICK: Normal View button (⊡) located near the bottom-left corner of the application window

6. CLICK: Previous Slide button (⊠) on the vertical scroll bar until slide 1 appears in the Slide pane

7. Using the Outline pane, let's change the text from "Go Wild!" to "Join us on the Wild Side!"
SELECT: the text "Go Wild!" on the first slide
TYPE: Join us on the Wild Side!

8. Using the Slide pane, let's edit the text on the second slide.
CLICK: Next Slide button (⊠) to display slide 2
SELECT: the word "adventure" in the first bulleted point
TYPE: outdoor
The item should now read "Specialists in outdoor vacations."

9. Let's delete the slide entitled "Special Group Rates."
CLICK: Next Slide button (⊠) on the vertical scroll bar until the fifth slide appears
CHOOSE: Edit, Delete Slide

10. Save the revised presentation and then print the presentation.

11. Close the "Outdoor" presentation.

1.7.2 Monashee Community College: Open House

In this exercise, you create a new presentation from a design template and add new slides.

1. To start a new presentation based on the "Artsy" design template, do the following:
CHOOSE: File, New command
CLICK: *Design Templates* tab
DOUBLE-CLICK: Artsy template
(*Note:* Select another suitable design template if "Artsy" isn't available).

2. Select the Title Slide layout for the first slide.

3. Let's add text to the slide.
TYPE: Computer Open House in the title placeholder
TYPE: Monashee Community College in the subtitle placeholder

4. To insert a new slide with a Bulleted List layout:
CLICK: New Slide button (⊠) on the Standard toolbar
SELECT: Bulleted List in the New Slide dialog box
CLICK: OK command button

5. To insert a title on the second slide:
TYPE: When? in the title placeholder

6. Type the following text in the bulleted list:
   `8:00 am – 6:00 pm`
   `Saturday, September 18, 1999`
7. Insert another new slide with a Bulleted List layout and then type `Where?` in the title placeholder.
8. Type the following text in the bulleted list:
   `Monashee Community College`
   `100 College Way`
   `Spokane, Washington`
9. Insert another new slide with a Bulleted List layout and then type `Why?` in the title placeholder.
10. Type the following text in the bulleted list:
    `Visit our new Computer Labs`
    `Hourly information sessions`
    `Computer course registration`
    `Free refreshments`
11. Save the presentation as "Monashee Open House" to your personal storage location.

1.7.3 Coldstream Corporation: Marketing Overview

In this exercise, you create a new presentation using the AutoContent Wizard, edit existing text, insert and delete slides, and switch views.

1. Launch the AutoContent Wizard using the File, New command.
2. Select the "Selecting a Product or Service" presentation from the "Sales/Marketing" category.
3. Select "On-screen presentation" as the output option.
4. Type `Coldstream Corporation` in the *Presentation title* text box.
5. Insert `Arena Proposal` in the *Footer* text box and then click the Finish command button to compile the presentation.
6. Edit the subtitle placeholder on the first slide to include the text `Prepared by:` followed by *your name*.
7. Delete slides 4 and 6.
8. Insert a slide that uses the Bulleted List layout after slide 2. (*Hint:* Display slide 2 in the Slide pane before inserting the slide.)

9. Edit the new slide by typing New Ways to Promote Business in the Title placeholder and Web-based services, Local advertising, and Door-to-door sales as bulleted items in the bulleted list placeholder.
10. Display the presentation in Slide Sorter view.
11. Save the presentation as "Coldstream Marketing" to your personal storage location.
12. Close the presentation.

1.7.4 Spiderman Web Marketing: Promotion

You will now open a previously created presentation and then edit, preview, and print the presentation.

1. Open the PPT174 presentation.
2. Save the presentation as "Spiderman" to your personal storage location.
3. Insert the text Selling Your Product on the World Wide Web in the subtitle placeholder of the first slide.
4. Insert a new slide that uses the Bulleted List layout after the first slide. Type Who Uses the WWW? in the title placeholder and the following text in the bulleted list:
Gender
Age
Education
Nationality
5. After the third slide, add a new slide with a bulleted list layout. Enter Further Benefits in the title placeholder. Type the following text in the bulleted list:
Easily updated
Customer interaction
Text, color, movement, sounds and music
Online transactions
6. Preview the presentation in shades of gray and then redisplay the presentation in color.
7. Save the revised presentation.
8. Print and then close the presentation.

1.7.5 On Your Own: Hobby

Using one of PowerPoint's design templates, create a new PowerPoint presentation on a topic or hobby that interests you. Your presentation should consist of one Title Slide followed by three Bulleted List Slides. The first slide should include the name of your hobby and your name. Suggestions for the following slides are (a) Why do I like my hobby?, (b) How to do my hobby, and (c) What does my hobby involve? Save your presentation as "Hobby" to your personal storage location.

1.7.6 On Your Own: Vacation

Create a presentation that tries to convince your audience (a relative, business associate, or other individual) why you need a vacation. Use your experience with PowerPoint to make the most compelling case possible. When you're finished, save the presentation as "Vacation" to your personal storage location and then print the presentation.

1.8 Case Problems: Tristar Development

After completing Chapter 1, Tina is eager to view her nephew's presentation and provide him with some feedback. Then she will edit the presentation and add several new slides. Finally, she will create a new presentation for her client, *Union Pipeline Limited*.

In the following case problems, assume the role of Tina and perform the same steps that she identifies. You may want to re-read the chapter opening before proceeding.

1. Tina opens her nephew's PowerPoint presentation entitled PPT180. She saves the presentation as "Budgies" to her personal storage location. Tina first uses the Slide Sorter view to preview Kenyon's presentation. Amazed at her quick progress in Power-Point, she practices using the Normal, Outline, and Slide views. Tina chuckles at the animations while using the Slide Show view. After closing the presentation, she is ready to respond to Kenyon's e-mail by answering the questions in his "Budgie Test." Tina closes the presentation and sends Kenyon the following e-mail:
    Dear Kenyon, I love your presentation! I learned a lot about budgies and here are my answers for your "Budgie Test".

2. Tina decides to use Kenyon's presentation for practice with adding and modifying slides. She first saves a copy of Kenyon's presentation as "Kenyon" to her personal storage location. After the first slide, Tina adds a new slide with a Title Slide layout. She enters **Approved by Tina Pusch** in the title place-holder, **Public Relations Coordinator** on the first line of the subtitle placeholder, and **Tristar Development** on the second line. Tina then saves the revised presentation.

3. Tina continues working on the "Kenyon" presentation, chang-ing the appearance of text and bullets. She adds a new slide before the final slide of the presentation. Using the Bulleted List layout, she types **Keep your Budgie away from:** in the title placeholder. In the bulleted list placeholder she types the following text:

    *   **Hungry cats**
    *   **Open windows**
    *   **Hot stoves**
    *   **Curious alligators!**

    Tina saves the revised presentation as "Kenyon Update" to her personal storage location and then prints and closes the presen-tation.

4. With an afternoon deadline quickly approaching, Tina begins working on a PowerPoint presentation for her client, *Union Pipeline Limited*. Using the AutoContent Wizard, she selects "Reporting Progress or Status" from the "Projects" category. She adds **Union Pipeline Limited** to the title placeholder. She then selects any existing text in the subtitle placeholder and types **Jonathon C. Union President and CEO**.

POWERPOINT

As Tina previews the Union Pipeline presentation in Normal and Slide Show views, she receives an important telephone call from Mr. Jonathon Union, the president of the company. He requests that she print an outline of the presentation and then fax it to him. Tina assures Mr. Union that she can immediately complete his request. After hanging up the telephone, Tina chooses File, Print and then selects Outline View from the *Print what* drop-down list. Relieved that she has completed her required tasks, she saves the presentation as "Union Status" before exiting PowerPoint.

Notes

Notes

Notes

Notes

MICROSOFT POWERPOINT 2000
Developing a Presentation

CHAPTER
TWO

Chapter Outline

Learning Objectives

After reading this chapter, you will be able to:

- Insert slides from other presentations and change slide order

- Apply different slide layouts and design templates

- Insert clip art, pictures, graphs, and organization charts

- Start and run slide shows

Case Study   Snowmelt Hydrology Research

Natasha Newman is a graduate student who is preparing to defend her master's thesis. Her topic, Snowmelt Hydrology Research, involves data that she has collected from the Arctic region. Natasha has experience creating text-based presentations, but would like to present her data in a more interesting format using graphs, organization charts, and photographs.

In this chapter, you and Natasha learn how to change a presentation to meet your needs, embellish a presentation with graphs, organization charts, and pictures, and deliver online presentations.

2.1 Managing Existing Slides

Instead of reinventing the wheel each time you need to create a presentation, PowerPoint makes it easy to reuse slides that you've created previously. Although you can copy and paste slides in Slide Sorter view, the more efficient method involves using the Slide Finder tool. In the following lessons, we describe how to use the Slide Finder tool and how to reorder slides.

2.1.1 Inserting Slides from Other Presentations

FEATURE
The **Slide Finder** tool shows the contents of presentations using slide snapshots. You then select the slides you want to insert in your presentation.

METHOD
1. CHOOSE: Insert, Slides From Files
2. CLICK: Browse button and then locate the presentation you want to insert slides from
3. DOUBLE-CLICK: the presentation you located in the previous step
   CLICK: Display
4. SELECT: one or more slides by clicking them
5. CLICK: Insert to insert a selection of slides, or
   CLICK: Insert All to insert all of a presentation's slides

PRACTICE

You will now open an existing presentation and then add slides to it from another presentation.

Setup: Ensure that no presentations are open in the application window.

1 Open the PPT210 presentation.

2 Before continuing, save the presentation as "Wireless" to your personal storage location. This presentation contains two slides.

3 In the next few steps, you're going to insert slides from another presentation in the "Wireless" presentation. New slides are inserted after the current slide. Let's add a new slide after the second slide in the presentation. To view the second slide:
CLICK: Next Slide (⬇) on the vertical scroll bar
The inserted slides will now be inserted after the second slide.

4 To insert slides from the PPT211 presentation in the current presentation:
CHOOSE: Insert, Slides From Files
The Slide Finder dialog box should now appear, as shown in Figure 2.1.

Figure 2.1

Slide Finder dialog box

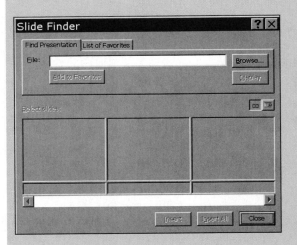

5 To locate the PPT211 student file:
CLICK: Browse command button

6 Use the *Look in* drop-down list or the Places bar to locate the PPT211 file.

7 DOUBLE-CLICK: PPT211 file
CLICK: Display command button to reveal the slides in the Slide Finder dialog box
Your screen should now appear similar to Figure 2.2.

Figure 2.2

Displaying slides in the Slide Finder dialog box

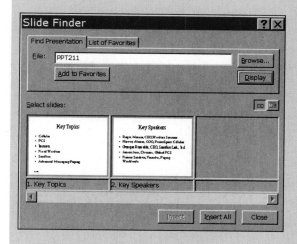

8 To insert the entire PPT211 presentation:
CLICK: Insert All command button

9 To close the Slide Finder dialog box:
CLICK: Close command button
The presentation now contains four slides. Note that the inserted slides adopted the same design as the first two slides.

10 Save the revised presentation.

2.1.2 Changing Slide Order

FEATURE
Once inserted in a presentation, it's easy to reorder slides in both the Outline pane and in Slide Sorter view. At the heart of the operation is a simple drag and drop.

METHOD
- To reorder slides in the Outline pane:
  DRAG: slide icon up or down to a new location
- To reorder slides in Slide Sorter view:
  DRAG: a slide to a new location

PRACTICE
You will now practice reordering slides.

POWERPOINT

Setup: Ensure that you've completed the previous lesson and that the "Wireless" presentation is displaying in Normal view.

1   Using the Outline pane, let's move slide 4 so that it is positioned before slide 3. To begin, locate the slide 4 icon in the Outline pane.

2   Let's see what happens when we click the slide 4 icon.
CLICK: slide 4 icon
Note that the slide's title and bulleted items are selected.

3   Your current objective is to drag the slide 4 icon upward in the Outline pane so that it is positioned above slide 3. As you drag the icon, the slide's title and bulleted items will move with it. A narrow horizontal bar will mark where the slide will be inserted when you release the mouse button.
DRAG: the slide 4 icon upward until the horizontal bar is one line above the slide 3 icon and title (Key Topics)
Your screen should now appear similar to Figure 2.3.

Figure 2.3

Reordering slides in the Outline pane

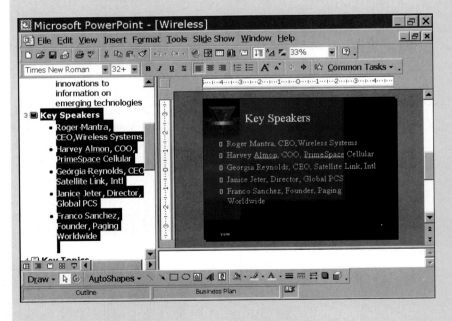

4   Now, let's practice changing slide order in Slide Sorter view. To begin:
CHOOSE: View, Slide Sorter

5 As you drag a slide in Slide Sorter view, a narrow vertical bar will mark where the slide will be inserted when you release the mouse button.
DRAG: the slide 3 thumbnail to the right of slide 4
The presentation has now been returned to its original order.

6 Save and then close the "Wireless" presentation.

2.1 Self Check   What is the the Slide Finder tool used for?

2.2   Changing Slide Layout and Design

The look of your presentation is determined by several factors including the current design template and slide layouts. In this module, we explore procedures for changing the layout and design of your presentations to suit your specific requirements and preferences.

2.2.1   Applying a Different Layout

FEATURE
You may find that an existing slide layout doesn't meet your needs. For example, in addition to your bulleted list placeholder, you may decide that you need a graph placeholder. In this case, you will want to change the existing slide layout to meet your new requirements.

METHOD
1.   CHOOSE: Format, Slide Layout
2.   DOUBLE-CLICK: an AutoLayout format

PRACTICE
You will now begin a presentation for a class project on current trends in technology. In the process you will practice changing slide layouts.

Setup: Ensure that no presentations are open in the application window.

1 To create a new presentation:
CHOOSE: File, New

2 To select a design template:
CLICK: *Design Templates* tab
DOUBLE-CLICK: Technology

3 In the New Slide dialog box, the Title Slide layout is already selected. To accept this selection:
CLICK: OK command button

4 To insert text in the title placeholder:
CLICK: the title placeholder
TYPE: CURRENT TRENDS

5 To insert text in the subtitle placeholder:
CLICK: the subtitle placeholder
TYPE: By
PRESS: ENTER
TYPE: Your Name
Your screen should now appear similar to Figure 2.4.

Figure 2.4

This slide uses the Title Slide layout

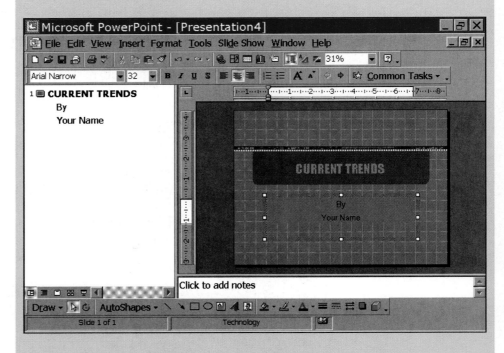

6 Let's add a second slide to the presentation.
CLICK: New Slide button (⬚) on the Standard toolbar

7 SELECT: Text & Chart (located in the second row, first column)
CLICK: OK command button
The inserted slide now includes placeholders for a title, bulleted list, and graph.

8 To add a title to the slide:
CLICK: title placeholder
TYPE: The Leading Trends

9 To add content to the slide:
CLICK: bulleted list placeholder (located on the left side of the slide)
TYPE: Connectivity
PRESS: ENTER
TYPE: Interactivity
PRESS: ENTER
TYPE: Online Access
Your screen should now appear similar to Figure 2.5.

Figure 2.5
This slide uses the
Text & Chart layout

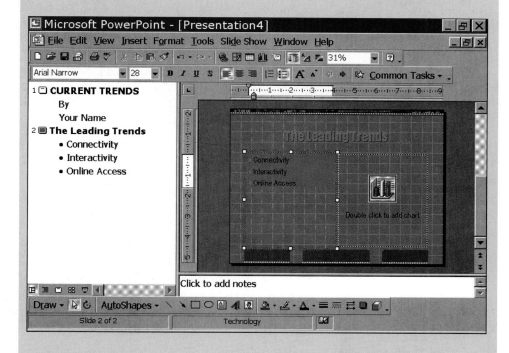

10 To change the layout of the second slide from the "Text & Chart" layout to the Bulleted List layout:
CHOOSE: Format, Slide Layout
CLICK: Bulleted List layout (located in the first row, second column)
CLICK: Apply command button
The slide was changed to conform to the Bulleted List layout. The text in the bulleted list appears larger and the graph placeholder no longer appears.

11 Save the presentation as "Current Trends" to your personal storage location.

2.2.2 Modifying an Existing Layout

FEATURE

Just about anything you place on a slide, such as text, a table, clip art, a graph, or a movie, is an *object*. As described in Chapter 1, *placeholders* mark the location of slide objects and provide instructions for editing them. When you choose a layout for a new or existing slide, PowerPoint inserts an arranged group of placeholders on the slide. You can move, resize, and delete object placeholders to suit your needs.

METHOD

- Select an object by positioning the mouse pointer over the object's placeholder until a four-headed arrow (✛) appears and then click.
- Move a selected object by dragging.
- Resize a selected object by dragging its sizing handles.
- Delete a selected object by pressing DELETE.

PRACTICE

You will now practice editing slide objects.

Setup: Ensure that you've completed the previous lesson in this module and that slide 2 in the "Current Trends" presentation is displaying in the application window.

1 Visually, the bulleted items are positioned too close to the left edge of the slide. Let's practice resizing the bulleted list placeholder and moving it to the right. To select the placeholder:
CLICK: in the bulleted list placeholder, near one of the bulleted items
The object should be surrounded with **sizing handles** (tiny boxes surrounding the object).

2 When you position the mouse pointer over a sizing handle, the pointer will change to a double-headed arrow. To resize the placeholder:
DRAG: the sizing handle in the bottom-right corner inward about two inches
(*Hint:* Use the slide ruler as your guide.)

3 To move the placeholder to the right, position the mouse pointer over one of the placeholder borders until a four-headed arrow (✛) appears.

4 DRAG: the placeholder to the right about 1.5 inches
Your screen should now appear similar to Figure 2.6.

Figure 2.6

The bulleted list placeholder
was resized and moved

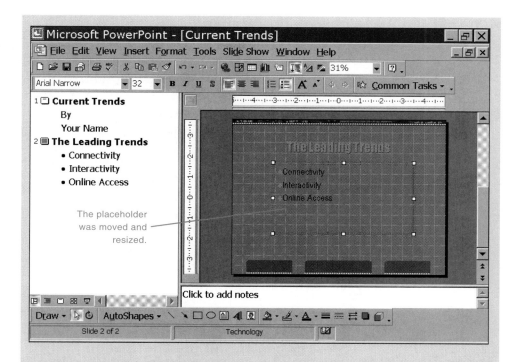

POWERPOINT

5 The placeholder should still be selected. To practice deleting the placeholder:
PRESS: **DELETE**
The contents of the placeholder are now deleted. To delete the placeholder itself:
PRESS: **DELETE** again

6 To undo the two previous deletions:
PRESS: the curved part of the Undo button (↶▾) twice

7 Save the revised presentation.

2.2.3 Changing an Existing Design Template

FEATURE
You learned how to create a new presentation from a design template in Chapter 1. Design templates determine what colors and text fonts are used in a presentation and the position of placeholders and other objects. By applying a design template to your presentation, you help give your presentation's slides a consistent look. You can apply one of PowerPoint's preset design templates or apply a design template from an existing presentation.

METHOD
- To apply one of PowerPoint's preset design templates:
  CHOOSE: Format, Apply Design Template
  DOUBLE-CLICK: a design template
- To apply a design template from an existing presentation:
  CHOOSE: Format, Apply Design Template
  CHOOSE: Presentations and Shows from the *Files of type* drop-down list
  DOUBLE-CLICK: a presentation file

PRACTICE
You will now practice applying design templates.

Setup: Ensure that you've completed the previous lessons in this module and that the "Current Trends" presentation is open.

1 Let's apply a design template to this presentation from a presentation named PPT223. To begin:
CHOOSE: Format, Apply Design Template
The contents of the Presentation Designs folder on your hard disk should appear, listing the design templates provided by PowerPoint.

2 To select a presentation file, rather than one of PowerPoint's template files:
CHOOSE: Presentations and Shows from the *Files of type* drop-down list

3 Using the *Look in* drop-down list or the Places bar, navigate to where your student files are stored.

4 DOUBLE-CLICK: PPT223
The design template used in the PPT223 presentation has now been applied to the current presentation. Your screen should now appear similar to Figure 2.7.

Figure 2.7

This design template was applied from the PPT223 presentation

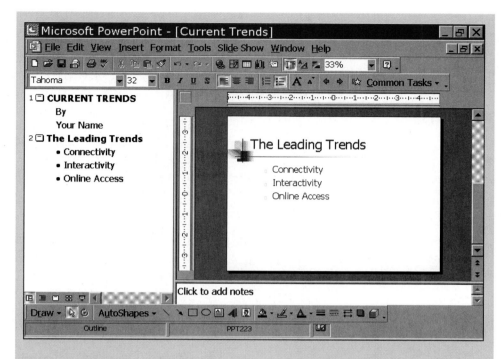

POWERPOINT

5 Now, let's apply one of PowerPoint's design templates to the presentation.
CHOOSE: Format, Apply Design Template

6 The templates in the Presentation Designs folder should be listed in the dialog box.
DOUBLE-CLICK: Factory
PowerPoint's "Factory" design template was applied to the presentation.

7 Save and then close the presentation.

2.2 Self Check What is the procedure for moving and resizing object placeholders?

2.3 Inserting Graphics Objects

A picture is worth a thousand words! Although this phrase is overused, its truth is undeniable. Graphics add personality to your presentations and often convey information more efficiently than text alone. In this module, you learn how to embellish your presentations with clip art and pictures, graphs, and organization charts.

2.3.1 Inserting Clip Art

FEATURE

The **Microsoft Clip Gallery** provides access to numerous images for inclusion in your presentations. **Clip art images** are computer graphics or pictures that you can insert into your documents, usually without having to pay royalties or licensing fees to the artist or designer. To make it easier for you to find that perfect image for conveying your message, clips are organized by category and you can search for clips based on typed keywords.

METHOD

Several methods exist for opening the Clip Gallery:
- DOUBLE-CLICK: a clip art placeholder, or
- CLICK: Insert Clip Art button ([⬚]) on the Drawing toolbar, or
- CHOOSE: Insert, Picture, Clip Art, or
- CHOOSE: Insert, Object and then double-click Microsoft Clip Gallery

To insert a clip:
1. CLICK: the clip you want to insert
2. CLICK: Insert clip button ([⬚]) on the shortcut menu

PRACTICE

You will now open a short presentation that currently contains three slides. Your objective is to locate clips for slides 1 and 3 of the presentation.

Setup: Ensure that no presentations are open in the application window.

1 Open the PPT231 data file.

2 Save the presentation as "PC Seminar" to your personal storage location.

3 In the remainder of this module, you won't be using the Outline pane. Therefore, to increase the size of the slide for more convenient editing, do the following:
CLICK: Slide view button ([⬚]) at the bottom of the Outline pane
Your screen should now appear similar to Figure 2.8. A computer-related graphic would greatly enhance this first slide. Let's use the Clip Gallery to locate an image.

Figure 2.8

"PC Seminar" presentation

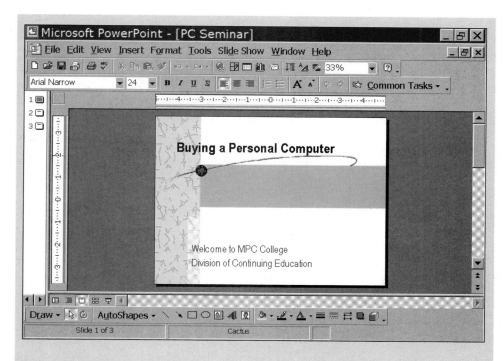

4 To locate an image clip for the first slide:
CHOOSE: Insert, Picture, Clip Art
The Insert ClipArt window should now appear.

5 To maximize the Insert ClipArt window
CLICK: the window's Maximize button (□)
Your screen should now appear similar to Figure 2.9.

Figure 2.9

Maximized Insert ClipArt
window

Clicking the Clips Online
button connects you to *Clip
Gallery Live*, a Web site
where you can find, preview,
and download additional
clips.

Categories of clips

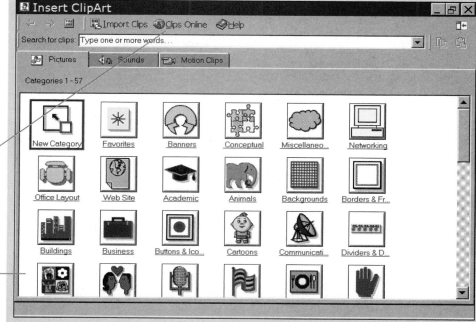

All the underlined words and phrases represent clip art categories. To display the contents of a category, you simply click the category name. To illustrate:
CLICK: Animals category
Your screen should now appear similar to Figure 2.10. (*Note:* Alternate clips may be available on your computer.)

Figure 2.10

Animals ClipArt
category

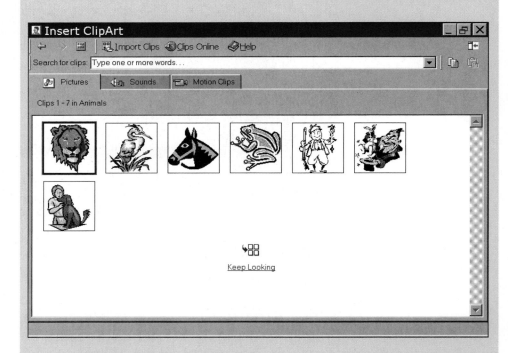

To return to the previous list of categories:
CLICK: Back button (⬅) on the toolbar

Let's locate a computer-related image based on a typed keyword.
CLICK: in the *Search for clips* text box
The existing text should be selected.
TYPE: computer
PRESS: ENTER
Your screen should now appear similar to Figure 2.11.

Figure 2.11

Search results for computer-related image clips

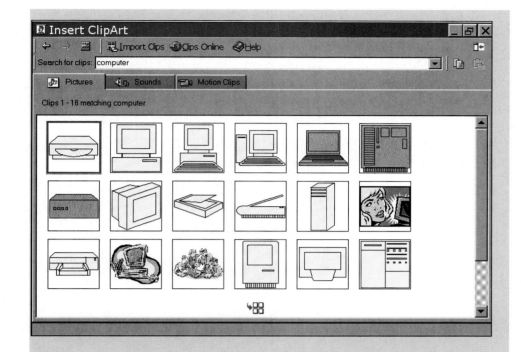

9 Practice pointing with the mouse at the different clips in the Clip Gallery window. Note that for each clip a yellow pop-up description appears detailing the name, dimension, and file type of the image.

10 When you click an image, a pop-up menu will appear. To illustrate:
CLICK: "computers" graphic (shown below)
The clip art image and associated pop-up menu appear below:

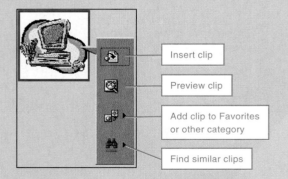

11 To insert the clip:
CLICK: Insert clip button (⬛)
Although the clip was inserted in your presentation, you won't be able to see it until you minimize or close the Insert ClipArt dialog box.

To close the dialog box:
CLICK: the window's Close button ([x])
Your screen should now appear similar to Figure 2.12. Notice that the Picture toolbar appears for changing the characteristics of the selected image.

Figure 2.12

Inserting a clip art image

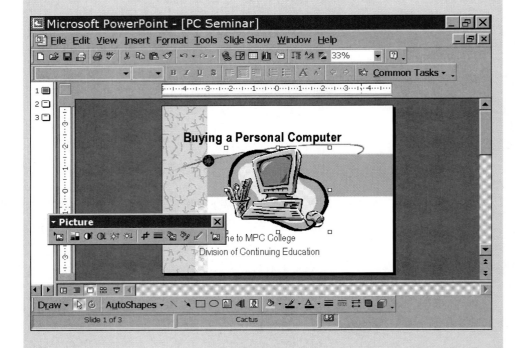

Since we're not going to use the Picture toolbar in this module, let's close it.
CLICK: the Picture toolbar's Close button ([x])
After you insert clip art and other graphics objects, you will often need to move, resize, or otherwise format them to fit the specific needs of your document. The methods for moving and resizing graphics objects are the same as for manipulating place-holders, a topic we discussed earlier in lesson 2.2.2. Since the graphic is somewhat large, you resize the image in the next step.

Resize and move the image so that your screen appears similar to Figure 2.13.

Figure 2.13

Moving and resizing a clip art image

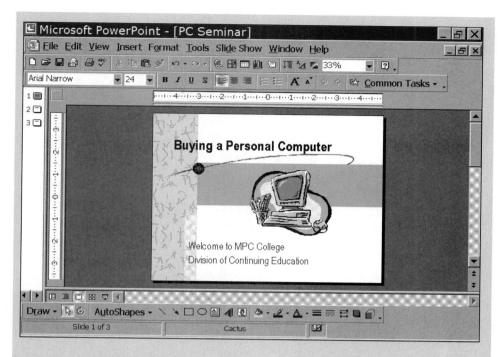

15 Let's insert another image on slide 3 of this presentation, but this time let's use the clip art placeholder. To display slide 3:
PRESS: Next Slide button (⬇) twice

16 To insert an image on this slide:
DOUBLE-CLICK: clip art placeholder

17 On your own, search for the clip pictured in Figure 2.14 and then insert it on the slide. (*Note:* If the clip pictured in Figure 2.14 isn't available, search for an alternate clip.) Move and resize the image as necessary.

Figure 2.14

Using the clip art placeholder

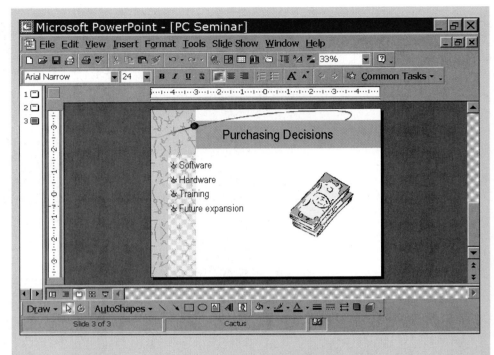

18 To select an alternate clip image for the current slide, do the following:
SELECT: the clip image
PRESS: `DELETE`
DOUBLE-CLICK: the clip art placeholder

19 On your own, search for an alternate clip for the current slide. Move and resize the image as necessary.

20 Save and then close the revised presentation.

2.3.2 Inserting Pictures

FEATURE

In PowerPoint, you can embellish your presentations with images from a variety of sources. To insert a picture from a file, choose Insert, Picture, From File from the menu and then double-click the file you want to insert.

METHOD
1. CHOOSE: Insert, Picture, From File
2. SELECT: the desired disk drive and filename
   CLICK: OK command button

PRACTICE

You will now practice inserting a picture object from a file.

Setup: Ensure that no presentations are open in the application window.

1 To begin a blank presentation:
CLICK: New button (⬚)
The New Slide dialog box appears.

2 DOUBLE-CLICK: Title Only layout (located in the third row, third column)

3 To increase the size of the slide for convenient editing:
CLICK: Slide view button (⬚) at the bottom of the Outline pane

4 CLICK: the title placeholder
TYPE: Two Boys

5 To insert a photograph named PPT232 from the student files location:
CHOOSE: Insert, Picture, From File
SELECT: *the location of your student files*
SELECT: PPT232 from the list box
CLICK: Insert command button
The picture is inserted on the slide and appears selected. Also, the Picture toolbar appears.

6 Move and resize the picture so that the slide appears similar to Figure 2.15. (*Note:* If the Picture toolbar is displaying, click its Close button (⬚).)

POWERPOINT

Figure 2.15

Inserting a picture from a file

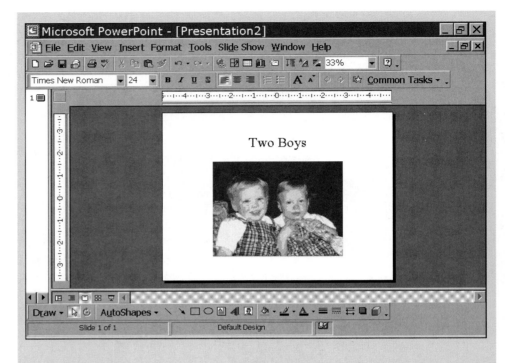

7 Save the presentation as "Two Boys" to your personal storage location.

8 Close the presentation.

2.3.3 Inserting Graphs

FEATURE

The **Microsoft Graph** mini-app helps you produce great-looking charts and graphs right from within PowerPoint! Graph does not replace a full-featured spreadsheet application like Microsoft Excel, but it does provide a more convenient tool for embedding simple charts into presentations.

METHOD

The following methods can be used to launch Microsoft Graph:

- CLICK: Insert Chart button (⬛) on the Standard toolbar, or
- DOUBLE-CLICK: graph placeholder, or
- CHOOSE: Insert, Chart from the menu, or
- CHOOSE: Insert, Object and then select Microsoft Graph

To edit an inserted graph:
DOUBLE-CLICK: the graph object

POWERPOINT

PRACTICE

You will now insert a graph on a slide by editing a graph placeholder.

Setup: Ensure that no presentations are open in the application window.

1 To begin a blank presentation:
CLICK: New button (☐)
The New Slide dialog box appears.

2 DOUBLE-CLICK: Chart layout (located in the second row, fourth column)

3 To increase the size of the slide for easy editing:
CLICK: Slide view button (☐) at the bottom of the Outline panel

4 CLICK: the title placeholder
TYPE: Grading Formula

5 To insert a graph:
DOUBLE-CLICK: the chart placeholder
The Graph datasheet appears in a separate window with sample information. Similar to using an electronic spreadsheet, you add and edit data in the datasheet that you want to plot on a graph. Figure 2.16 shows the datasheet as it first appears and how it will look after you edit it.

Figure 2.16

Editing the datasheet

Before

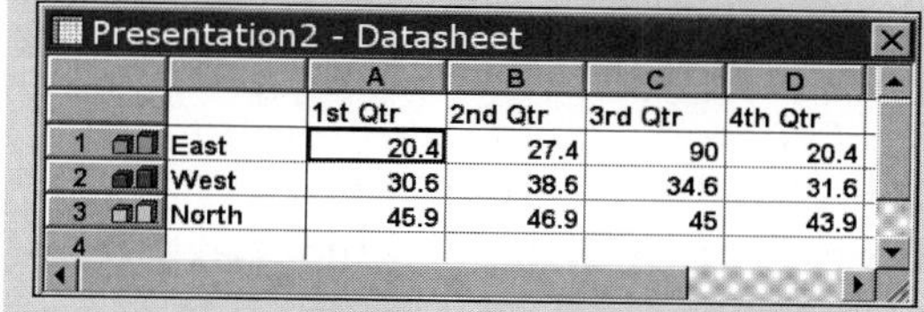

Presentation2 - Datasheet		A	B	C	D	
		1st Qtr	2nd Qtr	3rd Qtr	4th Qtr	
1	East	20.4	27.4	90	20.4	
2	West	30.6	38.6	34.6	31.6	
3	North	45.9	46.9	45	43.9	
4						

After

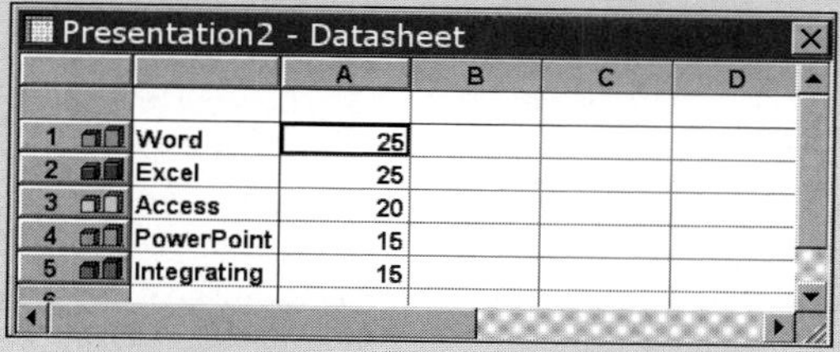

Presentation2 - Datasheet		A	B	C	D	
1	Word	25				
2	Excel	25				
3	Access	20				
4	PowerPoint	15				
5	Integrating	15				

6 In this step, you delete all the data that currently appears in the datasheet. To do this, you first select the entire datasheet by clicking the upper-left corner of the datasheet, directly below the Title bar. You then press the `DELETE` key.
CLICK: the upper-left corner of the datasheet (refer to Figure 2.17)
PRESS: `DELETE`

Figure 2.17
Deleting the contents
of the datasheet

Click here to select all the
cells in the datasheet

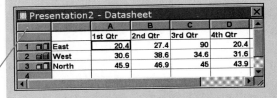

Presentation2 - Datasheet					
		A	B	C	D
		1st Qtr	2nd Qtr	3rd Qtr	4th Qtr
1	East	20.4	27.4	90	20.4
2	West	30.6	38.6	34.6	31.6
3	North	45.9	46.9	45	43.9
4					

7 To enter data into the datasheet, you click the cross-hair mouse pointer on the appropriate *cell* (the intersection of a row and a column) in the datasheet. In this step, you enter the titles.
CLICK: in the cell to the right of the number 1
TYPE: Word
PRESS: `ENTER`
The insertion point automatically moved to the cell below.
TYPE: Excel
PRESS: `ENTER`
TYPE: Access
PRESS: `ENTER`
TYPE: PowerPoint
PRESS: `ENTER`
TYPE: Integrating
PRESS: `ENTER`

8 Now you prepare to enter the data.
PRESS: `CTRL` + `HOME`
The insertion point automatically moved to where you will type in the first value (25).

9 To enter the data:
TYPE: 25
PRESS: `ENTER`
TYPE: 25
PRESS: `ENTER`
TYPE: 20
PRESS: `ENTER`
TYPE: 15
PRESS: `ENTER`
TYPE: 15
PRESS: `ENTER`

10 If you drag the bottom border of the datasheet window downward and then press CTRL + HOME, the datasheet should appear similar to the completed datasheet in Figure 2.16. (*Note:* You may have to use the scroll bar in the datasheet to view the headings.)

11 Let's display the graph on the slide:
CLICK: anywhere in the background of the presentation window
The graph is inserted automatically into your presentation. Your screen should now appear similar to Figure 2.18.

Figure 2.18

Inserting a graph

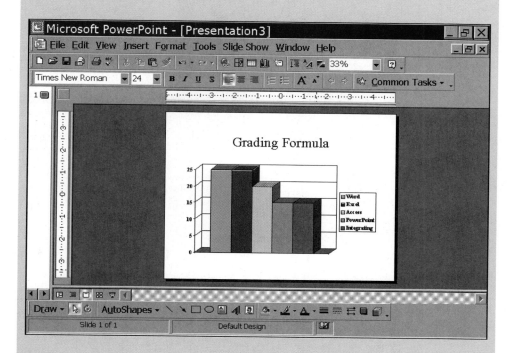

12 Once you've inserted a graph on a slide, you can edit it at any time by double-clicking the graph object to load Microsoft Graph. To illustrate, let's create a different type of chart:
DOUBLE-CLICK: the graph object
CHOOSE: Chart, Chart Type from the Menu bar
SELECT: Bar in the *Chart type* list box
CLICK: OK command button

13 To return to PowerPoint:
CLICK: anywhere in the background of the presentation window
Your screen should now appear similar to Figure 2.19.

POWERPOINT

Figure 2.19

A bar chart is
inserted on the slide

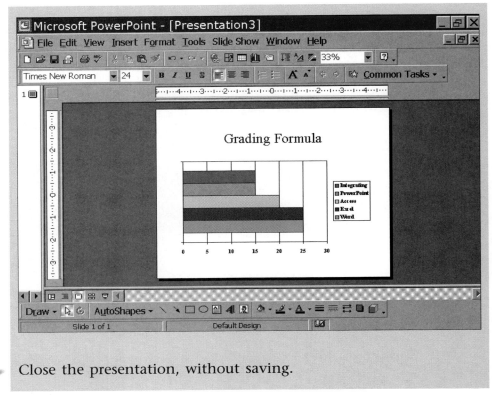

14 Close the presentation, without saving.

2.3.4 Inserting Organization Charts

FEATURE

An **organization chart** is a schematic drawing showing a hierarchy of formal relationships, such as the relationships among an organization's employees. **Microsoft Organization Chart** allows you to create organization charts and other hierarchical diagrams. PowerPoint provides several methods for inserting organization charts in your presentations.

METHOD

Several methods exist for launching Microsoft Organization Chart including:

- DOUBLE-CLICK: organization chart placeholder, or
- CHOOSE: Insert, Picture, Organization Chart from the menu, or
- CHOOSE: Insert, Object and then select MS Organization Chart

To edit an existing organization chart:
DOUBLE-CLICK: organization chart object

PRACTICE
You will now insert an organization chart on a slide by editing an organization chart placeholder.

Setup: Ensure that no presentations are open in the application window.

1 To begin a blank presentation:
CLICK: New button (🗋)
The New Slide dialog box appears.

2 DOUBLE-CLICK: Organization Chart layout (located in the second row, third column)

3 To increase the size of the slide for convenient editing, do the following:
CLICK: Slide view button (🖾) at the bottom of the Outline pane

4 CLICK: the title placeholder
TYPE: `Practice Chart`

5 To insert an organization chart:
DOUBLE-CLICK: the organization chart placeholder
Microsoft Organization Chart appears in a separate window.
(*Note:* If this application isn't stored on your computer, proceed to the next module.)

6 To maximize the Organization Chart window:
CLICK: Maximize button (🖾)
Your screen should now appear similar to Figure 2.20. You should see four boxes in the chart area. The topmost box should already be selected.

Figure 2.20

Microsoft Organization Chart
application window

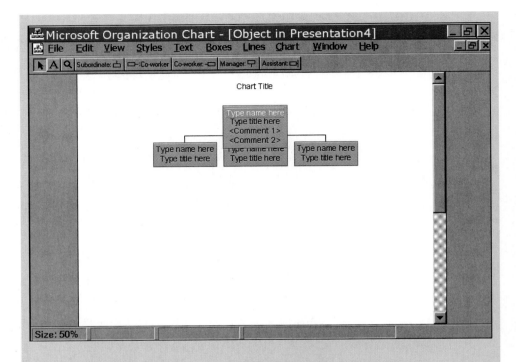

7 To edit the content of the organization chart boxes:
TYPE: *Your Name*
PRESS: ENTER
TYPE: Lead Instructor

8 CLICK: the far left box, located in the second row of the chart
TYPE: Feliberto Reyes
PRESS: ENTER
TYPE: Assistant Instructor

9 CLICK: the box in the center of the second row
TYPE: Frank Rogers
PRESS: ENTER
TYPE: Lab Assistant

10 CLICK: the box on the right of the second row
TYPE: Maritza James
PRESS: ENTER
TYPE: Lab Assistant

11 To embed the organization chart on the current slide:
CHOOSE: File, Exit and Return to Presentation
CLICK: Yes command button to update the presentation
The organization chart should now appear on the slide, as shown
in Figure 2.21.

Figure 2.21

Embedded organization chart

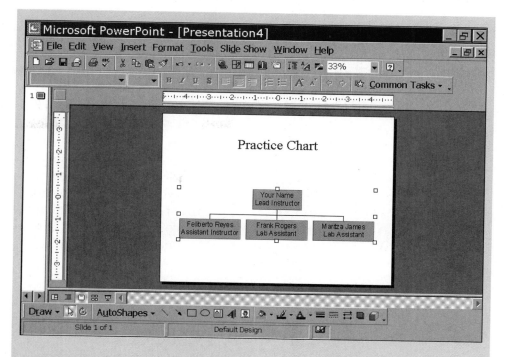

 12 Let's edit the organization chart to include a new box on the second level.
DOUBLE-CLICK: organization chart object

13 To add a new box to the chart:
CLICK: Subordinate button on the toolbar
CLICK: the box that contains your name
A new box appears on the second level.

14 Because the new box is already selected, do the following:
TYPE: Roxanna Adams
PRESS: ENTER
TYPE: Network Manager

15 To embed the revised chart on the current slide:
CHOOSE: File, Exit and Return to Presentation
CLICK: Yes command button to update the presentation

16 Close the presentation, without saving.

2.3 Self Check   What are organization charts used for?

In Addition
Inserting Pictures
from a Scanner

To insert a scanned picture on a slide, your computer must first be connected to a scanner. Choose Insert, Picture, From Scanner or Camera and then follow the instructions of your scanner.

2.4 Delivering Online Presentations

It's showtime! PowerPoint provides several ways to deliver a presentation. Whereas handouts, overhead transparencies, and 35mm slides constitute static delivery approaches, online presentations are more dynamic, often incorporating special multimedia effects that help maintain an audience's attention. In this module, we focus on delivering online presentations.

2.4.1 Starting and Running Slide Shows

FEATURE
PowerPoint provides several tools for assisting your delivery of online presentations. You access these tools by right-clicking a slide in Slide Show view. Among the available commands on the right-click menu are options for navigating the slide show, changing the characteristics of the mouse pointer, and ending the slide show. Keep in mind that when you switch to Slide Show view, your presentation will start with the current slide.

METHOD
- To start a slide show:
  SELECT: the slide you want to start on
  CHOOSE: View, Slide Show (or click 🖵)
- To access several tools for controlling running slide shows:
  RIGHT-CLICK: with the mouse in Slide Show view

PRACTICE
You will now open an existing presentation and then switch to Slide Show view. You will then practice using the right-click menu to control the running slide show.

Setup: Ensure that no presentations are open in the application window.

1 Open the PPT240 data file.

2 Save this four-slide presentation as "Getting to Know" to your personal storage location.

3 At this point, slide 1 is the current slide.
CHOOSE: View, Slide Show
The first slide should be displaying in Slide Show view.

4 To illustrate that you can start a presentation on any slide, let's exit Slide Show view, display slide 2, and then switch back to Slide Show view.
PRESS: ESC to exit Slide Show view
CLICK: Next Slide button (⬇) on the vertical scroll bar to display slide 2
CHOOSE: View, Slide Show
The second slide should be displaying in Slide Show view.

5 In Chapter 1, you learned several methods for navigating a presentation using the mouse and keyboard. For example, pressing the Space Bar will display the next slide and pressing the PgUp key displays the previous slide. In this lesson, we would like to explore some additional options that become available when you right-click a slide.
RIGHT-CLICK: anywhere on the current slide
The right-click menu shown to the right should now appear.

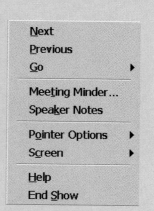

6 To move to the previous slide using the right-click menu:
CHOOSE: Previous
Slide 1 should now appear.

7 To see a listing of the slides in your presentation and then move to a specific slide:
RIGHT-CLICK: anywhere on the current slide
CHOOSE: Go, Slide Navigator
The Slide Navigator dialog box should now appear, as shown in Figure 2.22.

POWERPOINT

Figure 2.22

Slide Navigator dialog box

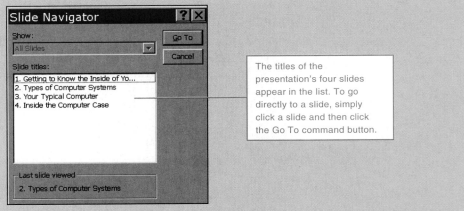

The titles of the presentation's four slides appear in the list. To go directly to a slide, simply click a slide and then click the Go To command button.

8 To display the third slide:
CLICK: "Your Typical Computer" title in the list box
CLICK: Go To command button
Slide 3 should now appear in Slide Show view.

9 To return to the previously viewed slide:
RIGHT-CLICK: anywhere on the current slide
CHOOSE: Go, Previously Viewed
Slide 1 should reappear in the window.

10 To change the pointer to a pen that you can write with on the screen:
RIGHT-CLICK: anywhere on the current slide
CHOOSE: Pointer Options
CHOOSE: Pen
The pen mouse pointer is now activated. You can draw on the screen by dragging the pen mouse pointer.

11 Let's emphasize the company name on the first slide by drawing a line under it with the pen mouse pointer.
DRAG: with the mouse under "Computers, Intl."
Your screen may now appear similar, but not identical, to Figure 2.23. (*Note:* You can change the pen color by choosing Pointer Options, Pen Color from the right-click menu.)

POWERPOINT

Figure 2.23

A line was drawn on this slide with the pen mouse pointer

12 To erase the inserted line:
RIGHT-CLICK: anywhere on the screen
CHOOSE: Screen, Erase Pen

13 In some presentations, an arrow will appear in the bottom-left corner of the screen. If you click this, the right-click menu will appear.
CLICK: arrow in the bottom-left corner of the window

14 To hide the arrow:
CHOOSE: Pointer Options, Hidden
The arrow should no longer appear in the left-hand corner.

15 To end the slide show using the right-click menu:
RIGHT-CLICK: anywhere on the screen
CHOOSE: End Show

16 Close the presentation.

2.4 Self Check   How can you go to a specific slide in Slide Show view?

2.5 Chapter Review

Once created, slides can be manipulated with ease. The Slide Finder tool enables you to use your favorite slides in other presentations and the Outline pane and Slide Sorter view provide convenient environments for reordering slides. You can apply alternate layouts to slides and modify existing layouts by manipulating the slide's placeholders. You can also modify the entire look of your slides by applying an alternate design template.

Besides text, several objects are commonly inserted on slides, including clip art, pictures, graphs, and organization charts. These objects are often more effective at conveying information than text by itself, and help keep your audience's attention. The chapter concluded with practice delivering online presentations using PowerPoint's right-click menu that you can access in Slide Show view.

2.5.1 Command Summary

Many of the commands and procedures appearing in this chapter are summarized in the following table.

Skill Set	To Perform This Task . . .	Do the Following . . .
Creating a Presentation	Insert slides from other presentations	CHOOSE: Insert, Slides From Files
Modifying a Presentation	Change slide order in the Outline pane	DRAG: the selected slide up or down
	Change slide order in Slide Sorter view	DRAG: the selected slide to a new location
	Apply a different layout	CHOOSE: Format, Slide Layout DOUBLE-CLICK: an AutoLayout
Customizing a Presentation	Apply one of PowerPoint's design templates	CHOOSE: Format, Apply Design Template DOUBLE-CLICK: a template
	Apply a template from another presentation	CHOOSE: Format, Apply Design Template CHOOSE: Presentations and Shows from the *Files of type* drop-down list DOUBLE-CLICK: a presentation file

Continued

Skill Set	To Perform This Task . . .	Do the Following . . .
Working with Visual Elements	Display the Clip Gallery	DOUBLE-CLICK: a clip art placeholder, or CLICK: Insert Clip Art button (▣) on the Drawing toolbar, or CHOOSE: Insert, Picture, Clip Art, or CHOOSE: Insert, Object and then double-click Microsoft Clip Gallery
	Add clip art	CLICK: a clip in the Clip Gallery CLICK: Insert clip button (▣) on the shortcut menu
	Insert a picture	CHOOSE: Insert, Picture, From File
	Insert a graph	CLICK: Insert Chart button (▣), or DOUBLE-CLICK: graph placeholder, or CHOOSE: Insert, Chart, or CHOOSE: Insert, Object and then select Microsoft Graph
	Modify a graph	DOUBLE-CLICK: graph object
	Insert an organization chart	DOUBLE-CLICK: organization chart placeholder, or CHOOSE: Insert, Picture, Organization Chart, or CHOOSE: Insert, Object and then select MS Organization Chart
	Modify an organization chart	DOUBLE-CLICK: organization chart object
Delivering a Presentation	Use on-screen navigation tools	RIGHT-CLICK: a slide in Slide Show view

POWERPOINT

2.5.2 Key Terms

This section specifies page references for the key terms identified in this session. For a complete list of definitions, refer to the Glossary provided immediately after the Appendix in this learning guide.

clip art image, *p. 64*

organization chart, *p. 76*

Microsoft Clip Gallery, *p. 64*

Microsoft Graph, *p. 72*

Microsoft Organization Chart, *p. 76*

sizing handles, *p. 60*

Slide Finder, *p. 53*

2.6 Review Questions

2.6.1 Short Answer

1. In the Clip Gallery, what information displays in a pop-up window when you click an image?
2. What is the Slide Finder tool used for?
3. What is Microsoft Graph used for?
4. Describe the process of inserting a picture from a file into your presentation.
5. What mouse action enables you to modify an existing organization chart?
6. In Slide Show view, what is the Slide Navigator tool used for?
7. How would you go about starting a slide show on the fourth slide in a presentation?
8. What is the procedure for reordering slides in the Outline pane?
9. Describe two methods for inserting an organization chart on a slide.
10. How would you go about applying a different layout to the current slide?

2.6.2 True/False

1. __F__ In the Clip Gallery, clips are organized by date.
2. __T__ Design templates can be applied from existing presentations.
3. __T__ You edit a graph placeholder by double-clicking.
4. __F__ Organization charts are often used to represent spreadsheet data.
5. __T__ You resize objects by dragging their sizing handles.
6. __F__ Before using the Slide Finder, you must display open presentations in Slide Sorter view.
7. __T__ To apply one of PowerPoint's design templates, choose Format, Apply Design Template from the Menu bar.
8. __T__ It's possible to change a slide's layout in Slide Show view.
9. __T__ Changing an existing slide layout may involve moving and resizing object placeholders.
10. __T__ In PowerPoint, you can apply a design template from an existing presentation.

2.6.3 Multiple Choice

1. Which of the following reveals a presentation using slide snapshots?
   a. design template
   b. Slide Finder
   c. Title Master
   d. Slide Master

2. To insert a picture file in your presentation:
   a. CHOOSE: Insert, Picture, From File
   b. CLICK: Insert Picture button
   c. CHOOSE: File, Insert
   d. All of the above

3. To insert slides from another presentation, use the:
   a. Slide Finder
   b. Slide Master
   c. Title Master
   d. All of the above

4. You can reorder slides in _____ .
   a. Slide view
   b. Outline pane
   c. Slide Sorter view
   d. Both b and c

5. To edit an organization chart on an AutoLayout slide, _____ the placeholder.
   a. click
   b. double-click
   c. drag
   d. None of the above

6. Which of the following tools could you use to map a hierarchy of relationships?
   a. Picture toolbar
   b. Microsoft Graph
   c. Microsoft Organization Chart
   d. All of the above

7. Once you've inserted a graph on a slide, you can edit it in the future by _____ .
   a. dragging
   b. clicking
   c. double-clicking
   d. None of the above

8. Which of the following should you use to create a bar chart?
   a. Microsoft Organization Chart
   b. Microsoft Graph
   c. Microsoft ClipArt Gallery
   d. None of the above

9. To change the overall look of a presentation, you should apply an alternate _____ .
   a. AutoLayout
   b. placeholder
   c. design template
   d. All of the above

10. To delete an existing clip art image:
    a. double-click the image
    b. select the image and press (DELETE)
    c. drag the image to outside the Slide pane
    d. All of the above

2.7 Hands-On Projects

2.7.1 Outdoor Adventure Tours: Skiing Tours

This exercise practices inserting a clip art object on a slide.

1. Begin a blank presentation using the New button ([D]).
2. In the New Slide dialog box:
   DOUBLE-CLICK: Title Only layout

3. Type **Total Skiing Tours** in the title placeholder.
4. To launch Microsoft Clip Gallery so that you can insert a clip
    art image on the slide:
    CHOOSE: Insert, Picture, Clip Art
5. To search for an image that relates to skiing:
    CLICK: in the *Search for clips* text box
    TYPE: **skiing** in the *Search for clips* text box
    PRESS: (ENTER)
    An appropriate image should now appear in
    the window, such as the one shown to the
    right. (*Note:* If no image appears, then search for an alternate
    image.)

[handwritten: Abby, Ben, Cloud]

6. To select the image:
    CLICK: the image
    CLICK: Insert clip button (⊡) from the pop-up menu
7. Close the Insert ClipArt window by clicking its Close (☒)
    button.
8. If necessary, move and resize the image.
9. Save the presentation as "Outdoor Skiing Tours" to your
    personal storage location.
10. Close the presentation.

2.7.2 Monashee Community College: Animation

In this exercise, you will reorder slides, change slide layouts, insert clip
art, and apply an alternate design template.

1. Open the PPT272 data file.
2. Save the presentation as "Monashee Animation" to your person-
    al storage location.
3. In the Outline pane, drag the slide 5 icon upward so that it is
    positioned before slide 4.
4. Let's change the layout of slide 4 from the bulleted list layout to
    the "Text & Clip Art" layout. First, ensure that slide 4 is display-
    ing in the Slide pane.
5. CHOOSE: Format, Slide Layout
    DOUBLE-CLICK: Text & Clip Art layout (located in the third
    row, first column)
6. To insert a clip art image on the slide:
    DOUBLE-CLICK: clip art placeholder
7. To search for the word "information":
    CLICK: in the *Search for clips* text box
    TYPE: **information**
    PRESS: (ENTER)
8. SELECT: the clip shown to the right
    CLICK: Insert clip button (⊡)
    (*Note:* If this clip isn't available on
    your computer, insert an alternate
    clip on the slide.)

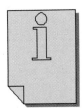

9. Resize the image so that it is about half its original size. Also,
    move the image so that it lines up opposite the bulleted list.

10. To apply an alternate design template to the presentation:
CHOOSE: Format, Apply Design Template
DOUBLE-CLICK: "Blends" template in the list box
11. Display slide 1 in the Slide pane. The title might look better if it's positioned higher on the slide.
12. DRAG: the title placeholder upward about one-half inch so that the entire title is above the horizontal line
13. Save and then close the revised presentation.

2.7.3 Coldstream Corporation: Executive Committee

In this exercise, you create a new presentation and then insert and edit an organization chart.

1. Start a new presentation and select the Title Slide layout.
2. Save the new presentation as "Coldstream Executive" to your personal storage location.
3. Type `Coldstream Corporation` for the title and `Executive Committee` for the subtitle.
4. Insert another new slide that includes a title placeholder and an organization chart layout.
5. Type `Executive Committee Members` in the title placeholder.
6. Create the following organization chart:

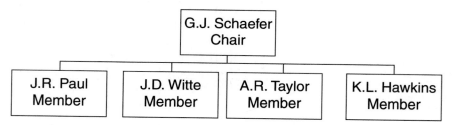

7. Display the organization chart on the slide.
8. Edit the organization chart to include two subordinates under "J.D. Witte": `D.E. Reid Secretary`; and `A.J. Epp Treasurer` as shown on nexgt page:

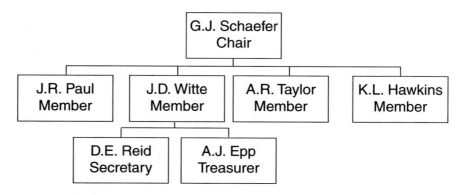

9. Adjust the size and position of the chart so that it is larger and centered beneath the title.
10. Apply the "Global" design template to the presentation.
11. Save your changes and close your presentation.

2.7.4 Spiderman Web Marketing: Technology

You will now add a photograph and a graph to an existing presentation.

1. Open the PPT274 presentation.
2. Save the presentation as "Spiderman Technology" to your personal storage location.
3. On the first slide, insert a photograph named PPT274a. (*Note:* If necessary, close the Picture toolbar.)
4. Move and resize the photo so that it fits in the large triangular white area beneath the title.
5. Insert a new slide that includes a title and a chart placeholder.
6. Type `Current Sales Breakdown` in the title placeholder and then double-click the chart placeholder to create the chart.
7. Edit the chart's datasheet to look like the following:

Solution-Spiderman Photo - Datasheet		A	B	C	D
		1998	1999		
1	Web-Based	2000	5500		
2	Mail Order	2200	1850		
3					
4					

8. Display the bar chart on the slide.
9. Move and resize the chart so that it fits in the black area of the slide.
10. Save and then print the revised presentation.

2.7.5 On Your Own: Wally's Widgets

Create a slide show that describes a fictitious company called "Wally's Widgets." The presentation should include five slides containing the information listed below:

- Wally's Widgets
  Address, phone number
  A photograph (stored in the PPT275 data file)
- Description of the product (features and benefits)
- Projected Sales (include a graph)
- Personnel (include an organization chart)
- Summary slide

Apply an appropriate design template to the presentation. Save your presentation as "Wally's Widgets" to your personal storage location.

2.7.6 On Your Own: Life as a Student

Create a true or fictitious presentation that describes your life as a student. Your presentation should include your course timetable in the form of a bulleted list. Your course grades should be presented in a graph, and the members of one of your study groups should be displayed in an organization chart. Insert the photograph named PPT276 or a scanned photograph of yourself. Save your presentation as "Student" to your personal storage location.

2.8 Case Problem: Snowmelt Hydrology Research

Now that Natasha has completed Chapter 2, she is ready to insert several objects into her PowerPoint presentation. After creating a title slide, Natasha will insert a graph, an organization chart, and a photograph.

In the following case problems, assume the role of Natasha and perform the same steps that she identifies. You may want to reread the chapter opening before proceeding.

1. Natasha creates a new presentation entitled "Thesis" and saves it to her personal storage location. On the first slide, she types `Spatial Variability in the Arctic Snowmelt Landscape` as the title and `presented by Natasha Newman` as the subtitle.

   Natasha decides to create a graph on the second slide that will visually compare her data. She inserts a second slide with the Chart layout. She types `Variability of Snow Distribution, Trail Valley Basin` in the title placeholder and then double-clicks the chart placeholder. Next, she edits the chart datasheet to include the following information:

	May 23	May 24
Snow Covered Area	93	66
Total # of Patches	54	75
Patch Fractal Dimension	34	36

   She experiments with several different chart types including Bar, Line, and Area charts. She prefers the 'Cone Chart' and the 'Column with a conical shape' sub-type (located in the first row, first column). She saves her changes.

2. In her thesis defense, Natasha would like to tell something about the different members in her research group. Using an organization chart on the third slide, she types `Snowmelt Research Group` in the title placeholder and creates the following organization chart:

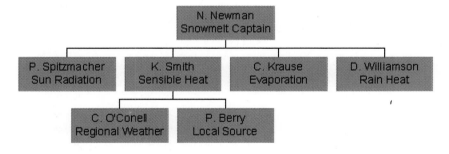

   She then saves the revised presentation.

3. Natasha has chosen the perfect photograph to include on her summary slide. She creates a final slide with the title `Field Measurement Difficulties` and inserts the photograph entitled PPT283. She moves and resizes the picture to fit nicely in the area beneath the horizontal border, and then saves her changes.

4. After experimenting with PowerPoint's selection of design templates, Natasha decides to apply the "Sunny Days" design template. She then reviews each slide in the presentation and moves and resizes placeholders to achieve the best visual result.

    After reviewing the presentation in Slide Show view, she decides to move slide 4 to before slide 3. She practices delivering her slide show, incorporating the use of the pen pointer and other options on the right-click menu. She saves her changes and is ready to defend her thesis!

Notes

Notes

ADVANTAGE SERIES

MICROSOFT®
ACCESS 2000

BRIEF EDITION

MICROSOFT ACCESS 2000
Working with Access

CHAPTER
ONE

Chapter Outline

Learning Objectives

After reading this chapter, you will be able to:

- Understand basic database terminology

- Describe the different components of the Access application window and the Database window

- Select commands and perform actions using the keyboard and mouse

- Open various database objects, including tables, queries, forms, and reports, for display

- View, edit, and print data in a datasheet

- Insert and delete records in a datasheet

- Open and close a database

Case Study

On-Track Seminars

Joanna Walsh just started a new job with On-Track Seminars, a company that specializes in career and life skills training. As an administrative assistant, Joanna knows that she is expected to answer phones, write and edit letters, and organize meetings. However, on her first day, Karen Chase, the office director, informs her of some additional expectations: "You will also be using Microsoft Access to manage our basic seminar information. Our instructors will call you if they have a problem or need to modify the database for any reason. Mostly you are required to look up student phone numbers to inform them when a seminar is cancelled." Fortunately, Joanna knows there is a course in Microsoft Access starting next week at the local community college, so she is not overly concerned by this new job requirement.

In this chapter, you and Joanna learn about managing information in desktop databases, how to use the different components and features of Microsoft Access, and how to display and edit the information stored in a database.

1.1 Getting Started with Access

Microsoft Access is a desktop database program that enables you to enter, store, analyze, and present data. For end users, power users, and software developers alike, Access provides easy-to-use yet powerful tools most often associated with higher-end **database management systems (DBMS)**. In fact, Access 2000 offers scalability never seen before in desktop database software. At the local or desktop level, Access can help you manage your personal information or collect data for a research study. At the corporate and enterprise level, Access can retrieve and summarize data stored on servers located throughout the world. Access also enables you to create and publish dynamic Web-based forms and reports for intranet and Internet delivery.

While this is not a database theory course, a familiarity with some basic terms will help you become more productive using Microsoft Access 2000. The word **database**, for example, refers to a collection of related information, such as a company's accounting data. The primary object in a database for collecting and storing data is called a **table**. As shown in Figure 1.1, tables are organized into rows and columns similar to an electronic spreadsheet. An individual entry in a table (for example, a person's name and address) is called a **record** and is stored as a horizontal row. Each record in a table is composed of one or more fields. A **field** holds a single piece of data. For example, the table in Figure 1.1 divides each person's record into vertical columns or fields for ID, Surname, Given, Address, City, and State.

Figure 1.1
Storing data in an Access table

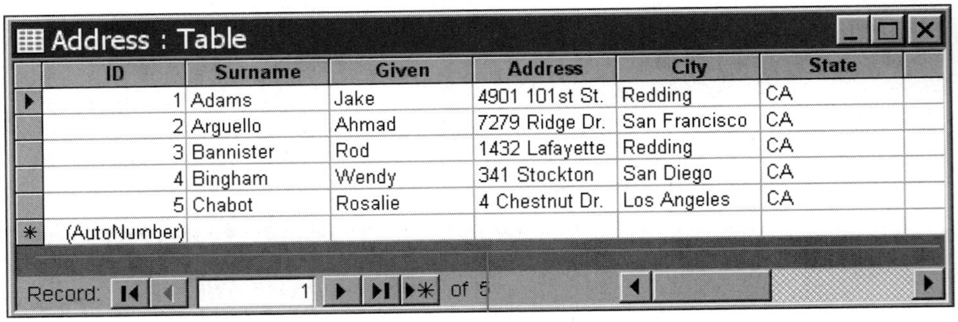
Address : Table
Record: 1 of 5
Each row represents a record
Each column represents a field

ID	Surname	Given	Address	City	State
1	Adams	Jake	4901 101st St.	Redding	CA
2	Arguello	Ahmad	7279 Ridge Dr.	San Francisco	CA
3	Bannister	Rod	1432 Lafayette	Redding	CA
4	Bingham	Wendy	341 Stockton	San Diego	CA
5	Chabot	Rosalie	4 Chestnut Dr.	Los Angeles	CA
(AutoNumber)					

1.1.1 Loading and Exiting Access

FEATURE
You load Access from the Windows Start menu, accessed by clicking the Start button (Start) on the taskbar. Because Access requires a significant amount of memory, you should always exit the application when you are finished doing your work. Most Windows applications allow you to close their windows by clicking on the Close button (☒) appearing in the top right-hand corner. You may also choose the File, Exit command.

METHOD
- To load Access:
  CLICK: Start button (Start)
  CHOOSE: Programs, Microsoft Access
- To exit Access:
  CHOOSE: File, Exit from the Access Menu bar

PRACTICE
After loading Microsoft Access using the Windows Start menu, you open an existing database file in this lesson.

Setup: Ensure that you have turned on your computer and that the Windows desktop appears.

1 Position the mouse pointer over the Start button (█Start) appearing in the bottom left-hand corner of the Windows taskbar and then click the left mouse button once. The Start pop-up menu appears as shown here.

2 Position the mouse pointer over the Programs menu option. Notice that you do not need to click the left mouse button to display the list of programs in the fly-out or cascading menu.

3 Move the mouse pointer horizontally to the right until it highlights an option in the Programs menu. You can now move the mouse pointer vertically within the menu to select an option.

4 Position the mouse pointer over the Microsoft Access menu option and then click the left mouse button once. After a few seconds, the Access application window and startup dialog box appear (Figure 1.2). Notice that a new button also appears on the taskbar at the bottom of your screen.

5 Leave the startup dialog box displayed and proceed to the next lesson.

Figure 1.2

Access application window and startup dialog box

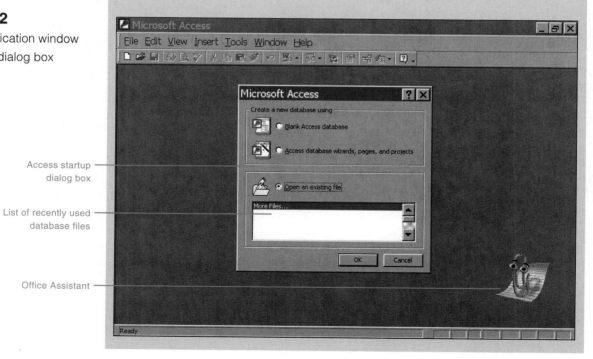

Access startup dialog box

List of recently used database files

Office Assistant

In Addition
Switching Among
Applications

Each application that you are currently working with is represented by a button on the taskbar. Switching between open applications on your desktop is as easy as clicking the appropriate taskbar button, like switching channels on a television set.

1.1.2 Opening a Database File at Startup

FEATURE
You use the Open dialog box to search for and retrieve existing database files that are stored on your local hard disk, a floppy diskette, a network server, or on the Web. If you want to load Access and an existing database at the same time, you can use the Open Office Document command on the Start menu. Or, if you have recently opened a database, you can launch Access and then double-click its file name in the startup dialog box.

METHOD
To display the Open dialog box at startup:
1. CLICK: *Open an existing file* option button in the startup dialog box
2. SELECT: More Files... in the list box area
3. CLICK: OK command button

To retrieve a database file using the Open dialog box:
1. SELECT: *the desired folder* from the Places bar or the *Look in* drop-down list box
2. DOUBLE-CLICK: *the desired file* from the list area

PRACTICE
Using the startup dialog box, you practice opening a database file.

Setup: Ensure that you have completed the previous lesson and that you have identified the location of your Advantage student data files.

1

To open an existing database using the startup dialog box:
CLICK: *Open an existing file* option button
SELECT: More Files... in the list box area
CLICK: OK command button
The Open dialog box appears, as shown in Figure 1.3.

Figure 1.3

Open dialog box

Lists the files that you have most recently worked with

The default working folder

Lists common desktop shortcuts

Lists shortcuts to your favorite files and folders

Lists files and folders stored on your intranet or Internet Web Server

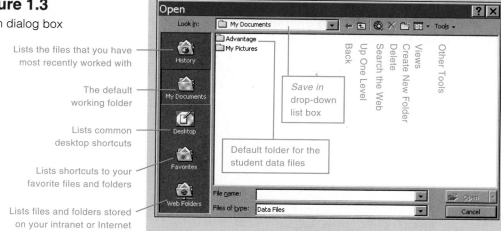

Important: In this guide, we refer to the files that have been created for you as the **student data files**. Depending on your computer or lab setup, these files may be located on a floppy diskette, in a folder on your hard disk, or on a network server. If necessary, ask your instructor or lab assistant where to find these data files. To download the Advantage Series' student data files from the Internet, visit McGraw-Hill's Information Technology Web site at:

http://www.mhhe.com/it

2 The **Places bar,** located along the left border of the dialog box, provides convenient access to commonly used storage locations. To illustrate, let's view the contents of some folders:
CLICK: History folder button (📁)
A list of recently opened Office documents appears.

3 To view the contents of the My Documents folder:
CLICK: My Documents button (📁)

4 Let's browse the local hard disk:
CLICK: down arrow attached to the Look in drop-down list box
SELECT: Hard Disk C:
The list area displays the folders and files stored in the root directory of your local hard disk.

5 To change how the files are displayed in the list area:
CLICK: down arrow beside the Views button (📊▾)
CHOOSE: Details
Each folder and file is presented on a single line with additional file information, such as its size, type, and last date modified.
(*Hint:* You can sort the folders and files in the list area by clicking on one of the column heading buttons.)

6 To select a multicolumn list format:
CLICK: down arrow beside the Views button (⊞▾)
CHOOSE: List

7 Now, using either the Places bar or the *Look in* drop-down list box:
SELECT: *the location of your Advantage student data files*
(*Note:* In this guide, we retrieve and save files to a folder named "Advantage" in the My Documents folder.)

8 Let's open one of the Access databases in this folder:
DOUBLE-CLICK: ACC100 in the list area
The Open dialog box disappears and the ACC100 database is loaded into the application window.

1.1.3 Touring Access

FEATURE
The **application window** (Figure 1.4) acts as a container for the *Database window* and for displaying the database objects that you will create and use in Access. It also contains several key interface components, including the *Windows icons*, *Menu bar*, *Toolbar*, and *Status bar*.

PRACTICE
In a guided tour, you now explore some of the interface features of the Access application window.

Setup: Ensure that you have completed the previous lessons and that the ACC100 Database window is displayed in the application window.

1 The Database window is best displayed as a floating window, although it may be maximized to cover the entire work area. You control the display of the application and Database windows by clicking their Title bar or Windows icons—Minimize (▬), Maximize (□), Restore (🗗), and Close (✖). Familiarize yourself with the components labeled in Figure 1.4.

Figure 1.4

Access application window

Menu bar

Database toolbar

Database window

Work area

Status bar

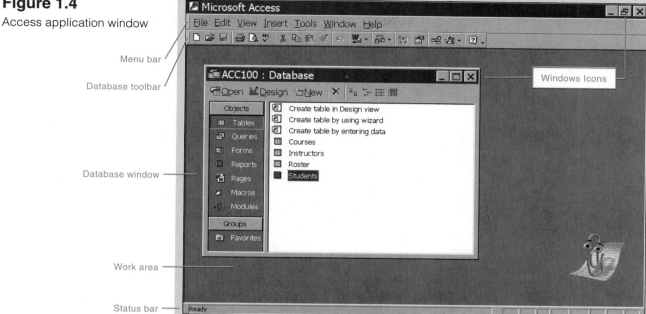

2 The Menu bar contains the Access menu commands. To execute a command, click once on the desired Menu bar option and then click again on the command. Commands that appear dimmed are not available for selection. Commands that are followed by an ellipsis (...) display a dialog box when selected. To practice using the menu:
CHOOSE: Help
(*Note:* This instruction directs you to click the left mouse button once on the Help option appearing in the Menu bar. All menu commands that you execute in this guide begin with the instruction "CHOOSE.")

3 To display other pull-down menus, move the mouse pointer to the left over other options in the Menu bar. As each option is highlighted, a pull-down menu appears with its associated commands.

4 To leave the Menu bar without making a command selection:
CLICK: in a blank portion of the Access work area

5 Access provides context-sensitive *right-click menus* for quick access to menu commands. Rather than searching for a command in the Menu bar, position the mouse pointer on a database object and right-click to display a list of commands applicable for that object.

To display the right-click menu for a table:
RIGHT-CLICK: Students in the list area of the Database window
The pop-up menu at the right should appear.

| Open |
| Design View |
| Print... |
| Print Preview |
| Cut |
| Copy |
| Save As... |
| Export... |
| Send To ▶ |
| Add to Group ▶ |
| Create Shortcut... |
| Delete |
| Rename |
| Properties |

6 To remove the right-click menu without making a selection:
PRESS: ESC

7 If the Office Assistant currently appears on your screen, do the following to temporarily hide it from view:
RIGHT-CLICK: *the character*
CHOOSE: Hide from the right-click menu
(*Note:* The character's name may also appear in the Hide command.)

1.1.4 Selecting Database Objects

FEATURE
The Access **Database window** is your command control center; it provides the interface to your database. The **Objects bar**, located along the left border, organizes the available database objects into seven categories named *Tables, Queries, Forms, Reports, Pages, Macros,* and *Modules*. Most of your time in this guide will be spent working with these objects in the Database window.

METHOD
To peruse the objects in a database:
CLICK: *category buttons* in the Objects bar

PRACTICE
In the Database window, you practice selecting objects for display.

Setup: Ensure that the ACC100 Database window is displayed, as shown in Figure 1.5.

1 Table objects are the primary element of a database and are used to store and manipulate data. A single database file may contain several tables. To display the contents of a table object, ensure that the *Tables* button in the Objects bar is selected and then do the following:
DOUBLE-CLICK: Students in the list area
The Students table appears in a row and column layout called a *datasheet*. You will learn how to navigate and manipulate the contents of a datasheet in the next module.

Figure 1.5

Access Database window

Database Window Toolbar

Objects Bar

Category Button

Groups Bar

New Object Shortcuts

Object List

List Area

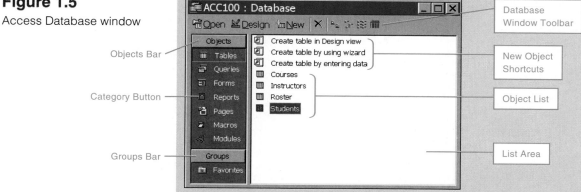

2 To close the Students datasheet:
CLICK: its Close button ([x])

3 A **query** is a question you ask of your database. The answer, which may draw data from more than one table in the database, typically displays a datasheet of records. To see a list of the stored queries:
CLICK: *Queries* button

4 The stored query in this database links and extracts data from the Courses and Instructors tables. To display the results of the query:
DOUBLE-CLICK: Courses Query in the list area

5 After reviewing the query, close the displayed datasheet:
CLICK: its Close button ([x])

6 Unlike a table's column and row layout, a **form** generally displays one record at a time. To see a list of the stored forms:
CLICK: *Forms* button

7 To display a form:
DOUBLE-CLICK: Student Input Form in the list area
Your screen should now appear similar to Figure 1.6.

Figure 1.6

Displaying a form object

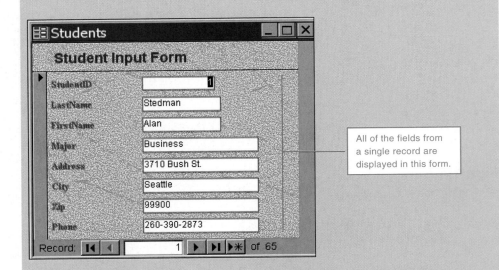

All of the fields from a single record are displayed in this form.

8 To close the Student Input Form:
CLICK: its Close button (☒)

9 While datasheets and forms are used to input and modify data, you create **reports** to present, summarize, and print data. To see a list of the stored reports in the database:
CLICK: *Reports* button

10 To view a report as it will appear when printed:
DOUBLE-CLICK: Students by Major in the list area
The report appears in the Print Preview window.

11 To close the Print Preview window:
CLICK: its Close button (☒)

12 To return to displaying the table objects:
CLICK: *Tables* button
(*Note:* If you are proceeding to the next module, keep the database open for use in the next lesson.)

In Addition
Additional Database Objects

The Objects bar lets you access a variety of database objects. Besides *Tables*, *Queries*, *Forms*, and *Reports*, the *Pages* category links to external Internet-ready database objects called *data access pages*. The *Macro* category stores objects that you use to automate frequently performed procedures. And for greater control, you can write code *modules* using Visual Basic for Applications (VBA), a subset of the Microsoft Visual Basic programming language.

1.1 Self Check   How do you close a window that appears in the Access work area?

1.2   Viewing and Printing Your Data

Much like an electronic worksheet, the data stored in a table object appears in rows and columns called a **datasheet**. Each row represents an individual record and each column represents a field. The intersection of a row and column is called a **cell**. This mode, called **Datasheet view**, lets you display and work with many records at once. In this module, you learn how to navigate, customize, and print datasheets.

1.2.1   Moving Around a Datasheet

FEATURE

To properly manage the data stored in a table object, you must know how to efficiently move the selection cursor to view all parts of a table. As with most Access features, there are mouse methods and there are keyboard methods for moving the cursor. You should try both methods and then select the one that appeals to you most.

METHOD

Keystroke	Task Description
↑, ↓	Moves to the previous or next record
←, →	Moves cursor to the left or to the right
CTRL + ↓	Moves to the bottom of a field column
CTRL + ↑	Moves to the top of a field column
PgUp, PgDn	Moves up or down one screen
HOME	Moves to the first (leftmost) field in a record
END	Moves to the last (rightmost) field in a record
CTRL + HOME	Moves to the top (first record and first field)
CTRL + END	Moves to the bottom (last record and last field)

PRACTICE

Using the Students table, you practice moving the cursor around a datasheet.

Setup: Ensure that the ACC100 Database window is displayed. If not, open the ACC100 database from your student data files location.

1 Ensure that the *Tables* button in the Objects bar is selected. To display the Students datasheet, do the following:
DOUBLE-CLICK: Students in the list area
The Students data table is loaded into the computer's memory and displayed in Datasheet view. Depending on your screen size, you may see more or fewer records than shown in Figure 1.7.

Figure 1.7
Students table displayed in Datasheet view

This triangular symbol appears in the current or active record.

Cursor

Navigation area for moving the cursor using a mouse

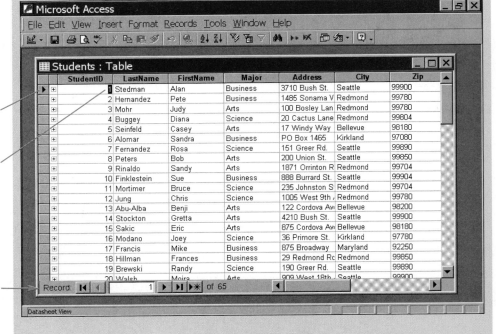

2 A flashing cursor appears in the leftmost field of the first record. To move to the last field in the current record:
PRESS: `END`
The cursor is positioned in the "Phone" column.

3 To move one field to the left and down to the fourth record:
PRESS: `←` once
PRESS: `↓` three times
(*CAUTION:* If pressing a cursor movement key does not yield the expected result, you may have activated Edit mode accidentally. To begin navigating between records and fields again, press `F2` or `ENTER` to end Edit mode.)

4 To move the cursor down by one screen at a time:
PRESS: PgDn twice

5 To move to the top of the datasheet:
PRESS: CTRL + HOME

6 Position the mouse pointer over the scroll box on the vertical scroll bar and then drag the scroll box downward. Notice that a yellow Scroll Tip appears identifying the current record number. When you see "Record: 25 of 65" in the Scroll Tip, release the mouse button. (*Note:* Although the window pans downward, this method does not move the cursor.)

7 For quick mouse selection, Access provides navigation buttons in the bottom left-hand corner of the Datasheet window. To demonstrate:
CLICK: Last Record button (⏭) to move to the bottom of the datasheet
CLICK: First Record button (⏮) to move to the top of the datasheet

8 Access allows you to open a number of Datasheet windows at the same time. To display another table, first make the Database window active:
CHOOSE: Window, ACC100 : Database

9 To display the Roster table:
DOUBLE-CLICK: Roster in the list area
The Roster Datasheet window appears overlapping the other two windows. Similar to the Students table, the Roster table contains a field named StudentID. This common field enables a link to be established between the two tables.

10 To display the Students datasheet once again:
CHOOSE: Window, Students : Table

11 Within the Students Datasheet window, you can display course and grade information from the Roster table using subdatasheets. A **subdatasheet** allows you to browse hierarchical and related data for a particular record. In a sense, a subdatasheet provides a picture-in-picture view of your data. To demonstrate, let's drill down and display the courses and grades for Rosa Fernandez:
CLICK: Expand button (⊞) in the left-hand column of StudentID 7
Your screen should now appear similar to Figure 1.8.

ACCESS

Figure 1.8

Displaying a subdatasheet

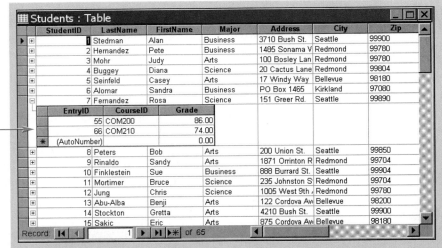

Displaying related records from the Roster table in a subdatasheet

12 Using the mouse, do the following:
CLICK: a cell in the first row of the subdatasheet
Notice that the record navigation area in the Datasheet window shows Record 1 of 2. Clicking the First Record (◄◄) or Last Record (►►) buttons will move the cursor in this subdatasheet only.

13 To collapse the subdatasheet:
CLICK: Collapse button (⊟) for StudentID 7
The record navigation area shows Record 1 of 65 once again.

14 On your own, expand the subdatasheets for three records in the Students Datasheet window. When finished, collapse all of the subdatasheets and then return to the top of the Students datasheet.

15 To close the Roster Datasheet window:
CHOOSE: Window, Roster : Table
CLICK: its Close button (☒)

16 Keep the Students Datasheet window open for use in the next lesson.

In Addition
Moving to a Specific Record Number

Access displays the current record number alongside the navigation buttons in the bottom left-hand corner of a Datasheet window. To move to a specific record in the datasheet or subdatasheet, click the mouse pointer once in this text box, type a record number, and then press **ENTER**. The cursor immediately moves to the desired record.

1.2.2 Adjusting Column Widths and Row Heights

FEATURE

By adjusting the column widths and row heights in a datasheet, you can enhance its appearance for both viewing and printing—similarly to how a document uses double-spacing to make text easier to read. To change the width of a column in Datasheet view, you drag its border line in the **field header area**. You can also have Access scan the contents of the column and recommend the best width. Rows behave somewhat differently. When you adjust a single row's height in the *record selection area*, Access updates all of the rows in a datasheet. Figure 1.9 labels the field header and record selection areas for a datasheet.

METHOD

- To change a column's width using the mouse:
  DRAG: its right border line in the field header area
- To change a column's width using the menu:
  SELECT: a cell in the column that you want to format
  CHOOSE: Format, Column Width
  TYPE: *the desired width*
- To change the default row height using the mouse:
  DRAG: its bottom border line in the record selection area
- To change the default row height using the menu:
  CHOOSE: Format, Row Height
  TYPE: *the desired height*

PRACTICE

In this lesson, you adjust column widths and row heights in a datasheet.

Setup: Ensure that the Students datasheet is displayed.

1 To select a cell in the Zip column:
PRESS: END
PRESS: ←

2 To begin, let's reduce the width of the Zip column using the menu:
CHOOSE: Format, Column Width
The Column Width dialog box appears, as shown here.

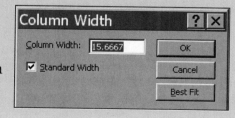

ACCESS

3 Although you can type the desired width, let's have Access calculate the best width for the column:
CLICK: Best Fit command button
The column's width is decreased automatically.

4 Now let's adjust the width of the Address column. In the field header area, position the mouse pointer over the border line between the Address and City fields. The mouse pointer changes shape when positioned correctly, as shown below.

Field Header Area
and mouse pointer

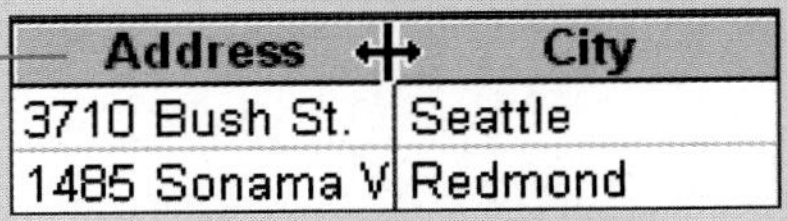

Address	⟷	City
3710 Bush St.	Seattle
1485 Sonama V	Redmond

5 CLICK: the border line and hold down the mouse button
DRAG: the mouse pointer to the right to increase the width (to approximately the beginning of the word "City")

6 You can also set the best-fit width for a column using the mouse. To adjust the width of the Major column:
DOUBLE-CLICK: the border line between Major and Address

7 To reposition the cursor:
PRESS: CTRL + HOME

8 To change the row height setting in the Datasheet window:
CHOOSE: Format, Row Height
TYPE: 18
CLICK: OK
All of the rows in the datasheet are updated to reflect the formatting change. Your worksheet should now appear similar to Figure 1.9.

9 Keep the datasheet open for use in the next lesson.

Figure 1.9

Formatting the
Datasheet window

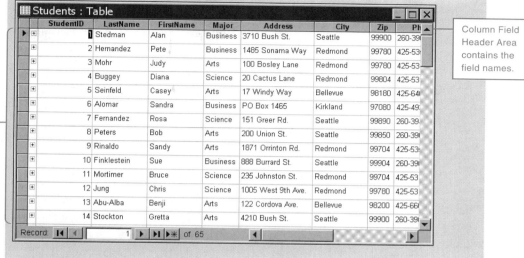

The Record Selection Area
contains row selector buttons.

Column Field
Header Area
contains the
field names.

1.2.3 Previewing and Printing

FEATURE
Before sending a datasheet to the printer, you can preview it using
a full-page display that resembles the printed output. In Preview
mode, you can move back and forth through the pages, zoom in
and out on desired areas, and modify page layout options such as
print margins and page orientation. Once you are satisfied with its
appearance, send it to the printer with a single mouse click.

METHOD
- To preview the current Datasheet window:
  CLICK: Print Preview button (▣), or
  CHOOSE: File, Print Preview
- To print the current Datasheet window:
  CLICK: Print button (▣), or
  CHOOSE: File, Print

PRACTICE
You now use the Print Preview mode to display the Students
datasheet.

Setup: Ensure that you have completed the previous lesson and that
the Students datasheet is displayed.

1 To preview how the datasheet will appear when printed:
CLICK: Print Preview button (▣) on the toolbar
The Datasheet window becomes the Print Preview window.

2 To preview the pages to print, click the navigation buttons at the bottom of the window. Let's practice:
CLICK: Next Page button (▶)
CLICK: Last Page button (▶|)
CLICK: First Page button (|◀)

3 To zoom in or magnify the Print Preview window, move the magnifying glass mouse pointer over the column headings, centered between the margins, and then click once. Your screen should now appear similar to Figure 1.10.

Figure 1.10
Previewing the Students
table for printing

Print Preview toolbar
replaces the Database
toolbar.

Navigation buttons for
moving among the
preview pages

4 To zoom back out on the page:
CLICK: anywhere on the page in the Print Preview window

5 You can change the page setup to landscape orientation in order to print more columns of data on each page. Do the following:
CHOOSE: File, Page Setup
CLICK: *Page* tab
The Page Setup dialog box appears as shown in Figure 1.11.

Figure 1.11

Page Setup dialog
box: *Page* tab

Select this tab to
specify margin
settings.

Select an option
button to specify
page orientation.

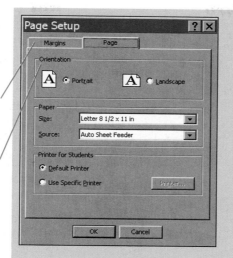

ACCESS

6. To change the page orientation:
SELECT: *Landscape* option button
CLICK: OK command button
Notice that the Print Preview window is dynamically updated.

7. On your own, zoom in and out on the Print Preview window
using the magnifying glass mouse pointer.

8. There are two ways to close the Print Preview window. First, you
can click the Close button (☒), which closes both the Print Preview window and the Students Datasheet window. Second, you
can click the Close command button in the Print Preview toolbar, which returns you to the Datasheet window. To return to
the Students datasheet:
CLICK: Close command button in the toolbar

9. Now let's close the Students Datasheet window:
CLICK: its Close button (☒)

10. Since you have made changes to the layout of the Datasheet
window, Access asks you to either save or discard the formatting
changes. Let's discard the changes for now:
CLICK: No command button
You should now see the Database window.

You can also preview and print database objects from the Database window. Do the following:
RIGHT-CLICK: Courses in the list area
CHOOSE: Print Preview
The Courses table object is displayed in a Print Preview window. (*Note:* To send the datasheet to the printer directly, choose the Print command from the right-click menu. It is a good idea, however, to preview a page first to ensure that it will print as expected.)

 To close the Print Preview window:
CLICK: its Close button ([×])

1.2 Self Check   Describe two methods to quickly move the cursor to the last record in a large datasheet

1.3   Manipulating Table Data

Maintaining a database is difficult work. Updating the contents of a table, adding and deleting records, and fixing mistakes can take a tremendous amount of time. Fortunately, Access provides some tools and features that can help you manipulate data productively. In this module, you learn to enter, edit, and delete data in Datasheet view.

1.3.1   Selecting and Editing Data

FEATURE
You can edit information either as you type or after you have entered data into a table. In Datasheet view, editing changes are made by selecting the data or cell and then issuing a command or typing. The editing changes are saved automatically when you move the cursor to another record.

METHOD

Some points to keep in mind when editing in Datasheet view:

- You can press `F2` to enter and end Edit mode for the current cell.
- If you start typing while data is selected, what you type replaces the selection.
- If the flashing insertion point is positioned in a cell but no data is selected, what you type will be inserted in the field.
- With the insertion point positioned in a cell, press `BACKSPACE` to remove the character to the left of the insertion point and press `DELETE` to remove the character to the right.

PRACTICE

In this lesson, you practice editing table data in the ACC100 database.

Setup: Ensure that the ACC100 Database window is displayed. If not, open the ACC100 database from your student data files location.

1 In the Database window, ensure that the *Tables* button in the Objects bar is selected. Then do the following:
DOUBLE-CLICK: Instructors in the list area
The Instructors Datasheet window is displayed.

2 To position the cursor in the Office column of the first record:
PRESS: ➡ three times
Notice that the entire cell entry "A220" is selected.

3 To update the Office number:
TYPE: B113
PRESS: `ENTER`
Notice that the new office number replaces the selection. When you press `ENTER`, the cursor moves to the first field of the next record.

4 Rather than replacing an entire entry, let's edit the contents of InstructorID 4. Position the I-beam mouse pointer to the right of the last name "Kunicki" and then click once. A flashing insertion point appears to the right of the trailing letter "i," which means that you are ready to edit the cell's contents. (*Hint:* You can also position the insertion point by first selecting the cell using the cursor keys and then pressing `F2` to enter Edit mode.)

ACCESS

5 To replace the final "i" in Kunicki with a "y," do the following:
PRESS: [BACKSPACE]
TYPE: y
Notice that a pencil icon (✐) appears in the row's selector button. This icon indicates that you have not yet saved the editing changes.

6 To complete the editing process:
PRESS: [ENTER]
The pencil icon remains displayed. (*Hint:* You can also press [F2] to toggle Edit mode on and off.)

7 To save the changes, you must move the cursor to another record:
PRESS: [↓]
The pencil icon disappears.

8 When you move the mouse pointer over a cell, it changes shape to an I-beam so that you may easily position the insertion point between characters. In order to select an entire cell for editing, you position the mouse pointer over the top or left grid line of a cell and click once. You know the mouse pointer is properly positioned when it changes shape to a cross. To select the contents of the LastName field for InstructorID 7, position the mouse pointer as shown below.

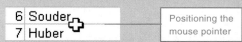

| 6 | Souder |
| 7 | Huber |

Positioning the mouse pointer

9 To select the cell:
CLICK: left mouse button once
The entire "Huber" cell is highlighted in reverse video.

10 Let's assume that Tessa got married recently and has decided to change her name. Do the following:
TYPE: Moss
The pencil icon appears in the row's selector button.

11 To save the changes:
PRESS: [↓] to move to the next record

In Addition
Saving Your Changes

Rather than moving to another row, you can save the changes you make to the current record by pressing [SHIFT] + [ENTER]. This keyboard shortcut allows you to write the changes permanently to the disk without having to move to another record.

1.3.2 Using the Undo Command

FEATURE

The **Undo command** allows you to reverse mistakes during editing. Unlike other Office products, Access does not offer a multiple undo capability. Therefore, you must remember to choose the command immediately after making a mistake.

METHOD

To reverse the last action performed:
- CHOOSE: Edit, Undo, or
- CLICK: Undo button (▣), or
- PRESS: CTRL + z

(*Note:* The command's name changes to reflect the action that may be reversed. For example, on the Edit pull-down menu, the command may read Undo Current Field/Record, Undo Delete, or Undo Saved Record.)

PRACTICE

Using the Undo command, you practice reversing common editing procedures.

Setup: Ensure that you have completed the previous lesson and that the Instructors datasheet is displayed.

1 You've just been informed that "Robert Harris" prefers to go by the name of "Bobby." Let's edit the table:
SELECT: the FirstName cell for InstructorID 5
The cell containing "Robert" is highlighted, as shown below.

Click the top or
left gridline to —
select the cell.

Kenyon	A310
Robert	B103
Manfred	B108

2 TYPE: Bobby
PRESS: ENTER
The cursor moves to the next field in the current record.

3 To undo the last edit using the Menu bar:
CHOOSE: Edit, Undo Current Field/Record
The contents revert back to "Robert," yet the cursor remains in the Office column.

ACCESS

4 To practice deleting a cell entry, let's remove the Office assignment for Anna Cortez:
SELECT: the Office cell for InstructorID 8, as shown below

Tessa	B104
Anna	A316
Simon	A319

5 To remove the entry:
PRESS: DELETE

6 To save the changes and move to the next record:
PRESS: ⬇

7 Even though this change has been saved and recorded to disk, Access lets you reverse the deletion. Do the following:
CLICK: Undo button (🔄)
(*Note:* In this step, clicking the toolbar button executes the Edit, Undo Saved Record command.)

In Addition
Using ESC to Undo Changes

Instead of choosing the Undo command from the menu, you can undo changes in the current field by pressing ESC once. Pressing ESC a second time will undo all of the changes made to the current record.

1.3.3 Adding Records

FEATURE
In Datasheet view, you typically add new records to the blank row appearing at the bottom of a datasheet. If the text "(AutoNumber)" appears in a cell, press ENTER, TAB, or ➡ to bypass the cell and move to the next field. Any cell containing an *AutoNumber* field is incremented automatically by Access when a new record is added to the table.

METHOD
Use any of the following methods to position the cursor in a blank row at the bottom of the datasheet, ready for inserting a new record:
● CLICK: New Record button (▶*) on the toolbar, or
● CLICK: New Record button (▶*) in the navigation bar, or
● CHOOSE: Insert, New Record from the Menu bar

PRACTICE

In this lesson, you insert two records into the Instructors datasheet.

Setup: Ensure that the Instructors datasheet is displayed.

1 To position the cursor at the bottom of the datasheet:
CLICK: New Record button (▶*) on the toolbar

2 Because the InstructorID column contains an AutoNumber entry:
PRESS: TAB to move to the next field
(*Note:* You can also press ENTER to move to the next field. The convention in this guide, however, is to use TAB to move the cursor forward and SHIFT + TAB to move the cursor backward.)

3 Let's enter the new record information:
TYPE: Joyce
PRESS: TAB
Notice that the AutoNumber entry for the InstructorID column is calculated and entered automatically.

4 To complete the entry:
TYPE: James
PRESS: TAB
TYPE: C230
Your screen should now appear similar to Figure 1.12. Notice that the pencil icon appears in the current row's selector button and that a new row was added, as denoted with an asterisk in its selector button.

Figure 1.12
Adding a new record

A pencil icon in a row selector button indicates that the current record has not yet been saved.

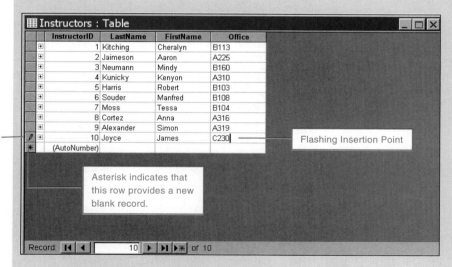

5 To save the record and move to the next row:
PRESS: TAB
(*Note:* Again, you can also press ENTER to move the cursor.)

ACCESS

6 On your own, add the following two records to the datasheet:

InstructorID: 11   InstructorID: 12
LastName: Melville   LastName: Conrad
FirstName: Herman   FirstName: Joseph
Office: C240   Office: C220

7 To return to the top of the datasheet:
PRESS: CTRL + HOME

1.3.4 Deleting Records

FEATURE
In Datasheet view, Access provides several methods for removing records from a table. To do so efficiently, however, you must learn how to select records. Using the mouse, you click and drag the pointer in the **record selection area**, sometimes called the *row selector buttons*. Refer to the diagram below for clarification on the parts of a Datasheet window.

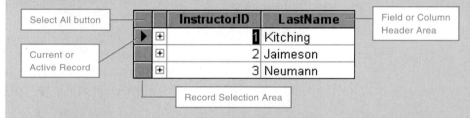

METHOD
1. SELECT: a record or group of records
2. CLICK: Delete Record button (⊠), or
   PRESS: DELETE, or
   CHOOSE: Edit, Delete Record

PRACTICE
You now practice selecting and removing records from a datasheet.

Setup: Ensure that the Instructors datasheet is displayed.

1 To begin, let's select all the records in the current datasheet:
CLICK: Select All button (▢) in the upper left-hand corner
All of the records should now appear in reverse video (white on black).

2 To remove the highlighting:
PRESS: HOME

3 To select record number 3, position the mouse pointer to the left of the desired record in the record selection area. The mouse pointer changes shape to a black horizontal right-pointing arrow (→). When positioned over the row selector button properly, click the left mouse button once to select the entire row.

4 Let's remove the selected record from the table:
CLICK: Delete Record button (⌧) on the toolbar
A confirmation dialog box appears, as shown in Figure 1.13. (*CAUTION:* Access displays this dialog box whenever you delete records. Click the Yes command button to permanently remove the record or click No to return the datasheet to its previous state.)

Figure 1.13

Removing records from a datasheet

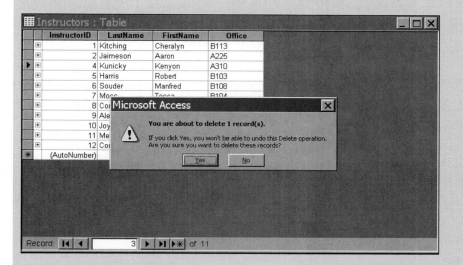

5 To confirm the deletion:
CLICK: Yes

6 You can also delete numerous records with a single command. To illustrate, click once in the record selection area for Manfred Souder's entry (InstructorID 6) and hold down the left mouse button. Then drag the mouse pointer downward to Anna Cortez's record (InstructorID 8). Release the mouse button to display the selected records.

7 To delete the selected records:
PRESS: DELETE
CLICK: Yes to confirm

8 To close the Instructors datasheet:
CLICK: its Close button (⊠)
You should now see the Database window for the ACC100 database.

To close the ACC100 database:
CLICK: its Close button ([X])

 To exit Access:
CHOOSE: File, Exit

1.3 Self Check   When does Access save the changes that you've made when editing a record?

1.4 Chapter Review

Microsoft Access is a full-featured database management application for desktop computers. Database software enables you to store and manipulate large amounts of data such as customer mailing lists. When you first open a database using Access, you are presented with a control center called the Database window. From this one window, you can create and display a variety of objects, including tables, forms, queries, and reports. In this chapter, you learned how to open a database, select database objects, and display and print the contents of a Datasheet window. In addition to navigating a datasheet, you learned to insert, modify, and delete records. You also practiced using the Undo command to reverse your mistakes.

1.4.1 Command Summary

Many of the commands and procedures appearing in this chapter are summarized in the following table.

Skill Set	To Perform This Task . . .	Do the Following . . .
Using Access	Launch Microsoft Access	CLICK: Start button ([Start]) CHOOSE: Programs, Microsoft Access
	Exit Microsoft Access	CLICK: its Close button ([X]), or CHOOSE: File, Exit
	Close a database	CLICK: its Close button ([X]), or CHOOSE: File, Close

Continued

Skill Set	To Perform This Task . . .	Do the Following . . .
Viewing and Organizing Information	Expand/collapse subdatasheets in a Datasheet window	CLICK: Expand button (⊞) CLICK: Collapse button (⊟)
	Adjust a column's width in in the field header area	DRAG: a column's right border line a datasheet
	Adjust the height of all rows in a datasheet	DRAG: a row's bottom border line in the record selection area
	Add a new record to a datasheet	CLICK: New Record buttons (▶* or ▶※)
	Delete selected record(s) from a datasheet	CLICK: Delete Record button (▧), or PRESS: DELETE
Working with Access	Select and open database objects using the Objects bar	CLICK: the desired object category DOUBLE-CLICK: the desired object
	Navigate to a specific record	CLICK: in the navigation text box TYPE: the desired record number PRESS: ENTER
	Toggle Edit mode on and off for editing a datasheet cell	PRESS: F2 Edit key
	Reverse or undo the most recent changes or mistakes	CLICK: Undo button (↶), or CHOOSE: Edit, Undo
	Save the editing changes to the current record	PRESS: SHIFT + ENTER
	Preview a datasheet for printing	CLICK: Print Preview button (◳), or CHOOSE: File, Print Preview
	Print a datasheet	CLICK: Print button (🖶), or CHOOSE: File, Print
	Change the page orientation for a printed document	CHOOSE: File, Page Setup CLICK: *Page* tab SELECT: *Portrait* or *Landscape*

ACCESS

1.4.2 Key Terms

This section specifies page references for the key terms identified in this chapter. For a complete list of definitions, refer to the Glossary at the end of this learning guide.

application window, *p. 10*

cell, *p. 15*

database, *p. 5*

database management system (DBMS), *p. 5*

Database window, *p. 12*

datasheet, *p. 15*

Datasheet view, *p. #15*

field, *p. 5*

field header area, *p. 19*

form, *p. 13*

Objects bar, *p. 12*

Places bar, *p. 9*

query, *p. 13*

record, *p. 5*

record selection area, *p. 30*

report(s), *p. 14*

subdatasheet, *p. 17*

table, *p. 5*

Undo command, *p. 27*

1.5 Review Questions

1.5.1 Short Answer

1. Provide examples of when you might use a database.
2. Define the following terms: *table*, *record*, and *field*.
3. What is an *object* in Microsoft Access? Provide examples.
4. Which database object is used to collect and store data?
5. Which database object displays in Preview mode when opened?
6. Why is the Database window referred to as a *control center*?
7. How do you select the contents of a cell in a datasheet?
8. How do you select all of the records displayed in a datasheet?
9. What is the procedure for adding a record in Datasheet view?
10. What is the procedure for deleting records in Datasheet view?

1.5.2 True/False

1. __F__ DBMS stands for Database Backup Management System.
2. __T__ When you first launch Access, the startup dialog box appears.
3. __F__ A *form* is a database object that displays multiple records in a column and row layout.
4. __T__ A *query* allows you to ask questions of your data and to combine information from more than one table.
5. __T__ The column widths of a datasheet cannot be adjusted once information has been entered into the cells.
6. _____ Changing the height of one row in a datasheet affects the height of every row.
7. __T__ If you want to fit more field columns on a single page, you can select landscape orientation for printing.
8. __T__ If you make a mistake while editing a field, you can press ⌈ESC⌉ to undo the error.
9. __F__ In a datasheet, the *record selection area* is the gray area at the top of each column.
10. __T__ Access allows you to delete several records at once.

1.5.3 Multiple Choice

1. Which of the following buttons does not appear in the Objects bar?
   a. Programs
   b. Modules
   c. Reports
   d. Forms

2. Which database object do you use to display information for one record at a time?
   a. table
   b. report
   c. form
   d. query

3. In a datasheet, the intersection of a row and column is called a:
   a. cell
   b. cursor
   c. form
   d. record

4. In a datasheet, what does each column represent?
    a. database
    b. table
    c. record
    ✓d. field

5. In a datasheet, which mouse pointer do you use to select a cell by clicking on its gridline?
    a. ▲
    b. ✛
    c. ⌛
    d. I

6. In a datasheet, which icon appears at the left side of a record while it is being edited?
    a. Pencil (✐)
    b. Asterisk (✳)
    c. Pointer (▶)
    d. Selector (▢)

7. When editing a record, which keystroke allows you to save the changes without leaving the current record?
    a. CTRL + ENTER
    b. CTRL + ALT
    c. ALT + ENTER
    d. SHIFT + ENTER

8. Which of the following will not reverse the last action performed?
    a. CHOOSE: Edit, Undo *command*
    b. CLICK: Undo button (↺)
    c. PRESS: CTRL + X
    d. PRESS: ESC

9. Any cell containing this type of field is incremented automatically by Access when a new record is added.
    a. AutoElevate
    b. AutoIncrement
    c. AutoNumber
    d. AutoValue

10. The row selector buttons in a datasheet are located in the:
    a. row selection area
    b. record selection area
    c. field selection area
    d. table selection area

1.6   Hands-On Projects

1.6.1 World Wide Imports: Sales Representatives

This exercise lets you practice fundamental database skills, such as opening a database, displaying a table, and navigating a datasheet.

1. Load Microsoft Access using the Windows Start menu.
2. To open an existing database using the startup dialog box:
    SELECT: *Open an existing file* option button
    SELECT: More Files... in the list box area
    CLICK: OK command button
3. Using either the Places bar or the *Look in* drop-down list box:
    SELECT: *the folder location* of your Advantage student data files
    DOUBLE-CLICK: ACC160 in the list area
    The Database window appears.
4. Ensure that the *Tables* button in the Objects bar is selected. Then do the following to display the Sales Reps table:
    DOUBLE-CLICK: 161 Sales Reps in the list area
    A table with 12 records and five field columns is displayed.
5. To move to second field of the third record:
    PRESS: ⬇ two times
    PRESS: ➡ once
    The cursor should now highlight the name "Louis."
6. Now move to the last record using the mouse:
    CLICK: Last Record button (⏭)
7. To quickly move to the top of the datasheet using the keyboard:
    PRESS: CTRL + HOME
8. Each sales rep at World Wide Imports is responsible for servicing specific customer accounts. You can display the customer accounts for each sales rep in a *subdatasheet*. To do so, let's drill down and display the customers assigned to Peter Fink (SalesRep A14):
    CLICK: Expand button (⊞) in the left-hand column of record 5
    Your screen should now appear similar to Figure 1.14.

ACCESS

Figure 1.14

Displaying the customers
assigned to a sales rep

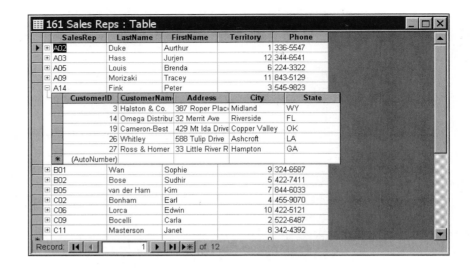

9. On your own, practice opening a few more subdatasheets. When you are finished, hide each subdatasheet by clicking the Collapse button (⊟) in the left-hand column.
10. To close the 161 Sales Reps Datasheet window: CLICK: its Close button (☒)

1.6.2 CyberWeb: Internet Accounts

In this exercise, you practice adjusting a datasheet's column widths and row heights before previewing it for printing.

1. Ensure that Access is loaded. Then open the data file named ACC160, if its Database window is not already displayed.
2. SELECT: *Tables* button in the Objects bar
DOUBLE-CLICK: 162 Internet Accounts
3. Let's adjust the width of the Address field column by having Access calculate its best width:
SELECT: any cell in the Address column
CHOOSE: Format, Column Width
CLICK: Best Fit command button
4. Now use the mouse to adjust the width of the Phone column. In the field header area, position the mouse pointer over the border line between the Phone and Amount fields.
CLICK: the border line and hold down the mouse button
DRAG: the mouse pointer to the left to decrease the width (to approximately the end of the word "Phone")
5. To set the best-fit width for the Zip column using the mouse:
DOUBLE-CLICK: the border line between Zip and Phone
6. On your own, adjust the width of the City column so that it is narrower.

7. To change the row height setting for all the rows in the
    datasheet:
    CHOOSE: Format, Row Height
    TYPE: **15**
    CLICK: OK

8. Now let's see what the datasheet would look like if it was
    printed:
    CLICK: Print Preview button (🔍) on the toolbar

9. On your own, zoom in and out on the Print Preview window
    using the magnifying glass mouse pointer.

10. If you have a printer connected to your computer, print the
    datasheet. Otherwise, proceed to step 11.
    CLICK: Print button (🖨) on the toolbar

11. To close the Print Preview window so that the 162 Internet
    Accounts datasheet remains displayed:
    CLICK: Close command button in the toolbar

12. To close the datasheet without saving the formatting changes:
    CLICK: its Close button (❌)
    CLICK: No command button

■ 1.6.3 Big Valley Mills: Forest Products

In this exercise, you edit data in an existing datasheet and practice
using the Undo command.

Setup: Ensure the ACC160 Database window is displayed.

1. SELECT: *Tables* button in the Objects bar
    DOUBLE-CLICK: 163 Products

2. To position the cursor in the Species column of the third
    record:
    PRESS: ⊕ two times
    PRESS: ➔ once

3. Let's change this cell value to match the standard abbrevia-
    tion. With the entry selected, enter the new data:
    TYPE: **DFIR**

4. To save the changes, move the cursor to the next record:
    PRESS: ⊕
    The pencil icon disappears.

5. Now let's edit the product code of record number 4. (*Hint:*
    Glance at the navigation bar in the Datasheet window to see
    the current record number.) Position the I-beam mouse pointer
    to the right of the product code "DF210S" and then click
    once. A flashing insertion point appears to the right of the
    letter "S."

6. To delete the final "S" in DF210S and save the change:
    PRESS: **[BACKSPACE]**
    PRESS: ⊕

7. SELECT: Grade cell for record 1 using the mouse
   (*Hint:* Position the mouse pointer over the cell's left gridline so that the pointer changes to a cross shape. Then click the left mouse button once to select the entire cell.)
8. Replace the cell's contents with the new Grade code "Utility" and then save the changes.
9. To move the cursor to the last field of the first record:
   PRESS: CTRL + ⬆
   PRESS: END
10. To delete the entry and save the change:
    PRESS: DELETE
    PRESS: ⬇
11. To reverse the deletion using the Menu bar:
    CHOOSE: Edit, Undo Saved Record
    (*Note:* Instead of using the menu, you could have clicked the Undo button (⬛) to achieve the same result.)
12. Close the Datasheet window.

1.6.4 Silverdale Festival: Contact List

You will now practice adding and deleting records in an existing table.

Setup: Ensure the ACC160 Database window is displayed.

1. Display the "164 Contacts" table object in Datasheet view.
2. To position the cursor at the bottom of the datasheet, ready for inserting a new record:
   CLICK: New Record button (⬛) on the toolbar
3. The first column contains an AutoNumber entry, so we can immediately move to the next field:
   PRESS: TAB
4. Let's start entering the new record information:
   TYPE: Silverdale Search and Rescue
   PRESS: TAB
   Notice that the AutoNumber entry for the ID column is calculated and entered automatically.
5. To continue filling out the record:
   TYPE: Amy McTell
   PRESS: TAB
   TYPE: P.O. Box 1359
   PRESS: TAB
   TYPE: Silverdale
   PRESS: TAB
   TYPE: 474-9636
   PRESS: TAB two times

6. On your own, add the following record to the datasheet:
   Volunteer Group: **Historical Society**
   Contact: **Craig Burns**
   Address: **3528 Pacific Ave.**
   City: **Silverdale**
   Phone 1: **945-6621**

7. To delete a record that was inadvertently entered twice, select ID 61 (which is also record number 61) using the record selection area. (*Hint:* The mouse pointer changes shape to a black horizontal right-pointing arrow (➡) when positioned properly.)

8. Let's remove the selected record from the table:
   CLICK: Delete Record button (📧) on the toolbar

9. To confirm the deletion:
   CLICK: Yes
   Notice that the values in the ID column now jump from 60 to 62. As you can see, an AutoNumber field, such as a record ID number, is just another table value; it does not have to match a record's number.

10. Close the Datasheet window.

1.6.5 On Your Own: Office Mart Inventory

To practice navigating and formatting a table's datasheet, open the table object named "165 Inventory" in the ACC160 database. Experiment with the various mouse and keyboard methods for moving the cursor in the datasheet. After you have familiarized yourself with the table, use the keyboard to reposition the cursor to the first field of the first record.

Resize the ProductID, Description, and Suggested Retail columns to their best fit. Adjust the Onhand and Cost columns to 12 characters. Change the height of all the rows to 14 points. Now, use Print Preview to see how the datasheet will look when it's printed. Change the page setup to landscape orientation so that all the columns fit on a single page, as shown in Figure 1.15. If they do not, adjust the widths of the remaining columns until they do. When you are satisfied with the appearance of the page, print a copy of the datasheet and exit Access without saving the changes to the layout.

Figure 1.15

Previewing a datasheet with a landscape print orientation

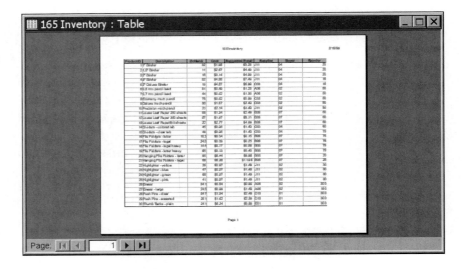

1.6.6 On Your Own: Sun Bird Resort

To practice manipulating table data, open the table object named "166 Patrons" in the ACC160 database.

Make the following editing changes:
- Change the spelling of guest ID 2 from "Neely" to "Neally"
- Change the Interest of guest ID 6 from "Tennis" to "Golf"
- Change the Hometown of guest ID 8 from "Clonkurry" to "Mount Isa"
- Change the Best Time of guest ID 22 to "11:30 AM"

Make the following addition:
Guest: `Ric Fernando`
Hometown: `Manila`
State: *(leave blank)*
Co: `PHI`
Interest: `Golf`
Room#: `B311`
#Stay: `1`
Best Time: `1:00 PM`

Finally, delete the record for guest ID 15. Once finished, close the Datasheet window, close the ACC160 database, and exit Microsoft Access.

1.7 Case Problems: On-Track Seminars

Joanna has been working at On-Track Seminars for several days now and is starting to become quite comfortable in her new job. In addition to her regular administrative duties, she is responsible for managing an Access database. Having never used database software before, she enrolled in an evening course on Microsoft Access at the local community college. Now she feels ready to open and view the contents of the company's database.

In the following case problems, assume the role of Joanna and perform the same steps that she identifies. You may want to re-read the chapter opening before proceeding.

1. Midway through the morning, Joanna receives a phone call from an agitated instructor. "Hello Joanna? My name is Mary Sterba and I teach the "Safety in the Workplace" seminars. Due to a family emergency, I can't make my TR145 seminar this Tuesday. Please call the students and ask if they can transfer into TR146 the following week."

    To start, Joanna loads the ACC170 database located in her Advantage student data files folder. From the Database window, she opens the Trainers table and locates Mary Sterba's record. She expands the subdatasheet for Mary's record and verifies that she is indeed scheduled to teach both the TR145 and TR146 seminars. Next she expands the subdatasheet for TR146, as shown in Figure 1.16, to ensure that it does not have more than 10 students registered. After collapsing the subdatasheet, she expands the TR145 subdatasheet in order to list the names and phone numbers of all students registered in the cancelled class. She will use the list to call the students and reschedule them into the next seminar. Having completed her first task using Access, Joanna closes the Trainers table.

ACCESS

Figure 1.16

Drilling down into a table's
data using subdatasheets

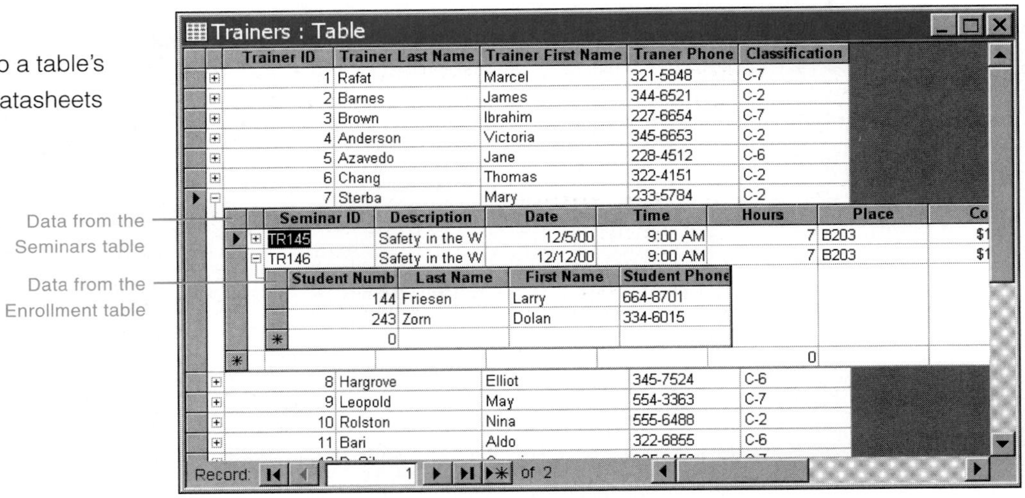

Data from the
Seminars table

Data from the
Enrollment table

2. Later that day, Karen Chase, the office director, asks Joanna to produce a printout of the currently scheduled seminars. Joanna opens the Seminars table in the ACC170 database and adjusts the column width of the Description field so that the entire title is visible. To provide some additional white space in the printout, she adjusts the height of all the rows to 16 points. Using Print Preview to view the datasheet, Joanna notices that not all columns fit on a single page. To compensate, she changes the page setup to use landscape orientation and adjusts the datasheet's column widths as necessary. When she is satisfied with the appearance of the datasheet, Joanna prints a copy for Karen. Then she closes the Seminars table without saving the formatting changes she has made.

3. Joanna phones the five students whose phone numbers she wrote down earlier that day and determines that they are all indeed able to switch to the later "Safety in the Workplace" seminar. To update the database, Joanna begins by opening the Enrollment table. She locates the five students' records and changes the Seminar ID for each record from TR145 to TR146. She then switches to the Database window and opens the Seminars table. To finish the task, Joanna deletes the record for Seminar TR145 and closes both datasheets.

4. Toward the end of the day, Joanna receives two phone calls from people wishing to register for seminars. After writing down the information, Joanna is ready to update the database. She opens the Enrollment table and adds two new records:

Student Number: **501**
Last Name: **Haldane**
First Name: **Chris**
Student Phone: **577-9685**
Seminar ID: **TR135**

Student Number: **502**
Last Name: **Zhou**
First Name: **Shih-Chang**
Student Phone: **345-6087**
Seminar ID: **TR146**

She saves the records and closes the datasheet. Then she closes the Database window and exits Microsoft Access.

NOTES

NOTES

NOTES

MICROSOFT ACCESS 2000
Creating a Database

CHAPTER
TWO

Chapter Outline

Learning Objectives

After reading this chapter, you will be able to:

- Create a new database using the Database Wizard

- Create a new database from scratch

- Define table objects for storing data

- Specify a primary key and indexes

- Rename, delete, and move fields

- Print a table's structure

[handwritten: F2 change info]

[handwritten: Due 11/28/00]

Case Study

Inland Transit

Inland Transit operates a fleet of trucks in the Pacific Northwest. Last week, Inland's management team asked their controller, Mike Lambert, to locate and summarize a variety of information about the business. After spending three days reviewing reports and searching through filing cabinets, Mike came to the realization that he needs a better information management system. He evaluates the leading database software programs and decides to use Microsoft Access to create a company database. Mike starts the process by laying out his design ideas on paper. He wants to ensure that all of the company's relevant business information is collected, stored, and readied for processing.

In this chapter, you and Mike learn about creating databases and tables using Microsoft Access. You also learn how to modify a table's design by adding and removing fields. Lastly, you use a special Access program called the Documenter to produce a printout of a table's structure.

2.1 Designing Your First Database

Desktop database software has existed since the first personal computer was introduced by IBM in the early 1980s. Since that time many database programs and applications have been developed for both personal and business use. Whatever your particular data management needs, rarely will you require a truly unique application. Refining or customizing an existing database application is a more common practice. Microsoft Access allows you to take advantage of what others before you have learned and accomplished. Using the Access wizards, you can develop an entire database application in less time than it takes to read this module.

[side tab: ACCESS]

[handwritten: Filters asking question suppose for female once get out list in you to make permanent do a query. It gets saved.]

2.1.1 Employing the Database Wizard

FEATURE

Access provides two main options for creating a new database. First, you can create an empty database structure and then populate it with objects. For example, in an inventory control system, you could create a new database and then add tables for Products, Suppliers, and Customers. Once completed, you would then create the data entry forms, product catalogs, and other reports. The second option is to use the **Database Wizard**. This wizard provides access to professionally designed templates for creating complete database applications. Each template contains tables, queries, forms, reports, and a main menu called a *switchboard* that makes the application's features easier to access.

METHOD

From the Access application window:
1. CLICK: New button (🗅), or
   CHOOSE: File, New
2. CLICK: *Databases* tab in the New dialog box
3. DOUBLE-CLICK: a database wizard (📰)

From the Access startup dialog box:
1. SELECT: *Access database wizards, pages, and projects* option button
2. DOUBLE-CLICK: a database wizard (📰) in the New dialog box

PRACTICE

Using the Access Database Wizard, you create an inventory control application from scratch.

Setup: Ensure that Access is loaded. If you are launching Access and the startup dialog box appears, click the Cancel command button to remove the dialog box from the application window.

1 To create a new database application:
CLICK: New button (🗅) on the toolbar

2 In the New dialog box that appears:
CLICK: *Databases* tab
A list of Database Wizard templates appear in the New dialog box as shown in Figure 2.1. (*Note:* If you haven't installed any database templates, you cannot perform the steps in this lesson.)

Figure 2.1

New dialog box:
Databases tab

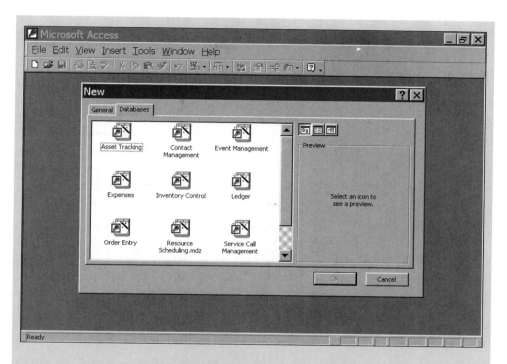

3 Using the appropriate Database Wizard template, let's create an inventory database application:
DOUBLE-CLICK: Inventory Control wizard (🖳)

4 In the File New Database dialog box that appears, use the Places bar or the *Save in* drop-down list box to select your personal storage location. Then, do the following:
TYPE: My Inventory in the *File name* text box
CLICK: Create command button
You should wait patiently as Access displays your new Database window and prepares the Database Wizard dialog box.

5 The opening screen of the Database Wizard dialog box provides information about the Inventory Control wizard. After reading its contents, proceed to the next step:
CLICK: Next >

6 Your first task in the Database Wizard, as shown in Figure 2.2, is to select optional fields for inclusion in the database. These fields appear in italic. On your own, click on the names listed in the *Tables in the database* list box. The field names for the selected table then appear in the *Fields in the table* list box.

ACCESS

Figure 2.2

Inventory Control
Database Wizard

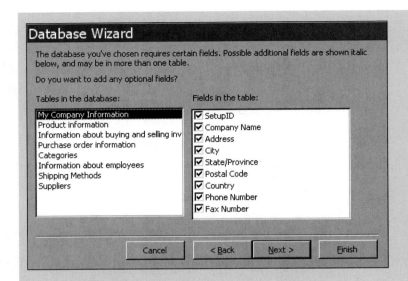

7 To proceed to the next step:
CLICK: [Next >]

8 To select a screen appearance for your forms, click on each option to see a preview and then:
SELECT: SandStone in the list box
CLICK: [Next >]

9 To select a page layout for your printed reports, click on each option to see a preview and then:
SELECT: Soft Gray
CLICK: [Next >]

10 You can also specify the title of the database and whether to include a logo or picture. To accept the default entries:
CLICK: [Next >]

11 At the finish line, you tell Access to create and display the database. Ensure that the *Yes, start the database* check box is selected and then do the following:
CLICK: [Finish]
The Database Wizard creates the database based on your selections. Depending on your system, this process can take a few minutes.

12 In this particular wizard, Access displays a dialog box asking you to furnish some company data. Using the [TAB] key to move forward through the text boxes, type your personal information. When finished:
CLICK: the Close button ([X]) for the dialog box to proceed

The Main Switchboard (Figure 2.3) for the Inventory Control application is displayed. On your own, click on the menu buttons to access and display the forms and reports created by the Database Wizard. Before proceeding, close the form or report Print Preview windows that appear by clicking their Close buttons (☒).

Figure 2.3

Main Switchboard for the
Inventory Control application

Menu buttons on the
Main Switchboard

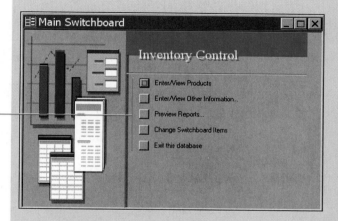

14 Let's examine the database objects that were created for this application. From the Menu bar:
CHOOSE: Window, My Inventory : Database

15 In the Database window, click on the various buttons in the Objects bar to view the table, query, form, and report objects. You may need to scroll the list area or adjust the size of the Database window to see all of the object names. When you are finished, close the application:
CLICK: its Close button (☒)
(*Note:* You can also choose the File, Close command.)
Notice that the Main Switchboard, which appears as a form object, also disappears when you close the Database window.

2.1.2 Planning a Database

FEATURE
Many people who have worked with computer databases can attest to the 90/10 rule of database design. Place 90 percent of your effort into designing a database properly in order to spend only 10 percent of your time maintaining it. As you can probably infer from this rule, many problems arising in database management are traceable to a faulty design. In this lesson, you learn some strategies for planning a well-designed database.

METHOD

Here are five steps to designing a better database:

1. *Determine your output requirements.* State your expectations in terms of the queries and reports desired from the application. It's often helpful to write out questions, such as "How many customers live in Kansas City?", and to sketch out reports on a blank piece of paper.

2. *Determine your input requirements.* From the output requirements, identify the data that must be collected, stored, and calculated. You should also review any existing paper-based forms used for data collection in order to get a better idea of what data is available.

3. *Determine your table structures.* Divide and group data into separate tables and fields for flexibility in searching, sorting, and manipulating data. Review the following example to see what fields can be separated out of a simple address:

Also ensure that each record can be identified using a unique code or field, such as Order Number or Customer ID. This code need not contain information related to the subject—a numeric field that is automatically incremented works fine.

4. *Determine your table relationships.* Rather than entering or storing the same information repeatedly, strive to separate data into multiple tables and then relate the tables using a common field. For example, in a table containing book information (Books), an AuthorID field would contain a unique code

that could be used to look up the author's personal data in a separate table (Authors). Without such a design, you would need to type an author's name and address each time you added one of their works to the Books table.

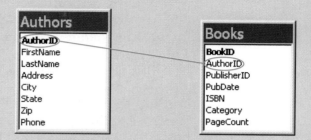

By incorporating common fields into your table structures, you can establish relationships amongst the tables for sharing data. This process, called *normalizing* your data, enhances your efficiency and reduces potential data redundancy and entry errors.

5. *Test your database application.* Add sample records to the table using both datasheets and forms, run queries, and produce reports to test whether the application is robust and accurate. In addition to ensuring the validity and integrity of data, you want the information to be readily accessible. *strong*

2.1.3 Starting a New Database

FEATURE
If you have specific requirements for a database application, you may choose to create a blank structure and then add the appropriate objects. Unlike other Office 2000 applications, such as Word and Excel, Access allows you to work with only one database at a time. Therefore, before starting a new database, you must ensure that there is no active database displayed in the application window's work area.

METHOD
1. CLICK: New (⬜), or
   CHOOSE: File, New
2. CLICK: *General* tab in the New dialog box
3. DOUBLE-CLICK: Database template (⬜)

PRACTICE
In this lesson, you create a new database file for storing table objects.

Setup: Ensure that Access is loaded and that there is no Database window displayed.

1 To create a new database:
CLICK: New button (⬚) on the toolbar

2 In the New dialog box that appears:
CLICK: *General* tab
DOUBLE-CLICK: Database template (🗐)

3 You use the File New Database dialog box (Figure 2.4) to select a storage location and file name for permanently saving the database structure. Using the Places bar or the *Save in* drop-down dialog box, select your personal storage location.

Figure 2.4

File New Database dialog box

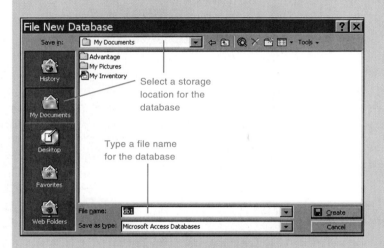

4 In the *File name* text box:
TYPE: My Phone Book
CLICK: Create command button
A new Database window appears in the work area. Notice that the Title bar reads "My Phone Book : Database" and that there are no objects, besides the New Object shortcuts, in the Database window.

5 To close the Database window:
CLICK: its Close button (☒)

2.1 Self Check What two objects are most closely associated with the output of a database application?

2.2 Creating a Simple Table

An Access database file is simply a container for storing database objects. Your first step in creating an application is to define the table objects for storing data. Each table in your database should be related on some level and contain information about a single topic or subject. In an automobile industry database, for example, one table may contain a list of car dealerships while another table contains a list of manufacturers. Although these tables deal with different subjects, they are related to the automobile industry. In this module, you learn two methods for quickly populating a database structure with table objects. What these methods may lack in power and flexibility, they make up for in ease of use and speed.

2.2.1 Creating a Table Using the Table Wizard

FEATURE

Access provides the **Table Wizard** to help you create a table structure, much like you created a complete application using the Database Wizard. Rather than defining a new table from scratch, you compile it by picking and choosing fields from existing personal and business tables. This method lets you quickly populate an empty database structure with reliable and usable table objects.

METHOD

In the Database window, select the *Tables* button and then:
- DOUBLE-CLICK: Create table by using wizard, or
- CLICK: New button (New) on the Database window toolbar
  DOUBLE-CLICK: Table Wizard in the New Table dialog box

PRACTICE

After displaying a new database, you create a table object using the Table Wizard.

Setup: Ensure that there is no Database window displayed.

1 To create a new database:
CLICK: New button ( ) on the toolbar
CLICK: *General* tab
DOUBLE-CLICK: Database template ( )

2 In the File New Database dialog box:
TYPE: My Business into the *File name* text box

ACCESS

3 Using the Places bar or the *Save in* drop-down dialog box, select your personal storage location. Then, do the following:
CLICK: Create command button
The "My Business" Database window will appear.

4 Your next step is to add table objects to the empty database structure. To use the Table Wizard, ensure that the *Tables* button is selected in the Objects bar and then do the following:
DOUBLE-CLICK: Create table by using wizard
The Table Wizard dialog box appears, as shown in Figure 2.5.

Figure 2.5

Table Wizard dialog box

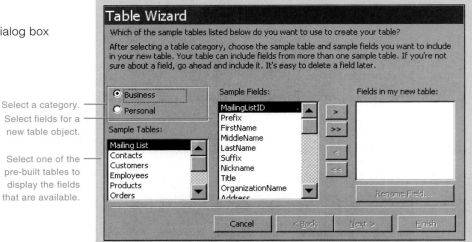

Select a category.
Select fields for a new table object.

Select one of the pre-built tables to display the fields that are available.

5 By default, the *Business* option button is chosen in the Table Wizard dialog box. And as a result, only business-related table structures appear in the *Sample Tables* list box. To view the Personal tables:
CLICK: *Personal* option button

6 On your own, scroll the *Sample Tables* list box to view the available table structures.

7 Let's create a new table to store the company's product information:
CLICK: *Business* option button
SELECT: Products in the *Sample Tables* list box
Notice that the fields for this table structure now appear in the *Sample Fields* list box.

8 In specifying the fields for a table, select individual fields using ⌐›⌐ and select all fields by clicking ⌐»⌐. For this step, let's include all of the suggested fields:
CLICK: Include All button (⌐»⌐)

9 To complete the wizard:
CLICK: [Finish]
The new table, called "Products," appears in a Datasheet window ready to accept data.

10 Close the Products Datasheet window. You should now see the Products table object in the Database window.

2.2.2 Creating a Table in Datasheet View

FEATURE

Using Datasheet view, you create a table by typing information into a blank datasheet, just as you would when entering data into an Excel worksheet. When you save the table, Access creates the table structure and assigns the proper data types to each field based on the information you've entered. This method lets novice users create tables without an in-depth understanding of table structures and data types.

METHOD

In the Database window, select the *Tables* button and then:
- DOUBLE-CLICK: Create table by entering data, or
- CLICK: New button ([New]) on the Database window toolbar
  DOUBLE-CLICK: Datasheet View in the New Table dialog box

PRACTICE

In this lesson, you create a new table in Datasheet view for storing supplier information.

Setup: Ensure that you have completed the previous lesson and that the My Business Database window is displayed.

1 To create a table using Datasheet view, ensure that the *Tables* button is selected in the Objects bar and then do the following:
DOUBLE-CLICK: Create table by entering data
A blank Datasheet window appears with several field columns and blank records.

2 Let's begin by renaming the column headings in the field header area:
DOUBLE-CLICK: Field1
TYPE: SupplierID
DOUBLE-CLICK: Field2
TYPE: Company
DOUBLE-CLICK: Field3
TYPE: Contact
DOUBLE-CLICK: Field4
TYPE: Phone
PRESS: ENTER
The cursor should now appear in the first field of the first record.

3 On your own, enter the records appearing in Figure 2.6.

Figure 2.6

Entering records in Datasheet view

Specify the field names by double-clicking and then typing in the field header area.

Enter sample records so that Access can determine the type of data you want stored.

4 To save and name the new table structure:
CLICK: Save button (⊞) on the toolbar
TYPE: Suppliers into the Save As dialog box
PRESS: ENTER or CLICK: OK

5 In the Alert dialog box that appears, Access offers to define a primary key for the table. A primary key holds a unique value for identifying, locating, and sorting records in a table. To accept the offer:
CLICK: Yes
After a few moments, Access displays the datasheet for the Suppliers table, complete with a new AutoNumber field in the left-hand column.

Close the Suppliers Datasheet window. You should now see the Suppliers table object in the Database window.

 Close the Database window.

2.2 Self Check   How do you specify the name of a field when creating a table in Datasheet view?

2.3 Using the Table Design View

If all of your database needs are satisfied by the templates found in the Database and Table Wizards, you are already on your way to developing robust desktop database applications. To unlock the real power behind Access, however, you must delve into the inner workings of an Access table structure. Using Design view, you create a table by specifying its properties, characteristics, and behaviors down to the field level. While this method requires the greatest understanding of database design, it is well worth the effort in terms of creating efficient custom table structures.

2.3.1 Creating a Table in Design View

FEATURE

Table Design view allows you to get down to the nuts and bolts of designing and constructing a table. In Design view, you create the table structure manually, specifying the field names, data types, and indexes. After some practice, you will find that this method affords the greatest power and flexibility in designing and modifying table objects.

METHOD

In the Database window, select the *Tables* button and then:
- DOUBLE-CLICK: Create table in Design view, or
- CLICK: New button (New) on the Database window toolbar
  DOUBLE-CLICK: Design View in the New Table dialog box

PRACTICE

In Design view, you create a new table structure in this lesson.

Setup: Ensure that there is no Database window displayed.

ACCESS

1 To create a new database:
CLICK: New button (🗅) on the toolbar
CLICK: *General* tab
DOUBLE-CLICK: Database template (📄)

2 In the File New Database dialog box:
TYPE: My Library into the *File name* text box

3 Using the Places bar or the *Save in* drop-down dialog box, select your personal storage location. Then, do the following:
CLICK: Create command button
The "My Library" Database window will appear.

4 Because tables are the foundation for all your queries, forms, and reports, you need to create at least one table before creating any other database object. To add a new table to the database:
CLICK: New button (🗔New) on the Database window toolbar
The New Table dialog box appears as shown in Figure 2.7.

Figure 2.7

New Table dialog box

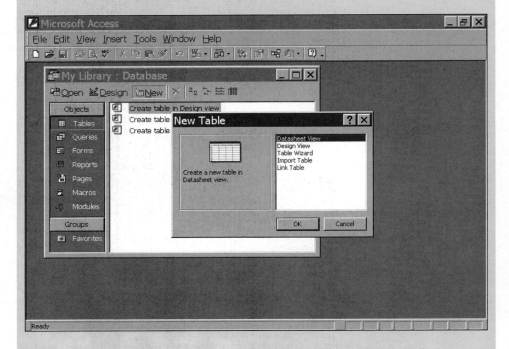

5 The New Table dialog box offers an alternative to selecting a New Object shortcut in the list area of the Database window. To proceed:
DOUBLE-CLICK: Design View

The table Design window, which is divided into a **Field Grid pane** and a **Field Properties pane**, appears in **Design view**. This window is used to add, delete, and rename fields for the table structure; set a field's data type; specify a field's properties or characteristics; and choose a primary key for organizing and sorting a table. The insertion point should now appear in the *Field Name* column. To define the first field in a table that will store information about the books you own:
TYPE: BookID
PRESS: TAB to move to the *Data Type* column
(*Note:* As with adding records, you may press TAB or ENTER to proceed from column to column.)

 By default, Access inserts "Text" as the data type for the BookID field. The data type you select determines the kind of values you can enter into the field. To view the other data type options, described further in Table 2.1, do the following:
CLICK: down arrow attached to the field
Your screen should now appear similar to Figure 2.8. (*CAUTION:* Although you can change the data type after you've entered data, you risk losing information if the data types aren't compatible.)

Figure 2.8

Displaying the data type options in Design view

Use the Field Grid pane to define the fields that you want in the table.

Use the Field Properties pane to specify field characteristics, such as size and display format.

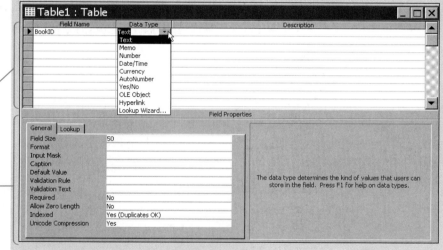

Table 2.1

Data Types

Type	Description
Text	Alphanumeric data, up to 255 characters. Used for entering text and numbers that are not required for calculation, such as zip codes and phone numbers.

Continued

Table 2.1
Data Types
Continued

Type	Description
Memo	Alphanumeric data, up to 64,000 characters. Used to store notes, comments, or lengthy descriptions.
Number	Numeric data that are used to perform mathematical calculations.
Date/Time	Dates and times.
Currency	Numeric data with a leading dollar sign. Used to store and calculate monetary values.
AutoNumber	Numeric value that increments automatically. Used for assigning a unique value to a record, which makes it a fantastic *primary key* field.
Yes/No	Logical or Boolean values for toggling (turning on and off) yes/no or true/false results.
OLE Object	Object Linking and Embedding (OLE) field for storing objects (Excel worksheets and Word documents), graphics, or other binary data up to one gigabyte (GB) in size.
Hyperlink	Text or numbers stored as a hyperlink address. Used to store Web site addresses, also called URLs, such as http://www.mhhe.com/it.
Lookup Wizard	A link to another table or to a static list of values for inserting data into the current table. Selecting this option launches a wizard.

8 For the BookID field's data type:
SELECT: AutoNumber
PRESS: `TAB`

9 The *Description* column allows you to store a helpful comment describing the contents of the field. This comment will also appear in the Status bar when you select the field in Datasheet view. To proceed:
TYPE: `Unique code generated by Access`
PRESS: `ENTER` to move to the next row

On you own, complete the Field Grid pane as displayed in Figure 2.9. Notice that the longer field names, such as PageCount, contain mixed case letters to enhance their readability. When finished, keep the table Design window displayed and proceed to the next lesson.

Figure 2.9
Completing the
Field Grid pane

Row Selection Area of
the Field Grid pane

Field Name	Data Type	Description
BookID	AutoNumber	Unique code generated by Access
ISBN	Text	International Standard Book Number
Title	Text	Main cover title
AuthorSurname	Text	Author's last name
AuthorGiven	Text	Author's first name
Publisher	Text	Publisher's name
PubYear	Number	Year published (i.e., 2000)
PageCount	Number	Total number of pages

In Addition
Field Naming Rules

Access provides specific rules for naming fields in a table. First, names cannot exceed 64 characters in length. Second, names should not contain special symbols or punctuation, such as a period or exclamation point. And lastly, names cannot begin with a space and, in our opinion, should not contain spaces. Descriptive single word names are best.

ACCESS

2.3.2 Assigning a Primary Key

FEATURE
As you create a table structure, you need to specify a field (or fields) that will uniquely identify each and every record in the table. This field, called the **primary key**, is used by Access in searching for data and in establishing relationships between tables. Once a field is defined as the primary key, its datasheet is automatically indexed, or sorted, into order by that field. Access also prevents you from entering a duplicate or **null value** into a primary key field. An **AutoNumber** data type automatically increments as each new record is added to a table, making this data type one of the best choices for a primary key.

METHOD
In table Design view:
1. SELECT: the desired field using the row selection area
2. CLICK: Primary Key button (🔑) on the toolbar, or
    CHOOSE: Edit, Primary Key

PRACTICE
You now assign a primary key field for the table created in the last lesson.

Setup: Ensure that you've completed the previous lesson and that the table Design window is displayed.

1 To select a field for the primary key:
CLICK: row selector button for BookID
(*Hint:* Position the mouse pointer in the row selection area of the Field Grid pane and click the row selector button next to the BookID field.)

2 To assign a primary key:
CLICK: Primary Key button ([🔑])
Your screen should now appear similar to Figure 2.10.

Figure 2.10

Setting the primary key

The primary key icon appears in the field's row selector button.

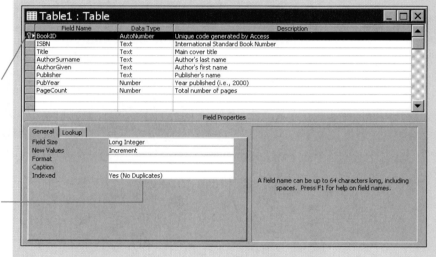

Notice that the field is indexed (sorted) and does not allow duplicate entries.

3 Now that you've assigned the primary key, you can save the table structure. Do the following:
CLICK: Save button ([💾])

4 In the Save As dialog box that appears:
TYPE: **Books**
CLICK: OK
Keep the table Design window displayed for use in the next lesson.

2.3.3 Defining and Removing Indexes

FEATURE

An **index**, like the primary key, is a special mechanism for dynamically organizing and ordering the data stored in a table. By defining indexes, you can speed up the search and sort operations for running queries and reports. However, you do not want to create indexes for all fields as this would slow down the common activities of adding and editing records. As a rule of thumb, just index the fields that you use frequently in searching for and sorting data, such as a Surname or Company Name field.

METHOD

To define an index in table Design view:
1. SELECT: the desired field using the row selection area
2. SELECT: *Indexed* text box in the Field Properties pane
3. CLICK: down arrow attached to the *Indexed* text box
4. SELECT: an indexing option

To remove an index in table Design view:
1. CLICK: Indexes button (📝) on the toolbar
2. RIGHT-CLICK: the desired field's row selection button
3. CHOOSE: Delete Rows

PRACTICE

In this lesson, you create two indexes to complement the primary key and remove an existing index that was created by Access.

Setup: Ensure that you've completed the previous lessons and that the Books table Design window is displayed.

1 In the Books table, you will most likely search for a book based on its title or author. Therefore, let's create indexes for these fields. To begin:
SELECT: Title in the Field Grid pane

2 Using the I-beam mouse pointer:
SELECT: *Indexed* text box in the Field Properties pane

3 With the flashing insertion point in the *Indexed* text box, you may select an indexing option from the drop-down list box. To proceed:
CLICK: down arrow attached to the *Indexed* text box
Your screen should now appear similar to Figure 2.11.

ACCESS

Figure 2.11

Setting an index

Select a field by clicking its row selector button.

Display the indexing options by clicking the attached arrow.

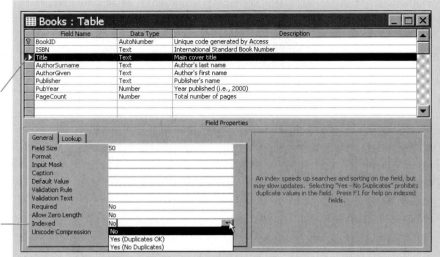

4 Because you do not want to limit the possibility of duplicate entries (different authors may have written a similarly entitled book):
SELECT: Yes (Duplicates OK)

5 Let's define another index for the table:
SELECT: AuthorSurname in the Field Grid pane
SELECT: *Indexed* text box in the Field Properties pane

6 From the drop-down list attached to the *Indexed* text box:
SELECT: Yes (Duplicates OK)

7 Save the table structure:
CLICK: Save button (⊞)
(*Note:* It's a good habit to save the table after each major change.)

8 To display the associated indexes for the Books table:
CLICK: Indexes button (▤⚡)
The Indexes window appears as shown in Figure 2.12.

Figure 2.12

Indexes window for the
Books table

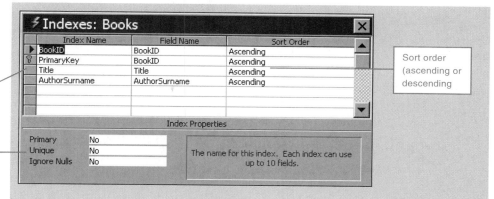

List of indexes

Index properties for
selected index

Sort order
(ascending or
descending)

9 As illustrated in Figure 2.12, Access automatically creates indexes for fields that contain the letters "ID" in their names. The BookID field, for example, is the primary key but also the name of an index. To remove this index:
RIGHT-CLICK: BookID row selector button

10 In the right-click menu that appears:
CHOOSE: Delete Rows
The BookID index is removed but the BookID primary key remains.

11 Close the Indexes window.

12 To clean up the Access work area, save and then close the table Design window. Lastly, close the My Library Database window.

In Addition
Setting Field
Properties

Every field in a table has a set of properties. A field property is a specific characteristic of a field or data type that enables you to provide greater control over how your data is entered, stored, displayed, and printed. Some common properties include *Field Size, Format, Decimal Places, Input Mask, Default Value, Required,* and *Indexed.* You set a field's properties using the Field Properties pane in the table Design window.

2.3 Self Check What is an AutoNumber field? Why is it useful as a primary key?

2.4 Modifying a Table

A database is a dynamic entity. It isn't uncommon to witness the initial design requirements for a database change once it is set in front of users. Fortunately Access enables you to modify a table's structure quickly and efficiently. Adding, deleting, and changing field specifications in table Design view is similar to editing records in a datasheet. Nonetheless, you should not perform structural changes hastily. When you modify a table's structure, you also affect the forms and reports that are based on the table.

2.4.1 Inserting and Deleting Fields

FEATURE

After displaying a table structure in Design view, you can easily add and remove fields. Adding a field is as simple as entering a field name and data type on a blank row in the Field Grid pane. Removing a field deletes the field from the Field Grid pane, but also deletes all of the data that is stored in the field.

METHOD

To insert a field in table Design view:
1. SELECT: an empty row in the Field Grid pane
2. Type a field name, select a data type, and enter a description.

To delete a field in table Design view:
1. RIGHT-CLICK: row selector of the field you want to remove
2. CHOOSE: Delete Rows

PRACTICE

In this lesson, you insert and remove fields in an existing table structure.

Setup: Ensure that there is no Database window displayed.

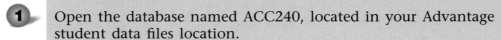 Open the database named ACC240, located in your Advantage student data files location.

This database contains a single table, named Books, that is based on the table structure you created in the last module. To display the table in Datasheet view:
DOUBLE-CLICK: Books

3 With the Datasheet window displayed:
CLICK: View–Design button () on the toolbar
(*Note:* Although the toolbar button is named View, we include the mode name "–Design" for clarity.)

4 Let's add a new field to the table structure that will store a reviewer's synopsis for each book. In the Field Grid pane:
CLICK: in the *Field Name* column of the next empty row
TYPE: `Synopsis`
PRESS: `TAB`

5 Since the contents of the field will be entered mostly in paragraph form, select Memo as the field's data type:
CLICK: down arrow attached to the *Data Type* cell
SELECT: Memo
PRESS: `TAB`

6 In the *Description* column:
TYPE: `Reviewer's synopsis or abstract`
PRESS: `ENTER`

7 To insert a new field between two existing fields, right-click the desired row selector button and then choose the Insert Rows command. Similarly you can delete an existing field using the right-click menu. To demonstrate, let's remove the PageCount field:
RIGHT-CLICK: row selector button for PageCount
Your screen should now appear similar to Figure 2.13.

Figure 2.13

Displaying a field's right-click menu

Right-click menu for the PageCount field

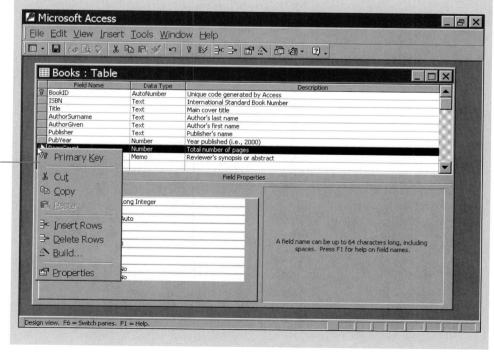

8 From the right-click menu:
CHOOSE: Delete Rows

9 To confirm that the deletion will also remove all the data in the field:
CLICK: Yes

10 Let's save and then view the table:
CLICK: Save button (⊞)
CLICK: View–Datasheet button (⊞)

11 To enter a brief synopsis for the first record:
PRESS: `END`
TYPE: `Another thrilling novel about Soviet and American attempts to develop a Strategic Defense Initiative (SDI). A CIA undercover confidant named the Cardinal provides a steady stream of Soviet secrets. Once compromised, however, Jack Ryan and John Clark, an ex-Navy SEAL, are given the task of pulling the Cardinal to safety.`
PRESS: `ENTER`

12 Close the Datasheet window.

2.4.2 Renaming and Moving Fields

FEATURE
In addition to modifying a table's structure, renaming and moving fields in Design view affects the display of a datasheet. You may have noticed that the columns in Datasheet view follow the field names and display order appearing in Design view. More importantly, however, you can speed up most database operations by moving frequently used fields (those used as primary keys or in indexes) to the top of a table structure.

METHOD
• To rename a field, edit the contents of the *Field Name* column as you would modify a cell entry in a datasheet.
• To move a field, click the field's row selector button and then drag it to the desired target location.

PRACTICE
You now practice renaming and moving fields in table Design view.

Setup: Ensure that the ACC240 Database window is displayed.

1. To display the Books table object in Design view:
   SELECT: Books in the list area
   CLICK: Design button (Design) on the Database window toolbar

2. Let's rename the Author fields. Using the I-beam mouse pointer:
   CLICK: to the right of "AuthorSurname" in the *Field Name* column
   The flashing insertion point should appear to the right of the name.

3. To remove the "Surname" portion of the cell entry:
   PRESS: BACKSPACE seven times

4. TYPE: **Last**
   PRESS: ↓
   The cell entry should now read "AuthorLast."

5. To remove the "Given" portion of the current entry:
   PRESS: F2 (Edit mode)
   PRESS: BACKSPACE five times
   TYPE: **First**
   PRESS: ↓
   The cell entry now reads "AuthorFirst."

6. Let's move the ISBN field below the AuthorFirst field. To begin:
   CLICK: row selector button for ISBN

7. Using the arrow mouse pointer:
   DRAG: row selector button for ISBN downward until a bold gridline appears below the AuthorFirst field

8. Release the mouse button. Your screen should now appear similar to Figure 2.14.

Field Name	Data Type	Description
BookID	AutoNumber	Unique code generated by Access
Title	Text	Main cover title
AuthorLast	Text	Author's last name
AuthorFirst	Text	Author's first name
ISBN	Text	International Standard Book Number
Publisher	Text	Publisher's name
PubYear	Number	Year published (i.e., 2000)
Synopsis	Memo	Reviewer's synopsis or abstract

Figure 2.14
Renaming and moving fields in table Design view

9. To save and then view the changes in Datasheet view:
   CLICK: Save button
   CLICK: View–Datasheet button
   Notice that the field header area displays the new field names in the modified field order.

10. Close the Datasheet window.

2.4.3 Printing a Table's Design Structure

FEATURE
Access provides a special tool called the **Documenter** that allows you to preview and print various design characteristics of your database objects, including a table's structure and field properties. This tool is especially useful when you are planning or revising a table's field specification.

METHOD
1. CHOOSE: Tools, Analyze, Documenter
2. CLICK: *Tables* tab
3. SELECT: the desired object or objects
4. CLICK: Options command button
5. SELECT: the desired options
6. CLICK: OK

PRACTICE
In this lesson, you prepare a documentation printout of the Books table.

Setup: Ensure that the ACC240 Database window is displayed.

1 To launch the Access Documenter:
CHOOSE: Tools, Analyze, Documenter
The Documenter window appears as shown in Figure 2.15.

Figure 2.15

Documenter window

Click the check box to include an object in the Documenter's report

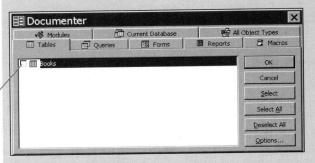

2 To print the design structure for the Books table object, ensure that the *Tables* tab is selected and then:
SELECT: Books check box so that a "✔" appears

3 To specify report options:
CLICK: Options command button
The Print Table Definition dialog box appears.

4 For this example, let's specify that only the table structure is printed. In the *Include for Table* area, remove all of the selections so that no "✔" appears in any of the check boxes.

5 In the *Include for Fields* area:
SELECT: *Names, Data Types, and Sizes* option button

6 In the *Include for Indexes* area:
SELECT: *Names and Fields* option button
CLICK: OK

7 To preview the report printout:
CLICK: OK

8 On your own, move, size, and scroll the Object Definition window to appear similar to Figure 2.16.

Figure 2.16

Object Definition Window

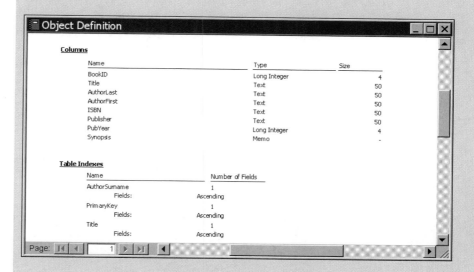

9 To print the documentation report:
CLICK: Print button (🖨) on the toolbar

10 Close the Object Definition window. Then, close the ACC240 Database window. Lastly, exit Microsoft Access.

2.4 Self Check   What happens to your table's data if you delete a field in table Design view?

2.5 Chapter Review

Access provides several tools to help novice users create new database applications. The Database Wizard offers a variety of professionally designed template solutions for common database problems. After you proceed through a few simple steps in the wizard, Access creates a comprehensive set of database objects, including tables, forms, and reports, that you can put to use immediately. If you prefer having more control, you can opt to create an empty database and then populate it with standard tables using the Table Wizard. Another straightforward method involves designing a table simply by entering data into a Datasheet window. And lastly, you can use Design view in order to develop a custom table object. In the table Design window, you add, delete, rename, move, and manipulate fields and indexes individually, in addition to specifying each field's properties and characteristics. In this chapter, you learned to design new database applications and to create and modify table objects.

2.5.1 Command Summary

Many of the commands and procedures appearing in this chapter are summarized in the following table.

Skill Set	To Perform This Task . . .	Do the Following . . .
Working with Access	Create a new empty database	CLICK: New button ( ) CLICK: *General* tab DOUBLE-CLICK: Database template ( )
	Create a comprehensive application using the Database Wizard	CLICK: New button ( ) CLICK: *Databases* tab DOUBLE-CLICK: a database wizard ( )
Viewing and Organizing Information	Switch from Datasheet view to Design view	CLICK: View – Design button ( )
	Switch from Design view to Datasheet view	CLICK: View – Datasheet button ( )
Building and Modifying Tables	Create a table using the Table Wizard	SELECT: *Tables* object button DOUBLE-CLICK: Create table by using wizard

Continued

Skill Set	To Perform This Task . . .	Do the Following . . .
	Create a table in Datasheet view	SELECT: *Tables* object button DOUBLE-CLICK: Create table by entering data
	Create a table in Design view	SELECT: *Tables* object button DOUBLE-CLICK: Create table in Design view
	Save the table structure in Design view	CLICK: Save button (⊟)
	Assign a primary key in Design view	SELECT: the desired field CLICK: Primary Key button (🔑)
	Add a new field in Design view	SELECT: an empty row in the Field Grid pane TYPE: *the field information*
	Remove a field in Design view	RIGHT-CLICK: row selector for the desired field CHOOSE: Delete Rows
	Move a field in Design view	DRAG: a field's row selector button to its new location
Refining Queries	Define an index in Design view	SELECT: the desired field SELECT: an indexing option in the *Indexed* property text box
	Display the Indexes window	CLICK: Indexes button (📝)
	Remove an index displayed in the Indexes window	RIGHT-CLICK: row selector for the desired Index field CHOOSE: Delete Rows
Using Access Tools	Launch the Documenter utility	CHOOSE: Tools, Analyze, Documenter

ACCESS

2.5.2 Key Terms

This section specifies page references for the key terms identified in this chapter. For a complete list of definitions, refer to the Glossary at the end of this learning guide.

AutoNumber, *p. 67*   Field Properties pane, *p. 64*

Database Wizard, *p. 52*   index, *p. 66*

Design view, *p. 64*   null value, *p. 67*

Documenter, *p. 76*   primary key, *p. 67*

Field Grid pane, *p. 64*   Table Wizard, *p. 59*

2.6 Review Questions

2.6.1 Short Answer

1. Name four Database Wizard templates that are available on your computer.
2. What is a switchboard?
3. Name the five steps to designing a better database.
4. Name three methods for creating a table in an Access database.
5. What are the two categories of Table Wizards?
6. What data storage types can be defined in a table structure?
7. What is the difference between the Text and Memo data types?
8. How does a primary key differ from an index?
9. When would you want to insert a row in a table structure?
10. Why must you be careful when changing a field's data type?

2.6.2 True/False

1. _T_ In creating a new database, you select either the *General* or *Wizards* tab in the New dialog box.
2. _T_ In the Database Wizard, the optional fields that you may select for inclusion appear in italic.
3. ____ The process of dividing related data into separate tables in order to reduce data redundancy is called *normalizing* your data.
4. ____ In Word and Excel, you can open multiple Database windows in the Access work area.

Something in excess
use of surplus words

5. _____ After selecting a sample table in the Table Wizard, you can specify only the fields that you want included in your new table.

6. _____ In table Design view, you define the names of fields in the Field Grid pane and select data types in the Field Properties pane.

7. _____ Field names cannot exceed 64 characters in length.

8. _____ What you type into the *Description* column of the Field Grid pane appears in the Title bar of a table's Datasheet window.

9. _____ Access prevents you from entering duplicate values into a primary key field.

10. _____ You print a table's structure the same way that you print a table's datasheet.

2.6.3   Multiple Choice

1. In an application created using the Database Wizard, the main menu is presented as a _____.
   a.   form, called a *switchboard*
   b.   report, called a *menu*
   c.   table, called a *switchboard*
   d.   query, called a *menu*

2. Which of the following is not a step presented in this chapter for designing a better database?
   a.   Determine your input requirements.
   b.   Test your database application.
   c.   Create your tables using wizards.
   d.   Determine your table structures.

3. You have the choice of either creating a table structure from scratch or using a(n) _____ to lead you through the process.
   a.   assistant
   b.   coach
   c.   relation
   d.   wizard

4. Which data type would you use to store the price of an item within an inventory table?
   a.   AutoNumber
   b.   Currency
   c.   Number
   d.   Text

5. Which data type would you use to store a phone number?
    a. Currency
    b. Memo
    c. Number
    d. Text

6. What determines a table's sort order in a datasheet?
    a. AutoNumber field
    b. field order
    c. index field
    d. primary key

7. To display a window showing the table's primary key and indexes:
    a. CLICK: Indexes button (⌨)
    b. CLICK: Primary Key button (🔑)
    c. CLICK: View – Datasheet button (▥)
    d. CLICK: View – Design button (✎)

8. To delete a field in Design view, you right-click the field's selector button and choose the following command:
    a. Delete Field
    b. Delete Rows
    c. Remove Field
    d. Remove Rows

9. You use this tool to generate a printout of a table's structure.
    a. Analyzer
    b. Designator
    c. Documenter
    d. Generator

10. When printing a table's structure, you use this dialog box to specify the desired options.
    a. Print Object Definition
    b. Print Table Definition
    c. Print Table Setup
    d. Print Setup Definition

2.7 Hands-On Projects

2.7.1 World Wide Imports: New Employee Database

This exercise lets you practice creating a new database and adding a table using the Table Wizard.

1. Load Microsoft Access using the Windows Start menu.
2. To create a new database using the startup dialog box:
    CLICK: *Blank Access database* option button
    CLICK: OK command button
3. In the File New Database dialog box:
    TYPE: `World Wide Payroll` into the *File name* text box
4. Using the Places bar or the *Save in* drop-down dialog box, select your personal storage location. Then, do the following:
    CLICK: Create command button
5. To use the Table Wizard, ensure that the *Tables* button is selected in the Objects bar and then do the following:
    DOUBLE-CLICK: Create table by using wizard
6. You will now create a new table to store World Wide Imports' employee records. Do the following:
    SELECT: *Business* option button, if it is not already selected
    SELECT: Employees in the *Sample Tables* list box
7. Let's start by including all of the suggested fields:
    CLICK: Include All button (>>)
8. Now let's remove an unnecessary field. First scroll to the end of the *Fields in my new table* list. Then do the following:
    SELECT: Photograph
    CLICK: Remove button (<)
9. On your own, remove the Notes and OfficeLocation fields.
10. To complete the wizard and open the "Employees" table in Datasheet view:
    CLICK: Finish
11. Close the Datasheet window.
12. Close the Database window.

2.7.2 CyberWeb: Internet Accounts

In this exercise, you practice creating two new tables in an existing database.

1. Open the database file named ACC270. Ensure that the *Tables* button in the Objects bar is selected.
2. To create a new table in Datasheet view:
    DOUBLE-CLICK: Create table by entering data

3. To start, rename the column headings in the field header area:
DOUBLE-CLICK: Field1
TYPE: `City`
DOUBLE-CLICK: Field2
TYPE: `AreaCode`
DOUBLE-CLICK: Field3
TYPE: `DialUp`
PRESS: `ENTER`
4. Now let's enter one record before saving the table:
TYPE: `Arjuna`
PRESS: `TAB`
TYPE: `555`
PRESS: `TAB`
TYPE: `533-1525`
5. To save and name the new table structure:
CLICK: Save button (🖫) on the toolbar
TYPE: `Cities` into the Save As dialog box
PRESS: `ENTER` or CLICK: OK
6. Access warns you that you have not yet defined a primary key. To have Access take care of this for you:
CLICK: Yes
7. Close the Datasheet window.
8. Now let's create a second table:
DOUBLE-CLICK: Create table in Design view
9. To define the fields in a table that will store information about CyberWeb's technical support personnel:
TYPE: `SupportID`
PRESS: `TAB` to move to the *Data Type* column
SELECT: AutoNumber
PRESS: `TAB`
TYPE: `Code to identify Tech Support`
PRESS: `ENTER` to move to the next row
10. On your own, add two more fields to the table. First, a "Name" field with a Text data type and the description "First and last name." Then, a "Local" field with a Number data type and the description "4-digit phone local."
11. To save the table structure, do the following:
CLICK: Save button (🖫)
12. Enter a name for the new table:
TYPE: `TechSupport`
CLICK: OK
13. When Access offers to create a primary key:
CLICK: Yes
14. Close the Datasheet window.

2.7.3 Big Valley Mills: Forest Products

In this exercise, you add a primary key to an existing table and then modify its indexes.

Setup: Ensure the ACC270 Database window is displayed.

1. Ensure that the *Tables* button in the Objects bar is selected.
2. To display a table in Datasheet view:
   DOUBLE-CLICK: 273 Orders in the list area
3. To display the table in Design view:
   CLICK: View – Design button (⊠▾)
4. First, let's make the OrderNumber field the primary key of the table:
   CLICK: row selector button for OrderNumber
   CLICK: Primary Key button (⌖)
   Notice that a key icon appears in the row selector button.
5. To speed up search operations for looking up a particular salesperson, let's create an index for this field. To begin:
   SELECT: SalesRep in the Field Grid pane
6. Using the I-beam mouse pointer:
   SELECT: *Indexed* text box in the Field Properties pane
   CLICK: down arrow attached to the *Indexed* text box
7. From the drop-down list attached to the *Indexed* text box:
   SELECT: Yes (Duplicates OK)
8. To display all the indexes for the table:
   CLICK: Indexes button (⊠)
9. Let's remove the OrderDate index:
   RIGHT-CLICK: row selector button for OrderDate
   CHOOSE: Delete Rows
10. Close the Indexes window.
11. To save the table structure:
    CLICK: Save button (⊟)
12. Close the Datasheet window.

2.7.4 Silverdale Festival: Contact List

In this exercise, you practice modifying the field structure of an existing table.

Setup: Ensure the ACC270 Database window is displayed.

1. To open the 274 Contacts table in Design view:
   SELECT: 274 Contacts in the list area
   CLICK: Design button (⊠Design) on the Database window toolbar

2. First, let's rename one of the fields. Using the I-beam mouse pointer:
   CLICK: to the right of "Contact" in the *Field Name* column

3. TYPE: `Name`
   PRESS: ⊕
   The cell entry should now read "ContactName."

4. You need to add a field to the table structure that stores the contact's email address. In the Field Grid pane:
   CLICK: in the *Field Name* column of the next empty row
   TYPE: `Email`
   PRESS: ⊕
   Notice that the Data Type field accepted the Text data type by default.

5. To delete a field using the right-click menu:
   RIGHT-CLICK: row selector button for Phone 2
   CHOOSE: Delete Rows

6. To confirm that the deletion will remove all of the data in the field:
   CLICK: Yes

7. Let's move the Phone 1 field below the Email field. To begin:
   CLICK: row selector button for Phone 1

8. Using the arrow mouse pointer:
   DRAG: row selector button for Phone 1 downward so that a bold gridline appears below the last field
   (*Note:* Remember to release the mouse button to drop the field.)

9. To save and then view the changes in Datasheet view:
   CLICK: Save button (🖫)
   CLICK: View–Datasheet button (🖳)
   Your screen should now appear similar to Figure 2.17.

10. Close the Datasheet window.

Figure 2.17

Modifying the structure of a table

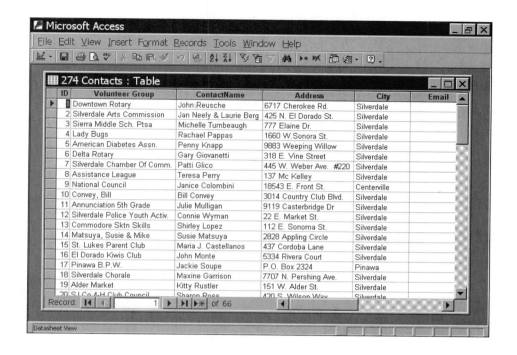

2.7.5 On Your Own: Office Mart Inventory

To practice making changes to a table's structure, open the 275 Inventory table in the ACC270 database. After changing to Design view, add a new field named Category between the existing Description and OnHand fields. Assign a data type of Number to the new field. Next, move the Reorder field so that it appears immediately after the OnHand field and then remove the SuggestedRetail field. To speed up your table search and sort operations, create an index for the Buyer field that allows duplicate entries. Finally, in the Indexes window, remove the extraneous index on ProductID that was created by Access. Make sure that you don't remove the primary key for this field. When you are finished, save the table changes and close the table Design window.

2.7.6 On Your Own: Sun Bird Resort

In this exercise, you practice creating a new table in the ACC270 database. If this database does not appear in the application window, open it now. Then, using Design view, add a new table named "Sun Packages" to the database. The table should contain the following fields, complete with data types and descriptions.

- *PackageID*: This field, which automatically increments by one each time a new record is added, contains a unique code that identifies each promotional package.
- *Description*: This text field stores the name of each package.
- *Price*: This field stores the suggested price in dollars for each package.
- *Nights*: This field stores the number of nights for accommodation.

Use the Documenter tool to print out the table's design structure. Then, close all windows and exit Microsoft Access.

2.8 Case Problems: Inland Transit

Having selected Microsoft Access, Mike Lambert, Inland's controller, focuses his attention on planning and designing a database. In order to reduce data redundancies, Mike splits the company information into three tables. The first table stores operational data for each truck in the fleet. The second table stores personnel data for each driver. The third and final table stores a detailed log of each delivery. Now Mike must launch Access, create a database structure, and initialize these tables.

In the following case problems, assume the role of Mike and perform the same steps that he identifies. You may want to re-read the chapter opening before proceeding.

1. To begin, Mike creates a new database from scratch. He names the database "Inland Transit" and then saves it to his *personal storage location*. Once the Database window appears, he proceeds to create the first table using the Table Wizard. After launching the wizard, Mike ensures that the *Business* option button is selected. He then scrolls the list of sample tables to find a suitable structure. From the list, Mike selects a table named "Assets" and then includes all of the fields for his new table. He then names the new table "Trucks" and lets Access set the primary key. Finally, Mike opens the table in Design view in order to rename three of the fields. In total, he changes "AssetID" to "TruckID," "AssetDescription" to "TruckDescription," and "AssetCategoryID" to "TruckCategoryID." He saves the changes to the table structure and closes the Trucks table.

2. Mike decides to create the second table in Datasheet view. After double-clicking the appropriate New Object shortcut, he renames the column headings in the empty datasheet to create the following fields:

- Name
- Address
- Phone
- Classification

Mike saves the new table object as "Drivers" and lets Access define a primary key. Then, Mike uses Design view to rename the new ID field, which Access has added to the table structure, to "DriverID." And, lastly, he saves the table structure and then closes the table Design window.

3. For the third table, Mike uses Design view to create the structure shown in Figure 2.18. As shown in the screen graphic, Mike makes the TripID field the primary key. He saves the table as "Trips" and closes the table Design window. Using the Access Documenter tool, he prints out the Trips table structure for later review.

Figure 2.18

Creating a table structure in Design view

Field Name	Data Type	Description
TripID	AutoNumber	Identifies the delivery
TruckID	Number	Identifies the truck
Date	Date/Time	Date of the trip
Destination	Text	Delivery destination
Miles	Number	Round trip mileage
DriverID	Number	Identifies the driver
LoadWeight	Number	Weight in pounds

4. Later the same day, Mike realizes he needs to make a few structural changes to some of the tables. He begins by opening the Trips table in Design view and creating an index for the Destination field. Using the Indexes window, he removes the extra index on the TripID field that Access automatically created. After closing the Indexes window, Mike adds a new text field named "Pickup" between the Data and Destination fields. He saves the changes and closes the table Design window.

For the Trucks table, Mike opens the table in Design view and deletes the DepartmentID and BarcodeNumber fields. He then moves the Make and Model fields to be the third and fourth fields respectively. Satisfied with the progress he has made in setting up Inland Transit's new database, Mike saves his changes and exits Microsoft Access.

NOTES

MICROSOFT ACCESS 2000
Organizing and Retrieving Data

CHAPTER
THREE

Chapter Outline

Learning Objectives

After completing this chapter, you will be able to:

- Enhance the display and printing of a datasheet using fonts and special effects

- Sort the contents of a datasheet into ascending and descending order

- Find a record by entering search criteria and using wildcard characters

- Filter the records displayed in a datasheet using Filter For Input, Filter By Selection, and Filter By Form

- Create a query using the Simple Query Wizard

Case Study

Can-Do Rentals

Ellie Floyd is the office supervisor for Can-Do Rentals, a rental and lease company that specializes in landscaping and gardening equipment. As well as managing the administrative and inside sales staff, Ellie's responsibilities have been extended recently to cover the company's record-keeping. The owner and manager of Can-Do Rentals, Sal Witherspoon, knows that Ellie recently completed a course in Microsoft Access. Because much of the record-keeping data is already stored in a database, Sal asks Ellie to open the company's database using Access and peruse its contents. Sal wants Ellie to become well versed in its operation so that she can eventually take over the day-to-day management of the database.

In this session, you and Ellie learn how to enhance a Datasheet window, organize and sort records in a datasheet, filter information for display, and develop a simple query. All of these techniques enable you to better organize and retrieve information.

3.1 Customizing Datasheet View

Access provides numerous options for customizing the appearance, or layout, of a datasheet. Because a datasheet is only an image of the underlying table, you can manipulate the datasheet's column widths, row heights, and field order without affecting the table structure itself. Exceptions to this rule are when you rename or delete a column. These changes flow through to the structural level of the table. Once the table is customized to your satisfaction, save the layout changes by clicking the Save button (🖫) on the toolbar. Otherwise, the modifications are discarded when you close the Datasheet window.

3.1.1 Formatting a Datasheet

> **FEATURE**
> You enhance the display and printing of a datasheet by applying fonts and special effects. Any changes that you make affect the entire datasheet but do not affect other database objects such as forms and reports. After formatting the datasheet to suit your needs, remember to save the layout changes for displaying the datasheet thereafter.

ACCESS

METHOD
- CHOOSE: Format, Font to select font characteristics
- CHOOSE: Format, Datasheet to apply special visual effects
- CLICK: Save button (◪) to save the layout changes, or CHOOSE: File, Save from the menu

PRACTICE
In this lesson, you format and then save an existing datasheet to appear with a custom font, color, and background.

Setup: Ensure that Access is loaded. If you are launching Access and the startup dialog box appears, click the Cancel command button to remove the dialog box from the application window.

1 Open the database file named ACC300, located in the Advantage student data files folder.

2 To open the Courses table in Datasheet view:
DOUBLE-CLICK: Courses in the list area
The Courses Datasheet window appears in the work area.

3 You can change the font characteristics of text displayed in a datasheet without affecting any other Datasheet window. To do so:
CHOOSE: Format, Font
The Font dialog box appears, as shown in Figure 3.1. In this one dialog box, you can change the font **typeface**, style, size, and text color.

Figure 3.1

Font dialog box

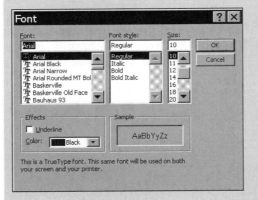

4 In the Font dialog box, make the following selections:
SELECT: Times New Roman in the *Font* list box
SELECT: Regular in the *Font style* list box
SELECT: 12 in the *Size* list box
SELECT: Navy in the *Color* drop-down list box
Notice that the *Sample* area in the dialog box displays an example of the current selections.

5 To accept the changes:
CLICK: OK
The Datasheet window is updated to display the font selections.

6 You can also enhance a datasheet by formatting the window characteristics such as gridlines and its background matting. To do so:
CHOOSE: Format, Datasheet
The Datasheet Formatting dialog box in Figure 3.2 is displayed. Notice that the options selected in the screen graphic are the default settings for a Datasheet window.

Figure 3.2

Datasheet Formatting
dialog box

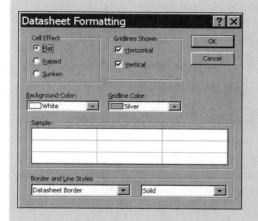

7 After selecting a few options, you can better appreciate the resulting changes by viewing the *Sample* area of the dialog box. To begin:
SELECT: *Raised* option button in the *Cell Effect* area
Notice that this selection nullifies the other options in the dialog box—they are no longer available for selection.

8 To specify other formatting enhancements, do the following:
SELECT: *Flat* option button in the *Cell Effect* area
SELECT: *Vertical* check box so that no "✔" appears
SELECT: Teal in the *Gridline Color* drop-down list box

9 In the *Border and Line Styles* area of the dialog box:
SELECT: Horizontal Gridline in the leftmost drop-down list box
SELECT: Dots in the rightmost drop-down list box
CLICK: OK
The Datasheet window now appears with teal dots separating records in the datasheet as horizontal gridlines.

10 To save the formatting changes to the datasheet:
CLICK: Save button (🖫) on the toolbar

ACCESS

3.1.2 Changing the Field Column Order

FEATURE
Access determines the column order displayed in a Datasheet window from the field order in the underlying table structure. You may want to modify the column order in order to display fields side by side or to perform a multiple-field sort operation. One way to change the column order is to modify the field order in table Design view. A less drastic and permanent method is to move fields by dragging their column headings in Datasheet view. This method does not affect the underlying table structure. Once the columns are positioned, you can save the field column order in the datasheet along with other customizing options.

METHOD
1. SELECT: the desired column in the field header area
2. DRAG: the column heading to its new location

PRACTICE
You now practice selecting and moving columns in a datasheet.

Setup: Ensure that you've completed the previous lesson and that the Courses Datasheet window is displayed.

1 Before moving fields in the datasheet, let's practice selecting columns and changing column widths. Do the following:
CLICK: CourseID in the field header area
Notice that the mouse pointer becomes a downward pointing arrow (↓) when positioned properly on the column heading. The entire column should now appear highlighted.

2 Using the horizontal scroll bar, scroll the window so that the last field column is visible:
CLICK: right scroll button (▶) until InstructorID appears

3 To change all of the columns in the datasheet at once:
PRESS: SHIFT and hold it down
CLICK: InstructorID in the field header area
All of the columns should now appear highlighted. (*Note:* Although not explicitly stated, you should release the SHIFT key after clicking on the InstructorID column heading.)

4 You can now update the columns to their best-fit widths. To do so:
CHOOSE: Format, Column Width
CLICK: Best Fit command button
PRESS: HOME to remove the highlighting

5 Let's practice moving columns in the datasheet. Using the horizontal scroll bar, scroll the window so that both the Faculty and DeptHead field columns are visible.

6 CLICK: DeptHead in the field header area

7 Position the white arrow mouse pointer ($\lambdabar$) over the field name. Then:
DRAG: DeptHead to the left so that the bold vertical gridline appears between the Faculty and MaxStudents field columns

8 Release the mouse button to complete the move operation.

9 To move two fields at the same time:
CLICK: Faculty in the field header area
PRESS: (SHIFT) and hold it down
CLICK: DeptHead in the field header area
Both columns should now appear highlighted.

10 You will now reposition the two field columns. Position the mouse pointer on one of the selected column headings. Then:
DRAG: Faculty (or DeptHead) to the left so that the bold vertical gridline appears between Title and StartDate

11 After releasing the mouse button:
PRESS: (HOME) to remove the highlighting
Your Datasheet window should now appear similar to Figure 3.3.

12 Save the layout changes by clicking the Save ($\boxed{\blacksquare}$) button.

Figure 3.3

Changing the field
column order

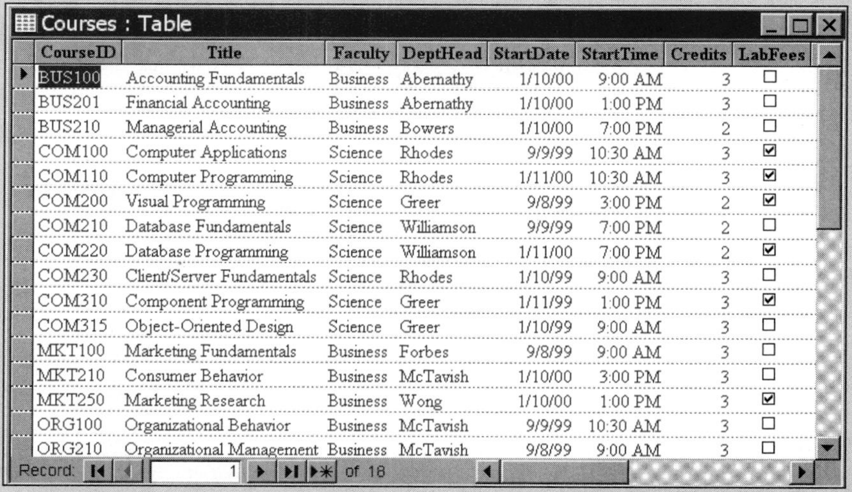

CourseID	Title	Faculty	DeptHead	StartDate	StartTime	Credits	LabFees
BUS100	Accounting Fundamentals	Business	Abernathy	1/10/00	9:00 AM	3	☐
BUS201	Financial Accounting	Business	Abernathy	1/10/00	1:00 PM	3	☐
BUS210	Managerial Accounting	Business	Bowers	1/10/00	7:00 PM	2	☐
COM100	Computer Applications	Science	Rhodes	9/9/99	10:30 AM	3	☑
COM110	Computer Programming	Science	Rhodes	1/11/00	10:30 AM	3	☑
COM200	Visual Programming	Science	Greer	9/8/99	3:00 PM	2	☑
COM210	Database Fundamentals	Science	Williamson	9/9/99	7:00 PM	2	☐
COM220	Database Programming	Science	Williamson	1/11/00	7:00 PM	2	☑
COM230	Client/Server Fundamentals	Science	Rhodes	1/10/99	9:00 AM	3	☐
COM310	Component Programming	Science	Greer	1/11/99	1:00 PM	3	☑
COM315	Object-Oriented Design	Science	Greer	1/10/99	9:00 AM	3	☐
MKT100	Marketing Fundamentals	Business	Forbes	9/8/99	9:00 AM	3	☐
MKT210	Consumer Behavior	Business	McTavish	1/10/00	3:00 PM	3	☐
MKT250	Marketing Research	Business	Wong	1/10/00	1:00 PM	3	☑
ORG100	Organizational Behavior	Business	McTavish	9/9/99	10:30 AM	3	☐
ORG210	Organizational Management	Business	McTavish	9/8/99	9:00 AM	3	☐

Courses : Table

Record: 1 of 18

3.1.3 Hiding and Unhiding Columns

FEATURE
Hiding columns in a datasheet is useful for temporarily restricting the display of sensitive data, such as salaries or commissions. You can also hide columns that you do not want displayed in a print-out or that you are thinking about deleting permanently. Whatever your reasons, Access makes it very easy to hide and unhide field columns in the Datasheet window.

METHOD
To hide a field column:
1. SELECT: the desired column in the field header area
2. CHOOSE: Format, Hide Columns

To unhide a field column:
1. CHOOSE: Format, Unhide Columns
2. SELECT: the desired columns in the Unhide Columns dialog box
3. CLICK: Close command button

PRACTICE
In this lesson, you hide and unhide columns in the active datasheet.

Setup: Ensure that you've completed the previous lessons and that the Courses Datasheet window is displayed.

1 Let's assume that you've been asked to print out the Courses datasheet. However, the last three columns in this datasheet are for administrative eyes only and should not be included. Therefore, you must hide the last three field columns before printing. To begin:
PRESS: (END) to move the cursor to the last field column

2 Fortunately, the three columns, MaxStudents, MinStudents, and InstructorID, appear next to one another in the datasheet. To select the three columns:
CLICK: MaxStudents in the field header area
PRESS: (SHIFT) and hold it down
CLICK: InstructorID in the field header area
Remember to release the (SHIFT) key after you click InstructorID.

3. To hide the selected columns:
CHOOSE: Format, Hide Columns
The columns disappear from displaying in the Datasheet window, although the data remains safe in the table object.

4. To specify how the datasheet will now print:
CHOOSE: File, Page Setup
CLICK: *Page* tab
SELECT: *Landscape* option button
CLICK: OK

5. To preview the datasheet:
CLICK: Print Preview button ([🔍]) on the toolbar

6. Using the magnifying glass mouse pointer, zoom in and out on the page. Notice that the hidden columns are not displayed in the Print Preview window.

7. To return to the Datasheet window:
CLICK: Close on the toolbar

8. To unhide the columns:
CHOOSE: Format, Unhide Columns
The dialog box in Figure 3.4 appears.

Figure 3.4

Unhide Columns dialog box

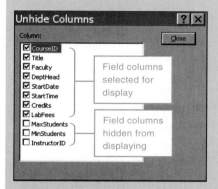

9. In the Unhide Columns dialog box:
SELECT: *MaxStudents* check box
SELECT: *MinStudents* check box
SELECT: *InstructorID* check box
CLICK: Close
Notice that the field columns are displayed once again.

10. Save the layout changes before proceeding.

ACCESS

3.1.4 Freezing and Unfreezing Columns

FEATURE

When navigating a large table with many columns, the Datasheet window scrolls automatically to accommodate your cursor movements. The farther right you move the cursor, the more the columns scroll away from view at the left. To more easily identify the current record, Access lets you freeze or lock in place one or more columns, such as a company name or product number, along the left edge of the Datasheet window.

METHOD

To freeze a field column:
1. SELECT: the desired column(s) in the field header area
2. CHOOSE: Format, Freeze Columns

To unfreeze columns in a datasheet:
CHOOSE: Format, Unfreeze All Columns

PRACTICE

In this lesson, you freeze and unfreeze columns in the active datasheet.

Setup: Ensure that you've completed the previous lessons and that the Courses Datasheet window is displayed.

1 Let's use the right-click menu to freeze the CourseID field column from scrolling off the screen. Do the following:
RIGHT-CLICK: CourseID in the field header
A shortcut menu appears, as displayed to the right.

2 To freeze the column in the Datasheet window:
CHOOSE: Freeze Columns

3 Now remove the column highlighting:
PRESS: (HOME)
Notice that a vertical gridline appears between the CourseID and Title field columns.

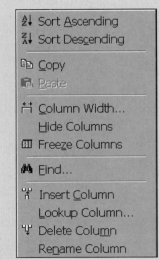

- Sort Ascending
- Sort Descending
- Copy
- Paste
- Column Width...
- Hide Columns
- Freeze Columns
- Find...
- Insert Column
- Lookup Column...
- Delete Column
- Rename Column

4 To demonstrate how you use the locked column feature:
PRESS: END to move to the last field column
The CourseID column remains displayed at the left side of the window. This command is especially useful for displaying datasheets that contain many fields.

5 To unfreeze the CourseID column:
CHOOSE: Format, Unfreeze All Columns

6 PRESS: HOME

7 Save the layout changes and then close the Datasheet window.

8 To prove that the formatting changes were indeed saved:
DOUBLE-CLICK: Courses in the list area
The Datasheet window appears with the same text and window formatting and field column order.

9 Close the Datasheet window.

3.1 Self Check Name two reasons for changing the field column order in a datasheet.

3.2 Sorting and Finding Data

ACCESS

Information is *processed data*. This processing can take several forms, from analyzing, organizing, and summarizing data to presenting data in charts and reports. In this module, you learn how to sort and arrange records into a precise and logical order. You also learn how to find and replace data stored in a table.

3.2.1 Sorting Records in a Datasheet

FEATURE
Records are displayed in the order that they are originally entered into a table, unless a primary key has been assigned. With a primary key, records are arranged and displayed according to the contents of the primary key field. Even so, Access allows you to rearrange the records appearing in a datasheet into ascending (0 to 9; A to Z) or descending (Z to A; 9 to 0) order by the contents of any field. Sorting is often your first step in extracting information from raw data. It allows you to better organize records and makes it easier to scan a datasheet for specific information.

METHOD
1. SELECT: the desired column(s) in Datasheet view
2. CLICK: Sort Ascending button (⬆) to sort in ascending order
   CLICK: Sort Descending button (⬇) to sort in descending order

PRACTICE
You now practice sorting a table into ascending and descending order.

Setup: Ensure that the ACC300 Database window is displayed.

1 To open the Students table in Datasheet view:
DOUBLE-CLICK: Students in the list area
Notice that the datasheet is displayed in order by StudentID, the primary key field.

2 To sort the records into order by surname:
CLICK: LastName in the field header area
CLICK: Sort Ascending button (⬆) on the toolbar
The datasheet is sorted immediately.

3 Instead of selecting the entire field column, you can position the cursor in any cell within the desired column for sorting. To illustrate:
CLICK: in any cell within the Zip field column
CLICK: Sort Descending button (⬇)

4 You can also sort a table by the contents of more than one column, if the columns are adjacent to one another. Access sorts a table starting with the values in the leftmost selected column and then, for identical values, the records are sorted further by the values appearing in the next column. For example, to sort the datasheet into order by Major and then surname, you must move the first or primary **sort key**, Major, to the left of the secondary sort key, LastName. To begin:
CLICK: Major in the field header area
DRAG: Major to the left of LastName
When you release the mouse button, the Major column appears between the StudentID and LastName columns.

5 Now you must select both columns. Since the Major column is already highlighted, do the following:
PRESS: SHIFT and hold it down
CLICK: LastName in the field header area

6 To sort the datasheet by the contents of these columns:
CLICK: Sort Ascending button (⬆)
The datasheet should appear similar to Figure 3.5.

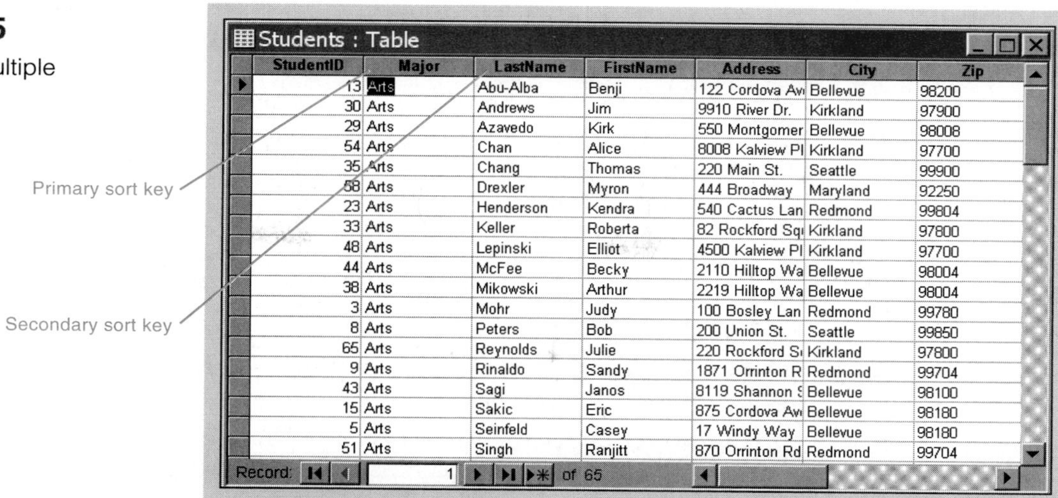

Figure 3.5

Sorting by multiple field columns

StudentID	Major	LastName	FirstName	Address	City	Zip
13	Arts	Abu-Alba	Benji	122 Cordova Av	Bellevue	98200
30	Arts	Andrews	Jim	9910 River Dr.	Kirkland	97900
29	Arts	Azavedo	Kirk	550 Montgomer	Bellevue	98008
54	Arts	Chan	Alice	8008 Kalview Pl	Kirkland	97700
35	Arts	Chang	Thomas	220 Main St.	Seattle	99900
58	Arts	Drexler	Myron	444 Broadway	Maryland	92250
23	Arts	Henderson	Kendra	540 Cactus Lan	Redmond	99804
33	Arts	Keller	Roberta	82 Rockford Sqt	Kirkland	97800
48	Arts	Lepinski	Elliot	4500 Kalview Pl	Kirkland	97700
44	Arts	McFee	Becky	2110 Hilltop Wa	Bellevue	98004
38	Arts	Mikowski	Arthur	2219 Hilltop Wa	Bellevue	98004
3	Arts	Mohr	Judy	100 Bosley Lan	Redmond	99780
8	Arts	Peters	Bob	200 Union St.	Seattle	99850
65	Arts	Reynolds	Julie	220 Rockford St	Kirkland	97800
9	Arts	Rinaldo	Sandy	1871 Orrinton R	Redmond	99704
43	Arts	Sagi	Janos	8119 Shannon S	Bellevue	98100
15	Arts	Sakic	Eric	875 Cordova Av	Bellevue	98180
5	Arts	Seinfeld	Casey	17 Windy Way	Bellevue	98180
51	Arts	Singh	Ranjitt	870 Orrinton Rd	Redmond	99704

Record: 1 of 65

Primary sort key

Secondary sort key

7 Using the vertical scroll bar, scroll the window down to where the values in the Major column change from Arts to Business. Notice that the student records appear sorted by surname within each major.

8 Close the Datasheet window without saving the changes.

3.2.2 Performing a Simple Search

FEATURE

The Find command in Access lets you search an entire table for the existence of a few characters, a word, or a phrase. With large tables, this command is especially useful for moving the cursor to a particular record for editing. Most commonly, the Find command is used to locate a single record. Filters and query objects, discussed later in this chapter, are best used to locate groups of records meeting a specific criteria.

METHOD

1. SELECT: a cell in the field column you want to search
2. CLICK: Find button (🔍) on the toolbar, or
   CHOOSE: Edit, Find
3. SELECT: desired search options

PRACTICE

In this lesson, you attempt to find data appearing in a datasheet.

Setup: Ensure that the ACC300 Database window is displayed.

ACCESS

1 Open the Students table in Datasheet view.

2 Finding data is much easier when the datasheet is sorted by the field in which you want to perform a search. To begin:
PRESS: ➡ to move the cursor to the LastName field column
CLICK: Sort Ascending button (🔄)

3 Let's find the record for Jimmy Kazo:
CLICK: Find button (🔍) on the toolbar

4 In the Find and Replace dialog box that appears:
TYPE: **Kazo** in the *Find What* combo box
Notice that the LastName field already appears selected in the *Look In* drop-down list box, as shown in Figure 3.6.

Figure 3.6

Find and Replace dialog box:
Find tab

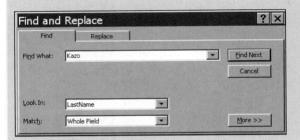

5 To proceed with the search:
CLICK: Find Next
The cursor moves down the column and stops on the first occurrence of "Kazo." (*Note*: The Find and Replace dialog box does not disappear. Therefore, it may be necessary to drag the dialog window out of the way by its Title bar in order to view the selected record.)

6 You can continue the search for more entries for Kazo:
CLICK: Find Next
A dialog box appears stating that no more matches were found.

7 To end the search:
CLICK: OK in the dialog box
CLICK: Cancel in the Find and Replace dialog box

8 To move the cursor back to the first record:
PRESS: (CTRL) + (HOME)

3.2.3 Specifying Search Patterns

FEATURE

Using the Find command, you can specify several options to control how a search is performed. You can also use **wildcard characters** to help locate words for which you are unsure of the spelling. These wildcards are also useful in defining search criteria for filters and queries.

METHOD

- Use the question mark (?) in place of a single character. For example, the search pattern "??S?" matches ROSI and DISC.
- Use the number symbol (#) in place of a single number. For example, the search pattern "##9" matches 349 and 109.
- Use the asterisk (*) to represent a group of characters. For example, the search pattern "Sm*" yields entries beginning with the letters "Sm," such as Smith, Smythe, and Smallwood. You can also use the asterisk in the middle of a search pattern.

PRACTICE

You now practice using wildcards in building search criteria.

Setup: Ensure that you've completed the previous lesson and that the Students datasheet is displayed.

1 Your objective in this lesson is to find all the students who live on Bush Street. To begin, select the Address column:
CLICK: Address in the field header area

2 CLICK: Find button (🔍)

3 In the Find and Replace dialog box:
TYPE: *Bush*
Notice that the existing value, Kazo, in the combo box is replaced by the new entry. This search criteria tells Access to find all occurrences of the word Bush anywhere within a cell entry.

4 To begin the search:
CLICK: Find Next
The cursor moves to record number 47.

ACCESS

5 To continue the search:
CLICK: Find Next to move the cursor to record number 53
CLICK: Find Next to move the cursor to record number 55
CLICK: Find Next
A dialog box appears stating that the search item was not found.

6 To accept the dialog box and proceed:
CLICK: OK

7 To cancel the search and return to the top of the datasheet:
CLICK: Cancel
PRESS: CTRL + HOME

3.2.4 Performing a Find and Replace

FEATURE
The Replace command in Access lets you perform a global find and replace operation to update the contents of an entire table. Using the same process as Find, you enter an additional value to replace all occurrences of the successful match. Replace is an excellent tool for correcting spelling mistakes and updating standard fields, such as telephone area codes.

METHOD
1. SELECT: a cell in the field column you want to search
2. CHOOSE: Edit, Replace
3. SELECT: desired search and replace options

PRACTICE
You now practice using the Find and Replace feature.

Setup: Ensure that you've completed the previous lesson and that the Students datasheet is displayed.

1 In the next few steps, you will replace the word "Science" in the Major field column with the word "CompSci." To begin:
CLICK: Major in the field header area

2 To proceed with the find and replace operation:
CHOOSE: Edit, Replace

3. On the *Replace* tab of the Find and Replace dialog box:
TYPE: **Science** in the *Find What* combo box
PRESS: TAB
TYPE: **CompSci** in the *Replace With* combo box
Your dialog box should now appear similar to Figure 3.7

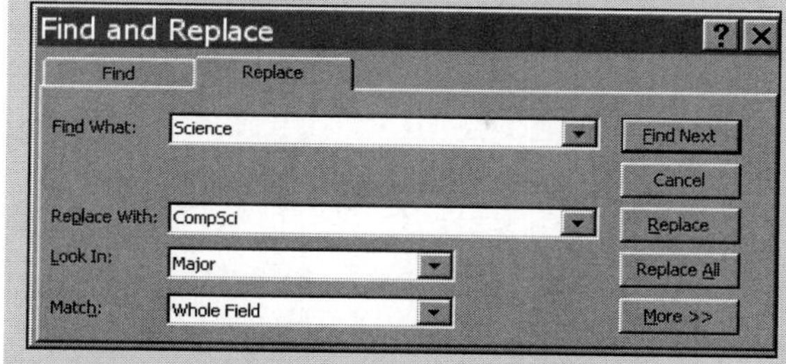

Figure 3.7
Find and Replace dialog box: *Replace* tab

4. If you want to check the values you are about to replace, click the Replace command button to proceed one change at a time. If, however, you want to change all of the values in a single step, do the following:
CLICK: Replace All

5. A confirmation dialog box appears:
CLICK: Yes to accept and remove the dialog box
CLICK: Cancel to remove the Find and Replace dialog box

6. Close the Datasheet window without saving the changes.

In Addition
Finding Spelling Mistakes

You can check the spelling of entries in a datasheet in the same way that you spell-check a word processing document. With the Datasheet window displayed, click the Spelling button ( ) on the toolbar. A dialog box appears for each word that the Spelling Checker does not recognize or believes to be misspelled. You can correct the spelling, ignore the entry, or add the word to a custom dictionary.

3.2 Self Check How do you perform a sort operation using more than one field column?

3.3 Using Filters

A **filter** is a technique that limits the display of records in a table using a simple matching criterion. Similar to a pasta strainer that lets water through but not the pasta, a filter allows only some records to pass through for display. Filtering is an excellent way to find a subset of records to work with that match a particular value or range of values. There are several methods available for filtering records in a table: **Filter For Input, Filter By Selection, Filter Excluding Selection,** and **Filter By Form.** In this module, you learn how to define, apply, and remove filters.

3.3.1 Filtering For Input

FEATURE
Filtering displays a subset of records from a table. The **Filter For Input** method allows you to specify which records are let through. To apply this filter, you display a field's right-click shortcut menu and then type a value into the Filter For: text box. The datasheet is filtered by finding matches to this value in the current field. You may return to viewing all of the records at any time by clicking the Apply/Remove Filter button (▽).

METHOD
1. RIGHT-CLICK: any cell in the desired field column
2. CHOOSE: Filter For:
3. TYPE: *filter criteria*

PRACTICE
In this lesson, you use the Filter For Input method to apply a filter.

Setup: Ensure that the ACC300 Database window is displayed.

1 Open the Students table in Datasheet view.

2 Let's apply a filter to the datasheet that displays only those students with a last name beginning with the letter "S." Do the following:
RIGHT-CLICK: Stedman in the LastName field column
Your screen should now appear similar to Figure 3.8.

Figure 3.8

Choosing the Filter
For Input command

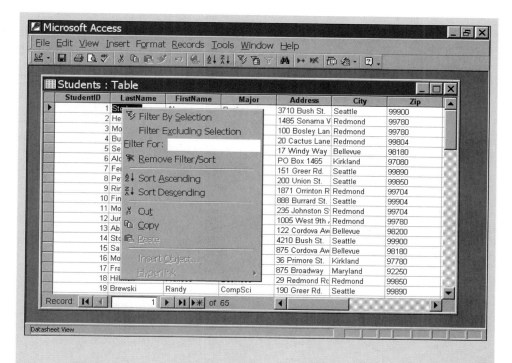

3 CHOOSE: Filter For:
A flashing insertion point should appear in the adjacent text
box.

4 In the Filter For: text box:
TYPE: s*
PRESS: ENTER
The datasheet (Figure 3.9) displays eight of the original 65
records.

Figure 3.9

A filtered datasheet

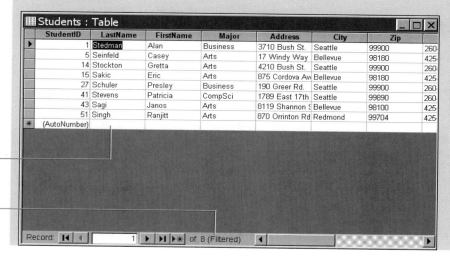

Displays only those
students with a last
name beginning with "s"

Displays only the
filtered results

5 Once filtered, you can sort the resulting subset of records using the appropriate toolbar buttons. To sort the filtered records:
CLICK: Sort Ascending button (⌷)
The datasheet now appears sorted by surname.

6 The Apply/Remove Filter button (⌷) on the toolbar acts as a toggle to turn on and off the current or active filter. To illustrate:
CLICK: Remove Filter button (⌷)

7 To reapply the last filter:
CLICK: Apply Filter button (⌷)
Notice that this toolbar button changes names depending on its toggle status.

8 Close the Datasheet window without saving the changes.

3.3.2 Filtering By Selection

FEATURE
Using the **Filter By Selection** method, you apply a filter based on a selected value from the datasheet. The selection may be an entire cell's contents or only a portion of the entry. Likewise, you use the **Filter Excluding Selection** method to display only those records that do not match the selected value.

METHOD
To apply a Filter By Selection:
1. SELECT: all or part of an existing field entry
2. CLICK: Filter By Selection button (⌷), or
    CHOOSE: Records, Filter, Filter By Selection

To apply a Filter Excluding Selection:
1. SELECT: all or part of an existing field entry
2. CHOOSE: Records, Filter, Filter Excluding Selection

PRACTICE
In this lesson, you use the Filter By Selection method to apply a filter.

Setup: Ensure that the ACC300 Database window is displayed.

1 Open the Students table in Datasheet view.

2 To display only those students living in the city of Redmond:
DOUBLE-CLICK: "Redmond" in any cell of the City field column

3 To create a filter based on the selected text:
CLICK: Filter By Selection button (⊽)
A subset of 10 records is displayed in the Datasheet window.

4 To remove the filter:
CLICK: Remove Filter button (⊽)

5 To display only those students who are <u>not</u> taking Arts as their major:
DOUBLE-CLICK: "Arts" in any cell of the Major field column
CHOOSE: Records, Filter, Filter Excluding Selection
A subset of 42 records is displayed in the Datasheet window.

6 To remove the filter:
CLICK: Remove Filter button (⊽)

7 To display only those students living in Seattle and taking Comp-Sci as their major, you apply more than one filter to the datasheet. To begin:
DOUBLE-CLICK: "CompSci" in any cell of the Major field column
CLICK: Filter By Selection button (⊽)
A subset of 20 records is displayed.

8 Without removing the filter:
DOUBLE-CLICK: "Seattle" in any cell of the City field column
CLICK: Filter By Selection button (⊽)
Now a subset of 11 records is displayed. These records match the criteria specified in the previous two filter selections.

9 To continue, let's filter out those students who live on Greer Road:
DOUBLE-CLICK: "Greer" in any cell of the Address field column
CLICK: Filter By Selection button (⊽)
Four students who live on Greer Road in Seattle are taking CompSci as their major.

10 Close the Datasheet window without saving the changes.

ACCESS

3.3.3 Filtering By Form

FEATURE

For more detailed filtering operations, you use the **Filter By Form** method to set multiple criteria. Unlike Filter For Input or Filter By Selection, a blank datasheet row appears in which you can enter or select the desired criteria. Once you have defined a filter, Access enables you to save it as a query object in the Database window.

METHOD

To apply a Filter By Form:
1. CLICK: Filter By Form button (📷), or
   CHOOSE: Records, Filter, Filter By Form
2. Enter the desired filtering criteria.
3. CLICK: Apply/Remove Filter button (▽)

To save a Filter By Form as a Query:
1. Display the Filter By Form window.
2. CLICK: Save As Query button (💾)

PRACTICE

In this lesson, you use the Filter By Form method to apply a filter.

Setup: Ensure that you've completed the previous lesson and that the Students datasheet is displayed.

1 Open the Students table in Datasheet view.

2 To use the Filter By Form method for filtering a datasheet:
CLICK: Filter By Form button (📷) on the toolbar
Your screen should now appear similar to Figure 3.10.

Figure 3.10

Creating a filter
using Filter By Form

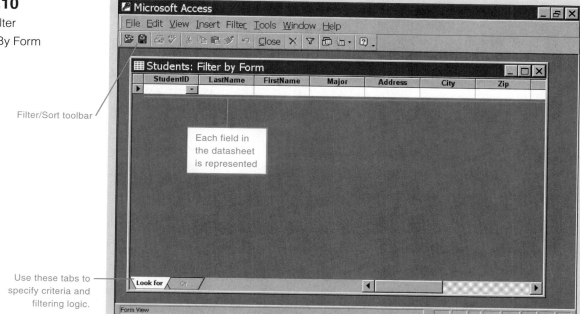

Filter/Sort toolbar

Use these tabs to
specify criteria and
filtering logic.

3 Let's display only those students living in Kirkland who are taking Arts as their major. To begin:
CLICK: Major cell once, immediately below the field header area
Notice that a down arrow appears next to the cell. You use this arrow to access a drop-down list of unique values taken from the datasheet.

4 CLICK: down arrow attached to the Major field
SELECT: Arts from the list of three values
The search criteria "Arts" is entered into the cell.

5 To specify the city criteria:
CLICK: City cell once
CLICK: down arrow attached to the City field
SELECT: Kirkland from the list of five values

6 To apply the filter and display the results:
CLICK: Apply Filter button ($\boxed{\triangledown}$)
A subset of six records is displayed.

7 To save this filter as a query object:
CLICK: Filter By Form button ($\boxed{\text{⊞}}$)
CLICK: Save As Query button ($\boxed{\text{⊟}}$)
TYPE: Kirkland Arts Students
PRESS: ENTER or CLICK: OK

ACCESS

8 To specify a new filter:
CLICK: Clear Grid button (⊠)
The existing filter criteria are removed from the window.

9 In addition to selecting values from the drop-down list, you can type values into the Filter By Form window. To illustrate, let's display only those students with a last name starting with the letter "m:"
CLICK: LastName cell once
TYPE: m*
CLICK: Apply Filter button (▽)
A subset of seven records is displayed.

10 Close the Datasheet window without saving the changes.

11 In the Database window:
CLICK: *Queries* button in the Objects bar
DOUBLE-CLICK: Kirkland Arts Students in the list area
A datasheet displaying the filtered results appears, as shown in Figure 3.11.

12 Close the Datasheet window and then:
CLICK: *Tables* button in the Objects bar

Figure 3.11

Displaying a query object
created using Filter By Form

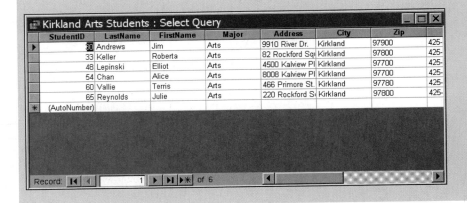

3.3 Self Check   In a personnel table, how would you display a subset of those employees working in the Accounting department?

3.4 Creating a Simple Query

A query is a question that you ask of your database, such as "How many customers live in Chicago?" or "What is the average age of employees in XYZ Corporation?" Using queries, you can prepare, view, analyze, and summarize your data. The results of a query may also be used when presenting data in forms and reports. And lastly, you can use special queries to perform advanced updating routines in your database.

Although similar to filters, queries differ in several significant areas. While both filters and queries allow you to retrieve and display a subset of records, queries also allow you to display data from multiple tables, control which fields display and in what order they appear, and perform calculations on selected field values. In addition, filters provide a temporary view of a subset of records while queries are saved as independent database objects. Use the following as a guideline—you *find* a record, *filter* a table, and *query* a database.

3.4.1 Creating a Query Using the Query Wizard

FEATURE
The **Simple Query Wizard** is a step-by-step tool that helps you retrieve data from one or more tables in a database. Unfortunately, the wizard does not allow you to specify search criteria or sort parameters. The type of query object created by the wizard is known as a **select query,** since you use it to select data for display. The results of the query are listed in a Datasheet window, sometimes referred to as a **dynaset.** Other types of queries include action queries for updating, adding, and deleting records in a database and parameter queries for accepting input from users.

METHOD
In the Database window, select the *Queries* button and then:
- DOUBLE-CLICK: Create query by using wizard, or
- CLICK: New button (New) on the Database window toolbar
  DOUBLE-CLICK: Simple Query Wizard in the New Query dialog box

PRACTICE
You now use the Simple Query Wizard to extract data from two tables for display in a single Datasheet window.

Setup: Ensure that the ACC300 Database window is displayed.

1. The options for creating a new query object are similar to the options for creating a new table object. You can start from scratch in query Design view or get helpful guidance from wizards. In the next few steps, you use the Simple Query Wizard to create a query. To begin:
CLICK: *Queries* button in the Objects bar

2. To launch the Simple Query Wizard:
DOUBLE-CLICK: Create query by using wizard
The dialog box in Figure 3.12 appears.

Figure 3.12
Simple Query Wizard
dialog box

Select a table in
order to specify
fields for display.

Select fields for
display in the query.

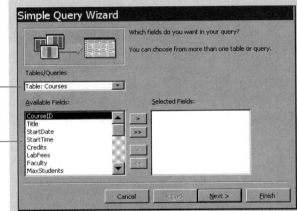

3. In order to display a listing of courses along with the instructor's name, you must select fields from two tables. To begin, ensure that "Table: Courses" is selected in the *Tables/Queries* drop-down list box.

4. In the *Available Fields* list box:
SELECT: CourseID
CLICK: Include button (>)
SELECT: Title
CLICK: Include button (>)

5. Now select a new table:
SELECT: Table: Instructors in the *Tables/Queries* drop-down list box
Notice that there are new fields displayed in the associated list box.

6. In the *Available Fields* list box:
SELECT: LastName
CLICK: Include button (>)
SELECT: FirstName
CLICK: Include button (>)

7 To proceed to the next step in the wizard:
CLICK: Next >

8 Now let's name the query:
TYPE: Course Listing Query
CLICK: Finish
Your screen should appear similar to Figure 3.13. Data in the first two columns is taken from the Courses table and data in the last two columns is taken from the Instructors table.

9 Close the Datasheet window for the Course Listing Query. Then, close the ACC300 Database window. And, lastly, exit Microsoft Access.

Figure 3.13

Creating a query using the Simple Query Wizard

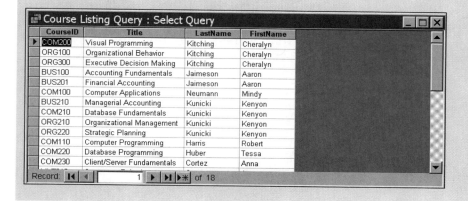

In Addition
Specifying Search Criteria in Queries

Querying a database involves more than limiting its display to specific fields. Using query Design view, you can create and modify queries to extract records from tables that meet a given criterion. You can also adjust the sorting order and perform calculations.

3.4 Self Check Name one way that a query's dynaset may differ from a table's datasheet.

3.5   Chapter Review

One of the primary advantages of using a computerized database is the ability to manipulate, retrieve, and display information quickly and easily. But making your information pleasing to read requires the ability to format and customize the results. Fortunately, you can spice up your datasheets by applying fonts, styles, and special effects. You can also improve your efficiency in working with a datasheet by moving, hiding, and freezing field columns in Datasheet view.

To help you turn raw data into information, the Sort, Find, and Filter commands enable you to organize, locate, and highlight records in a table. You can also use filters to limit the display of records in a table and queries to ask questions of your database. In addition to being able to draw data from multiple tables, queries enable you to specify complex search criteria and sort parameters. Queries are powerful database objects and the sole subject of more advanced chapters.

3.5.1   Command Summary

Many of the commands and procedures appearing in this chapter are summarized in the following table.

Skill Set	To Perform This Task . . .	Do the Following . . .
Viewing and Organizing Information	Enhance the text displayed in a datasheet using fonts and colors	CHOOSE: Format, Font
	Enhance the background and appearance of a Datasheet window	CHOOSE: Format, Datasheet
	Change the field column order in a datasheet	SELECT: the desired column DRAG: its column heading into position
	Hide a field column in a datasheet	SELECT: the desired column CHOOSE: Format, Hide Columns
	Unhide field columns in a datasheet	CHOOSE: Format, Unhide Columns SELECT: the columns to unhide
	Freeze or lock a field column into place in a datasheet	SELECT: the desired column CHOOSE: Format, Freeze Columns

Continued

Skill Set	To Perform This Task . . .	Do the Following . . .
	Unfreeze all of the locked columns in a datasheet	CHOOSE: Format, Unfreeze All Columns
	Save modifications and layout changes made to a datasheet	CLICK: Save button (▣), or CHOOSE: File, Save
	Sort a field column in a datasheet into ascending order	SELECT: the desired column CLICK: Sort Ascending button (▣)
	Sort a field column in a datasheet into descending order	SELECT: the desired column CLICK: Sort Descending button (▣)
	Find or locate a value or record in a datasheet	CLICK: Find button (▣), or CHOOSE: Edit, Find
	Replace an existing value in a datasheet with a new value	CHOOSE: Edit, Replace
	Filter a datasheet using the Filter For Input method	RIGHT-CLICK: a cell in the desired column CHOOSE: Filter For: TYPE: *a filter criteria*
	Filter a datasheet using the Filter By Selection method	SELECT: a datasheet entry CLICK: Filter By Selection button (▣)
	Filter a datasheet using the Filter Excluding Selection method	SELECT: a datasheet entry CHOOSE: Records, Filter, Filter Excluding Selection
	Filter a datasheet using the Filter By Form method	CLICK: Filter By Form button (▣) SELECT: the desired criteria
	Toggle a filter on or off	CLICK: Apply/Remove Filter button (▣)
	Saves the criteria entered using Filter By Form as a query object	CLICK: Save As Query button (▣)
	Create a query using the Simple Query Wizard	SELECT: *Queries* object button DOUBLE-CLICK: Create query by using wizard

3.5.2 Key Terms

This section specifies page references for the key terms identified in this chapter. For a complete list of definitions, refer to the Glossary at the end of this learning guide.

dynaset, *p. 115*

filter, *p. 108*

Filter By Form, *p. 108*

Filter By Selection, *p. 108*

Filter Excluding
Selection, *p. 108*

Filter For Input, *p. 108*

select query, *p. 115*

Simple Query Wizard, *p. 115*

sort key, *p. 102*

typeface, *p. 94*

wildcard characters, *p. 105*

3.6   Review Questions

3.6.1 Short Answer

1. Name the three *Cell Effect* options for formatting a datasheet.
2. What command allows you to lock one or more columns of a datasheet in place? Name two ways to execute this command.
3. What are the two primary options for sorting a list?
4. What are wildcards? Provide an example of how they are used.
5. Name four methods for filtering records in a table.
6. When would you use the Find command rather than applying a filter?
7. How do the Filter For Input and Filter By Selection methods differ?
8. When would you apply a filter rather than creating a query?
9. What are two limitations of the Simple Query Wizard?
10. What type of query is created by the Simple Query Wizard? What are two additional types of queries?

3.6.2 True/False

1. _T_ You can change the color of a datasheet's background.
2. _F_ In Datasheet view, click Save (🖫) to save your editing changes and click Save Layout (🗗▾) to save your formatting changes.
3. _T_ To sort a datasheet by more than one column, you must first ensure that the columns are positioned next to one another.

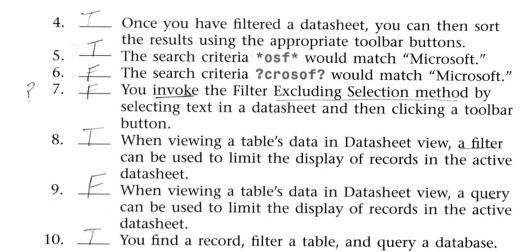

4. _I_ Once you have filtered a datasheet, you can then sort the results using the appropriate toolbar buttons.

5. _I_ The search criteria *osf* would match "Microsoft."

6. _F_ The search criteria ?crosof? would match "Microsoft."

? 7. _F_ You invoke the Filter Excluding Selection method by selecting text in a datasheet and then clicking a toolbar button.

take Part

8. _I_ When viewing a table's data in Datasheet view, a filter can be used to limit the display of records in the active datasheet.

9. _F_ When viewing a table's data in Datasheet view, a query can be used to limit the display of records in the active datasheet.

10. _I_ You find a record, filter a table, and query a database.

3.6.3 Multiple Choice

1. In the Datasheet Formatting dialog box, which of the following is not an option in the *Border and Line Styles* drop-down list box:
   a. Datasheet Border
   b. Datasheet Underline
   c. Horizontal Gridline
   d. Vertical Gridline

2. Which of the following is not an option for customizing a Datasheet window?
   a. Freeze one column
   b. Hide one column
   c. Change one row's height
   d. Change one column's width

3. Which of the following is not a command that is selectable from a field column's right-click menu?
   a. Hide Columns
   b. Unhide Columns
   c. Freeze Columns
   d. Sort Descending

4. The process of restricting the display of records in a table to those matching a particular criterion is called:
   a. filtering
   b. restricting
   c. sifting
   d. sorting

5. Which of the following is not a type of filter method described in this chapter?
    a. Filter By Example
    b. Filter By Form
    c. Filter By Selection
    d. Filter For Input

6. What is the name of the Access tool that simplifies the process of creating a query object?
    a. Database Wizard
    b. Simple Filter Wizard
    c. Simple Query Wizard
    d. Table Wizard

7. A collection of records matching the parameters of a query is sometimes called a:
    a. dynaset
    b. field
    c. table
    d. query

8. Which of the following criteria returns only those cities beginning with the letter "B?"
    a. =B
    b. B*
    c. B?
    d. B#

9. Which of the following criteria returns the name "Jones" as a match?
    a. *ne*
    b. J??nes
    c. J#s
    d. ?ne*

10. Which of the following statements is false?
    a. A filter operation limits records displayed in a datasheet.
    b. A query operation returns a Datasheet window of results.
    c. A sort operation modifies the natural order of data in a table.
    d. A find operation that is successful moves the cursor to the record.

3.7 Hands-On Projects

3.7.1 World Wide Imports: Customer Table

In this exercise, you enhance the appearance of a datasheet by applying fonts and specifying background special effects.

Setup: Ensure that Access is loaded. If you are launching Access and the startup dialog box appears, click the Cancel command button to remove the dialog box from the application window.

1. Open the database file named ACC370. Ensure that the *Tables* button in the Objects bar is selected.
2. To open a table in Datasheet view:
   DOUBLE-CLICK: 371 Customers in the list area
3. Let's change the font that is used to display the data. First, open the Font dialog box using the menu:
   CHOOSE: Format, Font
4. In the Font dialog box, make the following selections:
   SELECT: Courier New in the *Font* list box
   SELECT: Bold in the *Font style* list box
   SELECT: 11 in the *Size* list box
   SELECT: Maroon in the *Color* drop-down list box
   CLICK: OK
   The Datasheet window is modified to display using the new settings.
5. Now let's change the appearance of the datasheet's background:
   CHOOSE: Format, Datasheet
6. In the Datasheet Formatting dialog box:
   SELECT: *Raised* option button in the *Cell Effect* area
   CLICK: OK
7. To move the SalesRep column so that it appears beside the CustomerID field:
   CLICK: SalesRep in the field header area
8. Position the white arrow mouse pointer (⇖) over the field name. Then:
   DRAG: SalesRep to the left so that the bold vertical gridline appears between the CustomerID and CustomerName field columns
   (*Hint:* Remember to release the mouse button to drop the column into place.)
9. Finally, let's adjust some of the column widths:
   CLICK: CustomerName in the field header area
   PRESS: (SHIFT) and hold it down
   CLICK: City in the field header area
   Three columns should now appear selected.

ACCESS

10. To resize the three selected columns to their best-fit widths:
    CHOOSE: Format, Column Width
    CLICK: Best Fit command button
    PRESS: (HOME) to remove the highlighting
    Your Datasheet window should now appear similar to
    Figure 3.14.
11. Save the layout changes by clicking the Save (▣) button.
12. Close the Datasheet window.

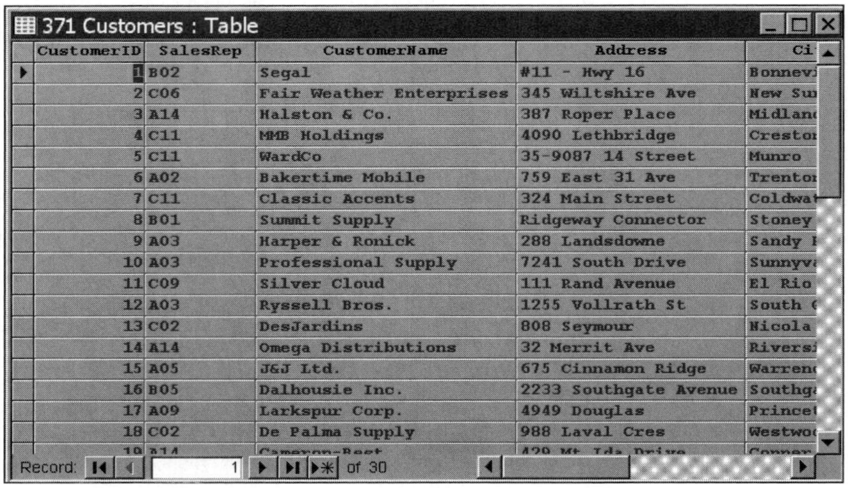

Figure 3.14

Applying fonts and
background effects
to a datasheet

CustomerID	SalesRep	CustomerName	Address	Ci
1	B02	Segal	#11 - Hwy 16	Bonnev
2	C06	Fair Weather Enterprises	345 Wiltshire Ave	New Su
3	A14	Halston & Co.	387 Roper Place	Midlan
4	C11	MMB Holdings	4090 Lethbridge	Cresto
5	C11	WardCo	35-9087 14 Street	Munro
6	A02	Bakertime Mobile	759 East 31 Ave	Trento
7	C11	Classic Accents	324 Main Street	Coldwa
8	B01	Summit Supply	Ridgeway Connector	Stoney
9	A03	Harper & Ronick	288 Landsdowne	Sandy
10	A03	Professional Supply	7241 South Drive	Sunnyv
11	C09	Silver Cloud	111 Rand Avenue	El Rio
12	A03	Ryssell Bros.	1255 Vollrath St	South
13	C02	DesJardins	808 Seymour	Nicola
14	A14	Omega Distributions	32 Merrit Ave	Rivers
15	A05	J&J Ltd.	675 Cinnamon Ridge	Warren
16	B05	Dalhousie Inc.	2233 Southgate Avenue	Southg
17	A09	Larkspur Corp.	4949 Douglas	Prince
18	C02	De Palma Supply	988 Laval Cres	Westwo

371 Customers : Table

Record: 14 ◄ 1 ► ►1 ►* of 30

3.7.2 CyberWeb: Internet Accounts

You now practice customizing a datasheet using the Freeze, Hide, and
Sort commands.

Setup: Ensure the ACC370 Database window is displayed.

1. Ensure that the *Tables* button in the Objects bar is selected
   and then:
   DOUBLE-CLICK: 372 Internet Accounts in the list area
2. First, let's freeze a column in the datasheet so that it is always
   visible when you scroll the window. Do the following:
   CLICK: Username in the field header
   CHOOSE: Format, Freeze Columns
   Notice that the column is moved to the far left of the
   Datasheet window.
3. To demonstrate the effect of freezing the Username column:
   PRESS: (END) to move to the last field column
   Notice that the Username column remains visible.
4. To unfreeze the column:
   PRESS: (HOME) to move to the first column
   CHOOSE: Format, Unfreeze All Columns

5. PRESS: (END) to move the cursor to the last field column
   Notice that the column is no longer locked into position.
6. In order to hide the last two columns, you must first select them:
   CLICK: Amount in the field header area
   PRESS: (SHIFT) and hold it down
   CLICK: BillingType in the field header area
7. To hide the selected columns:
   CHOOSE: Format, Hide Columns
   The Amount and BillingType columns are hidden from view but are not removed from the table.
8. To sort the records in the datasheet by city:
   CLICK: City in the field header area
   CLICK: Sort Ascending button (⬆) on the toolbar
   The records are grouped together into sorted order by the value appearing in the City field.
9. To preview what the datasheet looks like when sent to the printer:
   CLICK: Print Preview button (🔍) on the toolbar
10. On your own, use the magnifying glass mouse pointer to zoom in and out on the Print Preview window.
11. To close the Print Preview window:
    CLICK: Close command button in the toolbar
12. To unhide the columns:
    CHOOSE: Format, Unhide Columns
13. In the Unhide Columns dialog box:
    SELECT: *Amount* check box
    SELECT: *BillingType* check box
    CLICK: Close
14. Save the layout changes by clicking the Save (💾) button.
15. Close the Datasheet window.

3.7.3 Big Valley Mills: Forest Products

In this exercise, you sort data using more than one column and practice using the Find and Replace commands.

Setup: Ensure the ACC370 Database window is displayed.

1. Open the 373 Products table for display in Datasheet view.
2. You now perform a sort operation that orders the table by Category and then by ProductCode within each category. To begin:
   CLICK: Category in the field header area
   DRAG: Category field column to the left of ProductCode
3. To sort by category and then by product code:
   SELECT: Category and ProductCode field columns
   CLICK: Sort Ascending button (⬆) on the toolbar

4. Now let's find all of the products made from birch wood:
   PRESS: ➡ two times to move to the Species field column
   CLICK: Find button (🔍) on the toolbar

5. In the Find and Replace dialog box that appears:
   TYPE: `birch` in the *Find What* combo box
   CLICK: Find Next
   (*Note:* By default, the Find command is not case-sensitive.)

6. Use the Find Next button to determine if there are any other products made from birch. When you are finished, close the Find and Replace dialog box.

7. You now use the Replace command to replace all occurrences of the code "Dim." in the Category column with the code "Dimension:"
   PRESS: (CTRL) + (HOME) to move to the first field in the table
   CHOOSE: Edit, Replace

8. On the *Replace* tab of the Find and Replace dialog box:
   TYPE: `Dim.` in the *Find What* combo box
   PRESS: (TAB)
   TYPE: `Dimension` in the *Replace With* combo box
   CLICK: Replace All command button

9. When Access asks you to confirm the replacement:
   CLICK: Yes command button
   CLICK: Cancel to remove the Find and Replace dialog box

10. Close the datasheet without saving your changes.

3.7.4 Silverdale Festival: Contact List

You now use the Filter For Input and Filter By Selection methods to display only those records that match a specific criterion.

Setup: Ensure the ACC370 Database window is displayed.

1. Open the 374 Contacts table for display in Datasheet view.

2. To begin, you apply a filter so that only the records containing the word "Club" in the VolunteerGroup field column are displayed. Using the I-beam mouse pointer:
   RIGHT-CLICK: the first cell in the VolunteerGroup field column

3. In the right-click or shortcut menu that appears:
   CHOOSE: Filter For:
   TYPE: `*club*` in the Filter For: text box
   PRESS: (ENTER)
   How many groups have "Club" as part of their name?

4. To remove the *club* filter:
   CLICK: Remove Filter button (▽)

5. To display only those groups based in the city of Pinawa:
   DOUBLE-CLICK: "Pinawa" in any cell of the City field column
   CLICK: Filter By Selection button (▽)

Figure 3.16

Displaying the results
of a select query

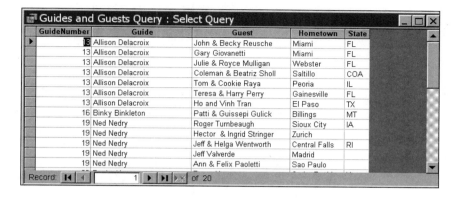

Before printing the dynaset, enhance the datasheet by applying formatting commands and preview the contents of the Datasheet window. Then, save the layout changes and close the datasheet. Lastly, close the Database window and exit Microsoft Access.

3.8 Case Problems: Can-Do Rentals

For the past week or so, Ellie Floyd, the office supervisor at Can-Do Rentals, has been familiarizing herself with the table objects in the company's Access database. Feeling confident that she now understands the nature of the table structures, she informs the owner, Sal Witherspoon, that she is ready to begin. Glad for the opportunity to escape the office, Sal provides Ellie with some afternoon work.

In the following case problems, assume the role of Ellie and perform the same steps that she identifies. You may want to re-read the chapter opening before proceeding.

1. To begin, Sal informs Ellie that he needs a formatted printout of Can-Do's equipment inventory. The data is stored in a table object named Equipment in the ACC380 database. While Sal thinks up other tasks for Ellie, she jots down a note to herself that Sal prefers all of his business correspondence and reports to appear using a 12-point Times New Roman font. She plans on opening the table in Datasheet view, applying the new font choice, and then removing the vertical gridlines from the Datasheet window. Just then Sal added to his preferences. In addition to hiding the DataPurchased field column, Sal wants the Cost column to be positioned as the last column in the datasheet. Ellie makes an additional note to preview the datasheet to ensure that the proper fields are hidden and positioned correctly. After printing the datasheet for Sal's review, Ellie closes it without saving the changes.

2. Next on his list, Sal asks Ellie to make some corrections to data stored in the Rentals table. She opens the datasheet and then sorts it into CustomerID sequence. Using the Find command, she locates the record for CustomerID 41. She changes the rental start date to 5/23/00 and the number of rental days to three (3). Then Ellie uses the Filter By Selection method to display and print only the records that have a status of "Active." After removing the filter, she uses the Find and Replace command to change any records that have a value of zero in the Days field to the minimum rental of one day. She closes the Datasheet window without saving the changes.

3. Before he leaves for the afternoon, Sal provides a list of questions for Ellie about Can-Do's customer base. To answer the questions, she must find, filter, and/or query the database. Using these filters, Ellie answers the following questions:

    • Which customers are not eligible for a discount, as determined by a zero value in the Discount field?
    • How many customers living in Pike Mountain have an account?
    • Which customer accounts are eligible for a discount of 10% on their rentals?
    • How many customers are from outside the city of Kelly?

4. Finally, Ellie uses the Simple Query Wizard to create a query that displays data from all three tables. She includes the following fields in the query and then saves it as "Customer Rentals Query."

Table	Field
Customers	Name
Rentals	StartDate
Rentals	Days
Rentals	Status
Equipment	Description

When the results are displayed, Ellie applies some formatting options, adjusts the column widths, and prints the Datasheet window. Then she closes all of the open windows, including ACC380, and exits Microsoft Access.

NOTES

NOTES

MICROSOFT ACCESS 2000
Presenting and Managing Data

CHAPTER
FOUR

Chapter Outline

Learning Objectives

After reading this chapter, you will be able to:

- Create new forms and reports using the AutoForm and AutoReport wizards

- Create new forms and reports using the Form and Report Wizards

- Navigate and edit data using a form

- Preview and print reports from the Database window

- Create a mailing labels report using the Label Wizard

- Rename, copy, and delete database objects

- Compact and repair a database file

Case Study

Lagniappe, Inc.

Janice Marchant is the western regional sales representative for Lagniappe, Inc., a New Orleans manufacturer of stylish travel gear. Although she has only worked for the company a short time, she enjoys the job and the challenges it presents. Janice works from her home in San Francisco with a notebook computer and fax machine, but meets once a month with the national sales manager, John Lucci. Like all of the sales representatives at Lagniappe, Janice is responsible for tracking sales to the company's preferred clientele using Microsoft Access. Now that she's getting the hang of entering data in Datasheet view, Janice wants to add a few form objects to facilitate data entry and enable her to focus on one customer at a time. She must also create and submit monthly reports listing the items that were sold and who purchased them. This information helps Lagniappe's management team forecast demand levels and predict next season's sale figures.

In this chapter, you and Janice learn to create forms to help you input data and to use reports to produce professional-looking printouts and Web pages. In addition to creating forms and reports using the Auto-Form and AutoReport Wizards, you employ the Form and Report Wizards for better controlling the layout of information. You also save a report as an HTML document and print out standard mailing labels. Lastly, you learn how to manage the database objects you create and how to compress an Access database file to improve performance and efficiency.

4.1 Creating a Simple Form

An alternative to working with numerous records in a datasheet is to focus your attention on a single record at a time using a form. Forms can also be customized to display multiple records and to link with data stored in other tables. Some forms that you may find useful in your database applications include data entry forms that resemble their paper counterparts, switchboard forms that provide menus of choices, and custom dialog boxes that gather input from users. Forms serve many purposes in Access and can enhance the productivity of both novice and expert users. In this module, you learn to create forms using the Access **form wizards.**

4.1.1 Creating a Form Using the AutoForm Wizards

FEATURE

An **AutoForm Wizard** provides the fastest and easiest way to create a new form. Requiring minimal information from you, the wizard analyzes a table's field structure, designs and builds the form, and then displays it in a **Form window**. There are actually three wizards from which to choose. First, the Columnar AutoForm Wizard displays data from one record in a single column, with each field appearing on a row. The Tabular AutoForm Wizard arranges data in a table format, with field labels as column headings and each row representing a record. Similarly, the Datasheet AutoForm Wizard creates a form of rows and columns resembling a datasheet. If you choose to create an AutoForm by clicking the New Object button (🖾▾), Access creates a columnar form based on the open or selected table or query.

METHOD

To create a columnar form quickly:
1. SELECT: a table or query object in the Database window
2. CLICK: New Object: AutoForm button (🖾▾)

To create a form using an AutoForm Wizard:
1. SELECT: *Forms* button in the Objects bar
2. CLICK: New button (🖾New) on the Database window toolbar
3. SELECT: a table or query from the drop-down list box
4. DOUBLE-CLICK: an AutoForm Wizard

PRACTICE

In this lesson, you create forms using the New Object button and the Tabular AutoForm Wizard.

Setup: Ensure that Access is loaded. If you are launching Access and the startup dialog box appears, click the Cancel command button to remove the dialog box from the application window.

1 Open the database file named ACC400, located in the Advantage student data files folder.

2 To have Access create a form automatically, ensure that the *Tables* button is selected in the Objects bar and then:
SELECT: Books in the table list area
(*Hint:* You do not need to open the Books table. Click once on the table object so that it appears highlighted.)

3 Once a table (or query) is selected:
CLICK: New Object: AutoForm button (🖾▾)
(*Hint:* The New Object button contains a list
of wizards used in creating database objects. If
the AutoForm image is not currently displayed
on the face of the New Object button, click
the attached down arrow to show the drop-
down list appearing to the right. Then select
the AutoForm command.)

🖾 AutoF**o**rm
🖉 AutoR**e**port
📑 **T**able
🖃 **Q**uery
🖾 **F**orm
📑 **R**eport
📑 **P**age
🖾 M**a**cro
🎇 M**o**dule
🖾 **C**lass Module

4 After a few seconds, Access displays the columnar form shown in Figure 4.1. Notice that
each field appears on a separate row in the Form window. You
learn how to navigate and manipulate data in a form later in
this module.

Figure 4.1

A columnar form displays
data for a single record

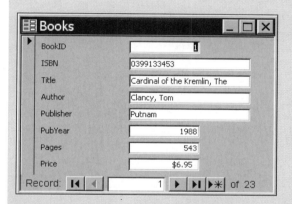

5 To close the form:
CLICK: its Close button (✖)

6 Access informs you that the form object has not yet been saved.
To proceed with saving and naming the form:
CLICK: Yes command button
TYPE: **Books — Columnar**
PRESS: **ENTER** or CLICK: OK

7 The new form object is stored in the *Forms* category of the Data-
base window. To view the object:
CLICK: *Forms* button in the Objects bar
DOUBLE-CLICK: Books - Columnar in the list area
The Form window appears as displayed previously.

8 Close the Form window.

ACCESS

9 To create a form using a tabular layout:
CLICK: *Tables* button in the Objects bar
SELECT: Books in the list area

10 To access the other AutoForm wizards:
CLICK: down arrow attached to the New Object button (▣)
CHOOSE: Form
The New Form dialog box appears, as shown in Figure 4.2.

Figure 4.2

New Form dialog box

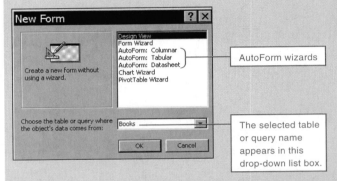

11 To create a new form using the Tabular AutoForm Wizard:
DOUBLE-CLICK: AutoForm: Tabular

12 After a few moments, the tabular form in Figure 4.3 is displayed.
Close the Form window without saving the changes.

Figure 4.3

A tabular form displays
numerous records at the
same time

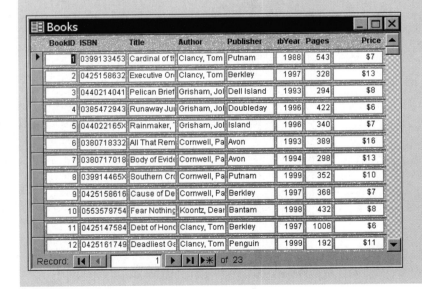

4.1.2 Creating a Form Using the Form Wizard

FEATURE

The Form Wizard provides a step-by-step approach to creating a form from scratch. Even experienced users find using the Form Wizard a handy way to get started building a new form. Whereas an AutoForm Wizard generates a complete form using a set of default values, the Form Wizard allows you to pick and choose options from a series of dialog boxes. Using the Form Wizard, you specify what fields to display on the form and how you want it to look. The layout options include Columnar, Tabular, Datasheet, and Justified. The columnar and justified layouts are suited to viewing a single record at a time and work especially well for tables with few fields. The tabular and datasheet layouts are best used to display numerous records at a time.

METHOD

In the Database window, select the *Forms* button and then:
- DOUBLE-CLICK: Create form by using wizard, or
- CLICK: New button ([New]) on the Database window toolbar
  SELECT: a table or query from the drop-down list box
  DOUBLE-CLICK: Form Wizard

PRACTICE

You now use the Form Wizard to create a standard form object.

Setup: Ensure that the ACC400 Database window is displayed.

1 As with other database objects, you may create a form from scratch in Design view or get helpful guidance from the Access wizards. You access the Form Wizard using the New Form dialog box or by double-clicking a shortcut in the Database window. To begin:
CLICK: *Forms* button in the Objects bar

2 To launch the Form Wizard:
DOUBLE-CLICK: Create form by using wizard
The dialog box in Figure 4.4 appears.

ACCESS

Figure 4.4

Form Wizard dialog box

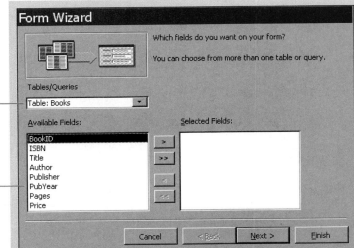

Select a table or query in order to specify fields for display.

Select fields for display on the form.

③ Let's create a form that displays the data from the Courses table:
SELECT: Table: Courses from the _Tables/Queries_ drop-down list box
Notice that the table's fields are displayed in the associated list box.

④ In the _Available Fields_ list box:
SELECT: Title
CLICK: Include button (▸)
Notice that the Title field is no longer displayed in the _Available Fields_ list box. (_Hint:_ You can double-click a field name to move it between the list boxes.)

⑤ Using the same process, add the Faculty, DeptHead, StartDate, and StartTime fields to the _Selected Fields_ list box, in the order specified.

⑥ To proceed to the next step in the wizard:
CLICK: Next >

⑦ In this step, you specify how to arrange the selected fields in the Form window. Notice that three of the four options (Columnar, Tabular, and Datasheet) mirror the AutoForm wizards. On your own, click the layout options one at a time to preview their formats. When you are ready to proceed:
SELECT: _Justified_ option button
CLICK: Next >

8 This step allows you to specify a formatting style for the form. On your own, click the style names appearing in the list box in order to preview their formats. When you are ready to proceed:
SELECT: Sumi Painting
CLICK: Next >
(Note: The next time you use the Form Wizard, the options selected here become the default selections.)

9 You may now specify the name of the form and whether to open the form for display or editing. Do the following:
TYPE: Courses – Form Wizard
CLICK: Finish
The Form window displays only the fields selected in the Form Wizard using a justified (wrapping) layout, as shown in Figure 4.5.

10 Close the Form window. Notice that the form name appears in the Database window.

Figure 4.5

A justified form created using the Form Wizard

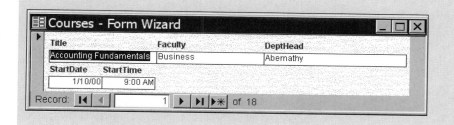

4.1.3 Navigating Data Using a Form

FEATURE
An Access form provides the same navigational buttons that you find at the bottom of a Datasheet window. Use these buttons, along with the arrow keys (described further below), to move through the records in a table. To move among the fields on a form, press the arrow keys (⬆ and ⬇) or use TAB to move forward and SHIFT + TAB to move backward. You can also move quickly to the top of a form using HOME and to the last field on a form using END.

METHOD

Button	Keystroke	Description
⏮	CTRL + HOME	Moves to the first field of the first record
◀	PgUp	Moves to the previous record
▶	PgDn	Moves to the next record
⏭	CTRL + END	Moves to the last field of the last record

PRACTICE
In this lesson, you use the AutoForm Wizard to create a form and practice navigating records in the Form window.

Setup: Ensure that the ACC400 Database window is displayed.

1 Let's begin by creating a new columnar form:
CLICK: *Tables* button in the Objects bar
SELECT: Courses in the list area

2 To launch the AutoForm Wizard:
CLICK: down arrow attached to the New Object button (🔠▾)
CHOOSE: AutoForm
The Courses Form window appears

3 To save the new form:
CLICK: Save button (💾)
TYPE: `Courses — AutoForm`
PRESS: ENTER or CLICK: OK

4 Using the form, let's display the last record in the table:
CLICK: Last Record button (⏭) at the bottom of the Form window
Notice that the record navigation area displays Record 18 of 18.

5 To move to record 15:
PRESS: PgUp three times

6 To move to the first field in the first record:
PRESS: CTRL + HOME

7 To move the cursor into the Title field:
PRESS: TAB

8 Let's use the Find command to locate all courses containing the word "database." Do the following:
CLICK: Find button (🔍)
TYPE: `database` in the *Find What* combo box
SELECT: Any Part of Field in the *Match* drop-down list box
CLICK: Find Next command button

9 Access moves the cursor to the first matching record. If the Find and Replace dialog box is covering the form, move the windows to appear similar to Figure 4.6.

Figure 4.6

Positioning windows in the work area

Database window
Form window
Record navigation area
Find and Replace dialog box

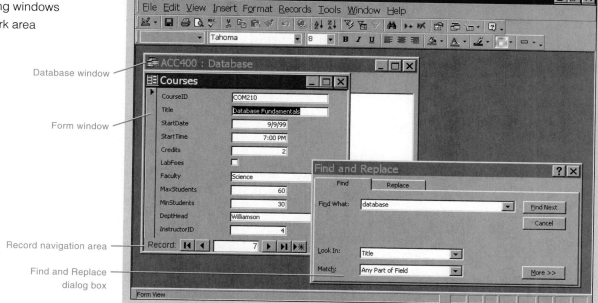

10 In the Find and Replace dialog box, continue the search:
CLICK: Find Next command button
The next record, Record 8, is displayed.

11 Close the Find and Replace dialog box.

12 Close the Form window.

ACCESS

4.1.4 Working With a Form

FEATURE
The methods for editing data in Form view are nearly identical to editing in Datasheet view. Nevertheless, many people find it easier to edit field data using a form, preferring the less cluttered interface and the ability to focus attention on a single record. After this lesson, you may also find it easier to add, delete, sort, and filter a table's records using a form.

METHOD
- CLICK: New Record button (⏭) to add a new record
- CLICK: Delete Record button (⏴) to remove a record
- CLICK: Sort Ascending button (⏺) to sort into ascending order
- CLICK: Sort Descending button (⏺) to sort into descending order
- CLICK: Print Preview button (🔍) to preview a form
- CLICK: Print button (🖨) to print a form

PRACTICE
You now practice sorting, adding, and deleting records, and previewing how a form will appear when printed.

Setup: Ensure that you've completed the previous lesson and that the ACC400 Database window is displayed.

1 Let's start by displaying the form that you created in the last lesson:
CLICK: *Forms* button in the Objects bar
DOUBLE-CLICK: Courses–AutoForm in the list area

2 Using `PgDn` and `PgUp`, navigate through the records and take notice of the CourseID sort order. Then sort the table's records into ascending order by course title:
PRESS: `CTRL`+`HOME` to move to the first field in the first record
PRESS: `TAB` to position the cursor in the Title field
CLICK: Sort Ascending button (⏺)

3 Using `PgDn` and `PgUp` once again, you see that the table is now sorted alphabetically by course title.

4 To add a new record to the table:
CLICK: New Record button (⏭) on the toolbar

5 Enter the data appearing below. Use the (TAB) key to move forward and (SHIFT)+(TAB) to move backward. As you type, notice the pencil icon (🖉) that appears in the record selection area of the form. When you reach the LabFees field, press the Spacebar to toggle the check box. In the last field, InstructorID, enter the value and then press (SHIFT)+(ENTER) to save the record. The pencil icon (🖉) disappears.

CourseID: ACC351   Faculty: Business
Title: Equity Management   MaxStudents: 20
StartDate: 1/15/00   MinStudents: 10
StartTime: 3:30 PM   DeptHead: Abernathy
Credits: 3   InstructorID: 2
LabFees: Yes

6 To delete a record from the table:
PRESS: (PgUp) until you reach record 14, Object-Oriented Design
CLICK: Delete Record button (🗷)
CLICK: Yes command button to confirm

7 To preview how a form will print:
CLICK: Print Preview button (🔍)

8 On your own, enlarge the Print Preview window and then use the magnifying glass mouse pointer to zoom in on the image. Your screen should appear similar to Figure 4.7.

Figure 4.7

Previewing a form

Each page contains as many records as possible, limited by the number of fields and form design.

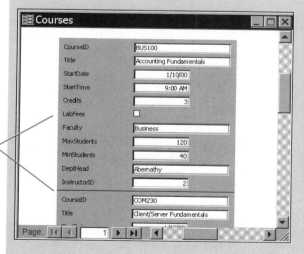

9 To return to the Form window:
CLICK: Close command button on the toolbar
Notice that the Form window maintains the same size as the Print Preview window.

10 Close the Form window.

ACCESS

4.1 Self Check   Name the layout options for designing a form using the Form Wizard.

4.2   Creating a Simple Report

A report provides a structured display format for presenting a table's data or a query's results. While most reports are designed for printing, you can also save reports as graphic snapshots or as Web pages. To capture and retain the attention of readers, each report may contain a variety of design elements such as fonts, lines, borders, colors, graphics, and white space. In addition to jazzing up reports, these elements combine with powerful features for summarizing data to present information clearly and concisely. Each day, people make important decisions using reports obtained from database management systems. Some potential uses for reports in a typical business database application include invoices, mailing labels, address books, product catalogs, and inventory listings. In this module, you learn to create reports using the Access **report wizards.**

4.2.1   Creating a Report Using the AutoReport Wizards

FEATURE

What AutoForm Wizards do for forms, AutoReport Wizards do for reports. Using an **AutoReport Wizard,** you can create a professionally designed report with the click of a button. Access provides two types of AutoReport wizards, Columnar and Tabular. Clicking the New Object button for a report (⊞▾) generates a relatively unattractive columnar report that presents data down a single column. The Tabular option, selected from the New Report dialog box, prepares a much nicer-looking report.

METHOD
To create a columnar report quickly:
1. SELECT: a table or query object in the Database window
2. CLICK: New Object: AutoReport button (🖼️▾)

To create a report using an AutoReport Wizard:
1. SELECT: *Reports* button in the Objects bar
2. CLICK: New button (⧉New) on the Database window toolbar
3. SELECT: a table or query from the drop-down list box
4. DOUBLE-CLICK: an AutoReport Wizard

PRACTICE
In this lesson, you create a columnar report using the AutoReport Wizard.

Setup: Ensure that the ACC400 Database window is displayed.

1 The first step is to select a table or query for which you want to produce a report. To begin:
CLICK: *Tables* button in the Objects bar
SELECT: Instructors in the list area
(*Hint:* You do not need to open the Instructors table. Click once on the table object so that it appears highlighted.)

2 To generate a report using the AutoReport Wizard:
CLICK: New Object: AutoReport button (🖼️▾)
(*Hint:* The New Object button contains a list of wizards used in creating database objects. If the AutoReport image is not currently displayed on the face of the New Object button, click the attached down arrow to show the drop-down list appearing to the right. Then select the AutoReport command.)

3 Access opens a columnar report in the Print Preview window. Each field from the Instructors table appears on a separate row in the report. On your own, use the magnifying glass mouse pointer to zoom in and out on the report (Figure 4.8).

Figure 4.8

A columnar report created using the AutoReport Wizard

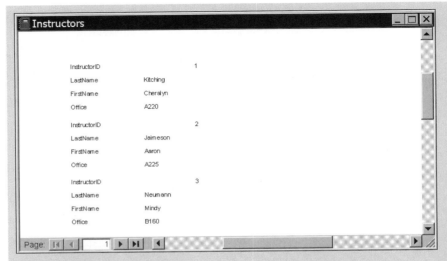

4 To close the report preview:
CLICK: its Close button ([X])

5 Access asks if you want to save the report. To proceed:
CLICK: Yes command button
TYPE: `Instructors — Columnar`
PRESS: ENTER or CLICK: OK

6 To view the new object:
CLICK: *Reports* button in the Objects bar
DOUBLE-CLICK: Instructors - Columnar in the list area
The report opens up into the Print Preview window.

7 Close the Print Preview window.

4.2.2 Creating a Report Using the Report Wizard

FEATURE

The Report Wizard lets you select options from a series of dialog boxes in constructing a new report. After selecting the fields to display, you determine grouping and subtotal levels, sorting options, and presentation styles. The three layout options include Columnar, Tabular, and Justified, similar to the options provided in the Form Wizard. Once a report has been created and saved, you can preview and print the report at any time.

METHOD

In the Database window, select the *Reports* button and then:
- DOUBLE-CLICK: Create report by using wizard, or
- CLICK: New button (New) on the Database window toolbar
  SELECT: a table or query from the drop-down list box
  DOUBLE-CLICK: Report Wizard

PRACTICE

You now use the Report Wizard to create a tabular report.

Setup: Ensure that the ACC400 Database window is displayed.

1 To launch the Report Wizard, ensure that the *Reports* button is selected in the Database window and then:
DOUBLE-CLICK: Create report by using wizard
The first dialog box of the Report Wizard appears. Notice the similarity between this dialog box and the Form Wizard in Figure 4.4.

2 To create a report that displays data from the Students table:
SELECT: Table: Students from the *Tables/Queries* drop-down list box

3 In the *Available Fields* list box, you select the fields to include:
DOUBLE-CLICK: LastName
DOUBLE-CLICK: FirstName
DOUBLE-CLICK: Major
DOUBLE-CLICK: GradYear
DOUBLE-CLICK: GPA

4 To proceed to the next step in the wizard:
CLICK: Next >

5 Access now provides the option of grouping records so that you may better organize your data and perform subtotal calculations. To group the student records by their selected major:
DOUBLE-CLICK: Major in the list box
As shown in Figure 4.9, the layout preview area is updated to help you visualize the grouping options selected.

Figure 4.9

Report Wizard dialog box:
Grouping Levels

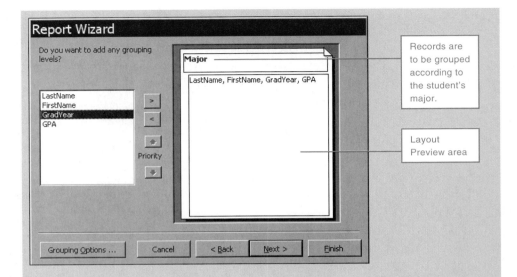

Report Wizard

Do you want to add any grouping levels?

LastName
FirstName
GradYear
GPA

Priority

Major

LastName, FirstName, GradYear, GPA

Records are to be grouped according to the student's major.

Layout Preview area

Grouping Options ...   Cancel   < Back   Next >   Finish

6 To proceed to the next step:
CLICK: Next >

7 In this step, you specify sorting options for the report. Since the report is already grouped (and, thus sorted) by major, let's sort the report alphabetically by name:
CLICK: down arrow attached to the first drop-down list box
SELECT: LastName
CLICK: down arrow attached to the second drop-down list box
SELECT: FirstName
(*Hint:* If desired, you can click the Sort Ascending button that appears to the right of each drop-down list box in order to toggle between ascending and descending order.)

8 If the selected table or query contains numeric or currency fields, you can also include summary calculations in the report. To illustrate:
CLICK: Summary Options command button
The Summary Options dialog box is displayed showing the fields that are eligible for performing calculations.

9 There are four summary calculations from which to choose. The Sum option totals record values stored in a field, while the Avg option calculates the arithmetic mean or average. The Min and Max options find the minimum and maximum values in a field, respectively. For those fields you sum, you can also calculate each record's percent share of the total value.

In the Students table, these calculations provide no real benefit toward better understanding the GradYear field. However, summarizing the student grade point averages might provide useful information. To proceed, complete the Summary Options dialog box to match the selections shown in Figure 4.10.

Figure 4.10

Report Wizard's Summary
Options dialog box

Select primary and
secondary sorting
levels for the report.

Select calculation
options for fields
with the number or
currency data type.

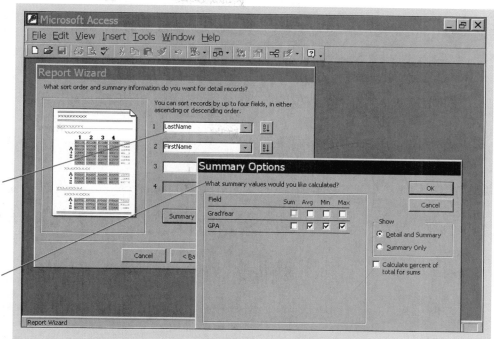

10 To accept the choices made in the Summary Options dialog box and proceed to the next step:
CLICK: OK
CLICK: Next >

11 In this step, you specify the desired layout and page orientation settings. For grouping data, the Report Wizard provides nice formats for separating and organizing the information. Do the following:
SELECT: *Outline 1* option button in the *Layout* area
SELECT: *Portrait* option button in the *Orientation* area
CLICK: Next >

12 A style is a formatting template that you can apply to a report. On your own, click on the style options in the list box to preview their formats. When you are ready to proceed:
SELECT: Corporate
CLICK: Next >

13 In the final step, you name the report and determine whether to preview it or perform additional modifications. Do the following:
TYPE: Students - By Major
SELECT: *Preview the report* option button
CLICK: Finish
The report is displayed in the Print Preview window.

ACCESS

14 To close the Print Preview window:
CLICK: its Close button (☒)
The new report object appears in the Database window. In the next lesson, you learn more about previewing and printing the report.

In Addition
Using Form and
Report Design Views

Although the form and report wizards let you immediately create usable objects, you may want to create a form or report from scratch or modify an existing object. Although not covered in this chapter, you can further customize forms and reports in Design view.

4.2.3 Previewing and Printing a Report

FEATURE
Whereas you open tables, queries, and forms, you **preview** reports. Double-clicking a report object in the Database window opens the report for display in a Print Preview window. In this mode, you can navigate pages, zoom in and out, and modify page setup options.

METHOD
After selecting the report object in the Database window:
- CLICK: Print Preview button (🔍) to preview the report, or
  CHOOSE: File, Print Preview
- CLICK: Print button (🖨) to print the report, or
  CHOOSE: File, Print
- CHOOSE: File, Page Setup to specify print options

PRACTICE
You now display and print a report using the Print Preview window.

Setup: Ensure that you've completed the previous lesson and that the *Reports* button is selected in the ACC400 Database window.

1 To display a report in Print Preview mode:
DOUBLE-CLICK: Students–By Major

2 Let's maximize the Print Preview window for a better view:
CLICK: its Maximize button (□)
Your screen should now appear similar to Figure 4.11.

Figure 4.11

Maximized Print
Preview window

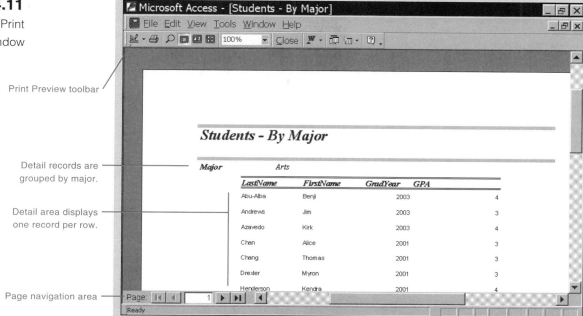

Print Preview toolbar

Detail records are
grouped by major.

Detail area displays
one record per row.

Page navigation area

3. On your own, move amongst the pages using the navigation buttons appearing at the bottom of the Print Preview window. When you are ready to proceed, return to Page 1 of the report.

4. To view two pages of the report side by side:
CLICK: Two Pages button (▥)
(*Hint:* You can also choose the View, Pages command.)

5. On your own, zoom in and out on different areas of the preview. Take special note of the summary calculations appearing at the end of a category grouping.

6. To view multiple pages:
CLICK: Multiple Pages button (▦)
SELECT: 1x3 Pages in the drop-down menu that appears

7. To return to the view shown in Figure 4.11:
CLICK: One Page button (▢)
CLICK: down arrow attached to the Zoom button (100% ▾)
SELECT: 100%
(*Hint:* You can also choose the View, Zoom command to change the magnification.)

8. To stop viewing the report and display the Database window:
CLICK: Database window button (▣)
Notice that the Print Preview window is restored to a window and is layered behind the Database window.

ACCESS

Close the Print Preview window.

 If a printer is attached to your computer, perform this step. Otherwise, proceed to the next lesson.
RIGHT-CLICK: Students–By Major
CHOOSE: Print
The report is sent directly to the printer.

4.2.4 Publishing a Report to the Web

FEATURE
The **World Wide Web** is an exciting medium for exchanging data. Using **Internet** technologies, the Web provides an easy-to-use multimedia interface for accessing information stored anywhere on the planet. Access makes it easy for you to tap the power of the Web. Once you've created a database object such as a table or report, you can export the object in **HTML** format, the standardized markup language of the Web. While it's true that such a document provides only a static representation or snapshot of a database, Access also provides several advanced tools for creating dynamic real-time Web applications.

METHOD
After selecting an object in the Database window:
1. CHOOSE: File, Export
2. TYPE: a file name for the Web document
3. SELECT: HTML documents in the *Save as type* drop-down list box
4. CLICK: Save command button

PRACTICE
In this lesson, you export a report object as an HTML document.

Setup: Ensure that you've completed the previous lessons and that the *Reports* button is selected in the ACC400 Database window.

 To export a report for publishing to the Web:
SELECT: Students–By Major
The object name must appear highlighted in the list area.

CHOOSE: File, Export
The Export Report dialog box appears.

3 In the *File name* text box:
TYPE: Students–Web Page

4 In the Places bar or the *Save in* drop-down list box:
SELECT: *your personal storage location*

5 In the *Save as type* drop-down list box
SELECT: HTML documents

6 To proceed with the export:
CLICK: Save command button

7 The HTML Output Options dialog box now displays on the screen. You use this dialog box to specify a template file that enhances the report's appearance, navigation, and formatting. To continue without specifying a template:
CLICK: OK

8 The export process creates one HTML document for each page of the report. You are then returned to the Database window. If you have access to Web browser software, you can open one of the pages for viewing. Click the hyperlinks appearing at the bottom of the page to navigate the report pages. Figure 4.12 provides an example of how the first page of the report is displayed using Internet Explorer.

Figure 4.12

Viewing a report page using Internet Explorer

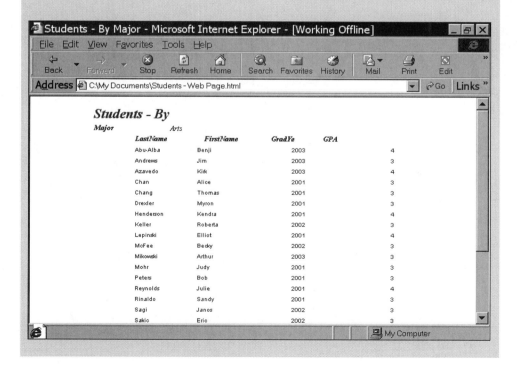

In Addition
Saving a Report
as a Snapshot

If you regularly need to print, photocopy, and distribute Access reports, consider sending a **report snapshot** instead. A snapshot, which is stored as a graphic metafile on a disk, contains a static image of each page in a report. To create a snapshot, select the desired report in the Database window and then choose the File, Export command. After specifying a name and storage location, select "Snapshot Format" as the file type. Once saved, you can distribute the snapshot file via electronic mail or post it to your Web site.

4.2 Self Check   What does the term "grouping data" refer to in a report?

4.3   Generating a Mailing Labels Report

Using your database to print mailing labels can save you a lot of time in preparing envelopes for greeting cards, birth announcements, or other special mailings. You can even keep track of your computer disks and files in a database and then prepare diskette labels (Avery Product Number 5296) using a report object. In this module, you learn to create and print mailing labels.

4.3.1 Creating a Report Using the Label Wizard

FEATURE
The Access **Label Wizard** provides an easy way for you to create a mailing labels report and print standard labels that fit on envelopes, packages, and diskettes.

METHOD
In the Database window, select the *Reports* button and then:
1.   CLICK: New button () on the Database window toolbar
2.   SELECT: a table or query from the drop-down list box
3.   DOUBLE-CLICK: Label Wizard

PRACTICE
You now create a mailing labels report for the Students table.

Setup: Ensure that the ACC400 Database window is displayed.

1   Let's generate mailing labels for the Students table. To begin, launch the Label Wizard:
SELECT: *Reports* button in the Objects bar
CLICK: New button () on the Database window toolbar

2 In the New Report dialog box:
SELECT: Students in the *Choose the table...*drop-down list box
DOUBLE-CLICK: Label Wizard
The first dialog box for the Label Wizard appears, as shown in
Figure 4.13. You use this dialog box to specify the label size and
format.

Figure 4.13

Label Wizard dialog box

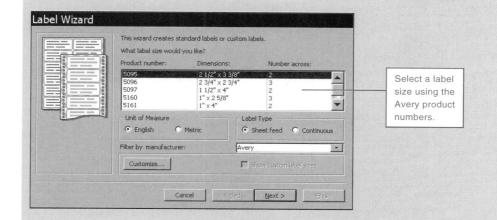

Select a label size using the Avery product numbers.

3 For a standard mailing labels report, ensure that Avery is selected
in the *Filter by manufacturer* drop-down list box and then:
SELECT: 5160 in the *Product number* column
CLICK: Next >

4 In this step, you select the font used for the labels. To accept the
default values and proceed:
CLICK: Next >

5 You now build the appearance of the label by entering text or
selecting fields. In the *Available fields* list box:
DOUBLE-CLICK: FirstName
PRESS: Spacebar
DOUBLE-CLICK: LastName
PRESS: ENTER
DOUBLE-CLICK: Address
PRESS: ENTER
DOUBLE-CLICK: City
TYPE: , (a single comma)
PRESS: Spacebar
DOUBLE-CLICK: State
PRESS: Spacebar
DOUBLE-CLICK: Zip
Your label should now appear similar to Figure 4.14.

ACCESS

Figure 4.14

Constructing a label

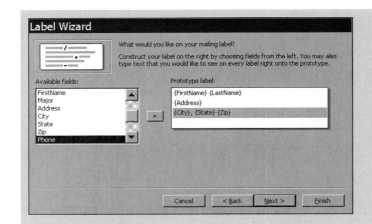

6 To proceed to the next step:
CLICK: Next >

7 To sort the mailing labels report by student name:
DOUBLE-CLICK: LastName in the *Available fields* list box
DOUBLE-CLICK: FirstName in the *Available fields* list box
CLICK: Next >

8 To accept the default selections in the wizard:
CLICK: Finish
After a few moments, the mailing labels report appears in the Print Preview window.

9 On your own, zoom in and out on pages in the Print Preview window.

10 Close the Print Preview window.

4.3 Self Check   How could you use table and report objects to print diskette labels?

4.4 Managing Database Objects

As you continue to use Access, you will create many databases and many database objects, and it is important that you know how to manage them properly. In this module, you learn to rename, copy, and delete database objects and to compress and repair a database file.

4.4.1 Renaming, Copying, and Deleting Objects

FEATURE

Similar to performing routine file management procedures using Windows Explorer, you can rename, copy, and delete the individual objects stored in a database. In a sense, the Access wizards make it too easy to create database objects. Especially true for novice users, it is common to find Database windows overflowing with trial editions of objects. In other words, users create a form or report using a wizard only to find that they would like to add a few improvements. Because it is often easier to create a new wizard-generated object than to edit the existing one, the Database window can become overpopulated quickly. To avoid capacity and performance issues, these trial objects should be deleted immediately.

METHOD

After right-clicking the desired database object:
- CHOOSE: Rename to rename an object
- CHOOSE: Cut to move an object, or CLICK: Cut button (⌧)
- CHOOSE: Copy to copy an object, or CLICK: Copy button (⌧)
- CHOOSE: Paste to paste an object, or CLICK: Paste button (⌧)
- CHOOSE: Delete to remove an object, or CLICK: Delete button (⌧)

PRACTICE

You now practice managing objects in the ACC400 database.

Setup: Ensure that the ACC400 Database window is displayed.

1 To begin, let's display the table objects:
CLICK: *Tables* button in the Objects bar

2 Let's practice adjusting the view options in the list area:
CLICK: Large Icons button (⌧) on the Database window toolbar
CLICK: Details button (⌧) to view additional information
CLICK: List button (⌧) to return to the standard view
(*Hint:* You can also change the order in which the objects are displayed by choosing the View, Arrange Icons command.)

3 To rename the Books table object to Fiction:
CLICK: the name "Books" once so that it appears highlighted
CLICK: the name "Books" again to enter Edit mode
(*Hint:* You can also select an object and press **F2** to enter Edit mode. Notice that you click the name and not the icon to rename an object.)

ACCESS

4 To rename the table object:
TYPE: Fiction
PRESS: ENTER

5 Let's create a copy of the Fiction object and name it Non-Fiction:
SELECT: Fiction
CLICK: Copy button (📋) on the toolbar
CLICK: Paste button (📋) on the toolbar
The dialog box in Figure 4.15 appears.

Figure 4.15

Paste Table As dialog box

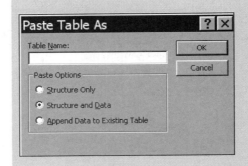

6 In the *Table Name* text box:
TYPE: Non-Fiction
SELECT: *Structure Only* check box
CLICK: OK command button
(*Note:* You copy the structure only since the data stored in the Fiction table is not required for the Non-Fiction table.)

7 To delete an object using the right-click menu:
RIGHT-CLICK: Non-Fiction
CHOOSE: Delete

8 In the confirmation dialog box:
CLICK: Yes command button
The table object is removed from the Database window.

4.4.2 Compacting and Repairing a Database

FEATURE
When you make several changes to a database, such as copying and deleting objects, it may become fragmented. Compacting a database reorganizes and packs the file more closely together, while repairing a database verifies the reliability of objects. An added benefit for those tables that contain AutoNumber fields, and where records have been deleted from the end of the table, is that compacting resets the field to the next sequential value. As a result, the next record added to the table will have an AutoNumber value that is one more than the last record in the table. In addition to saving disk space and resetting AutoNumber fields, compacting a database improves a database's performance.

METHOD
CHOOSE: Tools, Database Utilities, Compact and Repair Database

PRACTICE
In this lesson, you compact the ACC400 database file.

Setup: Ensure that the ACC400 Database window is displayed.

1 To compact and repair the ACC400 database:
CHOOSE: Tools, Database Utilities, Compact and Repair Database
The automated process begins, processes the database objects, and then ends rather quietly. You can witness its processing status by looking in the Status bar.

2 Close the ACC400 Database window. Then, exit Microsoft Access. (*Note*: If a warning dialog box appears regarding the Clipboard's contents, accept the dialog box and continue.)

ACCESS

In Addition
Backing Up
the Database

One of the most important tasks you can perform after creating and adding data to a database is to make a backup copy of it to another storage location. Most people back up a database, along with their other important data files, using "My Computer," Windows Explorer, or a specialized backup program. An Access database is stored in a file ending with the extension MDB or MDE. You can search for this file type using the Find, Files or Folders command on the Start (🔳Start) menu.

4.4 Self Check   Name two operating system tools that you can use to back up a database.

4.5 Chapter Review

The users of a database application are most familiar with its form and report objects. Forms are used in entering and editing data, while reports are used for presenting and displaying information. Besides offering a more attractive interface than datasheets, forms can help you focus your attention on a single record at a time. Reports, which also offer a variety of attractive layouts, are primarily meant for printing. It's uncommon to limit a report to previewing on-screen. Therefore, you must learn to match your printer's capabilities (color versus black-and-white, inkjet versus laser) with the report design and formatting options that are available. In this chapter, you learned to use the Access wizards to create forms, reports, and mailing labels. After experimenting with wizard-generated forms and reports, you also practiced renaming, copying, and deleting objects, and compacting and repairing a database.

4.5.1 Command Summary

Many of the commands and procedures appearing in this chapter are summarized in the following table.

Skill Set	To Perform This Task . . .	Do the Following . . .
Building and Modifying Forms	Create a new form using the AutoForm Wizard	SELECT: the desired table or query CLICK: New Object: AutoForm button (⚄▾)
	Create a new form using the Form Wizard	CLICK: *Forms* button in the Objects bar DOUBLE-CLICK: Create form by using wizard
Producing Reports	Create a new report using the AutoReport Wizard	SELECT: the desired table or query CLICK: New Object: AutoForm button (☑▾)
	Create a new report using the Report Wizard	CLICK: *Reports* button in the Object bar DOUBLE-CLICK: Create report by using wizard
	Create a new mailing labels report using the Label Wizard	CLICK: *Reports* button in the Object bar CLICK: New button (⬛New) DOUBLE-CLICK: Label Wizard

Continued

Skill Set	To Perform This Task . . .	Do the Following . . .
	Preview a report for printing	DOUBLE-CLICK: the report object, or CLICK: Print Preview button (🔍), or CHOOSE: File, Print Preview
	Print a report	CLICK: Print button (🖨), or CHOOSE: File, Print
Integrating with Other Applications	Export a report to HTML format for Web publishing	SELECT: the desired object CHOOSE: File, Export SELECT: HTML documents in the *Save as type* drop-down list box CLICK: Save command button
	Export a report as a snapshot file for e-mail and Web distribution	SELECT: the desired object CHOOSE: File, Export SELECT: Snapshot Format in the *Save as type* drop-down list box CLICK: Save command button
Working with Access	Rename a database object	RIGHT-CLICK: the desired object CHOOSE: Rename
	Copy a database object	CLICK: Copy button (📋) CLICK: Paste button (📋) SELECT: a paste option
	Delete a database object	RIGHT-CLICK: the desired object CHOOSE: Delete
Using Access Tools	Compact and repair a database	CHOOSE: Tools, Database Utilities CHOOSE: Compact and Repair Database
	Backup and restore a database	Use Windows Explorer or "My Computer" to perform copy, backup, and restore operations for an Access database file (extension .MDB)

ACCESS

4.5.2 Key Terms

This section specifies page references for the key terms identified in this chapter. For a complete list of definitions, refer to the Glossary at the end of this learning guide.

AutoForm Wizard, *p. 136*   Label Wizard, *p. 156*

AutoReport Wizard, *p. 146*   preview, *p. 152*

Form window, *p. 136*   report snapshot, *p. 156*

form wizards, *p. 135*   report wizards, *p. 146*

HTML, *p. 154*   World Wide Web, *p. 154*

Internet, *p. 154*

4.6   Review Questions

4.6.1 Short Answer

1. Why create forms for use in a database application?
2. Describe the three types of AutoForm Wizards.
3. List the form options available in the New Form dialog box.
4. When would you choose a columnar or justified form layout?
5. When would you choose a tabular or datasheet form layout?
6. Why create reports for use in a database application?
7. Describe the two types of AutoReport Wizards.
8. List the report options available in the New Report dialog box.
9. How would you prepare an Access report for publishing to the Web?
10. Describe two methods for removing objects in the Database window.

4.6.2 True/False

1. __T__ The default AutoForm Wizard is the Columnar AutoForm Wizard.
2. __T__ The Form Wizard allows you to specify a sorting order.
3. __F__ You can display data from more than one table in a form.
4. __F__ In the Form window, pressing (CTRL)+(END) moves the cursor to the last field in the current record.
5. __F__ The default AutoReport Wizard is the Tabular AutoReport Wizard.
6. __T__ The Report Wizard allows you to specify a sorting order.

7. __T__ The information that you want summarized in a report can be extracted from either a table or a query.

8. __F__ A tabular report prints several columns of information, with the field labels appearing down the left margin of the page.

9. __F__ In the Database window, you can copy a table object without duplicating the data stored in the table.

10. __T__ You should regularly compact a database using Windows Explorer.

4.6.3 Multiple Choice

1. A form is used to display data from which of the following objects:
   a. tables and queries
   b. tables and reports
   c. queries and reports
   d. tables only

2. Which form layout is produced by default when selecting the AutoForm option from the New Object button?
   a. Circular
   b. Columnar
   c. Singular
   d. Tabular

3. Which of the following best describes a tabular form layout?
   a. Data from a single record presented in a single column
   b. Data from numerous records presented in a single column
   c. Data from a single record presented in rows and columns
   d. Data from numerous records presented in rows and columns

4. Which of the following best describes a justified form layout?
   a. Data from a single record presented with stacked fields
   b. Data from numerous records presented with stacked fields
   c. Data from a single record presented in a single column
   d. Data from numerous records presented in rows and columns

5. Which of the following performs the same action as pressing (PgUp) in the Form window?
   a. CLICK: [|◄]
   b. CLICK: [◄]
   c. CLICK: [►] *Pg down*
   d. CLICK: [►|]

ACCESS

6. The Report Wizard provides the following options that are not available in the Form Wizard.
   a. Grouping and Filtering
   b. Outlining and Sorting
   c. Grouping and Sorting
   d. Outlining and Filtering

7. Which of the following is not a summary calculation available in the Summary Options dialog box of the Report Wizard?
   a. Avg
   b. Count
   c. Max
   d. Sum

8. This chapter discussed which two file format options for exporting a static report page for publishing to the Web?
   a. ASP and HTML
   b. HTML and Java
   c. MDB and MDE
   d. HTML and Snapshot

9. The Label Wizard enables you to create a report format using standard label sizes from this vendor.
   a. Avery
   b. Linux
   c. Microsoft
   d. Sun

10. Which of the following is <u>not</u> a paste option when copying a table object?
    a. Structure Only
    b. Structure and Data
    c. Structure, Forms, and Reports
    d. Append Data to Existing Table

4.7 Hands-On Projects

4.7.1 World Wide Imports: Forms and Reports

In this exercise, you create two new database objects for World Wide Imports. First, using the AutoForm Wizard, you create a columnar data entry form for the Customers table. Then, you create a tabular report using an AutoReport Wizard.

Setup: Ensure that Access is loaded. If you are launching Access and the startup dialog box appears, click the Cancel command button to remove the dialog box from the application window.

1. Open the database file named ACC470. Ensure that the *Tables* button in the Objects bar is selected.
2. To create a data entry form for the Customers table:
   SELECT: 471 Customers in the list area
   (*Hint:* Click once on the name of the table. Do not double-click.)
3. To have Access create a new columnar form:
   CLICK: New Object: AutoForm button (▣ ⋅)
   (*Hint:* If the AutoForm image is not displayed on the button face, click the attached down arrow and choose the AutoForm command.)
4. Let's save the new form:
   CLICK: Save button (▣)
   TYPE: **Customer Data Entry Form**
   PRESS: **ENTER** or CLICK: OK
5. To close the new form:
   CLICK: its Close button (☒)
6. Now your objective is to create a tabular report for the Customers table. To begin:
   CLICK: *Reports* button in the Objects bar
   CLICK: New button (▣New) on the Database window toolbar
7. In the New Report dialog box:
   SELECT: 471 Customers from the *Choose the table*...drop-down list box
   DOUBLE-CLICK: AutoReport: Tabular
   A new report is displayed in the Print Preview window.
8. On your own, use the magnifying glass mouse pointer to zoom in and out on the report page.
9. To close the report's Print Preview window:
   CLICK: its Close button (☒)
10. In the confirmation dialog box that appears, save the report:
    CLICK: Yes command button
    TYPE: **Customer AutoReport**
    PRESS: **ENTER** or CLICK: OK
    The new report object should appear in the Database window.

4.7.2 CyberWeb: Internet Accounts

CyberWeb's Internet Accounts table contains a listing of current user accounts for an Internet Service Provider. In this exercise, you create a report that groups and summarizes users according to where they live.

Setup: Ensure that the ACC470 Database window is displayed.

1. Ensure that the *Reports* button in the Objects bar is selected and then:
   DOUBLE-CLICK: Create report by using wizard

2. In the first step of the Report Wizard:
   SELECT: Table: 472 Internet Accounts from the *Tables/Queries*
   drop-down list box
3. Specify the fields that you want included in the report:
   DOUBLE-CLICK: Customer
   DOUBLE-CLICK: Username
   DOUBLE-CLICK: City
   DOUBLE-CLICK: Phone
   DOUBLE-CLICK: Amount
   CLICK: Next >
4. Specify a grouping level by city:
   DOUBLE-CLICK: City
   CLICK: Next >
5. Specify an alphabetical sort order by account name:
   SELECT: Username from the first drop-down list box
6. Now let's select a summary calculation to perform:
   CLICK: Summary Options command button
7. In the Summary Options dialog box:
   SELECT: *Sum* check box for the Amount field
   CLICK: OK
8. To specify a report layout and style:
   CLICK: Next >
   SELECT: *Align Left 1* option button in the *Layout* area
   SELECT: *Landscape* option button in the *Orientation* area
   CLICK: Next >
   SELECT: Soft Gray in the *Style* list box
9. To proceed to the last step in the wizard:
   CLICK: Next >
   TYPE: Internet Accounts By City
   CLICK: Finish
10. Maximize the report's Print Preview window and then:
    SELECT: 75% from the Zoom button (100% ▾)
    Your screen should appear similar to Figure 4.16.

Figure 4.16

Previewing a grouped and sorted report

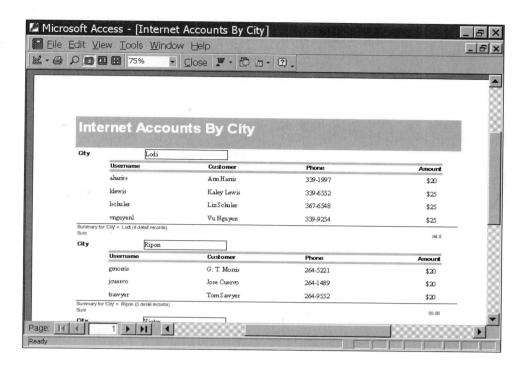

11. To print the report:
    CLICK: Print button (🖨)

12. Restore the Print Preview window by clicking its Restore button (🖳) and then close it by clicking its Close button (☒). (*Hint:* The Print Preview window's Restore button appears on the second row of Windows icons in the upper left-hand corner.)

4.7.3 Big Valley Mills: Forest Products

In this exercise, you practice creating and then working with a tabular form using the Form Wizard.

Setup: Ensure that the ACC470 Database window is displayed.

1. Display the form objects in the database using the Objects bar.
2. Launch the Form Wizard using the shortcut appearing in the list area.
3. In the Form Wizard dialog box:
   SELECT: Table: 473 Products in the *Tables/Queries* drop-down list box
   CLICK: Include All button (>>) to display all of the fields on the form
4. In the next two steps of the Form Wizard, select a *Tabular* layout and an Expedition style for the form.
5. In the last step of the wizard, enter the name "Products Tabular Form" and then open the form in Form view.

6. Enter the following data after clicking the New Record button
    (▶*):
    ProductCode: `DF99`
    Species: `DFIR`
    Size: `2  X  8`
    Grade: `Ungraded`
    Finish: `RGH`
    Category: `Dim.`
7. Move to the first field in the first record. Then:
    PRESS: `TAB` to move to the Species field column
8. Using the Sort Descending button (🔽) on the toolbar, sort the
    table into descending order by the Species column.
9. To filter the information displayed in the form:
    DOUBLE-CLICK: SYP in the Species field column
    CLICK: Filter By Selection button (🔽)
    Only records of the SYP species now appear in the new form.
10. Close the form by clicking its Close button (✖).

4.7.4 Silverdale Festival: Contact List

In this exercise, you create a mailing labels report for all the contacts
stored in Silverdale's table object.

Setup: Ensure that the ACC470 Database window is displayed.

1. Display the report objects in the database using the Objects bar.
2. To begin creating the mailing labels report:
    CLICK: New button (■New) on the Database window toolbar
    SELECT: 474 Contacts in the *Choose the table...* drop-down
    list box
    DOUBLE-CLICK: Label Wizard
    The first step of the wizard is displayed.
3. To use standard mailing labels for printing on a laser printer:
    SELECT: Avery 5160 in the *Product number* column
    SELECT: *Sheet feed* in the *Label Type* area
    CLICK: Next >
4. To adjust the typeface and font style:
    SELECT: Times New Roman in the *Font name* drop-down
    list box
    SELECT: 10 in the *Font size* drop-down list box
    SELECT: Normal in the *Font weight* drop-down list box
    CLICK: Next >

5. You build the label by adding fields from the *Available Fields* list box to the *Prototype label* area and by entering text. Do the following:
    DOUBLE-CLICK: Volunteer Group
    PRESS: (ENTER)
    TYPE: Attn:
    PRESS: Spacebar once
    DOUBLE-CLICK: Contact
    PRESS: (ENTER)
    Notice that you can input text directly onto the label.
6. Finish the label as it appears in Figure 4.17.

Figure 4.17

Designing mailing labels

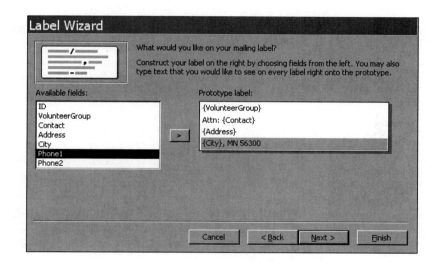

7. To proceed to the next step:
    CLICK: Next >
8. To sort the labels into order by city:
    DOUBLE-CLICK: City in the *Available fields* list box
    CLICK: Next >
9. In the last step of the wizard, enter the name "Volunteer Mailing Labels" and then display the report using the Print Preview window.
10. Print the report and then close the Print Preview window by clicking its Close button ([×]).

4.7.5 On Your Own: Office Mart Inventory

The Office Mart 475 Inventory table stores product information, including current stock levels, reorder quantities, costs, and suggested retail prices. Using the Form Wizard, create a justified form named "Inventory Input" to use for entering and editing data. To practice working with the form, enter the following records. (*Hint:* Access automatically adds the dollar signs to the Cost and SuggestedRetail values.) When you are finished, close the Form window.

ProductID: *(Autonumber)*
Description: **Push Pins**
OnHand: **45**
Cost: **$2**
SuggestedRetail: **$4**
Supplier: **E01**
Buyer: **01**
Reorder: **20**

ProductID: *(Autonumber)*
Description: **Project Folders**
OnHand: **112**
Cost: **$9**
SuggestedRetail: **$13**
Supplier: **B05**
Buyer: **07**
Reorder: **40**

Using the Report Wizard, create a report that calculates and displays the minimum and maximum values for the Cost and SuggestedRetail fields as grouped by supplier. Furthermore, sort the report by the product's description. In the last step of the wizard, name the report "Supplier Summary" and then view the report. Before closing the Print Preview window, send a copy of the report to the printer. And lastly, export the report to an HTML document named "Inventory" for posting to the company's internal Web server.

 ## 4.7.6 On Your Own: Sun Bird Resort

The Sun Bird Resort wants to make life easier for the front-counter clerks. To this end, they've asked you to create two data entry forms. Since the 476 Guides table contains only a few fields, create a tabular form named "Guides Data Entry" using the Tabular AutoForm Wizard. Then, for the 476 Patrons table, use the Form Wizard to create a columnar form named "Patrons Data Entry" and specify the Blends style. To test the usability of the forms, practice selecting records and editing data.

You've also been asked to create a report that includes all of the fields from the Patrons table and then groups the report according to interest. The report is to be sorted in order by the BestTime field. After specifying a layout and style, save the report as "Patrons By Interest." Then preview the report in the Print Preview window before sending it to the printer. When finished, close the ACC470 Database window and then exit Microsoft Access.

4.8   Case Problems: Lagniappe, Inc.

Lagniappe, Inc. manufactures and sells a limited line of travel luggage through boutiques in Seattle, San Francisco, Chicago, Boston, and New York. As the western regional sales representative, Janice is primarily responsible for servicing the repeat purchasers in San Francisco and Seattle. To keep in touch with the markets, her boss, John Lucci, has asked that Janice fax him monthly status reports. Since she must create these reports from scratch anyway, Janice decides to take this opportunity to also create form objects for her database.

In the following case problems, assume the role of Janice and perform the same steps that she identifies. You may want to re-read the
chapter opening before proceeding.

1. After launching Access, Janice opens the ACC480 database that
    is stored in her data files folder. Wanting to get a better feel for
    the forms Access can create, she uses the AutoForm Wizard to
    generate a columnar form for the Customers table. She saves
    the form as "Customers–AutoForm" and then practices moving
    through the records using the navigation buttons in the Form
    window. Feeling comfortable with her creation, she closes the
    Form window.

    Since the AutoForm Wizard did such a nice job with the form,
    Janice decides to create a new report. She selects the Customers
    table and launches the AutoReport Wizard using the toolbar. After
    perusing the report, she closes the window by clicking its Close
    button (⊠) and then saves the report as "Customers–AutoReport."
    After letting the report sink in for a few moments, Janice concedes
    that it's not quite what she had hoped for. After displaying the
    stored report objects, she uses the right-click menu to delete the
    AutoReport object from the Database window.

2. Being the adventurous type, Janice wants to create a new form
    layout for the Products table. To begin, she displays the form
    objects in the Database window and then double-clicks the
    "Create form by using wizard" shortcut. In the first step of the
    wizard, she selects the Products table and includes all of the
    fields. Then she specifies an International style for the form.
    Lastly, Janice names the new form "Products–Input Form" and
    opens it for display. After viewing the new form, she closes it
    by clicking its Close button (⊠).

3. Janice wants to send out a mailing to all of her preferred cus-
    tomers. Using the Customers table, she prepares a standard
    Avery 5160 mailing label. The font selected is Times New
    Roman with a 10-point font size. After specifying that the
    labels be sorted into ascending order by surname, she saves the
    report as "Customer Mailing." Figure 4.18 displays the results of
    the mailing labels report. Janice displays two pages in the Print
    Preview window and then sends the report to the printer.
    Lastly, she closes the Print Preview window to return to the
    Database window.

ACCESS

Figure 4.18

Previewing a mailing labels report

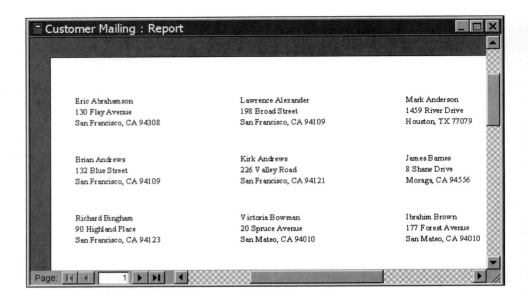

4. Janice's boss, John, commends her for the new reports, but would like to see her customers grouped by the product that they purchased. Janice knows that the Report Wizard can help her produce this report. After launching the wizard, she selects the Customers table and includes all of its fields for display in the report. Janice selects the ProductID field for grouping the contents of the report and the LastName field for sorting the report. She then selects a layout, page orientation, and style. In the last step of the Report Wizard, Janice names the report "Customers–By ProductID" and then opens it for display in the Print Preview window. Satisfied with the results, Janice prints and then closes the report.

"Janice, your reports look great!" John exclaims on the answering machine. "I'd like you to show Jose and Wendy how you produced these reports so quickly. They typically spend the last three days of each month compiling their reports." Janice is pleased that the reports have gone over so well. Rather than faxing them to Jose and Wendy, she decides to export the report as an HTML document. In the Database window, Janice selects the "Customers–By ProductID" report object and chooses the File, Export command. After locating her personal storage folder and selecting the "HTML Documents" format, she clicks the Save command button and bypasses the dialog box asking for an HTML template. She will inform her associates that they can preview the report after she finishes uploading it to her personal Web site. Lastly, she closes the ACC480 Database window and exits Microsoft Access.

NOTES

NOTES

MICROSOFT OFFICE 2000
Integrating Word and Excel

CHAPTER
ONE

Chapter Outline

Learning Objectives

After completing this chapter, you will be able to:

- Use the Office Clipboard to assemble a report

- Link Excel data to a Word document

- Embed Excel data in a Word document

- Move, resize, delete, and edit shared objects

- Enhance Word documents with new Excel worksheets and charts

Case Study

Riverdale Forest Products

Sam Houghton is the manager of the electrical division of a major lumber producing company called Riverdale Forest Products. He has worked there for several years, during which time he has become proficient using Word for creating memos, and Excel for tracking production levels. Sam would like to embellish his memos with supporting data from his Excel worksheets, however he doesn't want to have to retype any of the Excel data. Ideally, he would like to copy existing Excel data into his Word memos.

Forever cautious, Sam doesn't want to attempt any sharing of information between Word and Excel without first learning more about the process. His greatest fear is that he might damage his Excel worksheets.

In this chapter, you and Sam learn how to use the Office Clipboard to copy Office objects, and then paste, link, and embed them into different programs. You will manipulate the inserted objects, and then insert new Excel worksheets and charts in Word without launching Excel.

1.1 Using the Office Clipboard

In Microsoft Office 2000 applications, the Windows and Office Clipboards enable you to copy items from one location to another. Whereas the **Windows Clipboard** can store only a single item at once, the enhanced **Office Clipboard** can store up to 12 items. The Office Clipboard is ideal for assembling reports that require excerpts from multiple documents. For example, you can copy an Excel chart, an Access table, and a PowerPoint slide to the Office Clipboard and then paste the collection of items into a Word document.

1.1.1 Activating the Office Clipboard

FEATURE
The Office Clipboard is automatically activated when you copy two items without an intervening paste. You can also activate the Office Clipboard by right-clicking any Office toolbar and then selecting the Clipboard option. Each copied item is represented by a representative icon on the Clipboard toolbar. Note that the Windows Clipboard continues to work once the Office Clipboard is activated. The last item that was copied to the Office Clipboard will always be located in the Windows Clipboard.

METHOD
- Copy two items in sequence without an intervening paste, or
- RIGHT-CLICK: any Office toolbar
  SELECT: Clipboard

PRACTICE
In this lesson, you copy a range of worksheet cells and a chart from an existing Excel worksheet to the Office Clipboard.

Setup: Ensure that Word and Excel are installed on your computer.

1 Launch Word and then open the INT111 Word file.

2 Save the document as "Summary Memo" to your personal storage location.

3 Launch Excel and then open the INT111 Excel file.

4 Save the worksheet as "Orders Summary" to your personal storage location.

5 To display the Office Clipboard:
RIGHT-CLICK: any toolbar button
SELECT: Clipboard
The Clipboard toolbar should now appear.

6 When the Office Clipboard is empty, none of the buttons on the Clipboard toolbar will be available for selection. If your Clipboard isn't empty, do the following to clear the contents of the Office Clipboard now.
CLICK: Clear Clipboard button (🖾) on the Clipboard toolbar
Your screen should now appear similar to Figure 1.1. (*Note:* In Figure 1.1, the Clipboard toolbar has been dragged to the bottom-right corner of the worksheet.)

Figure 1.1

The empty Clipboard
toolbar is displayed

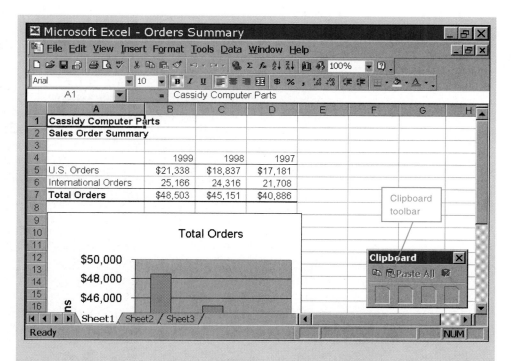

7 To copy the worksheet data to the Office Clipboard:
SELECT: cell range from A4 to D7
CLICK: Copy button (🖺) on the Standard toolbar
(*Note:* The Copy button on the Clipboard toolbar performs the identical function as the Copy button on the Standard toolbar.) An icon representing the Excel data now appears on the Clipboard toolbar. You should also see a dashed marquee around the cell range.

8 To select the chart:
CLICK: near the upper-left corner of the chart
The chart object should be surrounded with **sizing handles,** which are tiny boxes that surround the object. Later, you'll learn how to use these handles to resize an object.

9 To copy the chart to the Office Clipboard:
CLICK: Copy button (🖺) on the Standard toolbar
Two icons, representing the worksheet and the chart, should now appear on the Clipboard toolbar, as shown below:

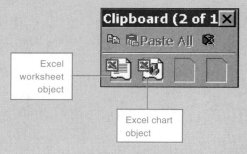

10 Continue to the next lesson.

INTEGRATING

1.1.2 Pasting and Clearing Clipboard Items

FEATURE

Whereas the contents of the Windows Clipboard are pasted by clicking the Paste button (⊞) on the Standard toolbar, the contents of the Office Clipboard are pasted using buttons on the Clipboard toolbar. Using the Clipboard toolbar, you can paste the items into any one of the Office 2000 applications individually or as a group. You can also clear the entire contents of the Office Clipboard with a button on the Clipboard toolbar.

METHOD

- CLICK: an item's icon on the Clipboard toolbar to paste an individual item
- CLICK: Paste All button (⊞Paste All) on the Clipboard toolbar to paste all items at once
- CLICK: Clear Clipboard icon (⊠) on the Clipboard toolbar to clear the entire contents of the Office Clipboard

PRACTICE

You will now paste the contents of the Office Clipboard into a Word briefing memo. You will then clear the contents of the Office Clipboard.

Setup: Ensure that you've completed the previous lesson. The "Summary Memo" should be open in Word and the "Orders Summary" worksheet should be open in Excel. The Excel window is the active window.

1 To display the "Summary Memo" document:
CLICK: "Summary Memo" Word button on the taskbar

2 To position the insertion point at the end of the memo:
PRESS: CTRL + END

3 Let's paste the entire contents of the Office Clipboard into the Word document:
CLICK: Paste All button (⊞Paste All) on the Clipboard toolbar

4 To view the results of the paste, let's move the insertion point to the top of the document and then zoom the screen to 50%:
PRESS: CTRL + HOME
CLICK: Zoom drop-down arrow (100% ▾) on the Standard toolbar
SELECT: 50%
Your screen should now appear similar to Figure 1.2.

Figure 1.2

"Summary Memo" document

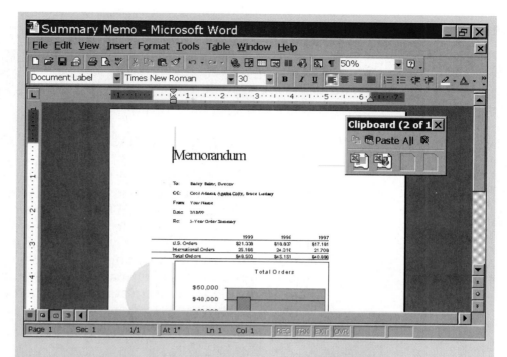

5 Before continuing, let's increase the zoom factor to 100%.
CLICK: Zoom drop-down arrow (100% ▼) on the Standard toolbar
SELECT: 100%

6 Save and then close the "Summary Memo" document.

7 Let's start a new document.
CLICK: New button (▢) on the Standard toolbar

8 If you click the Paste button (▣) on the Standard toolbar, the contents of the Windows Clipboard will appear in the document. Let's see what's stored in the Windows Clipboard.
CLICK: Paste button (▣) on the Standard toolbar
Note that the Windows Clipboard contains the chart—the last item you copied to the Office Clipboard.

9 Let's clear the contents of the Office Clipboard and then close the Clipboard toolbar:
CLICK: Clear Clipboard button (▣) on the Clipboard toolbar
CLICK: Close button (✖) on the Clipboard toolbar
(*Note:* If you close the Clipboard toolbar three times in a row without pasting one or all items on it, the Clipboard toolbar won't open again when you copy two clips in sequence. You'll have to activate the Clipboard toolbar by right-clicking a toolbar. With this action, the counter will be reset.)

10 Close the current document, without saving.

11 Close Word and Excel.

1.1 Self Check   What typically happens when you copy two items in sequence without an intervening paste?

1.2 Pasting, Linking, and Embedding

When you paste information from the Windows or Office Clipboards into a document, Office uses **HTML** (HyperText Markup Language) as its default data format. HTML, as you may already know, is the language of the World Wide Web. Microsoft selected HTML as the default data format so that your text formatting, tables, and other formats will remain unchanged when you copy items among the Office applications. There may be times, however, when you don't want to use HTML as the data format, such as when you don't want to retain your original formatting. In this case, you can use the Paste Special command and then select an alternate data format.

When sharing data among applications, not only do you have to consider the format of the shared data, but you also have to decide on how you want the source data (what you're copying) and the copied data to be related. Table 1.1 describes three ways to share data among Office 2000 applications. Each method involves copying the desired data from the **source document,** the document in which the data was first entered, into the **destination document,** or the document that receives the data.

Table 1.1

Three methods for sharing data among Office 2000 applications

Method	Description
Pasting	The simplest method for sharing information is to copy the desired data from the source document and then paste it into the destination document. **Pasting** data involves inserting a static representation of the source data into the destination document.
Linking	In **linking,** you not only paste the data, you also establish a dynamic link between the source and destination documents. Thereafter, making changes in the source document updates the destination document automatically.
Embedding	**Embedding** data involves inserting a source document into a destination document as an object. Unlike pasted data, an embedded object is fully editable within the client application. Unlike linked data, an embedded object does not retain a connection to its source document; everything is contained in the destination document.

In this module, we explore the methods of pasting, linking, and embedding data between applications.

1.2.1 Pasting Data from Word to Excel

FEATURE
Pasting is used to transfer data from one application to another. There is no linking of documents or embedding of objects when you paste data. The data is simply copied from the source document to the Clipboard and then inserted into the destination document.

METHOD
1. Copy data from a Word source document to the Clipboard.
2. Select the desired target location in the Excel worksheet.
3. CHOOSE: Edit, Paste, or
   CLICK: Paste button (📋)

PRACTICE
You will now practice pasting data from an existing Word document into an Excel worksheet.

Setup: Ensure that Word and Excel are installed on your computer.

1 Launch Word and then open the INT121 Word file.

2 Save the file as "Student Memo" to your personal storage location.

3 Launch Excel and open the INT121 Excel file.

4 Save the file as "Survey Results" to your personal storage location.

5 To switch back to Word:
CLICK: "Student Memo" Word button on the taskbar

6 The insertion point is currently blinking at the top of the document. To copy all the information located at the top of the document to the Clipboard:
SELECT: the five lines of information located at the top of the document
(*Hint:* Position the mouse pointer to the left of the first line. Then, press down and hold the left mouse button as you drag the mouse pointer downward over the five lines of information.)
CLICK: Copy button (📋) on the Standard toolbar

INTEGRATING

7 To make the Excel application window active:
CLICK: Microsoft Excel button on the taskbar

8 To insert the Word text into the worksheet:
SELECT: cell A1
CLICK: Paste button (⬛)
As shown in Figure 1.3, the data is automatically divided into separate cells. Also note that, because the default data format for pasted data is HTML, the formatting of the Word text is retained in the Excel worksheet.

Figure 1.3

Pasting data from a Word document into an Excel worksheet

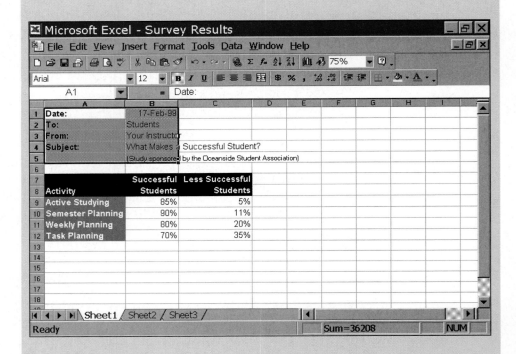

9 Save the revised worksheet and keep it open for the next lesson.

1.2.2 Linking Excel Data to a Word Document

FEATURE
You link files when the information you need from a source document is either maintained by other users or needs to be incorporated into multiple documents. Because Excel is largely an analysis tool for calculating and summarizing data, worksheets typically provide the source data for use in other documents. For successful linking to occur, the source documents must always be accessible, whether stored on the same computer as the destination document or via a network connection.

METHOD
1. Copy data from the Excel source document to the Clipboard.
2. In the Word destination document, position the insertion point where you want to insert the data.
3. CHOOSE: Edit, Paste Special
4. SELECT: *Paste link* option button
5. SELECT: a data format in the *As* list box
6. CLICK: OK command button

PRACTICE
Your objective in this lesson is to copy and link an Excel table into a Word document.

Setup: Ensure that you've completed the previous lesson in this module. The "Student Memo" document should be open in Word, and the "Survey Results" worksheet should be open in Excel. The Excel window is the active window.

1 Let's copy the "Activity" table to the Clipboard:
SELECT: cell range from A7 to C12
CLICK: Copy button ([🖺])

2 To display the Word "Student Memo" document:
CLICK: "Student Memo" Word button on the taskbar

3 To position the insertion point at the bottom of the document:
PRESS: [CTRL] + [END]

4 You will now paste the table into the memo document and establish a dynamic link between the source document, "Survey Results.xls," and the destination document, "Student Memo.doc." To begin:
CHOOSE: Edit, Paste Special from the Word menu
Microsoft Word's Paste Special dialog box appears, as shown in Figure 1.4. You can select the desired format for pasting the Clipboard contents from the *As* list box (Table 1.2). Note that "HTML Format" is the currently selected option.

INTEGRATING

Figure 1.4

Word's Paste Special
dialog box

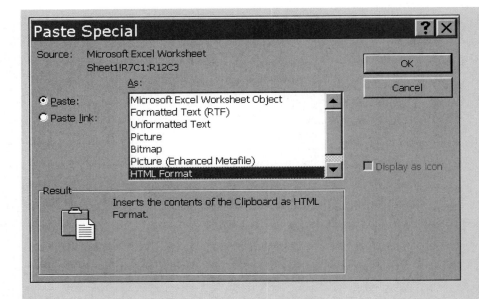

Table 1.2

Data Format
options

Data Format	Description
Microsoft Excel Worksheet Object	The data is inserted as an embedded Excel object that you can edit by double-clicking.
Formatted Text (RTF)	The data is inserted as an editable Word table.
Unformatted Text	The data is inserted as text, with no formatting applied.
Picture	The data is inserted as a picture object for printing on high-quality printers.
Bitmap	The data is inserted as a picture object for online viewing. This option takes up a lot of memory and disk space.
Picture (Enhanced Metafile)	The data is inserted as an enhanced metafile.
HTML Format	The data is inserted in an HTML format so that text attributes and other formatting are retained.

  To review the various data formats:
CLICK: once on each option in the *As* list box and read the
description appearing in the *Result* area

6 To insert the object using the HTML data format:
SELECT: HTML Format in the *As* list box

7 To establish a link between the source and the destination documents:
CLICK: *Paste link* option button
CLICK: OK command button
The information is inserted in the memo, and the link is established. Your screen should now appear similar to Figure 1.5.

Figure 1.5

Linking data from an Excel worksheet to a Word document

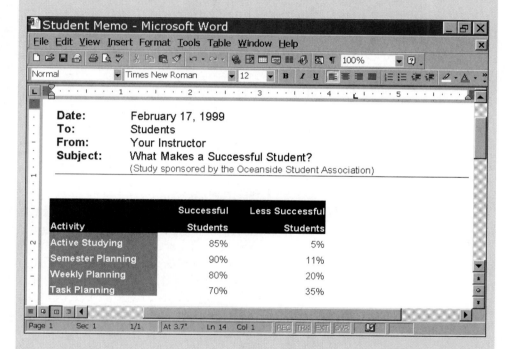

Student Memo - Microsoft Word

File Edit View Insert Format Tools Table Window Help

Normal Times New Roman 12 B I U 100%

Date:	February 17, 1999
To:	Students
From:	Your Instructor
Subject:	What Makes a Successful Student?
	(Study sponsored by the Oceanside Student Association)

Activity	Successful Students	Less Successful Students
Active Studying	85%	5%
Semester Planning	90%	11%
Weekly Planning	80%	20%
Task Planning	70%	35%

Page 1   Sec 1   1/1   At 3.7"   Ln 14   Col 1   REC TRK EXT OVR

8 Locate the value for Task Planning in the "Successful Students" column. Let's change this value from 70% to 90% in the Excel worksheet to demonstrate dynamic linking.
CLICK: Microsoft Excel button on the taskbar

9 With the worksheet displayed on the screen:
PRESS: ESC to remove the copy marquee
SELECT: cell B12
TYPE: 90%
PRESS: ENTER
You have now updated the worksheet source document.

INTEGRATING

10 To view the Word table:
CLICK: "Student Memo" Word button on the taskbar
Note that the value has been updated automatically in the table. Does dynamic linking work in the opposite direction? No, linking is a one-way relationship. If you change a value in the Word table, the Excel worksheet is not updated. And the next time that you update the worksheet, the changes that you made in the Word table will be overwritten!

11 Save the document as "Linked Memo" to your personal storage location.

12 Close the Word document.

1.2.3 Embedding Excel Data in a Word Document

FEATURE
Embedding data enables you to place a fully editable version of the source data into the destination document. Moreover, when editing an embedded object, you use the actual commands and tools of the original **server application** (the application that was used to create the data originally) from within the current application window. Understandably, a document containing embedded objects will require more disk space than one containing links.

METHOD
1. Copy data from the Excel source document to the Clipboard.
2. In the Word destination document, position the insertion point where you want to insert the data.
3. CHOOSE: Edit, Paste Special
4. SELECT: Microsoft Excel Worksheet Object in the *As* list box
5. CLICK: OK command button

PRACTICE
Your current objective is to insert and embed an Excel worksheet into a Microsoft Word document.

Setup: Ensure that you've completed the previous lessons in this module. No documents should be open in Word, and the "Survey Results" worksheet should be open in Excel. The Word window should be the active window.

1 In Word, open the "Student Memo" document from your personal storage location.

2 To position the insertion point at the end of the document:
PRESS: [CTRL] + [END]

3 To switch to Excel:
CLICK: Microsoft Excel button on the taskbar

4 To copy the desired information to the Clipboard:
SELECT: cell range from A7 to C12
CLICK: Copy button (⧉)

5 To switch back to Word:
CLICK: "Student Memo" Word button on the taskbar

6 To embed the worksheet object into the Word document:
CHOOSE: Edit, Paste Special
SELECT: Microsoft Excel Worksheet Object in the *As* list box
CLICK: OK command button
The object appears in the Word document with sizing handles. Any changes you make in the source document won't affect this embedded table.

7 In the next module, you learn more about editing linked and embedded objects. For now, save the document as "Embedded Memo" to your personal storage location.

8 Close Word and Excel.

In Addition
Manually Updating
Linked Objects

To specify that a linked object isn't updated each time you open the destination document, choose Edit, Links from the Menu bar and then select the Manual option button in the dialog box that appears. To manually update a linked object later, choose Edit, Links and then click the Update Now command button.

INTEGRATING

1.2 Self Check   When you paste data, what is the default data format?

1.3 Manipulating Shared Objects

Upon inserting an object in an Office document, you will most likely have to manipulate it to meet your specific needs. This module explores several techniques for manipulating shared objects.

1.3.1 Moving, Resizing, and Deleting Shared Objects

FEATURE

Once a linked or embedded object is inserted in an Office document, the object will appear surrounded with *sizing handles*, which appear as tiny boxes. You can also select an object that isn't currently selected by clicking the object once. Once selected, you can move and resize a shared object to fit the dimensions and layout of your document. You can also delete selected objects.

METHOD

- Select an object by positioning the mouse pointer over the object's placeholder until a four-headed arrow (✛) appears and then clicking.
- Move a selected object by dragging.
- Resize a selected object by dragging its sizing handles.
- Delete a selected object by pressing DELETE.

PRACTICE

You will now practice selecting, moving, resizing, and deleting an embedded object.

Setup: Ensure that Word and Excel are installed on your computer.

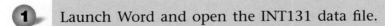 Launch Word and open the INT131 data file.

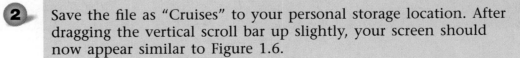 Save the file as "Cruises" to your personal storage location. After dragging the vertical scroll bar up slightly, your screen should now appear similar to Figure 1.6.

Figure 1.6

This Word document contains an embedded Excel worksheet

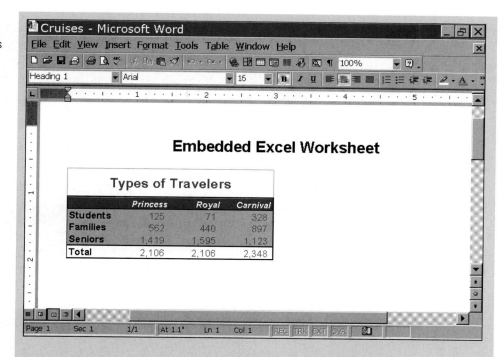

3 Let's practice resizing the embedded object and then centering it beneath the "Embedded Excel Worksheet" title.
CLICK: the Excel object
The object should be surrounded with sizing handles.

4 When you position the mouse pointer over a sizing handle, the pointer will change to a double-headed arrow. To resize the embedded object:
DRAG: the sizing handle in the bottom-right corner outward about an inch
(*Hint:* Use the Ruler as your guide.)

5 To move the object to the right, position the mouse pointer over the embedded object until a four-headed arrow (✛) appears.

6 DRAG: the object to the right until it is centered beneath the title
Your screen should now appear similar to Figure 1.7.

INTEGRATING

Figure 1.7

The object was resized and moved

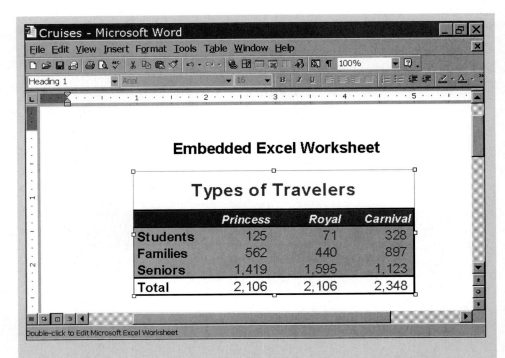

7 The object should still be selected. To practice deleting the object:

PRESS: DELETE

The object is now deleted.

8 To undo the previous action:

PRESS: the Undo button (⟲▾) once (not the drop-down arrow)

9 Save the revised document and keep it open for the next lesson.

1.3.2 Editing Shared Objects

FEATURE

A feature called *Visual Editing* makes it easy to update an embedded object in place. To edit an embedded object, such as an Excel table in Word, you simply double-click the object. Rather than being launched into the server application (Excel) to perform the changes, you remain where you are (Word) and the current application's menus and toolbars are replaced with those of the server application. In other words, you don't have to exit the current application to change the embedded object. In contrast, to edit a linked object, you must switch to the server application and then make your changes. By default, linked objects are updated automatically when the destination document is opened.

METHOD
- To edit an embedded object:
  DOUBLE-CLICK: the object and then make any necessary changes
  CLICK: outside the object when you're finished making changes
- To edit a linked object, switch to the server application and then make any necessary changes.

PRACTICE
You will now practice editing an embedded object. (*Note:* You practiced editing a linked object in lesson 1.2.2.)

Setup: Ensure that you've completed the previous lesson in this module and that the "Cruises" document is open in Word.

1 To modify the embedded worksheet that's located in the "Cruises" document:
DOUBLE-CLICK: the object
Your screen should now appear similar to Figure 1.8. Note that Word's Menu bar and toolbars are replaced by Excel's. Also, the embedded object itself is bounded by row and column frames, scroll bars, and sheet tabs.

Figure 1.8

Editing an embedded Excel object in Word

The hashed border indicates that you are editing the embedded object.

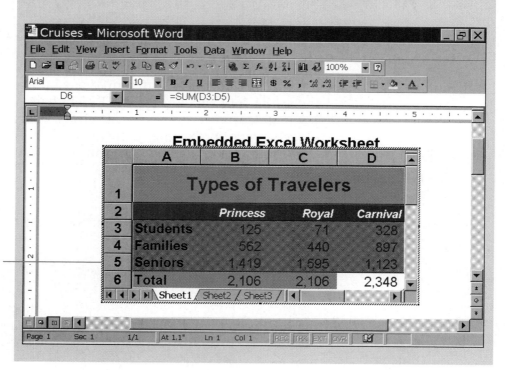

INTEGRATING

2 To practice editing an embedded object, you will now calculate a new total in the Princess column.
SELECT: cell B3
TYPE: 150
PRESS: ENTER
Note that the worksheet area recalculates as expected.

3 To finish editing the embedded object:
CLICK: the mouse pointer outside the object to deselect the object
The object's hashed border disappears, and you may now size and move it as before.

4 Save the revised document and then close Word.

1.3 Self Check   How would you go about resizing a shared object?

1.4 Inserting New Worksheets and Charts in Word

Not only can you insert existing objects in an Office document, but you can create new objects. To do this, you must choose Insert, Object and then select the type of object you want to insert. Office lets you create many different types of shared objects from scratch, including (but not limited to) Excel charts, Excel worksheets, Power-Point slides, PowerPoint presentations, and several Word objects. New objects are automatically embedded in the destination document. In this module, we explore inserting new worksheets and charts in a Word document.

1.4.1 Inserting a New Worksheet in Word

FEATURE
Although Word's table features are powerful, you may prefer to build the bulk of your tables in Excel, especially if your tables require extensive calculations. You can easily insert a new Excel worksheet into Word without launching Excel.

METHOD
1. Position the insertion point in the destination document.
2. CHOOSE: Insert, Object
3. DOUBLE-CLICK: Microsoft Excel Worksheet in the *Object type* list box
4. Without leaving Word, edit the object using the menus and tools of the object's source application.
5. CLICK: outside of the embedded object to return to Word

PRACTICE
You will now embed a new worksheet in a Word document.

Setup: Ensure that Word and Excel are installed on your computer.

1 Launch Word to display a new document in the application window.

2 CHOOSE: Insert, Object
CLICK: *Create New* tab

3 SELECT: Microsoft Excel Worksheet in the *Object type* list box
Your screen should now appear similar to Figure 1.9.

Figure 1.9

The Object dialog box

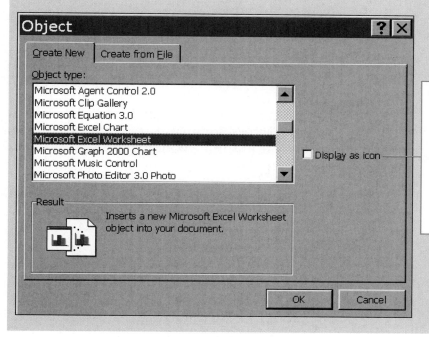

If you are concerned about file size, you may want to insert the new object as an icon that users can double-click in order to display the object. The icon takes up very little space in the document.

4 To proceed with embedding the new object:
CLICK: OK command button
Your screen should now appear similar to Figure 1.10. Note that Excel's Menu bar and Standard and Formatting toolbars have replaced Word's toolbars. (*Note:* You can also use the Insert Microsoft Excel Worksheet button (⊞) on Word's Standard toolbar to insert a new Excel worksheet.)

Figure 1.10

Embedding a new worksheet

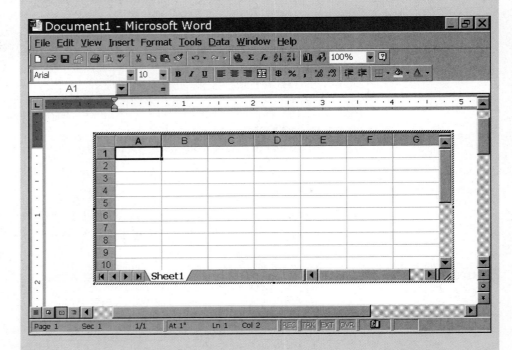

5 At this point, you would type your data into the worksheet and use Excel's commands to complete the worksheet. Because this isn't a lesson in building Excel worksheets, proceed with the next step.

6 To return to Word:
CLICK: outside of the embedded object
An empty table grid should have been inserted in the document.

7 Let's pretend that you now want to edit the Excel table. Since the object is embedded, you edit it by double-clicking.
DOUBLE-CLICK: the table grid
Note that Excel's toolbars are again activated.

8 Close the document window without saving.

1.4.2 Inserting a New Chart in Word

FEATURE
If you already know how to create charts in Excel and have access to Excel on your computer, you'll want to use it to create new charts instead of Microsoft Graph. **Microsoft Graph,** a charting and graphing tool, is one several mini-applications, called *applets*, that extend the capabilities of Office. Microsoft Excel, however, provides a more robust graphing environment.

METHOD
1. Position the insertion point in the destination document.
2. CHOOSE: Insert, Object
3. DOUBLE-CLICK: Microsoft Excel Chart in the *Object type* list box
4. Without leaving Word, edit the object using the menus and tools of the object's source application.
5. CLICK: outside of the embedded object to return to Word

PRACTICE
You will now embed a new chart in a Word document.

Setup: Ensure that you've completed the previous lesson in this module.

1 Display a new document in Word.

2 CHOOSE: Insert, Object
CLICK: *Create New* tab

3 SELECT: Microsoft Excel Chart in the *Object type* list box

4 To proceed with embedding the new object:
CLICK: OK command button
Your screen should now appear similar to Figure 1.11.

Figure 1.11

Embedding a new chart

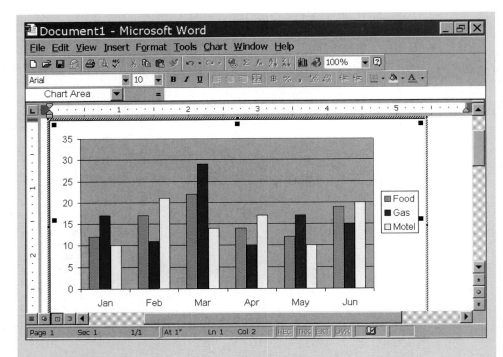

5 At this point, you would use Excel's Menu bar and Standard and Formatting toolbars to edit the chart according to your needs. Because this isn't a lesson in building Excel charts, proceed with the next step.

6 To return to Word:
CLICK: outside of the embedded object
The default chart should have been inserted in the document.

7 Close Word, without saving the revised document.

1.4 Self Check   What is the procedure for editing embedded objects?

1.5 Chapter Review

The Office Clipboard is an enhanced Windows Clipboard that lets you store up to 12 items at once. You can paste the items into any one of the Office 2000 applications individually or as a group. By default, pasted data is stored in an HTML data format, although you can change this setting using the Paste Special dialog box.

In Office, you share information through pasting, linking, and embedding. These three methods differ in how the source data and copied data are related. In this chapter, you used the pasting method to insert Word text in Excel, the linking method to insert a range of worksheet cells in Word, and the embedding method to insert a chart in Word. You also learned how to move, resize, edit, and delete shared objects.

1.5.1 Command Summary

Many of the commands and procedures appearing in this chapter are summarized in the following table.

Skill Set	To Perform this Task . . .	Do the Following . . .
Using the Office Clipboard	Display the Office Clipboard	RIGHT-CLICK: an existing toolbar button SELECT: Clipboard
	Paste the contents of the Office Clipboard as a group	CLICK: Paste All button (Paste All) on the Clipboard toolbar
	Clear the contents of the Office Clipboard	CLICK: Clear Clipboard button on the Clipboard toolbar
Pasting Data	Paste data from Word into Excel, once the data appears on the Clipboard	CHOOSE: Edit, Paste, or CLICK: Paste button
Linking Data	Insert links to existing Office 2000 data	SELECT: source information CLICK: Copy button and then position the insertion point in the destination document CHOOSE: Edit, Paste Special SELECT: *Paste link* option button SELECT: a data format in the *As* list box CLICK: OK command button
	Edit linked data that appears in the destination document	Switch to the server application and update the source document.

Continued

Skill Set	To Perform this Task . . .	Do the Following . . .
Embedding Data	Embed Excel data in Word, once the data appears on the Clipboard	CHOOSE: Edit, Paste Special SELECT: Microsoft Excel Worksheet Object in the *As* list box CLICK: OK command button
	Embed new Office 2000 objects, without using the Clipboard	CHOOSE: Insert, Object CLICK: *Create New* tab DOUBLE-CLICK: the desired object in the *Object type* list box
	Edit embedded data that appears in a destination document	DOUBLE-CLICK: the object and make your changes CLICK: outside of the object, when completed
Modifying Shared Objects	Resize an object	SELECT: the object DRAG: the object's sizing handles
	Move an object	DRAG: the object to a new location
	Delete an object	SELECT: the object PRESS: DELETE

1.5.2 Key Terms

This section specifies page references for the key terms identified in this chapter. For a complete list of definitions, refer to the Glossary at the end of this learning guide.

destination document, *p. 8*   pasting, *p. 8*

embedding, *p. 8*   server application, *p. 14*

HTML, *p. 8*   sizing handles, *p. 5*

linking, *p. 8*   source document, p. 8

Microsoft Graph, *p. 23*   Windows Clipboard, *p. 3*

Office Clipboard, *p. 3*

1.6   Review Questions

1.6.1   Short Answer

1. What is linking? Under what circumstances would you create links between documents?
2. How do embedded objects and linked objects differ?
3. Describe the general procedure for embedding a new Excel chart in a Word document.
4. What is the main difference between the Windows Clipboard and the Office Clipboard?
5. What are the three methods for sharing data among applications?
6. How would you go about deleting an embedded object?
7. How would you go about pasting the contents of the Office Clipboard as a group?
8. What is the procedure for clearing the contents of the Office Clipboard?
9. What is the procedure for editing a linked object?
10. How do you select linked and embedded objects?

1.6.2   True/False

1. _____ The destination document is the document that receives the data from another application.
2. _____ An embedded object is automatically updated when information in its source document changes.
3. _____ It's best to embed an object when the information needs to be updated by different people on a network.
4. _____ It is possible to embed either a new or existing object into a document.
5. _____ The Office Clipboard can store up to 12 items of information.
6. _____ By default, linked objects are updated automatically when the destination document is opened.
7. _____ Microsoft Graph provides charting capabilities superior to Microsoft Excel.
8. _____ The last item you copy to the Office Clipboard will always be located in the Windows Clipboard.
9. _____ Objects that you insert by choosing Insert, Object are automatically linked in the destination document.
10. _____ Using a method called *pasting*, a static representation of the source data is inserted in the destination document.

1.6.3 Multiple Choice

1. When sharing data in Office 2000, the _____ document is the document in which the data was first entered.
   a. source
   b. destination
   c. original
   d. primary

2. The _____ command is used to establish a link between a source document and a destination document.
   a. Tools, Link, Documents
   b. Tools, Link
   c. Edit, Link
   d. Edit, Paste Special

3. _____ is an Office 2000 feature that makes it easy to update embedded objects.
   a. Pasting
   b. Visual Editing
   c. Edit, Links
   d. Tools, Update, Links

4. Which of the following would be the most helpful when you are assembling the different components of a large document?
   a. Windows Clipboard
   b. Office Clipboard
   c. Visual Editing
   d. links

5. To enable automatic updates in destination documents, you must establish _____ between the source and destination documents.
   a. embedding
   b. objects
   c. relationships
   d. links

6. When you insert an Excel chart into a Word document:
   a. Word is the destination document
   b. Excel is the destination document
   c. The chart is the destination document
   d. The document is the source document

7. When you want to update the data in a linked worksheet range:
   a. DOUBLE-CLICK: the worksheet range object
   b. RIGHT-CLICK: the worksheet range and choose Edit Object
   c. Edit the data in the destination document
   d. Edit the data in the source document

8. When you want to update the data in an embedded worksheet range:
   a. DOUBLE-CLICK: the worksheet range object
   b. RIGHT-CLICK: the worksheet range and choose Edit Object
   c. Edit the data in the destination document
   d. Edit the data in the source document

9. It's possible to _____ embedded objects
   a. move
   b. resize
   c. delete
   d. all of the above

10. By default, data is pasted in a(n) _____ format
    a. RTF
    b. Enhanced Metafile
    c. Picture
    d. HTML

1.7 Hands-On Projects

1.7.1 Timberline Toys: Sales Summary

In this exercise, you copy two Excel items to the Office Clipboard and paste them into a Word document. You then practice clearing the Clipboard contents.

1. Launch Word and then open the INT171 Word File.
2. Save the document as "Toy Sales Letter" to your personal storage location.
3. Launch Excel and then open the INT171 Excel file.
4. Save the worksheet as "Toy Sales Data" to your personal storage location.
5. To display the Office Clipboard:
   RIGHT-CLICK: any toolbar button
   SELECT: Clipboard
   The Clipboard toolbar should now appear.

INTEGRATING

6. Let's clear any items in the Clipboard toolbar:
   CLICK: Clear Clipboard button (🗑) on the Clipboard toolbar

7. To copy a range of worksheet cells to the Office Clipboard:
   SELECT: cell range from A1 to E5
   CLICK: Copy button (📋) on the Standard toolbar
   An icon representing the Excel data should appear on the
   Clipboard toolbar, and a dashed marquee should appear
   around the cell range.

8. Let's select and copy the Excel chart to the Office Clipboard:
   CLICK: near the upper-right corner of the chart to select it
   CLICK: Copy button (📋) on the Clipboard toolbar
   Two icons, representing the worksheet and the chart, appear
   on the Clipboard toolbar.

9. To paste the contents of the Office Clipboard at the bottom of
   the Word "Toy Sales Letter" document:
   CLICK: "Toy Sales Letter" Word button on the taskbar, to display the Word document
   PRESS: (CTRL) + (END) to position the insertion point at the end
   of the document
   CLICK: Paste All button (📋Paste All) on the Clipboard toolbar, to
   paste both items at once

10. To clear the contents of the Office Clipboard and then close
    the Clipboard toolbar:
    CLICK: Clear Clipboard button (🗑) on the Clipboard toolbar
    CLICK: Close button (✖) on the Clipboard toolbar
    The "Toy Sales Letter" document should now appear similar to
    Figure 1.12.

Figure 1.12

"Toy Sales Letter" document

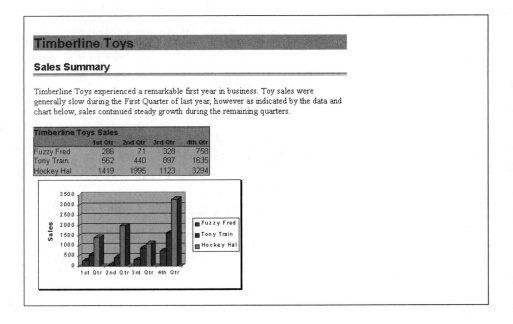

11. Save, print, and close the "Toy Sales Letter" document. Save and close the "Toy Sales Data" worksheet.
12. Close Word and Excel.

1.7.2 Down Under Exports: Chairman Letter

You will now practice inserting and linking an Excel chart to a Word document. You will then edit the Excel source data and observe the changes in the linked chart in Word.

1. Launch Word and then open the INT172 Word file.
2. Save the document as "Chairman Letter" to your personal storage location.
3. Launch Excel and then open the INT172 worksheet.
4. Save the worksheet as "Export Data" to your personal storage location.
5. To copy the blue Excel "Australian Investments" chart to the Clipboard:
   CLICK: near the upper-left corner of the blue chart to select it
   CLICK: Copy button (📇) on the Standard toolbar.
6. To indicate where to insert the object, let's return to Word and position the insertion point at the bottom of the "Chairman Letter" document:
   CLICK: "Chairman Letter" Word button on the taskbar
   PRESS: CTRL + END
7. To paste the Excel chart into the Word document and establish a dynamic link between the source document "Export Data.xls" and the destination document, "Chairman Letter.doc:"
   CHOOSE: Edit, Paste Special from the Word menu
   SELECT: *Paste link* option button
8. "Microsoft Excel Chart Object" should be highlighted in the *As* list box. To proceed:
   CLICK: OK command button
   Observe the inserted linked chart at the bottom of the destination document.
9. Let's make some alterations to the source document to demonstrate dynamic linking. To switch to Excel:
   CLICK: Excel button on the taskbar
10. With the worksheet displayed on the screen, let's change the 1999 Meat value from 333 to 9999 in the brown table:
    SELECT: cell C9
    TYPE: 9999
    PRESS: ENTER
    You have now updated the worksheet source document.
11. Save your changes in the "Export Data.xls" worksheet, replacing the previous version, and exit Excel.

12. To view the updated changes in Word:
    CLICK: "Chairman letter" Word button on the taskbar
    The linked chart should reflect the updated changes in the
    Excel source document.
13. Print, save and close the revised document, and then exit
    Word.

1.7.3 Maurizio Gourmet Ice Cream: Flavors

You will now practice inserting and manipulating shared objects in a
Word document.

1. Launch Word and open the INT173 Word file.
2. Save the document as "Flavors" to your personal storage location.
3. Launch Excel and open the INT173 Excel file.
4. Save the worksheet as "Ice Cream" to your personal storage
   location.
5. Select, copy, and embed the pink Excel table below the first
   heading of the Word document. (*Hint:* Choose Edit, Paste Special and then select "Microsoft Excel Worksheet Object" in the
   As list box.)
6. Select, copy, and link the pink Excel table below the second
   heading of the Word document. (*Hint:* Choose Edit, Paste Special and select the *Paste link* option button. Also, select
   "Microsoft Excel Worksheet Object" in the *As* list box.)
7. Resize both shared objects by dragging their bottom-right sizing handles outward about one inch.
8. Move both shared objects to the right margin.
9. Edit the embedded object by changing the Chocolate Deca-
   dence value from "527" to "1000."
10. Save, print, and then close the revised document.
11. Close Word and Excel.

1.7.4 Prologic Software: Conventions

In this exercise, you insert a new worksheet and a new chart into a
Word document without launching Excel. You then edit the embedded worksheet.

1. Launch Word. A blank document should be displaying.
2. Type the heading "Number of Prologic Software Conventions"
   at the top of the document followed by five blank lines.
3. Move your insertion point up two lines by pressing ⬆ twice.
4. Using the Insert, Object menu command, insert a new
   Microsoft Excel Worksheet object below the heading.
5. Insert the following data into the Excel worksheet.

New York	15
Chicago	10
Dallas	10
Phoenix	10

6. Return to Word by clicking outside the embedded object. Move the insertion point to the bottom of the document.
7. Insert a second heading, "Prologic Convention Expenses," below the embedded object, followed by several blank lines.
8. Using the Insert, Object menu command, insert a new Microsoft Excel Chart object below the second heading. (*Note:* Your going to leave the default chart unchanged.)
9. Return to Word by clicking outside the embedded chart.
10. In the first embedded object, change the Phoenix value from "10" to "14."
11. Save your document as "Prologic Conventions" to your personal storage location and then preview and print the document.
12. Close Word.

1.7.5 On Your Own: Favorites

In this exercise, you create and copy several Word items to the Office Clipboard and then insert them all at once into a new Excel worksheet. First create a new Word document entitled "Favorites" that lists your three favorite animals, followed by several blank lines, and then your three favorite colors. Ensure that no items are currently stored in the Office Clipboard. Select and copy the first three items to the Office Clipboard. Select and copy the last three items to the Office Clipboard. Launch Excel and paste both objects at once into a new worksheet. Save your Excel worksheet as "Favorites" to your personal storage location, and then print it.

1.7.6 On Your Own: Statistics

To practice pasting, linking, embedding, and manipulating objects in Word, create a simple table in Excel entitled "Cities" that lists three fictional cities and their corresponding populations. Create a new Word document and insert the title "Population." Copy the Excel table and paste it in the Word document. Below the pasted table in Word, copy and link the same Excel table. Then copy and embed the same table at the bottom of the document. Change a value in the source document and observe that only the linked object changes.

At the bottom of the Word document, type the title "Average Yearly Temperatures." Then, insert a new Excel worksheet below the title using the Insert, Object menu command. In the new Excel worksheet, list the same three cities you referenced earlier and their corresponding average-yearly temperatures. Save the Word document as "Statistics" and then preview and print your document.

1.8   Case Problems: Riverdale Forest Products

Now that Sam has learned several techniques for integrating Word and Excel, he is ready to practice embedding and linking Excel objects in his Word memos.

In the following case problems, assume the role of Sam and perform the same steps that he identifies. You may want to re-read the chapter opening before proceeding.

1.   Sam opens a Word memo to the Production General Manager entitled INT181 that explains the company's productivity over the past three months. He saves the memo as "Productivity" to his personal storage location. Rather than retyping the information, Sam decides to copy and paste data from an existing Excel worksheet into the memo. He launches Excel and opens the INT181.xls worksheet and saves it as "Jan-Mar.xls." Next, Sam displays the Office Clipboard and ensures that it doesn't contain any objects.

     Sam individually selects and copies the January, February, and March tables to the Office Clipboard. He returns to Word and moves the insertion point to the bottom of the document. He pastes the first table, enters a blank line, pastes the second table followed by a blank line, and then pastes the third table. After clearing the contents of the Office Clipboard, Sam prints and saves the revised memo and then closes Word. Finally, he closes Excel.

2.   Each month, Sam must also send the Personnel Manager, Harold Brock, a memo indicating the production days for each of Riverdale's plants. Sam opens a new document in Word and creates a memo to Harold, typing "April Productivity" as the subject of the memo.

     Sam opens the INT182.xls Excel document and saves it as "April.xls" to his personal storage location. Since several of the figures may change, Sam decides to link the April table into the Word document. Using the Paste Special command, he successfully copies and links the April table at the bottom of the Word document. Sam's memo now appears similar to Figure 1.13.

Figure 1.13

Memo to Harold Brock

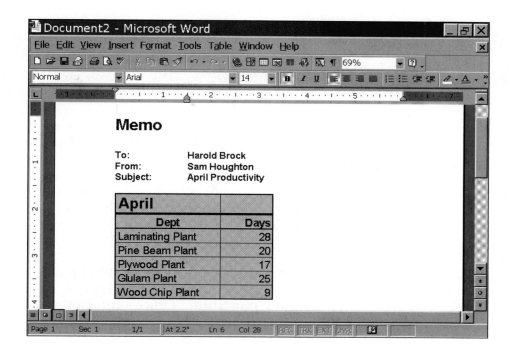

Prior to printing Harold's memo, Sam receives an e-mail message from the Wood Chip Plant indicating that their April production days totaled "29" rather than "9." Sam returns to the source document to make the correction, and then previews the destination document to ensure the change has been made. Sam saves his memo as "Personnel Memo" and prints a copy. Next, Sam closes Word before saving the Excel worksheet and exiting Excel.

3. Sam is ready to edit, delete, resize, and move shared objects in a Word document. He retrieves the INT183 Word document and saves it as "Conversions" to his personal storage location. Unsure of which table has been linked and which table has been embedded, Sam tries editing both tables. He deletes the linked table, and edits the embedded table to read "800/900" in the first row of the PLF column, rather than "600/900." He increases the size of the table and moves it so that it is centered between the margins. He saves and prints the Word document and then closes Word.

4. Sam must complete a memo to the Purchasing Department to order electrical wire for an upcoming sawmill installation. Sam opens the INT184 document that has already been started, and saves it as "Purchasing" to his personal storage location.

    Rather than launching Excel to create a worksheet, Sam uses the Insert, Object menu command to insert an Excel Worksheet at the bottom of the Word document. He adds the following data to the worksheet, and returns to the Word document.

INTEGRATING

Number	Size	Stranding
SD18	18	16/30
SD19	19	16/30
SD20	20	30/40

Fortunately, Sam notices an important omission and adds the following data to the fourth column of the table.

Amount
40 yds
20 yds
100 yds

He then saves and prints the memo before closing Word. On his way to the coffee machine, he smiles when thinking about how much time Office's integration capabilities will save him in the future.

MICROSOFT OFFICE 2000
Performing More Integration Tasks

CHAPTER
TWO

Chapter Outline

Learning Objectives

After completing this chapter, you will be able to:

- Create an outline in Word and then convert the outline to a PowerPoint presentation

- Copy PowerPoint slides to Word

- Copy an Excel chart to PowerPoint

- Export Access reports to Word

- Transfer an Excel list to Access

Case Study ## Wolfgang's Brewing Company

Wolfgang Paul is the owner of a successful brewing company. One of his marketing techniques involves delivering presentations at trade shows. In the past, Wolfgang has always created his presentations from scratch, even though much of their content already exists in Word documents. After a recent presentation, Wolfgang and a few other people began talking about Office 2000's integration capabilities. Since this is a topic that Wolfgang knew nothing about, he was the one asking the questions. "You mean, you can convert an existing Word document to a PowerPoint presentation? You can copy Excel charts into PowerPoint presentations? You can convert an Excel list into Access?" After hearing a string of "yes" responses, Wolfgang could think of many reasons why he should learn more about integrating Office applications.

In this chapter, you and Wolfgang learn how to convert a Word outline to a PowerPoint presentation. You also learn how to embed PowerPoint slides and presentations in Word, and embed an Excel chart in PowerPoint. Finally, you will export Access reports to Word, and transfer an Excel list to Access.

2.1 Creating a Presentation from a Word Document

When you need to create a long document such as a report, a term paper, or a book like this one, Word's Outline view can help you organize your thoughts. To switch to Outline view in Word, you choose View, Outline from the Menu bar or click the Outline View button (▤) located to the left of the horizontal scroll bar. A Word outline also provides a nice starting point for a PowerPoint presentation.

2.1.1 Creating an Outline in Word

FEATURE
Many writers like to begin the writing process by creating an outline. When you create a document from scratch in Outline view, Word automatically applies its default heading styles to the different levels in the outline. (*Note:* A Word *style* is collection of formatting commands that, when applied to text, change its appearance.) Pressing **ENTER** in Outline view inserts a heading at the same level. Clicking the Promote (◀) and Demote (▶) buttons on the Outlining toolbar enable you to change the current heading level.

INTEGRATING

METHOD

To switch to Outline view in Word:

- CHOOSE: View, Outline, or
- CLICK: Outline View button (🗐) located to the left of the horizontal scroll bar

To create an outline in Word:

- PRESS: ENTER to insert a new heading at the same level
- CLICK: Demote button (➡) to begin typing at a demoted (lower) level
- CLICK: Promote button (⬅) to begin typing at a promoted (higher) level

PRACTICE

You will now create an outline in Word.

Setup: Ensure that Word and PowerPoint are installed on your computer.

1 Launch Word. A new document should be displaying.

2 To switch to Outline view:
CHOOSE: View, Outline
The insertion point is blinking on the first line of the outline. Note that "Heading 1" appears in the Style box on the Formatting toolbar. Also note that a new toolbar, the Outlining toolbar, appears below the Formatting toolbar.

3 To begin typing your outline:
TYPE: Exploring the Internet
PRESS: ENTER to insert another heading

4 TYPE: Popular Internet Search Tools
PRESS: ENTER to insert another heading

5 To type at a demoted level:
CLICK: Demote button (➡) on the Outlining toolbar
Note that "Heading 2" now appears in the Style box on the Formatting toolbar.

6 TYPE: Yahoo!
PRESS: ENTER to insert another heading
TYPE: Infoseek
PRESS: ENTER to insert another heading
TYPE: AltaVista
PRESS: ENTER to insert another heading
TYPE: Excite
PRESS: ENTER to insert another heading

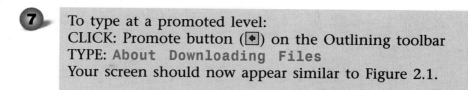

7

To type at a promoted level:
CLICK: Promote button (⬅) on the Outlining toolbar
TYPE: About Downloading Files
Your screen should now appear similar to Figure 2.1.

Figure 2.1

Sample Word outline

Outlining toolbar

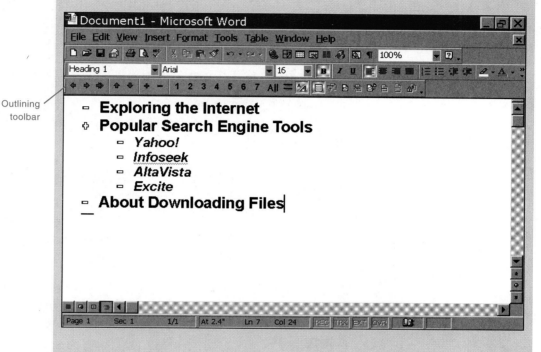

8

To view just the main headings in the outline:
CLICK: Show Heading 1 button (**1**) on the Outlining toolbar

9

To redisplay the entire outline:
CLICK: All button (**All**) on the Outlining toolbar
(*Note:* Since this outline only contains two heading levels, you could have also clicked the Show Heading 2 button (**2**) to display the entire outline.)

10

Save the document as "Internet Outline" to your personal storage location.

INTEGRATING

2.1.2   Converting a Word Outline to PowerPoint

FEATURE
If you've already created an outline in Word, you can transform it into a PowerPoint slide presentation in less time than it takes to send it to the printer.

METHOD
1. The headings in the Word document must be formatted with heading styles.
2. CHOOSE: File, Send To, Microsoft PowerPoint
3. Use PowerPoint to embellish the presentation.

PRACTICE
This exercise practices converting a Word outline to a PowerPoint presentation.

Setup: Ensure that you've completed the previous lesson and that the "Internet Outline" document is displaying in Word's Outline view.

1 To convert the Word outline to a PowerPoint presentation:
CHOOSE: File, Send To, Microsoft PowerPoint
After a few moments, the outline and presentation will appear in PowerPoint.

2 To apply the Title Slide layout to the first slide:
CHOOSE: Format, Slide Layout
CLICK: Title Slide layout in the Slide Layout dialog box
CLICK: Apply command button

3 To apply a design to the presentation:
CHOOSE: Format, Apply Design Template
SELECT: Blends template in the list box (or another available design template)
CLICK: Apply command button
Your screen should now appear similar to Figure 2.2.

Figure 2.2

Converting a Word outline into a PowerPoint presentation

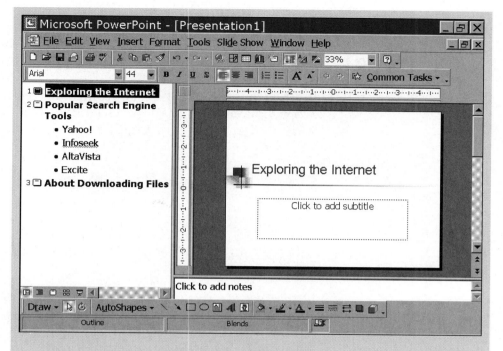

4 To display the short presentation as it will be seen by your audience:
CHOOSE: View, Slide Show
CLICK: with the mouse to proceed through the presentation

5 After you've viewed the three slides, the outline for the presentation will reappear.

6 Save the presentation as "Internet Presentation" to your personal storage location.

7 Close PowerPoint and Word.

2.1 Self Check Describe the procedure for converting a Word outline to a PowerPoint presentation.

INTEGRATING

2.2 Integrating PowerPoint with Word and Excel

In this module, we'll describe how to copy PowerPoint slides to a Word document and how to embellish a PowerPoint presentation with a chart created in Excel.

2.2.1 Copying PowerPoint Slides to Word

FEATURE
PowerPoint slides can be inserted in your Word reports to add visual interest.

METHOD
1. In PowerPoint, switch to Slide Sorter view and then copy a selection of slides to the Clipboard.
2. Switch to Word.
3. Position the insertion point where you want the object to be inserted.
4. CHOOSE: Edit, Paste Special
5. SELECT: a data type in the *As* list box
6. SELECT: *Paste* option button (the default selection) to embed the object, or
   SELECT: *Paste link* option button to link the object
7. CLICK: OK command button

PRACTICE
You will now open a four-slide presentation that addresses the topic of PC operating systems. You will then practice inserting slides from this presentation in a Word document.

Setup: Ensure that Word and PowerPoint are installed on your computer.

1 Launch Word. A new Word document should be displaying.

2 Launch PowerPoint and ensure that the application window is maximized.

3 In the PowerPoint startup dialog box:
SELECT: *Open an existing presentation* option
CLICK: OK command button

4 In the Open dialog box, locate your student files and then double-click the INT220 presentation.

5 Save a copy of the presentation as "OS" to your personal storage location.

6 To select slides in PowerPoint, you must switch to Slide Sorter view.
CHOOSE: View, Slide Sorter
Your screen should now appear similar to Figure 2.3. In this view mode, you see all the slides in the presentation in miniature.

Figure 2.3

Viewing PowerPoint
slides in Slide Sorter view

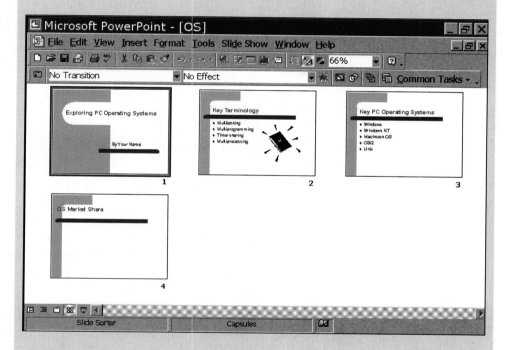

7 The first slide is currently selected, as indicated by the blue border surrounding the slide. To copy this slide to the Clipboard:
CLICK: Copy button (📋)
(*Note:* You select a slide in Slide Sorter view by clicking it. To select more than one slide at once, hold down the **SHIFT** key while clicking each slide.)

8 To switch to Word:
CLICK: its button on the Windows taskbar

9 To embed the slide in the Word document:
CHOOSE: Edit, Paste Special
Note that "Microsoft PowerPoint Slide Object" is selected in the *As* list box.

INTEGRATING

To proceed:
CLICK: OK
The slide is embedded in the document and appears selected (Figure 2.4). As with all embedded objects, you can edit the embedded slide by double-clicking. You can also move and resize the object as desired.

Figure 2.4

Embedding a slide in a Word document

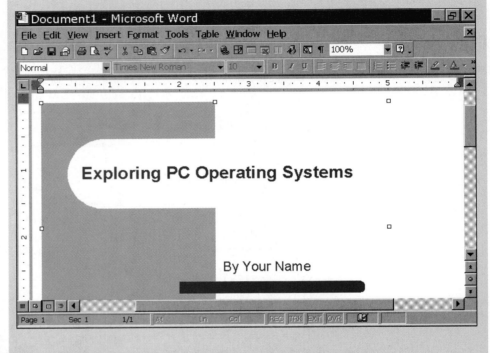

Close Word, without saving the current document.

2.2.2 Copying an Excel Chart to PowerPoint

FEATURE
As in Word, it's possible to link or embed an Excel workbook into a PowerPoint presentation. The source data from Excel is incorporated into the destination document (presentation).

METHOD
1. In Excel, copy the selected chart to the Clipboard.
2. Switch to PowerPoint.
3. Position the insertion point on the destination slide.
4. CHOOSE: Edit, Paste Special
5. SELECT: a data type in the *As* list box
6. SELECT: *Paste* option button to embed the object, or
    SELECT: *Paste link* option button to link the object
7. CLICK: OK command button

PRACTICE

You will now embed an existing Excel chart on the last slide in the "OS" presentation.

Setup: Ensure that PowerPoint and Excel are installed on your computer. The "OS" presentation should be displaying in Slide Sorter view in the PowerPoint application window.

1 In PowerPoint, let's select the final slide in the "OS" presentation and then switch to Normal view. To do this:
CLICK: Slide 4 in Slide Sorter view
CHOOSE: View, Normal
The fourth slide should be displaying in the Slide pane. Shortly, you will paste an Excel chart onto this slide.

2 Launch Excel and then open the INT222 workbook.

3 Save the worksheet as "Market Share" to your personal storage location. Your screen should now appear similar to Figure 2.5. Note that the chart is already selected.

Figure 2.5

Selected chart

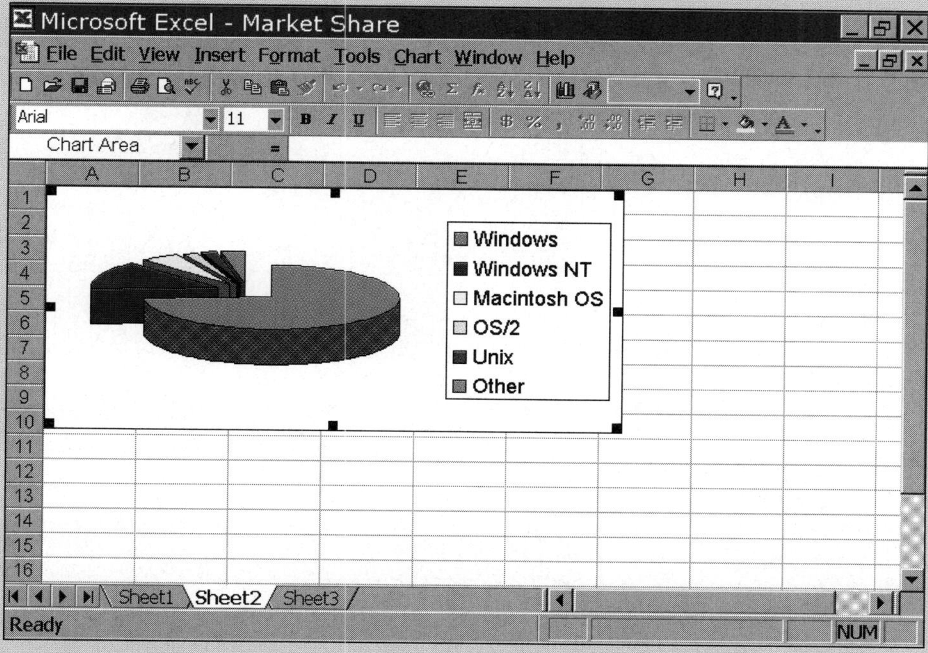

4 To copy the selected chart to the Clipboard:
CLICK: Copy button (⬚)

5 To switch to PowerPoint:
CLICK: its button on the Windows taskbar

INTEGRATING

6 The destination slide (slide 4) should be displaying in the Slide pane. To paste the Excel chart onto the slide:
CHOOSE: Edit, Paste Special
Note that "Microsoft Excel Chart Object" is selected in the *As* list box.
CLICK: OK

7 On your own, resize and move the chart object until your screen appears similar to Figure 2.6.

Figure 2.6

Embedded Excel chart

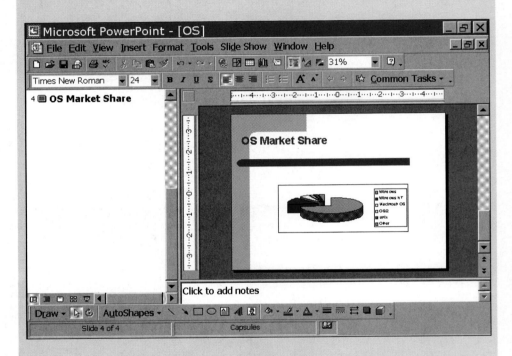

8 Save the presentation and then close PowerPoint.

9 Save the "Market Share" workbook and then close Excel.

2.2 Self Check   How would you go about editing an embedded PowerPoint slide?

2.3 Integrating Access with Word and Excel

Although Excel can successfully manage simple worksheet lists, it is not the best choice for managing large databases, performing complicated queries, and generating database-style reports. If you need the power of a database application to manage your worksheet list, consider transferring your Excel data into Access. Also, if you need more flexibility in terms of how your Access reports are formatted, consider converting them into a Word format for final polishing. In this module, we discuss both of these procedures.

2.3.1 Exporting Access Reports to Word

FEATURE

Although you can create nice-looking reports in Access, it can be difficult to customize them to your unique requirements. Since Word's formatting capabilities are easier to master, users often send their Access reports to Word for fine-tuning. Access reports that you export to Word are stored in an RTF (Rich Text Format) data format in a new document window.

METHOD

1. In Access, preview the report that you want to export to Word.
2. CLICK: OfficeLinks drop-down arrow (☒ ▾) on the Print Preview toolbar
3. SELECT: Publish It with MS Word

PRACTICE

This lesson practices sending an Access report to Word. In Word, you will increase the font size of the report data.

Setup: Ensure that Access and Word are installed on your computer.

1 Launch Access and open the INT230 database.

2 To display the "First Year Students" report, do the following:
CLICK: Reports button in the Objects bar

3 To preview the "First Year Students" report:
DOUBLE-CLICK: "First Year Students" report in the list area

INTEGRATING

4 To view more of the report at once:
CHOOSE: 75% from the Zoom drop-down list (100% ▾) on the Print Preview toolbar
With the report window maximized, your screen should now appear similar to Figure 2.7. Although the report looks pretty nice as is, let's send it to Word to increase the font size of the data.

Figure 2.7

"First Year Students" report in Access

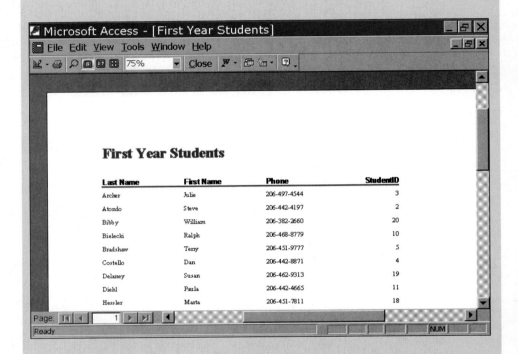

5 To send the "First Year Students" report to Word, do the following:
CLICK: OfficeLinks drop-down arrow (▾)
(*Note:* On your computer, the OfficeLinks button may appear dimmed.)
SELECT: Publish It with MS Word from the drop-down menu
After a few moments, the report will display in Word, looking very much as it did in Access. The file name assigned to the Word report is "First Year Students.rtf."

6 A portion of the title at the top of the Word document may have been truncated in the conversion to Word. If necessary, edit the title to read "First Year Students" rather than "First Year."

7 Let's increase the font size of all the columnar data, excluding the column headings:
SELECT: all the data beneath the headings in the Last Name, First Name, Phone, and StudentID columns

8 To enlarge the point size of the selected information:
CHOOSE: 12 from the Font Size drop-down list () on the
Formatting toolbar
After you move the insertion point to the top of the document,
your screen should appear similar to Figure 2.8.

Figure 2.8

Access report converted
to Word

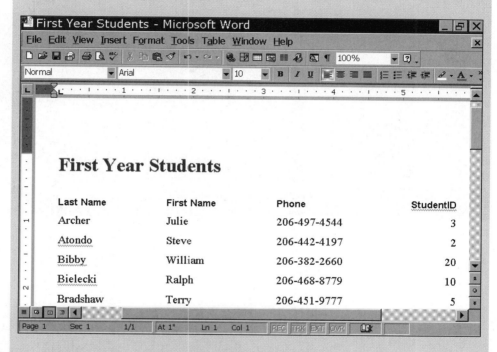

9 Save and then close the revised document.

10 Close Word.

11 In Access, the report should be displaying in Print Preview mode.
Before proceeding:
CLICK: the title bar to make Access the active application
CLICK: Close button on the Print Preview toolbar

In Addition
Mail Merging in Word with an Access Data Source

One of the most powerful features of word processing software is the ability to combine (merge) names and addresses with a standard document for printing. This process, called *mail merge,* can be a huge time-saver because it allows you to use a single document in printing personalized letters to numerous recipients. The merge process requires two files: the main document and the data source. The *main document* contains the standard text, graphics, and other objects that will stay the same from document to document. The *data source* contains the variable data, such as names and addresses, that will be fed into the main document. A data source is essentially a table composed of a *header row, records,* and *fields.*

Access databases work nicely as data sources because their data is stored in columns and rows. Although the process of mail merge may at first sound complicated, you can master it quickly, thanks in large part to the careful prompts of Word's Mail Merge Helper. The *Mail Merge Helper* assists you in your ultimate objective of producing form letters, envelopes, mailing labels, lists, or other types of merge documents.

2.3.2 Exporting a Worksheet List to Access

FEATURE
When a worksheet list becomes too large or complex for Excel to manage efficiently, use the Data, Convert to MS Access command to convert it to an Access database table. This command is available only after you install the **Access Links add-in** in Excel.

METHOD
1. In Excel, ensure that the Access Links add-in is installed. (To install the Access Links add-in, choose Tools, Add-Ins, and then select the *Access Links* check box.)
2. In Excel, open the workbook and then select the entire worksheet list or part of the list.
3. CHOOSE: Data, Convert to MS Access
4. Specify whether to store the table in a new or an existing database.
5. Complete the steps in Access' Import Spreadsheet Wizard.

PRACTICE
You will now practice converting an Excel worksheet list into an Access database.

Setup: After you've completed the previous lesson, ensure that the INT230 database is open in Access. Also, ensure that the Access Links program is installed in Excel.

1. Launch Excel and then open the INT232 worksheet. If necessary, maximize Excel's application window.

2. Save the worksheet as "Counselors" to your personal storage location. Since Access offers more powerful database management features than Excel, let's convert the "Counselors" worksheet into an Access table stored in the INT230 database.

3. To begin, you must select the worksheet range that you want to convert to Access. To select the range that is currently shaded:
SELECT: cell range from A1 to F16

4. Before you can convert a worksheet list into an Access table, you must have installed the Access Links Add-In program in Excel. Let's make sure that you have the necessary feature.
CHOOSE: Tools, Add-Ins
The Add-Ins dialog box will appear, as shown in Figure 2.9.

Figure 2.9

Viewing the Excel
Add-In Programs

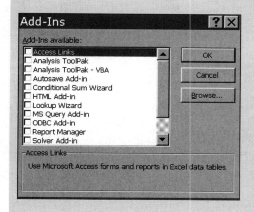

5. SELECT: *Access Links* check box so that a check mark "✔" appears
CLICK: OK command button
This Add-In provides three new commands at the bottom of Excel's Data drop-down menu: MS Access Form, MS Access Report, and Convert to MS Access.

6. To proceed with the conversion:
CHOOSE: Data, Convert to MS Access

7. To convert the Excel list to an existing Access database:
SELECT: *Existing database* option button

8. We now need to locate the existing Access database called INT230:
CLICK: Browse command button

9 In the Choose Database dialog box:
SELECT: the location of the student files
DOUBLE-CLICK: INT230
The Convert to Microsoft Access dialog box is displayed again with the selected database name appearing in the text box.

10 To proceed with the conversion:
CLICK: OK command button
In a few seconds, Access will appear as the active window and the Import Spreadsheet Wizard dialog box will display (Figure 2.10).

Figure 2.10

Import Spreadsheet
Wizard dialog box

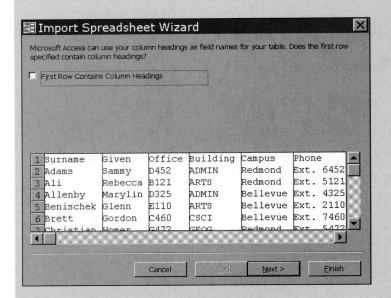

11 SELECT: *First Row Contains Column Headings* check box
Note that the headings now appear at the top of each column.

12 CLICK: Next command button

13 In this dialog box, you specify where to store your data. Do the following:
SELECT: *In a New Table* option button (the default selection)
CLICK: Next command button

14 You can now select which columns to import. By default, all columns will be imported. For our purposes, you will import all the data:
CLICK: Next command button

15 To improve performance and data reliability, you can have Access create a Primary key for your new table. To do so:
SELECT: *Let Access add primary key* option button (the default selection)
CLICK: Next command button

16 In this step, you name the table.
TYPE: `Counselors`
CLICK: Finish command button

17 A dialog box will appear after the importing process has completed.
CLICK: OK command button

18 When you are returned to the Database window, open the Counselors table in Datasheet view and then maximize the datasheet window. Your screen should now appear similar to Figure 2.11.

Figure 2.11

An Excel worksheet
converted to an Access table

19 Close Access.

20 Switch back to Excel and note that a message appears to the right of the selected worksheet range indicating that the worksheet list was converted to Access.

21 Save the "Counselors" worksheet and then exit Excel.

2.3 Self Check   When might you want to export a report created in Access to Word?

INTEGRATING

2.4   Chapter Review

PowerPoint integrates nicely with Word and Excel. Not only do your Word outlines provide a good starting point for PowerPoint presentations, but, using the techniques of linking and embedding, you can copy PowerPoint slides into Word and copy Excel charts into PowerPoint. Access also integrates well with Word and Excel. You can export an Access report to Word for final polishing and use Excel's Access Links add-in to convert an Excel list to Access.

2.4.1   Command Summary

Many of the commands and procedures appearing in this chapter are summarized in the following table.

Skill Set	To Perform this Task . . .	Do the Following . . .
Converting a Word Outline to a PowerPoint Presentation	Switch to Outline view in Word	CHOOSE: View, Outline, or CLICK: Outline View button (▣)
	Create an Outline in Word's Outline view	PRESS: **ENTER** to insert a new heading at the same level, or CLICK: Demote button (▶) to begin typing at a demoted (lower) level, or CLICK: Promote button (◀) to begin typing at a promoted (higher) level
	Send a Word outline to PowerPoint	CHOOSE: File, Send To, Microsoft PowerPoint from Word's Menu bar

Continued

Skill Set	To Perform this Task . . .	Do the Following . . .
Integrating PowerPoint with Word and Excel	Copy slides and presentations to Word	SELECT: a selection of slides in PowerPoint's Slide Sorter View CLICK: Copy button (🖻) and then switch to the destination location in Word CHOOSE: Edit, Paste Special from Word's Menu bar SELECT: a data type in the *As* list box SELECT: *Paste* or *Paste Link* option button CLICK: OK command button
	Copy an Excel chart to PowerPoint	SELECT: a chart in Excel CLICK: Copy button (🖻) and then switch to the destination slide in PowerPoint CHOOSE: Edit, Paste Special from Word's Menu bar SELECT: a data type in the *As* list box SELECT: *Paste* or *Paste Link* option button CLICK: OK command button
Integrating Access with Word and Excel	Export an Access report to Word	DOUBLE-CLICK: the Access report in Access' Database window to preview the report CLICK: OfficeLinks drop-down arrow (🗷▾) on the Print Preview toolbar SELECT: Publish It with MS Word
	Transfer a selected Excel worksheet list to Access	CHOOSE: Data, Convert to MS Access from Excel's Menu bar SELECT: whether to store the table in a new or an existing database and then follow the steps in Access' Import Spreadsheet Wizard

INTEGRATING

2.4.2 Key Terms

This section specifies page references for the key terms identified in this chapter. For a complete list of definitions, refer to the Glossary at the end of this learning guide.

Access Links add-in, *p. 52*

2.5   Review Questions

2.5.1 Short Answer

1. How must a Word document be formatted for successful conversion to PowerPoint?
2. What advantages does Word's Outline view provide?
3. How do you select more than one slide at once in PowerPoint's Slide Sorter view?
4. What is the procedure for exporting an Access report to Word?
5. When might you want to convert an Excel list into Access?
6. When might you want to copy a PowerPoint slide to Word?
7. What is the procedure for editing a chart that you've embedded in a PowerPoint slide?
8. After exporting an Access report to Word, what data format is used for the report in Word?
9. What command in Excel enables you to install the Access Links add-in?
10. Name the three commands that are provided by the Access Links add-in program.

2.5.2 True/False

1. ＿＿ You may only embed entire PowerPoint presentations in Word, not individual slides.
2. ＿＿ To use the Data, Convert to MS Access command in Excel, you must first install the Access Links add-in program.
3. ＿＿ When converting an Excel list to Access, you cannot possible to specify a primary key.
4. ＿＿ In Word's Outline view, you can promote or demote a heading with the click of a button.
5. ＿＿ After converting a Word outline to PowerPoint, you may apply a design template.
6. ＿＿ It's possible to move and resize an Excel chart that you've inserted in a PowerPoint slide.
7. ＿＿ In Word, it's possible to "collapse" a document so that just the main headings appear.

8. _____ In Outline view, Word automatically applies its own heading styles to the different levels in the outline.

9. _____ To link a PowerPoint slide in a Word document, choose Edit, Paste Special.

10. _____ No matter whether you're copying an Excel chart to PowerPoint or to Word, the procedure is basically the same.

2.5.3 Multiple Choice

1. The simplest way to convert a Word outline to a PowerPoint presentation is to choose:
   a. File, Send To, PowerPoint from the Word Menu bar
   b. Insert, Object, PowerPoint from the Word Menu bar
   c. Edit, Paste Special, PowerPoint slide presentation
   d. none of the above

2. For PowerPoint to easily convert a Word outline into representative slides, the Word document must be formatted using _____ .
   a. macros
   b. OLE objects
   c. fonts
   d. styles

3. Before selecting slides in PowerPoint to copy to Word, you must choose _____ in PowerPoint.
   a. View, Slide Sorter
   b. View, Outline
   c. Tools, Select slides
   d. View, OLE objects

4. When you place an Excel worksheet range into a PowerPoint slide:
   a. the workbook is the destination document
   b. the presentation is the destination document
   c. the presentation is the source document
   d. none of the above

5. Before transferring data between Excel and Access, you should:
   a. install the Access Links add-in program
   b. install the Text Import Wizard
   c. install the Import Spreadsheet Wizard
   d. all of the above

INTEGRATING

6. To transfer a worksheet list from Excel into Access, you should choose:
    a. Data, Convert List to Table
    b. Data, Convert to MS Access
    c. Data, Data Tracking
    d. Data, Template Wizard

7. To create an outline in Word, you must choose:
    a. File, Send To, Outline
    b. File, New, Outline
    c. View, Outline
    d. b or c

8. To embed an existing Excel chart in a PowerPoint presentation, you should choose:
    a. Edit, Paste Special
    b. View, Slide Sorter
    c. View, Outline
    d. Insert, Object

9. To export an Access report to Word:
    a. CHOOSE: File, Send To, MS Word
    b. CHOOSE: Data, Publish It with MS Word
    c. CLICK: OfficeLinks drop-down arrow
        CHOOSE: Publish It with MS Word
    d. all of the above

10. When importing an Excel list into Access, you are able to:
    a. select which columns to import
    b. name the imported table
    c. specify a primary key for the imported table
    d. all of the above

2.6   Hands-On Projects

2.6.1   Timberline Toys: Outline

In this exercise, you create a Word outline similar to Figure 2.16 and then convert the outline to a PowerPoint presentation.

Figure 2.16

"Toys Outline" document in Outline view

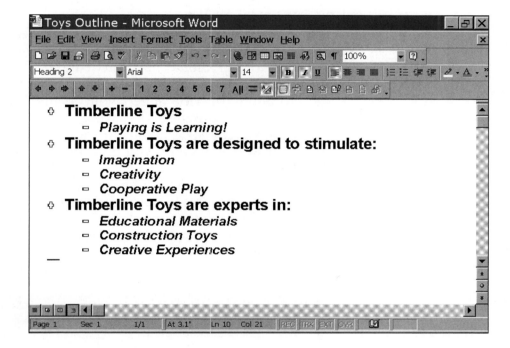

1. Launch Word. A new document should be displaying.
2. To switch to Outline view:
    CHOOSE: View, Outline
3. To begin typing your outline:
    TYPE: `Timberline Toys`
    PRESS: (ENTER) to insert another heading
4. To type at a demoted level:
    CLICK: Demote button (➡) on the Outlining toolbar
    TYPE: `Playing is Learning!`
    PRESS: (ENTER) to insert another heading
5. To type at a promoted level:
    CLICK: Promote button (⬅) on the Outlining toolbar
    TYPE: `Timberline Toys are designed to stimulate:`
    PRESS: (ENTER) to insert another heading
6. Type the following at a demoted level:
    TYPE: `Imagination`
    PRESS: (ENTER) to insert another heading
    TYPE: `Creativity`
    PRESS: (ENTER) to insert another heading
    TYPE: `Cooperative Play`
    PRESS: (ENTER) to insert another heading

7. Type the following at a promoted level:
   TYPE: `Timberline Toys are experts in:`

8. Type the following three items at a demoted level:
   TYPE: `Educational Materials`
   PRESS: ENTER to insert another heading
   TYPE: `Construction Toys`
   PRESS: ENTER to insert another heading
   TYPE: `Creative Experiences`

9. Save the outline as "Toys Outline" to your personal storage location.

10. To convert the Word outline to a PowerPoint presentation:
    CHOOSE: File, Send To, Microsoft PowerPoint
    PowerPoint should be launched and the converted Word outline should be displaying.

11. To apply the Title Slide layout to the first slide:
    CHOOSE: Format, Slide Layout
    CLICK: Title Slide layout in the Slide Layout dialog box
    CLICK: Apply command button

12. Let's apply a design to the presentation:
    CHOOSE: Format, Apply Design Template
    SELECT: Factory template in the list box (or another available design template)
    CLICK: Apply command button
    Your screen should appear similar to Figure 2.17.

Figure 2.17

PowerPoint presentation
created from a Word outline

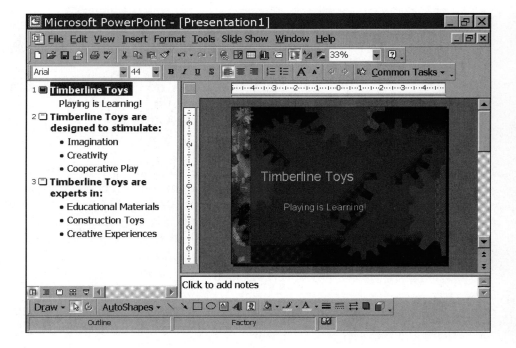

13. To view the slide show:
    CHOOSE: View, Slide Show
    CLICK: with the mouse to proceed through the presentation
14. Save the PowerPoint presentation as "Timberline Presentation" to your personal storage location.
15. Exit PowerPoint and Word.

2.6.2 Down Under Exports: Coal

You will now practice copying and embedding a PowerPoint slide into a Word document.

1. Launch Word. A new document should be displaying.
2. Launch PowerPoint and then open the INT262 presentation.
3. Save a copy of the presentation as "Coal Presentation" to your personal storage location.
4. To select slides in PowerPoint, first ensure PowerPoint's application window is maximized and then switch to Slide Sorter view:
   CHOOSE: View, Slide Sorter
5. Let's copy the second slide to the Clipboard:
   CLICK: second slide to select it
   CLICK: Copy button (⊞) on Standard toolbar
6. To switch to Word:
   CLICK: its button on the Windows taskbar
7. To embed the slide in the Word document:
   CHOOSE: Edit, Paste Special
8. Ensure "Microsoft PowerPoint Slide Object" is selected in the *As* list box.
   CLICK: OK command button
9. Let's try editing the embedded slide:
   DOUBLE-CLICK: slide
   Notice how Word's toolbars have changed.
10. Click outside the embedded slide to return to Word.
11. Save the Word document as "Coal Slide" and then print it.
12. Exit Word and PowerPoint.

2.6.3 Maurizio Gourmet Ice Cream: Restaurants

You will now practice exporting an Access report to Word. Once the report has been converted to Word, you will change the formatting.

1. Launch Access and open the INT263 database.
2. Click the Reports button in the Objects bar and double-click "Restaurant Report" in the list area to preview it.
3. View the report, adjusting the Zoom size if necessary.
4. Send the "Restaurant Report" to Word using the OfficeLinks drop-down arrow.

INTEGRATING

5. The Access report should open in Word.
6. Increase the font size of the column headings to 16 points and deselect the italics option.
7. Select the data beneath the headings and increase the font size to 10 points. The modified report appears in Figure 2.18.

Figure 2.18

Access report in Word

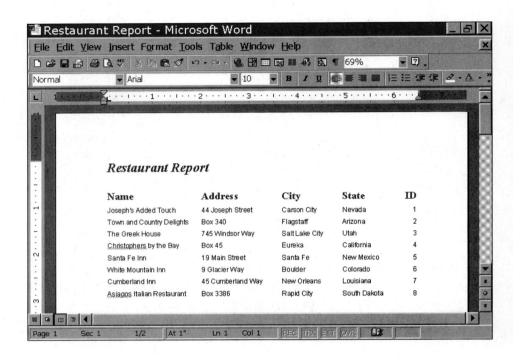

8. Save and print the Word document.
9. Close Word and Access.

2.6.4 Prologic Software: Development Teams

In this exercise, you transfer an Excel worksheet list to a new Access database and then print the resulting table.

1. Launch Excel and open the INT264 worksheet.
2. Save the worksheet as "Development Teams" to your personal storage location.
3. Using the Tools, Add-Ins menu command, ensure the Access Links program is installed in Excel.
4. Select the purple Excel worksheet list and convert it to Access using the Data, Convert to MS Access menu command.
5. Create a new database by selecting *New Database* option button.
6. Using the Import Spreadsheet Wizard, select the *First Row Contains Column Headings* check box.
7. To store the Excel data in a new table, select *In a New Table* option button.

8. When prompted to specify information about the fields you're importing, click the Next command button.
9. To have Access create a Primary key for the new table, select the *Let Access add primary key* option button.
10. Entitle the new table "Development" and then click the Finish command button.
11. Open the newly created Development table in Datasheet view and then print the table.
12. Close Access. Save and close the Excel "Development Teams" worksheet.

2.6.5 On Your Own: Web Training

In this exercise, you embed an entire PowerPoint presentation on the topic of Web-based training in a Word document. First, launch Word. Then, launch PowerPoint and open the INT265 file. Save this presentation as "Web Training" to your personal storage location. In Slide Sorter View, select the presentation's three slides. Then, copy and embed them in the Word document using the Edit, Paste Special menu command and selecting the *Display as icon* check box. Double-click the slide icon to view the entire slide show while in Word. Save the Word document as "Web Presentation" to your personal storage location. Exit Word and PowerPoint.

2.6.6 On Your Own: Ed's Exotic Emporium

Ed has asked you to assist him in exporting an Access report to Word, where he would like to embellish it. Open the INT266 Access database and preview the report entitled "Animal Report." Send the report to Word and save the newly created .rtf file as "Eds Animals." Add the title "Ed's Exotic Emporium Animal Inventory" to the top of the document. Increase the point size of the title to 22 points and then change the formatting of the rest of the document, particularly the headings and data, to your preference. Save and print the Word document. Close Word and Access.

INTEGRATING

2.7   Case Problems: Wolfgang's Brewing Company

Now that Wolfgang has completed Chapter 2, he is ready to begin integrating data between Word, Excel, PowerPoint, and Access. He is confident that his new understanding about integrating Office applications will assist him in creating a new presentation, a formatted report, and an inventory list.

In the following case problems, assume the role of Wolfgang and perform the same steps that he identifies. You may want to re-read the session opening before proceeding.

1. Wolfgang must prepare a presentation for an upcoming trade show. Rather than retyping the information, he decides to convert an existing Word outline into a PowerPoint presentation. Wolfgang opens the Word INT271 file and saves it as "Brewing" to his personal storage location.

    While in Outline View, Wolfgang decides to demote the second heading entitled "We're more than good taste." He also promotes the final heading "Beer Ingredients." Ready to convert the outline to PowerPoint, he uses the File, Send To, Microsoft PowerPoint menu command. He applies a Title Slide layout to the first slide using the Format, Slide Layout menu command. Finally, he applies the Cactus design template (or another appropriate design) to the presentation. After viewing the presentation, he saves it as "Brewers Trade Show." He saves and then closes the Word document, but leaves the PowerPoint presentation open for the next step.

2. Wolfgang would like to insert an Excel chart on the final slide of the "Brewers Trade Show" presentation. He first changes the slide layout of the final slide to "Title Only," using the Format, Slide Layout menu command.

    Wolfgang is ready to retrieve the previously created Excel chart. He launches Excel, opens the INT272 workbook, and saves it as "Ingredients." He selects and copies the green Excel chart and switches to the final slide of the PowerPoint presentation. Using the Edit, Paste Special menu command, he embeds the chart on the slide. He views the presentation and saves the revised version as "Trade Show Chart." Next, Wolfgang prints the last slide of the presentation. He then closes both the PowerPoint presentation and the Excel workbook.

3. Wolfgang has created a report in Access however he is not pleased with the formatting. He decides convert the report to Word and then make the necessary changes. Wolfgang launches Access and opens the INT273 database. He previews the "Machine Ingredients" report. Using the OfficeLinks drop-down arrow, Wolfgang selects Publish It with MS Word from the drop-down menu.

    Once the Access report has been converted to Word, Wolfgang increases the size of the "Machine Ingredients" heading to a 22-point, Times New Roman font. He adds italic formatting to the column headings and then changes the data under the headings to a 12-point, Times New Roman font. Pleased with the document's appearance, Wolfgang saves and prints it. He closes Word and Access.

4. Wolfgang has started a list in Excel, but now realizes it would be more useable in Access. After launching Excel, Wolfgang ensures that the Access Links add-in has been installed. He then launches Excel and opens the INT274 workbook and saves it as "Tank Inventory" to his personal storage location.

    Wolfgang selects the golden-colored list in the Excel worksheet and begins the conversion to Access using the Data, Convert to MS Access menu command. To create a new database in Access, Wolfgang selects the *New database* option button. Using the Import Spreadsheet Wizard, he selects the *First Row Contains Column Headings* check box. He stores the Excel data in a new table, and creates a Primary Key for the new table. Wolfgang entitles the new table "Inventory" and then opens it in Datasheet view.

    Finally, Wolfgang prints a copy of the Access table and then closes Access and Excel, saving the revised worksheet. Feeling a bit smug with his mastery of Office's integration features, Wolfgang decides it's time for a "coffee" break.

INTEGRATING

MICROSOFT OFFICE 2000
Extending Microsoft Office to the Web

CHAPTER
THREE

Chapter Outline

Learning Objectives

After completing this chapter, you will be able to:

- Insert hyperlinks in Office documents and browse with the Web toolbar

- Create HTML files of existing documents, worksheets, presentations, and databases

- Apply a Web theme and create a frames page in Word

- Create an interactive worksheet page and customize a presentation

- Post HTML files to Web servers

Case Study   ## Oasis Gardening

Cynthia Golanski has just been promoted to Marketing Director of Oasis Gardening, a gardening supply store with franchises around the world. The management of Oasis Gardening has been slow to acknowledge the existence of the Internet and the World Wide Web. Finally realizing the exciting international marketing potentials, they have asked Cynthia to create a presence for Oasis Gardening on the Web. Although Cynthia is comfortable with searching for information on the Web, she has never created Web pages.

In this chapter you and Cynthia learn how to insert hyperlinks in Office documents and browse with the Web toolbar. You will save existing Office documents to HTML and apply several techniques for customizing Web pages. Finally, you will learn how to post your HMTL files to a Web server.

3.1 Using Hyperlinks

The Internet, which is often referred to as the "mother of all networks," consists of thousands of smaller networks that link computers at academic, scientific, and commercial institutions around the world. The World Wide Web provides a visual interface for the Internet and lets you search for information by simply clicking on highlighted words and images, known as *hyperlinks*. Several features of the Web have been incorporated into Office 2000, including the ability to insert hyperlinks in your Office documents and create Web pages. The focus of this module is on inserting hyperlinks to other Office documents, locations on the Internet, and e-mail addresses.

3.1.1 Inserting Hyperlinks in Office Documents

FEATURE

To insert a hyperlink in an Office document to a Web page or e-mail address, simply type the address and then press the Space Bar or (ENTER) key. For example, when you type www.microsoft.com into a document and then press (ENTER), Word will automatically format it as a hyperlink. If you click the link, your browser software will launch and Microsoft's Home page will display. To insert a hyperlink to an existing Office file, you must use the Insert Hyperlink button (■). Once the hyperlink is inserted, you can easily edit it to meet your particular needs.

INTEGRATING

METHOD

- TYPE: a valid URL or e-mail address followed by pressing the Space Bar or (ENTER) key
- To insert a hyperlink to an existing file:
  CLICK: Insert Hyperlink button ([🔗])
  CLICK: File command button and then navigate to the file location
  DOUBLE-CLICK: file name
  CLICK: OK command button
- To edit a hyperlink:
  RIGHT-CLICK: hyperlink
  CHOOSE: Hyperlink, Edit Hyperlink

PRACTICE

You will now practice inserting and editing hyperlinks in a Word document.

Setup: Ensure that Office 2000 is installed on your computer and that no applications are currently open.

1 Launch Word. A new document should be displaying.

2 Let's type in a URL to McGraw-Hill's Information Technology Web site.
TYPE: `www.mhhe.com/it`
PRESS: (ENTER) twice
By default, Word formats hyperlinks using the Times New Roman font and the underline and blue attributes. The hyperlink should appear similar to the following:

www.mhhe.com/it

(*Note:* To turn automatic hyperlink formatting on or off, choose Tools, AutoCorrect and then click the *AutoFormat As You Type* tab. In the *Replace as you type* area, select or clear the *Internet and network paths with hyperlinks* check box.)

3 Point with the mouse to the inserted hyperlink. Note that the mouse pointer changed to a selection hand and that a description of the hyperlink, called a *ScreenTip*, appears above the pointer.

4 Let's insert a hyperlink to an existing Excel worksheet.
CLICK: Insert Hyperlink button ([🔗]) on the Standard toolbar
The Insert Hyperlink dialog box should now appear (Figure 3.1). By default, the *Existing File or Web Page* button is selected on the *Link to* bar on the left side of the dialog box.

Figure 3.1

Insert Hyperlink dialog box

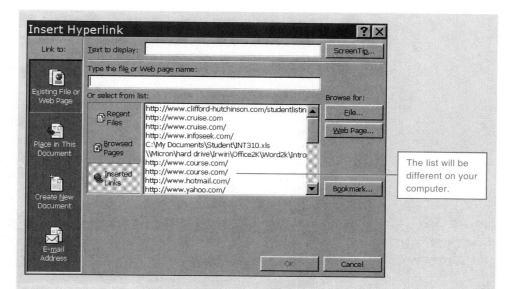

The list will be different on your computer.

5 ▸ To browse for the INT310 Excel file:
CLICK: File button on the right side of the dialog box

6 ▸ Using the *Look in* drop-down list or Places bar, navigate to where the student files are stored.

7 ▸ DOUBLE-CLICK: INT310
The current path and file name should now appear in both text boxes in the dialog box.

8 ▸ To proceed with inserting the hyperlink:
CLICK: OK command button
The hyperlink and associated ScreenTip appear below. (*Note:* The directory path may be different on your computer.)

C:\My Documents\Student\INT310.xls

C:\My Documents\Student\INT310.xls

9 ▸ Let's rename the hyperlink text so that it doesn't include the directory path. Do the following:
RIGHT-CLICK: the INT310 hyperlink
CHOOSE: Hyperlink, Edit Hyperlink
SELECT: the text in the *Text to display* text box at the top of the dialog box
TYPE: `INT310 student file`
CLICK: OK command button
The hyperlink and associated ScreenTip should now appear similar to the following:

C:\My Documents\Student\INT310.xls

INT310 student file

INTEGRATING

10 Save the current document as "Practice Web" to your personal storage location.

11 Let's see what happens when we click the "INT310 student file" link.
CLICK: "INT310 student file" hyperlink
The INT310 worksheet should have opened into Excel's application window. The Web toolbar should be displaying below the Formatting toolbar (Figure 3.2). In the next lesson, you'll use the Web toolbar to help navigate among hyperlinks.

Figure 3.2

Hyperlinking to the
INT310 worksheet

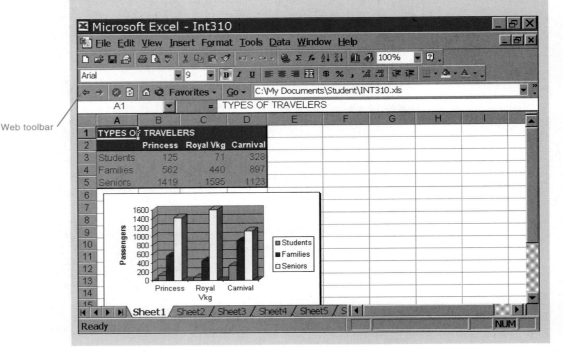

Web toolbar

3.1.2 Browsing with the Web Toolbar

FEATURE
The **Web toolbar** helps you to navigate hyperlinks locally and on the World Wide Web. In addition to the frequently used Back (⬅) and Start Page (⌂) buttons, this toolbar stores a history of links that you have visited. You can also use the toolbar to open, search, and keep track of your favorite Office and Web documents. The Web toolbar appears automatically when you activate a hyperlink, but you can also display it manually by right-clicking an existing toolbar and choosing the Web option.

METHOD

Some common procedures for browsing using the Web toolbar include:

- CLICK: Back button (⬅) to display the previously viewed document, according to the link history that tracks the locations you've visited
- CLICK: Forward button (➡) to display the next document, according to your position in the link history
- CLICK: Start Page button (⌂) to display your Home page
- To open a Web site:
  CLICK: Go button (Go ▾)
  CHOOSE: Open
  TYPE: Web address
  PRESS: ENTER

PRACTICE

You will now practice using the Web toolbar to browse backward and forward and to open a Web site.

Setup: Ensure that you've completed the previous lesson. Excel should be the active application, and the INT310 worksheet should be displaying. To perform all the steps in this lesson, your computer must be able to connect to the Internet and have browser software installed.

1 Let's return to the "Practice Web" document:
CLICK: Back button (⬅) on the Web toolbar
The "INT310 student file" hyperlink now appears in a different color. This is Office's way of reminding you that you've already visited that hyperlink.

2 If the Web toolbar doesn't currently appear in the "Practice Web" document, do the following:
RIGHT-CLICK: an existing toolbar
CHOOSE: Web from the right-click menu

3 The Forward button (➡) is now enabled because you have just browsed backward. To move forward to the INT310 Excel worksheet:
CLICK: Forward button (➡) on the Web toolbar

4 Let's practice opening a Web site using the Web toolbar.
CLICK: Go button (Go ▾) on the Web toolbar
CHOOSE: Open option
The dialog box in Figure 3.3 should now appear. (*Note:* You can also type Web addresses into the Address drop-down list on the Web toolbar.)

INTEGRATING

Figure 3.3

Open Internet Address
dialog box

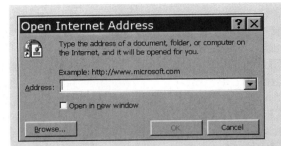

5 Since the topic of "cruise ships" is relevant to the INT310 worksheet, let's open a Web site dedicated to finding low rates on cruise ships. (*Note:* To successfully perform this step, your computer must be able to connect to the Internet.)
TYPE: www.cruise.com
CLICK: OK command button
After connecting to the Internet, the "cruise.com" Web site should open in your browser window.

6 To browse back to the INT310 worksheet:
CLICK: Back button in your browser window

7 To browse back to the "Practice Web" document:
CLICK: Back button (⇐) on Excel's Web toolbar

8 Let's display your computer's Start page, also called a *Home page*. When you click the Start Page button (⌂), your Home page will load into Word's application window and not, as you might expect, into your browser's application window. An example of a Home page might be your personal or corporate Web site or another site that you find interesting. (*Note:* To specify a Start page, use your browser software or the Web toolbar's Go, Start Page command.)
CLICK: Start Page button (⌂)
After several moments, your computer's Start page should open into Word's application window.

9 To prepare for future lessons, let's hide the Web toolbar in Word.
RIGHT-CLICK: an existing toolbar
CHOOSE: Web

10 Close any documents that are currently open in Word and then close Word.

11 Switch to Excel and then hide the Web toolbar before closing the application.

In Addition
Searching the Web

To display a search page where you can enter keywords for locating information on the Web, click the Search the Web button () on the Web toolbar. After connecting to the Internet, the "Pick a Search Engine" page will display in your browser with hyperlinks to many common search engines. When you click a hyperlink, your chosen search engine will display in a framed area on the left side of the screen. To proceed, enter your search criteria in the left frame and view your search results in the right frame.

3.1 Self Check   Provide an example of when you might use a hyperlink in an Office document to access information on the Web.

3.2 Saving Existing Documents to HTML

For most of us, knowing how to browse the Web and search for information are all the skills we require for using the World Wide Web. We have little interest in learning the "ins and outs" of programming in HTML. Fortunately, with Office 2000 you can create Web pages from your existing Office 2000 documents without knowing anything about HTML, and most, if not all, of your document's original formatting will be retained. Nicer yet, the HTML file can be returned to its original file format without losing its unique features and formatting. In this module, we explore creating Web pages from existing Office documents.

3.2.1 Saving Word, Excel, and PowerPoint Documents to HTML

FEATURE
Using Office 2000, publishing to the Web could hardly be easier. Simply choose File, Save as Web Page to convert your work to HTML. With very few exceptions, all the features of your Word, Excel, and PowerPoint documents will be retained in the HTML version. Note that, in the process of saving to HTML, you're given the opportunity to change the title of the Web page. The importance of this title is that it will display in the browser software's Title bar when you view the Web page.

INTEGRATING

METHOD
- To preview how a document or a worksheet will appear as a Web page:
  CHOOSE: File, Web Page Preview
- To save a document, worksheet, or presentation to HTML and change the title of the resulting Web page:
  CHOOSE: File, Save as Web Page
  CLICK: Change Title command button
  TYPE: *the new title*
  CLICK: OK command button
  CLICK: Save command button

PRACTICE
You will now save an existing PowerPoint presentation to HTML and then change the title of the Web page.

Setup: Ensure that Office 2000 is installed on your computer.

1 Launch PowerPoint and then open the INT321 data file.

2 Save the file as "Travel" to your personal storage location.

3 To preview how the presentation will appear in a Web browser:
CHOOSE: File, Web Page Preview
After a few moments, the presentation will appear in your Web browser.

4 If necessary, maximize the browser window. Figure 3.4 shows the presentation displayed using Internet Explorer. Note that "Travel" appears in the Title bar of the browser window. Shortly, you will change the Web title to be "Travel Tips by Rosalyn Peters."

Figure 3.4

Viewing a presentation
as a Web page

Navigate the online
presentation by clicking the
slide titles in the navigation
frame.

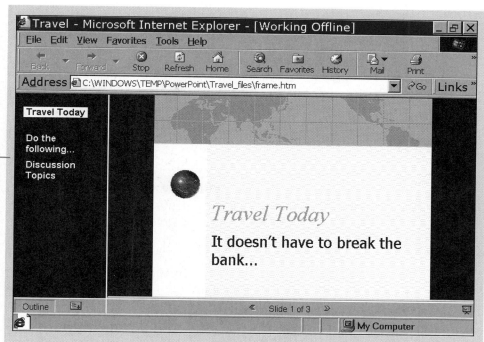

5 To view the slides, click their titles in the left window frame.

6 To switch back to PowerPoint:
CLICK: its button on the Windows taskbar

7 To save the current presentation as a Web page:
CHOOSE: File, Save as Web Page
The Save As dialog box appears with some additional options, as
shown in Figure 3.5. Note that "Web Page" appears as the file
type in the *Save as type* drop-down list box.

Figure 3.5

Save As dialog box
for a Web page

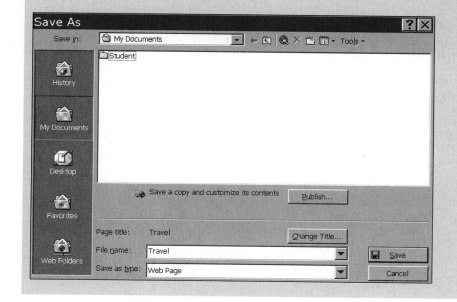

INTEGRATING

8 To change the title of the Web page:
CLICK: Change Title command button

9 In the Set Page Title dialog box:
TYPE: Travel Tips by Rosalyn Peters
CLICK: OK command button

10 Using the *Save in* drop-down list box or the Places bar:
SELECT: *your storage location*, if not already selected

11 To proceed with the conversion to HTML:
CLICK: Save command button
The document is saved as "Travel.htm" to your personal storage location.

12 To preview the presentation again to see if the Web title appears in the Title bar:
CHOOSE: File, Web Page Preview
The text "Travel Tips by Rosalyn Peters" should appear in the Title bar.

13 Close the browser window by clicking its Close button ([X]).

14 Close Microsoft PowerPoint.

| **In Addition** Web Editing | If you are using Internet Explorer 5.0 or later, you can easily edit an HTML document that you created in Office 2000 by choosing "Edit with Microsoft Application for Windows" from Explorer's File menu. The *HTML* document will then open in its source application (Word, Excel, or PowerPoint). After editing the HTML file and then saving your changes, close the source application. Then, click the Refresh button in the Explorer window to view the revised page. |

3.2.2 Displaying an Access Table on the Web

FEATURE

In Office 2000, publishing a database to the Web involves a different procedure from publishing a document, worksheet, or presentation. To view an Access database on the Web, you must use a database object called a **data access page.** Data access pages are interactive Web pages that enable you to view and edit data managed in an Access 2000 database. Because these pages are stored in HTML files that are separate from the database files, they can be stored locally, on a network server, or on a Web server. Note that you must be using Internet Explorer 5.0 or later to edit data displayed on a data access page. Otherwise, you will be able only to view, not change, the Access data.

METHOD

- To create a data access page using Access's Data Access Page Wizard:
  CLICK: Pages button in the Objects bar
  DOUBLE-CLICK: "Create data access page by using wizard" object in the list area
  SELECT: a table from the *Tables/Queries* drop-down list
  CLICK: Finish command button after completing all the steps presented by the wizard
- To preview the data access page in your browser:
  CLICK: Pages button in the Objects bar
  DOUBLE-CLICK: the page object in the list area
  CHOOSE: File, Web Page Preview

PRACTICE

You will now use a wizard to create a data access page for an existing database table and then preview the page in your browser.

Setup: Ensure that you've completed the previous lessons in this module and that Access and Internet Explorer 5.0 (or later) are installed on your computer.

1 Launch Access and then open the INT322 database.

2 CLICK: Pages button in the Object bar
Your screen should now appear similar to Figure 3.6.

Figure 3.6

INT322 database

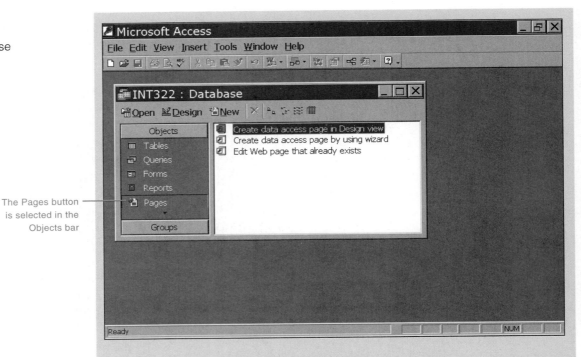

The Pages button
is selected in the
Objects bar

3 To launch the Data Access Page Wizard:
DOUBLE-CLICK: "Create data access page by using wizard" object
in the list area
The initial wizard screen should appear (Figure 3.7).

Figure 3.7

Page Wizard dialog box

If the current database
contains more than one
table, you may have to
select the table that
contains the data you want
to display on the Web page.

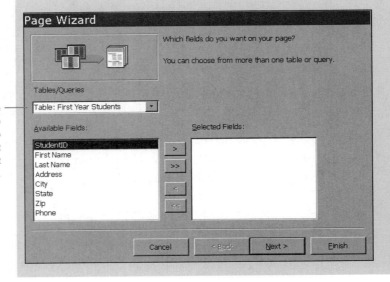

4 Since this database contains only one table, you don't have to select a table from the *Tables/Queries* drop-down list. To incorporate all the fields from the selected table on the data access page:
CLICK: >> in the dialog box
CLICK: Next command button
All of the fields should have been moved to the right into the *Selected Fields* list box.

5 You can now specify a grouping level for the data displayed on the data access page. To leave the settings unchanged:
CLICK: Next command button

6 You can now specify a sorting order for the table data. To leave the settings unchanged:
CLICK: Next command button

7 On this next page, you must specify a title for the data access page.
TYPE: Student Listing

8 To open, rather than modify, the data access page:
SELECT: *Open the page* option button
CLICK: Finish command button
The data access page should now appear similar to Figure 3.8. This is similar to how the data access page will appear in your browser. To navigate the table, you can use the navigation bar that appears beneath each record.

Figure 3.8

Data access page

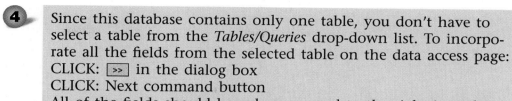

Student Listing : Data Access Page	
StudentID	1
First Name	Craig
Last Name	Sawchuk
Address	3501 Maple Valley Dr.
City	Bellevue
State	WA
Zip	98004
Phone	206-451-1919

First Year Students 1 of 31

9 To save the data access page:
CLICK: Save button (🖫) on the toolbar
The data access page will be saved as "First Year Students.htm" to the default "My Documents" folder.

INTEGRATING

10 Let's preview the data access page in your browser.
CHOOSE: File, Web Page Preview
Figure 3.9 shows the data access page in Internet Explorer. Any changes you make to the data will automatically be reflected in the underlying "First Year Students" table in the INT322 database.

Figure 3.9

Previewing the data access page in Internet Explorer

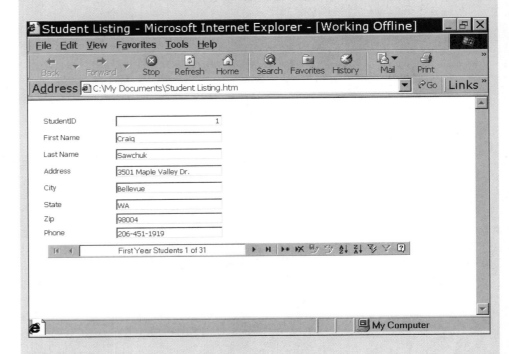

11 Close the browser window.

12 In Access, close the "Student Listing" window. The INT322 database should still be open in Access.

13 To prepare for the next lesson, let's minimize the Access application window to the taskbar.
CLICK: Minimize button (▢) in Access' Title bar

3.2 Self Check   What procedure must you use to convert a document, worksheet, or presentation to HTML?

3.3 Preparing Web Pages Using Office

Office provides several features for customizing Web pages. For example, you can apply Web themes to your Word documents and divide a document into frames for easy navigation. You can add interactivity to an Excel worksheet so that others can edit it online and customize the appearance and location of the navigation buttons that appear during a Web presentation. In the following lessons, you prepare and customize a Word document, Excel worksheet, and PowerPoint presentation for publication on the Web.

3.3.1 Applying Web Themes to Word Documents

FEATURE
Office includes more than 30 themes for optimizing the look of your documents in Word and on the Web. A theme determines what colors and text fonts are used in a document, as well as the appearance of other graphical elements such as bullets and horizontal lines.

METHOD
1. CHOOSE: Format, Theme from Word's Menu bar
2. SELECT: a theme in the *Choose a Theme* list box
3. CLICK: OK command button

PRACTICE
You will now apply a Web theme to an existing Word document.

Setup: Ensure that Office 2000 is installed on your computer.

1 Launch Word and then open the INT331 data file.

2 Save the file as "Office2K and the Web" to your personal storage location and then scroll down through the document to become familiar with its contents.

3 Let's apply a Web theme to this document.
CHOOSE: Format, Theme from Word's Menu bar

4 To view some of the different themes, click their names in the *Choose a Theme* list box. Before continuing:
CLICK: Artsy in the *Choose a Theme* list box
The Theme dialog box should now appear similar to Figure 3.10.

Figure 3.10

Theme dialog box

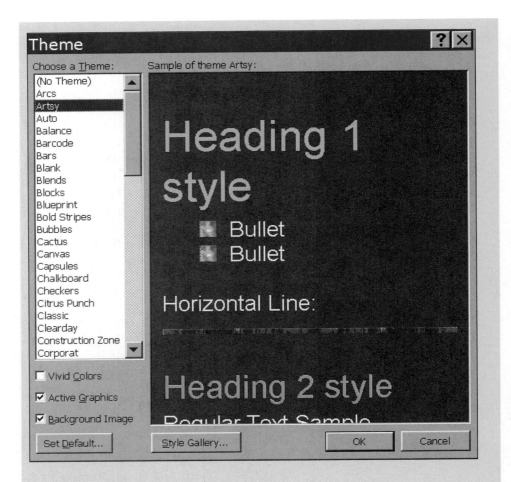

5 To apply this theme to the document:
CLICK: OK command button
With the insertion point at the top of the document, your screen should now appear similar to Figure 3.11.

Figure 3.11

Applying a Web theme

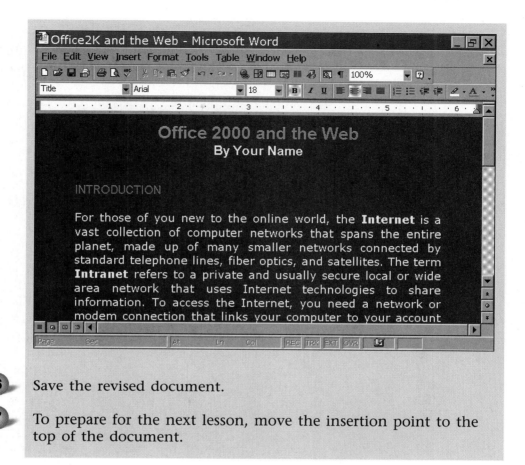

6 Save the revised document.

7 To prepare for the next lesson, move the insertion point to the top of the document.

3.3.2 Creating a Framed Table of Contents in Word

FEATURE

Using Word, it's possible to create a separate area on a Web page for offsetting a document's table of contents, and hyperlinks to other pages on a Web site. These areas are called **frames,** and a page that holds one or more frames is called a **frames page.** If the headings in your document are formatted with Word's heading styles, you can easily create a framed table of contents for a document. Most often, a frames page includes a narrow frame on the left and a larger frame to its right. In this case, when you click a hyperlink in the left frame, the information you're interested in will appear in the right frame.

METHOD
1. CHOOSE: Format, Frames, Table of Contents in Frame
   (*Note:* The frames page will display in a new document
   window.)
2. Edit the hyperlinks in the table of contents frame, as
   necessary.
3. Save the frames page.

PRACTICE
You will now create a new frames page that includes a table of
contents frame on the left side of the screen and the "Office 2K
and the Web" document on the right.

Setup: Ensure that you've completed the previous lesson. Word
should be the active application, and the insertion point should be
positioned at the top of the "Office 2K and the Web" document.

1 To create a table of contents frame for this current document:
CHOOSE: Format, Frames, Table of Contents in Frame
Your screen should now appear similar to Figure 3.12. Note that
the frames page is located in a new document window. The
hyperlinks in the newly added frame correspond to the
document's three main headings. Since these hyperlinks appear
to be running together, we're going to insert blank lines between
them shortly. Also note that the Frames toolbar is now displaying. This toolbar provides another means for inserting and deleting frames. Since we won't be using this toolbar, we'll close it in
the next step.

Figure 3.12

Adding a table of contents
frame

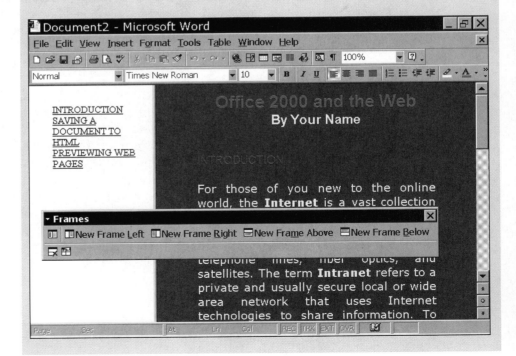

2 To close the Frames toolbar:
CLICK: its Close button (☒)

3 Let's insert a space between the three hyperlinks in the left frame. To do this, you will need to click to the right of each heading. If you click the heading itself, the hyperlink will execute. To insert a blank line after the "INTRODUCTION" hyperlink:
CLICK: to the right of the "INTRODUCTION" hyperlink
PRESS: ENTER to insert a blank line
A blank line should have been inserted after the "INTRODUCTION" hyperlink.

4 To insert a blank line after the "SAVING A DOCUMENT TO HTML" hyperlink:
CLICK: to the right of the "SAVING A DOCUMENT TO HTML" hyperlink
PRESS: ENTER to insert a blank line
Your screen should now appear similar to Figure 3.13.

Figure 3.13

Editing the hyperlink area in the left frame

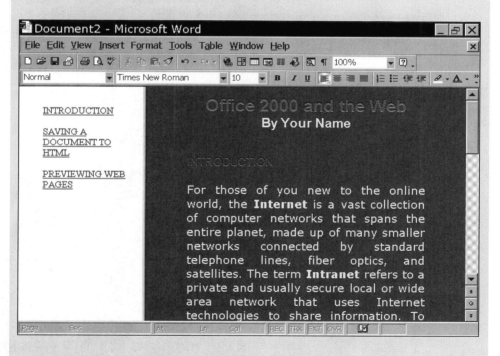

5 Save the frames page as "Frames Page" to your personal storage location.

6 Practice navigating the "Frames Page" document using the table of contents frame.

7 Close Word.

INTEGRATING

3.3.3 Creating an Interactive Worksheet Page

FEATURE

Using Office 2000, the Excel worksheets, charts, and PivotTables that you publish to the Web can be much more than static snapshots. Office 2000 employs three components, called *Web components*, for publishing interactive spreadsheets, charts, and PivotTables to the Web. This lesson focuses on the **Spreadsheet component,** which makes it possible for anyone to update a worksheet through their familiar browsers much as if it were being viewed in Excel. This capability is extremely valuable when corporate data must be made available to large numbers of people for updating. To return a worksheet that has been updated in a browser to Excel, you must export the data to a new Excel worksheet.

METHOD

- To create an interactive worksheet page:
  CHOOSE: File, Save as Web Page
  SELECT: *Selection: Sheet* option button in the *Save* area
  SELECT: *Add interactivity* check box
  CLICK: Publish command button and then customize the current settings
  CLICK: Publish command button again to accept the current selections
- To export the changed worksheet from the browser window back to Excel:
  CLICK: Export to Excel button (⊞) on the worksheet object's toolbar

PRACTICE

You will now add interactivity to an Excel worksheet.

Setup: Ensure that Office 2000 is installed on your computer.

1 Launch Excel and then open the INT333 worksheet.

2 Save the worksheet as "Highlights" to your personal storage location.

3 Let's save this worksheet as a Web page and enable interactivity.
CHOOSE: File, Save as Web Page

4 Do the following to enable interactivity:
SELECT: *Selection: Sheet* option button
SELECT: *Add interactivity* check box
The Save As dialog box should now appear similar to Figure 3.14.

Figure 3.14

Save As dialog box

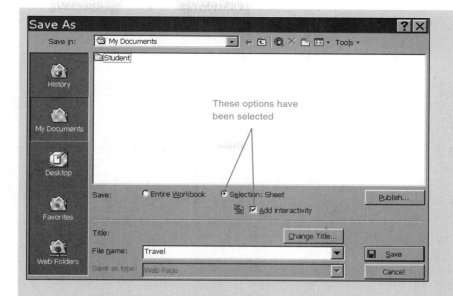

5 If you click the Save command button right now, the HTML worksheet will be saved to the My Documents folder with the default title "Page.htm." To specify an alternate path or file name, you must click the Publish command button.

CLICK: Publish command button

The Publish as Web Page dialog box should now appear (Figure 3.15).

Figure 3.15

Publish as Web Page

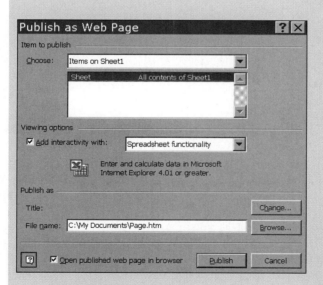

6 To change the default file name from "Page.htm" to "Highlights.htm:"

SELECT: the "Page.htm" in the *File name* text box

TYPE: Highlights.htm

INTEGRATING

7 To see how the worksheet will look in your browser upon saving the worksheet:
SELECT: *Open published web page in browser* check box
CLICK: Publish command button
Figure 3.16 shows the "Highlights.htm" document in Internet Explorer. You may need to maximize the browser window.

Figure 3.16

Viewing the interactive worksheet in Internet Explorer

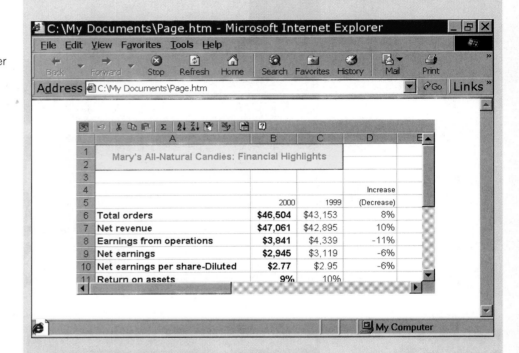

8 Let's say that the Total orders amount in the year 2000 column is incorrect. To change this amount:
SELECT: cell B6
TYPE: 52000
PRESS: ENTER and note that the formula in the Increase/Decrease column recalculated
To export this changed worksheet back to Excel, you can use the Export to Excel button (▦), located on the top border of the worksheet object.

9 Close the browser window.

10 Close Excel, saving your changes.

In Addition
Publishing Interactive
Charts and PivotTables
to the Web

Office's *Chart component* enables you to publish an Excel chart to the Web that automatically updates as its underlying worksheet data changes. The *PivotTable component* provides a way for users to perform such tasks as sorting, filtering, grouping, and totaling tables and lists through their Web browsers. Both of these components can be enabled through the *Add interactivity* check box in the Save As dialog box.

3.3.4 Customizing a Web Presentation

FEATURE
When you save a presentation to HTML, PowerPoint automatically creates a frame for navigating the presentation and a frame for viewing any associated notes pages. You have control over several features of your published presentation including whether to display the notes frame, what colors are used in the navigation pane, and whether animated effects should be visible in the browser window.

METHOD
1. CHOOSE: File, Save as Web Page
2. To customize the presentation:
    CLICK: Publish command button
    SELECT: options in the Publish as Web Page dialog box
    CLICK: Web Options command button, and then customize the current selections on the *General* tab
    CLICK: OK command button
3. To save the customized presentation to HTML:
    CLICK: Publish command button

PRACTICE
You will now practice customizing an existing presentation for publishing on the Web.

Setup: Ensure that Office 2000 is installed on your computer.

1 Launch PowerPoint and then open the INT334 presentation.

2 Save the presentation as "RCMelon Clothing" to your personal storage location.

3 Let's preview the presentation in your browser.
CHOOSE: File, Web Page Preview
Figure 3.17 shows how the presentation will appear using Internet Explorer. (*Note:* You may need to maximize the browser window.)

INTEGRATING

Figure 3.17

Previewing a PowerPoint presentation in Internet Explorer

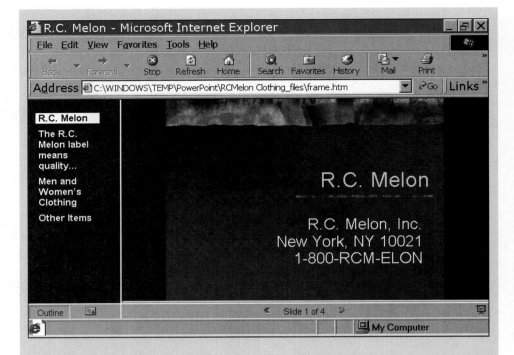

4 Let's customize the presentation so that a white background appears in the navigation bar and in the slide area. To return to PowerPoint:
CLICK: PowerPoint button on the Windows taskbar

5 To initiate the "Save as Web page" command:
CHOOSE: File, Save as Web Page
The Save As dialog box should now appear.

6 To customize the contents of the presentation:
CLICK: Publish command button
The Publish as Web Page dialog box should open.

7 To change the look of the navigation bar:
CLICK: Web Options command button
The Web Options dialog box should now appear (Figure 3.18).

Figure 3.18

Web Options dialog box

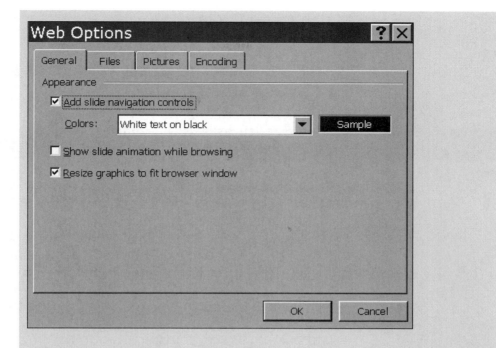

8 SELECT: "Black text on white" from the *Colors* drop-down list
CLICK: OK command button
CLICK: Publish command button
The presentation should immediately display in the browser window. Figure 3.19 shows the presentation in Internet Explorer. Note that the navigation frame and presentation are now offset by a white background.

Figure 3.19

Viewing the customized PowerPoint presentation in Internet Explorer

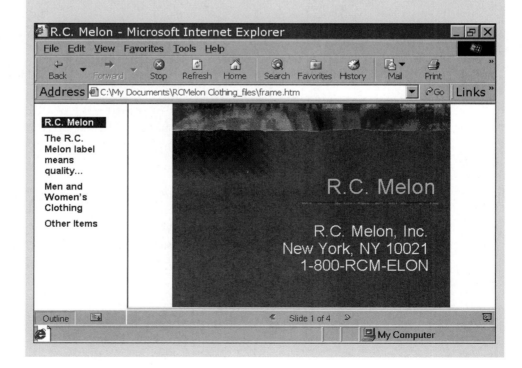

9   Close the browser window.

10   Close PowerPoint.

3.3 Self Check   What are frames used for on Web pages?

3.4   Posting Files to Web Servers

To make your Office 2000 Web pages available for others to see using their browsers, you can use the Save As dialog box to post (or copy) them to a special computer, called a **Web server.** The server computer must support *Web Folders*, a Windows system extension that enables users to browse Web servers using the familiar Explorer windows and Open and Save As dialog boxes. Before you can post files to a Web server, you must locate a Web server that supports Web Folder extensions and determine what your user name and password are. To perform both of these activities, talk to your system administrator or *Internet Service Provider (ISP)*, which is a company that rents Web space. In this module, you create a Web folder and then save an HTML file to the folder.

3.4.1   Creating a Web Folder

FEATURE
A **Web folder** that you create is essentially a shortcut to a location on your designated Web Server. By double-clicking the Web Folder icon (🖳) in the Save As dialog box, you can begin browsing your Web server. Similarly, by double-clicking the My Computer (🖳) or Network Neighborhood (🖳) icons, you can begin browsing your local hard drive or network computer.

METHOD
1. DOUBLE-CLICK: My Computer icon (🖳) on the Windows desktop
2. DOUBLE-CLICK: Web Folders icon (🖳)
3. DOUBLE-CLICK: Add Web Folder icon and then follow the instructions in the Add Web Folder wizard

PRACTICE

You will now create a Web folder. If you don't have access to a Web server, you should review, rather than perform, the following practice steps.

Setup: Ensure that Office 2000 is installed on your computer and that you have access to a Web server.

1 To create a Web folder:
DOUBLE-CLICK: My Computer icon (🖳) on the Windows desktop

2 Locate the Web Folders icon (🖳) in the My Computer window and then:
DOUBLE-CLICK: Web Folders icon (🖳)

3 In the Web Folders window:
DOUBLE-CLICK: Add Web Folder icon
The Add Web Folder wizard is launched. Your screen should now appear similar to Figure 3.20.

Figure 3.20
Add Web Folder wizard

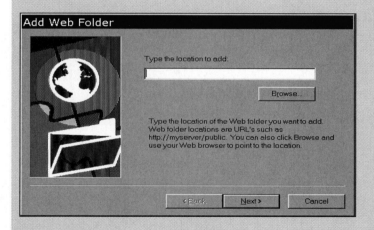

Add Web Folder

Type the location to add:

[   ]

Browse...

Type the location of the Web folder you want to add. Web folder locations are URL's such as http://myserver/public. You can also click Browse and use your Web browser to point to the location.

< Back   Next >   Cancel

4 You must now identify a location, or Web address, on your Web server for the new Web folder.
TYPE: *a Web server address*
CLICK: Next command button
(*Note:* At this point, the Add Web Folder wizard will check that your chosen Web server supports Web Folder extensions.)

5 You must now name the Web folder.
TYPE: *Web folder name (for example, "Sarah's Web Page")*
CLICK: Finish command button
A Web Folder icon, with the name you assigned, should be displaying in the Web Folders window.

6 Close the Web Folders window by clicking its Close button (☒).

3.4.2   Saving a File to a Web Folder

FEATURE

Saving a file to a Web folder is as easy as saving a file to your local hard drive. After you navigate to the desired Web folder, simply click the Save command button to transfer the open file.

METHOD

1. CHOOSE: File, Save As, or
   CHOOSE: File, Save as Web Page
2. CLICK: Web Folders button on the Places bar
3. DOUBLE-CLICK: the desired Web folder in the list area
4. CLICK: Save command button

PRACTICE

You will now save a Web page that contains a collection of hyperlinks to a Web server. If you don't have access to a Web server or don't have a password and username, you should review, rather than perform, the following practice steps.

Setup: Ensure that you've completed the previous lesson.

1 Launch Word and the open the INT342 document. This document is already stored in an HTML format.

2 Save this document as "Hyperlinks" to your personal storage location. This document maintains a list of hyperlinks that may be of interest to college students.

3 To save the Web page to a Web server:
CHOOSE: File, Save As

4 To save the page to the Web Folder you created in the previous lesson:
CLICK: Web Folders button in the Places bar
DOUBLE-CLICK: the desired Web Folder in the list area to the right
At this point, your computer will need to connect to the Internet.

5 Next, you will be prompted to provide your user name and password. Figure 3.21 provides an example of this dialog box. If you know your user name and password, type them in now and then click the OK command button when you're finished. After a few moments, the contents of the selected Web Folder will appear. If the Web Folder is new, it will be empty. Figure 3.22 shows the contents of a Web Folder named "Practice Web."

Figure 3.21

Enter Network Password dialog box

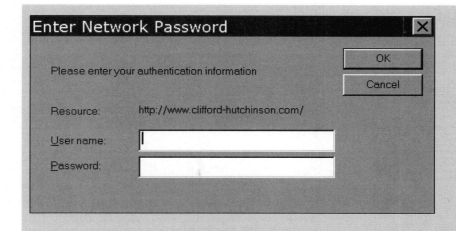

Figure 3.22

Viewing the contents of the "Practice Web" Web folder located on a Web server

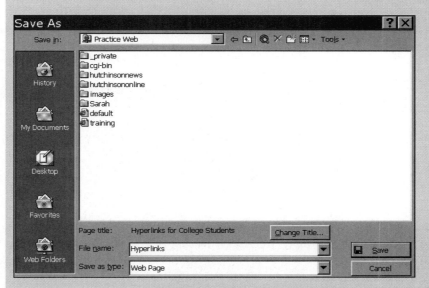

6 To execute the Save command:
CLICK: Save command button
A dialog box will display briefly indicating that the file is being transferred from your computer to the Web server.

7 To view the posted page in your browser, launch your browser software. Then, type the following into the Address bar: server computer name, a slash (/), and the posted file name followed by the ".htm" extension.
TYPE: *address in the Address bar* (for example, www.clifford-hutchinson.com/hyperlinks.htm)
PRESS: **ENTER**
Figure 3.23 shows the "Hyperlinks" page displaying in Internet Explorer after the page was copied to the "www.clifford-hutchinson.com" Web location.

Figure 3.23

The Web page was copied to the Web server

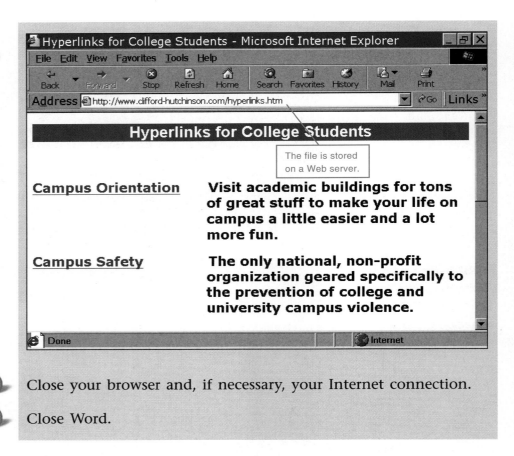

8 Close your browser and, if necessary, your Internet connection.

9 Close Word.

In Addition
Using Office's Web
Discussion Feature

Using Office 2000, you can participate in an online discussion, called a **Web discussion,** via a Web server that supports Office's discussion server extensions. This feature makes it possible for team members to share their comments about a posted Office document or Web page in a Discussion pane on the bottom of the screen. For example, you might use this feature to obtain feedback from employees about an Employee Handbook you've posted on the local Intranet. After obtaining the correct settings from your system administrator or ISP, to participate in a Web discussion choose Tools, Online Collaboration, Web Discussions from the Word, Excel, or PowerPoint Menu bar.

3.4 Self Check   What is the purpose for posting a file to a Web server?

3.5 Chapter Review

Office 2000 was developed to allow nontechnical users to take advantage of all that the Web has to offer. And, by all accounts, Microsoft has succeeded in delivering a software suite that is truly Web-enabled. For example, you can easily create hyperlinks in existing Office documents that lead to other Office documents and to locations on the Web. You can save your existing Office documents to HTML without losing the look and features of your original documents. Further, you can customize your Word pages with themes and frames, add interactivity to Excel worksheets, and customize the appearance of the navigation pane in PowerPoint. Once you've finalized a Web page, you can post it to a Web server using the same procedure that you would use to save it to your local hard drive or company network.

3.5.1 Command Summary

Many of the commands and procedures appearing in this chapter are summarized in the following table.

Skill Set	To Perform this Task . . .	Do the Following . . .
Working with Hyperlinks	Insert a hyperlink to a Web or an E-mail address	TYPE: *Web or e-mail address* PRESS: **ENTER** (or the Space Bar)
	Insert a hyperlink to an existing file	CLICK: Insert Hyperlink button (🔗) CLICK: File command button DOUBLE-CLICK: file name CLICK: OK command button
	Edit a hyperlink	RIGHT-CLICK: hyperlink CHOOSE: Hyperlink, Edit Hyperlink
	Browse using the Web toolbar	CLICK: Back button (⬅) to display the previously viewed document CLICK: Forward button (➡) to display the next document CLICK: Start Page button (🏠) to display your chosen Home page

Continued

INTEGRATING

Skill Set	To Perform this Task . . .	Do the Following . . .
Working with Word	Save a Word document to HTML	CHOOSE: File, Save as Web Page
	Apply a theme	CHOOSE: Format, Theme
	Create a table-of-contents frames page	CHOOSE: Format, Frames, Table of Contents in Frame
Working with Excel	Save an Excel worksheet to HTML	CHOOSE: File, Save as Web Page
	Create an interactive worksheet	CHOOSE: File, Save as Web Page SELECT: *Selection: Sheet* option button SELECT: *Add interactivity* check box CLICK: Publish command button CLICK: Publish command button
Working with PowerPoint	Save a PowerPoint presentation to HTML	CHOOSE: File, Save as Web Page
	Customize a Web presentation	CHOOSE: File, Save as Web Page CLICK: Publish command button CLICK: Web Options command button
Working with Access	Create a data access page	CLICK: Pages button in the Objects bar DOUBLE-CLICK: "Create data access page by using wizard" object in the list area and then follow the wizard prompts
	Preview a data access page in your browser	CLICK: Pages button in the Objects bar DOUBLE-CLICK: the page object in the list area CHOOSE: File, Web Page Preview

Continued

Skill Set	To Perform this Task . . .	Do the Following . . .
Posting Files to Web Servers	Create a Web folder	DOUBLE-CLICK: My Computer icon (🖳) DOUBLE-CLICK: Web Folders icon (🖳) DOUBLE-CLICK: Add Web Folder icon and then follow the wizard prompts
	Save and open pages on Web servers	CLICK: Web Folders button on the Places bar in the Open or Save As dialog box DOUBLE-CLICK: the desired Web folder in the list area CLICK: Save (or Open) command button

3.5.2 Key Terms

This section specifies page references for the key terms identified in this chapter. For a complete list of definitions, refer to the Glossary at the end of this learning guide.

Web toolbar, *p. 74*   Spreadsheet component, *p. 90*

data access page, *p. 81*   Web folder, *p. 96*

frames, *p. 87*   Web server, *p. 96*

frames page, *p. 87*   Web discussion, *p. 100*

3.6 Review Questions

3.6.1 Short Answer

1. What is the procedure for editing a hyperlink?
2. What function do the Back (⬅) and Forward (➡) buttons on the Web toolbar perform?
3. What is a Web folder?
4. What is a Web server?
5. When saving an Office document to HTML, what is the purpose for the Change Title command button in the Save As dialog box?
6. What is a data access page?

7. In Word, what are themes?
8. What is the procedure for creating a hyperlink to a Web address?
9. In Office 2000, what is the Web toolbar used for?
10. In Office 2000, what Web activity does the Spreadsheet component enable?

3.6.2 True/False

1. _____ The File, Web Page Preview command is available in Word, Excel, Access, and PowerPoint.
2. _____ When you save a PowerPoint presentation to HTML, PowerPoint automatically creates a frame for navigating the presentation.
3. _____ To create a hyperlink to an existing file name, simply type in the file name path and file name into your Office document.
4. _____ A data access page is an Excel feature for displaying worksheet data.
5. _____ A page that holds frames is called a *frames page*.
6. _____ Once you add a frame to a Word document, it's impossible to change the contents of the frame.
7. _____ Office's Spreadsheet component enables you to share data between Word and Excel.
8. _____ A Web folder is essentially a shortcut to a location on a Web server.
9. _____ There's no way to rename an inserted hyperlink using Office 2000.
10. _____ A data access page is stored in a file that's separate from its underlying database.

3.6.3 Multiple Choice

1. To convert a Word document to HTML, choose:
   a. File, Convert
   b. File, Export
   c. File, Format
   d. File, Save as Web Page

2. Which of the following procedures inserts a hyperlink to an existing file name?
   a. CHOOSE: Hyperlink, Edit Hyperlink
   b. CHOOSE: Hyperlink, Format Hyperlink
   c. CLICK: Insert Hyperlink button (🖳)
   d. all of the above

3. Which of the following can be used to navigate documents?
    a. frames
    b. hyperlinks
    c. Web toolbar
    d. all of the above

4. Which of the following enables you to view Access data on a Web page?
    a. data access page
    b. frames
    c. Web toolbar
    d. hyperlinks

5. Office's Spreadsheet component enables you to:
    a. change a worksheet when viewing it in your browser
    b. publish interactive worksheets
    c. copy a worksheet into Word
    d. Both a and b

6. What must you know before you can post pages to a Web server?
    a. your user name and password
    b. whether the Web server supports frames
    c. whether the Web server supports Web Folder extensions
    d. Both a and c

7. In Word, which of the following changes the overall look of a document?
    a. frame
    b. theme
    c. table of contents
    d. none of the above

8. Which of the following can you use to divide a Web page into areas?
    a. frame
    b. theme
    c. table of contents
    d. none of the above

9. By selecting the _____ check box in the Save As dialog box, you can publish interactive worksheets.
    a. *Selection: Sheet* option button
    b. *Add interactivity* check box
    c. *Spreadsheet component* check box
    d. none of the above

10. When publishing PowerPoint presentations to the Web, you have control over:
    a. whether a frames page displays
    b. what colors are used in the navigation frame
    c. whether animated effects should be visible in the browser window
    d. all of the above

3.7 Hands-On Projects

3.7.1 Timberline Toys: Hyperlinks

In this exercise, you insert and edit hyperlinks in a Word document.

1. Launch Word.
2. Save the blank document as "Toys Hyperlinks" to your personal storage location.
3. Let's type a URL to the Fisher-Price Toys home page:
   TYPE: www.fisher-price.com
   PRESS: ENTER
   Notice how the text has changed to the Times New Roman font with blue and underline attributes, indicating that it is a hyperlink.
4. Point with the mouse to the inserted hyperlink. Note how the mouse pointer has changed to a selection hand and a *ScreenTip* appears above the pointer.
5. To move the insertion point down a few more lines:
   PRESS: ENTER twice
6. Let's insert a hyperlink to an existing Word document.
   CLICK: Insert Hyperlink button (🔳) on the Standard toolbar
7. To browse for the INT371 Word document:
   CLICK: File button on the right side of the dialog box
8. Using the *Look in* drop-down list or Places bar, navigate to where the student files are stored.
   DOUBLE-CLICK: INT371
   The current path and file name should now appear in both text boxes of the dialog box.
9. To proceed with inserting the hyperlink:
   CLICK: OK command button
   The hyperlink and associated ScreenTip should appear in your document.
10. Let's save the current document and rename the hyperlink text.
    RIGHT-CLICK: the INT371 hyperlink
    CHOOSE: Hyperlink, Edit Hyperlink
    SELECT: the text in the *Text to display* text box at the top of the dialog box
    TYPE: Career Opportunities
    CLICK: OK command button

11. Save the document and let's try the new hyperlink.
    CLICK: Save button (⊟) on Standard toolbar
    CLICK: "Career Opportunities" hyperlink
    The INT371 Word document should have opened and the Web
    toolbar should be displaying below the Formatting toolbar.
12. Close Word.

3.7.2 Down Under Exports: Australia

You will first insert a hyperlink in a Word document. Then, you will
use the Web toolbar to browse backward and forward and to open a
Web site.

1. Launch Word and open the INT372 file. Save the document as
   "Browsing" to your personal storage location.
2. Let's replace the text "Investments in Australia" with a hyperlink to an Excel worksheet.
   SELECT: the text "Investments in Australia"
   CLICK: Insert Hyperlink button (🔖) on the Standard toolbar
3. To browse for the INT372.xls Excel worksheet:
   CLICK: File button on the right side of the dialog box
4. Using the *Look in* drop-down list or Places bar, navigate to
   where the student files are stored.
5. To proceed with inserting the hyperlink:
   DOUBLE-CLICK: INT372.xls
   The current path and file name should now appear in the second text box below *Type the file or Web page name.*
   CLICK: OK command button
   Notice how the font and attributes have changed, indicating a
   hyperlink.
6. Let's try the new hyperlink.
   CLICK: "Investments in Australia" hyperlink
   The INT372 Excel worksheet should have opened into Excel's
   application window, and the Web toolbar should be displaying
   below the Formatting toolbar.
7. Let's practice browsing backward and forward using the Web
   toolbar.
   To return to the "Browsing" document in Word:
   CLICK: Back button (⬅) on the Web toolbar in Excel
   Notice the "Investments in Australia" hyperlink has changed
   color to indicate that we have already visited this link.

INTEGRATING

8. Let's practice opening a Web site using the Web toolbar. (*Note:* To successfully perform this step, your computer must be able to connect to the Internet.)
   PRESS: (CTRL)+(END) to move your insertion point to the end of the document
   CLICK: Go button ([Go ▾]) on the Web toolbar
   CHOOSE: Open option
   TYPE: www.australia.com
   CLICK: OK command button
   After connecting to the Internet, the "www.australia.com" Web site should open in your browser window

9. To return to the "Browsing" document in Word:
   CLICK: Back button ([←]) on the browser toolbar

10. Notice the Forward button ([→]) is now enabled.
    CLICK: Forward button ([→]) to return to the "www.australia.com" Web site
    CLICK: Back button ([←]) to return to the "Browsing" document

11. Let's visit the "www.tasmania.com" Web site:
    CLICK: "www.tasmania.com" hyperlink in the "Browsing" document

12. To return to the "Browsing" document:
    CLICK: Back button ([←])

13. Save and close the Word document. Close all other windows.

3.7.3   Maurizio Gourmet Ice Cream: History

You will now practice saving an existing Word document to HTML and applying a Web theme. You will then change the title of the Web page as it will appear in a Web browser.

1. Launch Word and open the INT373 document.
2. Save the document as "History" to your personal storage location.
3. Preview how the document will appear in a Web browser using the File, Web Page Preview menu command.
4. Return to the "History" document in Word.
5. To add more visual interest to this page, select Format, Theme from Word's Menu bar.
6. Experiment with the different themes, by clicking their names in the *Choose a Theme* list box. Select an appropriate design of your choice.
7. Save the Word document as a Web page using the File, Save as Web Page menu command. While in the Save As dialog box, use the Change Title command button to change the title of the Web page to "How We Started."
8. Using the File, Web Page Preview menu command, preview the document once again to view the new theme and the new Web title. Return to Word.

9. Save and print the Word document. Close Word and the browser window.

3.7.4 Prologic Software: Employee Orientation

In this exercise, you publish a PowerPoint presentation to the Web and then customize the presentation so that a white background appears in the navigation bar and in the slide area.

1. Launch PowerPoint and then open the INT374 presentation.
2. Save the presentation as "Orientation" to your personal storage location.
3. Use the File, Web Page Preview command to preview the presentation in your Web browser. View each of the presentation slides by clicking the headings in the left frame.
4. Return to PowerPoint and select the File, Save as Web Page command.
5. In the Publish as Web Page dialog box, change the look of the navigation bar by clicking the Web Options command button, and selecting "Black text on white" from the *Colors* drop-down list.
6. View the presentation directly in the Web browser by clicking the *Open published Web page in browser* check box in the Publish as Web Page dialog box.
7. Close the Web browser, the presentation, and PowerPoint.

3.7.5 On Your Own: Tanya's Used Cars

In this exercise, you publish an Access database to the Web using the Data Access Page Wizard. Launch Access and open the INT375 database. Click the Pages button in the Object bar to and then launch the "Create data access page by using wizard" object. Select the "Used Cars" table from the *Tables/Queries* drop-down list. Incorporate all the fields from the "Used Cars" table. Type the title "Car Inventory" for the data access page and select the *Open the page* option button. Prior to publishing the database to the Web, preview the data access page in your browser and then close the browser window. In Access, close the "Car Inventory" window, saving your changes. Minimize the INT375 database to the taskbar in preparation for the next exercise.

INTEGRATING

3.7.6 On Your Own: Posting to A Web Server

Tanya has asked to you post her "Car Inventory" file (created in the previous exercise) to a Web server. Ensure that the INT375 database is open in Access and the Access application is minimized. If you have access to a Web server and know your user name and password, create a Web folder on the server (if one doesn't exist already) and then post the "Car Inventory" data access page to the server. Then, view the posted page in your browser and navigate the database table. After closing your browser, switch to Access and close the application.

3.8 Case Problems: Oasis Gardening

Now that Cynthia has completed Chapter 3, she is ready to tackle the world, and the World Wide Web. Cynthia has numerous Office documents that she would like to extend to the Web. First Cynthia will create a Word document that contains hyperlinks to other Office files and a Web site, and then she will practice browsing using the Web toolbar. She will then customize a Word document to include a frame, before publishing the document to the Web. Finally, she will create an interactive Excel worksheet page that all Oasis Gardening employees can access using their browsers.

In the following case problems, assume the role of Cynthia and perform the same steps that she identifies. You may want to re-read the chapter opening before proceeding.

1. Cynthia would like her marketing staff to have instant access to several Office documents and Web sites. An obvious solution would be the creation of a Word document that contains these important links. Cynthia creates a new document in Word and saves it as "Oasis Links" to her personal storage location. At the top of the document she types the heading "Oasis Gardening-Popular Links" followed by several blank lines.

    Cynthia launches Excel, opens the INT381 worksheet and saves it as "Campaigns" to her personal storage location. She then launches PowerPoint, opens the INT381 presentation and saves it as "Marketing Plan." Next, Cynthia switches back to the Word document.

Using the Insert Hyperlink button (▨), Cynthia creates a hyperlink to the Excel "Campaigns" file. She adds several blank lines to the document and then creates a hyperlink to the PowerPoint "Marketing Plan" file. As a third link she types the URL "www.gardening.com" below the two previous hyperlinks. She then uses her Web toolbar to practice browsing back and forth between each of these hyperlinks. She decides to change the Excel hyperlink name to "Marketing Campaigns" and the PowerPoint hyperlink to "Oasis Marketing Plan." Finally, she returns to the "Oasis Links" Word document and prints it. She closes all the other files and windows.

2. Cynthia is ready to publish an existing Word document to the Web. She opens the INT382 Word document and saves it as "Plants" to her personal storage location. Using the File, Web Page Preview command, Cynthia previews how the document will appear in a Web browser. Cynthia returns to Word and decides to add more formatting to this page by using the Format, Theme command. She selects an interesting style to match the document's content. She then saves the document as HTML using the File, Save as Web Page command.

   Cynthia returns to the Save As Web Page dialog box to change the title of the Web page from "Plants" to "Oasis Gardening Plant Varieties." She previews the document in her Web browser once again to ensure the title has changed, and then returns to Word. She prints the "Plants.htm" file and leaves it open for the next exercise. She closes the Web browser.

3. Since the headings of the previously created "Plants" document are formatting with Word's heading styles, Cynthia decides to create a framed table of contents. Using the Format, Frames, Table of Contents in Frame command, Cynthia inserts a framed table of contents to the left of the document.

   To make the table of contents easier to read, Cynthia adds blank lines between the topic headings. She experiments by clicking on each of the table of content's hyperlinks. Pleased with the ease of converting a document to the Web and adding a table of contents, Cynthia saves the revised file as "Plants TOC." She closes all the documents and open applications.

4. Cynthia would like to create an interactive Excel worksheet page to be used by all Oasis Gardening employees. She launches Excel and opens the INT384 worksheet. She saves the worksheet as "Promotions" to her personal storage location. To make the worksheet interactive, Cynthia uses the File, Save as Web Page command. To enable interactivity she selects the *Selection: Sheet* option button, and the *Add interactivity* check box within the dialog box. To specify an alternate file name, Cynthia clicks the Publish command button and changes the file name from "Path.htm" to "Promotional Materials.htm." She also selects the *Open published web page in browser* check box prior to clicking the Publish command button.

While viewing the worksheet in her Web browser, Cynthia is informed that the "Watering Cans" amount for the East Marketing region is incorrect. Working in the Web browser, she changes the amount in cell B9 from 7,000 to 10,000. She verifies that the totaled amount in cell B12 has been recalculated. Cynthia prints a copy from the Web browser and then closes the Web browser. She saves the Excel worksheet and closes Excel. Cynthia is eager to demonstrate to the management team how Oasis Gardening has blossomed and is now extending Office 2000 programs to the Web.

Answers to Self Check Questions

1.1 Self Check   How do you remove a right-click menu from view? Press ⟨ESC⟩.

1.2 Self Check   How would you insert a word in the middle of a sentence? Position the insertion point where you want to insert the word and then begin typing.

1.3 Self Check   What procedure enables you to undo several actions at once? Click the Undo drop-down arrow and then select the actions you want to undo.

1.4 Self Check   In the Open and Save As dialog boxes, how do the List and Details views differ? List view and Details view both provide a list of filenames, however Details view also provides information about the file size, file type, and when the file was last modified.

1.5 Self Check   What is the procedure for printing your work? Click the Print button (🖨) to send your work directly to the printer or choose File, Print to display the Print dialog box. Using the Print dialog box, you can specify what to print and how many copies to produce.

2.1 Self Check   How do you move directly to the end of a document using the keyboard? Press ⟨CTRL⟩ + ⟨END⟩.

2.2 Self Check   What is the procedure for selecting the entire document? Press ⟨CTRL⟩ and hold it down. Then, click once in the Selection bar.

2.3 Self Check   How would you go about boldfacing and underlining existing text? Select the text and then click the Bold (**B**) and Underline (U) buttons.

2.4 Self Check   How do you display a document's hidden symbols? Click the Show/Hide button (¶).

3.1 Self Check   What is the different between Normal and Print Layout view? In Normal view, you view your text without margins. Print Layout view displays your document exactly as it will appear when printed.

3.2 Self Check   What is the procedure for replacing text in a document? Choose Edit, Replace and then specify the text you're searching for and the replacement text.

3.3 Self Check   How would you go about moving text to the Clipboard? Select the text and then click the Cut button (✄).

3.4 Self Check   What is the procedure for adding a word to Word's custom dictionary? Click the Add command button in the Spelling and Grammar dialog box.

4.1 Self Check   In inches, how wide are the left and right margins by default? By default, the left and right margins are 1.25 inches wide.

4.2 Self Check   How do you insert page numbers in a document? Choose Insert, Page Numbers. Or, if you're displaying the Header and Footer toolbar, click the Insert Page Number button (🔢).

4.3 Self Check   What are page borders used for? Page borders extend around the perimeter of the page and are used to enhance a document's appearance.

4.4 Self Check   Why might you want to convert a Word document to HTML? You must convert your documents to HTML before you can post them on a Web site or your company's Intranet.

Glossary

adaptive menus   The dynamic menu bars and toolbars that are personalized to the way you work. Microsoft Office 2000 watches the tasks that you perform in an application and then displays only those commands and buttons that you use most often.

application window   In Microsoft Windows, each running application program appears in its own application window. These windows can be sized and moved anywhere on the Windows desktop.

AutoCorrect   A software feature that corrects common typing and spelling mistakes automatically as you type. It also enables you to enter complex symbols quickly and easily.

bullets   The symbols used to set apart points in a document. Bullets are typically round dots and appear in paragraphs with a hanging indent.

Click and Type   A software feature that lets you position the insertion point by simply double-clicking in the blank area of your document. Available in Print Layout and Web Layout views.

drag and drop   A software feature that allows you to copy and move information by dragging information from one location to another using the mouse.

End of Document Marker   The black horizontal bar that appears at the end of a Word document. You cannot move the insertion point beyond this marker.

font(s)   All the characters of one size in a particular *typeface;* includes numbers, punctuation marks, and uppercase and lowercase letters.

footer(s)   Descriptive information (such as page number and date) that appears at the bottom of each page of a document.

Format Painter   In Microsoft Office 2000, a software feature that enables you to copy only the formatting attributes and styles from one location to another.

gutter   In Word, the gutter is where pages are joined together in a bound document.

header(s)   Descriptive information (such as page number and data) that appears at the top of each page of a document.

HTML   An acronym for Hypertext Markup Language, which is the standardized markup language used in creating documents for display on the World Wide Web.

hyperlinks   In terms of Internet technologies, a text string or graphics that when clicked take you to another location, either within the same document or to a separate document stored on your computer, an Intranet resource, or onto the Internet.

insertion point   The vertical flashing bar in Word that indicates your current position in the document. The insertion point shows where the next typed characters will appear.

Internet   A worldwide network of computer networks that are interconnected by standard telephone lines, fiber optics, and satellites.

Intranet   A private local or wide area network that uses Internet protocols and technologies to share information within an institution or corporation.

justification   Refers to how a paragraph is aligned within the left and right indent markers (left, centered, right, or justified).

landscape orientation   Describes how a page is printed. Letter-size paper with a landscape orientation measures 11 inches wide by 8.5 inches high. Legal-size paper with a landscape orientation measures 14 inches wide by 8.5 inches high.

leaders   The symbols, lines, dots, or dashes that fill the gap between text and tab stops.

Office Clipboard   A program, in Office 2000, that allows you to copy and move information within or among Office 2000 applications. Unlike the Windows Clipboard, the Office Clipboard can store up to 12 items and then paste them all at once.

paragraph mark   The symbol (¶) at the end of a paragraph that stores all of Word's paragraph formatting information.

Places bar   The strip of icon buttons appearing in the Open and Save As dialog boxes that allow you to display the most common areas for retrieving and storing files using a single mouse click.

portrait orientation   Describes how a page is printed. Letter-size paper with a portrait orientation measures 8.5 inches wide by 11 inches high. Legal-size paper with a landscape orientation measures 8.5 inches wide by 14 inches high.

Redo command	Enables you to redo one or more actions after they have been undone.
Repeat command	Repeats the last action you performed.
Selection bar	The leftmost column of the document window. The Selection bar provides shortcut methods for selecting text in a document using the mouse.
Spelling and Grammar command	A proofing tool that analyzes your document all at once for spelling and grammar errors and reports the results
template	A document that has been saved to a special file and location so that it may be used again and again as a model for creating new documents.
thesaurus	A proofing tool that provides quick access to synonyms and antonyms for a given word or phrase. A synonym is a word that has the same meaning as another word. An antonym has the opposite meaning.
Undo command	A command that makes it possible to reverse up to the last 16 commands or actions performed.
Windows Clipboard	A program, in Windows, that allows you to copy and move information within an application or among applications. The Windows Clipboard temporarily stores the information in memory before you paste the data in a new location.
wizard	A program or process whereby a series of dialog boxes lead you step-by-step through performing a procedure.
word processing	Preparation of a document using a microcomputer.
word wrap	When the insertion point reaches the right-hand margin of a line, it automatically wraps to the left margin of the next line; the user does not have to press `ENTER` at the end of each line.
World Wide Web	A visual interface to the Internet based on *hyperlinks*. Using Web browser software, you click on hyperlinks to navigate resources on the Internet.

Index

Answers to Self Check Questions

1.1 Self Check How do you turn the adaptive menus feature on or off? Choose the Tools, Customize command and then ensure that no "✔" appears in the *Menus show recently used commands first* check box.

1.2 Self Check Explain why a phone number is not considered a numeric value in an Excel worksheet. Although it contains numbers, a phone number is never used to perform mathematical calculations.

1.3 Self Check Why is worksheet editing such a valuable skill? Most worksheets in use today are revisions and updates of older worksheets. As a novice user, you often spend more time updating existing worksheets than constructing new ones.

1.4 Self Check In the Open and Save As dialog boxes, how do the List and Details views differ? What two other views are accessible from the Views button? The List view uses a multi-column format. The Details view displays one file per row. Furthermore, the Details view displays other information, including the file size, type, and modification date. The two other views are Properties and Preview.

2.1 Self Check Which of the "Auto" features enables you to sum a range of values and display the result in the Status bar? AutoCalculate

2.2 Self Check Which method would you use to copy several non-adjacent worksheet values for placement into a single column? The Office Clipboard would provide the fastest method. After displaying the Clipboard toolbar, you would clear the Clipboard and collect up to 12 items in the desired sequence. Then, you would move to the target range and paste these items into a single column.

2.3 Self Check Why must you be careful when deleting rows or columns? Because if you delete the entire row or column, you may inadvertently delete data that exists further down a column or further across a row. Ensure that a row or column is indeed empty before deleting it.

3.1 Self Check What is the basic difference between using the Underline button (U) and the Borders button ( )? When you apply an underline to a cell, only the words in the cell appear underlined. When you apply a border underline to a cell, the entire cell is underlined. Also, borders may be applied to each side of a cell, such as top, bottom, left, and right.

EXCEL

3.2 Self Check — How might you ensure formatting consistency among related worksheets and workbooks? Use the same predefined AutoFormat style to format data in all of the worksheets.

3.3 Self Check — How does the Print Preview display mode differ from the Web Page Preview display mode? Print Preview appears in the Excel application window and displays the workbook as it will appear when printed. Web Page Preview uses the computer's default Web browser to display an HTML rendering of the current worksheet.

3.4 Self Check — How would you create a custom footer that displayed your name against the left page border and your company's name against the right page border? In the Page Setup dialog box, you would click the Custom Footer command button on the *Header/Footer* tab. Then, you would enter your name into the left text box and your company's name into the right text box of the Footer dialog box.

4.1 Self Check — Why is "AD1999" an unacceptable name for a cell range? You cannot name a cell range using an actual cell reference on the worksheet.

4.2 Self Check — When might you use the Formula Palette or Paste Function dialog box to enter a function into the worksheet? If you need help entering the arguments in the correct order or if you cannot remember a function's name or proper syntax, you can use these tools to refresh your memory or to assist you in completing the task.

4.3 Self Check — What must you do when selecting the print range for a worksheet that contains an embedded chart? Because charts do not appear in cells on a worksheet, you must ensure to select the print range to include these graphic objects. For example, select the cells that appear underneath the embedded chart that you want to print.

Glossary

absolute cell address　Cell reference in a worksheet that does not adjust when copied to other cells. You make a cell address absolute by placing dollar signs ($) before the column letter and row number, such as $C$4.

adaptive menus　The dynamic menu bars and toolbars that are personalized to the way you work. Microsoft Office 2000 watches the tasks that you perform in an application and then displays only those commands and buttons that you use most often.

application window　In Windows, each running application program appears in its own application window. These windows may be sized and moved anywhere on the Windows desktop.

arguments　The parameters used in entering a function according to its *syntax*. Arguments may include text, numbers, formulas, functions, and cell references.

AutoCalculate　In Excel, a software feature that sums the selected range of cells and displays the result in the Status bar.

AutoComplete　In Excel, a software feature that assists you in entering data into a worksheet by filling in letters from existing entries in the column as you type.

AutoFill　In Excel, a software feature that enables you to copy and extend a formula or data series automatically in a worksheet.

AutoFit　In Excel, a software feature that calculates the optimal row height or column width based on existing data in the worksheet.

AutoFormat　A software feature that applies professionally designed formatting styles to your documents.

AutoSum　A software feature that automatically inserts a formula for adding values from a surrounding row or column of cells.

bar chart　A chart that compares one data element to another data element using horizontal bars. Similar to a *column chart*.

cell　The intersection of a column and a row.

cell address　The location of a cell on a worksheet given by the intersection of a column and a row. Columns are labeled using letters. Rows are numbered. A cell address combines the column letter with the row number (for example, B9 or DF134.)

EXCEL

cell alignment	The positioning of data entered into a worksheet cell in relation to the cell borders.
cell pointer	The cursor on a worksheet that points to a cell. The cell pointer is moved using the arrow keys or the mouse.
cell range	One or more cells in a worksheet that together form a rectangle.
chart sheet	A sheet tab or page within a workbook file that is used to create, modify, and display a chart graphic.
Chart Wizard	A linear step progression of dialog boxes that leads you through creating a chart in Excel.
column chart	A chart that compares one data element with another data element and can show variations over a period of time.
document window	In Excel, each open *workbook* appears in its own document window. These windows may be sized and moved anywhere within the application window.
drag and drop	A software feature that allows you to copy and move information by dragging information from one location to another using the mouse.
embedded chart	A chart that is placed on the draw layer of a worksheet.
fill handle	The small black square that is located in the bottom right-hand corner of a cell or cell range. You use the fill handle to create a series or to copy cell information.
font(s)	All the characters of one size in a particular *typeface*; includes numbers, punctuation marks, and uppercase and lowercase letters.
footer(s)	Descriptive information (such as page number and date) that appears at the bottom of each page of a document.
Format Painter	A software feature that enables you to copy only the formatting attributes and styles from one location to another.
formula	A mathematical expression that typically defines the relationships among various cells in a worksheet or table.
Formula Palette	The dialog box, appearing beneath the Formula bar, that provides assistance for entering a function's *arguments* using the correct syntax.
functions	Built-in shortcuts that can be used in formulas to perform calculations.
gridlines	The lines on a worksheet that assist the user in lining up the cell pointer with a particular column letter or row number.
header(s)	Descriptive information (such as page number and data) that appears at the top of each page of a document.

HTML   An acronym for Hypertext Markup Language, which is the standardized markup language used in creating documents for display on the World Wide Web.

hyperlinks   In terms of Internet technologies, a text string or graphics that when clicked take you to another location, either within the same document or to a separate document stored on your computer, an intranet resource, or onto the Internet.

in-cell editing   In Excel, the feature that enables you to revise text labels, numbers, dates, and other entries directly within a cell. To activate in-cell editing, you double-click a cell.

Internet   A worldwide network of computer networks that are interconnected by standard telephone lines, fiber optics, and satellites.

intranet   A private local or wide area network that uses Internet protocols and technologies to share information within an institution or corporation.

line chart   A chart that plots trends or shows changes over a period of time.

macro virus   A malicious program that attaches itself to a document or template and performs instructions that may damage files on your computer.

margins   Space between the edge of the paper and the top, bottom, left, and right edges of the printed document.

mixed cell address   Cell reference in a worksheet that includes both *relative* and *absolute cell references*. For example, the address C$4 provides a "relative" column letter and an "absolute" row number.

Name box   The text box appearing at the left-hand side of the Formula bar that displays the current cell address and that enables you to navigate quickly to any cell location in the worksheet.

natural language formula   In Excel, a type of *formula* that allows you to use the column and row labels within a worksheet in building a mathematical expression.

Office Clipboard   A program, in Microsoft Office 2000, that allows you to copy and move information within or among Office 2000 applications. Unlike the Windows Clipboard, the Office Clipboard can store up to 12 items and then paste them all at once.

pie chart   A chart that shows the proportions of individual components compared to the whole.

Places bar   The strip of icon buttons appearing in the Open and Save As dialog boxes that allow you to display the most common areas for retrieving and storing files using a single mouse click.

EXCEL

range name A name that is given to a range of cells in the worksheet. This name can then be used in formulas and functions to refer to the cell range.

Redo command A command that makes it possible to reverse the effects of an Undo command.

relative cell address Default cell reference in a worksheet that automatically adjusts when copied to other cells.

series A sequence of numbers or dates that follows a mathematical or date pattern.

scatter plot chart A chart that shows how one or more data elements relate to another data element. Also called *XY charts.*

syntax The rules, structure, and order of *arguments* used in entering a formula or function.

template A workbook or document that has been saved to a special file and location so that it may be used again and again as a model for creating new documents.

typeface(s) The shape and appearance of characters. There are two categories of typefaces: serif and sans serif. Serif type (for example, Times Roman) is more decorative and, some say, easier to read than sans serif type (for example, Arial).

Undo command A command that makes it possible to reverse up to the last 16 commands or actions performed.

Windows Clipboard A program, in Windows, that allows you to copy and move information within an application or among applications. The Windows Clipboard temporarily stores the information in memory before you paste the data in a new location.

wizard A program or process whereby a series of dialog boxes lead you step-by-step through performing a procedure.

workbook The disk file that contains the *worksheets* and *chart sheets* that you create in Excel.

worksheet A sheet tab or page within a workbook file that is used to create, modify, and display a worksheet grid of columns and rows.

World Wide Web A visual interface to the Internet based on *hyperlinks.* Using Web browser software, you click on hyperlinks to navigate resources on the Internet.

XY charts Charts that show how one or more data elements relate to another data element. Also called *scatter plot diagrams.*

Index

EXCEL

Answers to Self Check Questions

1.1 Self Check — What is an adaptive menu? This type of menu displays only the most commonly-used commands. By default, the adaptive-menu feature is enabled in all Office 2000 applications.

1.2 Self Check — What is the difference between Slide Sorter and Slide Show view? In Slide Sorter view, you view several slides at once in the application window. In Slide Show view, you view an individual slide outside the application window.

1.3 Self Check — In the Save As dialog box, what is the Places bar used for? The Places bar provides convenient access to commonly used storage locations.

1.4 Self Check — What procedure enables you to print multiple copies of a presentation? Choose File, Print and then specify an alternate value in the *Number of copies* spin box.

2.1 Self Check — What is the Slide Finder tool used for? The Slide Finder tool is used to insert slides from other presentations into the current presentation.

2.2 Self Check — What is the procedure for moving and resizing object placeholders? To move a placeholder, position the mouse pointer over the placeholder until a four-headed arrow appears. Then drag the placeholder to a new location. You resize placeholders by dragging the object's sizing handles.

2.3 Self Check — What are organization charts used for? Organization charts are used to show a hierarchy of formal relationships.

2.4 Self Check — How can you go to a specific slide in Slide Show view? Right-click anywhere on the slide and then choose Go, Slide Navigator from the right-click menu. Then, click the slide you want to display and click the Go To command button.

Glossary

adaptive menus The dynamic menu bars and toolbars that are personalized to the way you work. Office 2000 watches the tasks that you perform in an application and then displays only those commands and buttons that you use most often.

application window In Microsoft Windows, each running application program appears in its own application window. These windows can be sized and moved anywhere on the Windows desktop.

AutoContent Wizard A PowerPoint feature that assists you in beginning new presentations by providing content and design suggestions.

AutoFit feature With this feature enabled, PowerPoint automatically resizes placeholders to accommodate inserted text.

AutoLayout A preset slide layouts. PowerPoint provides twenty-four AutoLayouts from which you can choose.

design template A presentation whose background, color schemes, typefaces, and other formatting options can be applied to another presentation.

Normal view In this view mode, the Outline, Slide, and Notes panes appear. This view mode provides one place for viewing the different parts of your presentation.

Notes pane Visible in Normal view, this location is used for typing reminder notes and information you want to share with your audience.

Outline pane In PowerPoint, this location is used for typing text and rearranging a presentation.

Outline view This view mode enlarges the Outline pane to fill most of the screen.

placeholder Marks the location of a slide object and provides instructions for editing the object.

Places bar The strip of icon buttons appearing in the Open and Save As dialog boxes that allow you to display the most common areas for retrieving and storing files using a single mouse click.

Slide pane In PowerPoint, this location is used for seeing how your slide will look and for editing the slide directly.

Slide Show view	In this view mode, your presentation is displayed as an on-screen slide show, complete with transitions and special effects.
Slide Sorter view	This mode for viewing a presentation displays multiple slides at once using small thumbnail representations. This mode gives you an immediate feeling for the continuity or flow of a presentation.
Slide view	This view mode enlarges the Slide pane to fill most of the screen.
clip art image	Computer graphic that you can insert into your document to make it more interesting or entertaining.
organization chart	Schematic drawing showing a hierarchy of formal relationships.
Microsoft Clip Gallery	The location where clip art, sound and movie clips are stored and organized for all Microsoft Office applications.
Microsoft Graph	An Office 2000 mini-application that lets you create charts and graphs for insertion in the current document.
Microsoft Organization Chart	An Office 2000 mini-application for creating organization charts that you can embed in the current document.
sizing handles	The tiny boxes that surround a selected object. You drag the sizing handles to resize an object.
Slide Finder	Tool used for inserting slides from existing presentations in the current presentation. The contents of presentations are displayed using slide snapshots.

POWERPOINT

Index

POWERPOINT

Answers to Self Check Questions

1.1 Self Check How do you close a window that appears in the Access work area? Click on its Close button (⊠).

1.2 Self Check Describe two methods to quickly move the cursor to the last record in a large datasheet. Here are three methods. First, you can use the cursor movement keys `CTRL`+`↓` or `CTRL`+`END` to move the cursor to the last record. Second, you can use the mouse to click the Last Record button (⏭). And, third, you can scroll the window by dragging the vertical scroll box and then click in a field of the last record. (*Note:* You must click in the record's row in order to move the cursor. Otherwise, you simply scroll the window.)

1.3 Self Check When does Access save the changes that you've made when editing a record? Editing changes to a record are saved permanently to disk when the cursor is moved to another record or when the user presses the `SHIFT`+`ENTER` combination.

2.1 Self Check What two objects are most closely associated with the output of a database application? Query objects (the questions you ask of a database) and Report objects (the structured printed output from a database).

2.2 Self Check How do you specify the name of a field when creating a table in Datasheet view? You double-click the column name in the field header area and then type the desired field name.

2.3 Self Check What is an AutoNumber field? Why is it useful as a primary key? An AutoNumber field is a data type that automatically increments a numeric value each time a new record is added to a table. It is useful as a primary key since it already supplies a unique field value for identifying each record in a table.

2.4 Self Check What happens to your table's data if you delete a field in table Design view? The table data that is stored in the field is removed along with the field definition in Design view.

3.1 Self Check Name two reasons for changing the field column order in a datasheet. Some reasons for changing the field order include customizing a datasheet's appearance for printing, displaying fields side-by-side in a datasheet, and arranging columns for performing multiple-field sort operations.

3.2 Self Check How do you perform a sort operation using more than one field column? You must first ensure that the columns are adjacent to one another. The leftmost column should contain the primary or first sort key. The next column(s) provides the secondary sort level(s). You must then select all of the columns involved in the sort operation and click the appropriate Sort button on the toolbar.

3.3 Self Check   In a personnel table, how would you display a subset of those employees working in the Accounting department? Using Filter For Input, you enter "Accounting" as the criterion. Using Filter By Selection, you select "Accounting" from the datasheet. Using Filter By Form, you select "Accounting" from the drop-down list attached to the department field. You then apply and remove the filter by clicking on the Apply/Remove Filter button (▽) on the toolbar.

3.4 Self Check   Name one way that a query's dynaset may differ from a table's datasheet. A query's dynaset may display results from two or more tables in the same Datasheet window.

4.1 Self Check   Name the layout options for designing a form using the Form Wizard. Columnar, Tabular, Datasheet, and Justified.

4.2 Self Check   What does the term "grouping data" refer to in a report? You can arrange data so that it appears combined into categories in a report. The categories are based on field values and appear sorted into ascending order, by default. Grouping data also enables you to prepare subtotal calculations.

4.3 Self Check   How could you use table and report objects to print diskette labels? You store the diskette names, titles, and other information in a table and then use a mailing labels report to print the information using the Avery 5296 diskette label.

4.4 Self Check   Name two operating system tools that you can use to back up a database. Windows Explorer and "My Computer"

ACCESS

Glossary

application window
In Windows, each running application program appears in its own application window. These windows may be sized and moved anywhere on the Windows desktop.

AutoForm Wizard
An Access wizard that creates a form automatically, using all of the fields from the selected table object in the Database window. There are three types of AutoForm Wizards: Columnar, Tabular, and Datasheet.

AutoNumber
A field data type that provides a unique value for each record automatically. The three types of AutoNumber fields include sequential (incremented by one), random, and replication. You cannot delete or modify the values generated for an AutoNumber field.

AutoReport Wizard
An Access wizard that creates a columnar or tabular report automatically, using all of the fields from the selected table or query object in the Database window. There are two types of AutoReport Wizards: Columnar and Tabular.

cell
In a datasheet, the intersection of a column (field) and a row (record).

database
A collection of related data. In Access, a database includes a collection of objects—tables, queries, reports, forms, and other objects.

database management system (DBMS)
A software tool that lets you create and maintain an information database.

Database window
The control center for an Access database. Using the *Objects* bar, categorizes and lists the objects stored in a database.

Database Wizard
In Access, a software feature for creating a complete database application based on professionally designed database templates.

datasheet
A window used for displaying multiple records from a table using an electronic spreadsheet layout of horizontal rows and vertical columns.

Datasheet view
The method or mode of displaying table data using a datasheet.

Design view
Each database object in Access may be opened in display mode or Design view mode. You use Design view to define table structures, construct queries, build forms, and design reports.

Documenter   In Access, a tool for documenting and printing the design characteristics of a database object.

dynaset   In previous versions of Access, the result of a query. A dynaset is displayed as a table in Datasheet view of the records matching the query parameters.

field   A single item, or column, of information in a *record.*

Field Grid pane   In table Design view, the top portion of the window where you specify field names, data types, and descriptions.

field header area   In an Access Datasheet window, the top frame or border area that contains the field names as column headings.

Field Properties   In table Design view, the bottom portion of the window where you specify field properties and characteristics.

filter   The process or method of temporarily restricting the display of records in a table to those that match a particular search criterion or pattern.

Filter By Form   In Access, a command that returns a subset of records from a table matching a filter specification.

Filter By Selection   In Access, a command that returns a subset of records from a table matching the selected value in a datasheet.

Filter Excluding Selection   In Access, a command that returns a subset of records from a table not matching the selected value in a datasheet.

Filter For Input   In Access, a command that returns a subset of records from a table matching a filter specification that you enter in a right-click menu's text box.

form   A database object used for displaying table data one record at a time.

Form window   In Access, a window that displays a form object.

form wizards   Access tools that simplify the process of creating a form.

HTML   An acronym for Hypertext Markup Language, which is the standardized markup language used in creating documents for display on the World Wide Web.

index   A feature of a table object that allows you to pre-sort a table based on key values. Indexes speed up searching, sorting, and other database operations. (*Note:* The primary key is indexed automatically.)

ACCESS

Internet A worldwide network of computer networks that are interconnected by standard telephone lines, fiber optics, and satellites.

Label Wizard An Access wizard that creates a mailing labels report based on the size, shape, and formatting of standard mailing labels.

null value Nothing; an empty or zero-length string.

Objects bar The strip of icon buttons appearing in the Database window that allows you to display a particular category of database objects.

Places bar The strip of icon buttons appearing in the Open and Save As dialog boxes that allow you to display the most common areas for retrieving and storing files using a single mouse click.

preview The act of displaying on-screen a document, worksheet, or report prior to sending it to the printer. An on-screen preview window displays a *soft copy* of a document, while the printer prepares the *hard copy.*

primary key A field whose values uniquely identify each record in a table. The primary key provides the default sort order for a table and is used to establish connections to and relationships with other tables.

query A database object that you use to ask a question of your data. The results from a query are typically displayed using a *datasheet.*

record An individual entry, or row, in a *table.* A record contains one or more *fields.*

record selection area The row frame area located to the left of the first column in a *datasheet.* Used for selecting records.

report snapshot A Windows graphic metafile that stores an accurate representation, including fonts, graphics, and colors, of each page in a report. You do not need Access installed on your computer to view a report snapshot. Instead, you can use the free Microsoft Snapshot Viewer to open, view, and print snapshots.

report wizards Access tools that simplify the process of creating a report.

report(s) A database object used for viewing, compiling, summarizing, and printing information.

select query A type of query object that lets you ask questions of your database, retrieve data from multiple tables, sort the data, and display the results in a datasheet.

Simple Query Wizard In Access, a software feature that simplifies the process of creating a query.

sort key   The field or column used to sort the contents of a datasheet.

subdatasheet   An extension of a datasheet that provides a picture-in-picture display of related or hierarchical data.

table   A database object used to collect and store data relating to a particular subject or topic.

Table Wizard   In Access, a software feature that simplifies the process of creating a table.

typeface   The shape and appearance of characters. There are two categories of typefaces: serif and sans serif. Serif type (for example, Times Roman) is more decorative and, some say, easier to read than sans serif type (for example, Arial).

Undo command   A command that makes it possible to reverse the last command or action performed.

wildcard characters   Special symbols that are used to represent other alphanumeric characters in search, filter, and query operations. You can use the question mark (?) to represent any single character and the asterisk (*) to represent any group of characters.

World Wide Web   A visual interface to the Internet based on hyperlinks. Using Web browser software, you click on hyperlinks to navigate resources on the Internet.

ACCESS

Index

ACCESS

Answers to Self Check Questions

1.1 Self Check — What typically happens when you copy two items in sequence without an intervening paste? The Office Clipboard will appear.

1.2 Self Check — When you paste data, what is the default data format? HTML.

1.3 Self Check — How would you go about resizing a shared object? To resize a shared object, select the object and then drag its sizing handles inward or outward.

1.4 Self Check — What is the procedure for editing embedded objects? Double-click the embedded object and then make your changes. Click outside the object when you're finished.

2.1 Self Check — Describe the procedure for converting a Word outline to a PowerPoint presentation. Choose File, Send To, Microsoft PowerPoint from Word's Menu bar.

2.2 Self Check — How would you go about editing an embedded PowerPoint slide? Double-click an embedded slide to edit it.

2.3 Self Check — When might you want to export a report created in Access to Word? Exporting Access reports to Word is useful when you want to customize the report using a variety of formatting commands to your particular needs.

3.1 Self Check — Provide an example of when you might use a hyperlink in an Office document to access information on the Web. If your document will be read onscreen, hyperlinks can enhance your reader's understanding of the current topic. For example, if your topic concerns travel in Asia, include a link to Web site that specializes in Asian tours and another that specializes in Asian history.

3.2 Self Check — What procedure must you use to convert a document, worksheet, or presentation to HTML? Choose File, Save as Web Page from the Menu bar in Word, Excel, or PowerPoint.

3.3 Self Check — What are frames used for on Web pages? Frames are used to offset links to a document's table of contents or other parts of a Web site.

3.4 Self Check — What is the purpose for posting a file to a Web server? Before others can view your file using their Web browsers, you must post (or copy) the file to a Web server.

INTEGRATING

Glossary

Access Links add-in An Excel add-in that enables you to translate Excel data into Access forms, reports, and tables.

data access page Interactive Web pages that enable you to view and edit data managed in an Access 2000 database.

destination document An Office document that contains data copied from another application.

embedding A method for sharing data in Office 2000 application. Embedded data is fully editable within the destination document and doesn't retain a connection to its source document.

frames Separate area on a Web page for offsetting hyperlinks to a document's table of contents or other pages on a Web site.

frames page Document or Web page that contains frames.

HTML An acronym for Hypertext Markup Language, which is the standardized markup language used in creating documents for display on the World Wide Web.

linking A method for sharing data in Office 2000 application. In linking, you not only paste the data, you also establish a dynamic link between the source and destination documents.

Microsoft Graph Shared mini-application in Microsoft Office for producing charts and graphs without leaving Word.

Office Clipboard A program, in Office 2000, that allows you to copy and move information within or among Office 2000 applications. Unlike the Windows Clipboard, the Office Clipboard can store up to 12 items and then paste them all at once.

pasting A method for sharing data in Office 2000 application. Pasting data involves inserting a static representation of the source data into the destination document.

server application When sharing data among Office applications, this term refers to the application that was used to create the shared data.

sizing handles The tiny boxes that surround a selected object.

source document Original document in which information is created for transfer to a destination document.

Spreadsheet component	Office 2000 Web component for publishing interactive worksheets on the Web.
Web discussion	Feature of Office 2000 for sharing comments about Office documents over the Web.
Web folder	Shortcut to a Web-server location.
Web server	Computer for storing Web pages.
Web toolbar	Office 2000 toolbar for navigating hyperlinks locally and on the World Wide Web.
Windows Clipboard	A program, in Windows, that allows you to copy and move information within an application or among applications. The Windows Clipboard temporarily stores the information in memory before you paste the data in a new location.

INTEGRATING

Index

INTEGRATING

Appendix: Microsoft Windows Quick Reference

Using the Mouse and Keyboard

Microsoft Windows provides a graphical environment for working in your application, such as Microsoft Word, Excel, Access, or Power-Point. As you work with Windows applications, you will find that there are often three different ways to perform the same command. The most common methods for performing commands include:

- Menu

  Choose a command from the Menu bar or from a right-click menu.
- Mouse

  Position the mouse pointer over a toolbar button and then click once.
- Keyboard

  Press a keyboard shortcut (usually CTRL + *letter*).

Although you may use a Windows application with only a keyboard, much of a program's basic design relies on using a mouse. Regardless of whether your mouse has two or three buttons, you will use the left or primary mouse button for selecting screen objects and menu commands and the right or secondary mouse button for displaying right-click menus.

The most common mouse actions include:

- Point

  Slide the mouse on your desk to position the tip of the mouse pointer over the desired object on the screen.
- Click

  Press down and release the left mouse button quickly. Clicking is used to select a screen object, activate a toolbar command, and choose menu commands.
- Right-Click

  Press down and release the right mouse button. Right-clicking the mouse pointer on a screen object displays a context-sensitive menu.
- Double-Click

  Press down and release the mouse button twice in rapid succession. Double-clicking is used to select screen objects or to activate an embedded object for editing.
- Drag

  Press down and hold the mouse button as you move the mouse pointer across the screen. When the mouse pointer reaches the desired location, release the mouse button. Dragging is used to select a group of screen objects and to copy or move data.

You may notice that the mouse pointer changes shape as you move it over different parts of the screen. Each mouse pointer shape has its own purpose and may provide you with important information. There are four primary mouse shapes that appear in Windows applications:

⌐k	arrow	Used to choose menu commands and click toolbars buttons.
⌛	hourglass	Informs you that the application is occupied and requests that you wait.
I	I-beam	Used to set the position of the insertion point and to modify and edit text.
👆	hand	Used to select hyperlinks in the Windows-based Help systems, in Microsoft Office documents, and on the Web.

Aside from being the primary input device for entering information, the keyboard offers shortcut methods for performing some common commands and procedures.

Starting Windows

Because Windows is an operating system, it is loaded into the computer's memory when you first turn on the computer. To start Windows, you must do the following:

1. Turn on the power switches to the computer and monitor. After a few seconds, the Windows desktop will appear. (*Note*: If you are attached to a network, a dialog box may appear asking you to enter your User name and Password. Enter this information now or ask your instructor for further instructions.)
2. A Welcome dialog box may appear providing information about the operating system's major features. If the Welcome dialog box appears on your screen:
CLICK: Close button (☒) in the top right-hand corner of the Welcome window
3. If additional windows appear open on your desktop:
CLICK: Close button (☒) in the top right-hand corner of each window

Parts of a Dialog Box

A dialog box is a common mechanism in Windows applications for collecting information before processing a command. In a dialog box, you indicate the options you want to use and then click the OK button when you're finished. Dialog boxes are also used to display messages or to ask for the confirmation of commands. The following shows an example of the Print dialog box, which is similar across Windows applications.

Print dialog box

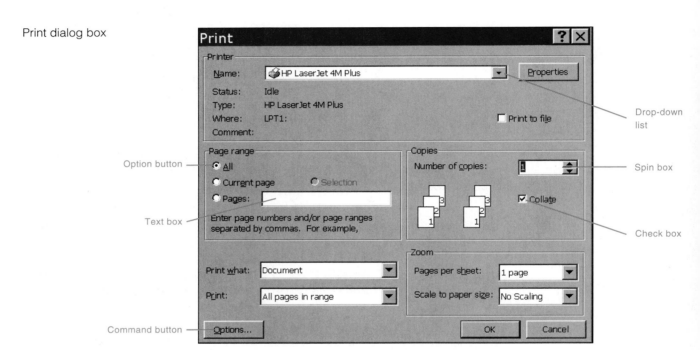

A dialog box uses several types of controls or components for collecting information. We describe the most common components in the following table.

Dialog box components

Name	Example	Action
Check box	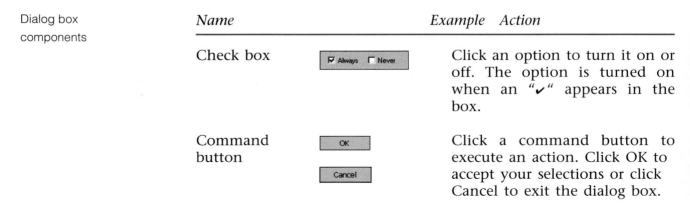	Click an option to turn it on or off. The option is turned on when an "✔" appears in the box.
Command button		Click a command button to execute an action. Click OK to accept your selections or click Cancel to exit the dialog box.

Drop-Down list box	Make a choice from the list that appears when you click the down arrow next to the box; only the selected choice is visible.
List box	Make a choice from the scrollable list; several choices, if not all, are always visible.
Option button	Select an option from a group of related options.
Slide box	Drag the slider bar to make a selection, like using a radio's volume control.
Spin box	Click the up and down arrows to the right of the box until the number you want appears.
Tab	Click a named tab at the top of the window to access other pages of options in the dialog box.
Text box	Click inside the text box and then type the desired information.

Most dialog boxes provide a question mark icon (?) near the right side of the Title bar. If you have a question about an item in the dialog box, click the question mark and then click the item to display a pop-up help window. To remove the help window, click on it once.

Getting Help

Windows applications, such as Microsoft Office 2000 applications, provide a comprehensive library of online documentation. This section describes these help features and how to find more detailed information.

Obtaining Context-Sensitive Help

In Windows applications, you can often retrieve context-sensitive help for menu options, toolbar buttons, and dialog box items. *Context-sensitive help* refers to a program's ability to present helpful information reflecting your current position in the program. The help information is presented concisely in a small pop-up window that you can remove with the click of the mouse. This type of help lets you access information quickly and then continue working without interruption. The following table describes some methods for accessing context-sensitive help while working in Windows applications.

Displaying context-sensitive Help information

To display...	Do this...
A description of a dialog box item	Click the question mark button ([?]) in a dialog box's Title bar and then click an item in the dialog box. Alternatively, you can often right-click a dialog box item and then choose the What's This? command from the shortcut menu.
A description of a menu command	Choose the Help, What's This? command from the menu and then choose a command using the question mark mouse pointer. Rather than executing the command, a helpful description of the command appears in a pop-up window.
A description of a toolbar button	Point to a toolbar button to display a pop-up label called a ToolTip.

Getting Help in Office 2000

Getting Help from the Office Assistant

In Office 2000 applications, the Office Assistant is your personal computer guru and is available by default when your application is first installed. When you need to perform a task that you're unsure of, simply click the Assistant character and then type a phrase such as "How do I obtain help" in the Assistant balloon. The Assistant analyzes your request and provides a resource list of suggested topics, as shown to the right. Simply click a topic to obtain additional information.

What would you like to do?
- Ways to get assistance while you work
- How to obtain the Microsoft Office 2000/Visual Basic Programmer's Guide
- Microsoft Download Library (MSDL)
- None of the above, look for more help on the Web

How do I obtain help

Options   Search

The Assistant also watches your keystrokes and mouse clicks as you work and offers suggestions and shortcuts to make you more productive and efficient. If you find the Office Assistant to be distracting, you can turn it off by choosing "Hide the Office Assistant" from the Help menu. To redisplay it, simply choose "Microsoft *Application* Help" or "Show the Office Assistant" from the Help menu.

Getting Help from the Help Window

You may prefer to obtain a complete topical listing of your application's Help system. To do this, you must first disable the Office Assistant by clicking the Options button in the Assistant balloon, clearing the *Use the Office Assistant* check box, and then pressing (ENTER). Once the Office Assistant is disabled, simply choose "Microsoft *Application* Help" from the Help menu to display the Help window. If the *Contents*, *Answer Wizard*, and *Index* tabs don't appear, click Show (⬓) in the window's toolbar.

The Help window, shown below, provides three different tools, each on its own tab, to help you find the information you need quickly and easily. You can read the Help information you find onscreen or print it out for later reference by clicking the Print button (🖨) in the window's toolbar. To close the Help window, click its Close button (✖).

Example Help window

The Contents tab is currently selected. Use this tab to display the Table of Contents for the entire Help system.

The Answer Wizard tab enables you to obtain help information by typing in questions.

The Index tab displays enables you to display topics by selecting keywords or typing in words and phrases.

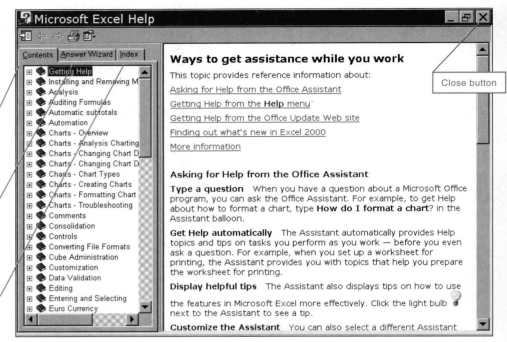

Getting Help from the Office Update Web Site

Microsoft's Office Update Web site provides additional technical support and product enhancements. You can access this site from any Office application by choosing "Office on the Web" from the Help menu.